4000 1416

KU-796-861

PREFACE

Since the first edition of this book appeared in early 1987 the volume of Community legislation in the field of competition law has more than doubled. Significant developments have also taken place on the domestic front with new primary as well as secondary legislation, although the broad statutory framework of UK competition law has remained largely unchanged. Fundamental reform by Parliament of the domestic law in this area seems set to come but is not likely to begin much before the close of 1991 nor (if it is to be spread across more than one Act of Parliament) end much before 1993.

No change has been made in the basic format of the book. Part I covers the main UK legislative material and is subdivided between, on the one hand, the key statutes (in the form in which they appear up to and including the coming into force of relevant provisions of the Companies Act 1989) and, on the other, a number of statutory instruments including recent orders concerning restrictive covenants in share or business sale agreements, the supply of beer, and the implementation of primary legislation on merger control at both UK and EEC levels.

Provisions of a competition law nature to be found in sectoral or, more particularly, privatisation legislation have not been reproduced in this work, although references to such legislation have been made in footnotes where thought appropriate.

In Part II the EEC material begins with the relevant provisions of the Treaty of Rome and includes all the main regulations and directives in force at 31 August 1990 (including the republished version of the Merger Control Regulation), together with notices issued by the Commission. In this latter respect omissions from the first edition have been corrected by the inclusion of the Notice which accompanied Regulations 1983/83 and 1984/83, the current Notice on Agreements of Minor Importance and two early notices issued by the Commission in 1968.

In this edition it has also been decided to include in an Appendix the proposals of the Commission for further legislation in the air transport, sea transport and insurance sectors. These are intended to alert the reader to these developments in prospect and to indicate the Commission's thinking in the matters to which they relate. It must not be assumed that legislation or guidance will appear in this form (or at all) and the reader should be careful to check the current status and content of this material.

Garth Lindrup   September 1990

CONTENTS

PART II   EEC LEGISLATION

Appendix

Index

PART I

UK LEGISLATION

A   ACTS OF PARLIAMENT

FAIR TRADING ACT 1973
(1973 c 41)

ARRANGEMENT OF SECTIONS

PART I

INTRODUCTORY

PART II

REFERENCES TO CONSUMER PROTECTION ADVISORY COMMITTEE

(not reproduced in this work)

PART III

ADDITIONAL FUNCTIONS OF DIRECTOR FOR PROTECTION OF CONSUMERS

(not reproduced in this work)

PART IV

FUNCTIONS OF DIRECTOR AND COMMISSION IN RELATION TO MONOPOLY SITUATIONS AND UNCOMPETITIVE PRACTICES

Powers for Director to require information

Monopoly references

R.T.C. LIBRARY, LETTERKENNY

PART V

MERGERS

Newspaper merger references

Other merger references

Restriction on power to make merger reference where prior notice has been given

Undertakings as alternative to merger reference

Supplementary

PART VI

REFERENCES TO COMMISSION OTHER THAN MONOPOLY AND MERGER REFERENCES

PART VII

PROVISIONS RELATING TO REFERENCES TO ADVISORY COMMITTEE OR TO COMMISSION

PART VIII

ADDITIONAL PROVISIONS RELATING TO REFERENCES TO COMMISSION

PART IX

AMENDMENTS OF RESTRICTIVE TRADE PRACTICES ACTS

PART X

EXTENSION OF ACT OF 1956 TO AGREEMENTS RELATING TO SERVICES

(repealed)

PART XI

PYRAMID SELLING AND SIMILAR TRADING SCHEMES

(not reproduced in this work)

PART XII

MISCELLANEOUS AND SUPPLEMENTARY PROVISIONS

*An Act to provide for the appointment of a Director General of Fair Trading
and of a Consumer Protection Advisory Committee, and to confer on the
Director General and the Committee so appointed, on the Secretary of State,
on the Restrictive Practices Court and on certain other courts new functions
for the protection of consumers; to make provision, in substitution for the
Monopolies and Restrictive Practices (Inquiry and Control) Act 1948 and
the Monopolies and Mergers Act 1965, for the matters dealt with in those*

Acts and related matters, including restrictive labour practices; to amend the Restrictive Trade Practices Act 1956 and the Restrictive Trade Practices Act 1968, to make provision for extending the said Act of 1956 to agreements relating to services, and to transfer to the Director General of Fair Trading the functions of the Registrar of Restrictive Trading Agreements; to make provision with respect to pyramid selling and similar trading schemes; to make new provision in place of section 30(2) to (4) of the Trade Descriptions Act 1968; and for purposes connected with those matters. [25 July 1973]

PART I
INTRODUCTORY

1. Director General of Fair Trading

(1) The Secretary of State shall appoint an officer to be known as the Director General of Fair Trading (in this Act referred to as "the Director") for the purpose of performing the functions assigned or transferred to the Director by or under this Act.

(2) An appointment of a person to hold office as the Director shall not be for a term exceeding five years; but previous appointment to that office shall not affect eligibility for re-appointment.

(3) The Director may at any time resign his office as the Director by notice in writing addressed to the Secretary of State; and the Secretary of State may remove any person from that office on the ground of incapacity or misbehaviour.

(4) Subject to subsections (2) and (3) of this section, the Director shall hold and vacate office as such in accordance with the terms of his appointment.

(5) The Director may appoint such staff as he may think fit, subject to the approval of the Minister for the Civil Service as to numbers and as to terms and conditions of service.

(6) The provisions of Schedule 1 to this Act shall have effect with respect to the Director. **[1]**

2. General functions of Director

(1) Without prejudice to any other functions assigned or transferred to him by or under this Act, it shall be the duty of the Director, so far as appears to him to be practicable from time to time, —

    (*a*) to keep under review the carrying on of commercial activities in the United Kingdom which relate to goods supplied to consumers in the United Kingdom or produced with a view to their being so supplied, or which relate to services supplied for consumers in the United Kingdom, and to collect information with respect to such activities, and the persons by whom they are carried on, with a view to his becoming aware of, and ascertaining the circumstances relating to, practices which may adversely affect the economic interests of consumers in the United Kingdom, and

    (*b*) to receive and collate evidence becoming available to him with respect to such activities as are mentioned in the preceding paragraph and which appears to him to be evidence of practices which may adversely affect the interests (whether they are economic interests or interests with respect to health, safety or other matters) of consumers in the United Kingdom.

(2) It shall also be the duty of the Director, so far as appears to him to be practicable from time to time, to keep under review the carrying on of commercial activities in the United Kingdom, and to collect information with respect to those activities, and the persons by whom they are carried on, with a view to his becoming aware of, and ascertaining the circumstances relating to, monopoly situations or uncompetitive practices.

(3) It shall be the duty of the Director, where either he considers it expedient or he is requested by the Secretary of State to do so, –

(a) to give information and assistance to the Secretary of State with respect to any of the matters in respect of which the Director has any duties under subsections (1) and (2) of this section, or

(b) subject to the provisions of Part II of this Act in relation to recommendations under that Part of this Act, to make recommendations to the Secretary of State as to any action which in the opinion of the Director it would be expedient for the Secretary of State or any other Minister to take in relation to any of the matters in respect of which the Director has any such duties.

(4) It shall also be the duty of the Director to have regard to evidence becoming available to him with respect to any course of conduct on the part of a person carrying on a business which appears to be conduct detrimental to the interests of consumers in the United Kingdom and (in accordance with the provisions of Part III of this Act) to be regarded as unfair to them, with a view to considering what action (if any) he should take under Part III of this Act.

(5) It shall be the duty of the Director to have regard to the needs of regional development and to the desirability of dispersing administrative offices from London in making decisions on the location of offices for his staff.   **[2]**

3. Consumer Protection Advisory Committee

(section not reproduced in this work)   **[3]**

4. The Monopolies and Mergers Commission

(1) The Commission established under section 1 of the Monopolies and Restrictive Practices (Inquiry and Control) Act 1948 by the name of the Monopolies and Restrictive Practices Commission, and subsequently renamed the Monopolies Commission, shall as from the commencement of this Act be known as the Monopolies and Mergers Commission, and shall continue to exist by that name for the purpose of performing the functions assigned to that Commission (in this Act referred to as "the Commission") by or under this Act.

(2) There shall be not less than ten and (subject to the next following subsection) not more than twenty-five regular members of the Commission, who shall be appointed by the Secretary of State.

(3) The Secretary of State may by order made by statutory instrument increase the maximum number of regular members of the Commission to such number as he may think fit.[1]

(4) The provisions of Schedule 3 to this Act shall have effect with respect to the Commission.   [4]

NOTE
1 The maximum number of regular members of the Commission is now 50; see the Monopolies and Mergers Commission (Increase in Membership) Order 1989, SI 1989 No 1240.

5. Principal functions of Commission

(1) Without prejudice to any other functions assigned to the Commission by or under this Act, it shall be the duty of the Commission, subject to and in accordance with the following provisions of this Act, to investigate and report on any question which may be referred to the Commission under this Act —

(*a*) with respect to the existence, or possible existence, of a monopoly situation, or

(*b*) with respect to a transfer of a newspaper or of newspaper assets (within the meaning of Part V of this Act), or

(*c*) with respect to the creation, or possible creation, of a merger situation qualifying for investigation (within the meaning of Part V of this Act).

(2) It shall be the duty of the Director, for the purpose of assisting the Commission in carrying out an investigation on a reference made to them under this Act, to give to the Commission —

(*a*) any information which is in his possession and which relates to matters falling within the scope of the investigation, and which is either requested by the Commission for that purpose or is information which in his opinion it would be appropriate for that purpose to give to the Commission without any such request, and

(*b*) any other assistance which the Commission may require, and which it is within his power to give, in relation to any such matters;

and the Commission, for the purpose of carrying out any such investigation, shall take account of any information given to them for that purpose under this subsection.

(3) In this Act "monopoly reference" means any reference to the Commission under this Act which falls within paragraph (*a*) of subsection (1) of this section; "merger reference" (subject to section 63 of this Act) means any reference to the Commission under this Act which falls within paragraph (*b*) or paragraph (*c*) of that subsection; and "monopoly situation" (except in sections 6 to 8 of this Act) means circumstances in which, in accordance with the following provisions of this Part of this Act, a monopoly situation is for the purposes of this Act to be taken to exist in relation to any matters specified in section 6(1), section 7(1) or section 8 of this Act.   [5]

6. Monopoly situation in relation to supply of goods

(1) For the purposes of this Act a monopoly situation shall be taken to exist in

relation to the supply of goods of any description in the following cases, that is to say, if —

(a) at least one-quarter of all the goods of that description which are supplied in the United Kingdom are supplied by one and the same person, or are supplied to one and the same person, or

(b) at least one-quarter of all the goods of that description which are supplied in the United Kingdom are supplied by members of one and the same group of interconnected bodies corporate, or are supplied to members of one and the same group of interconnected bodies corporate, or

(c) at least one-quarter of all the goods of that description which are supplied in the United Kingdom are supplied by members of one and the same group consisting of two or more such persons as are mentioned in sub-section (2) of this section, or are supplied to members of one and the same group consisting of two or more such persons, or

(d) one or more agreements are in operation, the result or collective result of which is that goods of that description are not supplied in the United Kingdom at all.

(2) The two or more persons referred to in subsection (1)(c) of this section, in relation to goods of any description, are any two or more persons (not being a group of interconnected bodies corporate) who whether voluntarily or not, and whether by agreement or not, so conduct their respective affairs as in any way to prevent, restrict or distort competition in connection with the production or supply of goods of that description, whether or not they themselves are affected by the competition and whether the competition is between persons interested as producers or suppliers or between persons interested as customers of producers or suppliers. **[6]**

NOTE
References in s 6 to the United Kingdom are to be taken to include references to a part of the United Kingdom: Competition Act 1980, s 11(2).

7. Monopoly situation in relation to supply of services

(1) For the purposes of this Act a monopoly situation shall be taken to exist in relation to the supply of services of any description in the following cases, that is to say, if —

(a) the supply of services of that description in the United Kingdom is, to the extent of at least one-quarter, supply by one and the same person, or supply for one and the same person, or

(b) the supply of services of that description in the United Kingdom is, to the extent of at least one-quarter, supply by members of one and the same group of interconnected bodies corporate, or supply for members of one and the same group of interconnected bodies corporate, or

(c) the supply of services of that description in the United Kingdom is, to the extent of at least one-quarter, supply by members of one and the same group consisting of two or more such persons as are mentioned in subsection (2) of this section, or supply for members of one and the same group consisting of two or more such persons, or

(d) one or more agreements are in operation, the result or collective result of which is that services of that description are not supplied in the United Kingdom at all.

(2) The two or more persons referred to in subsection (1)(c) of this section, in relation to services of any description, are any two or more persons (not being a group of interconnected bodies corporate) who whether voluntarily or not, and whether by agreement or not, so conduct their respective affairs as in any way to prevent, restrict or distort competition in connection with the supply of services of that description, whether or not they themselves are affected by the competition, and whether the competition is between persons interested as persons by whom, or as persons for whom, services are supplied.

(3) In the application of this section for the purposes of a monopoly reference, the Commission, or the person or persons making the reference, may, to such extent as the Commission, or that person or those persons, think appropriate in the circumstances, treat services as supplied in the United Kingdom if the person supplying the services —

(a) has a place of business in the United Kingdom, or

(b) controls the relevant activities from the United Kingdom, or

(c) being a body corporate, is incorporated under the law of Great Britain or of Northern Ireland,

and may do so whether or not those services would otherwise be regarded as supplied in the United Kingdom.   **[7]**

NOTE
  References in s 7 to the United Kingdom are to be taken to include references to a part of the United Kingdom: Competition Act 1980, s 11(2).

8. Monopoly situation in relation to exports

(1) For the purposes of this Act a monopoly situation shall be taken to exist in relation to exports of goods of any description from the United Kingdom in the following cases, that is to say, if —

(a) at least one-quarter of all the goods of that description which are produced in the United Kingdom are produced by one and the same person, or

(b) at least one-quarter of all the goods of that description which are produced in the United Kingdom are produced by members of one and the same group of interconnected bodies corporate;

and in those cases a monopoly situation shall for the purposes of this Act be taken to exist both in relation to exports of goods of that description from the United Kingdom generally and in relation to exports of goods of that description from the United Kingdom to each market taken separately.

(2) In relation to exports of goods of any description from the United Kingdom generally, a monopoly situation shall for the purposes of this Act be taken to exist if —

(a) one or more agreements are in operation which in any way prevent or restrict, or prevent, restrict or distort competition in relation to, the export of goods of that description from the United Kingdom, and

(*b*) that agreement is or (as the case may be) those agreements collectively are operative with respect to at least one-quarter of all the goods of that description which are produced in the United Kingdom.

(3) In relation to exports of goods of any description from the United Kingdom to any particular market, a monopoly situation shall for the purposes of this Act be taken to exist if —

(*a*) one or more agreements are in operation which in any way prevent or restrict, or prevent, restrict or distort competition in relation to, the supply of goods of that description (whether from the United Kingdom or not) to that market, and

(*b*) that agreement is or (as the case may be) those agreements collectively are operative with respect to at least one-quarter of all the goods of that description which are produced in the United Kingdom. **[8]**

9. Monopoly situation limited to part of United Kingdom

(1) For the purposes of a monopoly reference, other than a reference relating to exports of goods from the United Kingdom, the person or persons making the reference may, if it appears to him or them to be appropriate in the circumstances to do so, determine that consideration shall be limited to a part of the United Kingdom.

(2) Where such a determination is made, then for the purposes of that monopoly reference the provisions of sections 6 and 7 of this Act, or such of those provisions as are applicable for those purposes, shall have effect as if, wherever those provisions refer to the United Kingdom, they referred to that part of the United Kingdom to which, in accordance with that determination, consideration is to be limited.

(3) The preceding provisions of this section shall have effect subject to subsection (4) of section 50 of this Act in cases to which that subsection applies. **[9]**

10. Supplementary provisions relating to ss 6 to 9

(1) In the application of any of the provisions of sections 6 to 9 of this Act for the purposes of a monopoly reference, those provisions shall have effect subject to the following provisions of this section.

(2) No account shall for those purposes be taken of any provisions of an agreement in so far as they are provisions by virtue of which it is an agreement to which [the Act of 1976] applies.[1]

(3) In relation to goods or services of any description which are the subject of different forms of supply —

(*a*) references in paragraphs (*a*) to (*d*) of subsection (1), and in subsection (2), of section 6 or in section 8(3) of this Act to the supply of goods, or (*b*) references in paragraphs (*a*) to (*d*) of subsection (1), and in subsection (2), of section 7 of this Act to the supply of services,

shall for those purposes be construed in whichever of the following ways the Commission, or the person or persons making the monopoly reference, think appropriate in all the circumstances, that is to say, as references to any of those forms of supply taken separately, to all those forms of supply taken together, or to any of those forms of supply taken in groups.

(4) For the purposes of subsection (3) of this section the Commission, or the person or persons making the monopoly reference in question, may treat goods or services as being the subject of different forms of supply whenever the transactions in question differ as to their nature, their parties, their terms or their surrounding circumstances, and the difference is one which, in the opinion of the Commission, or the person or persons making the reference, ought for the purposes of that subsection to be treated as a material difference.

(5) For the purposes of a monopoly reference made by the Director, subsections (3) and (4) of this section shall have effect subject to section 50(3) and (4) of this Act.

(6) In determining, for the purposes of a monopoly reference, whether the proportion of one-quarter mentioned in any provision of section 6, section 7 or section 8 of this Act is fulfilled with respect to goods or services of any description, the Commission, or the person or persons making the reference, shall apply such criterion (whether it be value or cost or price or quantity or capacity or number of workers employed or some other criterion, of whatever nature) or such combination of criteria as may appear to them or him to be most suitable in all the circumstances.

(7) The criteria for determining when goods or services can be treated, for the purposes of a monopoly reference, as goods or services of a separate description shall be such as the person or persons making the reference may think most suitable in the circumstances.

(8) In construing the provisions of section 7(3) and section 9 of this Act and the provisions of subsections (1) to (7) of this section, the purposes of a monopoly reference shall be taken to include the purpose of enabling the Director, or the Secretary of State or any other Minister, to determine in any particular circumstances —

(*a*) whether a monopoly reference could be made under Part IV of this Act, and

(*b*) if so, whether in those circumstances such a reference could be made by the Director,

and references in those provisions to the person or persons making a monopoly reference shall be construed accordingly.   **[10]**

AMENDMENT
1 Words in sub-s (2) substituted by RTPA 1976, Sch 5.

11. Meaning of "complex monopoly situation"

(1) In this Act "complex monopoly situation" means circumstances in which, in accordance with the preceding provisions of this Act, a monopoly situation is for the purposes of this Act to be taken to exist in relation to the supply of goods or services of any description, or in relation to exports of goods of any description from the United Kingdom, by reason that the condition specified in paragraph (*c*) or in paragraph (*d*) of section 6(1) or of section 7(1) of this Act is fulfilled, or that the conditions specified in subsection (2) or in subsection (3) of section 8 of this Act are fulfilled.

(2) Any reference in the preceding subsection to paragraph (*c*) or paragraph (*d*) of section 6(1) or of section 7(1) of this Act shall be construed as including a reference to that paragraph as modified by section 9(2) of this Act.　　**[11]**

12. Powers of Secretary of State in relation to functions of Director

(1) The Secretary of State may give general directions indicating considerations to which the Director should have particular regard in determining the order of priority in which—

    (*a*) matters are to be brought under review in the performance of his duty under section 2(1) of this Act, or

    (*b*) classes of goods or services are to be brought under review by him for the purpose of considering whether a monopoly situation exists or may exist in relation to them.

(2) The Secretary of State may also give general directions indicating—

    (*a*) considerations to which, in cases where it appears to the Director that a practice may adversely affect the interests of consumers in the United Kingdom, he should have particular regard in determining whether to make a recommendation to the Secretary of State under section 2(3)(*b*) of this Act, or

    (*b*) considerations to which, in cases where it appears to the Director that a consumer trade practice may adversely affect the economic interests of consumers in the United Kingdom, he should have particular regard in determining whether to make a reference to the Advisory Committee under Part II of this Act, or

    (*c*) considerations to which, in cases where it appears to the Director that a monopoly situation exists or may exist, he should have particular regard in determining whether to make a monopoly reference to the Commission under Part IV of this Act.

(3) The Secretary of State, on giving any directions under this section, shall arrange for those directions to be published in such manner as the Secretary of State thinks most suitable in the circumstances.　　**[12]**

PART II

REFERENCES TO CONSUMER PROTECTION ADVISORY COMMITTEE

(not reproduced in this work)

PART III

ADDITIONAL FUNCTIONS OF DIRECTOR FOR PROTECTION OF CONSUMERS

(not reproduced in this work)

PART IV

FUNCTIONS OF DIRECTOR AND COMMISSION IN RELATION TO MONOPOLY
SITUATIONS AND UNCOMPETITIVE PRACTICES

Powers for Director to require information

44. General power for Director to require information

(1) Where it appears to the Director that there are grounds for believing—

(a) that a monopoly situation may exist in relation to the supply of goods
or services of any description, or in relation to exports of goods of any
description from the United Kingdom, and

(b) that in accordance with the following provisions of this Part of this Act
he would not be precluded from making a monopoly reference to the
Commission with respect to the existence or possible existence of that
situation,

the Director, for the purpose of assisting him in determining whether to
make a monopoly reference with respect to the existence or possible existence
of that situation, may exercise the powers conferred by the next following
subsection.

(2) In the circumstances and for the purpose mentioned in the preceding subsection the Director may require any person who supplies or produces goods of
the description in question in the United Kingdom, or to whom any such goods
are supplied in the United Kingdom, or (as the case may be) any person who
supplies services of that description in the United Kingdom, or for whom any
such services are so supplied, to furnish to the Director such information as the
Director may consider necessary with regard to—

(a) the value, cost, price or quantity of goods of that description supplied
or produced by that person, or of goods of that description supplied
to him, or (as the case may be) the value, cost, price or extent of the
services of that description supplied by that person or of the services
of that description supplied for him, or

(b) the capacity of any undertaking carried on by that person to supply,
produce or make use of goods of that description, or (as the case may
be) to supply or make use of services of that description, or

(c) the number of persons employed by that person wholly or partly on work
related to the supply, production or use of goods of that description,
or (as the case may be) the supply or use of services of that description.

[13]

NOTES
1 This section is applied with modifications by the Competition Act 1980, s 2(5).

2 For the purpose of enabling the Director General of Fair Trading to establish whether a person's conduct is excluded from being an anti-competitive practice under the Competition Act 1980 this section and s 46 are applied with modifications by the Anti-Competitive Practices (Exclusions) Order 1980, below.

3 By the Telecommunications Act 1984, s 50(2) the functions of the Director General of Fair Trading under this section and s 45 and his functions under ss 50, 52, 53, 86 and 88 of this Act, so far as relating to monopoly situations which exist or may exist in relation to commercial activities connected with telecommunications are transferred to the Director General of Telecommunications (so as to be exercisable concurrently with the Director General of Fair Trading); and the references in Part IV and ss 86, 88 and 133 of this Act to the Director are construed accordingly.

4 The functions of the Director General of Fair Trading under this section and s 45 of this Act, and his functions under ss 50, 52, 53, 86 and 88 of this Act, so far as relating to monopoly situations which exist in relation to commercial activities connected with the supply of water or the provision of sewerage services, are transferred to the Director General of Water Services, so as to be exercisable concurrently with the Director General of Fair Trading; and references in Pt IV (ss 44 – 56) and in ss 86, 88 and 133 of this Act to the Director, are to be construed accordingly; see the Water Act 1989, s 28(2).

5 The functions of the Director General of Fair Trading under this section and s 45 of this Act, and his functions under ss 50, 52, 53, 86 and 88 of this Act, so far as relating to monopoly situations which exist or may exist in relation to commercial activities connected with the generation, transmission or supply of electricity, are transferred to the Director General of Electricity Supply so as to be exercisable concurrently with the Director General of Fair Trading, and references in Pt IV (ss 44 – 56) and in ss 86, 88 and 133 of this Act are to be construed accordingly; see the Electricity Act 1989, s 43(2).

As to the furnishing of false or misleading information, generally, to the Director under this Part, see s 93B of this Act, as inserted by the Companies Act 1989, s 151.

45. Special power to require information with respect to complex monopoly situations

(1) Where it appears to the Director that there are grounds for believing —

 (a) that a complex monopoly situation may exist in relation to the supply of goods or services of any description, or in relation to exports of goods of any description from the United Kingdom, and

 (b) that in accordance with the following provisions of this Part of this Act he would not be precluded from making a monopoly reference to the Commission with respect to the existence or possible existence of that situation,

the Director may formulate proposals for requiring specified persons to furnish information to him in accordance with the proposals for the purpose of assisting him in determining whether to make a monopoly reference with respect to the existence or possible existence of that situation.

(2) The persons specified in any such proposals shall be persons appearing to the Director to be, or to be included among, those who, in relation to the production or supply of goods or to the supply of services of the description in question, or in relation to exports from the United Kingdom of goods of the description in question, —

 (a) may be parties to any such agreement as is mentioned in paragraph (d) of section 6(1) or paragraph (d) of section 7(1) of this Act (or mentioned in either of those paragraphs as modified by section 9(2) of this Act) or may be parties to any such agreement as is mentioned in subsection (2) or subsection (3) of section 8 of this Act, or

(b) may be conducting their respective affairs as mentioned in section 6(2) or in section 7(2) of this Act.

(3) Any such proposals shall also specify the description of goods or services in question, and —

(a) in a case falling within paragraph (a) of subsection (2) of this section, shall indicate the particular respects in which it appears to the Director that any agreement in question may be such an agreement as is referred to in that paragraph, or

(b) in a case falling within paragraph (b) of that subsection, shall indicate the particular respects in which it appears to the Director that the persons specified in the proposals may be conducting their respective affairs in a manner referred to in that paragraph,

and shall state what information the Director proposes that the persons specified in the proposals should be required to furnish for the purpose of indicating whether, in those respects, they are parties to such an agreement, or are so conducting their respective affairs, and, if so, of indicating in what circumstances they are parties to such an agreement or are so conducting their affairs.

(4) Where the Director has formulated proposals under this section, he may submit those proposals to the Secretary of State for approval; and if the Secretary of State approves the proposals, with or without modifications, the Director may require any person specified in the proposals to furnish to the Director such information as the Director may specify in accordance with the proposals, or, if the proposals have been approved with modifications, in accordance with the proposals as so modified.   **[14]**

NOTE
    See notes 3, 4 and 5 to s 44.

46. Supplementary provisions as to requirements to furnish information

(1) Any power conferred on the Director by the preceding provisions of this Part of this Act to require a person to furnish information shall be exercisable by notice in writing served on that person.

(2) Any person who refuses or wilfully neglects to furnish to the Director information required by such a notice shall be guilty of an offence and shall be liable on summary conviction to a fine not exceeding [level 5 on the standard scale][1].

(3) . . .[2]   **[15]**

NOTE
    See notes 1, 2, 4 and 5 to s 44.

AMENDMENTS
    1 The reference to level 5 on the standard scale is substituted by virtue of the Criminal Justice Act 1982, ss 38, 46.
    2 Sub-s (3) repealed by the Companies Act 1989, ss 153, 212, Sch 20, para 1, Sch 24, as from 1 April 1990.

Monopoly references

47. General provisions as to monopoly references

(1) A monopoly reference —

    (*a*) shall specify the description of goods or services to which it relates;

    (*b*) in the case of a reference relating to goods, shall state whether it relates to the supply of goods or to exports of goods from the United Kingdom or to both; and

    (*c*) if, for the purposes of the reference, consideration is to be limited to a part of the United Kingdom, shall specify the part of the United Kingdom to which consideration is to be limited,

and (subject to the next following subsection) shall be framed in one or other of the ways specified in section 48 or section 49 of this Act.

(2) A monopoly reference (whether it falls within section 48 or within section 49 of this Act) may be so framed as to require the Commission to exclude from consideration, or to limit consideration to, —

    (*a*) such agreements as are mentioned in paragraph (*d*) of section 6(1) or paragraph (*d*) of section 7(1) of this Act (or in either of those paragraphs as modified by section 9(2) of this Act) or as are mentioned in subsection (2) or subsection (3) of section 8 of this Act, or

    (*b*) agreements or practices whereby persons conduct their affairs as mentioned in section 6(2) or section 7(2) of this Act,

or to exclude from consideration, or to limit consideration to, such one or more agreements or practices falling within paragraph (*a*) or paragraph (*b*) of this subsection as are specified in the reference.   **[16]**

48. Monopoly reference limited to the facts

A monopoly reference may be so framed as to require the Commission only to investigate and report on the questions whether a monopoly situation exists in relation to the matters set out in the reference in accordance with section 47 of this Act and, if so, —

    (*a*) by virtue of which provisions of sections 6 to 8 of this Act that monopoly situation is to be taken to exist;

    (*b*) in favour of what person or persons that monopoly situation exists;

    (*c*) whether any steps (by way of uncompetitive practices or otherwise) are being taken by that person or those persons for the purpose of exploiting or maintaining the monopoly situation and, if so, by what uncompetitive practices or in what other way; and

    (*d*) whether any action or omission on the part of that person or those persons is attributable to the existence of the monopoly situation and, if so, what action or omission and in what way it is so attributable;

and a monopoly reference so framed is in this Act referred to as a "monopoly reference limited to the facts".   **[17]**

400014 16 .

49. Monopoly reference not limited to the facts

(1) A monopoly reference may be so framed as to require the Commission to investigate and report on the question whether a monopoly situation exists in relation to the matters set out in the reference in accordance with section 47 of this Act and, if so, to investigate and report —

    (a) on the questions mentioned in paragraphs (a) to (d) of section 48 of this Act, and

    (b) on the question whether any facts found by the Commission in pursuance of their investigations under the preceding provisions of this subsection operate, or may be expected to operate, against the public interest.

(2) A monopoly reference may be so framed as to require the Commission to investigate and report on the questions whether a monopoly situation exists in relation to the matters set out in the reference in accordance with section 47 of this Act and, if so, —

    (a) by virtue of which provisions of sections 6 to 8 of this Act that monopoly situation is to be taken to exist;

    (b) in favour of what person or persons that monopoly situation exists; and

    (c) whether any action or omission on the part of that person or those persons in respect of matters specified in the reference for the purposes of this paragraph operates, or may be expected to operate, against the public interest.

(3) For the purposes of subsection (2)(c) of this section any matter may be specified in a monopoly reference if it relates to any of the following, that is to say —

    (a) prices charged, or proposed to be charged, for goods or services of the description specified in the reference;

    (b) any recommendation or suggestion made as to such prices;

    (c) any refusal to supply goods or services of the description specified in the reference;

    (d) any preference given to any person (whether by way of discrimination in respect of prices or in respect of priority of supply or otherwise) in relation to the supply of goods or services of that description;

and any matter not falling within any of the preceding paragraphs may be specified for those purposes in a monopoly reference if, in the opinion of the person or persons making the reference, it is of a kind such that (if a monopoly situation is found to exist) that matter might reasonably be regarded as a step taken for the purpose of exploiting or maintaining that situation or as being attributable to the existence of that situation.

(4) A monopoly reference framed in either of the ways mentioned in subsections (1) and (2) of this section is in this Act referred to as a "monopoly reference not limited to the facts".   [18]

50. Monopoly references by Director

(1) Where it appears to the Director that a monopoly situation exists or may exist in relation to —

(*a*) the supply of goods of any description, or

(*b*) the supply of services of any description, or

(*c*) exports of goods of any description from the United Kingdom, either generally or to any particular market,

the Director, subject to section 12 of this Act and to the following provisions of this section, may if he thinks fit make a monopoly reference to the Commission with respect to the existence or possible existence of such a monopoly situation.

(2) No monopoly reference shall be made by the Director with respect to the existence or possible existence of a monopoly situation in relation to the supply of goods or services of any description specified in Part I of Schedule 5 or in Part I of Schedule 7 to this Act.

(3) Notwithstanding anything in subsections (3) and (4) of section 10 of this Act —

(*a*) for the purposes of any monopoly reference made by the Director the supply of goods or services of any description specified in the first column [. . .] of Part II of Schedule 7 to this Act in any manner specified in relation to that description of goods or services in the second column of Part II of the relevant Schedule shall be taken to be a separate form of supply, and

(*b*) any monopoly reference made by the Director in relation to the supply of goods or services of any such description shall be limited so as to exclude that form of supply.

(4) For the purposes of any monopoly reference made by the Director in relation to goods of any description specified in the first column of Part III of Schedule 7 to this Act —

(*a*) the supply of goods of that description in Northern Ireland in any manner specified in relation to that description of goods in the second column of that Part of that Schedule shall be taken to be a separate form of supply, and, notwithstanding anything in section 10(3) and (4) of this Act, any monopoly reference so made in relation to the supply of goods of any such description in Northern Ireland shall be limited so as to exclude that form of supply, and

(*b*) for the purposes of any such monopoly reference the Director shall so exercise his powers under section 9 of this Act as to comply with the requirements of the preceding paragraph.

(5) The Secretary of State may by order made by statutory instrument vary any of the provisions of Schedule 7 to this Act, either by adding one or more further entries or by altering or deleting any entry for the time being contained in it; and any reference in this Act to that Schedule shall be construed as a reference to that Schedule as for the time being in force.

(6) On making a monopoly reference to the Commission, the Director shall send a copy of it to the Secretary of State; and if, before the end of the period of fourteen days from the day on which the reference is first published in the Gazette in accordance with section 53 of this Act, the Secretary of State directs the Commission not to proceed with the reference, —

(a) the Commission shall not proceed with that reference, but

(b) nothing in the preceding paragraph shall prevent the Commission from proceeding with any subsequent monopoly reference, notwithstanding that it relates wholly or partly to the same matters.   [19]

NOTES

1 See notes 3, 4 and 5 to s 44, above.

2 See further, as to the powers exercisable in consequence of report of Monopolies and Mergers Commission, the Patents Act 1977, s 51, as substituted by the Copyright, Designs and Patents Act 1988, s 295, Sch 5, para 14.

3 For an order under sub-s (5) see the Monopoly References (Alteration of Exclusions) Order 1984, below.

AMENDMENT

Words in sub-s (3)(a) repealed by the Telecommunications Act 1984, s 109(6), Sch 1.

51. Monopoly references by Ministers

(1) Subject to the following provisions of this section, the Secretary of State, or the Secretary of State and any other Minister acting jointly, where it appears to him or them that a monopoly situation exists or may exist in relation to—

(a) the supply of goods of any description, or

(b) the supply of services of any description, or

(c) exports of goods of any description from the United Kingdom, either generally or to any particular market,

may, if the Secretary of State (or, in the case of joint action by the Secretary of State and another Minister, each of them) thinks fit, make a monopoly reference to the Commission with respect to the existence or possible existence of such a monopoly situation.

(2) Where it appears to the Secretary of State that a monopoly situation exists or may exist as mentioned in the preceding subsection, and that the goods or services in question are of a description specified in Part I of, [. . .]¹, Schedule 5 or Schedule 7 to this Act, the Secretary of State shall not make a monopoly reference with respect to the existence or possible existence of that situation except jointly with such one or more of the Ministers mentioned in the next following subsection as appear to him to have functions directly relating—

(a) to the supply of goods or services of that description in the area (whether consisting of the whole or part of the United Kingdom) in relation to which the question arises, or

(b) to exports of goods of that description from the United Kingdom,

as the case may be.

(3) The Ministers referred to in subsection (2) of this section are the Secretary of State for Scotland, the Secretary of State for Wales, the Secretary of State for Northern Ireland, the Secretary of State for the Environment, the Minister of Agriculture, Fisheries and Food, the Minister of Agriculture for Northern Ireland, the Minister of Commerce for Northern Ireland. . . .²

(4) Where it appears to the Secretary of State that a monopoly situation exists or may exist as mentioned in subsection (1) of this section in relation to the supply in Northern Ireland of goods of a description specified in the first column of

Part III of Schedule 7 to this Act, the Secretary of State shall not make a monopoly reference with respect to the existence or possible existence of that situation except jointly with the Minister of Agriculture for Northern Ireland.   **[20]**

NOTES

1 See Competition Act 1980, s 21 as to the power of the Secretary of State to make a monopoly reference acting alone.

2 See note 2 to s 50, above.

AMENDMENTS

1 Words in sub-s (2) repealed by the Telecommunications Act 1984, s 109(6), Sch 7.

2 Words in sub-s (3) repealed by the Ministry of Posts and Telecommunications (Dissolution) Order 1974.

52. Variation of monopoly reference

(1) Subject to the following provisions of this section, the Director may at any time vary a monopoly reference made by him, and the Secretary of State (or, in the case of a monopoly reference made by the Secretary of State jointly with one or more other Ministers, the Secretary of State and that Minister or those Ministers acting jointly) may vary a monopoly reference made by him or them.

(2) A monopoly reference not limited to the facts shall not be varied so as to become a monopoly reference limited to the facts; but (subject to the following provisions of this section) a monopoly reference limited to the facts may be varied so as to become a monopoly reference not limited to the facts, whether the Commission have already reported on the reference as originally made or not.

(3) A monopoly reference made by the Director shall not be varied so as to become a reference which he is precluded from making by any provisions of section 50 of this Act.

(4) On varying a monopoly reference made by him, the Director shall send a copy of the variation to the Secretary of State; and if, before the end of the period of fourteen days from the day on which the variation is first published in the Gazette in accordance with the next following section, the Secretary of State directs the Commission not to give effect to the variation, –

   (a) the Commission shall proceed with the reference as if that variation had not been made, but

   (b) nothing in the preceding paragraph shall prevent the Commission from proceeding with any subsequent monopoly reference, or from giving effect to any subsequent variation, notwithstanding that it relates wholly or partly to the matters to which that variation related.

(5) In this section and in sections 53 to 55 of this Act "Minister" includes the Minister of Agriculture for Northern Ireland and the Minister of Commerce for Northern Ireland.   **[21]**

NOTE

See notes 3, 4 and 5 to s 44, above.

53. Publication of monopoly references and variations, and of directions relating to them

(1) On making a monopoly reference, or a variation of a monopoly reference,

the Director or, as the case may be, the Secretary of State (or, in the case of a monopoly reference or variation made by the Secretary of State acting jointly with one or more other Ministers, the Secretary of State and that Minister or those Ministers acting jointly) shall arrange for the reference or variation to be published in full in the Gazette, and shall arrange for the reference or variation to be published in such other manner as he or they may think most suitable for bringing it to the attention of persons who, in his or their opinion, would be affected by it.

(2) Where the Secretary of State gives a direction under section 50(6) of this Act with respect to a monopoly reference, or gives a direction under section 52(4) of this Act with respect to a variation of a monopoly reference, the Secretary of State shall arrange for the direction to be published in the Gazette and otherwise in the same manner as the monopoly reference or variation was published in accordance with the preceding subsection.

(3) In this section "the Gazette" means the London, Edinburgh and Belfast Gazettes, except that, in relation to a monopoly reference under which consideration is limited to a particular part of the United Kingdom in accordance with section 9 of this Act (including a reference under which consideration is required to be so limited by section 50(4)(*b*) of this Act), it means such one or more of those Gazettes as are appropriate to that part of the United Kingdom.

(4) In sections 50 and 52 of this Act any reference to publication in the Gazette is a reference to publication in the London Gazette, the Edinburgh Gazette or the Belfast Gazette, whichever first occurs.   [22]

NOTE
    See notes 3, 4 and 5 to s 44, above.

54. Report of Commission on monopoly reference

(1) A report of the Commission on a monopoly reference —

   (*a*) if the reference was made by the Director, shall be made to the Secretary of State, and

   (*b*) in any other case, shall be made to the Minister or Ministers by whom the reference was made.

(2) In making their report on a monopoly reference, the Commission shall include in it definite conclusions on the questions comprised in the reference, together with —

   (*a*) such an account of their reasons for those conclusions, and

   (*b*) such a survey of the general position with respect to the subject-matter of the reference, and of the developments which have led to that position,

as in their opinion are expedient for facilitating a proper understanding of those questions and of their conclusions.

(3) Where, on a monopoly reference not limited to the facts, the Commission find that a monopoly situation exists and that facts found by the Commission in pursuance of their investigations under subsection (1) or subsection (2) of section

49 of this Act operate, or may be expected to operate, against the public interest, the report shall specify those facts, and the conclusions to be included in the report, in so far as they relate to the operation of those facts, shall specify the particular effects, adverse to the public interest, which in their opinion those facts have or may be expected to have; and the Commission—

(a) shall, as part of their investigations, consider what action (if any) should be taken for the purpose of remedying or preventing those adverse effects, and

(b) may, if they think fit, include in their report recommendations as to such action.

(4) In paragraph (a) of subsection (3) of this section the reference to action to be taken for the purpose mentioned in that paragraph is a reference to action to be taken for that purpose either—

(a) by one or more Ministers (including Ministers of departments of the Government of Northern Ireland) or other public authorities, or

(b) by the person or (as the case may be) one or more of the persons in whose favour, in accordance with the findings of the Commission, the monopoly situation in question exists.

(5) Where, on a monopoly reference not limited to the facts, the Commission find—

(a) that a monopoly situation exists, and

(b) that the person (or, if more than one, any of the persons) in whose favour it exists is a party to an agreement to which [the Act of 1976][1] applies,

the Commission, in making their report on that reference, shall exclude from their consideration the question whether the provisions of that agreement, in so far as they are provisions by virtue of which it is an agreement to which that Act applies, operate, or may be expected to operate, against the public interest; and subsection (3) of this section, in so far as it refers to facts found by the Commission in pursuance of their investigations, shall have effect subject to the provisions of this subsection. **[23]**

NOTE
See notes 4 and 5 to s 44, above.

AMENDMENT
1 Words in sub-s (5)(b) substituted by RTPA 1976, Sch 5.

55. Time-limit for report on monopoly reference

(1) A monopoly reference shall specify a period within which the Commission are to report on the reference; and, if a report of the Commission on the reference—

(a) is not made before the end of the period so specified, or

(b) if one or more extended periods are allowed under the next following subsection, is not made before the end of that extended period or of the last of those extended periods, as the case may be,

the reference shall cease to have effect and no action, or (if action has already been taken) no further action, shall be taken in relation to that reference under this Act.

(2) Directions may be given —

(*a*) in the case of a monopoly reference made by the Director or by the Secretary of State otherwise than jointly with one or more Ministers, by the Secretary of State, or

(*b*) in the case of a monopoly reference made by the Secretary of State jointly with one or more other Ministers, by the Secretary of State and that Minister or those Ministers acting jointly,

allowing to the Commission such extended period for the purpose of reporting on the reference as may be specified in the directions, or, if the period has already been extended once or more than once by directions under this subsection, allowing to the Commission such further extended period for that purpose as may be so specified.   **[24]**

NOTE
  See notes 4 and 5 to s 44, above.

56. Order of appropriate Minister on report on monopoly reference

(1) The provisions of this section shall have effect where a report of the Commission on a monopoly reference not limited to the facts has been laid before Parliament in accordance with the provisions of Part VII of this Act, and the conclusions of the Commission set out in the report, as so laid, —

(*a*) include conclusions to the effect that a monopoly situation exists and that facts found by the Commission in pursuance of their investigations under section 49 of this Act operate, or may be expected to operate, against the public interest, and

(*b*) specify particular effects, adverse to the public interest, which in their opinion those facts have or may be expected to have.

(2) In the circumstances mentioned in the preceding subsection the appropriate Minister may (subject to subsection (6) of this section) by order made by statutory instrument exercise such one or more of the powers specified in Parts I and II of Schedule 8 to this Act as he considers it requisite to exercise for the purpose of remedying or preventing the adverse effects specified in the report as mentioned in the preceding subsection; and those powers may be so exercised to such extent and in such manner as the appropriate Minister considers requisite for that purpose.

(3) In determining whether, or to what extent or in what manner, to exercise any of those powers, the appropriate Minister shall take into account any recommendations included in the report of the Commission in pursuance of section 54(3)(*b*) of this Act and any advice given by the Director under section 88 of this Act.

(4) Subject to the next following subsection, in this section "the appropriate Minister" means the Secretary of State.

(5) Where, in any such report as is mentioned in subsection (1) of this section,

the person or one of the persons specified as being the person or persons in whose favour the monopoly situation in question exists is a body corporate fulfilling the following conditions, that is to say—

(a) that the affairs of the body corporate are managed by its members, and
(b) that by virtue of an enactment those members are appointed by a Minister,

then for the purpose of making any order under this section in relation to that body corporate (but not for the purpose of making any such order in relation to any other person) "the appropriate Minister" in this section means the Minister by whom members of that body corporate are appointed.

(6) In relation to any such body corporate as is mentioned in subsection (5) of this section, the powers exercisable by virtue of subsection (2) of this section shall not include the powers specified in Part II of Schedule 8 to this Act**[25]**

NOTE
See notes 4 and 5 to s 44, above.

ORDERS UNDER THIS SECTION.
The Restriction on Agreements (Manufacturers and Importers of Motor Cars) Order 1982, SI 1982 No 1146, the Restriction on Agreement and Conduct (Tour Operators) Order 1987, SI 1987 No 1131, the Restriction on Conduct (Specialist Advertising Services) Order 1988, SI 1988 No 1017, and the Films (Exclusivity Agreements) Order 1989, SI 1989 No 271, the Supply of Beer (Loan Ties, Licensed Premises and Wholesale Prices) Order 1989, SI 1989 No 2258, the Supply of Beer (Tied Estate) Order 1989, SI 1989 No 2390. By virtue of s 139(2), Sch 11, para 1 post, the Monopolies and Restrictive Practices (Dental Goods) Order 1951, SI 1951 No 1200, the Monopolies and Restrictive Practices (Imported Hardwood and Softwood Timber) Order 1960, SI 1960 No 1211, and the Restriction on Agreements (Estate Agents) Order 1970, SI 1970 No 1696, have effect as if made under this section.

PART V

MERGERS

Newspaper merger references

57. Meaning of "newspaper", "transfer of newspaper or of newspaper assets" and related expressions

(1) In this Part of this Act—

(a) "newspaper" means a daily, Sunday or local (other than daily or Sunday) newspaper circulating wholly or mainly in the United Kingdom or in a part of the United Kingdom;
(b) "newspaper proprietor" includes (in addition to an actual proprietor of a newspaper) any person having a controlling interest in a body corporate which is a newspaper proprietor, and any body corporate in which a newspaper proprietor has a controlling interest;

and any reference to the newspapers of a newspaper proprietor includes all newspapers in relation to which he is a newspaper proprietor and, in the case of a body corporate, all newspapers in relation to which a person having a controlling interest in that body corporate is a newspaper proprietor.

(2) In this Part of this Act "transfer of a newspaper or of newspaper assets" means any of the following transactions, that is to say—

(a) any transaction (whether involving a transfer or not) by virtue of which a person would become, or would acquire the right to become, a newspaper proprietor in relation to a newspaper;

(b) any transfer of assets necessary to the continuation of a newspaper as a separate newspaper (including goodwill or the right to use the name of the newspaper);

(c) any transfer of plant or premises used in the publication of a newspaper, other than a transfer made without a view to a change in the ownership or control of the newspaper or to its ceasing publication;

and "the newspaper concerned in the transfer", in relation to any transaction falling within paragraph (a), paragraph (b) or paragraph (c) of this subsection, means the newspaper in relation to which (as mentioned in that paragraph) the transaction is or is to be effected.

(3) In this Part of this Act "average circulation per day of publication", in relation to a newspaper, means its average circulation for the appropriate period, ascertained by dividing the number of copies to which its circulation amounts for that period by the number of days on which the newspaper was published during that period (circulation being calculated on the basis of actual sales in the United Kingdom of the newspaper as published on those days); and for the purposes of this subsection "the appropriate period" —

(a) in a case in which an application is made for consent under the next following section, means the period of six months ending six weeks before the date of the application, or

(b) in a case in which a transfer or purported transfer is made without any such application for consent, means the period of six months ending six weeks before the date of the transfer or purported transfer.

(4) For the purposes of this section a person has a controlling interest in a body corporate if (but only if) he can, directly or indirectly, determine the manner in which one-quarter of the votes which could be cast at a general meeting of the body corporate are to be cast on matters, and in circumstances, not of such a description as to bring into play any special voting rights or restrictions on voting rights.   [26]

58. Prohibition of certain newspaper mergers

(1) Subject to the following provisions of this section, a transfer of a newspaper or of newspaper assets to a newspaper proprietor whose newspapers have an average circulation per day of publication amounting, together with that of the newspaper concerned in the transfer, to 500,000 or more copies shall be unlawful and void, unless the transfer is made with written consent given (conditionally or unconditionally) by the Secretary of State.

(2) Except as provided by subsections (3) and (4) of this section and by section 60(3) of this Act, the consent of the Secretary of State under the preceding subsection shall not be given in respect of a transfer until after the Secretary of State has received a report on the matter from the Commission.

(3) Where the Secretary of State is satisfied that the newspaper concerned in the transfer is not economic as a going concern and as a separate newspaper, then—

(a) if he is also satisfied that, if the newspaper is to continue as a separate newspaper, the case is one of urgency, he may give his consent to the transfer without requiring a report from the Commission under this section;

(b) if he is satisfied that the newspaper is not intended to continue as a separate newspaper, he shall give his consent to the transfer, and shall give it unconditionally, without requiring such a report.

(4) If the Secretary of State is satisfied that the newspaper concerned in the transfer has an average circulation per day of publication of not more than 25,000 copies, he may give his consent to the transfer without requiring a report from the Commission under this section.

(5) The Secretary of State may by order made by statutory instrument provide, subject to any transitional provisions contained in the order, that for any number specified in subsection (1) or subsection (4) of this section (whether as originally enacted or as previously varied by an order under this subsection) there shall be substituted such other number as is specified in the order.

(6) In this section "satisfied" means satisfied by such evidence as the Secretary of State may require. [27]

59. Newspaper merger reference

(1) Where an application is made to the Secretary of State for his consent to a transfer of a newspaper or of newspaper assets, the Secretary of State, subject to the next following subsection, shall, within one month after receiving the application, refer the matter to the Commission for investigation and report.

(2) The Secretary of State shall not make a reference to the Commission under the preceding subsection in a case where—

(a) by virtue of subsection (3) of section 58 of this Act he is required to give his consent unconditionally without requiring a report from the Commission under this section, or

(b) by virtue of subsection (3) or subsection (4) of that section he has power to give his consent without requiring such a report from the Commission, and determines to exercise that power,

or where the application is expressed to depend on the operation of subsection (3) or subsection (4) of that section.

(3) On a reference made to them under this section (in this Act referred to as a "newspaper merger reference") the Commission shall report to the Secretary of State whether the transfer in question may be expected to operate against the public interest, taking into account all matters which appear in the circumstances to be relevant and, in particular, the need for accurate presentation of news and free expression of opinion. [28]

60. Time-limit for report on newspaper merger reference

(1) A report of the Commission on a newspaper merger reference shall be made before the end of [such period (not being longer than three months beginning with the date of the reference) as may be specified in the]¹ reference or of such further period (if any) as the Secretary of State may allow for the purpose in accordance with the next following subsection.

(2) The Secretary of State shall not allow any further period for a report on such a reference except on representations made by the Commission and on being satisfied that there are special reasons why the report cannot be made within the [period specified in the newspaper merger reference]¹; and the Secretary of State shall allow only one such further period on any one reference, and no such further period shall be longer than three months.

(3) If on such a reference the Commission have not made their report before the end of the period specified in [the newspaper merger reference]¹ or of any further period allowed under subsection (2) of this section, the Secretary of State may, without waiting for the report, give his consent to the transfer to which the reference relates.   **[29]**

AMENDMENTS
1 Words in sub-ss (1)-(3) substituted by the Companies Act 1989, s 153, Sch 20, para 2, but not in relation to any newspaper merger reference made before 16 November 1989.

61. Report on newspaper merger reference

(1) In making their report on a newspaper merger reference, the Commission shall include in it definite conclusions on the questions comprised in the reference, together with—

(a) such an account of their reasons for those conclusions, and

(b) such a survey of the general position with respect to the transfer of a newspaper or of newspaper assets to which the reference relates, and of the developments which have led to that position,

as in their opinion are expedient for facilitating a proper understanding of those questions and of their conclusions.

(2) Where on such a reference the Commission find that the transfer of a newspaper or of newspaper assets in question might operate against the public interest, the Commission shall consider whether any (and, if so, what) conditions might be attached to any consent to the transfer in order to prevent the transfer from so operating, and may, if they think fit, include in their report recommendations as to such conditions.   **[30]**

62. Enforcement provisions relating to newspaper mergers

(1) Any person who is knowingly concerned in, or privy to, a purported transfer of a newspaper or of newspaper assets which is unlawful by virtue of section 58 of this Act shall be guilty of an offence.

(2) Where under that section the consent of the Secretary of State is given to

a transfer of a newspaper or of newspaper assets, but is given subject to one or more conditions, any person who is knowingly concerned in, or privy to, a breach of that condition, or of any of those conditions, as the case may be, shall be guilty of an offence.

(3) A person guilty of an offence under this section shall be liable, on conviction on indictment, to imprisonment for a term not exceeding two years or to a fine or to both.

(4) No proceedings for an offence under this section shall be instituted —

(a) in England or Wales, except by, or with the consent of, the Director of Public Prosecutions, or

(b) in Northern Ireland, except by, or with the consent of, the Director of Public Prosecutions for Northern Ireland.   **[31]**

Other merger references

63. Merger references to which ss 64 to 75 apply

(1) Sections 64 [to 75K of this Act shall not have effect in relation to]¹ newspaper merger references; and accordingly in those sections "merger reference" shall be construed —

(a) as not including a reference made under section 59 of this Act, but

(b) as including any merger reference relating to a transfer of a newspaper or of newspaper assets, if the reference is made under section 64 or section 75 of this Act in a case falling within section 59(2) of this Act.

(2) In the following provisions of this Part of this Act "enterprise" means the activities, or part of the activities, of a business.   **[32]**

AMENDMENTS
1 Words substituted by the Companies Act 1989, s 153, Sch 20, para 3, as from 16 November 1989.

64. Merger situation qualifying for investigation

(1) A merger reference may be made to the Commission by the Secretary of State where it appears to him that it is or may be the fact that two or more enterprises (in this section referred to as "the relevant enterprises"), of which one at least was carried on in the United Kingdom or by or under the control of a body corporate incorporated in the United Kingdom, have, at a time or in circumstances falling within subsection (4) of this section, ceased to be distinct enterprises, and that either —

(a) as a result, the condition specified in subsection (2) or in subsection (3) of this section prevails, or does so to a greater extent, with respect to the supply of goods or services of any description, or

(b) the value of the assets taken over exceeds [£30 million]¹.

(2) The condition referred to in subsection (1)(a) of this section, in relation to the supply of goods of any description, is that at least one-quarter of all the

goods of that description which are supplied in the United Kingdom, or in a substantial part of the United Kingdom, either —

(*a*) are supplied by one and the same person or are supplied to one and the same person, or

(*b*) are supplied by the persons by whom the relevant enterprises (so far as they continue to be carried on) are carried on, or are supplied to those persons.

(3) The condition referred to in subsection (1)(*a*) of this section, in relation to the supply of services of any description, is that the supply of services of that description in the United Kingdom, or in a substantial part of the United Kingdom, is, to the extent of at least one-quarter, either —

(*a*) supply by one and the same person, or supply for one and the same person, or

(*b*) supply by the persons by whom the relevant enterprises (so far as they continue to be carried on) are carried on, or supply for those persons.

(4) For the purposes of subsection (1) of this section enterprises shall be taken to have ceased to be distinct enterprises at a time or in circumstances falling within this subsection if either —

(*a*) they did so not earlier than six months before the date on which the merger reference relating to them is to be made, or

(*b*) they did so under or in consequence of arrangements or transactions which were entered into without prior notice being given to the Secretary of State or to the Director of material facts about the proposed arrangements or transactions and in circumstances in which those facts had not been made public, and notice of those facts was not given to the Secretary of State or to the Director or made public more than six months before the date mentioned in the preceding paragraph.

(5) In determining whether to make a merger reference to the Commission the Secretary of State shall have regard, with a view to the prevention or removal of uncertainty, to the need for making a determination as soon as is reasonably practicable.

(6) On making a merger reference, the Secretary of State shall arrange for it to be published in such manner as he thinks most suitable for bringing it to the attention of persons who in his opinion would be affected by it.

(7) The Secretary of State may by order made by statutory instrument provide, subject to any transitional provisions contained in the order, that for the sum specified in subsection (1)(*b*) of this section (whether as originally enacted or as previously varied by an order under this subsection) there shall be substituted such other sum (not being less than 5 million) as is specified in the order.

(8) The fact that two or more enterprises have ceased to be distinct enterprises in the circumstances described in subsection (1) of this section (including in those circumstances the result specified in paragraph (*a*), or fulfilment of the condition specified in paragraph (*b*), of that subsection) shall, for the purposes of this Act, be regarded as creating a merger situation qualifying for investigation; and in this Act "merger situation qualifying for investigation" and any reference to the creation of such a situation shall be construed accordingly.

(9) In this section "made public" means so publicised as to be generally known or readily ascertainable.   **[33]**

NOTE

Where, on a reference under this section or s 75, the Commission's report concludes that a merger situation operating against the public interest exists in relation to patented products, as to relief available in respect of the patent; see the Patents Act 1977, s 51(3), as substituted by the Copyright, Designs and Patents Act 1988, s 295, Sch 5, para 14.

A merger reference may be made under this section in a case in which the relevant enterprises ceased to be distinct enterprises at a time and in circumstances not falling within sub-s (4) if by reason of Council Regulation (EEC) No 4064/89 of 21 December 1989 on the Control of Concentrations between Undertakings or anything done under or in accordance with that Regulation the reference could not have been made earlier than six months before the date on which it is to be made: the EEC Merger Control (Consequential Provisions) Regulations 1990, SI 1990 No 1563 in force with effect on or after 21 September 1990.

AMENDMENT

1 The sum specified in para (*b*) of s 64(1) was increased from £15 million to £30 million with effect from 26 July 1984: Merger References (Increase in Value of Assets) Order 1984, SI 1984 No 932.

65. Enterprises ceasing to be distinct enterprises

(1) For the purposes of this Part of this Act any two enterprises shall be regarded as ceasing to be distinct enterprises if either —

> (*a*) they are brought under common ownership or common control (whether or not the business to which either of them formerly belonged continues to be carried on under the same or different ownership or control), or
>
> (*b*) either of the enterprises ceases to be carried on at all and does so in consequence of any arrangements or transaction entered into to prevent competition between the enterprises.

(2) For the purposes of the preceding subsection enterprises shall (without prejudice to the generality of the words "common control" in that subsection) be regarded as being under common control if they are —

> (*a*) enterprises of interconnected bodies corporate, or
>
> (*b*) enterprises carried on by two or more bodies corporate of which one and the same person or group of persons has control, or
>
> (*c*) an enterprise carried on by a body corporate and an enterprise carried on by a person or group of persons having control of that body corporate.

(3) A person or group of persons able, directly or indirectly, to control or materially to influence the policy of a body corporate, or the policy of any person in carrying on an enterprise, but without having a controlling interest in that body corporate or in that enterprise, may for the purposes of subsections (1) and (2) of this section be treated as having control of it.

(4) For the purposes of subsection (1)(*a*) of this section, in so far as it relates to bringing two or more enterprises under common control, a person or group of persons may be treated as bringing an enterprise under his or their control if —

> (*a*) being already able to control or materially to influence the policy of the person carrying on the enterprise, that person or group of persons acquires a controlling interest in the enterprise or, in the case of an enterprise carried on by a body corporate, acquires a controlling interest in that body corporate, or

(*b*) being already able materially to influence the policy of the person carrying on the enterprise, that person or group of persons becomes able to control that policy. [34]

66. Time when enterprises cease to be distinct

(1) Where under or in consequence of the same arrangements or transaction, or under or in consequence of successive arrangements or transactions between the same parties or interests, successive events to which this subsection applies occur within a period of two years, then for the purposes of a merger reference those events may, if the Secretary of State [or the Commission][1] thinks fit, be treated as having occurred simultaneously on the date on which the latest of them occurred.

(2) The preceding subsection applies to any event whereby, under or in consequence of the arrangements or the transaction or transactions in question, any enterprises cease as between themselves to be distinct enterprises.

(3) For the purposes of subsection (1) of this section any arrangements or transactions may be treated by the Secretary of State [or the Commission][1] as arrangements or transactions between the same interests if it appears to him to be appropriate that they should be so treated, having regard to the persons who are substantially concerned in them.

(4) Subject to the preceding provisions of this section [and to section 66A of this Act][1], the time at which any two enterprises cease to be distinct enterprises, where they do so under or in consequence of any arrangements or transaction not having immediate effect, or having immediate effect in part only, shall be taken to be the time when the parties to the arrangements or transaction become bound to such extent as will result, on effect being given to their obligations, in the enterprises ceasing to be distinct enterprises.

(5) In accordance with subsection (4) of this section (but without prejudice to the generality of that subsection) for the purpose of determining the time at which any two enterprises cease to be distinct enterprises no account shall be taken of any option or other conditional right until the option is exercised or the condition is satisfied. [35]

AMENDMENT
1 Words added by the Companies Act 1989, s 153, Sch 20, paras 4, 10, although not in relation to any merger reference made before 16 November 1989.

[66A. Obtaining control by stages

(1) Where an enterprise is brought under the control of a person or group of persons in the course of two or more transactions (referred to in this section as a "series of transactions") falling within subsection (2) of this section, those transactions may, if the Secretary of State or, as the case may be, the Commission thinks fit, be treated for the purposes of a merger reference as having occurred simultaneously on the date on which the latest of them occurred.

(2) The transactions falling within this subsection are—

(*a*) any transaction which —
  (i) enables that person or group of persons directly or indirectly to control or materially to influence the policy of any person carrying on the enterprise,
  (ii) enables that person or group of persons to do so to a greater degree, or
  (iii) is a step (whether direct or indirect) towards enabling that person or group of persons to do so, and
(*b*) any transaction whereby that person or group of persons acquires a controlling interest in the enterprise or, where the enterprise is carried on by a body corporate, in that body corporate.

(3) Where a series of transactions includes a transaction falling within subsection (2)(*b*) of this section, any transaction occurring after the occurrence of that transaction is to be disregarded for the purposes of subsection (1) of this section.

(4) Where the period within which a series of transactions occurs exceeds two years, the transactions that may be treated as mentioned in subsection (1) of this section are any of those transactions that occur within a period of two years.

(5) Sections 65(2) to (4) and 77(1) and (4) to (6) of this Act apply for the purposes of this section to determine whether an enterprise is brought under the control of a person or group of persons and whether a transaction falls within subsection (2) of this section as they apply for the purposes of section 65 of this Act to determine whether enterprises are brought under common control.

(6) In determining for the purposes of this section the time at which any transaction occurs, no account shall be taken of any option or other conditional right until the option is exercised or the condition is satisfied.]   [36]

AMENDMENT

This section was inserted by the Companies Act 1989, s 150(1) in relation to any merger reference made on or after 16 November 1989.

67. Valuation of assets taken over

(1) The provisions of this section shall have effect for the purposes of section 64(1)(*b*) of this Act.

(2) Subject to subsection (4) of this section, the value of the assets taken over —

(*a*) shall be determined by taking the total value of the assets employed in, or appropriated to, the enterprises which cease to be distinct enterprises, except
  [(i) any enterprise which remains under the same ownership and control, or
  (ii) if none of the enterprises remains under the same ownership and control, the enterprise having the assets with the highest value, and][1]
(*b*) shall be so determined by reference to the values at which, on the enterprises ceasing to be distinct enterprises or (if they have not then done so) on the making of the merger reference to the Commission, the assets

stand in the books of the relevant business, less any relevant provisions for depreciation, renewals or diminution in value.

(3) For the purposes of subsection (2) of this section any assets of a body corporate which, on a change in the control of the body corporate or of any enterprise of it, are dealt with in the same way as assets appropriated to any such enterprise shall be treated as appropriated to that enterprise.

(4) Where in accordance with subsection (1) of section 66 [or subsection (1) of section 66A]¹ of this Act events to which [either of those subsections]¹ applies are treated as having occurred simultaneously, subsection (2) of this section shall apply with such adjustments as appear to the Secretary of State or to the Commission to be appropriate.   [37]

AMENDMENT
1 Sub-ss (2)(*a*), (4) amended by the Companies Act 1989, s 153, Sch 20, paras 5, 10, although not in relation to any merger reference made before 16 November 1989.

68. Supplementary provisions as to merger situations qualifying for investigation

(1) In relation to goods or services of any description which are the subject of different forms of supply—

(*a*) references in subsection (2) of section 64 of this Act to the supply of goods, or

(*b*) references in subsection (3) of that section to the supply of services,

shall be construed in whichever of the following ways appears to the Secretary of State or the Commission, as the case may be, to be appropriate in all the circumstances, that is to say, as references to any of those forms of supply taken separately, to all those forms of supply taken together, or to any of those forms of supply taken in groups.

(2) For the purposes of the preceding subsection the Secretary of State or the Commission may treat goods or services as being the subject of different forms of supply whenever the transactions in question differ as to their nature, their parties, their terms or their surrounding circumstances, and the difference is one which, in the opinion of the Secretary of State or of the Commission, as the case may be, ought for the purposes of that subsection to be treated as a material difference.

(3) For the purpose of determining whether the proportion of one-quarter mentioned in subsection (2) or subsection (3) of section 64 of this Act is fulfilled with respect to goods or services of any description, the Secretary of State or the Commission, as the case may be, shall apply such criterion (whether it be value or cost or price or quantity or capacity or number of workers employed or some other criterion, of whatever nature) or such combination of criteria as may appear to the Secretary of State or the Commission to be most suitable in all the circumstances.

(4) The criteria for determining when goods or services can be treated, for the purposes of section 64 of this Act, as goods or services of a separate description shall be such as in any particular case the Secretary of State [or, as the case may

be, the Commission]¹ thinks most suitable in the circumstances of that case.

[38]

AMENDMENT
1 Sub-s (4) amended by the Companies Act 1989, s 153, Sch 20, paras 6, 10, but not in relation to any merger reference made before 16 November 1989.

69. Different kinds of merger references

(1) Subject to the following provisions of this Part of this Act, on a merger reference the Commission shall investigate and report on the questions—

(a) whether a merger situation qualifying for investigation has been created, and

(b) if so, whether the creation of that situation operates, or may be expected to operate, against the public interest.

(2) A merger reference may be so framed as to require the Commission, in relation to the question whether a merger situation qualifying for investigation has been created, to exclude from consideration paragraph (a) of subsection (1) of section 64 of this Act, or to exclude from consideration paragraph (b) of that subsection, or to exclude one of those paragraphs if the Commission find the other satisfied.

(3) In relation to the question whether any such result as is mentioned in section 64(1)(a) of this Act has arisen, a merger reference may be so framed as to require the Commission to confine their investigation to the supply of goods or services in a specified part of the United Kingdom.

(4) A merger reference may require the Commission, if they find that a merger situation qualifying for investigation has been created, to limit their consideration thereafter to such elements in, or possible consequences of, the creation of that situation as may be specified in the reference, and to consider whether, in respect only of those elements or possible consequences, the situation operates, or may be expected to operate, against the public interest. **[39]**

70. Time-limit for report on merger reference

(1) Every merger reference shall specify a period (not being longer than six months beginning with the date of the reference) within which a report on the reference is to be made; and a report of the Commission on a merger reference shall not have effect, and no action shall be taken in relation to it under this Act, unless the report is made before the end of that period or of such further period (if any) as may be allowed by the Secretary of State in accordance with the next following subsection.

(2) The Secretary of State shall not allow any further period for a report on a merger reference except on representations made by the Commission and on being satisfied that there are special reasons why the report cannot be made within the period specified in the reference; and the Secretary of State shall allow only one such further period on any one reference, and no such further period shall be longer than three months. **[40]**

NOTE
This section is applied by the Competition Act 1980, ss 7(6), 11(9) and, with modifications, to licence modification references to the Commission under the Telecommunications Act 1984, s 13.

71. Variation of certain merger references

(1) Subject to the following provisions of this section, the Secretary of State may at any time vary a merger reference . . .[1]

(2) . . .[1]

(3) Without prejudice to the powers of the Secretary of State under section 70 of this Act, a merger reference shall not be varied so as to specify a period within which a report on the reference is to be made which is different from the period specified in the reference in accordance with that section.   [41]

AMENDMENT
1 Words omitted from sub-s (1) and sub-s (2) repealed by the Companies Act 1989, ss 153, 212, Sch 20, paras 7, 10, Sch 24, except in relation to any merger reference made before 16 November 1989.

72. Report of Commission on merger reference

(1) In making their report on a merger reference, the Commission shall include in it definite conclusions on the questions comprised in the reference, together with—

(a) such an account of their reasons for those conclusions, and
(b) such a survey of the general position with respect to the subject-matter of the reference, and of the developments which have led to that position,

as in their opinion are expedient for facilitating a proper understanding of those questions and of their conclusions.

(2) Where on a merger reference the Commission find that a merger situation qualifying for investigation has been created and that the creation of that situation operates or may be expected to operate against the public interest (or, in a case falling within subsection (4) of section 69 of this Act, find that one or more elements in or consequences of that situation which were specified in the reference in accordance with that subsection so operate or may be expected so to operate) the Commission shall specify in their report the particular effects, adverse to the public interest, which in their opinion the creation of that situation (or, as the case may be, those elements in or consequences of it) have or may be expected to have; and the Commission—

(a) shall, as part of their investigations, consider what action (if any) should be taken for the purpose of remedying or preventing those adverse effects, and
(b) may, if they think fit, include in their report recommendations as to such action.

(3) In paragraph (a) of subsection (2) of this section the reference to action to be taken for the purpose mentioned in that paragraph is a reference to action to be taken for that purpose either—

(a) by one or more Ministers (including Ministers or departments of the Government of Northern Ireland) or other public authorities, or

(b) by one or more persons specified in the report as being persons carrying on, owning or controlling any of the enterprises which, in accordance with the conclusions of the Commission, have ceased to be distinct enterprises. **[42]**

73. Order of Secretary of State on report on merger reference

(1) The provisions of this section shall have effect where a report of the Commission on a merger reference has been laid before Parliament in accordance with the provisions of Part VII of this Act, and the conclusions of the Commission set out in the report, as so laid, —

(a) include conclusions to the effect that a merger situation qualifying for investigation has been created and that its creation, or particular elements in or consequences of it specified in the report, operate or may be expected to operate against the public interest, and

(b) specify particular effects, adverse to the public interest, which in the opinion of the Commission the creation of that situation, or (as the case may be) those elements in or consequences of it, have or may be expected to have.

(2) In the circumstances mentioned in the preceding subsection the Secretary of State may by order made by statutory instrument exercise such one or more of the powers specified in Parts I and II of Schedule 8 to this Act as he may consider it requisite to exercise for the purpose of remedying or preventing the adverse effects specified in the report as mentioned in the preceding subsection; and those powers may be so exercised to such extent and in such manner as the Secretary of State considers requisite for that purpose.

(3) In determining whether, or to what extent or in what manner, to exercise any of those powers, the Secretary of State shall take into account any recommendations included in the report of the Commission in pursuance of section 72(2)(b) of this Act and any advice given by the Director under section 88 of this Act. **[43]**

74. Interim order in respect of merger reference

(1) Where a merger reference has been made to the Commission, . . .¹ then, with a view to preventing action to which this subsection applies, the Secretary of State, subject to subsection (3) of this section, may by order made by statutory instrument —

(a) prohibit or restrict the doing of things which in his opinion would constitute action to which this subsection applies, or

(b) impose on any person concerned obligations as to the carrying on of any activities or the safeguarding of any assets, or

(c) provide for the carrying on of any activities or the safeguarding of any assets either by the appointment of a person to conduct or supervise the conduct of any activities (on such terms and with such powers as may be specified or described in the order) or in any other manner, or (*d*) exercise any of the powers which, by virtue of [paragraphs 12 and 12A]¹ of Schedule 8 to this Act, are exercisable by an order under section 73 of this Act.

(2) In relation to a merger reference the preceding subsection applies to any action which might prejudice the reference or impede the taking of any action under this Act which may be warranted by the Commission's report on the reference.

(3) No order shall be made under this section in respect of a merger reference after whichever of the following events first occurs, that is to say—

(*a*) the time (including any further period) allowed to the Commission for making a report on the reference expires without their having made such a report;

(*b*) the period of forty days beginning with the day on which a report of the Commission on the reference is laid before Parliament expires.

(4) An order under this section made in respect of a merger reference (if it has not previously ceased to have effect) shall cease to have effect on the occurrence of whichever of those events first occurs, but without prejudice to anything previously done under the order.

(5) Subsection (4) of this section shall have effect without prejudice—

(*a*) to the operation, in relation to any such order, of section 134(1) of this Act, or

(*b*) to the operation of any order made under section 73 of this Act which exercises the same or similar powers to those exercised by the order under this section.   **[44]**

AMENDMENT
1 Sub-s (1) amended by the Companies Act 1989, ss 153, 212, Sch 20, paras 8, 10, Sch 24 although not in relation to any merger reference made before 16 November 1989.

75. Reference in anticipation of merger

(1) A merger reference may be made to the Commission by the Secretary of State where it appears to him that it is or may be the fact that arrangements are in progress or in contemplation which, if carried into effect, will result in the creation of a merger situation qualifying for investigation.

(2) Subject to the following provisions of this section, on a merger reference under this section the Commission shall proceed in relation to the prospective and (if events so require) the actual results of the arrangements proposed or made as, in accordance with the preceding provisions of this Part of this Act, they could proceed if the arrangements in question had actually been made, and the results in question had followed immediately before the date of the reference under this section.

(3) A merger reference under this section may require the Commission, if they find that a merger situation qualifying for investigation has been created, or will be created if the arrangements in question are carried into effect, to limit their consideration thereafter to such elements in, or possible consequences of, the

creation of that situation as may be specified in the reference, and to consider whether, in respect only of those elements or possible consequences, the situation might be expected to operate against the public interest.

(4) In relation to a merger reference under this section, sections 66, [66A][1], 67, 69, 71, 72, 73 and 74 of this Act shall apply subject to the following modifications, that is to say —

[(*a*) section 66 shall apply, where an event by which any enterprises cease as between themselves to be distinct enterprises will occur if the arrangements are carried into effect, as if the event had occurred immediately before the date of the reference;

(*aa*) section 66A shall apply, where a transaction falling within subsection (2) of that section will occur if the arrangements are carried into effect, as if the transaction had occurred immediately before the date of the reference;

(*b*) in section 67(4) the references to subsection (1) of section 66 and subsection (1) of section 66A shall be construed as references to those subsections as modified in accordance with paragraph (*a*) or (*aa*) of this subection;][1]

(*c*) in section 69, subsection (1) shall be construed as modified by subsection (2) of this section; in subsections (2) and (3) any reference to the question whether a merger situation qualifying for investigation has been created, or whether a result mentioned in section 64(1)(*a*) of this Act has arisen, shall be construed as including a reference to the question whether such a situation will be created or such a result will arise if the arrangements in question are carried into effect; and subsection (4) of that section shall not apply;

(*d*) in section 71, in section 72(2) and in section 74(1), the references to section 69(4) of this Act shall be construed as references to subsection (3) of this section; and

(*e*) in section 73(1), the reference to conclusions to the effect that a merger situation qualifying for investigation has been created shall be construed as including a reference to conclusions to the effect that such a situation will be created if the arrangements in question are carried into effect.

[(4A) Where a merger reference is made under this section, it shall be unlawful, except with the consent of the Secretary of State under subsection (4C) of this section —

(*a*) for any person carrying on any enterprise to which the reference relates or having control of any such enterprise or for any subsidiary of his, or

(*b*) for any person associated with him or for any subsidiary of such a person,

directly or indirectly to acquire, at any time during the period mentioned in subsection (4B) of this section, an interest in shares in a company if any enterprise to which the reference relates is carried on by or under the control of that company.

(4B) The period referred to in subsection (4A) of this section is the period beginning with the announcement by the Secretary of State of the making of the merger reference concerned and ending —

(*a*) where the reference is laid aside at any time, at that time,

(*b*) where the time (including any further period) allowed to the Commission for making a report on the reference expires without their having made such a report, on the expiration of that time,

(*c*) where a report of the Commission on the reference not including such conclusions as are referred to in section 73(1)(*b*) of this Act is laid before Parliament, at the end of the day on which the report is so laid,

(*d*) where a report of the Commission on the reference including such conclusions is laid before Parliament, at the end of the period of forty days beginning with the day on which the report is so laid,

and where such a report is laid before each House on different days, it is to be treated for the purposes of this subsection as laid on the earlier day.

(4C) The consent of the Secretary of State—

(*a*) may be either general or special,

(*b*) may be revoked by the Secretary of State, and

(*c*) shall be published in such way as, in the opinion of the Secretary of State, to give any person entitled to the benefit of it an adequate opportunity of getting to know of it, unless in the Secretary of State's opinion publication is not necessary for that purpose.

(4D) Section 93 of this Act applies to any contravention or apprehended contravention of subsection (4A) of this section as it applies to a contravention or apprehended contravention of an order to which section 90 of this Act applies.

(4E) Subsections (4F) to (4K) of this section apply for the interpretation of subsection (4A).

(4F) The circumstances in which a person acquires an interest in shares include those where—

(*a*) he enters into a contract to acquire the shares (whether or not for cash),

(*b*) not being the registered holder, he acquires a right to exercise, or to control the exercise of, any right conferred by the holding of the shares, or

(*c*) he acquires a right to call for delivery of the shares to himself or to his order or to acquire an interest in the shares or assumes an obligation to acquire such an interest,

but does not include those where he acquires an interest in pursuance of an obligation assumed before the announcement by the Secretary of State of the making of the merger reference concerned.

(4G) The circumstances in which a person acquires a right mentioned in subsection (4F) of this section—

(*a*) include those where he acquires a right or assumes an obligation the exercise or fulfilment of which would give him that right, but

(*b*) does not include those where he is appointed as proxy to vote at a specified meeting of a company or of any class of its members or at any adjournment of the meeting or he is appointed by a corporation to act as its representative at any meeting of the company or of any class of its members, and references to rights and obligations in this subsection and subsection (4F) of this section include conditional rights and conditional obligations.

(4H) Any reference to a person carrying on or having control of any enterprise includes a group of persons carrying on or having control of an enterprise and any member of such a group.

(4J) Sections 65(2) to (4) and 77(1) and (4) to (6) of this Act apply to determine whether any person or group of persons has control of any enterprise and whether persons are associated as they apply for the purposes of section 65 of this Act to determine whether enterprises are brought under common control.

(4K) "Subsidiary" has the meaning given by section 736 of the Companies Act 1985, but that section and section 736A of that Act also apply to determine whether a company is a subsidiary of an individual or of a group of persons as they apply to determine whether it is a subsidiary of a company and references to a subsidiary in subsections (8) and (9) of Section 736A as so applied are to be read accordingly.

(4L) In this section—

"company" includes any body corporate, and

"share" means share in the capital of a company, and includes stock.

(4M) Nothing in subsection (4A) of this section makes anything done by a person outside the United Kingdom unlawful unless he is—

(a) a British citizen, a British Dependent Territories citizen, a British Overseas citizen or a British National (Overseas),

(b) a body corporate incorporated under the law of the United Kingdom or of a part of the United Kingdom, or

(c) a person carrying on business in the United Kingdom, either alone or in partnership with one or more other persons.]²

(5) If, in the course of their investigations on a merger reference under this section, it appears to the Commission that the proposal to make arrangements such as are mentioned in the reference has been abandoned, the Commission—

(a) shall, if the Secretary of State consents, lay the reference aside, but

(b) shall in that case furnish to the Secretary of State such information as he may require as to the results until then of the investigations.

[45]

NOTE
1 Sub-s (4) amended by the Companies Act 1989, s 153, Sch 20, paras 9, 10.
2 Sub-ss (4A)-(4M) inserted by s 149(1), (2) of the 1989 Act.
These amendments have effect in relation to any merger reference made on or after 16 November 1989.

[Restriction on power to make merger reference where prior notice has been given]

[75A. General rule where notice given by acquirer and no reference made within period for considering notice

(1) Notice may be given to the Director by a person authorised by regulations

to do so of proposed arrangements which might result in the creation of a merger situation qualifying for investigation.

(2) The notice must be in the prescribed form and state that the existence of the proposal has been made public.

(3) If the period for considering the notice expires without any reference being made to the Commission with respect to the notified arrangements, no reference may be made under this Part of this Act to the Commission with respect to those arrangements or to the creation or possible creation of any merger situation qualifying for investigation which is created in consequence of carrying those arrangements into effect.

(4) Subsection (3) of this section is subject to sections 75B(5) and 75C of this Act.

(5) A notice under subsection (1) of this section is referred to in sections 75B to 75F of this Act as a "merger notice".]   **[46]**

NOTE
  This section and ss 75B – F were inserted by the Companies Act 1989, s 146, as from 1 April 1990.
REGULATIONS UNDER THIS SECTION
  The Merger (Prenotification) Regulations 1990, SI 1990 No 501 were made partly under sub-s (1) above, and partly under ss 75C(1)(*c*), 75D(1), (2)(*b*) – (*h*), (3), (4) and 75E, below.

[75B. The role of the Director

(1) The Director shall, when the period for considering any merger notice begins, take such action as he considers appropriate to bring the existence of the proposal, the fact that the merger notice has been given and the date on which the period for considering the notice may expire to the attention of those who in his opinion would be affected if the arrangements were carried into effect.

(2) The period for considering a merger notice is the period of twenty days, determined in accordance with subsection (9) of this section, beginning with the first day after —

  (*a*) the notice has been received by the Director, and
  (*b*) any fee payable to the Director in respect of the notice has been paid.

(3) The Director may, and shall if required to do so by the Secretary of State, by notice to the person who gave the merger notice —

  (*a*) extend the period mentioned in subsection (2) of this section by a further ten days, and
  (*b*) extend that period as extended under paragraph (*a*) of this subsection by a further fifteen days.

(4) The Director may by notice to the person who gave the merger notice request him to provide the Director within such period as may be specified in the notice with such information as may be so specified.

(5) If the Director gives to the person who gave the merger notice (in this subsection referred to as "the relevant person") a notice stating that the Secretary of State is seeking undertakings under section 75G of this Act, section 75A(3) of this Act does not prevent a reference being made to the Commission unless —

(a) after the Director has given that notice, the relevant person has given a notice to the Director stating that he does not intend to give such undertakings, and

(b) the period of ten days beginning with the first day after the notice under paragraph (a) of this subsection was received by the Director has expired.

(6) A notice by the Director under subsection (3), (4) or (5) of this section must either be given to the person who gave the merger notice before the period for considering the merger notice expires or be sent in a properly addressed and pre-paid letter posted to him at such time that, in the ordinary course of post, it would be delivered to him before that period expires.

(7) The Director may, at any time before the period for considering any merger notice expires, reject the notice if —

(a) he suspects that any information given in respect of the notified arrangements, whether in the merger notice or otherwise, by the person who gave the notice or any connected person is in any material respect false or misleading,

(b) he suspects that it is not proposed to carry the notified arrangements into effect,

(c) any prescribed information is not given in the merger notice or any information requested by notice under subsection (4) of this section is not provided within the period specified in the notice; or,

(d) it appears to him that the notified arrangements are, or if carried into effect would result in, a concentration with a Community dimension within the meaning of Council Regulation (EEC) No 4064/89 of 21 December 1989 on the control of concentrations between undertakings.

(8) If —

(a) under subsection (3)(b) of this section the period for considering a merger notice has been extended by a further fifteen days, but

(b) the Director has not made any recommendation to the Secretary of State under section 76(b) of this Act as to whether or not it would in the Director's opinion be expedient for the Secretary of State to make a reference to the Commission with respect to the notified arrangements,

then, during the last five of those fifteen days, the power of the Secretary of State to make a reference to the Commission with respect to the notified arrangements is not affected by the absence of any such recommendation.

(9) In determining any period for the purposes of subsections (2), (3) and (5) of this section no account shall be taken of —

(a) Saturday, Sunday, Good Friday and Christmas Day, and

(b) any day which is a bank holiday in England and Wales.] **[47]**

NOTE
See the note to s 75A, above.

[75C. Cases where power to refer unaffected

(1) Section 75A(3) of this Act does not prevent any reference being made to the Commission if —

(*a*) before the end of the period for considering the merger notice, it is rejected by the Director under section 75B(7) of this Act,

(*b*) before the end of that period, any of the enterprises to which the notified arrangements relate cease to be distinct from each other,

(*c*) any information (whether prescribed information or not) that —

(i) is, or ought to be, known to the person who gave the merger notice or any connected person, and

(ii) is material to be notified arrangements;

is not disclosed to the Secretary of State or the Director by such time before the end of that period as may be specified in regulations,

(*d*) at any time after the merger notice is given but before the enterprises to which the notified arrangements relate cease to be distinct from each other, any of those enterprises ceases to be distinct from any enterprise other than an enterprise to which those arrangements relate,

(*e*) the six months beginning with the end of the period for considering the merger notice expires without the enterprises to which the notified arrangements relate ceasing to be distinct from each other,

(*f*) the merger notice is withdrawn, or

(*g*) any information given in respect of the notified arrangements, whether in the merger notice or otherwise, by the person who gave the notice or any connected person is in any material respect false or misleading.

(2) Where —

(*a*) two or more transactions which have occurred or, if any arrangements are carried into effect, will occur may be treated for the purposes of a merger reference as having occurred simultaneously on a particular date, and

(*b*) subsection (3) of section 75A of this Act does not prevent such a reference with respect to the last of those transactions,

that subsection does not prevent such a reference with respect to any of those transactions which actually occurred less than six months before —

(i) that date, or

(ii) the actual occurrence of another of those transactions with respect to which such a reference may be made (whether or not by virtue of this subsection).

(3) In determining for the purposes of subsection (2) of this section the time at which any transaction actually occurred, no account shall be taken of any option or other conditional right until the option is exercised or the condition is satisfied.]   **[48]**

NOTE
See the note to s 75A, above.

REGULATIONS UNDER THIS SECTION
See the note to s 75A, above.

[75D. Regulations

(1) The Secretary of State may make regulations for the purposes of sections 75A to 75C of this Act.

(2) The regulations may, in particular —

(a) provide for section 75B(2) or (3) or section 75C(1)(e) of this Act to apply as if any reference to a period of days or months were a reference to a period specified in the regulations for the purposes of the provision in question,

(b) provide for the manner in which any merger notice is authorised or required to be given, rejected or withdrawn, and the time at which any merger notice is to be treated as received or rejected,

(c) provide for the manner in which any information requested by the Director or any other material information is authorised or required to be provided or disclosed, and the time at which such information is to be treated as provided or disclosed,

(d) provide for the manner in which any notice under section 75B of this Act is authorised or required to be given,

(e) provide for the time at which any notice under section 75B(5)(a) of this Act is to be treated as received,

(f) provide for the address which is to be treated for the purposes of section 75B(6) of this Act and of the regulations as a person's proper address,

(g) provide for the time at which any fee is to be treated as paid, and

(h) provide that a person is, or is not, to be treated, in such circumstances as may be specified in the regulations, as acting on behalf of a person authorised by regulations to give a merger notice or a person who has given such a notice.

(3) The regulations may make different provision for different cases.

(4) Regulations under this section shall be made by statutory instrument.]

[49]

NOTE
See the note to s 75A, above.
REGULATIONS UNDER THIS SECTION
See the note to s 75A, above.

[75E. Interpretation of sections 75A to 75D

In this section and sections 75A to 75D of this Act —

"connected person", in relation to the person who gave a merger notice, means —

(a) any person who, for the purposes of section 77 of this Act, is associated with him, or

(b) any subsidiary of the person who gave the merger notice or of any person so associated with him,

"merger notice" is to be interpreted in accordance with section 75A(5) of this Act,
"notified arrangements" means the arrangements mentioned in the merger notice or arrangements not differing from them in any material respect,

"prescribed" means prescribed by the Director by notice having effect for the time being and published in the London, Edinburgh and Belfast Gazettes,
"regulations" means regulations under section 75D of this Act, and
"subsidiary" has the meaning given by section 75(4K) of this Act,

and references to the enterprises to which the notified arrangements relate are references to those enterprises that would have ceased to be distinct from one another if the arrangements mentioned in the merger notice in question had been carried into effect at the time when the notice was given.]   **[50]**

NOTE
See the note to s 75A, above.
REGULATIONS UNDER THIS SECTION
See the note to s 75A, above.

[75F. Power to amend sections 75B to 75D

(1) The Secretary of State may, for the purpose of determining the effect of giving a merger notice and the steps which may be or are to be taken by any person in connection with such a notice, by regulations made by statutory instrument amend sections 75B to 75D of this Act.

(2) The regulations may make different provision for different cases and may contain such incidental and supplementary provisions as the Secretary of State thinks fit.

(3) No regulations shall be made under this section unless a draft of the regulations has been laid before and approved by resolution of each House of Parliament.]   **[51]**

NOTE
See the note to s 75A, above.

[Undertakings as alternative to merger reference]

[75G. Acceptance of undertakings

(1) Where—

  (*a*) the Secretary of State has power to make a merger reference to the Commission under section 64 or 75 of this Act,
  (*b*) the Director has made a recommendation to the Secretary of State under section 76 of this Act that such a reference should be made, and
  (*c*) the Director has (in making that recommendation or subsequently) given advice to the Secretary of State specifying particular effects adverse to the public interest which in his opinion the creation of the merger situation qualifying for investigation may have or might be expected to have,

the Secretary of State may, instead of making a merger reference to the Commission, accept from such of the parties concerned as he considers appropriate undertakings complying with subsections (2) and (3) of this section to take specified action which the Secretary of State considers appropriate to remedy or prevent the effects adverse to the public interest specified in the advice.

(2) The undertakings must provide for one or more of the following—

(a) the division of a business by the sale of any part of the undertaking or assets or otherwise (for which purpose all the activities carried on by way of business by any one person or by any two or more interconnected bodies corporate may be treated as a single business),

(b) the division of a group of interconnected bodies corporate, and

(c) the separation, by the sale of any part of the undertaking or assets concerned or other means, of enterprises which are under common control otherwise than by reason of their being enterprises of interconnected bodies corporate.

(3) The undertakings may also contain provision—

(a) preventing or restricting the doing of things which might prevent or impede the division or separation,

(b) as to the carrying on of any activities or the safeguarding of any assets until the division or separation is effected,

(c) for any matters necessary to effect or take account of the division or separation, and

(d) for enabling the Secretary of State to ascertain whether the undertakings are being fulfilled.

(4) If the Secretary of State has accepted one or more undertakings under this section, no reference may be made to the Commission with respect to the creation or possible creation of the merger situation qualifying for investigation by reference to which the undertakings were accepted, except in a case falling within subsection (5) of this section.

(5) Subsection (4) of this section does not prevent a reference being made to the Commission if material facts about the arrangements or transactions, or proposed arrangements or transactions, in consequence of which the enterprises concerned ceased or may cease to be distinct enterprises were not—

(a) notified to the Secretary of State or the Director, or

(b) made public,

before the undertakings were accepted.

(6) In subsection (5) of this section "made public" has the same meaning as in section 64 of this Act.] **[52]**

NOTE
This section and ss 75H, 75J, 75K together with the cross heading before this section were inserted by the Companies Act 1989, s 147, as from 16 November 1989.

[75H. Publication of undertakings

(1) The Secretary of State shall arrange for—

(a) any undertaking accepted by him under section 75G of this Act,

(b) the advice given by the Director for the purposes of subsection (1)(c) of that section in any case where such an undertaking has been accepted, and

(c) any variation or release of such an undertaking,

to be published in such manner as he may consider appropriate.

(2) In giving advice for the purposes of section 75G(1)(c) of this Act the Director shall have regard to the need for excluding, so far as practicable, any matter to which subsection (4) of this section applies.

(3) The Secretary of State shall exclude from any such advice as published under this section—

(a) any matter to which subsection (4) of this section applies and in relation to which he is satisfied that its publication in the advice would not be in the public interest, and

(b) any other matter in relation to which he is satisfied that its publication in the advice would be against the public interest.

(4) This subsection applies to—

(a) any matter which relates to the private affairs of an individual, where publication of that matter would or might, in the opinion of the Director or the Secretary of State, as the case may be, seriously and prejudicially affect the interests of that individual, and

(b) any matter which relates specifically to the affairs of a particular body of persons, whether corporate or unincorporate, where publication of that matter would or might, in the opinion of the Director or the Secretary of State, as the case may be, seriously and prejudicially affect the interests of that body, unless in his opinion the inclusion of that matter relating specifically to that body is necessary for the purposes of the advice.

(5) For the purposes of the law relating to defamation, absolute privilege shall attach to any advice given by the Director for the purposes of section 75G(1)(c) of this Act.]   **[53]**

NOTE
See the note to s 75G, above.

[75J. Review of undertakings

Where an undertaking has been accepted by the Secretary of State under section 75G of this Act, it shall be the duty of the Director—

(a) to keep under review the carrying out of that undertaking, and from time to time consider whether, by reason of any change of circumstances, the undertaking is no longer appropriate and either—

(i) one or more of the parties to it can be released from it, or

(ii) it needs to be varied or to be superseded by a new undertaking, and

(b) if it appears to him that the undertaking has not been or is not being fulfilled, that any person can be so released or that the undertaking needs to be varied or superseded, to give such advice to the Secretary of State as he may think proper in the circumstances.]   **[54]**

[75K. Order of Secretary of State where undertaking not fulfilled

(1) The provisions of this section shall have effect where it appears to the Secretary of State that an undertaking accepted by him under section 75G of this Act has not been, is not being or will not be fulfilled.

(2) The Secretary of State may by order made by statutory instrument exercise such one or more of the powers specified in paragraphs 9A and 12 to 12C and Part II of Schedule 8 to this Act as he may consider it requisite to exercise for the purpose of remedying or preventing the adverse effects specified in the advice given by the Director for the purposes of section 75G(1)(c) of this Act; and those powers may be so exercised to such extent and in such manner as the Secretary of State considers requisite for that purpose.

(3) In determining whether, or to what extent or in what manner, to exercise any of those powers, the Secretary of State shall take into account any advice given by the Director under section 75J(b) of this Act.

(4) The provision contained in an order under this section may be different from that contained in the undertaking.

(5) On the making of an order under this section, the undertaking and any other undertaking accepted under section 75G of this Act by reference to the same merger situation qualifying for investigation are released by virtue of this section.   **[55]**

NOTE
See the note to 75G, above

Supplementary

76. Functions of Director in relation to merger situations

[(1)]¹ It shall be the duty of the Director —

    (a) to take all such steps as are reasonably practicable for keeping himself informed about actual or prospective arrangements or transactions which may constitute or result in the creation of merger situations qualifying for investigation, and

    (b) to make recommendations to the Secretary of State as to any action under this Part of this Act which in the opinion of the Director it would be expedient for the Secretary of State to take in relation to any such arrangements or transactions.

[(2) In exercising his duty under this section the Director shall take into consideration any representations made to him by persons appearing to him to have a substantial interest in any such arrangements or transactions or by bodies appearing to him to represent substantial numbers of persons who have such an interest.]¹   **[56]**

AMENDMENT

1 Section as originally enacted numbered sub-s (1), and sub-s (2) added, by the Companies Act 1989, s 153, Sch 20, para 11, as from 16 November 1989.

77. Associated persons

(1) For the following purposes, that is to say—

(a) for the purpose of determining under section 57(1) of this Act whether a person is a newspaper proprietor and, if so, which newspapers are his newspapers;

(b) for the purpose of determining under section 65 of this Act whether any two enterprises have been brought under common ownership or common control; and

(c) for the purpose of determining what activities are carried on by way of business by any one person, in so far as that question arises in the application, by virtue of an order under section 73 of this Act, of paragraph 14 of Schedule 8 to this Act,

associated persons, and any bodies corporate which they or any of them control, shall (subject to the next following subsection) be treated as one person.

(2) The preceding subsection shall not have effect—

(a) for the purpose mentioned in paragraph (a) of that subsection so as to exclude from section 58 of this Act any case which would otherwise fall within that section, or

(b) for the purpose mentioned in paragraph (b) of the preceding subsection so as to exclude from section 65 of this Act any case which would otherwise fall within that section.

(3) A merger reference other than a newspaper merger reference (whether apart from this section the reference could be made or not) may be so framed as to exclude from consideration, either altogether or for any specified purpose or to any specified extent, any matter which, apart from this section, would not have been taken into account on that reference.

(4) For the purposes of this section the following persons shall be regarded as associated with one another, that is to say—

(a) any individual and that individual's husband or wife and any relative, or husband or wife of a relative, of that individual or of that individual's husband or wife;

(b) any person in his capacity as trustee of a settlement and the settlor or grantor and any person associated with the settlor or grantor;

(c) persons carrying on business in partnership and the husband or wife and relatives of any of them;

(d) any two or more persons acting together to secure or exercise control of a body corporate or other association or to secure control of any enterprise or assets.

(5) The reference in subsection (1) of this section to bodies corporate which associated persons control shall be construed as follows, that is to say—

(*a*) in its application for the purpose mentioned in paragraph (*a*) of that subsection, "control" in that reference means having a controlling interest within the meaning of section 57(4) of this Act, and

(*b*) in its application for any other purpose mentioned in subsection (1) of this section, "control" in that reference shall be construed in accordance with section 65(3) and (4) of this Act.

(6) In this section "relative" means a brother, sister, uncle, aunt, nephew, niece, lineal ancestor or descendant (the stepchild or illegitimate child of any person, or anyone adopted by a person, whether legally or otherwise, as his child, being taken into account as a relative or to trace a relationship in the same way as that person's child); and references to a wife or husband shall include a former wife or husband and a reputed wife or husband. **[57]**

PART VI

REFERENCES TO COMMISSION OTHER THAN MONOPOLY AND MERGER REFERENCES

78. General references

(1) The Secretary of State, or the Secretary of State and any other Minister acting jointly, may at any time require the Commission to submit to him or them a report on the general effect on the public interest —

(*a*) of practices of a specified class which, in his or their opinion, are commonly adopted as a result of, or for the purpose of preserving, monopoly situations, or

(*b*) of any specified practices which appear to him or them to be uncompetitive practices.

(2) The Secretary of State, or the Secretary of State and any other Minister acting jointly, may also at any time require the Commission to submit to him or them a report on the desirability of action of any specified description for the purpose of remedying or preventing effects, adverse to the public interest, which result or might result from monopoly situations or from any such practices as are mentioned in the preceding subsection.

(3) The matters to be taken into consideration by the Commission on any reference under this section shall not include any provisions of any agreement in so far as they are provisions by virtue of which it is an agreement to which [the Act of 1976]¹ applies. **[58]**

AMENDMENT
1 Words in sub-s (3) substituted by RTPA 1976, Sch 5.

79. References as to restrictive labour practices

(1) The Secretary of State, or the Secretary of State and any other Minister acting jointly, may at any time refer to the Commission the questions —

(*a*) whether a practice of a description specified in the reference exists and, if so, whether it is a restrictive labour practice, and

(b) if it exists and is a restrictive labour practice, whether it operates or may be expected to operate against the public interest and, if so, what particular effects, adverse to the public interest, it has or may be expected to have.

(2) A reference under this section may refer those questions to the Commission either —

(a) in relation to commercial activities in the United Kingdom generally, or

(b) in relation to such commercial activities in the United Kingdom as consist of the supply of goods of a description specified in the reference, or of the supply of services of a description so specified, or of the export from the United Kingdom of goods of a description so specified.

(3) The Commission shall examine any questions referred to them under this section and shall report to the Minister or Ministers who referred them to the Commission.

(4) For the purposes of their functions under subsection (3) of this section the Commission shall disregard anything which appears to them to have been done, or omitted to be done, in contemplation or furtherance of an industrial dispute within the meaning of the Industrial Relations Act 1971.

(5) In this section "restrictive labour practice" means any practice whereby restrictions or other requirements, not being restrictions or requirements relating exclusively to rates of remuneration, operate in relation to the employment of workers in any commercial activities in the United Kingdom or in relation to work done by any such workers, and are restrictions or requirements which —

(a) could be discontinued without thereby contravening the provisions of an enactment or of any instrument having effect by virtue of an enactment, and

(b) are not necessary for, or are more stringent than is necessary for, the efficient conduct of those activities.   [59]

80. Variation of reference under Part VI

A reference made under this Part of this Act may at any time be varied by the Minister or Ministers by whom the reference was made.   [60]

PART VII

PROVISIONS RELATING TO REFERENCES TO ADVISORY COMMITTEE OR TO COMMISSION

81. Procedure in carrying out investigations

(1) The Advisory Committee, in carrying out an investigation on a reference to which section 17 of this Act applies, and the Commission, in carrying out an investigation on a reference made to them under this Act (whether it is a monopoly reference or a merger reference or a reference under Part VI of this Act), —

(a) shall take into consideration any representations made to them by persons appearing to them to have a substantial interest in the subject-matter of the reference, or by bodies appearing to them to represent substantial numbers of persons who have such an interest, and

(b) unless in all the circumstances they consider it not reasonably necessary or not reasonably practicable to do so, shall permit any such person or body to be heard orally by the Advisory Committee or the Commission, as the case may be, or by a member of the Committee or of the Commission nominated by them for that purpose.

(2) Subject to subsection (1) of this section, the Advisory Committee or the Commission may determine their own procedure for carrying out any investigation on a reference under this Act, and in particular may determine —

(a) the extent, if any, to which persons interested or claiming to be interested in the subject-matter of the reference are allowed to be present or to be heard, either by themselves or by their representatives, or to cross-examine witnesses or otherwise take part in the investigation, and

(b) the extent, if any, to which the sittings of the Advisory Committee or of the Commission are to be held in public.

(3) In determining their procedure under subsection (2) of this section, and, in the case of the Commission, in exercising any powers conferred on them by section 85 of this Act, the Advisory Committee or the Commission, as the case may be, shall act in accordance with any general directions which may from time to time be given to them by the Secretary of State.

(4) The Secretary of State shall lay before each House of Parliament a copy of any directions given by him under subsection (3) of this section.   **[61]**

82. General provisions as to reports

(1) In making any report under this Act the Advisory Committee or the Commission shall have regard to the need for excluding, so far as that is practicable, —

(a) any matter which relates to the private affairs of an individual, where the publication of that matter would or might, in their opinion, seriously and prejudicially affect the interests of that individual, and

(b) any matter which relates specifically to the affairs of a particular body of persons, whether corporate or unincorporate, where publication of that matter would or might, in the opinion of the Advisory Committee or of the Commission, as the case may be, seriously and prejudicially affect the interests of that body, unless in their opinion the inclusion of that matter relating specifically to that body is necessary for the purposes of the report.

(2) For the purposes of the law relating to defamation, absolute privilege shall attach to any report of the Advisory Committee or of the Commission under this Act.

(3) Subject to the next following subsection, if —

(a) on a reference to the Advisory Committee under this Act, or

(b) on a reference to the Commission, other than a monopoly reference limited to the facts, a member of the Advisory Committee or of the Commission, as the case may be, dissents from any conclusions contained in the report on the reference as being conclusions of the Committee or of the Commission, the report shall, if that member so desires, include a statement of his dissent and of his reasons for dissenting.

(4) In relation to a report made by a group of members of the Commission in pursuance of paragraph 10 or paragraph 11 of Schedule 3 to this Act, subsection (3) of this section shall have effect subject to paragraph 14(1) of that Schedule.   **[62]**

NOTES

1 This section is applied by the Telecommunications Act 1984, s 14(3).

2 Any relevant statement contained in a report of the Commission laid before Parliament under this Part of the Act is prima facie evidence of the matters stated for the purposes of proceedings under the Patents Act 1977, ss 48–51; see s 53(2) of that Act (but note the amendment of s 53(2) by the Copyright, Designs and Patents Act 1988, s 295, Sch 5, para 15, as from a day to be appointed).

83. Laying before Parliament and publication of reports

(1) [Subject to subsection (1A) below][1] The Minister or Ministers to whom any report of the Advisory Committee on a reference to which section 17 of this Act applies, or any report of the Commission under this Act, is made shall lay a copy of the report before each House of Parliament, and shall arrange for the report to be published in such manner as appears to the Minister or Ministers to be appropriate.

[(1A) The Minister or Ministers to whom a report of the Commission on a monopoly reference is made shall not lay a copy of the report before either House of Parliament unless at least twenty-four hours before doing so he transmits or they transmit to every person named in the report as a person in whose favour a monopoly situation exists a copy of the report in the form in which it is laid (or by virtue of subsection (2) below is treated as being laid) before each House of Parliament.][2]

(2) If such a report is presented by command of Her Majesty to either House of Parliament otherwise than at or during the time of a sitting of that House, the presentation of the report shall for the purposes of this section be treated as the laying of a copy of it before that House by the Minister or Ministers to whom the report was made.

(3) If it appears to the Minister or Ministers to whom any report of the Advisory Committee or of the Commission under this Act is made that the publication of any matter in the report would be against the public interest, the Minister or Ministers shall exclude that matter from the copies of the report as laid before Parliament and from the report as published under this section.

[(3A) Without prejudice to subsection (3) above, if the Minister or Ministers to whom any such report is made consider that it would not be in the public interest to disclose —

(a) any matter contained in the report relating to the private affairs of an individual whose interests would, in the opinion of the Minister or

Ministers, be seriously and prejudicially affected by the publication of that matter, or

(b) any matter contained in the report relating specifically to the affairs of a particular person whose interests would, in the opinion of the Minister or Ministers, be seriously and prejudicially affected by the publication of that matter,

the Minister or Ministers shall exclude that matter from the copies of the report as laid before Parliament and from the report as published under this section.][3]

(4) Any reference in this Act to a report of the Advisory Committee or of the Commission as laid before Parliament shall be construed as a reference to the report in the form in which copies of it are laid (or by virtue of subsection (2) of this section are treated as having been laid) before each House of Parliament under this section. **[63]**

AMENDMENTS

1 Words in sub-s (1) inserted by Competition Act 1980, s 22.

2 Sub-s (1A) inserted by Competition Act 1980, s 22.

3 Sub-s (3A) inserted by the Companies Act 1989, s 153, Sch 20, para 12 in relation to any report made on or after 16 November 1989.

PART VIII

ADDITIONAL PROVISIONS RELATING TO REFERENCES TO COMMISSION

84. Public interest

(1) In determining for any purposes to which this section applies whether any particular matter operates, or may be expected to operate, against the public interest, the Commission shall take into account all matters which appear to them in the particular circumstances to be relevant and, among other things, shall have regard to the desirability—

(a) of maintaining and promoting effective competition between persons supplying goods and services in the United Kingdom;

(b) of promoting the interests of consumers, purchasers and other users of goods and services in the United Kingdom in respect of the prices charged for them and in respect of their quality and the variety of goods and services supplied;

(c) of promoting, through competition, the reduction of costs and the development and use of new techniques and new products, and of facilitating the entry of new competitors into existing markets;

(d) of maintaining and promoting the balanced distribution of industry and employment in the United Kingdom; and

(e) of maintaining and promoting competitive activity in markets outside the United Kingdom on the part of producers of goods, and of suppliers of goods and services, in the United Kingdom.

(2) This section applies to the purposes of any functions of the Commission under this Act other than functions to which section 59(3) of this Act applies.

[64]

NOTE
This section is applied by the Competition Act 1980, ss 7(6), 11(9).

85. Attendance of witnesses and production of documents

(1) For the purposes of any investigation on a reference made to them under this Act the Commission may, by notice in writing signed on their behalf by any of their members or by their secretary, —

    (a) require any person to attend at a time and place specified in the notice, and to give evidence to the Commission or a member of the Commission nominated by them for the purpose, or

    (b) require any person to produce, at a time and place specified in the notice, to the Commission or to any person nominated by the Commission for the purpose, any documents which are specified or described in the notice and which are documents in his custody or under his control and relating to any matter relevant to the investigation, or

    (c) require any person carrying on any business to furnish to the Commission such estimates, returns or other information as may be specified or described in the notice, and specify the time, the manner and the form in which any such estimates, returns or information are to be furnished.

(2) For the purposes of any such investigation the Commission, or a member of the Commission nominated by them for that purpose, may take evidence on oath, and for that purpose may administer oaths.

(3) No person shall be compelled for the purpose of any such investigation to give any evidence or produce any document which he could not be compelled to give or produce in civil proceedings before the court or, in complying with any requirement for the furnishing of information, to give any information which he could not be compelled to give in evidence in such proceedings.

(4) No person shall be required, in obedience to a notice under subsection (1) of this section, to go more than ten miles from his place of residence unless the necessary expenses of his attendance are paid or tendered to him.

(5) . . .[1]

(6) Any person who —

    (a) wilfully alters, suppresses or destroys any document which he has been required by any such notice to produce, . . .[1]

    (b) . . .[1]

shall be guilty of an offence and liable on summary conviction to a fine not exceeding [the prescribed sum][2] or, on conviction on indictment, to imprisonment for a term not exceeding two years or to a fine or to both.

[(7) If any person (referred to in subsection (7A) of this section as "the defaulter") refuses or otherwise fails to comply with any notice under subsection (1) of this section, any one of those who, in relation to the investigation in question, are performing the functions of the Commission may certify that fact in writing to the court and the court may enquire into the case.

(7A) If, after hearing any witness who may be produced against or on behalf of the defaulter and any statement which may be offered in defence, the court is satisfied that the defaulter did without reasonable excuse refuse or otherwise fail to comply with the notice, the court may punish the defaulter (and, in the case of a body corporate, any director or officer) in like manner as if the defaulter had been guilty of contempt of court.]¹

(8) In this section "the court" —

(a) in relation to England and Wales, means the High Court;
(b) in relation to Scotland, means the Court of Session; and
(c) in relation to Northern Ireland, means the High Court or a judge of the High Court.   [65]

NOTE
   This section is applied by the Competition Act 1980, ss 3(8), 7(6), 11(9) and, with modifications, to licence modification references to the Commission under the Telecommunications Act 1984, s 13.

AMENDMENTS
   1 Sub-ss (5), (6)(b) repealed and new sub-ss (7), (7A) substituted for the original sub-s (7) by the Companies Act 1989, s 153, Sch 20, para 13, as from 1 April 1990 (sub-ss (5), (6)(b) are also repealed and, additionally, the word omitted preceding sub-s (6)(b), by s 212 of, and Sch 24 to, that Act).
   2 The reference to the prescribed sum is substituted by virtue of the Magistrates' Courts Act 1980, s 32(2).

86. Director to receive copies of reports

(1) Subject to the next following subsection, a copy of every report of the Commission on a monopoly reference, or on a merger reference other than a newspaper merger reference, shall be transmitted by the Commission to the Director; and the Minister or Ministers to whom any such report is made shall take account of any advice given to him or them by the Director with respect to a report of which a copy is transmitted to the Director under this section.

(2) The preceding subsection shall not apply to a report made on a monopoly reference, where the reference was made by a Minister or Ministers and (by virtue of any of the provisions of section 50 of this Act) could not have been made by the Director.

(3) In this section "Minister" includes the Minister of Agriculture for Northern Ireland and the Minister of Commerce for Northern Ireland.   [66]

NOTE
   See notes 3, 4 and 5 to s 44.

87. Supplementary provisions as to laying reports before Parliament

(1) Where under section 83 of this Act the Secretary of State lays before Parliament a copy of a report of the Commission on a newspaper merger reference, then —

(a) if before laying it the Secretary of State has consented to the transfer of a newspaper or of newspaper assets to which the report relates, he shall annex a copy of that consent to the copy of the report laid before Parliament, or (*b*) if he subsequently consents to that transfer, he shall thereupon lay before Parliament a copy of that consent.

(2) Where the persons to whom a report of the Commission is made under this Act include the Minister of Agriculture for Northern Ireland, that Minister shall lay a copy of the report before the Senate and House of Commons of Northern Ireland and shall arrange for it to be published in Northern Ireland in such manner as appears to him to be appropriate.

(3) If a report to which subsection (2) of this section applies is presented by command of the Governor of Northern Ireland to the Senate or House of Commons of Northern Ireland otherwise than at or during the time of a sitting of the Senate or of that House, as the case may be, the presentation of the report shall for the purposes of that subsection be treated as the laying of a copy of it before the Senate or that House as required by that subsection.   **[67]**

88. Action by Director in consequence of report of Commission on monopoly or merger reference

(1) Where a report of the Commission on a monopoly reference, or on a merger reference other than a newspaper merger reference, as laid before Parliament, –

   (*a*) in the case of a monopoly reference, sets out such conclusions as are mentioned in section 56(1) of this Act, or
   (*b*) in the case of a merger reference, sets out such conclusions as are mentioned in section 73(1) or in section 75(4)(*e*) of this Act,

and a copy of the report is transmitted to the Director under section 86 of this Act, it shall be the duty of the Director, [to comply with any request of the appropriate Minister or Ministers to consult with any persons mentioned in the request (referred to below in this section as "the relevant parties")][1] with a view to obtaining from them undertakings to take action indicated in the request made to the Director as being action requisite, in the opinion of the appropriate Minister or Ministers, for the purpose of remedying or preventing the adverse effects specified in the report.

(2) The Director shall report to the appropriate Minister or Ministers the outcome of his consultations under the preceding subsection; and if any undertaking is given by any of the relevant parties to take action indicated in the request made to the Director as mentioned in that subsection (in this section referred to as an "appropriate undertaking") the Minister to whom the undertaking is given shall furnish particulars of it to the Director.

[(2A) Where –
   (*a*) an undertaking is given under this section after the commencement of this subsection, or
   (*b*) an undertaking given under this section is varied or released after that time,
the Minister to whom the undertaking is or was given shall cause the undertaking or, as the case may be, the variation or release to be published in such manner as the Minister may consider appropriate.][1]

(3) Where in his consultations under subsection (1) of this section the Director

seeks to obtain an appropriate undertaking from any of the relevant parties, and either —

(a) he is satisfied that no such undertaking is likely to be given by that party within a reasonable time, or

(b) having allowed such time as in his opinion is reasonable for the purpose, he is satisfied that no such undertaking has been given by that party,

the Director shall give such advice to the appropriate Minister or Ministers as he may think proper in the circumstances (including, if the Director thinks fit, advice with respect to the exercise by the appropriate Minister or Ministers of his or their powers under section 56 or section 73 of this Act, as the case may be).

(4) Where the Director has made a report under subsection (2) of this section, and particulars of an undertaking given by any of the relevant parties have been furnished to the Director in accordance with that subsection, it shall be the duty of the Director —

(a) to keep under review the carrying out of that undertaking, and from time to time to consider whether, by reason of any change of circumstances, [the undertaking is no longer appropriate and either the relevant parties (or any of them) can be released from the undertaking or the undertaking][1] needs to be varied or to be superseded by a new undertaking, and

(b) if it appears to him [that any person can be so released or that an undertaking][1] has not been or is not being fulfilled, or needs to be varied or superseded, to give such advice to the appropriate Minister or Ministers as he may think proper in the circumstances.

(5) Where, in consequence of a report of which a copy is transmitted to the Director under section 86 of this Act, an order is made under section 56 or section 73 of this Act in relation to any of the matters to which the report relates, it shall be the duty of the Director to keep under review the action (if any) taken in compliance with that order, and from time to time to consider whether, by reason of any change of circumstances, the order should be varied [or revoked][1] or should be superseded by a new order, and —

(a) if it appears to him that the order has in any respect not been complied with, to consider whether any action (by way of proceedings in accordance with section 93 of this Act or otherwise) should be taken for the purpose of securing compliance with the order, and (where in his opinion it is appropriate to do so) to take such action himself or give advice to any Minister or other person by whom such action might be taken, or

(b) if it appears to him that the order needs to be varied [or revoked][1], or to be superseded by a new order, to give such advice to the appropriate Minister or Ministers as he may think proper in the circumstances.

(6) In this section . . .[1] in relation to a report of the Commission, "the appropriate Minister or Ministers" means the Minister or Ministers to whom the report is made, "undertaking" means an undertaking given to that Minister or to one of those Ministers, as the case may be, and, in subsections (3) and (5) of this section, the references to section 73 of this Act shall be construed as including references to that section as applied by section 75(4) of this Act.   **[68]**

NOTES
[1] See notes 3, 4 and 5 to s 44.
[2] See the Competition Act 1980, s 29(1).
AMENDMENTS
1 All amendments and repeals are made to this section by the Companies Act 1989, ss 153, 212, Sch 20, para 14, Sch 24, although not in relation to any report made before 16 November 1989.

89. Interim order after report of Commission under s 54 or s 72

(1) The provisions of this section shall have effect where —

[(*a*) in the circumstances specified in subsection (1) of any of the following sections —

  (i) sections 56, 73 and 75K of this Act, and

  (ii) section 10 of the Competition Act 1980,

  the Secretary of State makes, has made, or has under consideration the making of, an order under the section in question exercising any of the powers specified in Schedule 8 to this Act, or

(*b*) in the circumstances specified in subsection (1) of section 12 of the Competition Act 1980 the Secretary of State makes, has made, or has under consideration the making of, an order under subsection (5) of that section exercising any of those powers;][1]

and in those provisions "the principal order" means the order which the Secretary of State makes, or has it under consideration to make, as mentioned in paragraph (*a*) or paragraph (*b*) of this subsection.

(2) With a view to achieving the purpose for which any of the powers specified in . . .[1] of that Schedule are, or are proposed to be, exercised by the principal order, the Secretary of State may by order made by statutory instrument exercise any of the powers mentioned in the next following subsection.

(3) An order under this section may —

(*a*) prohibit or restrict the doing of things which, in the opinion of the Secretary of State, might impede the operation of the principal order or, where it has not yet been made, might be an impediment to making it;

(*b*) impose on any person concerned obligations as to the carrying on of any activities or the safeguarding of any assets;

[(*bb*) require any person to furnish any such information to the Director as may be specified or described in the order;][1]

(*c*) provide for the carrying on of any activities or the safeguarding of any assets either by the appointment of a person to conduct or supervise the conduct of any activities (on such terms and with such powers as may be specified or described in the order under this section) or in any other manner.   **[69]**

AMENDMENTS
1 All amendments and repeals are made to this section by the Companies Act 1989, ss 153, 212, Sch 20, para 15, Sch 24 (and sub-ss (1) – (3) as amended have effect in relation to any order under this section after 16 November 1989, whether the principal order was made before or after that date.

90. General provisions as to orders under ss 56, 73, 74 and 89

(1) This section applies to any order under section 56, section 73, section 74 [, 75K]¹ or section 89 of this Act.

(2) Any such order declaring anything to be unlawful may declare it to be unlawful either for all persons or for such persons as may be specified or described in the order.

(3) Nothing in any such order shall have effect so as to apply to any person in relation to his conduct outside the United Kingdom unless that person is —

(a) a citizen of the United Kingdom and Colonies, or
(b) a body corporate incorporated under the law of the United Kingdom or of a part of the United Kingdom, or
(c) a person carrying on business in the United Kingdom, either alone or in partnership with one or more other persons,

but, in the case of a person falling within paragraph (a), paragraph (b) or paragraph (c) of this subsection, any such order may extend to acts or omissions outside the United Kingdom.

(4) An order to which this section applies may extend so as to prohibit the carrying out of agreements already in existence on the date on which the order is made.

[(5) Nothing in any order to which this section applies shall have effect so as to —

(a) cancel or modify conditions in licences granted —

(i) under a patent granted under the Patents Act 1949 or the Patents Act 1977 or a European patent (UK) (within the meaning of the Patents Act 1977), or
(ii) in respect of a design registered under the Registered Designs Act 1949,

by the proprietor of the patent or design, or
(b) require an entry to be made in the register of patents or the register of designs to the effect that licences under such a patent or such a design are to be available as of right.]¹

(6) Nothing in any such order shall affect the conduct of a board established under a scheme made under the Agricultural Marketing Act 1958 [or under the Agricultural Marketing (Northern Ireland) Order 1982]².

(7) An order to which this section applies may authorise the Minister making the order to give directions to a person specified in the directions, or to the holder for the time being of an office so specified in any company or association, —

(a) to take such steps within his competence as may be specified or described in the directions for the purpose of carrying out, or securing compliance with, the order, or
(b) to do or refrain from doing anything so specified or described which he might be required by the order to do or refrain from doing,

and may authorise that Minister to vary or revoke any directions so given.

[70]

NOTE
  S 90 extended, with the exception of sub-s (2), by the Competition Act 1980, s 10(4)(*a*), and with the exception of sub-ss (2) and (3), by s 12(6)(*a*) of that Act.

AMENDMENTS
  1 Sub-s (1) amended and sub-s (5) substituted by the Companies Act 1989, s 153, Sch 20, para 16, as from 16 November 1989.
  2 Sub-s (6) amended by the Agricultural Marketing (Northern Ireland) Order 1982, SI 1982 No 1080.

91. Procedure relating to orders to which s 90 applies

(1) No order to which section 90 of this Act applies and which exercises any of the powers specified in Part II of Schedule 8 to this Act, and no order varying or revoking any such order, shall be made unless a draft of the order has been laid before Parliament and approved by a resolution of each House of Parliament; and the provisions of Schedule 9 to this Act shall have effect with respect to the procedure to be followed before laying before Parliament a draft of any such order.

(2) Before making any order under section 56 or section 73 of this Act other than any such order as is mentioned in the preceding subsection, the Minister proposing to make the order shall publish, in such manner as appears to him to be appropriate, a notice —

(*a*) stating his intention to make the order;
(*b*) indicating the nature of the provisions to be embodied in the order; and
(*c*) stating that any person whose interests are likely to be affected by the order, and who is desirous of making representations in respect of it, should do so in writing (stating his interest and the grounds on which he wishes to make the representations) before a date specified in the notice (that date being not earlier than the end of the period of thirty days beginning with the day on which publication of the notice is completed);

and the Minister shall not make the order before the date specified in the notice in accordance with paragraph (*c*) of this subsection and shall consider any representations duly made to him in accordance with the notice before that date.

[71]

NOTE
  Sub-s (2) extended by the Competition Act 1980, ss 10(4)(*b*), 12(6)(*b*).

92. Investigation of company or association with reference to order to which s 90 applies

(1) For the purpose of determining whether to make an order to which section 90 of this Act applies whereby any powers are to be exercised in relation to a company or association, or for the purpose of obtaining information on which to exercise by or under any such order any powers in relation to a company or association, the Secretary of State may appoint an inspector to investigate and report to him on any such matters falling within the next following subsection as are specified or described in the appointment.

[(2) The matters which may be so specified or described are any matters which in the case of a company registered under the Companies Act 1985 (or the previous corresponding legislation) —

(a) could in accordance with sections 432 and 433 of that Act be investigated by an inspector appointed under section 432, or

(b) could in accordance with section 442 of that Act, or in accordance with any provisions as applied by section 443(1), be investigated by an inspector appointed under section 442.

(3) For purposes connected with any investigation made by an inspector appointed under this section —

(a) sections 434 to 436 of the Companies Act 1985 (or those sections as applied by section 443(1)) shall have effect as they do for the purposes of any investigation under section 432 or 442 of that Act, and

(b) the provisions of that Act referred to in this and the last preceding subsection shall be taken to extend throughout the United Kingdom.]¹

[72]

AMENDMENT

1 Sub-ss (2) and (3) substituted by the Companies Consolidation (Consequential Provisions) Act 1985, s 30, Sch 2.

93. Enforcement of orders to which s 90 applies

(1) No criminal proceedings shall, by virtue of the making of an order to which section 90 of this Act applies, lie against any person on the grounds that he has committed, or aided, abetted, counselled or procured the commission of, or conspired or attempted to commit, or incited others to commit, any contravention of the order.

(2) Nothing in the preceding subsection shall limit any right of any person to bring civil proceedings in respect of any contravention or apprehended contravention of any such order, and (without prejudice to the generality of the preceding words) compliance with any such order shall be enforceable by civil proceedings by the Crown for an injunction or interdict or for any other appropriate relief.

(3) If any person makes default in complying with any directions given under section 90(7) of this Act, the court may, on the application of the Secretary of State, make an order requiring him to make good the default within a time specified in the order, or, if the directions related to anything to be done in the management or administration of a company or association, requiring the company or association or any officer of it to do so.

(4) Any order of the court under subsection (3) of this section may provide that all the costs or expenses of or incidental to the application for the order shall be borne by any person in default or by any officers of a company or association who are responsible for its default.

(5) In this section "the court" —

(a) in relation to England and Wales, means the High Court;

(b) in relation to Scotland, means the Court of Session; and

(c) in relation to Northern Ireland, means the High Court or a judge of the High Court.   [73]

NOTE
S 93 extended by the Competition Act 1980, ss 10(4)(c), 12(6)(c).

[93A. Enforcement of undertakings

(1) This section applies where a person (in this section referred to as "the responsible person") has given an undertaking which—

(a) has been accepted by the Secretary of State under section 75G of this Act,
(b) has been accepted by the appropriate Minister or Ministers under section 88 of this Act after the commencement of this section, or
(c) has been accepted by the Director under section 4 or 9 of the Competition Act 1980 after that time.

(2) Any person may bring civil proceedings in respect of any failure, or apprehended failure, of the responsible person to fulfil the undertaking, as if the obligations imposed by the undertaking on the responsible person had been imposed by an order to which section 90 of this Act applies.]   [74]

NOTE
This section was inserted by the Companies Act 1989, s 148, as from 16 November 1989.

[93B. False or misleading information

(1) If a person furnishes any information—

(a) to the Secretary of State, the Director or the Commission in connection with any of their functions under Parts IV, V, VI or this Part of this Act or under the Competition Act 1980, or
(b) to the Commission in connection with the functions of the Commission under the Telecommunications Act 1984 or the Airports Act 1986,

and either he knows the information to be false or misleading in a material particular, or he furnishes the information recklessly and it is false or misleading in a material particular, he is guilty of an offence.

(2) A person who—

(a) furnishes any information to another which he knows to be false or misleading in a material particular, or
(b) recklessly furnishes any information to another which is false or misleading in a material particular,

knowing that the information is to be used for the purpose of furnishing information as mentioned in subsection (1)(a) or (b) of this section, is guilty of an offence.

(3) A person guilty of an offence under subsection (1) or (2) of this section is liable—

(*a*) on summary conviction, to a fine not exceeding the statutory maximum, and

(*b*) on conviction on indictment, to imprisonment for a term not exceeding two years or to a fine or to both.

(4) Section 129(1) of this Act does not apply to an offence under this section.]

[75]

NOTE

This section was inserted by the Companies Act 1989, s 151, as from 16 November 1989.

PART IX

AMENDMENTS OF RESTRICTIVE TRADE PRACTICES ACTS

94. Transfer of functions of Registrar to Director

(1) Subject to the transitional provisions having effect by virtue of section 139 of this Act, the functions of the Registrar of Restrictive Trading Agreements are hereby transferred to the Director, and the office of Registrar of Restrictive Trading Agreements is hereby abolished.

(2) . . .[1]   **[76]**

AMENDMENT

1 Sub-s (2) repealed by Resale Price Act 1976, Sch 3.

95. Agreements as to prices to be recommended or suggested for resale of goods . . . **[77]**

AMENDMENT

Section repealed by RTPA 1976, Sch 6, and replaced by RTPA 1976, ss 6(1)(*b*), 7(1)(*b*).

96. Subscriptions to trade associations . . . **[78]**

AMENDMENT

Section repealed by RTPA 1976, Sch 6, and replaced by RTPA 1976, s 6(4).

97. "Trade association" not to include certain approved societies . . . **[79]**

AMENDMENT

Section repealed by RTPA 1976, Sch 6, and replaced by RTPA 1976, s 32(1).

98. Wholesale co-operative societies . . . **[80]**

AMENDMENT

Section repealed by RTPA 1976, Sch 6, and replaced by RTPA 1976, s 32(1) – (4), (6), (7).

99. Agreements relating to coal or steel . . . **[81]**

AMENDMENT

Section repealed by RTPA 1976, Sch 6, and replaced by RTPA 1976, s 9(1), (2).

100. Agreements to comply with standards of performance . . .   [82]
AMENDMENT
Section repealed by RTPA 1976, Sch 6, and replaced by RTPA 1976, s 9(5).

101. Patent or design pooling agreements . . .   [83]
AMENDMENT
Section repealed by RTPA 1976, Sch 6, and replaced by RTPA 1976, Sch 3, paras 5(1), (4) – (8).

102. Particulars of export agreements to be furnished to Director . . .   [84]
AMENDMENT
Section repealed by RTPA 1976, Sch 6, and replaced by RTPA 1976, ss 25, 36(5), (6).

103. Examination on oath of certain employees etc . . .   [85]
AMENDMENT
Section repealed by RTPA 1976, Sch 6, and replaced by RTPA 1976, s 37(3), (5), (6).

104. Extension of certain powers of Restrictive Practices Court . . .   [86]
AMENDMENT
Section repealed by RTPA 1976, Sch 6, and replaced by RTPA 1976, ss 2(2) – (4), 35(4), (5).

105. Interim orders of Restrictive Practices Court . . .   [87]
AMENDMENT
Section repealed by RTPA 1976, Sch 6, and replaced by RTPA 1976, s 3.

106. Industrial and provident societies etc . . .   [88]
AMENDMENT
Section repealed by RTPA 1976, Sch 6, and replaced by RTPA 1976, s 43(1).

PART X
EXTENSION OF ACT OF 1956 TO AGREEMENTS RELATING TO SERVICES . . .[1]
AMENDMENT
1 Part X repealed by RTPA 1976, Sch 6, and replaced by RTPA 1976, ss 1(1), 11(1), (2), 14(1).

108. Order bringing under control information agreements relating to services . . .   [89]
AMENDMENT
Section repealed by RTPA 1976, Sch 6, and replaced by RTPA 1976, ss 1(1), 12(1), 14(1), 12(2).

109. Designated services . . .   [90]
AMENDMENT
Section repealed by RTPA 1976, Sch 6, and replaced by RTPA 1976, ss 13(1), 43(1), 13(2), (3).

110. Supplementary provisions as to orders under s 107 or s 108 . . .   [91]
AMENDMENT
Section repealed by RTPA 1976, Sch 6, and replaced by RTPA 1976, s 14(2) – (6).

111. Procedure in relation to orders under s 107 or s 108 . . . **[92]**

AMENDMENT

Section repealed by RTPA 1976, Sch 6, and replaced by RTPA 1976, s 15.

112. Provisions as to certain associations . . . **[93]**

AMENDMENT

Section repealed by RTPA 1976, Sch 6, and replaced by RTPA 1976, ss 16(1) – (6), 32(1), (5), 43(1).

113. Matters to be treated as equivalent to restrictions for purposes of s 107 . . . **[94]**

AMENDMENT

Section repealed by RTPA 1976, Sch 6, and replaced by RTPA 1976, s 17(1) and (2).

114. Provisions to be disregarded . . . **[95]**

AMENDMENT

Section repealed by RTPA 1976, Sch 6, and replaced by RTPA 1976, s 18(1) – (6).

115. Excepted agreements . . . **[96]**

AMENDMENT

Section repealed by RTPA 1976, Sch 6, and replaced by RTPA 1976, Sch 3, paras 1(3), 7, 5(1) and (9), 5(4), 8, 9(1), s 18(7), and Sch 3, paras 5(5) – (8), 9(1), (2).

116. Application of provisions of Acts of 1956 and 1968 . . . **[97]**

AMENDMENT

Section repealed by RTPA 1976, Sch 6, and replaced by various sections of the RTPA 1976.

117. Interpretation of Part X and Schedule 10 . . . **[98]**

AMENDMENT

Section repealed by RTPA 1976, Sch 6, and replaced by RTPA 1976, ss 20, 43(1) – (4).

PART XI

PYRAMID SELLING AND SIMILAR TRADING SCHEMES

(not reproduced in this work)

PART XII

MISCELLANEOUS AND SUPPLEMENTARY PROVISIONS

124. Publication of information and advice

(1) With respect to any matter in respect of which the Director has any duties under section 2(1) of this Act, he may arrange for the publication, in such form and in such manner as he may consider appropriate, of such information and advice as it may appear to him to be expedient to give to consumers in the United Kingdom.

(2) In arranging for the publication of any such information or advice, the Director shall have regard to the need for excluding, so far as that is practicable, –

(*a*) any matter which relates to the private affairs of an individual, where the publication of that matter would or might, in the opinion of the Director, seriously and prejudicially affect the interests of that individual, and

(*b*) any matter which relates specifically to the affairs of a particular body of persons, whether corporate or unincorporate, where publication of that matter would or might, in the opinion of the Director, seriously and prejudicially affect the interests of that body.

(3) Without prejudice to the exercise of his powers under subsection (1) of this section, it shall be the duty of the Director to encourage relevant associations to prepare, and to disseminate to their members, codes of practice for guidance in safeguarding and promoting the interests of consumers in the United Kingdom.

(4) In this section "relevant association" means any association (whether incorporated or not) whose membership consists wholly or mainly of persons engaged in the production or supply of goods or in the supply of services or of persons employed by or representing persons so engaged and whose objects or activities include the promotion of the interests of persons so engaged.   **[99]**

NOTE
By virtue of the Telecommunications Act 1984, s 109(1) and Sch 4, para 57(1), the Director General of Fair Trading is to consult with the Director General of Telecommunications before publishing under sub-s (1) of this section any information or advice which the Director General of Telecommunications has power to publish under s 48(1) of the Act of 1984.

125. Annual and other reports of Director

(1) The Director shall, as soon as practicable after the end of the year 1974 and of each subsequent calendar year, make to the Secretary of State a report on his activities, and the activities of the Advisory Committee and of the Commission, during that year.

(2) Every such report shall include a general survey of developments, during the year to which it relates, in respect of matters falling within the scope of the Director's duties under any enactment (including any enactment contained in this Act, other than this section) [and shall set out any directions given to the Director under section 2(2) of the Consumer Credit Act 1974 during that year][1].

(3) The Secretary of State shall lay a copy of every report made by the Director under subsection (1) of this section before each House of Parliament, and shall arrange for every such report to be published in such manner as he may consider appropriate.

(4) The Director may also prepare such other reports as appear to him to be expedient with respect to such matters as are mentioned in subsection (2) of this section, and may arrange for any such report to be published in such manner as he may consider appropriate.

(5) In making any report under this Act the Director shall have regard to the need for excluding, so far as that is practicable, any such matter as is specified in paragraph (*a*) or paragraph (*b*) of section 124(2) of this Act.

(6) For the purposes of this section any period between the commencement of this Act and the end of the year 1973 shall be treated as included in the year 1974.

[100]

AMENDMENT
1 Words added to sub-s (2) by the Consumer Credit Act 1974, s 5.

126. Special provisions relating to patents . . . **[101]**

AMENDMENT
Section repealed by Patents Act 1977, s 132(7).

127. Additional power to make orders under Agricultural Marketing Act 1958

The following section shall be inserted in the Agricultural Marketing Act 1958 after section 19: —

"19A. — (1) The provisions of this section shall have effect where a report made by the Monopolies and Mergers Commission under section 54 of the Fair Trading Act 1973, as laid before Parliament, contains conclusions to the effect —

  (*a*) that certain matters indicated in the report operate, or may be expected to operate, against the public interest, and

  (*b*) that those matters consist of or include any provision of a scheme or any act or omission of a board administering a scheme.

(2) In the circumstances mentioned in subsection (1) of this section, the Minister shall have the like power to make orders under section 19 of this Act as if those conclusions of the Monopolies and Mergers Commission —

  (*a*) had been to the effect that the provision of the scheme in question, or the act or omission of the board to which those conclusions relate, were contrary to the interests of consumers of the regulated product, and

  (*b*) had been contained in a report of a committee of investigation."

[102]

128. Order superseded by declaration of Restrictive Practices Court . . . [103]

AMENDMENT
Section repealed by RTPA 1976, Sch 6, and replaced by RTPA 1976, s 40(3).

129. Time-limit for prosecutions

(1) No prosecution for an offence under this Act shall be commenced after the expiration of three years from the commission of the offence or one year from its discovery by the prosecutor, whichever is the earlier.

(2) Notwithstanding anything in [section 127(1) of the Magistrates' Courts Act 1980],[1] a magistrates' court may try an information for an offence under this Act if the information was laid within twelve months from the commission of the offence.

(3) Notwithstanding anything in section 23 of the Summary Jurisdiction (Scotland) Act 1954, summary proceedings in Scotland for an offence under this Act may be commenced within twelve months from the commission of the offence, and subsection (2) of the said section 23 shall apply for the purposes of this subsection as it applies for the purposes of that section.

(4) In the application of this section to Northern Ireland, for the references

in subsection (2) to [section 127(1) of the Magistrates' Courts Act 1980][1] and to the trial and laying of an information there shall be substituted respectively references to [Article 19(1) of the Magistrates' Courts (Northern Ireland) Order 1981][2] and to the hearing and determination and making of a complaint [and if in that subsection for the words "an offence under this Act" there were substituted the words "an offence under section 30(1) or 46(2) of this Act"].[3] **[104]**

NOTE
See RTPA 1976, s 41(4)–(7).

AMENDMENTS
1 Words in sub-ss (2) and (4) substituted by the Magistrates' Courts Act 1980, s 154, Sch 7, para 119.
2 Words in sub-s (4) substituted by the Magistrates' Courts (Northern Ireland) Order 1981.
3 Words in sub-s (4) added by the Criminal Justice (Northern Ireland) Order 1980.

130. Notice to Director of intended prosecution

(1) Where a local weights and measures authority in England or Wales proposes to institute proceedings for an offence under section 23 of this Act, or for an offence under the Trade Descriptions Act 1968, other than an offence under section 28(5) or section 29 of that Act [or for an offence under any provision made by or under Part III of the Consumer Protection Act 1987][1], it shall, as between the authority and the Director, be the duty of the authority to give to the Director notice of the intended proceedings, together with a summary of the facts on which the charges are to be founded, and to postpone institution of the proceedings until either —

   (a) twenty-eight days have elapsed since the giving of that notice, or
   (b) the Director has notified the authority that he has received the notice and the summary of the facts.

(2) In relation to offences under the Trade Descriptions Act 1968, the preceding subsection shall have effect subject to the transitional provisions having effect by virtue of section 139 of this Act.   **[105]**

AMENDMENT
1 Sub-s (1) amended by the Consumer Protection Act 1987, s 48, Sch 4, para 3, as from 1 March 1989.

131. Notification of convictions and judgments to Director

(1) Where in any criminal proceedings a person is convicted of an offence by or before a court in the United Kingdom, or a judgment is given against a person in civil proceedings in any such court, and it appears to the court —

   (a) having regard to the functions of the Director under Part III of this Act [or under the Estate Agents Act 1979],[1] that it would be expedient for the conviction or judgment to be brought to his attention, and
   (b) that it may not be brought to his attention unless arrangements for the purpose are made by the court,

the court may make arrangements for that purpose notwithstanding that the proceedings have been finally disposed of by the court.

(2) In this section "judgment" includes any order or decree, and any reference to the giving of a judgment shall be construed accordingly.   **[106]**

AMENDMENT
1 Words in sub-s (1)(*a*) added by the Estate Agents Act 1979, s 9(5).

132. Offences by bodies corporate

(1) Where an offence under section 23, section 46, section 85(6) [, section 93B][1] or Part XI of this Act, which has been committed by a body corporate, is proved to have been committed with the consent or connivance of, or to be attributable to any neglect on the part of, any director, manager, secretary or other similar officer of the body corporate, or any person who was purporting to act in any such capacity, he as well as the body corporate shall be guilty of that offence and be liable to be proceeded against and punished accordingly.

(2) Where the affairs of a body corporate are managed by its members, sub-section (1) of this section shall apply in relation to the acts and defaults of a member in connection with his functions of management as if he were a director of the body corporate. **[107]**

AMENDMENT
Sub-s (1) amended by the Companies Act 1989, s 153, Sch 20, para 17, as from 1 April 1990.

133. General restrictions on disclosure of information

(1) Subject to subsections (2) to (4) of this section, no information with respect to any particular business which has been obtained under or by virtue of the provisions (other than Part II) of this Act . . .[1] shall, so long as that business continues to be carried on, be disclosed without the consent of the person for the time being carrying on that business.

(2) The preceding subsection does not apply to any disclosure of information which is made —

(*a*) for the purposes of facilitating the performance of any functions of the Director, [the Director General of Telecommunications,] [the Director General of Gas Supply], [the Civil Aviation Authority], [the Director General of Water Services], [the Director General of Electricity Supply], the Commission, the Secretary of State or any other Minister under this Act, the [Restrictive Trade Practices Act 1956 or the Restrictive Trade Practices Act 1968] [the Estate Agents Act 1979] [the Competition Act 1980] [or the Telecommunications Act 1984] [or Chapter XIV of Part I of the Financial Services Act 1986] [or the Airports Act 1986] [the Control of Misleading Advertisements Regulations 1988] [or the Water Act 1989] [or the Electricity Act 1989],[2] or

(*b*) in pursuance of a Community obligation within the meaning of the European Communities Act 1972.

(3) Subsection (1) of this section does not apply to any disclosure of information which is made for the purposes of any proceedings before the Restrictive Practices Court or of any other legal proceedings, whether civil or criminal, under this Act, the [Restrictive Trade Practices Act 1956 or the Restrictive Trade Practices Act 1968][3] [or the Control of Misleading Advertisements Regulations 1988][4].

(4) Nothing in subsection (1) of this section shall be construed —

(a) as limiting the matters which may be included in, or made public as part of, a report of the Advisory Committee or of the Commission;

(b) as limiting the particulars which may be entered or filed in, or made public as part of, the register . . .¹

(c) as applying to any information which has been made public as part of such a report or as part of that register.

(5) Any person who discloses any information in contravention of this section shall be guilty of an offence and shall be liable —

(a) on summary conviction, to a fine not exceeding [⁵],

(b) on conviction on indictment, to imprisonment for a term not exceeding two years or to a fine or to both.

(6) In this section references to this Act shall be construed as including references to any enactment repealed by this Act.   [108]

NOTES
See RTPA 1976, s 41(1), (2), (3).
See notes 4 and 5 to s 44, above.

AMENDMENTS
1 Words in sub-ss (1) and (4)(b) repealed by RTPA 1976, Sch 6.
2 Words in sub-s (2)(a) added or substituted by the Telecommunications Act 1984, s 109(1), Sch 4, para 57(3), the RTPA 1976, Sch 5, the Estate Agents Act 1979, s 10(4)(a), the Competition Act 1980, s 19(4)(c), the Gas Act 1986, s 67(1), Sch 7, para 15(3), the Airports Act 1986, s 83(1), Sch 4, para 3, the Financial Services Act 1986, s 182, Sch 13, para 1, the Control of Misleading Advertisements Regulations 1988, SI 1988 No 915, the Water Act 1989, s 190(1), Sch 25, para 45(3) and the Electricity Act 1989, s 112(1), Sch 16, para 16(1), (4).
3 Words in sub-s (3) substituted by RTPA 1976, Sch 5.
4 Added by SI 1988 No 915, reg 7(6)(a).
5 The maximum fine under sub-s (5) is now the prescribed sum under the Magistrates' Courts Act 1980, s 32(2), ie £2,000.

134. Provisions as to orders

(1) Any statutory instrument whereby any order is made under any of the preceding provisions of this Act, other than a provision which requires a draft of the order to be laid before Parliament before making the order, or whereby any regulations are made under this Act, shall be subject to annulment in pursuance of a resolution of either House of Parliament.

(2) Any power conferred by any provision of this Act to make an order by statutory instrument shall include power to revoke or vary the order by a subsequent order made under that provision.   [109]

NOTE
See RTPA 1976, s 42.

135. Financial provisions

(1) The Secretary of State shall pay all remuneration, allowances or other sums payable under this Act to or in respect of persons who are or have been members of the Advisory Committee or the Commission, and shall defray —

(a) all expenses duly incurred by the Commission in the payment of remuneration or allowances payable under this Act to staff of the Commission, and

(b) to such amount as the Secretary of State with the approval of the Minister for the Civil Service may determine, all other expenses duly incurred by the Advisory Committee or the Commission.

(2) There shall be defrayed out of moneys provided by Parliament—

(a) all expenses incurred by the Secretary of State in consequence of the provisions of this Act;

(b) any expenses incurred in consequence of those provisions by any other Minister of the Crown or government department, not being a Minister or department of the Government of Northern Ireland;

(c) the remuneration of, and any travelling or other allowances payable under this Act to, the Director and any staff of the Director, any other sums payable under this Act to or in respect of the Director, and any expenses duly incurred by the Director or by any of his staff in consequence of the provisions of this [or any other]¹ Act;

(d) any increase attributable to this Act in the sums payable out of moneys so provided under the Superannuation Act 1972.

(3) . . .² **[110]**

AMENDMENTS
1 Words in sub-s (2)(c) added by the Competition Act 1980, s 32(2).
2 Sub-s (3) repealed by the Northern Ireland (Modification of Enactments—No 1) Order 1973, SI 1973 No 2163.

136. Powers of Parliament of Northern Ireland . . . **[111]**

AMENDMENT
Section repealed by Statute Law (Repeals) Act 1977.

137. General interpretation provisions

(1) In this Act—

"the Act of 1948" means the Monopolies and Restrictive Practices (Inquiry and Control) Act 1948;
["the Act of 1976" means the Restrictive Trade Practices Act 1976];¹
"the Act of 1964" means the Resale Prices Act 1964 (repealed);
"the Act of 1965" means the Monopolies and Mergers Act 1965;
"the Act of 1968" means the Restrictive Trade Practices Act 1968 (repealed);
"assignment", in relation to Scotland, means assignation;
"contract of employment" means a contract of service or of apprenticeship, whether it is express or implied, and (if it is express) whether it is oral or in writing;
"scale" (where the reference is to the scale on which any services are, or are to be, made available, supplied or obtained) means scale measured in terms of money or money's worth or in any other manner.

(2) Except in so far as the context otherwise requires, in this Act . . .² the following expressions have the meanings hereby assigned to them respectively, that is to say—

"the Advisory Committee" means the Consumer Protection Advisory Committee;

"agreement" means any agreement or arrangement, in whatever way and in whatever form it is made, and whether it is, or is intended to be, legally enforceable or not;

"business" includes a professional practice and includes any other undertaking which is carried on for gain or reward or which is an undertaking in the course of which goods or services are supplied otherwise than free of charge;

"commercial activities in the United Kingdom" means any of the following, that is to say, the production and supply of goods in the United Kingdom, the supply of services in the United Kingdom and the export of goods from the United Kingdom;

"the Commission" means the Monopolies and Mergers Commission;

"complex monopoly situation" has the meaning assigned to it by section 11 of this Act;

"consumer" (subject to subsection (6) of this section) means any person who is either —

(*a*) a person to whom goods are or are sought to be supplied (whether by way of sale or otherwise) in the course of a business carried on by the person supplying or seeking to supply them, or

(*b*) a person for whom services are or are sought to be supplied in the course of a business carried on by the person supplying or seeking to supply them,

and who does not receive or seek to receive the goods or services in the course of a business carried on by him;

"the Director" means the Director General of Fair Trading;

"enactment" includes an enactment of the Parliament of Northern Ireland;

"goods" includes buildings and other structures, and also includes ships, aircraft and hovercraft, . . .[3]

"group" (where the reference is to a group of persons fulfilling specified conditions, other than the condition of being interconnected bodies corporate) means any two or more persons fulfilling those conditions, whether apart from fulfilling them they would be regarded as constituting a group or not;

"merger reference" has the meaning assigned to it by section 5(3) of this Act;

"merger situation qualifying for investigation" has the meaning assigned to it by section 64(8) of this Act;

"Minister" includes a government department but shall not by virtue of this provision be taken to include the establishment consisting of the Director and his staff, and, except where the contrary is expressly provided, does not include any Minister or department of the Government of Northern Ireland;

"monopoly reference" and "monopoly situation" have the meanings assigned to them by section 5(3) of this Act;

"newspaper merger reference" has the meaning assigned to it by section 59(3) of this Act;

"practice" means any practice, whether adopted in pursuance of an agreement or otherwise;

"price" includes any charge or fee, by whatever name called;

"produce", in relation to the production of minerals or other substances, includes getting them, and, in relation to the production of animals or fish, includes taking them;

"supply", in relation to the supply of goods, includes supply by way of sale, lease, hire or hire-purchase, and, in relation to buildings or other structures, includes the construction of them by a person for another person;

"uncompetitive practices" means practices having the effect of preventing, restricting or distorting competition in connection with any commercial activities in the United Kingdom;

"worker" (subject to subsection (7) of this section) has the meaning assigned to it by section 167 of the Industrial Relations Act 1971.

(3) In the provisions of this Act . . .² "the supply of services" does not include the rendering of any services under a contract of employment but . . .²—

    (a) includes the undertaking and performance for gain or reward of engagements (whether professional or other) for any matter other than the supply of goods, and

    (b) includes both the rendering of services to order and the provision of services by making them available to potential users, [and

    (c) includes the making of arrangements for a person to put or keep on land a caravan (within the meaning of Part 1 of the Caravan Sites and Control of Development Act 1960) other than arrangements by virtue of which the person may occupy the caravan as his only or main residence],⁴ [and

    (d) includes the making of arrangements for the use by public service vehicles (within the meaning of the Public Passenger Vehicles Act 1981) of a parking place which is used as a point at which passengers on services provided by means of such vehicles may be taken up or set down],⁵

and any reference in those provisions to services supplied or to be supplied, or to services provided or to be provided, shall be construed accordingly.

(4) . . .³

(5) For the purposes of the provisions of this Act . . .², any two bodies corporate are to be treated as interconnected if one of them is a body corporate of which the other is a subsidiary (within the meaning of [section 736 of the Companies Act 1985])⁶ or if both of them are subsidiaries (within the meaning of that section) of one and the same body corporate; and in those provisions "interconnected bodies corporate" shall be construed accordingly, and "group of interconnected bodies corporate" means a group consisting of two or more bodies corporate all of whom are interconnected with each other.

(6) For the purposes of the application of any provision of this Act in relation to goods or services of a particular description or to which a particular practice

applies, "consumers" means persons who are consumers (as defined by subsection (2) of this section) in relation to goods or services of that description or in relation to goods or services to which that practice applies.

(7) For the purposes of the application of this Act to Northern Ireland, the definition of "worker" in subsection (2) of this section shall apply as if the Industrial Relations Act 1971 extended to Northern Ireland but, in section 167(2)(*a*) of that Act, references to general medical services, pharmaceutical services, general dental services or general ophthalmic services provided under the enactments mentioned in that subsection were references to the corresponding services provided in Northern Ireland under the corresponding enactments there in force.

(8) Except in so far as the context otherwise requires, any reference in this Act to an enactment shall be construed as a reference to that enactment as amended or extended by or under any other enactment, including this Act.   **[112]**

NOTE
    See RTPA 1976, s 20, Sch 3, para 5(9) and s 43(1), (5). See also the Telecommunications Act 1984, s 106(1).

AMENDMENTS
    1 Words in sub-s (1) substituted by RTPA 1976, Sch 5.
    2 Words in sub-ss (1), (2), (3), (4) and (5) repealed by RTPA 1976, Sch 6.
    3 Words omitted repealed by the Electricity Act 1989, s 112(4), Sch 18.
    4 Para (*c*) inserted in sub-s (3) by the Competition Act 1980, s 23.
    5 Para (*d*) inserted in sub-s (3) by the Transport Act 1985, s 116 (1) with effect from 1 April 1986. The Transport Act 1985 (Commencement No 3) Order 1986, SI 1986 No 414.
    6 Words in sub-s (5) substituted by the Companies Consolidation (Consequential Provisions) Act 1985, s 30, Sch 2.

138. Supplementary interpretation provisions

(1) This section applies to the following provisions of this Act, that is to say, section 2(4), Parts II and III, section 137(6), and the definition of "consumer" contained in section 137(2).

(2) For the purposes of any provisions to which this section applies it is immaterial whether any person supplying goods or services has a place of business in the United Kingdom or not.

(3) For the purposes of any provisions to which this section applies any goods or services supplied wholly or partly outside the United Kingdom, if they are supplied in accordance with arrangements made in the United Kingdom, whether made orally or by one or more documents delivered in the United Kingdom or by correspondence posted from and to addresses in the United Kingdom, shall be treated as goods supplied to, or services supplied for, persons in the United Kingdom.

(4) In relation to the supply of goods under a hire-purchase agreement, a credit-sale agreement or a conditional sale agreement, the person conducting any antecedent negotiations, as well as the owner or seller, shall for the purposes of any provisions to which this section applies be treated as a person supplying or seeking to supply the goods.

[(5) In subsection (4) of this section, the following expressions have the meanings given by, or referred to in, section 189 of the Consumer Credit Act 1974 –

"antecedent negotiations"
"conditional sale agreement"
"credit-sale agreement"
"hire-purchase agreement"].[1]

(6) In any provisions to which this section applies—

(a) any reference to a person to or for whom goods or services are supplied shall be construed as including a reference to any guarantor of such a person, and

(b) any reference to the terms or conditions on or subject to which goods or services are supplied shall be construed as including a reference to the terms or conditions on or subject to which any person undertakes to act as such a guarantor;

and in this subsection "guarantor", in relation to a person to or for whom goods or services are supplied, includes a person who undertakes to indemnify the supplier of the goods or services against any loss which he may incur in respect of the supply of the goods or services to or for that person.

(7) For the purposes of any provisions to which this section applies goods or services supplied by a person carrying on a business shall be taken to be supplied in the course of that business if payment for the supply of the goods or services is made or (whether under a contract or by virtue of an enactment or otherwise) is required to be made. **[113]**

AMENDMENT
1 Sub-s (5) substituted by the Consumer Credit Act 1974, s 192(3)(a), Sch 4 Part I, para 37.

139. Amendments, repeals and transitional provisions

(1) Subject to the transitional provisions and savings contained in Schedule 11 to this Act—

(a) the enactments specified in Schedule 12 to this Act shall have effect subject to the amendments specified in that Schedule (being minor amendments or amendments consequential upon the preceding provisions of this Act), and

(b) the enactments specified in Schedule 13 to this Act are hereby repealed to the extent specified in the third column of that Schedule.

(2) The provisions of Schedule 11 to this Act shall have effect for the purposes of this Act. **[114]**

140. Short title, citation, commencement and extent

(1) This Act may be cited as the Fair Trading Act 1973.

(2) . . .[1]

(3) This Act shall come into operation on such day as the Secretary of State may by order made by statutory instrument appoint; and different dates may be so appointed for, or for different purposes of, any one or more of the provisions of this Act (including, in the case of section 139 of this Act, the amendment

or repeal of different enactments specified in Schedule 12 or Schedule 13 to this Act or of different provisions of any enactment so specified).

(4) Where any provision of this Act, other than a provision contained in Schedule 11, refers to the commencement of this Act, it shall be construed as referring to the day appointed under this section for the coming into operation of that provision.

(5) This Act extends to Northern Ireland.   [115]

AMENDMENT
1 Sub-s (2) repealed by RTPA 1976, Sch 6.

SCHEDULES
SCHEDULE 1
Section 1
DIRECTOR GENERAL OF FAIR TRADING

1. There shall be paid to the Director such remuneration, and such travelling and other allowances, as the Secretary of State with the approval of the Minister for the Civil Service may determine.

2. In the case of any such holder of the office of the Director as may be determined by the Secretary of State with the approval of the Minister for the Civil Service, there shall be paid such pension, allowance or gratuity to or in respect of him on his retirement or death, or such contributions or payments towards provision for such a pension, allowance or gratuity, as may be so determined.

3. If, when any person ceases to hold office as the Director, it appears to the Secretary of State with the approval of the Minister for the Civil Service that there are special circumstances which make it right that he should receive compensation, there may be paid to him a sum by way of compensation of such amount as may be so determined.

4. *In the House of Commons Disqualification Act 1957, in Part III of Schedule 1 (other disqualifying offices) there shall (at the appropriate place in alphabetical order) be inserted the following entry: —*

   "Director General of Fair Trading";

and the like amendment shall be made in the Part substituted for the said Part III by Schedule 3 to that Act in its application to the Senate and House of Commons of Northern Ireland.[1]

5. The Director shall have an official seal for the authentication of documents required for the purposes of his functions.

6. The Documentary Evidence Act 1868 shall have effect as if the Director were included in the first column of the Schedule to that Act, as if the Director and any person authorised to act on behalf of the Director were mentioned in the second column of that Schedule, and as if the regulations referred to in that Act included any document issued by the Director or by any such person.

7. Anything authorised or required by or under this Act or any other enactment to be done by the Director, other than the making of a statutory instrument, may be done by any member of the staff of the Director who is authorised generally or specially in that behalf in writing by the Director.   [116]

AMENDMENT

1 Para 4 repealed as respects the House of Commons by the House of Commons Disqualification Act 1975, s 10(2), Sch 3, and as respects the Northern Ireland Assembly by the Northern Ireland Assembly Disqualification Act 1975, s 5(2), Sch 3, Part I, and replaced as noted in the destination tables to those Acts.

SCHEDULE 2

Section 3

CONSUMER PROTECTION ADVISORY COMMITTEE

(not reproduced in this work)

SCHEDULE 3

Section 4

THE MONOPOLIES AND MERGERS COMMISSION

PART I

STATUS, TERMS OF OFFICE, AND STAFF

Status of Commission

1. Members of the Commission in their capacity as such shall not be regarded as servants or agents of the Crown or as enjoying any status, immunity or privilege of the Crown.

Tenure of office of regular members

2. — (1) Subject to the following provisions of this paragraph, a regular member of the Commission shall hold and vacate office as such in accordance with the terms of his appointment.

(2) A person shall not be appointed to be a regular member of the Commission for a term exceeding five years; but previous membership shall not affect eligibility for re-appointment.

(3) A regular member of the Commission may at any time resign his membership by notice in writing addressed to the Secretary of State.

(4) The Secretary of State may remove a regular member of the Commission on the ground of incapacity or misbehaviour.

Appointment and tenure of office of chairman and deputy chairmen

3. — (1) There shall be a chairman of the Commission appointed from among the regular members by the Secretary of State; and the Secretary of State may appoint not more than three other regular members to be deputy chairmen.

(2) The chairman or a deputy chairman may at any time resign his office as such by notice in writing addressed to the Secretary of State.

(3) The Secretary of State may remove a chairman or deputy chairman of the Commission on the ground of incapacity or misbehaviour.

(4) If the chairman or a deputy chairman of the Commission ceases to be a regular member of the Commission, he shall also cease to be chairman or, as the case may be, a deputy chairman.

Staff

4. The Commission shall have a secretary, who shall be a person appointed by the Commission with the approval of the Secretary of State.

5. The Commission may appoint such other staff as the Commission think fit, subject to the approval of the Secretary of State and of the Minister for the Civil Service as to numbers and as to terms and conditions of service.

Remuneration and allowances

6. There shall be paid to the members of the Commission such remuneration, and such travelling and other allowances, as in the case of any of those members the Secretary of State may determine with the approval of the Minister for the Civil Service.

7. There shall be paid to the staff of the Commission such remuneration, and such travelling and other allowances, as the Commission may determine with the approval of the Secretary of State and of the Minister for the Civil Service.

General provisions as to sums payable on retirement or death of members

8. As regards any member of the Commission in whose case the Secretary of State may so determine with the approval of the Minister for the Civil Service, the Secretary of State shall pay such pension, allowance or gratuity to or in respect of him, or make such payments towards the provision of such a pension, allowance or gratuity, as may be so determined.

9. If, when any person ceases to be a member of the Commission, it appears to the Secretary of State that there are special circumstances which make it right that he should receive compensation, the Secretary of State may pay him a sum by way of compensation of such amount as he may determine with the approval of the Minister for the Civil Service.   **[117]**

PART II

PERFORMANCE OF FUNCTIONS OF COMMISSION

10. — (1) If the chairman of the Commission so directs —

(a) the functions of the Commission in relation to any investigation under this Act, in so far as those functions have not been performed before the direction is given, or

(b) the functions of the Commission in relation to the making of a report required of them under Part VI of this Act,

shall be performed through a group of not less than [three][1] regular members of the Commission selected by the chairman of the Commission [or, where the functions to be performed through the group relate to a newspaper merger reference, not less than [three][1] members, being, in that event, the additional members (if any) appointed by the Secretary of State under paragraph 22 of this Schedule for the purposes of the reference and such regular members of the Commission as the chairman may select].[2]

[(1A) Where no direction has been made under sub-paragraph (1) hereof with respect to the investigation on a merger reference the chairman of the Commission may perform the functions of the Commission under section 75(5) of this Act in relation to that reference and anything done by or in relation to the chairman in, or in connection with, the performance of those functions shall have the same effect as if it had been done by or in relation to the Commission.][1]

(2) In the following provisions of this Part of this Schedule "group" means a group of members of the Commission selected under this paragraph, and "the chairman" (except where the reference is expressly to the chairman of a group) means the chairman of the Commission.

11. Where, after a direction under paragraph 10 of this Schedule has been given with respect to the investigations on a monopoly reference or on a merger reference, the reference is varied under section 52 of this Act or, in the case of a merger reference, under section 71 of this Act, the functions of the Commission in relation to those investigations shall be performed either through the group specified in that direction, or through another group, or by the Commission as a whole, as the chairman may direct.

12. The chairman may appoint one of the members of a group to act as chairman of the group.

13.—(1) Where during the proceedings of a group—

(a) a member of the group ceases to be a member of the Commission, or
(b) the chairman is satisfied that a member of the group will be unable for a substantial period to perform his duties as a member of the group,

the chairman may appoint any member of the Commission to be a member of the group in his place.

(2) The chairman may also at any time appoint any member of the Commission to be an additional member of a group, whether the person so appointed was or was not a member of the Commission at the time when the group was originally selected.

14.—(1) At the invitation of the chairman of a group, any member of the Commission who is not a member of the group may attend meetings or otherwise take part in the proceedings of the group, except that such a member shall not be entitled—

(a) to vote at any such meeting or in any such proceedings, or
(b) to have a statement of his dissent from a conclusion of the group included in a report made by them.

(2) Nothing in the preceding sub-paragraph shall be taken to prevent a group or a member of a group from consulting any member of the Commission with respect to any matter or question with which the group is concerned.

15. In determining their procedure, and in exercising any powers conferred on the Commission by this Act, a group shall comply with any special or general directions which may be given to them by the Commission, as well as with any directions given to the Commission by the Secretary of State.

16.—(1) Subject to the next following sub-paragraph, anything done by or in relation to a group in, or in connection with, the performance of functions required by a direction under paragraph 10 or paragraph 11 of this Schedule to be performed by the group shall have the same effect as if it had been done by or in relation to the Commission.

(2) For the purposes of sections 56 and [73]³ of this Act, . . .⁴ and of section 19A of the Agricultural Marketing Act 1958 [and of Articles 23 and 42 of the Agricultural Marketing (Northern Ireland) Order 1982],⁵ a conclusion contained in a report of the Commission shall be disregarded if the report is made through a group and the conclusion is not that of at least two-thirds of the members of the group.

17. The quorum necessary—

(a) for any meeting of the Commission held for the final settling of a report of the Commission shall be not less than two-thirds of the regular members of the Commission, and

(b) for any other meeting of the Commission shall be such as the Commission may from time to time determine.

18. The quorum necessary for a meeting of a group shall be such as the group may from time to time determine.

19. In the case of an equality of votes on any question at a meeting of the Commission or of a group the chairman, or the chairman of the group, as the case may be, shall have a second or casting vote.

20. At any time when the chairman is absent or otherwise incapable of acting, or there is a vacancy in the office of chairman,—

(a) such one of the deputy chairmen of the Commission as the Secretary of State may direct, or in default of any such direction such one of them as they may agree, or

(b) if there is only one deputy chairman of the Commission the deputy chairman,

may perform any of the functions of the chairman.

21. At any time when every person who is chairman or deputy chairman of the Commission is absent or otherwise incapable of acting, or there is no such person, such member of the Commission as the Secretary of State may direct, or in default of any such direction such member of the Commission as the Commission may agree, may perform any of the functions of the chairman.

22. For the purposes of a newspaper merger reference the Secretary of State may appoint [one, two, or three]¹ additional members of the Commission, from a panel maintained by the Secretary of State for the purpose of making such appointments; and if any functions of the Commission in relation to that reference are performed through a group, any additional members appointed under this paragraph for the purposes of the reference shall be members of the group in addition to the members selected by the chairman.

[118]

NOTES

1 Part II is applied by the Competition Act 1980, ss 7(6), 11(9).

2 The Secretary of State may make modifications in Part II by order; see Competition Act 1980, s 24.

AMENDMENTS

1 Sub-s (1) amended and sub-s (1A) inserted by the Monopolies and Mergers Commission (Performance of Functions) Order 1989, SI 1989 No 122, as from 31 January 1989.

2 Words in paras 10(1) and 22 added or substituted by the Monopolies and Mergers Commission (Membership of Groups for Newspaper Merger References) Order 1982, SI 1982 No 1889 with effect from 3 January 1983.

3 Substituted by the Companies Act 1989, s 153, Sch 20, para 18, although not in relation to any report made before 16 November 1989.

4 Words in para 16(2) repealed by the Patents Act 1977, s 132 and Sch 6.
5 Words in para 16(2) substituted by the Agricultural Marketing (Northern Ireland) Order 1982.

SCHEDULE 4

Sections 14 and 109
SERVICES EXCLUDED FROM SECTIONS 14 AND 109

1. Legal services (that is to say, the services of barristers, advocates or solicitors in their capacity as such).

2. Medical services (that is to say, the provision of medical or surgical advice or attendance and the performance of surgical operations).

3. Dental services (that is to say, any services falling within the practice of dentistry within the meaning of the Dentists Act [1984].¹

4. Ophthalmic services (that is to say, the testing of sight).

5. Veterinary services (that is to say, any services which constitute veterinary surgery within the meaning of the Veterinary Surgeons Act 1966).

6. Nursing services (that is to say, any services which constitute nursing within the meaning of the Nurses Act 1957, the Nurses (Scotland) Act 1951 or the Nurses and Midwives Act (Northern Ireland) 1970).

7. The services of midwives, physiotherapists or chiropodists in their capacity as such.

8. The services of architects in their capacity as such.

9. Accounting and auditing services (that is to say, the making or preparation of accounts or accounting records and the examination, verification and auditing of financial statements).

10. *The services of patent agents (within the meaning of the [Patents Act 1977],¹ in their capacity as such.*

[10A. The services of persons carrying on for gain in the United Kingdom the business of acting as agents or other representatives of other persons for the purpose of applying for or obtaining European patents or for the purpose of conducting proceedings in relation to applications for or otherwise in connection with such patents before the European Patent Office or the comptroller and whose names appear on the European list (within the meaning of *section 84(7) of the Patents Act 1977)*, in their capacity as such persons].²

11. The services of parliamentary agents entered in the register in either House of Parliament as agents entitled to practise both in promoting and in opposing Bills, in their capacity as such parliamentary agents.

12. The services of surveyors (that is to say, of surveyors of land, of quantity surveyors, of surveyors of buildings or other structures and of surveyors of ships) in their capacity as such surveyors.

13. The services of professional engineers or technologists (that is to say, of persons practising or employed as consultants in the field of —

    (a) civil engineering;
    (b) mechanical, aeronautical, marine, electrical or electronic engineering;
    (c) mining, quarrying, soil analysis or other forms of mineralogy or geology;

(*d*) agronomy, forestry, livestock rearing or ecology;
(*e*) metallurgy, chemistry, biochemistry or physics; or
(*f*) any other form of engineering or technology analogous to those mentioned in the preceding sub-paragraphs),

in their capacity as such engineers or technologists.

14. Services consisting of the provision —

(*a*) of primary, secondary or further education within the meaning of the Education Act 1944, the Education (Scotland) Acts 1939 to 1971 or the Education and Libraries (Northern Ireland) Order 1972, or
(*b*) of university or other higher education not falling within the preceding sub-paragraph.

15. The services of ministers of religion in their capacity as such ministers.   **[119]**

NOTE
See RTPA 1976, s 13.

AMENDMENTS
1 The references to 1984 in para 3 and to the Patents Act 1977 in para 10 substituted by the Dentists Act 1984 and the Patents Act 1977 respectively.
2 Para 10A inserted by the Patents Act 1977, s 132(6), Sch 5, para 7 and amended by the Administration of Justice Act 1985, s 60(2)(*a*), (6).

PROSPECTIVE AMENDMENT
As from a day to be appointed, the Copyright, Designs and Patents Act 1988, s 303(1), Sch 7, para 15 makes the following amendments:
   (i) for para 10 above there is substituted:
      "10. The services of registered patent agents (within the meaning of Part V of the Copyright, Designs and Patents Act 1988) in their capacity as such."
   (ii) for the words in italics in para 10A, there is substituted "Part V, of the Copyright, Designs and Patents Act 1988."

SCHEDULE 5
Sections 16, 50 and 51
GOODS AND SERVICES REFERRED TO IN SECTION 16
(not reproduced in this work)

SCHEDULE 6
Section 17
MATTERS FALLING WITHIN SCOPE OF PROPOSALS UNDER SECTION 17
(not reproduced in this work)

SCHEDULE 7
Sections 50 and 51
GOODS AND SERVICES (IN ADDITION TO THOSE IN SCHEDULE 5) WHOLLY OR PARTLY EXCLUDED FROM SECTION 50

PART I
GOODS AND SERVICES WHOLLY EXCLUDED
1 Raw cane or beet sugar.
2 Sugar beet.
3 Hops.

4 *Water.*[1]

5 Port facilities (as defined by section 92(1) of the Transport Act 1962).

6 Air navigation services (as defined by section 64(1) of the Civil Aviation Act 1971).

7 [International carriage by air, otherwise than on a charter flight (that is to say, a flight on which the whole capacity of the aircraft is available for purchase by one or more charterers for his or their own use or for resale)].[2]

8 The provision by programme contractors of programmes for transmission (whether by way of television or of sound broadcasting) by the Independent Broadcasting Authority [(including, by virtue of section 14(5) of the Broadcasting Act 1981, the provision by teletext contractors of teletext transmissions for transmission by that Authority)].[3]

[9 The provision of a licensed cable programme service].[4]   **[120]**

AMENDMENTS

1 Para 4 repealed as to England and Wales by the Water Act 1989, s 190(1),(3), Sch 25, para 45(4), Sch 27, Pt I.

2 Para 7 substituted by the Monopoly References (Alteration of Exclusions) Order 1984, SI 1984 No 1887 with effect from 1 January 1985.

3 Para 8 amended by the Broadcasting Act 1981, s 65(1).

4 Para 9 added by the Cable and Broadcasting Act 1984, s 57(1), Sch 5, para 29.

PART II

GOODS AND SERVICES PARTLY EXCLUDED

Description of goods or services	*Form of supply excluded*
9 Liquid cows' milk.	Supply otherwise than in containers in which milk is put up for purposes of retail sale.
10 Refined sugar.	Supply otherwise than by way of retail sale.
11 Fleece wool.	Supply under a scheme for the time being in force under the Agricultural Marketing Act 1958.
12 Potatoes to which no process of manufacture (other than dressing or dyeing) has been applied.	Supply which is neither— (a) supply by way of retail sale, other than any such supply by the producer of the goods, nor (b) supply to a person purchasing the goods for the purpose of selling them by retail.
13 . . .[1]	**[121]**

AMENDMENTS

Para 13 repealed by the Airports Art 1986, s 83(5), Sch 6, Pt II.

PART III

GOODS PARTLY EXCLUDED IN RELATION TO NORTHERN IRELAND ONLY

Description of goods	*Form of supply excluded*
14 Live pigs.	Supply for slaughter.
15 Fresh uncured carcases or parts of carcases of pigs.	Supply otherwise than by way of retail sale. **[122]**

SCHEDULE 8
Sections 56, 73, 74, 77, 89 and 91
POWERS EXERCISABLE BY ORDERS UNDER SECTIONS 56 AND 73

PART I

POWERS EXERCISABLE IN ALL CASES

1. Subject to paragraph 3 of this Schedule, an order under section 56 or section 73 of this Act (in this Schedule referred to as an "order") may declare it to be unlawful, except to such extent and in such circumstances as may be provided by or under the order, to make or to carry out any such agreement as may be specified or described in the order.

2. Subject to the next following paragraph, an order may require any party to any such agreement as may be specified or described in the order to terminate the agreement within such time as may be so specified, either wholly or to such extent as may be so specified.

3.—(1) An order shall not by virtue of paragraph 1 of this Schedule declare it to be unlawful to make any agreement in so far as, if made, it would be an agreement to which [the Act of 1976][1] would apply.

(2) An order shall not by virtue of paragraph 1 or paragraph 2 of this Schedule declare it to be unlawful to carry out, or require any person to terminate, an agreement in so far as it is an agreement to which [the Act of 1976][1] applies.

(3) An order shall not by virtue of either of those paragraphs declare it to be unlawful to make or to carry out, or require any person to terminate, an agreement in so far as, if made, it would relate, or (as the case may be) in so far as it relates, to the terms and conditions of employment of any workers, or to the physical conditions in which any workers are required to work.

(4) In this paragraph "terms and conditions of employment" has the meaning assigned to it by section 167(1) of the Industrial Relations Act 1971.

4. An order may declare it to be unlawful, except to such extent and in such circumstances as may be provided by or under the order, to withhold or to agree to withhold or to threaten to withhold, or to procure others to withhold or to agree to withhold or threaten to withhold, from any such persons as may be specified or described in the order, any supplies or services so specified or described or any orders for such supplies or services (whether the withholding is absolute or is to be effectual only in particular circumstances).

5. An order may declare it to be unlawful, except to such extent and in such circumstances as may be provided by or under the order, to require, as a condition of the supplying of goods or services to any person,—

(a) the buying of any goods, or
(b) the making of any payment in respect of services other than the goods or services supplied, or
(c) the doing of any other such matter as may be specified or described in the order.

6. An order may declare it to be unlawful, except to such extent and in such circumstances as may be provided by or under the order,—

(a) to discriminate in any manner specified or described in the order between any persons in the prices charged for goods or services so specified or described, or
(b) to do anything so specified or described which appears to the appropriate Minister to amount to such discrimination,

or to procure others to do any of the things mentioned in sub-paragraph (*a*) or sub-paragraph (*b*) of this paragraph.

7. An order may declare it to be unlawful, except to such extent and in such circumstances as may be provided by or under the order, —

(*a*) to give or agree to give in other ways any such preference in respect of the supply of goods or services, or the giving of orders for goods or services, as may be specified or described in the order, or

(*b*) to do anything so specified or described which appears to the appropriate Minister to amount to giving such preference,

or to procure others to do any of the things mentioned in sub-paragraph (*a*) or sub-paragraph (*b*) of this paragraph.

8. An order may declare it to be unlawful, except to such extent and in such circumstances as may be provided by or under the order, to charge for goods or services supplied prices differing from those in any published list or notification, or to do anything specified or described in the order which appears to the appropriate Minister to amount to charging such prices.

9. An order may require a person supplying goods or services to publish a list of or otherwise notify prices, with or without such further information as may be specified or described in the order.

[9A. —(1) An order may require a person supplying goods or services to publish —

(*a*) any such accounting information in relation to the supply of the goods or services, and

(*b*) any such information in relation to —
(i) the quantities of goods or services supplied, or
(ii) the geographical areas in which they are supplied,

as may be specified or described in the order.

(2) In this paragraph "accounting information", in relation to a supply of goods or services, means information as to —

(*a*) the costs of the supply, including fixed costs and overheads.

(*b*) the manner in which fixed costs and overheads are calculated and apportioned for accounting purposes of the supplier, and

(*c*) the income attributable to the supply.][2]

10. —(1) Subject to the following provisions of this paragraph, an order may, to such extent and in such circumstances as may be provided by or under the order, regulate the prices to be charged for any goods or services specified or described in the order.

(2) An order shall not exercise the power conferred by the preceding sub-paragraph in respect of goods or services of any description unless the matters specified in the relevant report as being those which in the opinion of the Commission operate, or may be expected to operate, against the public interest relate, or include matters relating, to the prices charged for goods or services of that description.

(3) In this paragraph "the relevant report", in relation to an order, means the report of the Commission in consequence of which the order is made, in the form in which that report is laid before Parliament.

11. An order may declare it to be unlawful, except to such extent and in such circumstances as may be provided by or under the order, for any person, by publication or otherwise, to notify, to persons supplying goods or services, prices recommended or suggested as appropriate to be charged by those persons for those goods or services.

12. – (1) An order may prohibit or restrict the acquisition by any person of the whole or part of the undertaking or assets of another person's business, or the doing of anything which will or may have a result to which this paragraph applies, or may require that, if such an acquisition is made or anything is done which has such a result, the persons concerned or any of them shall thereafter observe any prohibitions or restrictions imposed by or under the order.

(2) This paragraph applies to any result which consists in two or more bodies corporate becoming interconnected bodies corporate.

(3) Where an order is made in consequence of a report of the Commission under section 72 of this Act, or is made under section 74 of this Act, this paragraph also applies to any result (other than that specified in sub-paragraph (2) of this paragraph) which, in accordance with section 65 of this Act, consists in two or more enterprises ceasing to be distinct enterprises.

[12A. An order may require any person to furnish any such information to the Director as may be specified or described in the order.

12B. An order may require any activities to be carried on separately from any other activities.

12C. An order may prohibit or restrict the exercise of any right to vote exercisable by virtue of the holding of any shares, stock or securities.]²

13. In this Part of this Schedule "the appropriate Minister", in relation to an order, means the Minister by whom the order is made.   **[123]**

NOTE
Part I extended by the Competition Act 1980, s 10(2)(*b*), 4(*d*) and extended, with the exception of para 10, by s 12(5), (6)(*d*) of that Act.

AMENDMENT
1 Words in para 3(1) and (2) substituted by RTPA 1976, Sch 5.
2 Paras 9A, 12A – 12C inserted by the Companies Act 1989, s 153, Sch 20, para 19, as from 16 November 1989.

PART II

POWERS EXERCISABLE EXCEPT IN CASES FALLING WITHIN SECTION 56(6)

14. An order may provide for the division of any business by the sale of any part of the undertaking or assets or otherwise (for which purpose all the activities carried on by way of business by any one person or by any two or more interconnected bodies corporate may be treated as a single business), or for the division of any group of interconnected bodies corporate, and for all such matters as may be necessary to effect or take account of the division, including –

(*a*) the transfer or vesting of property, rights, liabilities or obligations;
(*b*) the adjustment of contracts, whether by discharge or reduction of any liability or obligation or otherwise;
(*c*) the creation, allotment, surrender or cancellation of any shares, stock or securities;
(*d*) the formation or winding up of a company or other association, corporate or unincorporate, or the amendment of the memorandum and articles or other instruments regulating any company or association;
(*e*) the extent to which, and the circumstances in which, provisions of the order affecting a company or association in its share capital, constitution or other matters may be altered by the company or association, and the registration under any enactment of the order by companies or associations so affected;
(*f*) the continuation, with any necessary change of parties, of any legal proceedings.

15. In relation to an order under section 73 of this Act, the reference in paragraph 14 of this Schedule to the division of a business as mentioned in that paragraph shall be construed as including a reference to the separation, by the sale of any part of any undertaking or assets concerned or other means, of enterprises which are under common control otherwise than by reason of their being enterprises of interconnected bodies corporate.   **[124]**

SCHEDULE 9

Section 91

PROCEDURE PRELIMINARY TO LAYING DRAFT OF ORDER TO WHICH
SECTION 91(1) APPLIES

1. The provisions of this Schedule shall have effect where the Secretary of State proposes to lay before Parliament a draft of any such order as is mentioned in section 91(1) of this Act.

2. The Secretary of State shall cause notice of his intention to lay a draft of the order before Parliament to be published in the London Gazette, the Edinburgh Gazette and the Belfast Gazette and in two or more daily newspapers (other than local newspapers), and shall not lay a draft of the order until the end of the period of forty-two days beginning with the day on which the publication of the notice in accordance with this paragraph is completed.

3. A notice under this Schedule shall—

   (a) state that it is proposed to lay a draft of the order before Parliament;
   (b) indicate the nature of the provisions to be embodied in the order;
   (c) name a place where a copy of the draft will be available to be seen at all reasonable times; and
   (d) state that any person whose interests are likely to be affected by the order, and who is desirous of making representations in respect of it, should do so in writing (stating his interest and the grounds on which he wishes to make the representations) before the date on which the period mentioned in paragraph 2 of this Schedule is due to expire (specifying that date).

4. The Secretary of State shall consider any representation that is duly made with respect to the draft order and is not withdrawn, and, at any time after the date specified in the notice in accordance with sub-paragraph (d) of paragraph 3 of this Schedule, may lay the draft order . . .[1]   **[125]**

AMENDMENT
1 Words omitted from para 4 repealed by the Companies Act 1989, ss 153, 212, Sch 20, para 20, Sch 24, in relation to the laying of any draft order under this paragraph after 16 November 1989 whether the notice was published before or after that time.

SCHEDULE 10

Sections 116, 117

MODIFICATIONS OF ACTS OF 1956 AND 1968 IN RELATION TO SERVICES . . .[1]   **[126]**

AMENDMENT
1 Sch 10 repealed by RTPA 1976, Sch 6.

SCHEDULE 11

Sections 139, 140

TRANSITIONAL PROVISIONS AND SAVINGS

General provisions

1. – (1) Subject to the following provisions of this Schedule, in so far as anything done under an enactment repealed by this Act could have been done under a corresponding provision of this Act, it shall not be invalidated by the repeal but shall have effect as if done under that provision.

(2) In relation to the Commission (by whichever of the names mentioned in section 4(1) of this Act it was for the time being called) sub-paragraph (1) of this paragraph applies, in particular, to any appointment of a member of the Commission (including any appointment, or extension of the term of service, of a chairman or deputy chairman of the Commission) or of any of the staff of the Commission, any reference made to the Commission, any proceedings or report of the Commission on such a reference, and any order made in consequence of any such report.

(3) A provision of this Act shall, for the purposes of this Schedule, be regarded as corresponding to an enactment repealed by this Act if (notwithstanding that it differs, whether to a small extent or substantially, from that enactment) it fulfils in this Act a purpose similar to that which that enactment fulfilled in the repealed enactments; and any reference in this Schedule to provisions of the repealed enactments corresponding to any provisions of this Act shall be construed accordingly.

(4) In this Schedule "the repealed enactments" means the enactments repealed by this Act, and "the commencement of this Act", where that expression occurs in any provision of this Schedule, –

(a) if the same day is appointed under section 140 of this Act for the repeal of all those enactments, means the day so appointed, or

(b) if different days are appointed under that section for the repeal of different enactments, means such day as may be specified for the purposes of this sub-paragraph in an order made by the Secretary of State by statutory instrument;

and different days may be so specified in relation to different provisions of this Schedule.

2. For the purposes of the operation of paragraph 1 of this Schedule, anything done by or in relation to the Board of Trade shall be treated as having been done by or in relation to the Secretary of State, whether apart from this paragraph it would fall to be so treated or not.

3. Without prejudice to any express amendment made by this Act, where an Act (whether passed before, or in the same Session as, this Act) or any document refers, either expressly or by implication, to an enactment repealed by this Act, the reference shall, except where the context otherwise requires, be construed as, or as including, a reference to any corresponding provision of this Act.

4. Where any period of time specified in an enactment repealed by this Act is current at the commencement of this Act, and there is a corresponding provision in this Act, this Act shall have effect as if that corresponding provision had been in force when that period began to run.

5. Without prejudice to paragraph 1 of this Schedule, any reference in this Act (whether express or implied) to a thing done or required or authorised to be done, or omitted to be done, or to an event which has occurred, under or for the purposes of or by reference to or in contravention of any provisions of this Act shall, except where the context otherwise requires, be construed as including a reference to the corresponding thing done or

required or authorised to be done, or omitted, or to the corresponding event which occurred, as the case may be, under or for the purposes of or by reference to or in contravention of any corresponding provisions of the repealed enactments.

6. Nothing in this Act shall affect the repealed enactments in their operation in relation to offences committed before the commencement of this Act.

Reference made to Commission before commencement of Act

7. – (1) Any reference made to the Commission under the repealed enactments, and any report of the Commission made before the commencement of this Act on any such reference, shall have effect in accordance with paragraph 1 of this Schedule if made in accordance with such of the repealed enactments as were applicable to it, and shall so have effect notwithstanding that the reference or report was not made in accordance with the corresponding provisions of this Act.

(2) In the case of any such reference on which the Commission have not made their report before the commencement of this Act –

(a) any proceedings of the Commission on that reference after the commencement of this Act shall be conducted in accordance with the repealed enactments as if they had not been repealed, and

(b) any report of the Commission on that reference shall be made in accordance with those enactments and not in accordance with any corresponding provisions of this Act;

but nothing in this sub-paragraph shall be construed as excluding the operation of any provisions of this Act relating to any functions of the Director in relation to the Commission, to the transmission to the Director of copies of reports of the Commission, or to any other action authorised or required to be taken in relation to or in consequence of a report made by the Commission.

(3) In particular, but without prejudice to the generality of the preceding sub-paragraphs, any reference, proceedings or report to which either of those sub-paragraphs applies shall have effect, or shall be conducted or made, as mentioned in that sub-paragraph notwithstanding that the reference or report related or relates to the question whether conditions to which the Act of 1948 applied prevailed or prevail, and not to the existence or possible existence of a monopoly situation within the meaning of this Act.

(4) For the purposes of the operation of sub-paragraph (2) of this paragraph in relation to a report made by the Commission after the commencement of this Act, section 29(1) of the Act of 1956 (whereby conditions to which the Act of 1948 applied were not to be considered to prevail by reason of any agreement to which Part I of the Act of 1956 applied) shall be construed as if section 6(1) of the Act of 1956 had been originally enacted as amended by section 95 of this Act.

Report of Commission made before 5th August 1965

8. An order made under section 56 of this Act in consequence of a report made by the Commission before the commencement of the Act of 1965 shall not exercise any of the powers specified in Part II of Schedule 8 to this Act; and accordingly the powers conferred by section 89 of this Act shall not be exercisable in consequence of any such report.

Undertaking given in consequence of report on reference made under repealed enactments

9.—(1) This paragraph applies to any undertaking given to a Minister which is certified by the Secretary of State to have been given in relation to matters dealt with in a report made by the Commission on a reference under section 2 of the Act of 1948 or on a reference under section 6 of the Act of 1965 and which either—

(*a*) was given before the commencement of this Act, or

(*b*) is given after the commencement of this Act in a case where no request under subsection (1) of section 88 of this Act has been made to the Director to carry out consultations in accordance with that subsection.

(2) A copy of any certificate given by the Secretary of State under the preceding subparagraph shall be furnished to the Director; and the Minister to whom any such undertaking was or is given shall furnish particulars of it to the Director.

(3) Subsection (4) of section 88 of this Act shall have effect in relation to any undertaking to which this paragraph applies as if—

(*a*) it were an undertaking of which particulars have been furnished to the Director under subsection (2) of that section, and

(*b*) any reference in subsection (4) of that section to the report of the Director were a reference to a report made by the Commission as mentioned in sub-paragraph (1) of this paragraph.

(4) The preceding provisions of this paragraph shall have effect without prejudice—

(*a*) to the duty of the Commission under section 86 of this Act to transmit to the Director copies of reports which were made by the Commission before the commencement of this Act and which, by virtue of paragraphs 1 and 7 of this Schedule, have effect as if made under this Act, or

(*b*) to any duty of the Director, where requested by the appropriate Minister or Ministers to do so with respect to any such report, to carry out such consultations as are mentioned in section 88(1) of this Act.

NOTE
See Competition Act 1980, s 29(1).

Functions of Director in relation to orders made under Acts of 1948 and 1965

10. Subsection (5) of section 88 of this Act shall have effect in relation to any order which was made under section 10 of the Act of 1948 or under section 3 or section 6 of the Act of 1965 and which, by virtue of paragraph 1 of this Schedule, has effect as if made under this Act, as that subsection has effect in relation to orders made under this Act in the circumstances specified in that subsection.

Provisions consequential upon transfer of functions from Registrar to Director

11.—(1) Except as provided by paragraph 15 of this Schedule, in relation to any time after the commencement of this Act, anything which has before the commencement of this Act been done by or in relation to the Registrar shall have effect as if it had been done by or in relation to the Director.

(2) Sub-paragraph (1) of this paragraph applies, in particular, to any regulations made by the Registrar, any register kept or document issued by the Registrar, any particulars furnished to the Registrar, and any application to or proceedings before the Restrictive Practices Court, or any other court, tribunal or authority, made or instituted by or against the Registrar or to which the Registrar was otherwise a party; and any such proceedings, if pending at the commencement of this Act, may accordingly be continued by or against the Director, or with the Director being otherwise treated as a party to them, as the circumstances may require, and for the purpose of so continuing them anything done by or in relation to the Registrar in connection with any such proceedings shall be treated as having been done by or in relation to the Director.

(3) In this Schedule "the Registrar" means the Registrar of Restrictive Trading Agreements.

Particulars of export agreements

12. . . .

AMENDMENT
Para 12 repealed by RTPA 1976, Sch 6, and replaced by RTPA 1976, Sch 4, para 7.

Restrictive Trade Practices Act 1968, s 11

13. . . .

AMENDMENT
Para 13 repealed by RTPA 1976, Sch 6, and replaced by RTPA 1976, Sch 4, para 8.

Pension benefits

14. The repeal by this Act of the following enactments, that is to say, Part II of Schedule 1 to the Act of 1965 and section 3(4)(*d*) of the Superannuation (Miscellaneous Provisions) Act 1967, shall not affect the operation of those enactments in relation to any person who was appointed to be chairman or deputy chairman of the Commission before the commencement of this Act; and, in relation to any such person, a recommendation made under paragraph 5 of that Schedule shall have effect whether made before or after the commencement of this Act.

15. — (1) The repeal by this Act of subsections (7) and (8) of section 1 of the Act of 1956 shall not affect the operation of those subsections in relation to any person who was appointed to be the Registrar before the commencement of this Act; and, in relation to any such person, a determination made under subsection (7) of that section shall have effect whether made before or after the commencement of this Act.

(2) Paragraph 11 of this Schedule shall not have effect for the purposes of the operation of subsection (7) or subsection (8) of section 1 of the Act of 1956 in accordance with the preceding sub-paragraph.

Trade Descriptions Act 1968, s 30

16. The repeal by this Act of subsections (2) to (4) of section 30 of the Trade Descriptions Act 1968 shall not affect the operation of those subsections in their application to any case where a notice under subsection (2) of that section, or a certificate under subsec-

tion (4) of that section or a document purporting to be such a certificate, has been given
or issued before the commencement of this Act; and the duty imposed by section 130(1)
of this Act shall not apply where such a notice has been so given.   **[127]**

*(Sch 12 contains miscellaneous amendments and Sch 13 lists the enactments repealed
by this Act.)*

THE RESTRICTIVE TRADE PRACTICES ACT 1976
(1976 c 34)

ARRANGEMENT OF SECTIONS

PART I

REGISTRATION AND JUDICIAL INVESTIGATION OF RESTRICTIVE AGREEMENTS

PART II

GOODS

PART III

SERVICES

PART IV

GENERAL

Proceedings

Registration

Exemptions

Enforcement

PART V

MISCELLANEOUS AND SUPPLEMENTAL

An Act to consolidate the enactments relating to restrictive trade practices
[22 July 1976]

PART I

REGISTRATION AND JUDICIAL INVESTIGATION OF RESTRICTIVE
AGREEMENTS

1. Registration of agreements and Court's jurisdiction

(1) Every agreement to which this Act applies by virtue of —

(*a*) section 6 below (restrictive agreements as to goods);
(*b*) an order under section 7 below (information agreements as to goods);
(*c*) an order under section 11 below (restrictive agreements as to services);
(*d*) an order under section 12 below (information agreements as to services);

is subject to registration under this Act.

(2) The Director General of Fair Trading ("the Director") continues charged
with the duty —

(*a*) of compiling and maintaining a register of agreements subject to registration under this Act;
(*b*) of entering or filing in the register such particulars as may be prescribed
by regulations made under section 27 below of any such agreement,
being —

(i) particulars duly furnished to him under this Act by parties to the
agreement; or
(ii) documents or information obtained by him under this Act;

(*c*) of taking proceedings before the Restrictive Practices Court ("the
Court") in respect of the agreements of which particulars are from time
to time entered or filed in the register; but this paragraph is subject to —

(i) such directions as may be given by the Secretary of State as to the
order in which those proceedings are to be taken;
(ii) section 21 below (Director's duties as to proceedings for
investigation).

(3) The Court has jurisdiction, on the Director's application in respect of an
agreement of which particulars are for the time being registered under this Act,
to declare whether or not any restrictions or information provisions by virtue
of which this Act applies to the agreement are contrary to the public interest:
but this jurisdiction is subject to paragraphs 6(2) and 9(2) of Schedule 3 to this Act.

[128]

NOTES

The application of this Act is excluded by the following enactments in relation to the agreements
therein specified: the Agriculture (Miscellaneous Provisions) 1968, s 45; the Plant Varieties and Seeds
Act 1964, s 8 (and see further s 6(1) post); the Agriculture Act 1967, s 9(11); the Energy Act 1976,
s 5; the Participation Agreements Act 1978, s 1; the Competition Act 1980, ss 29, 30(2); the Gas
Act 1986, s 62; the Financial Services Act 1986, s 125; the Insolvency Act 1986, s 428; the Companies
Act 1989, s 47(1), Sch 14, para 9, and the Electricity Act 1989, s 100(2) – (5).

For the power of the Restrictive Practices Court to declare whether an agreement is one to which
this Act applies and if so whether or not it is subject to registration, see s 26(2) post (and see also
s 26(3),(4) post).

In making certain reports the Monopolies and Mergers Commission are to exclude from their
consideration the question whether the provisions of an agreement to which this Act applies operate,

or might be expected to operate, against the public interest; see the Telecommunications Act 1984, s 14(2), the Airports Act 1986, s 45(3), the Gas Act 1986, s 25(2), the Electricity Act 1989, s 13(2), and the Water Act 1989, s 17(2).

As to the suspension of declarations under sub-s(3) above, see the Competition Act 1980, ss 25,26.

By the Merchant Shipping (Liner Conferences) Act 1982, s 11, no account is to be taken of any restriction described in s 11(2) of that Act for the purposes of this Act, and no agreement shall, so far as it relates to any such restriction, be unenforceable by virtue of any rule of law about unreasonable restraint of trade.

2. Restrictions against public interest and consequent Court orders

(1) Where under section 1(3) above any restrictions or information provisions by virtue of which this Act applies to an agreement are found by the Court to be contrary to the public interest, the agreement shall be void in respect of those restrictions or those information provisions.

(2) Without prejudice to subsection (1) above, the Court may on the Director's application, make such order as appears to the Court to be proper for restraining all or any of those mentioned in subsection (3) below—

> (*a*) from giving effect to, or enforcing or purporting to enforce, the agreement in respect of those restrictions or those information provisions;
>
> (*b*) from making any other agreement (whether with the same parties or with other parties) to the like effect; or
>
> (*c*) where such an agreement as is mentioned in paragraph (*b*) above has already been made, from giving effect to that agreement or enforcing or purporting to enforce it.

(3) Those who may be restrained by an order of the Court under subsection (2) above are—

> (*a*) the persons party to the agreement who carry on business within the United Kingdom;
>
> (*b*) a trade association or a services supply association of which any such person is a member; or
>
> (*c*) any person acting on behalf of any such association.

(4) Where any of the parties to an agreement against whom an order under subsection (2) is made is a member of a trade association or of a services supply association, the order may include provisions for restraining the association and any person acting on behalf of the association from procuring or assisting any such party to do anything which would be a contravention of the order in its application to him.

(5) Where—

> (*a*) any restriction accepted under a term implied by virtue of section 8(2) below in an agreement for the constitution of a trade association;
>
> (*b*) any information provision made under a term implied by virtue of section 8(4) below in an agreement for the constitution of a trade association;
>
> (*c*) any restriction accepted under a term implied by virtue of section 16(3) below in an agreement for the constitution of a services supply association;
>
> (*d*) any information provision made under a term implied by virtue of

section 16(5) below in an agreement for the constitution of a services supply association;

is found by the Court to be contrary to the public interest, the Court may (without prejudice to its powers under this section) make such order as appears to the Court to be proper for restraining the association or any person acting on behalf of the association from making any recommendation to which that term would apply.

(6) The powers of the Court under this and the preceding section are not affected by the determination of an agreement effected after the commencement of the proceedings, and where an agreement is varied after the commencement of the proceedings, the Court may make a declaration and, if it thinks fit, an order under subsection (2) or subsection (5) above, either in respect of the agreement as at the commencement of the proceedings or in respect of the agreement as varied, or both.   **[129]**

3. Interim orders of the Court

(1) Where the Director has made an application under section 1(3) above, he may apply to the Court for an interim order under this section —

  (a) at any time before the Court has made an order under section 2(2) above in respect of the agreement, and

  (b) whether before or after the Court has made a declaration under section 1(3) in respect of the agreement.

(2) An application under this section shall specify the restrictions or information provisions which appear to the Director, in relation to the agreement to which the application relates —

  (a) to be restrictions or information provisions such as are mentioned in section 1(3), and

  (b) to be contrary to the public interest, and

  (c) to be restrictions or information provisions in respect of which, in accordance with the following provisions of this section, it would be appropriate for an interim order to be made.

(3) If on an application under this section the Court is satisfied that the following conditions are fulfilled in relation to all or any of the restrictions or information provisions specified in the application —

  (a) that they are restrictions or information provisions such as are mentioned in section 1(3);

  (b) that they could not reasonably be expected to be shown to fall within any of paragraphs (a) to (h) of section 10(1) below or any of paragraphs (a) to (h) of section 19(1) below, as the case may be; and

  (c) that the operation of the restrictions or information provisions, during the period likely to elapse before an order can be made in respect of them under section 2(2), is likely to cause material detriment to the public or a section of the public generally, or to a particular person who is not a party to the agreement;

the Court may, if it thinks fit, make an interim order specifying the restrictions or information provisions in relation to which the Court is satisfied that those conditions are fulfilled.

(4) Any such interim order may exercise, in respect of the restrictions or information provisions specified in the order, any powers which could be exercised in respect of them by an order under section 2(2) if those restrictions or those information provisions had been found by the Court to be contrary to the public interest.

(5) At any time when any such interim order is in force the Court, on the application of the Director or of any person who is subject to or entitled to the benefit of any restriction or information provision specified in the order, may discharge the order and substitute for it any interim order which could have been made on the original application under this section.

(6) An interim order made under this section in respect of an agreement ceases to have effect on the occurrence of whichever of the following first occurs—

(*a*) the termination of such period, or the happening of such event, as may be specified for that purpose in the order;

(*b*) the discharge of the order by the Court;

(*c*) a declaration by the Court that the restrictions or information provisions specified in the interim order are not contrary to the public interest;

(*d*) the final determination by the Court of an application under section 2(2) in respect of that agreement. **[130]**

4. Variation of the Court's decisions

(1) The Court, upon application made in accordance with this section, may—

(*a*) discharge any previous declaration of the Court in respect of any restriction or information provision, and any order made by the Court in pursuance of that declaration, and

(*b*) substitute such other declaration, and make such order in pursuance of that declaration,

as appears to the Court to be proper at the time of the hearing of the application.

(2) The provisions of section 10 below or of section 19 below, as the case may be, apply with the necessary modifications in relation to proceedings on an application under this section as they apply in relation to the proceedings mentioned in those sections.

(3) An application under this section may be made by the Director or by any person who is, or was at the time of the previous determination of the Court, subject to or entitled to the benefit of the restriction or information provision in question.

(4) No application shall be made under this section except with the leave of the Court, and such leave shall not be granted except upon prima facie evidence of a material change in the relevant circumstances.

(5) Notwithstanding anything in subsection (4) above, leave to make an application under this section for the discharge of a declaration or order of the

Court made before the commencement of the Restrictive Trade Practices Act 1968 (25 November 1968) may, if the applicant proposes to rely on paragraph (*h*) of section 10(1) below, be granted upon prima facie evidence of the relevance of that paragraph to the application.

(6) This section does not apply in relation to any order made under section 3 above.   **[131]**

5. The European Communities

(1) This Act applies to an agreement notwithstanding that it is or may be void by reason of any directly applicable Community provision, or is expressly authorised by or under any such provision; but this subsection is subject to subsection (2) and section 34 below.

(2) The Court —

   (*a*) may decline or postpone the exercise of its jurisdiction under sections 1 and 2 above, or

   (*b*) may, notwithstanding subsection (2) of section 4 above exercise its jurisdiction under that section,

if and in so far as it appears to the Court right so to do having regard to the operation of any directly applicable Community provision or to the purpose and effect of any authorisation or exemption granted in relation to such a provision.

                                                                              [132]

PART II

GOODS

6. Restrictive agreements as to goods

(1) This Act applies to agreements (whenever made) between two or more persons carrying on business within the United Kingdom in the production or supply of goods, or in the application to goods of any process of manufacture, whether with or without other parties, being agreements under which restrictions are accepted by two or more parties in respect of any of the following matters —

   (*a*) the prices to be charged, quoted or paid for goods supplied, offered or acquired, or for the application of any process of manufacture to goods;

   (*b*) the prices to be recommended or suggested as the prices to be charged or quoted in respect of the resale of goods supplied;

   (*c*) the terms or conditions on or subject to which goods are to be supplied or acquired or any such process is to be applied to goods;

   (*d*) the quantities or descriptions of goods to be produced, supplied or acquired;

   (*e*) the processes of manufacture to be applied to any goods, or the quantities or descriptions of goods to which any such process is to be applied; or

   (*f*) the persons or classes of persons to, for or from whom, or the areas or places in or from which, goods are to be supplied or acquired, or any such process applied.

(2) For the purposes of subsection (1) above it is immaterial—

(a) whether any restrictions accepted by parties to an agreement relate to the same or different matters specified in that subsection, or have the same or different effect in relation to any matter so specified, and

(b) whether the parties accepting any restrictions carry on the same class or different classes of business.

(3) For the purposes of this Part of this Act an agreement which—

(a) confers privileges or benefits only upon such parties as comply with conditions as to any such matters as are described in subsection (1)(a) to (f) above; or

(b) imposes obligations upon parties who do not comply with such conditions;

shall be treated as an agreement under which restrictions are accepted by each of the parties in respect of those matters.

(4) Without prejudice to subsection (3) above, an obligation on the part of any party to an agreement to make payments calculated by reference—

(a) to the quantity of goods produced or supplied by him, or to which any process of manufacture is applied by him; or

(b) to the quantity of materials acquired or used by him for the purpose of or in the production of any goods or the application of any such process to goods;

being payments calculated, or calculated at an increased rate, in respect of quantities of goods or materials exceeding any quantity specified in or ascertained in accordance with the agreement, shall be treated for the purposes of this Act as a restriction in respect of the quantities of those goods to be produced or supplied, or to which that process is to be applied.

This subsection does not apply to any obligation on the part of any person to make payments to a trade association of which he is a member, if the payments are to consist only of bona fide subscriptions for membership of the association.

[133]

NOTE

For the purpose of determining whether an agreement containing financing terms is one to which this Act applies, see RTPA 1977, s 2(2). See also s 2(3) of that Act for the power of the Secretary of State to specify certain matters to be disregarded in determining whether an agreement is governed by the Act.

7. Information agreements as to goods

(1) The Secretary of State may by statutory instrument make an order directing that this Act shall apply to information agreements (whenever made) of any class described in the order; and in this section "information agreement" means an agreement between two or more persons carrying on within the United Kingdom any such business as is described in section 6(1) above, whether with or without

other parties, being an agreement under which provision is made for or in relation to the furnishing by two or more parties to each other or to other persons (whether parties or not) of information in respect of any of the following matters —

(a) the prices charged, quoted or paid or to be charged, quoted or paid for goods which have been or are to be supplied, offered or acquired or for the application of any process of manufacture to goods;

(b) the prices to be recommended or suggested as the prices to be charged or quoted in respect of the resale of goods supplied;

(c) the terms or conditions on or subject to which goods have been or are to be supplied or acquired or any such process has been or is to be applied to goods;

(d) the quantities or descriptions of goods produced, supplied or acquired or to be produced, supplied or acquired;

(e) the costs incurred or to be incurred in producing, supplying or acquiring goods or in applying any such process to goods;

(f) the processes of manufacture which have been or are to be applied to any goods or the quantities or descriptions of goods to which any such process has been or is to be applied;

(g) the persons or classes of persons to or for whom goods have been or are to be supplied, or from or for whom goods have been or are to be acquired, or for whom any such process has been or is to be applied;

(h) the areas or places in or from which goods have been or are to be supplied or acquired or in which any such process has been or is to be applied to goods.

(2) For the purposes of subsection (1) above it is immaterial —

(a) whether any information provisions made by the parties to an agreement relate to the same or different matters specified in that subsection, or have the same or different effect in relation to any matter so specified, and

(b) whether the parties by whom any information is to be furnished carry on the same class or different classes of business.

(3) An order under this section may describe the classes of information agreements to which it applies by reference to one or more of the following matters —

(a) the trade or industry in which the persons to whom the information provision made by the agreement applies are engaged, or the class of business carried on by such persons;

(b) the character of the information provision made by the agreement, or the goods, processes, transactions, areas, places or other matters with respect to which that provision relates;

(c) any other features which appear to the Secretary of State to be expedient.

[(3A) An order under this section may specify matters (in addition to those mentioned in section 9) which are to be disregarded in determining whether an agreement is one to which this Act applies by virtue of the order].[1]

(4) No order shall be made under this section unless a draft of the order has been laid before, and approved by resolution of each House of Parliament.

(5) The Secretary of State shall, before laying before Parliament the draft of an order under this section for applying this Act in relation to information agreements of any class, publish in such manner as he thinks appropriate a notice—

(a) describing the classes of agreements to which the proposed order would apply; and

(b) specifying a period (not being less than 28 days) within which representations with respect to the proposed order may be made to the Secretary of State;

and in settling the draft to be laid before Parliament shall take into consideration any such representations received by him within that period. **[134]**

NOTES
The Restrictive Trade Practices (Information Agreements) Order 1969, SI 1969 No 1842, as amended by the Restrictive Trade Practices Act 1977, s 3(3), Schedule, Pt II has effect as if made under this section by virtue of s 44 of, and Sch 4, para 1(1) to, this Act.

AMENDMENT
1 Sub-s (3A) added by RTPA 1977, s 3(1).

8. Trade associations

(1) This Act has effect in relation to an agreement made by a trade association as if the agreement were made between all persons who are members of the association or are represented on it by such members and, where any restriction is accepted or information provision made in the agreement on the part of the association, as if the like restriction or the like information provision were accepted or made by each of those persons.

(2) Where—

(a) specific recommendations (whether express or implied) are made by or on behalf of an association to its members, or to any class of its members, and

(b) those recommendations are as to the action to be taken or not to be taken by them in relation to any particular class of goods or process of manufacture in respect of any matters described in section 6(1) above,

this Act has effect in relation to the agreement for the constitution of the association (notwithstanding any provision in the agreement to the contrary) as if that agreement contained the term mentioned in subsection (3) below.

(3) The term referred to in subsection (2) above is one by which each such member, and any person represented on the association by any such member, agrees to comply with those recommendations and with any subsequent recommendations made to them by or on behalf of the association as to the action to be taken by them in relation to the same class of goods or process of manufacture and in respect of the same matters.

(4) In the case of an order under section 7 above, where—

(a) specific recommendations (whether express or implied) are made by or on behalf of an association to its members, or to any class of its members, and

(b) those recommendations are as to the furnishing of information in relation to any particular class of goods or process of manufacture in respect of any matters described in subsection (1) of that section,

this Act has effect in relation to the agreement for the constitution of the association (notwithstanding any provision in the agreement to the contrary) as if that agreement contained the term mentioned in subsection (5) below.

(5) The term referred to in subsection (4) above is one by which each such member, and any person represented on the association by any such member, agrees to comply with those recommendations and with any subsequent recommendations made to them by or on behalf of the association as to the furnishing of information in relation to the same class of goods or process of manufacture and in respect of the same matters.   [135]

9. Provisions to be disregarded under Part II

(1) In determining whether an agreement is an agreement to which this Act applies by virtue of this Part, where—

(a) the parties to the agreement are or include two or more bodies to which this subsection applies, and

(b) restrictions or information provisions relating to coal or steel, or relating to both coal and steel, are accepted or made, as the case may be, under the agreement by two or more such bodies, whether the restrictions so accepted or the information provisions so made by those bodies are the same restrictions or different restrictions or are the same information provisions or different information provisions,

no account shall be taken of any such restriction or information provision which is accepted or made under the agreement by a body to which this subsection applies, whether that restriction or information provision is also accepted or made by any other party to the agreement or not.

(2) Subsection (1) above applies to any body which, in accordance with Article 80 of the ECSC Treaty, constitutes an undertaking for the purposes of Articles 65 and 66 of that Treaty, and in that subsection "coal" and "steel" have the meanings assigned to them respectively by Annex I to that Treaty.

(3) In determining whether an agreement for the supply of goods or for the application of any process of manufacture to goods is an agreement to which this Act applies by virtue of this Part, no account shall be taken of any term which relates exclusively to the goods supplied, or to which the process is applied, in pursuance of the agreement.

(4) Where any such restrictions as are described in section 6(1) above are accepted or any such information provisions as are described in section 7(1) above are made as between two or more persons by whom, or two or more persons to or for whom, goods are to be supplied, or the process applied, in pursuance of the agreement, subsection (3) above shall not apply to those restrictions or to those information provisions unless accepted or made in pursuance of a previous agreement—

(a) in respect of which particulars have been registered under this Act; or (*b*) which is exempt from registration by virtue of an order under section 29 (agreements important to the national economy) or section 30 (agreements holding down prices) below.

(5) In determining whether an agreement is an agreement to which this Act applies by virtue of this Part, no account shall be taken of any term by which the parties or any of them agree to comply with or apply, in respect of the production, supply or acquisition of any goods or the application to goods of any process of manufacture —

    (*a*) standards of dimension, design, quality or performance, or

    (*b*) arrangements as to the provision of information or advice to purchasers, consumers or users,

being either standards or arrangements for the time being approved by the British Standards Institution or standards or arrangements prescribed or adopted by any trade association or other body and for the time being approved by order of the Secretary of State made by statutory instrument.

(6) In determining whether an agreement is an agreement to which this Act applies by virtue of this Part, no account shall be taken of any restriction or information provision which affects or otherwise relates to the workers to be employed or not employed by any person, or as to the remuneration, conditions of employment, hours of work or working conditions of such workers.

In this subsection "worker" means a person who has entered into or works under a contract with an employer whether the contract be by way of manual labour, clerical work, or otherwise, be express or implied, oral or in writing, and whether it be a contract of service or of apprenticeship or a contract personally to execute any work or labour.

(7) Any reference in Schedule 3 to this Act to —

    (*a*) such restrictions as are described in section 6(1) above, or

    (*b*) such information provisions as are described in section 7(1) above,

shall be construed, in relation to any agreement, as not including references to restrictions or information provisions of which, by virtue of any provision of this section, account cannot be taken in determining whether the agreement is one to which this Act applies by virtue of this Part, or of restrictions accepted or information provisions made by any term of which account cannot be so taken.

[136]

ORDERS UNDER THIS SECTION

The Restrictive Trade Practices (Approval of Standards and Arrangements) Order 1983, SI 1983 No 382, as amended by SI 1984 No 1269, and SI 1986 No 614; the Restrictive Trade Practices (Approval of Standards and Arrangements) Order 1984, SI 1984 No 2031; the Restrictive Trade Practices (Standards and Arrangements) Order 1990, SI 1990 No 888.

By virtue of s 44 and Sch 4, para 1(1) post, the Restrictive Practices (Approval of Arrangements) No 1 Order 1969, SI 1969 No 226, has effect as if made under this section.

10. Presumption under Part II as to the public interest

(1) For the purposes of any proceedings before the Court under Part I of this Act, a restriction accepted or information provision made in pursuance of an

agreement to which this Act applies by virtue of this Part shall be deemed to be contrary to the public interest unless the Court is satisfied of any one or more of the following circumstances —

(a) that the restriction or information provision is reasonably necessary, having regard to the character of the goods to which it applies, to protect the public against injury (whether to persons or to premises) in connection with the consumption, installation or use of those goods;

(b) that the removal of the restriction or information provision would deny to the public as purchasers, consumers or users of any goods other specific and substantial benefits or advantages enjoyed or likely to be enjoyed by them as such, whether by virtue of the restriction or information provision itself or of any arrangements or operations resulting therefrom;

(c) that the restriction or information provision is reasonably necessary to counteract measures taken by any one person not party to the agreement with a view to preventing or restricting competition in or in relation to the trade or business in which the persons party thereto are engaged;

(d) that the restriction or information provision is reasonably necessary to enable the persons party to the agreement to negotiate fair terms for the supply of goods to, or the acquisition of goods from, any one person not party thereto who controls a preponderant part of the trade or business of acquiring or supplying such goods, or for the supply of goods to any person not party to the agreement and not carrying on such a trade or business who, either alone or in combination with any other such person, controls a preponderant part of the market for such goods;

(e) that, having regard to the conditions actually obtaining or reasonably foreseen at the time of the application, the removal of the restriction or information provision would be likely to have a serious and persistent adverse effect on the general level of unemployment in an area, or in areas taken together, in which a substantial proportion of the trade or industry to which the agreement relates is situated;

(f) that, having regard to the conditions actually obtaining or reasonably foreseen at the time of the application, the removal of the restriction or information provision would be likely to cause a reduction in the volume or earnings of the export business which is substantial either in relation to the whole export business of the United Kingdom or in relation to the whole business (including export business) of the said trade or industry;

(g) that the restriction or information provision is reasonably required for purposes connected with the maintenance of any other restriction accepted or information provision made by the parties, whether under the same agreement or under any other agreement between them, being a restriction or information provision which is found by the Court not to be contrary to the public interest upon grounds other than those specified in this paragraph, or has been so found in previous proceedings before the Court; or

(h) that the restriction or information provision does not directly or indirectly restrict or discourage competition to any material degree in any relevant trade or industry and is not likely to do so;

and is further satisfied (in any such case) that the restriction or information provision is not unreasonable having regard to the balance between those circumstances and any detriment to the public or to persons not parties to the agreement (being purchasers, consumers or users of goods produced or sold by such parties, or persons engaged or seeking to become engaged in the trade or business of selling such goods or of producing or selling similar goods) resulting or likely to result from the operation of the restriction or the information provision.

(2) In this section—

  (a) "purchasers", "consumers" and "users" include persons purchasing, consuming or using for the purpose or in the course of trade or business or for public purposes; and

  (b) references to any one person include references to any two or more persons being interconnected bodies corporate or individuals carrying on business in partnership with each other. **[137]**

NOTE

  This section was extended to proceedings under the Competition Act 1980, s 26, by s 26(9) of that Act.

PART III

SERVICES

11. Restrictive agreements as to services

(1) The Secretary of State may by statutory instrument make an order in respect of a class of services described in the order (in this Act referred to, in relation to an order under this section, as "services brought under control by the order") and direct by the order that this Act shall apply to agreements (whenever made) which—

  (a) are agreements between two or more persons carrying on business within the United Kingdom in the supply of services brought under control by the order, or between two or more such persons together with one or more other parties; and

  (b) are agreements under which restrictions, in respect of matters specified in the order for the purposes of this paragraph, are accepted by two or more parties.

(2) The matters which may be specified in such an order for the purposes of subsection (1)(b) above are any of the following—

  (a) the charges to be made, quoted or paid for designated services supplied, offered or obtained;

  (b) the terms or conditions on or subject to which designated services are to be supplied or obtained;

  (c) the extent (if any) to which, or the scale (if any) on which, designated services are to be made available, supplied or obtained;

(*d*) the form or manner in which designated services are to be made available, supplied or obtained;

(*e*) the persons or classes of persons for whom or from whom, or the areas or places in or from which, designated services are to be made available or supplied or are to be obtained.   **[138]**

NOTE

See the Transport Act 1985, ss 115, 116 (agreements between road passenger transport operators and agreements as to the use of bus stations) with effect from 26 July 1986: Transport Act 1985 (Commencement No 4) Order 1986, SI 1986 No 1088. See also the Merchant Shipping (Liner Conferences) Act 1982, s 11(5).

ORDER UNDER THIS SECTION

By virtue of s 44 and Sch 4, para 1(1) post, the Restrictive Trade Practices (Services) Order 1976, SI 1976 No 98, as amended by the Restrictive Trade Practices Act 1977, s 1(3), Schedule, Pt I, by SI 1985 No 2044, by the Transport Act 1985, ss 115(1), 139(5), by SI 1986 No 2204, and by SI 1989 No 1082, has effect as if made under this section.

12. Information agreements as to services

(1) The Secretary of State may by statutory instrument make an order in respect of a class of services described in the order (in this Act referred to, in relation to an order under this section, as "services brought under control by the order") and direct by the order that this Act shall apply to agreements (whenever made) which—

(*a*) are agreements between two or more persons carrying on business within the United Kingdom in the supply of services brought under control by the order, or between two or more such persons together with one or more other parties; and

(*b*) are agreements under which provision is made for or in relation to the furnishing by two or more parties to each other or to other persons (whether parties or not) of information with respect to matters specified in the order for the purposes of this paragraph.

(2) The matters which may be specified in such an order for the purposes of subsection (1)(*b*) above are any of the following—

(*a*) the charges made, quoted or paid or to be made, quoted or paid for designated services which have been or are to be supplied, offered or obtained;

(*b*) the terms or conditions on or subject to which designated services have been or are to be supplied or obtained;

(*c*) the extent (if any) to which, or the scale (if any) on which, designated services have been or are to be made available, supplied or obtained;

(*d*) the form or manner in which designated services have been or are to be made available, supplied or obtained;

(*e*) the costs incurred or to be incurred in making available, supplying or obtaining designated services;

(*f*) the persons or classes of persons for whom or from whom, or the areas or places in or from which, designated services have been or are to be made available or supplied or have been or are to be obtained.

                                                            [139]

13. Designated services

(1) In relation to any order made under section 11 or section 12 above, "designated services" in this Act means services of any class described in the order as being designated services.

(2) Subject to subsection (3) below, a class of services described in any such order as being designated services may consist wholly or partly of services brought under control by the order or wholly or partly of other services, and may be described so as to consist —

(a) of services of one or more descriptions specified in that behalf in the order, or

(b) of all services except services of one or more descriptions so specified,

and different classes of services may be so described in relation to different matters specified in the order for the purposes of section 11(1)(b) or section 12(1)(b) above, as the case may be.

(3) A class of services described in such an order as being designated services shall not include any of the services specified in Schedule 1 to this Act.

[140]

14. Supplementary provisions as to orders under Part III

(1) A class of services described in an order under section 11 or section 12 above as being the services brought under control by the order may consist —

(a) of services of one or more descriptions specified in that behalf in the order; or

(b) of all services except services of one or more descriptions so specified; or

(c) of all services without exception.

(2) An order under section 11 or section 12 may limit the operation of the order to agreements fulfilling such conditions (in addition to those mentioned in section 11 or section 12, as the case may be) as may be specified in the order [and may specify matters (in addition to those mentioned in section 18) which are to be disregarded for the purpose of determining whether an agreement is one to which this Act applies by virtue of the order].[2]

(3) In particular, but without prejudice to the generality of subsection (2) above, an order under section 12 may limit the operation of the order to agreements under which the provision for the furnishing of information (as mentioned in subsection (1)(b) of that section) is provision of a kind specified in the order or provides for the furnishing of information of a kind so specified.

(4) Subject to subsection (2) above —

(a) for the purposes of any order under section 11 it is immaterial whether any restrictions accepted by parties to an agreement relate to the same or to different matters specified in the order for the purposes of subsection (1)(b) of that section, or have the same or a different effect in relation to any matter so specified, and

(b) for the purposes of any order under section 12 it is immaterial whether any information provision made by an agreement relates to the same or to different matters specified in the order for the purposes of sub-section (1)(*b*) of that section,

and it is immaterial for those purposes whether the parties accepting any restrictions, or the parties by whom any information is to be furnished, as the case may be, carry on the same class or different classes of business.

(5) Where, at a time when an order under section 11 or section 12 (in this subsection referred to as "the earlier order") is in force, another order (in this subsection referred to as "the subsequent order") is made under the same section, the subsequent order may provide that —

(*a*) for the purposes of the earlier order; or
(*b*) for the purposes of the subsequent order; or
(*c*) for the purposes of both orders;

the condition specified in section 11(1)(*a*) or in section 12(1)(*a*), as the case may be, shall be treated as fulfilled in relation to an agreement if it is an agreement to which the parties are or include one person carrying on business in the United Kingdom in the supply of services brought under control by the earlier order and one person carrying on business within the United Kingdom in the supply of services brought under control by the subsequent order.

This subsection has effect without prejudice to any power to vary any order made under section 11 or section 12.

(6) In the following provisions of this Part of this Act "the relevant provisions", in relation to an order under section 11 or section 12 above, means the provisions of this Act as they have effect in relation to that order.   **[141]**

AMENDMENT
1 Words in sub-s (2) added by RTPA 1977, s 1(1).

15. Procedure as to orders under Part III

(1) No order shall be made under section 11 or section 12 above unless a draft of the order has been laid before Parliament and approved by a resolution of each House of Parliament.

(2) Before laying before Parliament a draft of any such order, the Secretary of State shall publish in such manner as he thinks appropriate a notice —

(*a*) describing the classes of services which, if the order is made, will be services brought under control by the order and will be designated services in relation to the order respectively;
(*b*) indicating the nature of any limitation to be imposed by the order under section 14(2) or (3) above; and
(*c*) specifying a period (not being less than 28 days) within which representations with respect to the proposed order may be made to the Secretary of State.

(3) In settling the draft to be laid before Parliament the Secretary of State shall take into consideration any representations with respect to the proposed order which may be received by him within the period specified in the notice in accordance with subsection (2)(*c*) above.   **[142]**

16. Services supply associations

(1) For the purposes of any order made under section 11 or section 12 above, and for the purposes of the relevant provisions, subsections (2) to (6) below have effect in relation to any association (whether incorporated or not) if —

(a) its membership consists wholly or mainly of persons (in this subsection referred to as "members affected by the order") who are either engaged in the supply of services brought under control by the order or are employed by or represent persons so engaged; and

(b) its objects or activities include the promotion of the interests of persons engaged in the supply of those services who are either members affected by the order or are persons represented by such members.

(2) The relevant provisions have effect in relation to any agreement made by an association described in subsection (1) above ("services supply association") —

(a) as if the agreement were made between all persons who are members of the association or are represented on it by members of the association, and

(b) where any restriction is accepted under the agreement by the association, or any information provision is made in the agreement by the association, as if the like restriction were accepted by, or (as the case may be) the like provision were made by, each of the persons who are members of the association or are so represented.

(3) In the case of an order under section 11, where —

(a) specific recommendations (whether express or implied) are made by or on behalf of the association to its members, or to any class of its members, and

(b) those recommendations are as to the action to be taken or not to be taken by them in relation to any particular class of services in respect of any matters specified in the order for the purposes of subsection (1)(b) of that section,

the relevant provisions have effect in relation to the agreement for the constitution of the association (notwithstanding any provision in the agreement to the contrary) as if that agreement contained the term mentioned in subsection (4) below.

(4) The term referred to in subsection (3) above is one by which each such member, and any person represented on the association by any such member, agrees to comply with those recommendations and with any subsequent recommendations made to them by or on behalf of the association as to the action to be taken by them in relation to the same class of services and in respect of the same matters.

(5) In the case of an order under section 12 above, where —

(a) specific recommendations (whether express or implied) are made by or on behalf of the association to its members, or to any class of its members, and

(b) those recommendations are as to the furnishing of information in relation to any particular class of services in respect of any matters specified in the order for the purposes of subsection (1)(*b*) of that section,

the relevant provisions have effect in relation to the agreement for the constitution of the association (notwithstanding any provision in the agreement to the contrary) as if that agreement contained the term mentioned in subsection (6) below.

(6) The term referred to in subsection (5) above is one by which each such member, and any person represented on the association by any such member, agrees to comply with those recommendations and with any subsequent recommendations made to them by or on behalf of the association as to the furnishing of information in relation to the same class of services and in respect of the same matters.   **[143]**

NOTE

As to recommendations by services supply associations, see Competition Act 1980, s 27.

17. Matters equivalent to restrictions for purposes of s 11

(1) For the purposes of any order made under section 11 above, and for the purposes of the relevant provisions, an agreement which —

(*a*) confers privileges or benefits only upon such parties as comply with conditions as to any such matters as are mentioned in subsection (2) of that section; or

(*b*) imposes obligations upon parties who do not comply with such conditions;

shall be treated as an agreement under which restrictions are accepted by each of the parties in respect of those matters.

(2) Without prejudice to subsection (1) above, an obligation on the part of any party to an agreement to make payments calculated by reference to the extent to which, or the scale on which —

(*a*) any designated services are made available or supplied by him; or

(*b*) any services are obtained by him for the purpose of making available or supplying any designated services;

if the payments are calculated, or calculated at an increased rate, in respect of an extent or scale exceeding an extent or scale specified in or ascertained in accordance with the agreement, shall be treated for the purposes mentioned in subsection (1) as a restriction in respect of the extent or scale of the designated services to be made available or supplied.

This subsection does not apply to any obligation on the part of any person to make payments to a services supply association of which he is a member, if the payments are to consist only of bona fide subscriptions for membership of the association.   **[144]**

18. Provisions to be disregarded under Part III

(1) The following provisions of this section have effect for the purpose of determining whether an agreement is one to which this Act applies by virtue of an order under section 11 or section 12 above.

(2) Subject to subsections (3) and (4) below, no account shall for that purpose be taken of any term which relates exclusively to the services supplied in pursuance of the agreement in question.

(3) Where —

    (*a*) the order referred to in subsection (1) above is an order under section 11, and

    (*b*) any of the restrictions accepted as mentioned in subsection (1)(*b*) of that section are accepted as between two or more persons by whom, or two or more persons for whom, designated services are to be supplied in pursuance of the agreement,

subsection (2) above does not apply to any term of the agreement which imposes those restrictions unless they are accepted in pursuance of a previous agreement in respect of which particulars have been registered under this Act by virtue of this Part.

(4) Where —

    (*a*) the order referred to in subsection (1) is an order under section 12, and

    (*b*) the term referred to in subsection (2) is one by which provision is made for the furnishing of information as mentioned in subsection (1)(*b*) of that section by two or more persons by whom, or two or more persons for whom, designated services are to be supplied in pursuance of the agreement,

subsection (2) does not apply to that term unless it is included in the agreement in pursuance of a previous agreement of which particulars have been registered under this Act by virtue of this Part.

(5) For the purpose mentioned in subsection (1) no account shall be taken of any term by which the parties or any of them agree to comply with or apply, in respect of making available, supplying or obtaining any designated services —

    (*a*) any standards (whether being standards of performance in the provision of the services or standards of dimension, design, quality or performance in respect of goods used in providing them) which are either standards approved for the time being by the British Standards Institution or standards prescribed or adopted by an association or other body and for the time being approved by an order made by the Secretary of State by statutory instrument; or

    (*b*) any arrangements either approved by the British Standards Institution, or prescribed or adopted and approved by an order of the Secretary of State, as mentioned in the preceding paragraph, as to the provision of information or advice to persons for whom designated services are supplied or agreed to be supplied.

(6) For the purpose mentioned in subsection (1) no account shall be taken of any restriction which affects or relates to any of the matters mentioned in section 9(6) above (which relates to employment and to terms and conditions of employment) or of any information provision with respect to any of those matters.

(7) Any reference in Schedule 3 to this Act—

(a) to restrictions accepted in respect of matters specified in an order under section 11 for the purposes of subsection (1)(b) of that section; or

(b) to information provisions made with respect to matters specified in an order under section 12 for the purposes of subsection (1)(b) of that section;

shall be construed, in relation to any agreement, as not including anything of which, by virtue of this section, account cannot be taken for the purpose mentioned in subsection (1).   **[145]**

ORDER UNDER THIS SECTION
The Restrictive Trade Practices (Standards and Arrangements) Order 1990, SI 1990 No 888.

19. Presumption under Part III as to the public interest

(1) For the purposes of any proceedings before the Court under Part I of this Act, a restriction accepted or information provision made in pursuance of an agreement to which this Act applies by virtue of this Part shall be deemed to be contrary to the public interest unless the Court is satisfied of any one or more of the following circumstances—

(a) that the restriction or information provision is reasonably necessary having regard to the character of the services to which it applies, to protect the public against injury (whether to persons or to premises) in connection with the use of those services or in connection with the consumption, installation or use of goods in relation to which those services are supplied;

(b) that the removal of the restriction or information provision would deny to the public as users of any services, or as [vendors][1] purchasers, consumers or users of any goods [or other property][1] in relation to which any services are supplied, other specific and substantial benefits or advantages enjoyed or likely to be enjoyed by them as such, whether by virtue of the restriction or information provision itself or of any arrangements or operations resulting therefrom;

(c) that the restriction or information provision is reasonably necessary to counteract measures taken by any one person not party to the agreement with a view to preventing or restricting competition in or in relation to the trade or business in which the persons party thereto are engaged;

(d) that the restriction or information provision is reasonably necessary to enable the persons party to the agreement to negotiate fair terms for the supply of services to, or for obtaining services from, any one person not party thereto who controls a preponderant part of the trade or business of supplying such services, or for the supply of services to any person not party to the agreement and not carrying on such a trade or business who, either alone or in combination with any other such person, controls a preponderant part of the market for such services;

(e) that, having regard to the conditions actually obtaining or reasonably foreseen at the time of the application, the removal of the restriction or information provision would be likely to have a serious and persistent adverse effect on the general level of unemployment in an area, or in areas taken together, in which a substantial proportion of the trade or industry to which the agreement relates is situated;

(*f*) that, having regard to the conditions actually obtaining or reasonably foreseen at the time of the application, the removal of the restriction or information provision would be likely to cause a reduction in the volume or earnings of the export business which is substantial either in relation to the whole export business of the United Kingdom or in relation to the whole business (including export business) of the said trade or industry;

(*g*) that the restriction or information provision is reasonably required for purposes connected with the maintenance of any other restriction accepted or information provision made by the parties, whether under the same agreement or under any other agreement between them, being a restriction or information provision which is found by the Court not to be contrary to the public interest upon grounds other than those specified in this paragraph, or has been so found in previous proceedings before the Court; or

(*h*) that the restriction or information provision does not directly or indirectly restrict or discourage competition to any material degree in any relevant trade or industry and is not likely to do so;

and is further satisfied (in any such case) that the restriction or information provision is not unreasonable having regard to the balance between those circumstances and any detriment to the public or to persons not parties to the agreement (being users of services supplied by such parties, or persons engaged or seeking to become engaged in any business of supplying such services or of making available or supplying similar services, or being [vendors]¹ purchasers, consumers or users of goods [or other property]¹ in relation to which any such services or similar services are supplied) resulting or likely to result from the operation of the restriction or information provision.

(2) In this section —

(*a*) ["vendors"]¹ "purchasers", "consumers" and "users" include persons [selling]¹ purchasing, consuming or using for the purpose or in the course of trade or business or for public purposes; and

(*b*) references to any one person include references to any two or more persons being interconnected bodies corporate or individuals carrying on business in partnership with each other.   **[146]**

NOTE
  This section extended to proceedings under the Competition Act 1980, s 26, by s 26(9) of that Act.
AMENDMENT
  1 Words in sub-ss (1) and (2) added by the Competition Act 1980, s 28.

20. Interpretation of Part III

In this Part of this Act —

"business" includes a professional practice;

"the relevant provisions" has the meaning given by section 14(6) above; "scale" (where the reference is to the scale on which any services are, or are to be, made available, supplied or obtained) means scale measured in terms of money or money's worth or in any other manner; "service"—

(a) does not include the application to goods of any process of manufacture or any services rendered to an employer under a contract of employment (that is, a contract of service or of apprenticeship, whether it is express or implied, and, if it is express, whether it is oral or in writing), but, with those exceptions,

(b) includes engagements (whether professional or other) which for gain or reward are undertaken and performed for any matter other than the production or supply of goods, [and

(c) includes arrangements for the use by public service vehicles (within the meaning of the Public Passenger Vehicles Act 1981) of a parking place which is used as a point at which passengers on services provided by means of such vehicles may be taken up or set down],[1]

and any reference to the supply of services or to supplying, obtaining or offering services or to making services available shall be construed accordingly.   [147]

AMENDMENT
1 Para (c) inserted by the Transport Act 1985, s 116(2), with effect from 26 July 1986: Transport Act (Commencement No 4) Order 1986, SI 1986 No 1088.

PART IV

GENERAL

Proceedings

21. Director's duties as to proceedings for investigation

(1) The Director may refrain from taking proceedings before the Court—

(a) in respect of an agreement if and for so long as he thinks it appropriate so to do having regard to the operation of any directly applicable Community provision and to the purpose and effect of any authorisation or exemption granted in relation to such a provision;

(b) where an agreement—

(i) of which particulars are entered or filed in the register pursuant to this Act has been determined (whether by effluxion of time or otherwise); or

(ii) has been so determined in respect of all restrictions accepted or information provisions made under that agreement.

(2) If it appears to the Secretary of State, upon the Director's representation, that the restrictions accepted or information provisions made under an

agreement of which particulars are so entered or filed are not of such significance as to call for investigation by the Court, the Secretary of State may give directions discharging the Director from taking proceedings in the Court in respect of that agreement during the continuance in force of the directions.

(3) The Secretary of State may at any time upon the Director's representation withdraw any directions given by him under subsection (2) above if satisfied that there has been a material change of circumstances since the directions were given.

[148]

22. Rules of procedure

(1) Without prejudice to the generality of section 9(1) of the Restrictive Practices Court Act 1976, rules[1] made under that subsection may provide—

    (a) for enabling a single application to be made to the Court in respect of a number of related agreements, or separate applications made in respect of related agreements to be heard together;

    (b) for enabling the Court to determine in a summary way any issue arising in relation to an agreement where it appears to the Court that the relevant provisions of the agreement and the circumstances of the case are substantially similar to the provisions and circumstances considered, in relation to any other agreement, in any previous proceedings before the Court;

    (c) for enabling the Court to make an order for the payment by any party to proceedings under sections 1, 2 and 4 above of costs in respect of proceedings in which he is guilty of unreasonable delay, or in respect of any improper, vexatious, prolix or unnecessary proceedings or any other unreasonable conduct on his part.

(2) The Court—

    (a) does not have power to order the payment of costs by any party to proceedings under sections 1, 2 and 4 above except so far as may be provided by rules made in pursuance of subsection (1)(c) above; but

    (b) without prejudice to section 9(3) of the Restrictive Practices Court Act 1976, the Court has power in exercise of its jurisdiction under sections 26, 35 and 37 below to order the payment of costs by any party to proceedings before the Court. **[149]**

NOTE
1 See the Restrictive Practices Court Rules 1976, SI 1976 No 1897, as amended by SI 1982 No 871.

Registration

23. General provisions as to the register

(1) The register for the purposes of this Act shall be kept by the Director—

    (a) at such premises within the United Kingdom; and
    (b) in such form;

as he may determine.

(2) The Director shall cause notice of —

(a) any declaration made under section 1(3) above;
(b) any order made under section 2 above;

to be entered in the register.

(3) Regulations made under section 27 below shall provide for the maintenance of a special section of the register, and for the entry or filing in that section of such particulars as the Secretary of State may direct, being —

(a) particulars containing information the publication of which would in the Secretary of State's opinion be contrary to the public interest;
(b) particulars containing information as to any secret process of manufacture (or, in relation to Part III of this Act, any secret process) or as to the presence, absence or situation of any mineral or other deposits or as to any other similar matter, being information the publication of which in the Secretary of State's opinion would substantially damage the legitimate business interests of any person.

(4) The register, other than the special section, shall be open to public inspection during such hours and subject to payment of such fee as may be prescribed by regulations made under section 27.

(5) Any person may, upon payment of such fee as may be prescribed by regulations made under section 27, require the Director to supply to him a copy of or extract from any particulars entered or filed in the register, other than the special section, certified by the Director to be a true copy or extract.

(6) No process for compelling the production of the register or of any other document kept by the Director shall issue from any court except with the leave of the court, and any such process if issued shall bear a statement that it is issued with the leave of the court.

(7) A copy of or extract from any document entered or filed in the register, certified under the hand of the Director or an officer authorised to act on his behalf (whose official position it shall not be necessary to prove), shall in all legal proceedings be admissible in evidence as of equal validity with the original.

[150]

24. Particulars and time for registration

(1) In respect of every agreement which is subject to registration under this Act the following particulars shall be furnished to the Director —

(a) the names and addresses of the persons who are parties to the agreement; and
(b) the whole of the terms of the agreement, whether or not relating to any such restriction or information provision as is described in this Act.

(2) The additional provisions contained in Schedule 2 to this Act have effect as to the particulars to be furnished in respect of —

(a) an agreement which is subject to registration under this Act; and
(b) the variation or determination of such an agreement;

and such particulars shall in the cases specified in the first column of the Table in paragraph 5(1) of that Schedule be furnished within the time specified in the second column of that Table.

(3) In relation to an agreement to which this Act —

    (*a*) has effect by virtue of section 8 above as if it were an agreement between members of a trade association, or persons represented on the trade association by such members;

    (*b*) has effect by virtue of section 16 above as if it were an agreement between members of a services supply association, or persons represented on the services supply association by such members;

references in this section and Schedule 2 to the parties to the agreement include references to those members or persons, and in relation to an agreement in which a term is implied by virtue of section 8(2) or (4) above, or section 16(3) or (5) above, as the case may be, the reference in this section to the terms of the agreement includes a reference to that term, and references in this section and Schedule 2 to an agreement shall be construed accordingly.   **[151]**

25. Particulars of export agreements

Section 24 above has effect in relation to an agreement which is or becomes one to which this Act would apply but for —

    (*a*) paragraph 6(1) of Schedule 3 to this Act, where the agreement relates to exports from the United Kingdom, or

    (*b*) paragraph 9(1) of that Schedule,

as if that agreement were subject to registration under this Act.   **[152]**

26. Court's power to rectify the register, etc

(1) The Court may, on the application of any person aggrieved, order the register to be rectified by the variation or removal of particulars included in the register in respect of any agreement.

(2) The Court may, on the application of —

    (*a*) any person party to an agreement; or

    (*b*) the Director, in respect of an agreement of which particulars have been furnished to him under this Act;

declare whether or not the agreement is one to which this Act applies, and if so whether or not it is subject to registration under this Act.

(3) Where application is made under subsection (2) above by a party to an agreement before the expiry of the time within which, if the agreement is subject to registration under this Act, particulars are required to be furnished under section 24 above, then —

    (*a*) if particulars of the agreement have not been so furnished before the commencement of the proceedings, that time shall be extended by a time equal to the time during which the proceedings and any appeal therein are pending, and such further time, if any, as the Court may direct; and

(b) if particulars have been so furnished, the Director shall not enter or file particulars of the agreement in the register during the time during which the proceedings and any appeal therein are pending.

(4) Notice of an application to the Court under this section shall be served, in accordance with rules of court[1] —

(a) in the case of an application by a person other than the Director, on the Director;

(b) in the case of an application by the Director, on the parties to the agreement or such of them as may be prescribed or determined by or under the rules;

and a party on whom notice is so served shall be entitled, in accordance with such rules, to appear and be heard on the application.   [153]

NOTE

1 See the Restrictive Practices Court Rules 1976, SI 1976 No 1897, rr 54–56.

27. Regulations for registration

(1) Subject to the provisions of this Act, the Director may make regulations for the purposes of registration under this Act and for purposes connected therewith, and in particular, but without prejudice to the generality of the foregoing provision —

(a) for requiring that —

(i) in respect of an agreement he is furnished with information as to any steps taken, or decision given, under or for the purpose of any directly applicable Community provision affecting the agreement; and

(ii) the information so given or such part, if any of it, as may be provided by the regulations is included in the particulars to be entered or filed in the register under section 1(2)(b) above;

(b) for regulating the procedure to be followed in connection with the furnishing of particulars, information and documents under section 24 above and section 36 below;

(c) for excluding from the particulars to be furnished or from the particulars to be entered in the register under this Act —

(i) such details as to parties or other persons, prices (or, in relation to Part III of this Act, charges) terms or other matters as are material for the purpose only of defining the particular application of continuing restrictions accepted or information provisions made under agreements of which particulars are so entered;

(ii) particulars of such variations as may be specified in the regulations, being variations the registration of which is in the Director's opinion unnecessary for the purposes of this Act;

(d) for prescribing the form of any notice, certificate or other document

to be given, made or furnished under the provisions of this Act;
(e) for regulating the inspection of the register or of any document kept by the Director;
(f) for prescribing anything authorised or required by this Act to be prescribed by regulations made under this section.

(2) Nothing in regulations made by virtue of subsection (1)(c) above shall affect the Director's power under section 36(3) to require the furnishing of further documents or information by any such person as is mentioned in section 36(3).

(3) Any regulations made under this section prescribing a fee for inspection of the register or for the supply of copies of or extracts from particulars entered or filed in the register, shall be made with the approval of the Treasury.

(4) The Director's power to make regulations under this section is exercisable by statutory instrument, and the Statutory Instruments Act 1946 shall apply to such regulations as it applies to regulations made by a Minister of the Crown within the meaning of that Act.   [154]

REGULATIONS UNDER THIS SECTION
The Registered Restrictive Trading Agreements (Inspection and Copy) (Fees) Regulations 1977, SI 1977 No 612, and the Registration of Restrictive Trading Agreements Regulations 1984, SI 1984 No 392 (made under this section and s 23). In addition, by virtue of s 44 and Sch 4, para 1(1), above post, the Registration of Restrictive Trading Agreements (EEC Documents) Regulations 1973, SI 1973 No 950, have effect as if made under this section and s 23, above.

Exemptions

28. Excepted agreements

This Act does not apply to the agreements described in Schedule 3 to this Act.
[155]

29. Agreements important to the national economy

(1) If it appears to the Secretary of State, on consideration of an agreement proposed to be made by any parties, that the conditions set out in subsection (2) below are complied with in respect of the proposed agreement, he may, by order made on or before the conclusion of the agreement, approve the agreement for the purposes of this section; and any agreement so approved shall be exempt from registration under this Act during the continuance in force of the order.

(2) The conditions for the making of an order under subsection (1) above in respect of an agreement (in this section referred to as the conditions of exemption) are —

(a) that the agreement is calculated to promote the carrying out of an industrial or commercial project or scheme of substantial importance to the national economy;
(b) that its object or main object is to promote efficiency in a trade or industry or to create or improve productive capacity in an industry;
(c) that the object cannot be achieved or achieved within a reasonable time

except by means of the agreement or of an agreement for similar purposes;

(*d*) that no restrictions are accepted or information provisions made under the agreement other than such as are reasonably necessary to achieve that object; and

(*e*) that the agreement is on balance expedient in the national interest.

(3) In considering the national interest for the purposes of subsection (2)(*e*) above the Secretary of State shall take into account any effects which an agreement is likely to have on persons not parties thereto as purchasers, consumers or users of any relevant goods or, in relation to an agreement to which this Act applies by virtue of an order under section 11 or section 12 above, as users of any relevant services.

(4) An order under this section shall continue in force for such period as may be specified therein, which may be extended by subsequent order of the Secretary of State: but the period so specified or extended shall not exceed the period which appears to the Secretary of State sufficient for the purposes for which the order was made.

(5) An order under this section approving an agreement may be revoked by order of the Secretary of State at any time after the expiry of one year from the day on which the first-mentioned order was made if it appears to him —

(*a*) that the object or main object of the agreement has not been or is not likely to be achieved, or that any other condition or exemption is no longer satisfied in respect of the agreement; or

(*b*) that the agreement is used for purposes other than those for which it was approved;

and may be so revoked at any time if the Secretary of State becomes aware of circumstances by reason of which, if known to him at the material time, the agreement would not have been approved.

The Secretary of State shall not make an order by virtue of paragraph (*a*) or paragraph (*b*) of this subsection unless he has given to each of the parties at least 28 days' notice of his intention to make the order.

(6) The Secretary of State shall —

(*a*) lay before each House of Parliament a copy of any order made under this section and of the agreement to which the order relates; and

(*b*) make available for public inspection a copy of any such agreement.

(7) Subsection (6) above shall not apply —

(*a*) to an agreement which varies an agreement previously approved under this section; or

(*b*) to an order approving such an agreement;

if in the Secretary of State's opinion the variation does not substantially affect the operation of restrictions accepted or information provisions made under the agreement previously approved.   **[156]**

30. Agreements holding down prices

(1) A competent authority may by order approve for the purposes of this section any agreement made at the request of the competent authority, or any term included at their request in any agreement, being an agreement or term which relates exclusively —

    (*a*) to the prices to be charged in connection with transactions of any description and is designed either to prevent or restrict increases or to secure reductions in those prices; or

    (*b*) in relation to an agreement to which this Act applies by virtue of an order under section 11 or section 12 above, to the charges to be made in connection with transactions of any description and is designed either to prevent or restrict increases or to secure reductions in those charges.

(2) Where an agreement is approved by order under this section, the agreement shall be exempt from registration under this Act during the continuance in force of the order; and where a term of an agreement is so approved, that term, and any restrictions accepted or information provisions made thereunder, shall during the continuance in force of the order be disregarded for all purposes in determining whether this Act applies to the agreement.

(3) An order under this section shall continue in force for such period as may be specified therein, which may be extended by subsequent order of the competent authority: but the period so specified shall not exceed two years, and shall not be extended by more than two years at a time.

(4) An order under this section may at any time be revoked by order of the competent authority if it appears to that authority that the relevant agreement or term is used for purposes other than those for which it was approved.

(5) A competent authority shall make available for public inspection a copy of any agreement or term of an agreement approved by order under this section.

(6) The competent authorities for the purposes of this section are the Secretary of State, and the Minister of Agriculture, Fisheries and Food. **[157]**

31. Supplementary provisions for ss 29 and 30

(1) Sections 29 and 30 above apply, with the necessary modifications, in relation to any recommendation made by or on behalf of a trade association or a services supply association as they apply in relation to an agreement; and where any such recommendation is approved by order under either of those sections —

    (*a*) subsection (2) or subsection (4) of section 8 above;

    (*b*) subsection (3) or subsection (5) of section 16 above;

shall not apply in relation to the recommendation during the continuance in force of the order.

(2) In the case of an order under section 29 approving a recommendation by or on behalf of a trade association or of a services supply association, as the case may be —

(*a*) the requirement of subsection (5) of that section as to the giving of notice of intention to revoke the order shall be treated as a requirement to give such notice as is there mentioned to the association; and

(*b*) any notice under that subsection which is required to be given to a trade association or to a services supply association or to each of the members of such an association shall be treated as duly so given if it is given either —

(i) to the association; or

(ii) to the secretary, manager or other similar officer of the association.

(3) An order under section 29 or section 30 made before the conclusion of the agreement or issue of the recommendation to which it relates may be made subject to conditions —

(*a*) as to the time within which the agreement is to be concluded or the recommendation issued; and

(*b*) as to the furnishing of copies of the agreement or recommendation to the Secretary of State or other competent authority.

(4) There may be omitted from the copies of any agreement, term of an agreement or recommendation to be laid before Parliament under section 29, and to be made available for public inspection under that section or section 30, the particulars mentioned in subsection (5) below.

(5) The particulars referred to in subsection (4) above are such as would, in the opinion of the Secretary of State or other competent authority, fall to be entered in the special section of the register referred to in section 23(3) above if the relevant agreement were subject to registration under this Act.

(6) If any agreement, term of an agreement or recommendation approved by order under section 29 or section 30 is subsequently varied, the order shall cease to have effect unless the variation is also approved by order under section 29 or section 30, as the case may be; and a variation may be so approved if (and only if) the agreement, term or recommendation could be so approved as varied.

(7) The approval by order under section 29 or section 30 of an agreement or recommendation made by or on behalf of a trade association or a services supply association shall not be affected by any change in the persons who are members of the association or are represented on the association by such members, but without prejudice to the power of the Secretary of State or other competent authority to revoke the order under section 29 or section 30.

(8) No order made by the Court in proceedings under this Act for restraining any person from making an agreement or recommendation, and no corresponding undertaking given to the Court in such proceedings, shall be construed as extending to an agreement or recommendation which is exempt from registration by virtue of an order under section 29 or section 30.

(9) In any proceedings before the Court under sections 1 and 2 above in respect of an agreement, the fact that the agreement has or has not at any time been the subject of an order under section 29 or section 30 shall not be treated as relevant to the question whether any restrictions accepted or information provisions made under the agreement are contrary to the public interest.   **[158]**

32. Wholesale co-operative societies

(1) The Secretary of State may approve under this section any industrial and provident society which in his opinion fulfils the following conditions—

(a) that it carries on business in the production or supply of goods or in the supply of services or in the application to goods of any process of manufacture;

(b) that its shares are wholly or mainly held by industrial and provident societies; and

(c) that those societies are retail societies or societies whose shares are wholly or mainly held by retail societies;

and a society which is for the time being so approved shall not be treated as a trade association or a services supply association.

(2) An approval given in respect of a society under this section (if it has not been previously withdrawn) expires at the end of the period of two years beginning with the date on which it was given or, if that period is extended (once or more than once) under subsection (3) below, at the end of that period as so extended, or further extended, as the case may be.

(3) The Secretary of State may extend or, if it has already been extended under this subsection, may further extend the period of two years referred to in subsection (2) above by such period, not exceeding two years, as he may specify.

(4) The Secretary of State may at any time withdraw an approval given in respect of a society under this section if it appears to him—

(a) that the society has made an agreement which would have been subject to registration under this Act if the approval had not been given, or that such a recommendation as is mentioned in section 8(2) or (4) above has been made by or on behalf of the society; and

(b) that the agreement or recommendation has such adverse effects on competition that it should not be precluded from being investigated by the Court under the provisions of this Act.

(5) In relation to a society which is for the time being approved under this section but which, in consequence of an order made under section 11 or section 12 above, is a society to which the provisions of section 16 above would apply if it were not so approved, subsection (4) above has effect as if in that subsection—

(a) any reference to an agreement which would have been subject to registration under this Act if the approval had not been given included a reference to an agreement which would in those circumstances have been subject to such registration by virtue of the order; and

(b) any reference to such a recommendation as is mentioned in section 8(2) or (4) included a reference to such a recommendation as is mentioned in section 16(3) or (5).

(6) On the expiry or withdrawal of an approval given in respect of a society under this section, the provisions of this Act shall have effect in relation to agreements and recommendations made by the society during the currency of the approval as if the society had not been approved under this section.

(7) In this section—

"industrial and provident society" means a society registered or deemed to be registered under the Industrial and Provident Societies Acts 1965 to 1975 or under the Industrial and Provident Societies Act (Northern Ireland) 1969; "retail society" means a society which carries on business in the sale by retail of goods for the domestic or personal use of individuals dealing with the society, or in the provision of services for such individuals.   **[159]**

33. Agricultural and forestry associations, and fisheries associations

(1) Subject to the provisions of this section, this Act does not apply to an agreement between members of an association to which this section applies, or between such an association and any other person, whether a member of the association or not, by reason only of any restriction accepted or treated as accepted, or any information provision made or treated as made, by the association, or by members of the association or of any constituent association, for the purposes of or in connection with—

(a) the marketing or preparation for market by the association of produce produced by members of the association on land occupied by them and used for agriculture or forestry (with or without similar produce not so produced); or

(b) the marketing or preparation for market by the association of fish or shellfish caught or taken by members of the association in the course of their business (with or without fish or shellfish not so caught or taken); or

(c) the supply by the association to the members of goods required for the production of that produce on that land, or for the catching or taking of fish or shellfish in the course of that business, as the case may be; or

(d) the production of produce or the catching or taking of fish or shellfish, as the case may be, by members of the association; or

(e) the supply of produce, or the supply of fish or shellfish, as the case may be, by members of the association;

and in determining whether any such agreement is an agreement to which this Act applies, no account shall be taken of any such restriction or information provision.

(2) This section applies—

(a) to any association in the case of which the conditions specified in subsection (3) below are satisfied where the association is—

(i) of persons occupying land used for agriculture or forestry or both;
(ii) of persons engaged in the business of catching or taking fish or shellfish;

(b) to any association of the associations referred to in paragraph (a) above which—

(i) satisfies the condition specified in paragraph (a) of subsection (3) below; and

(ii) would satisfy the condition specified in paragraph (c) of subsection (3) if references in that paragraph to members of the association included references to members of constituent associations;

(c) to any co-operative association (whether or not the conditions specified in paragraphs (a) to (c) of subsection (3) are satisfied) which has as its object or primary object to assist its members —

   (i) in the carrying on of the businesses of agriculture or forestry or both on land occupied by them; or

   (ii) in the carrying on of businesses consisting in the catching or taking of fish or shellfish.

(3) The conditions referred to in subsection (2) above are that —

(a) the association is or is deemed to be registered under the Industrial and Provident Societies Acts 1965 to 1975 or, being a company within the meaning of the [Companies Act 1985][1], contains in its memorandum or articles of association such provisions as may be prescribed by order of the Ministers with respect to the number of members, numbers of shares held by members, distribution of profits, voting rights or other matters;

(b) at least 90 per cent of the voting power is attached to shares held by persons occupying land used for agriculture or forestry or both, or by persons engaged in the business of catching or taking fish or shellfish, as the case may be; and

(c) the only business, or the principal business, carried on by the association is one or more of the following —

   (i) the marketing or preparation for market of produce produced by members of the association on land occupied by them and used for agriculture or forestry or both (with or without similar produce not so produced);

   (ii) the marketing or preparation for market of fish or shellfish caught or taken by members of the association in the course of their business (with or without fish or shellfish not so caught or taken);

   (iii) the supply to the members of goods required for the production of that produce on that land, or for the catching or taking of fish or shellfish in the course of that business, as the case may be;

   (iv) in the case of an association of persons occupying land for forestry, the carrying out of forestry operations for the members on that land.

References in this subsection to the Industrial and Provident Societies Acts 1965 to 1975, and the [Companies Act 1985],[1] include references respectively to the Industrial and Provident Societies Act (Northern Ireland) 1969 and the [Companies (Northern Ireland) Order 1986][2].

(4) The Ministers may by order made by statutory instrument direct that the exemption provided by subsection (1) shall not apply —

(a) in relation to agreements of such classes as may be prescribed by the order; or (*b*) in relation to agreements, or agreements of any class, made by associations of such classes as may be so prescribed;

and any such order may apply to agreements made before as well as after the coming into force of the order.

(5) In this section —

"agriculture" has the meaning given by the Agriculture Act 1947 and the Agriculture (Scotland) Act 1948;
"co-operative association" has the meaning given by section 340(8) and (9) of the Income and Corporation Taxes Act 1970, and references to members of a co-operative association include references to members of any such association which is a member of that association;
"forestry" includes the processing of wood for sale, but not the manufacture of articles of wood;
"the Ministers" means —

(*a*) the Minister of Agriculture, Fisheries and Food and the Secretaries of State respectively concerned with agriculture in Scotland and Northern Ireland, acting jointly; but
(*b*) in the case of functions exercisable in relation to associations falling within paragraph (*c*) of subsection (2) above and concerned only with forestry in Wales "Secretary of State" shall be substituted for "Minister of Agriculture, Fisheries and Food";

"produce" means anything (whether live or dead) produced in the course of agriculture or forestry.

(6) Without prejudice to the responsibilities of the Secretaries of State respectively concerned with agriculture in Scotland and Northern Ireland, the discharge of any functions as functions exercisable by virtue of subsection (5) above by the Secretary of State shall belong to the Secretary of State for Wales; but nothing in this subsection shall be taken —

(*a*) to prejudice any powers exercisable in relation to the functions of Ministers of the Crown and government departments by virtue of Her Majesty's prerogative, or
(*b*) to affect the power of any Secretary of State to perform any functions of that office in place of the Secretary of State entrusted with the discharge of those functions.   **[160]**

NOTE
See below, the Anti-Competitive Practices (Exclusions) Order 1980, Art 2(a), Sch 1, para 7. For an order under sub-ss (3)(*a*) and (4), see now the Agricultural and Forestry Associations Order 1982, SI 1982 No 569.

AMENDMENTS
1 Substituted by the Companies Consolidation (Consequential Provisions) Act 1985, s 30, Sch 2.
2 Substituted by the Companies Consolidation (Consequential Provisions) (Northern Ireland) Order 1986, SI 1986 No 1035.

34. Authorisations for purposes of ECSC Treaty

An agreement is exempt from registration under this Act so long as there is in force in relation to that agreement an authorisation given for the purpose of any provision of the ECSC Treaty relating to restrictive trade practices.

[161]

Enforcement

35. Failure to register

(1) If particulars of an agreement which is subject to registration under this Act are not duly furnished within the time required by section 24 above, or within such further time as the Director may, upon application made within that time, allow—

    (*a*) the agreement is void in respect of all restrictions accepted or information provisions made thereunder; and

    (*b*) it is unlawful for any person party to the agreement who carries on business within the United Kingdom to give effect to, or enforce or purport to enforce, the agreement in respect of any such restrictions or information provisions.

(2) No criminal proceedings lie against any person on account of a contravention of subsection (1)(*b*) above; but the obligation to comply with that paragraph is a duty owed to any person who may be affected by a contravention of it and any breach of that duty is actionable accordingly subject to the defences and other incidents applying to actions for breach of statutory duty.

(3) Without prejudice to any right which any person may have by virtue of subsection (2) above to bring civil proceedings in respect of an agreement affected by subsection (1)(*b*), the Court may, upon the Director's application, make such order as appears to the Court to be proper for restraining all or any of those mentioned in subsection (4) below from giving effect to, or enforcing or purporting to enforce—

    (*a*) the agreement in respect of any restrictions or information provisions;

    (*b*) other agreements in contravention of subsection (1) above;

and nothing in subsection (2) prevents the enforcement of any such order by appropriate proceedings.

(4) Those who may be restrained by an order of the Court under subsection (3) above are—

    (*a*) any person party to the agreement who carries on business within the United Kingdom;

    (*b*) a trade association or a services supply association of which any such person is a member; or

    (*c*) any person acting on behalf of any such association.

(5) Where an order is made under subsection (3) against any party to an agreement and that party is a member of a trade association or a services supply association, the order may include provisions for restraining the association, and any person acting on its behalf, from procuring or assisting that party to do anything which would be a contravention of the order in its application to him.

(6) In relation to an agreement for the constitution of a trade association or a services supply association which is subject to registration in consequence of the making of a recommendation to which—

(a) subsection (2) or subsection (4) of section 8 above;

(b) subsection (3) or subsection (5) of section 16 above;

applies, the Court's power under subsection (3) includes power to make such order as appears to the Court to be proper for restraining the association or any person acting on its behalf from making other such recommendations.

(7) Where any issue, whether of law or of fact or partly of law and partly of fact, has been finally determined on an application under subsection (3) above in respect of an agreement, then in any proceedings brought in respect of that agreement by virtue of subsection (2) above in which the same issue arises—

(a) any finding of fact relevant to that issue which was made on the application shall be evidence (and in Scotland sufficient evidence) of that fact; and

(b) any decision on a question of law relevant to that issue which was given on the application shall be binding on the court in so far as the material facts found in those proceedings are the same as were found on the application.

(8) Where an agreement which is subject to registration under this Act is varied so as to extend or add to the restrictions accepted or information provisions made under the agreement, the provisions of this section apply, with the necessary modifications, in relation to the variation as they apply in relation to an original agreement which is subject to registration under this Act.   **[162]**

NOTE
  Provisions relating to applications under this section are contained in the Restrictive Practices Court Rules 1976, SI 1976 No 1897, rr 54–56.

36. Director's power to obtain information

(1) If the Director has reasonable cause to believe that a person being—

(a) a person carrying on within the United Kingdom any such business as is described in section 6(1) above; or

(b) a trade association, the members of which consist of or include persons carrying on business as so described, or representatives of such persons; or

(c) a person carrying on within the United Kingdom any business of supplying services brought under control by an order under section 11 or section 12 above; or

(d) an association which, in relation to such an order, is a services supply association;

is or may be party to an agreement subject to registration under this Act, he may give to that person such notice as is described in subsection (2) below.

(2) The notice referred to in subsection (1) above may require any person mentioned in paragraphs (a) to (d) of that subsection to notify the Director (within

such time as may be specified in the notice) whether that person is party to any agreement relating to —

(*a*) any such matters as are described in paragraphs (*a*) to (*f*) of section 6(1); or

(*b*) any such matters as are described in paragaphs (*a*) to (*h*) of section 7(1) above; or

(*c*) matters specified in the relevant order for the purposes of section 11(1)(*b*) above; or

(*d*) matters specified in the relevant order for the purposes of section 12(1)(*b*) above;

and if so to furnish to the Director such particulars of the agreement as may be specified in the notice.

(3) The Director may give notice to any person by whom particulars are furnished under section 24 above in respect of an agreement, or to any other person being party to the agreement, requiring him to furnish such further documents or information in his possession or control as the Director considers expedient for the purposes of or in connection with the registration of the agreement.

(4) In the case of —

(*a*) any such trade association as is mentioned in subsection (1)(*b*) above; or

(*b*) any such services supply association as is mentioned in subsection (1)(*d*) above;

a notice may be given under subsection (1) by the Director either to the association or to the secretary, manager or other similar officer of the association.

For the purposes of this section any such trade association or services supply association shall be treated as party to any agreement to which members of the association, or persons represented on the association by such members, are parties as such.

(5) In subsection (1) the reference to an agreement subject to registration under this Act shall, in relation to Part II, be construed as including a reference to any agreement which —

(*a*) relates to exports from the United Kingdom; and

(*b*) would, but for paragraph 6(1) of Schedule 3 to this Act, be an agreement subject to registration under this Act.

(6) In subsection (1) the reference to an agreement subject to registration under this Act shall, in relation to Part III, be construed as including a reference to any agreement which would, but for paragraph 9(1) of Schedule 3, be an agreement subject to registration under this Act. **[163]**

37. Court's power to order examination on oath

(1) In any case in which the Director has given notice to any person under section 36 above the Court may on the Director's application order that person to attend and be examined on oath in accordance with this section concerning the matters in respect of which the Director has given notice to him under that section.

(2) Where an order is made under this section for the attendance and examination of any person —

(a) the Director shall take part in the examination and for that purpose may be represented by solicitor or counsel;

(b) the person examined shall answer all such questions as the Court may put or allow to be put to him, but may at his own cost employ a solicitor with or without counsel, who shall be at liberty to put to him such questions as the Court may deem just for the purpose of enabling him to explain or qualify any answers given by him;

(c) notes of the examination shall be taken down in writing and shall be read over to or by, and signed by, the person examined, and may thereafter be used in evidence against him;

(d) the Court may require the person examined to produce any such particulars, documents or information in his possession or control as may be specified in the notice given by the Director as aforesaid.

(3) Where notice under section 36 has been given to a body corporate, an order may be made under this section for the attendance and examination —

(a) of any director, manager, secretary or other officer of that body corporate; or

(b) of any other person who is employed by the body corporate and appears to the Court to be likely to have particular knowledge of any of the matters in respect of which the notice was given.

(4) In any case referred to in subsection (3) above —

(a) the reference in subsection (1) above to matters in respect of which the Director has given notice to the person examined shall be construed as a reference to matters in respect of which notice was given to the body corporate; and

(b) in paragraph (d) of subsection (2) above and in paragraph (c) so far as it relates to evidence, references to the person examined shall include references to the body corporate.

(5) The provisions of subsections (3) and (4) above have effect —

(a) in relation to a trade association which is not incorporated;

(b) in relation to a services supply association which is not incorporated;

as those provisions have effect in relation to a body corporate.

(6) Nothing in this section shall be taken to compel the disclosure by a barrister, advocate or solicitor of any privileged communication made by or to him in that capacity, or the production by him of any document containing any such communication.   **[164]**

NOTE

Provisions relating to applications under this section are contained in the Restrictive Practices Courts Rules 1976, SI 1976 No 1897, r 57.

38. Offences in connection with registration

(1) A person who fails without reasonable excuse to comply with a notice duly

given to him under section 36 above is guilty of an offence and liable on summary conviction to a fine not exceeding . . .[1]

(2) If a person who furnishes or is required to furnish any particulars, documents or information under this Act—

(a) makes any statement, or furnishes any document, which he knows to be false in a material particular; or

(b) recklessly makes any statement, or furnishes any document, which is false in a material particular; or

(c) wilfully alters, suppresses or destroys any document which he is required to furnish as aforesaid;

he is guilty of an offence under this section.

(3) A person guilty of an offence mentioned in subsection (2) above is liable—

(a) on summary conviction to imprisonment for a term not exceeding three months or to a fine not exceeding . . .[2] or to both such imprisonment and such a fine; or

(b) on conviction on indictment to imprisonment for a term not exceeding two years or to a fine, or to both such imprisonment and a fine.

(4) If any default in respect of which a person is convicted of an offence under subsection (1) above continues after the conviction, that person is guilty of a further offence and liable on summary conviction to a fine—

(a) not exceeding . . .[1]; or

(b) not exceeding £10 for every day on which the default continues within the three months next following his conviction for the first-mentioned offence;

whichever is the greater.

(5) For the purposes of subsection (4) above a default in respect of the furnishing of any particulars, documents or information shall be deemed to continue until the particulars, documents or information have been furnished.

(6) Where an offence under this section committed by a body corporate is proved to have been committed with the consent or connivance of, or to be attributable to any neglect on the part of, any director, manager, secretary or other similar officer of the body corporate or any person who was purporting to act in any such capacity, he as well as the body corporate is guilty of that offence and liable to be proceeded against and punished accordingly.

(7) In this section "director", in relation to a body corporate established by or under any enactment for the purpose of carrying on under national ownership any industry or part of an industry or undertaking, being a body corporate whose affairs are managed by its members, means a member of that body corporate. **[165]**

AMENDMENTS

1 In sub-ss (1) and (4)(a) the maximum fine is increased to the current amount at level 3 on the standard scale by the Criminal Justice Act 1982, s 38.

2 The maximum fine which may be imposed under sub-s (3)(a) is the prescribed sum under the Magistrates' Courts Act 1980, s 32(2).

39. Proceedings and venue in respect of offences

(1) No proceedings for an offence under the preceding provisions of this Act shall be instituted —

(a) in England and Wales except by or with the consent of the Director of Public Prosecutions or the Director;

(b) in Northern Ireland except by or with the consent of the Attorney General for Northern Ireland or the Director.

(2) Any information relating to an offence under the preceding provisions of this Act may be tried by a magistrates' court or by a court of summary jurisdiction in Northern Ireland, if it is laid at any time —

(a) within three years after the commission of the offence; and

(b) within twelve months after the date on which evidence sufficient in the opinion of the Director of Public Prosecutions, the Attorney General for Northern Ireland or the Director, as the case may be, to justify the proceedings comes to his knowledge;

notwithstanding anything in [section 127(1) of the Magistrates' Courts Act 1980] or in [article 19(1) of the Magistrates' Courts (Northern Ireland) Order 1981].

(3) Proceedings in Scotland for an offence against the preceding provisions of this Act may be commenced at any time —

(a) within three years after the commission of the offence; and

(b) within twelve months after the date on which evidence sufficient in the Director's opinion to justify a report to the Lord Advocate with a view to consideration of the question of proceedings comes to the Director's knowledge;

notwithstanding anything in section 23 of the Summary Jurisdiction (Scotland) Act 1954.

(4) For the purposes of subsections (2) and (3) above, a certificate of the ꞈ Director of Public Prosecutions, the Attorney General for Northern Ireland or the Director, as the case may be, as to the date on which such evidence as aforesaid came to his knowledge shall be conclusive evidence.

(5) An offence under section 38 above may be tried by a court having jurisdiction either in the county or place in which the offence was actually committed or in any county or place in which the alleged offender carries on business.

(6) For the purposes of article 7(2) of the Prosecution of Offences (Northern Ireland) Order 1972 (which relates to consents to prosecutions by the Director of Public Prosecutions for Northern Ireland) subsections (1) and (2) above shall be treated as if they were in force before the coming into operation of that order.   **[166]**

PART V

MISCELLANEOUS AND SUPPLEMENTAL

40. Order under s 56 of Fair Trading Act 1973

(1) The Court may, upon application made by any person who desires to make an agreement —

(a) which, if made, would be an agreement to which this Act applies, and

(b) is one the making of which is unlawful by virtue of any order in force under section 56 of the Fair Trading Act 1973 or having effect as if made under that section,

declare whether or not any restrictions or information provisions by virtue of which this Act would apply to the agreement (not being such restrictions or information provisions as are described in paragraphs (b) to (d) of paragraph 6(1) of Schedule 3 to this Act) are contrary to the public interest.

(2) The provisions of section 2(1) to (4) above apply with the necessary modifications in relation to any such declaration as they apply in relation to a finding under that section.

(3) Where an application is made to the Court under subsection (1) above and —

(a) on that application the Court makes a declaration under that subsection in relation to a restriction proposed to be accepted or an information provision proposed to be made under an agreement, and

(b) by virtue of an order under section 56 of the 1973 Act which is for the time being in force, the making or carrying out of an agreement under which that restriction was accepted or that information provision was made would be unlawful,

the order under section 56 of the 1973 Act shall cease to have effect in so far as it renders unlawful the making or carrying out of an agreement under which that restriction is accepted or that information provision is made.

(4) The Director shall be the respondent to any application made under this section; and the provisions of section 10 or section 19 above apply with the necessary modifications in relation to proceedings on any such application as they apply in relation to the proceedings mentioned in that section.   [167]

41. Disclosure of information

(1) Subject to subsection (2) below, no information with respect to any particular business which has been obtained under or by virtue of the provisions of this Act shall, so long as that business continues to be carried on, be disclosed without the consent of the person for the time being carrying on that business; but this subsection does not apply to any disclosure of information which is made —

(a) for the purpose of facilitating the performance of any functions of the Director, [the Director General of Telecommunications], [the Director General of Gas Supply,] [the Civil Aviation Authority,] [the Director

General of Water Services,] [the Director General of Electricity Supply],[1] the Monopolies and Mergers Commission, the Secretary of State or any other Minister under this Act or the Fair Trading Act 1973 [or the Estate Agents Act 1979] [or the Competition Act 1980] [or the Telecommunications Act 1984] [or Chapter XIV of Part I of the Financial Services Act 1986] [or the Gas Act 1986] [or the Airports Act 1986] [or the Control of Misleading Advertisements Regulations 1988] [or the Water Act 1989] [or the Electricity Act 1989][1];

(b) in pursuance of a Community obligation;

(c) for the purposes of any proceedings before the Court or of any other legal proceedings, whether civil or criminal, under this Act or the Fair Trading Act 1973 [or the Control of Misleading Advertisements Regulations 1988][1].

(2) Nothing in subsection (1) above shall be construed—

(a) as limiting the particulars which may be entered or filed in, or made public as part of, the register under this Act; or

(b) as applying to any information which has been made public as part of that register.

(3) Any person who discloses any information in contravention of this section is guilty of an offence and liable—

(a) on summary conviction, to a fine not exceeding . . .[2]

(b) on conviction on indictment, to imprisonment for a term not exceeding two years or to a fine or to both.

(4) No prosecution for an offence under this section shall be commenced after the expiry of three years from the commission of the offence or one year from its discovery by the prosecutor, whichever is the earlier.

(5) Notwithstanding anything in [section 127(1) of the Magistrates' Courts Act 1980],[3] a magistrates' court may try an information for an offence under this section if the information was laid within twelve months from the commission of the offence.

(6) Notwithstanding anything in section 23 of the Summary Jurisdiction (Scotland) Act 1954, summary proceedings in Scotland for an offence under this section may be commenced within twelve months from the commission of the offence, and subsection (2) of the said section 23 applies for the purposes of this subsection as it applies for the purposes of that section.

(7) In the application of this section to Northern Ireland, for the references in subsection (5) above to [section 127(1) of the Magistrates' Courts Act 1980][3] and to the trial and laying of an information there shall be substituted respectively references to [article 19(1) of the Magistrates' Courts (Northern Ireland) Order 1981][4] and to the hearing and determination and making of a complaint.

[168]

AMENDMENTS
1 Additions to sub-s (1) made by the Telecommunications Act 1984, s 109(1), Sch 4, para 65, the Estate Agents Act 1979, s 10(4)(c), the Competition Act 1980, s 19(4)(e), the Gas Act 1986, s 67(1), Sch 7, para 23, the Airports Act 1986, s 83(1), Sch 4, para 5, the Control of Misleading

Advertisements Regulations 1988, SI 1988 No 915, the Financial Services Act 1986, s 182, Sch 13, para 2, the Water Act 1989, s 190(1), Sch 25, para 53, and the Electricity Act 1989, s 112(1), Sch 16, para 19.

2 The maximum fine under sub-s (3)(*a*) is increased to level 5 on the standard scale by the Criminal Justice Act 1982, s 38.

3 Words in sub-ss (5) and (7) substituted by the Magistrates' Courts Act 1980, s 154, Sch 7, para 141.

4 Words in sub-s (7) substituted by the Magistrates' Courts (Northern Ireland) Order 1981.

42. Orders and regulations

(1) Any statutory instrument by which —

(*a*) an order is made under section 18(5) or section 33(4) above; or
(*b*) regulations are made under section 27(1) above;

is subject to annulment in pursuance of a resolution of either House of Parliament.

(2) Any power conferred by a preceding provision of this Act to make an order by statutory instrument includes power to revoke or vary that order by a subsequent order made under that provision. **[169]**

43. Interpretation and construction

(1) In this Act —

"agreement" includes any agreement or arrangement, whether or not it is or is intended to be enforceable (apart from any provision of this Act) by legal proceedings, and references in this Act to restrictions accepted or information provisions made under an agreement shall be construed accordingly;

"the Court" means the Restrictive Practices Court;

"designated services" has the meaning given by section 13(1) above;

"the Director" means the Director General of Fair Trading appointed under the Fair Trading Act 1973;

"goods" includes ships and aircraft, minerals, substances and animals (including fish), and references to the production of goods include references to the getting of minerals and the taking of such animals;

"information provision" includes a provision for or in relation to the furnishing of information;

"interconnected bodies corporate" means bodies corporate which are members of the same group, and for the purposes of this definition "group" means a body corporate and all other bodies corporate which are its subsidiaries —

(*a*) within the meaning of [section 736 of the Companies Act 1985] (or for companies in Northern Ireland, [Article 4 of the Companies (Northern Ireland) Order 1986]; or

(*b*) in the case of an industrial and provident society, within the meaning of section 15 of the Friendly and Industrial and Provident Societies Act 1968 (or for industrial and provident societies in Northern Ireland, section 47 of the Industrial and Provident Societies Act (Northern Ireland) 1969);

"price" includes a charge of any description;

"restriction" includes a negative obligation, whether express or implied and whether absolute or not;

"services supply association" means such an association as is described in section 16(1) above;

"supply" includes supply by way of lease or hire, and "acquire" shall be construed accordingly;

"trade association" means a body of persons (whether incorporated or not) which is formed for the purpose of furthering the trade interests of its members, or of persons represented by its members.

(2) For the purposes of —

(*a*) sections 6 to 9 above, and Schedule 3 to this Act except for paragraph 5(4) to (8) of that Schedule;

(*b*) Part III of this Act except as is provided by section 19(2) above;

any two or more interconnected bodies corporate, or any two or more individuals carrying on business in partnership with each other, shall be treated as a single person.

(3) This Act applies to the construction or carrying out of buildings, structures and other works by contractors, as it applies to the supply of goods, and for the purposes of this Act any buildings, structures or other works so constructed or carried out shall be deemed to be delivered at the place where they are constructed or carried out.

(4) For the purposes of this Act a person shall not be deemed to carry on a business within the United Kingdom by reason only of the fact that he is represented for the purposes of that business by an agent within the United Kingdom.

(5) Any reference in this Act to any other enactment is a reference to that enactment as amended, or extended or applied by or under any other enactment, including this Act.   **[170]**

NOTE

This section applied and extended by the Competition Act 1980, s 33(3).

AMENDMENTS

Sub-s(1)(a) amended by the Companies Consolidation (Consequential Amendments) Act 1986, s 30, Sch 2 and the Companies Consolidation (Consequential Provisions) (Northern Ireland) Order 1986, SI 1986 No 1035.

44. Consequential amendments, repeals and transitional provisions

The provisions of Schedule 4 to this Act have effect; and subject to the transitional provisions and savings contained in that Schedule —

(*a*) the enactments specified in Schedule 5 to this Act have effect subject to the amendments (being amendments consequent on the provisions of this Act) specified in that Schedule, and

(*b*) the enactments specified in Schedule 6 to this Act are hereby repealed to the extent specified in the third column of that Schedule,

but nothing in this Act shall be taken as prejudicing the operation of section 38 of the Interpretation Act 1889 (which relates to the operation of repeals).

[171]

45. Short title, extent and commencement

(1) This Act may be cited as the Restrictive Trade Practices Act 1976.

(2) This Act extends to the Northern Ireland.

(3) This Act shall come into operation on such day as the Secretary of State may by order made by statutory instrument appoint.   **[172]**

SCHEDULES

SCHEDULE 1
Section 13
SERVICES EXCLUDED FROM SECTION 13 (DESIGNATED SERVICES)

1. Legal services (that is to say, the services of barristers, advocates or solicitors in their capacity as such).

2. Medical services (that is to say, the provision of medical or surgical advice or attendance and the performance of surgical operations).

3. Dental services (that is to say, any services falling within the practice of dentistry within the meaning of the Dentists Act [1984]).[1]

4. Ophthalmic services (that is to say, the testing of sight).

5. Veterinary services (that is to say, any services which constitute veterinary surgery within the meaning of the Veterinary Surgeons Act 1966).

6. [The services of nurses].[2]

7. The services of midwives, physiotherapists or chiropodists in their capacity as such.

8. The services of architects in their capacity as such.

9. Accounting and auditing services (that is to say, the making or preparation of accounts or accounting records and the examination, verification and auditing of financial statements).

[9A. Insolvency services within the meaning of section 428 of the Insolvency Act 1986].[3]

10. *The services of patent agents (within the meaning of [the Patents Act 1977][4]), in their capacity as such.*

[10A. The services of persons carrying on for gain in the United Kingdom the business of acting as agents or other representatives for or obtaining European patents or for the purpose of conducting proceedings [in relation to applications for or otherwise][5] in connection with such patents before the European Patent Office or the comptroller and whose names appear on the European list (within the meaning of *section 84(7) of the Patents Act 1977*), in their capacity as such persons].[4]

11. The services of parliamentary agents entered in the register in either House of Parliament as agents entitled to practise both in promoting and in opposing Bills, in their capacity as such parliamentary agents.

12. The services of surveyors (that is to say, of surveyors of land, of quantity surveyors, of surveyors of buildings or other structures and of surveyors of ships) in their capacity as such surveyors.

13. The services of professional engineers or technologists (that is to say, of persons practising or employed as consultants in the field of—

(a) civil engineering;

(b) mechanical, aeronautical, marine, electrical or electronic engineering;

(c) mining, quarrying, soil analysis or other forms of mineralogy or geology;

(d) agronomy, forestry, livestock rearing or ecology;

(e) metallurgy, chemistry, biochemistry or physics; or

(f) any other form of engineering or technology analogous to those mentioned in the preceding sub-paragraphs);

in their capacity as such engineers or technologists.

14. Services, consisting of the provision—

(a) of primary, secondary or further education within the meaning of the Education Act 1944, the Education (Scotland) Acts 1939 to 1971 or the Education and Libraries (Northern Ireland) Order 1972, or

(b) of university or other higher education not falling within the preceding sub-paragraph.

15. The services of ministers of religion in their capacity as such ministers.

[173]

AMENDMENTS

1 The date in square brackets was substituted by the Dentists Act 1984, s 54(1), Sch 5, para 7.

2 Para 6 substituted by the Nurses, Midwives and Health Visitors Act 1979, s 23(4), Sch 7, para 27.

3 Para 9A (as inserted by the Insolvency Act 1985, s 217(4)) was substituted by the Insolvency Act 1986, s 439(2), Sch 14.

4 Para 10A inserted, and the words in square brackets in para 10 substituted, by the Patents Act 1977, s 132(6), Sch 5, para 8.

5 Words inserted by the Administration of Justice Act 1985, s 60(2), (a), (b).

PROSPECTIVE AMENDMENT

As from a day to be appointed, the Copyright, Designs and Patents Act 1988, s 303(1), Sch 7, para 15 makes the following amendments:

(i) for para 10 above there is substituted:

"10. The services of registered patent agents (within the meaning of Part V of the Copyright, Designs and Patents Act 1988) in their capacity as such."

(ii) for the words in italics in para 10A, there is substituted "Part V, of the Copyright, Designs and Patents Act 1988."

SCHEDULE 2

Section 24

FURNISHING OF PARTICULARS OF AGREEMENTS

1.—(1) Subject to paragraph 2 below, the duty to furnish particulars in respect of an agreement which at any time is subject to registration shall not be affected by any subsequent variation or determination of the agreement.

(2) If at any time after an agreement has become subject to registration it is varied (whether in respect of the parties or in respect of the terms) or determined otherwise than by effluxion of time, particulars of the variation or determination shall be furnished to the Director.

2.—(1) The following provisions of this paragraph apply where an agreement becomes subject to registration after it is made.

(2) If, before the expiry of the time within which, apart from this paragraph, particulars would be required to be furnished in respect of the agreement, and before particulars have been so furnished, the agreement is determined (whether by effluxion of time or otherwise), section 24(1) above and paragraph 1 above shall cease to apply to the agreement.

(3) If, before the expiry of that time and before particulars have been furnished in respect of the agreement, the agreement is varied, the particulars to be furnished under section 24 shall be particulars of the agreement as varied, and paragraph 1 above shall not apply in relation to the variation.

3. Particulars of an agreement shall—

(a) in so far as the agreement, or any variation or determination of it, is made by an instrument in writing, be furnished by the production of the original or a true copy of the instrument;

(b) in so far as the agreement, or any variation or determination of it, is not made by an instrument in writing, be furnished by the production of a memorandum in writing signed by the person by whom the particulars are furnished.

4.—(1) Particulars may be furnished by or on behalf of any person who is party to the agreement or, as the case may be, was party thereto immediately before its determination.

(2) Where such particulars are duly furnished by or on behalf of any such person the provisions of section 24 and this Schedule shall be deemed to be complied with on the part of all such persons.

5.—(1) The following Table shows the time within which particulars of agreements and any variation or determination of an agreement, are to be furnished under section 24 and this Schedule:—

TABLE

Description of agreement	Time for registering particulars
(a) Agreement made on or after 25th November 1968, other than an agreement to which (b) to (j) below apply.	Before the date on which any restriction accepted or information provision made under the agreement takes effect, and in any case within 3 months from the day on which the agreement is made.
(b) Agreement approved by order under section 29 or section 30 above which becomes subject to registration by virtue of the expiry or revocation of that order.	Within 1 month from the day on which the agreement becomes so subject.
(c) Agreement which becomes subject to registration by virtue of the revocation of an order under section 9(5) above.	Within 1 month from the day on which the agreement becomes so subject.
(d) Agreement which becomes subject to registration by virtue of an order under section 7 above coming into force after the making of the agreement.	Within 3 months from the day on which the agreement becomes so subject.
(e) Agreement which becomes subject to registration by virtue of an order under section 11 or section 12 above coming into force after the making of the agreement.	Within 3 months from the day on which the agreement becomes so subject.

Description of agreement	*Time for registering particulars*
(*f*) Agreement whether made before on or after 25th November 1968 which becomes subject to registration by virtue of a variation on or after that date [not being a variation which becomes subject to registration by virtue of an order under section 11 or 12 above.][1]	Within the time which would apply under (*a*) above if the agreement were made on the day on which it becomes so subject.
(*g*) Agreement which becomes subject to registration by virtue of the expiry or withdrawal of an approval given under section 32 above.	Within 3 months from the day on which the agreement becomes so subject.
(*h*) Agreement which was subject to registration on 25th November 1968, of which particulars had not been duly furnished.	Within 3 months from 25th November 1968.
(*i*) Variation on or after 25th November 1968 of an agreement (whether made before or after that date) being a variation which extends or adds to the restrictions accepted or information provisions made under the agreement [other than a variation to which (ii) below applies].[1]	Within the time which would apply under (*a*) above in the case of an agreement made on the day of the variation.
(*ii*) Variation of an agreement being a variation which extends or adds to the restrictions accepted or information provisions made under the agreement and which becomes subject to registration by virtue of the revocation or variation of an order made under section 11 or 12 above].[1]	Within 1 month from the day on which the variation becomes so subject.
(*j*) Any other variation of an agreement, and the determination of an agreement.	Within 3 months from the day of the variation or determination.

(2) Any reference in the second column of the Table in this paragraph to a period calculated from a specified day is a reference to the period in question inclusive of that day.   **[174]**

AMENDMENT
1 Words and additional paragraph inserted by Competition Act 1980, s 27(4).

SCHEDULE 3

Section 28

EXCEPTED AGREEMENTS

Agreements for statutory purposes

1. — (1) This Act does not apply to an agreement which is expressly authorised by an enactment, or by any scheme, order or other instrument made under an enactment.

(2) This Act does not apply to an agreement which constitutes or forms part of a scheme certified by the Secretary of State under Chapter V of Part XIV of the Income and Corporation Taxes Act 1970 (which relates to schemes for rationalising industry).

(3) Sub-paragraphs (1) and (2) above have effect in relation to any agreement notwithstanding any order under section 11 or section 12 above.

Exclusive dealing

2. This Act does not apply to an agreement for the supply of goods between two persons, neither of whom is a trade association, being an agreement to which no other person is party and under which no such restrictions as are described in section 6(1) above are accepted or no such information provisions as are described in section 7(1) above are made other than restrictions accepted or provision made for the furnishing of information —

   (a) by the party supplying the goods, in respect of the supply of goods of the same description to other persons; or
   (b) by the party acquiring the goods, in respect of the sale, or acquisition for sale, of other goods of the same description.

Know-how about goods

3. This Act does not apply to an agreement between two persons (neither of whom is a trade association) for the exchange of information relating to the operation of processes of manufacture (whether patented or not) where —

   (a) no other person is party to the agreement; and
   (b) no such restrictions as are described in section 6(1) above are accepted or no such information provisions as are described in section 7(1) above are made under the agreement except in respect of the descriptions of goods to be produced by those processes or to which those processes are to be applied.

Trade marks

4. – (1) This Act does not apply to an agreement made in accordance with regulations approved by the Secretary of State under section 37 of the Trade Marks Act 1938 (which makes provision as to certification trade marks) authorising the use of such a trade mark, being an agreement under which no such restrictions as are described in section 6(1) above are accepted or no such information provisions as are described in section 7(1) above are made other than restrictions or information provisions permitted by those regulations.

(2) This Act does not apply to an agreement —

   (a) between the registered proprietor of a trade mark (other than a certification trade mark) [or of a service mark]¹ and a person authorised by the agreement to use the mark subject to registration as a registered user under section 28 of the Trade Marks Act 1938 (which makes provision as to registered users); and
   (b) under which no such restrictions as are described in section 6(1) [or 11(2)]¹ are accepted or no such information provisions as are described in section 7(1) [or 12(2)]¹ are made except in respect of —

      (i) the descriptions of goods bearing the mark which are to be produced or supplied; or
      (ii) the processes of manufacture to be applied to such goods or to goods to which the mark is to be applied [or

(iii) the kinds of services in relation to which the mark is to be used which are to be made available or supplied; or

(iv) the form or manner in which services in relation to which the mark is used are to be made available or supplied; or

(v) the descriptions of goods which are to be produced or supplied in connection with the supply of services in relation to which the mark is to be used; or

(vi) the process of manufacture to be applied to goods which are to be produced or supplied in connection with the supply of services in relation to which the mark is to be used].[1]

Patents and registered designs

5.—(1) Subject to sub-paragraphs (4) to (8) below, this Act does not apply—

(a) to a licence granted by the proprietor or a licensee of a patent or registered design, or by a person who has applied for a patent or for the registration of a design;

(b) to an assignment of a patent or registered design, or of the right to apply for a patent or for the registration of a design; or

(c) to an agreement for such a licence or assignment;

being a licence, assignment or agreement such as is described in sub-paragraph (2) or sub-paragraph (3) below.

(2) The licence, assignment or agreement referred to in sub-paragraph (1) above is in relation to Part II of this Act one under which no such restrictions as are described in section 6(1) above are accepted or no such information provisions as are described in section 7(1) above are made except in respect of—

(a) the invention to which the patent or application for a patent relates, or articles made by the use of that invention; or

(b) articles in respect of which the design is or is proposed to be registered and to which it is applied;

as the case may be.

(3) The licence, assignment or agreement referred to in sub-paragraph (1) above is in relation to Part III of this Act one under which—

(a) in the case of an order under section 11 above, no restrictions in respect of matters specified in the order for the purposes of subsection (1)(b) of that section are accepted except in respect of the invention to which the patent or application for a patent relates; or

(b) in the case of an order under section 12 above, no information provision with respect to matters specified in the order for the purposes of subsection (1)(b) of that section is made except in respect of that invention.

(4) No licence, assignment or agreement is by virtue of sub-paragraph (1) above precluded from being an agreement to which this Act applies if—

(a) it is a patent or design pooling agreement; or

(b) it is a licence, assignment or agreement granted or made in pursuance (directly or indirectly) of a patent or design pooling agreement.

(5) In this paragraph, subject to sub-paragraph (8) below, "patent or design pooling agreement" means an agreement—

(a) to which the parties are or include at least three persons (in this and the following sub-paragraph the "principal parties") each of whom has an interest in one or more patents or registered designs, and

(b) by which each of the principal parties agrees, in respect of patents or registered designs in which he has an interest, or in respect of patents or registered designs in which he has or may during the currency of the agreement acquire an interest, to grant such an interest as is mentioned in sub-paragraph (6) below.

(6) The grant referred to in sub-paragraph (5) above is—

(a) of an interest in one or more such patents or registered designs to one or more of the other principal parties, or to one or more of those parties and to other persons; or

(b) of an interest in at least one such patent or registered design to a third person for the purpose of enabling that person to grant an interest in it to one or more of the other principal parties, or to one or more of those parties and to other persons;

and "interest", in relation to a patent or registered design, means an interest as proprietor or licensee of the patent or registered design or an interest consisting of such rights as a person has by virtue of having applied for a patent or for the registration of a design or by virtue of having acquired the right to apply for a patent or for the registration of a design.

(7) For the purposes of sub-paragraphs (4) to (6) above, a licence, assignment or agreement—

(a) shall be taken to be granted or made directly in pursuance of a patent or design pooling agreement if it is granted or made in pursuance of provisions of that agreement such as are mentioned in sub-paragraph (6)(a); and

(b) shall be taken to be granted or made indirectly in pursuance of a patent or design pooling agreement if it is granted or made by a third person to whom an interest has been granted in pursuance of provisions of that agreement such as are mentioned in sub-paragraph (6)(b).

(8) In relation to any interest held by or granted to any two or more persons jointly, sub-paragraphs (5) and (6) apply as if those persons were one person by whom the interest is held or to whom it is granted, and accordingly those persons shall be treated for the purposes of those sub-paragraphs as together constituting one party.

(9) In this paragraph, references—

(a) to an assignment mean, in relation to Scotland, an assignation;

(b) to the registration of designs have effect only in relation to Part II.

Copyrights

[5A(1) This Act does not apply to:—

(a) a licence granted by the owner or a licensee of any copyright;

(b) an assignment of any copyright; or

(c) an agreement for such a licence or assignment;

being a licence, assignment or agreement such as is described in sub-paragraph (2) or sub-paragraph (3) below.

(2) The licence, assignment or agreement referred to in sub-paragraph (1) above is in relation to Part II of this Act one under which no such restrictions as are described in section 6(1) above are accepted or no such information provisions as are described

in section 7(1) above are made except in respect of the work or other subject-matter in which the copyright subsists or will subsist.

(3) The licence, assignment or agreement referred to in sub-paragraph (1) above is in relation to Part III of this Act one under which: —

(a) in the case of an order under section 11 above, no restrictions in respect of matters specified in the order for the purposes of subsection (1)(b) of that section are accepted except in respect of the work or other subject-matter in which the copyright subsists or will subsist; or

(b) in the case of an order under section 12 above, no information provision with respect to matters specified in the order for the purposes of subsection (1)(b) of that section is made except in respect of that work or other subject-matter.

(4) In relation to Scotland references in this paragraph to an assignment mean an assignation.]²

Design right

[5B — (1) This Act does not apply to: —

(a) a licence granted by the owner or a licensee of any design right;

(b) an assignment of design right or

(c) an agreement for such a licence or assignment,

if the licence, assignment or agreement is one under which no such restrictions as are described in section 6(1) above are accepted, or no such information provisions as are described in section 7(1) above are made, except in respect of articles made to the design; but subject to the following provisions.

(2) Sub-paragraph (1) does not exclude a licence, assignment or agreement which is a design pooling agreement or is granted or made (directly or indirectly) in pursuance of a design pooling agreement.

(3)In this paragraph a "design pooling agreement" means an agreement —

(a) to which the parties are or include at least three persons (the "principal parties") each of whom has an interest in one or more design rights, and

(b) by which each principal party agrees, in respect of design right in which he has, or may during the currency of the agreement acquire, an interest to grant an interest (directly or indirectly) to one or more of the other principal parties, or to one or more of those parties and to other persons.

(4) In this paragraph —

"assignment", in Scotland, means assignation; and
"interest" means an interest as owner or licensee of design right.

(5) This paragraph applies to an interest held by or granted to more than one person jointly as if they were one person.

(6) References in this paragraph to the granting of an interest to a person indirectly are to its being granted to a third person for the purpose of enabling him to make a grant to the person in question.]³

Agreements as to goods with overseas operation

6. — (1) This Act does not apply to an agreement in the case of which all such

restrictions as are described in section 6(1) above, or all such information provisions as are described in section 7(1) above, relate exclusively—

    (*a*) to the supply of goods by export from the United Kingdom;

    (*b*) to the production of goods, or the application of any process of manufacture to goods, outside the United Kingdom;

    (*c*) to the acquisition of goods to be delivered outside the United Kingdom and not imported into the United Kingdom for entry for home use; or

    (*d*) to the supply of goods to be delivered outside the United Kingdom otherwise than by export from the United Kingdom;

and subsections (2) and (4) of section 8 above do not apply in relation to recommendations relating exclusively to those matters.

(2) The Court's jurisdiction mentioned in section 1(3) above does not extend to restrictions or to information provisions in respect of matters described in paragraphs (*b*) to (*d*) of sub-paragraph (1) above.

Exclusive supply of services

7. This Act does not apply to an agreement to which there are no parties other than one person who agrees to supply services and another person for whom they are to be supplied, where neither of those persons is, in relation to any order under Part III of this Act, a services supply association and, except in respect of the supply of services of the same description to, or obtaining services of the same description from, other persons—

    (*a*) in the case of an order under section 11 above, no restrictions are accepted under the agreement by those parties in respect of matters specified in the order for the purposes of subsection (1)(*b*) of that section; or

    (*b*) in the case of an order under section 12 above, no information provision is made under the agreement with respect to matters specified in the order for the purposes of subsection (1)(*b*) of that section.

Know-how about services

8. This Act does not apply to an agreement between two persons (neither of whom is a services supply association) for the exchange of information relating to techniques or processes to be applied in the provision of designated services where—

    (*a*) no other person is party to the agreement; and

    (*b*) all such restrictions as are mentioned in section 11(1)(*b*) above which are accepted under the agreement relate exclusively to the form or manner in which services incorporating those techniques or processes are to be made available or supplied.

Agreements for supplying services with overseas operation

9.—(1) This Act does not apply to an agreement where—

    (*a*) in the case of an order under section 11 above, all such restrictions as are accepted under the agreement in respect of matters specified in the order for the purposes of subsection (1)(*b*) of that section (or, in a case falling within section 16(3) above, all the recommendations referred to in that subsection) relate to the supply of services outside the United Kingdom or to the supply of services to persons or in relation to property (of any description, whether movable or immovable) outside the United Kingdom; or (*b*) in the case of an order under section 12 above, all such provision as is made under the agreement for or in relation to the furnishing of information with respect to matters specified in the order for the purposes of subsection (1)(*b*) of that section (or, in a case falling within section 16(5), every such recommendation as is referred to in that subsection) relates to the supply of services as mentioned in paragraph (*a*) above.

(2) The Court's jurisdiction mentioned in section 1(3) above does not extend to restrictions or to information provisions —

(*a*) in respect of the supply of services outside the United Kingdom; or
(*b*) in respect of the supply of services to persons or in relation to property (of any description, whether movable or immovable) outside the United Kingdom.

[175]

AMENDMENTS
1 Para 4(2) amended by the Patents, Designs and Marks Act 1986, s 2(3), Sch 2, para 8.
2 Para 5A inserted by Competition Act 1980, s 30.
3 Para 5B inserted by the Copyrights, Designs and Patents Act 1988, s 303(1), Sch 7, para 18(1),(3).

SCHEDULE 4

Section 44

TRANSITIONAL PROVISIONS AND SAVINGS

General provisions

1. — (1) In so far as anything done under an enactment repealed by this Act could have been done under a corresponding provision of this Act it shall not be invalidated by the repeal but shall have effect as if done under that provision.

(2) Without prejudice to sub-paragraph (1) above, any reference in this Act (whether express or implied) to a thing done or required or authorised to be done, or omitted to be done, or to an event which has occurred, under or for the purposes of or by reference to or in contravention of any provisions of this Act shall, except where the context otherwise requires, be construed as including a reference to the corresponding thing done or required or authorised to be done, or omitted, or to the corresponding event which occurred, as the case may be, under or for the purposes of or by reference to or in contravention of any corresponding provisions of the repealed enactments.

2. Where a document refers expressly or by implication to an enactment repealed by this Act the reference shall (except where the context otherwise requires) be construed as a reference to the corresponding provision of this Act.

3. Where any period of time specified in an enactment repealed by this Act is current at the commencement of this Act, and there is a corresponding provision in this Act, this Act shall have effect as if that corresponding provision had been in force when that period began to run.

Insignificant agreements under the
Restrictive Trade Practices Act 1956, s 12

4. — (1) Directions under section 12 of the Restrictive Trade Practices Act 1956 in force at the commencement of this Act for the removal from the register of particulars of such agreements as appeared to be of no substantial economic significance continue to have effect by virtue of this paragraph.

(2) Sub-paragraph (1) above does not affect the operation in relation to the agreement

of paragraph 1 of Schedule 2 to this Act; and where any such agreement is varied as mentioned in that paragraph—

   (a)   the particulars to be furnished thereunder shall include all such particulars as would be required in the case of an original agreement in the terms of the agreement as varied;

   (b)   the directions referred to in sub-paragraph (1) shall cease to have effect, but without prejudice to the Secretary of State's power to give further directions under section 21(2) above.

Section 18(2) of the Restrictive Trade Practices Act 1956

5.   Nothing in this Act affects the right of a person to make an application to the Court in a case where an order is in force against that person under section 18(2) of the Restrictive Trade Practices Act 1956.

Disclosure of information

6.   Section 41 above applies in relation to information obtained under or by virtue of—

   (a)   the Restrictive Trade Practices Act 1956;

   (b)   the Restrictive Trade Practices Act 1968;

so that section applies in relation to information obtained under or by virtue of this Act.

Particulars of certain export agreements

7.   Any particulars furnished to the Board of Trade or to the Secretary of State under section 31(1) of the Restrictive Trade Practices Act 1956 shall be treated as if they had been furnished to the Director under sections 24 and 25 above.

Restrictive Trade Practices Act 1968, s 11

8.   An agreement which—

   (a)   was made before the commencement of this Act by a society at a time when it was approved for the purposes of section 11 of the Restrictive Trade Practices Act 1968 (wholesale co-operative societies), and

   (b)   by virtue of that approval was not subject to registration under Part I of the Restrictive Trade Practices Act 1956,

shall, notwithstanding the repeal of that section (by the Fair Trading Act 1973), not be subject to registration under this Act.   **[176]**

SCHEDULE 5

Section 44

CONSEQUENTIAL AMENDMENTS

(not reproduced in this work)

SCHEDULE 6

Section 44

REPEALS

(not reproduced in this work)

THE RESTRICTIVE TRADE PRACTICES ACT 1977
(1977 c 19)

An Act to provide for the disregard of certain matters in determining whether an agreement is one to which the Restrictive Trade Practices Act 1976 applies; and for connected purposes   [30 June 1977]

1. Agreements as to services

(1) At the end of section 14(2) of the Restrictive Trade Practices Act 1976 (supplementary provisions as to orders under Part III) there shall be added the words "and may specify matters (in addition to those mentioned in section 18) which are to be disregarded for the purposes of determining whether an agreement is one to which this Act applies by virtue of the order".

(2) Section 110(1) of the Fair Trading Act 1973 (which was replaced by section 14(2) of the Act of 1976) shall be deemed to have been enacted with a corresponding addition, and accordingly the amendment made by subsection (1) above shall be deemed to have had effect from the commencement of the Act of 1976.

(3) The Restrictive Trade Practices (Services) Order 1976 (which was made under the Act of 1973 and now has effect as if made under, and as referring to provisions of, the Act of 1976) shall have effect and be deemed always to have had effect as if it had been made with the addition of the Article set out in Part I of the Schedule to this Act.   **[177]**

2. Restrictive agreements as to goods

(1) In this section "financing terms" means provisions for any of the following, that is to say —

    (*a*) the making or continuation of a loan;

    (*b*) the granting or continuation of any form of credit or of facilities for credit;

    (*c*) the supply of any property by way of lease or hire (with or without the option to acquire the ownership of the property);

    (*d*) the assumption of any liability in the event of a person's default; and

    (*e*) the granting of any right to resort to any property in the event of a person's default.

(2) Subject to the following provisions of this section, where an agreement, whenever made, contains financing terms, paragraphs (3) and (4) of the Article set out in Part I of the Schedule to this Act apply —

    (*a*) for the purpose of determining whether the agreement is one to which the Restrictive Trade Practices Act 1976 applies by virtue of section 6 of that Act; and

    (*b*) if the agreement was made before the commencement of that Act, also for the purpose of determining whether it was one to which Part I of the Restrictive Trade Practices Act 1956 applied;

and in those paragraphs as so applying "financing terms" has the same meaning as in this section.

(3) The Secretary of State may by statutory instrument make an order specifying matters (in addition to those mentioned in section 9 of the Act of 1976) which are to be disregarded for the purpose of determining whether an agreement is one to which that Act applies by virtue of section 6 of that Act.

(4) An order under this section may vary or repeal subsections (1) and (2) above so far as they relate to the Act of 1976 and may be varied or revoked by a subsequent order under this section.

(5) No order shall be made under this section unless a draft of the order has been laid before, and approved by resolution of, each House of Parliament.

[178]

ORDER UNDER THIS SECTION
The Restrictive Trade Practices (Sale and Purchase and Share Subscription Agreements) (Goods) Order 1989, SI 1989 No 1081.

3. Information agreements as to goods

(1) In section 7 of the Restrictive Trade Practices Act 1976 (information agreements as to goods) the following shall be inserted after subsection (3): —

"(3A) An order under this section may specify matters (in addition to those mentioned in section 9) which are to be disregarded in determining whether an agreement is one to which this Act applies by virtue of the order".

(2) Section 5 of the Restrictive Trade Practices Act 1968 (which was replaced by section 7 of the Act of 1976) shall be deemed to have been enacted with a corresponding addition, and accordingly the amendment made by subsection (1) above shall be deemed to have had effect from the commencement of the Act of 1976.

(3) The Restrictive Trade Practices (Information Agreements) Order 1969 (which was made under the Act of 1968 and now has effect as if made under, and as referring to provisions of, the Act of 1976) shall have effect and be deemed always to have had effect as if it had been made with the addition of the Article set out in Part II of the Schedule to this Act.   **[179]**

4. Citation and extent

(1) This Act may be cited as the Restrictive Trade Practices Act 1977.

(2) This Act and the Restrictive Trade Practices Act 1976 may be cited together as the Restrictive Trade Practices Acts 1976 and 1977.

(3) This Act extends to Northern Ireland.   **[180]**

SCHEDULE

ARTICLE ADDED TO RESTRICTIVE TRADE PRACTICES
(SERVICES) ORDER 1976 AND RESTRICTIVE TRADE
PRACTICES (INFORMATION AGREEMENTS) ORDER 1969

PART I

ARTICLE ADDED TO ORDER OF 1976

4. — (1) In this Article "financing terms" means provisions for any of the following, that is to say—

(a) the making or continuation of a loan;
(b) the granting or continuation of any form of credit or of facilities for credit;
(c) the supply of any property by way of lease or hire (with or without the option to acquire the ownership of the property);
(d) the assumption of any liability in the event of a person's default; and
(e) the granting of any right to resort to any property in the event of a person's default.

(2) Where an agreement contains financing terms the following provisions apply for the purpose of determining whether the agreement is one to which Part I of the Restrictive Trade Practices Act 1956 applies by virtue of this order.

(3) No account shall be taken of any restriction the sole purpose of which is either or both of the following—

(a) to maintain a person's ability to discharge any liability incurred by him under or in connection with the financing terms; and
(b) to protect a person against the consequences of another person's default in discharging such a liability.

(4) If the financing terms relate to the doing of anything outside the United Kingdom by a person who neither resides nor carries on a business within the United Kingdom, no account shall be taken of any restriction which is accepted only—

(a) by him; or
(b) by one or more other such persons; or
(c) by him and one or more other such persons.   [181]

PART II

ARTICLE ADDED TO ORDER OF 1969

4. — (1) In this Article "financing terms" means provisions for any of the following, that is to say—

(a) the making or continuation of a loan;
(b) the granting or continuation of any form of credit or of facilities for credit;
(c) the supply of any property by way of lease or hire (with or without the option to acquire the ownership of the property);
(d) the assumption of any liability in the event of a person's default; and
(e) the granting of any right to resort to any property in the event of a person's default.

(2) Where an agreement contains financing terms the following provisions apply for the purpose of determining whether the agreement is one to which Part I of the Restrictive Trade Practices Act 1956 applies by virtue of this order.

(3) No account shall be taken of any provision for or in relation to the furnishing of information if the sole purpose of the provision is to enable either or both of the following to be assessed —

(*a*) the ability of any person who has incurred or may incur a liability under or in connection with the financing terms to discharge that liability; and

(*b*) the observance by such a person of any terms of the agreement.

(4) If the financing terms relate to the doing of anything outside the United Kingdom by a person who neither resides nor carries on a business within the United Kingdom, no account shall be taken of any provision requiring information to be furnished only —

(*a*) by him; or

(*b*) by one or more other such persons; or

(*c*) by him and one or more other such persons.   **[182]**

THE RESTRICTIVE PRACTICES COURT ACT 1976
(1976 c 33)

ARRANGEMENT OF SECTIONS

An Act to consolidate certain enactments relating to the Restrictive Practices Court   **[22 July 1976]**

1. The Court

(1) The Restrictive Practices Court ("the Court") established by the Restrictive Trade Practices Act 1956 shall continue in being by that name as a superior court of record.

(2) The Court shall consist of the following members —

(*a*) five nominated judges; and

(*b*) not more than ten appointed members.

(3) Of the nominated judges one, to be selected by the Lord Chancellor, shall be President of the Court.

(4) The Court shall have an official seal which shall be judicially noticed.
[183]

2. Judges of the Court

(1) The nominated judges of the Court shall be—

(a) three puisne judges of the High Court nominated by the Lord Chancellor;

(b) one judge of the Court of Session nominated by the Lord President of that Court;

(c) one judge of the Supreme Court of Northern Ireland nominated by the Lord Chief Justice of Northern Ireland.

(2) A judge of any court who is nominated under this section shall not be required to sit in any place outside the jurisdiction of that court, and shall be required to perform his duties as a judge of that court only when his attendance on the Restrictive Practices Court is not required.

(3) In the case of the temporary absence or inability to act of a nominated judge, the Lord Chancellor, the Lord President of the Court of Session, or the Lord Chief Justice of Northern Ireland (as the case may be) may nominate another judge of the same court to act temporarily in his place, and a judge so nominated shall, when so acting, have all the functions of the judge in whose place he acts.

(4) No judge shall be nominated under this section except with his consent.
[184]

3. Non-judicial members

(1) The other members of the Court ("appointed members") may be appointed by Her Majesty on the recommendation of the Lord Chancellor, and any person recommended for appointment shall be a person appearing to the Lord Chancellor to be qualified by virtue of his knowledge of or experience in industry, commerce or public affairs.

(2) An appointed member shall hold office for such period (not less than three years) as may be determined at the time of his appointment, and shall be eligible for reappointment, but—

(a) he may at any time by notice in writing to the Lord Chancellor resign his office;

(b) the Lord Chancellor may, if he thinks fit, remove any appointed member for inability or misbehaviour, or on the ground of any employment or interest which appears to the Lord Chancellor incompatible with the functions of a member of the Court.

(3) In the case of the temporary absence or inability to act of an appointed member, the Lord Chancellor may appoint a temporary member, being a person appearing to him to be qualified as provided in subsection (1) above, to act in place of that member; and a temporary member shall, when so acting, have all the functions of an appointed member.   [185]

4. Provision for additional judges or members

(1) The Lord Chancellor may—

    (*a*) after consultation with the Lord President of the Court of Session and the Lord Chief Justice of Northern Ireland, by order increase the number of nominated judges of the Court;

    (*b*) with the approval of the Minister for the Civil Service, by order increase the maximum number of appointed members;

and sections 1 to 3 above, as to the number of judges and members, have effect subject to any order in force under this section.

(2) Orders under this section shall be made by statutory instrument; and an order shall be of no effect until it is approved by resolution of each House of Parliament.   **[186]**

5. Pay and pensions of non-judicial members

(1) There may be paid to the appointed members of the Court, and to any temporary member, such remuneration as the Lord Chancellor may, with the approval of the Minister for the Civil Service, determine.

(2) In the case of any such holder of the office of appointed member as may be determined by the Lord Chancellor acting with that approval, there shall be paid such pension, allowance or gratuity to or in respect of him on his retirement or death, or such contributions or other payments towards provision for such a pension, allowance or gratuity as may be so determined.

(3) As soon as may be after the making of any determination under subsection (2) above the Lord Chancellor shall lay before each House of Parliament a statement of the amount of the pension, allowance or gratuity or contributions or other payments, as the case may be, payable in pursuance of the determination.   **[187]**

6. Administration

(1) The Lord Chancellor may appoint such officers and servants of the Court as he may, with the approval of the Minister for the Civil Service as to numbers and conditions of service, determine.

(2) The principal civil service pension scheme within the meaning of section 2 of the Superannuation Act 1972 and for the time being in force applies, with the necessary adaptations, to officers and servants of the Court as to other persons employed in the civil service of the State.

(3) The central office of the Court shall be in London.

(4) Subject to its rules, the Court may sit at such times and in such place or places in any part of the United Kingdom as may be most convenient for the determination of proceedings before it.

(5) When sitting in public in London, the Court shall sit at the Royal Courts of Justice or at such other place as the Lord Chancellor may appoint.

(6) The Court may sit either as a single court or in two or more divisions concurrently and either in private or in public.   **[188]**

7. Hearing and judgment

(1) For the hearing of any proceedings the Court shall consist of a presiding judge and at least two other members, except that in the case of proceedings involving only issues of law the Court may instead consist of a single member being a judge.

(2) On the hearing of any proceedings, the opinion of the judge or judges sitting as members of the Court upon any question of law shall prevail; but subject to this the decision of the Court shall be taken by all the members sitting, or, in the event of a difference of opinion, by the votes of the majority of the members.

In the event of an equality of votes, the presiding judge shall be entitled to a second or casting vote.

(3) The judgment of the Court in any proceedings shall be delivered by the presiding judge.   **[189]**

8. Right of audience

(1) Every person who has the right of audience at the trial of an action in the High Court or in the Court of Session, or in proceedings preliminary to such a trial, shall have the like right at the hearing of any application to the Court, whether sitting in England and Wales or in Scotland, or in proceedings preliminary to such a hearing, as the case may be.

(2) Every person who has the right of audience at the trial of an action in the High Court of Northern Ireland, or in proceedings preliminary to such trial, shall have the like right at the hearing of any application to the Court when sitting in Northern Ireland, or in proceedings preliminary to such a hearing, as the case may be.   **[190]**

9. Procedure

(1) The procedure in or in connection with any proceedings before the Court and, subject to the approval of the Treasury, the fees chargeable in respect of such proceedings, shall be such as may be determined by rules made by the Lord Chancellor.

Rules under this section shall be made by statutory instrument subject to annulment in pursuance of a resolution of either House of Parliament.

(2) Without prejudice to the generality of subsection (1) above, rules made under that subsection may provide —

(a) with respect to the persons to be made respondents to any application to the Court;

(b) with respect to the place at which the Court is to sit for the purposes of any proceedings;

(c) with respect to the evidence which may be required or admitted in any proceedings;

(d) for securing, by means of preliminary statements of facts and contentions, and by the production of documents, the administration of interrogatories and other methods of discovery, that all material facts and considerations are brought before the Court by all parties to any proceedings, including the Director General of Fair Trading.

(3) In relation to the attendance and examination of witnesses, the production and inspection of documents, the enforcement of its orders, and all other matters incidental to its jurisdiction, the Court shall have the like powers, rights, privileges and authority —

(a) in England and Wales, as the High Court;

(b) in Scotland, as the Court of Session; and

(c) in Northern Ireland, as the High Court of Northern Ireland.

(4) No person shall be punished for contempt of the Court except by or with the consent of a judge who is a member of the Court.   **[191]**

RULES UNDER THIS SECTION
The following rules have been made under this section or under this section as extended by either of the enactments mentioned in the last previous note: the Restrictive Practices Court Rules 1976, SI 1976 No 1897, as amended by SI 1982 No 871; the Restrictive Practices Court (Protection of Consumers) Rules 1976, SI 1976 No 1898; and the Restrictive Practices Court (Resale Prices) Rules 1976, SI 1976 No 1899.

10. Appeal

(1) Subject to and in accordance with this section, an appeal lies from any decision or order of the Court —

(a) in the case of proceedings in England and Wales, to the Court of Appeal;

(b) in the case of proceedings in Scotland, to the Court of Session; and

(c) in the case of proceedings in Northern Ireland, to the Court of Appeal in Northern Ireland.

(2) In proceedings under Part III of the Fair Trading Act 1973 (consumer protection) the appeal lies on a question of fact or on a question of law.

(3) In proceedings other than those referred to in subsection (2) above —

(a) the appeal lies on a question of law only and the Court's decision on a question of fact is final; and

(b) the appeal —

(i) to the Court of Appeal, or to the Court of Appeal in Northern Ireland, is by way of case stated; and

(ii) to the Court of Session, is by way of stated case.   **[192]**

11. Consequential amendment, savings and repeals

(1) . . .[1]

(2) In so far as anything done under an enactment repealed by this Act could have been done under a corresponding provision of this Act, it is not invalidated by the repeal but has effect as if done under that provision.

(3) The enactments mentioned in the Schedule to this Act are hereby repealed to the extent specified in the third column of that Schedule. **[193]**

AMENDMENT
1 Sub-s (1) repealed by the Judicial Pensions Act 1981, s 36, Sch 4.

12. Short title, extent and commencement

(1) This Act may be cited as the Restrictive Practices Court Act 1976.

(2) This Act extends to Northern Ireland.

(3) This Act shall come into operation on such day as the Lord Chancellor may appoint by order made by statutory instrument. **[194]**

SCHEDULE

Section 11

REPEALS

(not reproduced in this work)

THE RESALE PRICES ACT 1976
(1976 c 53)

ARRANGEMENT OF SECTIONS

PART I

PROHIBITION OF COLLECTIVE RESALE PRICE MAINTENANCE

PART II

INDIVIDUAL MINIMUM RESALE PRICE MAINTENANCE

Prohibition of individual resale price maintenance

Applications to the Restrictive Practices Court in relation to exemptions

PART III

GENERAL AND SUPPLEMENTAL

An Act to consolidate those provisions of the Resale Prices Act 1964 still having effect, Part II of the Restrictive Trade Practices Act 1956, and related enactments; and to repeal the provisions of the Resale Prices Act 1964 and the Restrictive Trade Practices Act 1968 which have ceased to have any effect [26 October 1976]

PART I

PROHIBITION OF COLLECTIVE RESALE PRICE MAINTENANCE

1. Collective agreement by suppliers

(1) It is unlawful for any two or more persons carrying on business in the United Kingdom as suppliers of any goods to make or carry out any agreement or arrangement by which they undertake —

(*a*) to withhold supplies of goods for delivery in the United Kingdom from dealers (whether party to the agreement or arrangement or not) who resell or have resold goods in breach of any condition as to the price at which those goods may be resold;

(*b*) to refuse to supply goods for delivery in the United Kingdom to such dealers except on terms and conditions which are less favourable than those applicable in the case of other dealers carrying on business in similar circumstances; or

(c) to supply goods only to persons who undertake or have undertaken –

    (i) to withhold supplies of goods as described in paragraph (a) above; or

    (ii) to refuse to supply goods as described in paragraph (b) above.

(2) It is unlawful for any two or more such persons to make or carry out any agreement or arrangement authorising –

    (a) the recovery of penalties (however described) by or on behalf of the parties to the agreement or arrangement from dealers who resell or have resold goods in breach of any such condition as is described in paragraph (a) of subsection (1) above; or

    (b) the conduct of any domestic proceedings in connection therewith.

[195]

2. Collective agreement by dealers

(1) It is unlawful for any two or more persons carrying on business in the United Kingdom as dealers in any goods to make or carry out any agreement or arrangement by which they undertake –

    (a) to withhold orders for supplies of goods for delivery in the United Kingdom from suppliers (whether party to the agreement or arrangement or not) –

        (i) who supply or have supplied goods otherwise than subject to such a condition as is described in paragraph (a) of section 1(1) above; or

        (ii) who refrain or have refrained from taking steps to ensure compliance with such conditions in respect of goods supplied by them;

        or,

    (b) to discriminate in their handling of goods against goods supplied by such suppliers.

(2) It is unlawful for any two or more such persons to make or carry out any agreement or arrangement authorising –

    (a) the recovery of penalties (however described) by or on behalf of the parties to the agreement or arrangement from such suppliers; or

    (b) the conduct of any domestic proceedings in connection therewith.

[196]

3. Recommendations

It is unlawful for any person carrying on business in the United Kingdom as a supplier of or dealer in any goods to make to any other person carrying on such a business any recommendation to act in such a manner that, if there were an agreement between those persons so to act, the agreement would be unlawful by virtue of section 1 or section 2 above.   **[197]**

4. Associations

Sections 1 to 3 above apply in relation to an association the members of which consist of or include persons carrying on business in the United Kingdom as suppliers of or dealers in any goods, or representatives of such persons, as they apply in relation to a person so carrying on business.   **[198]**

5. Exclusive dealing

A contract for the sale of goods to which not more than two persons are party is not unlawful under this Part of this Act by reason only of undertakings by the purchaser in relation to the goods sold and by the vendor in relation to other goods of the same description.   **[199]**

6. Discounts and part exchanges

For the purposes of this Part of this Act a condition—

(*a*) as to the amount of discount which may be allowed on the resale of any goods, or

(*b*) as to the price which may be paid on the resale of any goods for other goods taken by way of exchange,

shall be treated as a condition as to the price at which goods may be resold.   **[200]**

7. Hire-purchase agreements

The provisions of Schedule 1 to this Act, which relate to hire-purchase agreements, have effect for the purposes of this Part of this Act.   **[201]**

8. Interpretation of Part I

(1) In this Part of this Act—

"goods" includes ships and aircraft, minerals, substances and animals (including fish);
"price" includes a charge of any description;
"supply" includes supply by way of lease or hire, and "acquire" shall be construed accordingly.

(2) This Part applies to the construction or carrying out of buildings, structures and other works by contractors, as it applies to the supply of goods, and for the purposes of this Part any buildings, structures or other works so constructed or carried out shall be deemed to be delivered at the place where they are constructed or carried out.

(3) For the purposes of this Part a person shall not be deemed to carry on a business within the United Kingdom by reason only of the fact that he is represented for the purposes of that business by an agent within the United Kingdom.

(4) For the purposes of any provision of this Part referring to two or more or not more than two persons, two or more persons being interconnected bodies

corporate or individuals carrying on business in partnership with each other shall be treated as a single person. **[202]**

PART II

INDIVIDUAL MINIMUM RESALE PRICE MAINTENANCE

Prohibition of individual resale price maintenance

9. Minimum resale prices maintained by contract or agreement

(1) Any term or condition —

(*a*) of a contract for the sale of goods by a supplier to a dealer, or

(*b*) of any agreement between a supplier and a dealer relating to such a sale,

is void in so far as it purports to establish or provide for the establishment of minimum prices to be charged on the resale of the goods in the United Kingdom.

(2) It is unlawful for a supplier of goods (or for an association or person acting on behalf of such suppliers) —

(*a*) to include in a contract for sale or agreement relating to the sale of goods a term or condition which is void by virtue of this section;

(*b*) to require, as a condition of supplying goods to a dealer, the inclusion in a contract or agreement of any such term or condition, or the giving of any undertaking to the like effect;

(*c*) to notify to dealers, or otherwise publish on or in relation to any goods, a price stated or calculated to be understood as the minimum price which may be charged on the resale of the goods in the United Kingdom.

Paragraph (*a*) does not affect the enforceability of a contract of sale or other agreement, except in respect of the term or condition which is void by virtue of this section.

Paragraph (*c*) is not to be construed as precluding a supplier (or an association or person acting on behalf of a supplier) from notifying to dealers or otherwise publishing prices recommended as appropriate for the resale of goods supplied or to be supplied by the supplier. **[203]**

10. Patented articles under s 9

(1) Section 9 above applies to patented articles (including articles made by a patented process) as it applies to other goods.

(2) Notice of any term or condition which is void by virtue of section 9, or which would be so void if included in a contract of sale or agreement relating to the sale of any such article, is of no effect for the purpose of limiting the right of a dealer to dispose of that article without infringement of the patent.

(3) Nothing in section 9 and in this section affects the validity, as between the parties and their successors, of any term or condition —

    (*a*) of a licence granted by the proprietor of a patent or by a licensee under
        any such licence; or
    (*b*) of any assignment of a patent,

so far as it regulates the price at which articles produced or processed by the
licensee or assignee may be sold by him.

    (4) References in this section to patented articles include references to —

    (*a*) articles protected [by design right or] by the registration of a design, and
    (*b*) articles protected by plant breeders' rights or a protective direction under
        Schedule 1 to the Plant Varieties and Seeds Act 1964,

and references in this section to a patent shall be construed accordingly.

[204]

AMENDMENT
  Sub-s (4)(*a*) amended by the Copyright, Designs and Patents Act 1988, s 303(1), Sch 7, para 19.

11. Minimum resale prices maintained by other means

(1) It is unlawful for a supplier to withhold supplies of any goods from a dealer
seeking to obtain them for resale in the United Kingdom on the ground that the
dealer —

    (*a*) has sold in the United Kingdom at a price below the resale price goods
        obtained, either directly or indirectly, from that supplier, or has supplied
        such goods, either directly or indirectly, to a third party who had done
        so; or
    (*b*) is likely, if the goods are supplied to him, to sell them in the United
        Kingdom at a price below that price, or supply them, either directly or
        indirectly, to a third party who would be likely to do so.

(2) In this section "the resale price", in relation to a sale of any description,
means —

    (*a*) any price notified to the dealer or otherwise published by or on behalf
        of a supplier of the goods in question (whether lawfully or not) as the
        price or minimum price which is to be charged on or is recommended
        as appropriate for a sale of that description; or
    (*b*) any price prescribed or purporting to be prescribed for that purpose
        by a contract or agreement between the dealer and any such supplier.

    (3) Where under this section it would be unlawful for a supplier to withhold
supplies of goods it is also unlawful for him to cause or procure any other supplier
to do so.
[205]

12. Meaning of "withhold supplies" in relation to Part II

(1) For the purposes of this Part of this Act a supplier of goods shall be treated
as withholding supplies of goods from a dealer —

    (*a*) if he refuses or fails to supply those goods to the order of the dealer;
    (*b*) if he refuses to supply those goods to the dealer except at prices, or on

terms or conditions as to credit, discount or other matters, which are significantly less favourable than those at or on which he normally supplies those goods to other dealers carrying on business in similar circumstances; or

(c) if, although he contracts to supply the goods to the dealer, he treats him in a manner significantly less favourable than that in which he normally treats other such dealers in respect of times or methods of delivery or other matters arising in the execution of the contract.

(2) For the purposes of this Part a supplier shall not be treated as withholding supplies of goods on any such ground as is mentioned in section 11(1) above if, in addition to that ground, he has other grounds which, standing alone, would have led him to withhold those supplies.

(3) If in proceedings brought against a supplier of goods in respect of a contravention of section 11 it is proved that supplies of goods were withheld by the supplier from a dealer, and it is further proved—

(a) that down to the time when supplies were so withheld the supplier was doing business with the dealer or was supplying goods of the same description to other dealers carrying on business in similar circumstances, and

(b) that the dealer, to the knowledge of the supplier, had within the previous six months acted as described in section 11(1)(a), or had indicated his intention to act as described in paragraph (b) of that subsection in relation to the goods in question,

it shall be presumed, unless the contrary is proved, that the supplies were withheld on the ground that the dealer had so acted or was likely so to act.

This subsection does not apply where the proof that supplies were withheld consists only of evidence of requirements imposed by the supplier in respect of the time at which or the form in which payment was to be made for goods supplied or to be supplied.   **[206]**

13. Exception for measures against loss leaders

(1) It is not unlawful by virtue of section 11 above for a supplier to withhold supplies of any goods from a dealer, or to cause or procure another supplier to do so, if he has reasonable cause to believe that within the previous twelve months the dealer or any other dealer to whom the dealer supplies goods has been using as loss leaders any goods of the same or a similar description, whether obtained from that supplier or not.

(2) The reference in this section to the use of goods as loss leaders is a reference to a resale of the goods effected by the dealer, not for the purpose of making a profit on the sale of those goods, but for the purpose of attracting to the establishment at which the goods are sold customers likely to purchase other goods or otherwise for the purpose of advertising the business of the dealer.

(3) A sale of goods shall not be treated for the purposes of this section as the use of those goods as loss leaders—

(a) where the goods are sold by the dealer at a genuine seasonal or clearance sale, not having been acquired by the dealer for the purpose of being resold as mentioned in this section; or

(b) where the goods are resold as mentioned in this section with the consent of the manufacturer of the goods or, in the case of goods made to the design of a supplier or to the order and bearing the trade mark of a supplier, of that supplier.   **[207]**

Applications to the Restrictive Practices Court in relation to exemptions

14. Exemption of goods by the Court

(1) Upon an application under section 16 or section 17 below the Restrictive Practices Court ("the Court") may make an order in accordance with this section directing that goods of any class shall be exempted goods for the purposes of this Part of this Act.

(2) The order referred to in subsection (1) above may be made if it appears to the Court that in default of a system of maintained minimum resale prices applicable to those goods —

(a) the quality of the goods available for sale, or the varieties of the goods so available, would be substantially reduced to the detriment of the public as consumers or users of those goods; or

(b) the number of establishments in which the goods are sold by retail would be substantially reduced to the detriment of the public as such consumers or users; or

(c) the prices at which the goods are sold by retail would in general and in the long run be increased to the detriment of the public as such consumers or users; or

(d) the goods would be sold by retail under conditions likely to cause danger to health in consequence of their misuse by the public as such consumers or users; or

(e) any necessary services actually provided in connection with or after the sale of the goods by retail would cease to be so provided or would be substantially reduced to the detriment of the public as such consumers or users;

and in any such case that the resulting detriment to the public as consumers or users of the goods in question would outweigh any detriment to them as such consumers or users (whether by the restriction of competition or otherwise) resulting from the maintenance of minimum resale prices in respect of the goods.

In this section —

"necessary services", in relation to goods, means services which, having regard to the character of the goods, are required to guard against the risk of injury, whether to persons or to premises, in connection with the consumption, installation or use of the goods, or are otherwise reasonably necessary for the benefit of consumers or users; and

"consumers" and "users" include persons consuming or using for the
purpose or in the course of trade or business or for public purposes.

[208]

15. Who may apply to the Court

An application to the Court under section 16 or section 17 below may be made
by —

- (a) the Director General of Fair Trading ("the Director");
- (b) any supplier of goods of the class in question; or
- (c) any trade association whose members consist of or include such
  suppliers.   [209]

16. New applications

(1) Upon an application under this section the Court may make an order under
section 14 above directing that goods of any class specified in the order other
than goods in respect of which —

- (a) a reference has been made under section 5 of the Resale Prices Act 1964,
  or
- (b) a previous application has been made under this section,

shall be exempted goods for the purposes of this Part of this Act.

(2) No application shall be made under this section except with the Court's
leave, and that leave shall not be granted except upon prima facie evidence of
facts upon which an order could be made in accordance with section 14 in respect
of the goods in question, or could be so made if any detriment to the public resulting from the maintenance of minimum resale prices were disregarded.   [210]

17. Court's power to review its decisions

(1) Upon an application under this section the Court may —

- (a) discharge any order previously made by the Court directing that goods
  of any class shall be exempted goods;
- (b) make an order under section 14 above directing that goods of any class
  shall be exempted goods for the purposes of this Act where the Court
  has in respect of that class of goods previously refused to make such
  an order or has previously discharged such an order.

(2) No application shall be made under this section except with the Court's
leave, and that leave shall not be granted except upon prima facie evidence of
a material change in the relevant circumstances since the Court's last decision
in respect of the goods in question.   [211]

18. Facts found under the Restrictive Trade Practices Act 1976

Upon an application under section 16 or section 17 above in respect of goods
of any class which have been the subject of proceedings in the Court under Part
I of the Restrictive Trade Practices Act 1976 (or under Part I of the Restrictive

Trade Practices Act 1956) the Court may treat as conclusive any finding of fact made in those proceedings, and shall do so unless prima facie evidence is given of a material change in the relevant circumstances since those proceedings.

[212]

19. Effect of exemption order

Where an exemption order is made under section 14 above —

    (*a*) section 9 above does not apply in relation to any contract of sale or other agreement relating to exempted goods of the class specified in the order, or anything done in relation to such goods; and

    (*b*) notwithstanding section 11 above, a supplier may withhold supplies of any such goods from a dealer seeking to obtain them for resale in the United Kingdom on the ground that the dealer —

        (i) has sold in the United Kingdom at a price below the resale price (which means the same in this paragraph as in section 11) exempted goods obtained, either directly or indirectly, from that supplier or has supplied such goods, either directly or indirectly to a third party who had done so, or

        (ii) is likely, if the exempted goods are supplied to him, to sell them in the United Kingdom at a price below that price, or supply them, either directly or indirectly, to a third party who would be likely to do so. **[213]**

20. Discharge of exemption order

Where, by virtue of a decision of the Court under section 17(1)(*a*) above, section 9 above takes effect, that section, so far as it affects the validity of any term or condition of a contract or agreement for or relating to the sale of any goods, or the effect of notice of any term or condition so relating, applies to contracts and agreements made and notices given before as well as after that section takes effect, and —

    (*a*) for the purposes of the jurisdiction of any court to grant an injunction in proceedings pending at the time when section 9 takes such effect, that section shall be treated as if it had taken effect before the cause of action arose; and

    (*b*) any injunction granted or undertaking given before section 9 takes such effect in or for the purpose of any proceedings shall be of no effect in so far as it would operate to require compliance with any term or condition which is void, or notice of which is invalidated, by virtue of that section. **[214]**

21. Supplementary provisions as to applications to the Court

(1) Rules made by virtue of section 9(1) of the Restrictive Practices Court Act 1976 in relation to an application under this Part of this Act shall include provisions —

(*a*) for enabling the Court, on the application of the Director or of any party interested, to give directions with respect to the goods to be included in or excluded from any application under this Part of this Act;

(*b*) for securing that retailers, and trade associations representing employees in the distributive trades, who —

    (i) have an interest in any such application, and

    (ii) have given notice to the Director within such time and in such manner as may be prescribed by the rules,

are entitled, whether in consequence of a representation order or otherwise, to be represented before the Court in the proceedings.

(2) Without prejudice to the generality of section 9(1) of the Restrictive Practices Court Act 1976, rules made under that subsection in relation to an application under this Part of this Act may provide —

(*a*) for enabling a single application to be made to the Court in respect of a number of related classes of goods, or separate applications made in respect of related classes, to be heard together;

(*b*) for enabling the Court to determine in a summary way any issue arising in relation to a class of goods where it appears to the Court that the class of goods and the circumstances of the case are substantially similar to the class of goods and circumstances considered in any previous proceedings before the Court;

(*c*) for enabling the Court to make an order for the payment by any party of costs in respect of proceedings in which he is guilty of unreasonable delay, or in respect of any improper, vexatious, prolix or unnecessary proceedings or any other unreasonable conduct on his part.

(3) The Court does not have power to order the payment of costs by any party to proceedings on an application under this Part of this Act, except —

(*a*) so far as may be the case under rules made as provided by subsection (2) above;

(*b*) as is provided by subsection (4) below.

(4) The Court may order the payment by the Director of all or any of the following costs incurred by any other party —

(*a*) costs incurred on an application under section 16 above in respect of any issue determined in favour of that party, being an issue which in the Court's opinion substantially corresponds with an issue so determined in proceedings in respect of an agreement of which particulars are entered or filed in the register under the Restrictive Trade Practices Act 1976 (or under the Restrictive Trade Practices Act 1956);

(*b*) costs incurred on an application under section 17 above in respect of an issue determined in favour of that party.   **[215]**

RULES UNDER THIS SECTION

The Restrictive Practices Court (Resale Prices) Rules 1976, SI 1976 No 1899 are made partly under this section.

Miscellaneous

22. Listing of the Court's orders as to goods

The Director shall publish lists of the classes of goods in respect of which the Court has made, refused to make or discharged orders under this Part of this Act. **[216]**

23. Statutory schemes

Nothing in this Part of this Act applies to an agreement which is expressly authorised by an enactment, or by a scheme, order or other instrument made under an enactment, or to anything done pursuant to any such agreement, scheme, order or instrument. **[217]**

24. Interpretation of Part II

(1) In this Part of this Act—

"dealer" means a person carrying on a business of selling goods, whether by wholesale or by retail;
"supplier" means a person carrying on a business of selling goods other than a business in which goods are sold only by retail;
"trade association" means a body of persons (whether incorporated or not) which is formed for the purpose of furthering the trade interests of its members or the persons represented by its members.

(2) Where—

(a) the dealer referred to in section 11(1)(a) above, or in section 13(1) above, or
(b) the supplier referred to in section 11(1)(a),

is one of a group of interconnected bodies corporate the reference includes a reference to any other dealer or, as the case may be, any other supplier who is also a member of that group. **[218]**

PART III

GENERAL AND SUPPLEMENTAL

25. Contravention of and compliance with the Act

(1) No criminal proceedings lie against any person on the ground that he has committed, or aided, abetted, counselled or procured the commission of, or conspired or attempted to commit, or incited others to commit, any contravention of sections 1 and 2 and sections 9 and 11 above.

(2) Without prejudice to the right of any person to bring civil proceedings by virtue of subsection (3) below, compliance with those sections shall be enforceable by civil proceedings on behalf of the Crown for an injunction or other appropriate relief.

(3) The obligation to comply with those sections is a duty owed to any person who may be affected by a contravention of them, and any breach of that duty is actionable accordingly (subject to the defences and other incidents applying to actions for breach of statutory duty). **[219]**

26. Individual resale price maintenance enforceable in certain cases

(1) The provisions of this section shall —

(*a*) apply where goods are sold by a supplier subject to a condition which is not unlawful under this Act as to the price at which those goods may be resold; and

(*b*) be interpreted as if they were provisions of Part I of this Act.

(2) Where goods are sold by a supplier subject to such a condition, either generally or by or to a specified class or person, that condition may be enforced by the supplier against any person —

(*a*) who is not party to the sale, and

(*b*) who subsequently acquires the goods with notice of the condition,

as if that person had been party to the sale.

(3) A condition shall not be enforceable by virtue of this section —

(*a*) in respect of the resale of any goods —

(i) by a person who acquires those goods otherwise than for the purpose of resale in the course of business; or

(ii) by any person who acquires them, whether immediately or not, from such a person;

(*b*) in respect of the resale of any goods —

(i) pursuant to an order of any court; or

(ii) by way of execution or distress; or

(iii) by any person who acquires them, whether immediately or not, after such resale.

(4) Nothing in this section shall be construed as enabling any person to enforce a condition imposed in pursuance of any restriction which is declared by an order of the Court for the time being in force under the Restrictive Trade Practices Act 1976 (or under the Restrictive Trade Practices Act 1956) to be contrary to the public interest.

(5) The court may, upon proof that goods sold by the plaintiff have been resold by the defendant in breach of a condition which is enforceable against him by virtue of this section, grant an injunction restraining the defendant from reselling in breach of any such condition any goods sold or to be sold by the plaintiff, whether of the same description as the goods proved to have been resold as described above or of any other description.

This subsection is without prejudice to any other relief which may be granted in proceedings against any person in respect of a breach or apprehended breach of such a condition. **[220]**

27. Interpretation of the Act

In this Act —

"the Court" means the Restrictive Practices Court;
"the Director" means the Director General of Fair Trading;
"interconnected bodies corporate" means bodies corporate which are members of the same group, and for the purposes of this definition "group" means a body corporate and all other bodies corporate which are its subsidiaries —

(a) within the meaning of [section 736 of the Companies Act 1985][1]; or

(b) for companies in Northern Ireland, within the meaning of [Article 4 of the Companies (Northern Ireland) Order 1986][2]; or

(c) (in the case of an industrial and provident society) within the meaning of section 15 of the Friendly and Industrial and Provident Societies Act 1968 or section 47 of the Industrial and Provident Societies Act (Northern Ireland) 1969, as the case may be.   **[221]**

AMENDMENTS
1 Substituted by the Companies Consolidation (Consequential Provisions) Act 1985, s 30, Sch 2.
2 Substituted by the Companies Consolidation (Consequential Provisions) (Northern Ireland) Order 1986, SI 1986 No 1035.

28. Application to Scotland

In the application of this Act to Scotland —

"assignment" means "assignation";
"defendant" means "defender";
"injunction" means "interdict";
"plaintiff" means "pursuer".   **[222]**

29. Transitional provisions, savings and repeals

(1) The provisions of Schedule 2 to this Act have effect for the purposes of the Act.

(2) The enactments specified in Part I of Schedule 3 to this Act (consequential repeals) and Part II of that Schedule (repeals of provisions of the Resale Prices Act 1964 and the Restrictive Trade Practices Act 1968 which have ceased to have any effect) are hereby repealed to the extent specified in the third column of that Schedule.

(3) Nothing in this Act shall be taken as prejudicing the operation of section 38 of the Interpretation Act 1889 (which relates to the operation of repeals).   **[223]**

30. Short title, extent and commencement

(1) This Act may be cited as the Resale Prices Act 1976.

(2) This Act extends to Northern Ireland.

(3) This Act shall come into operation on such day as the Secretary of State may appoint by order made by statutory instrument.　　　　　**[224]**

SCHEDULES
SCHEDULE 1

Section 7

HIRE-PURCHASE AGREEMENTS UNDER PART I

Hire-purchase agreements before amendment by the Consumer Credit Act 1974

1.—(1) *This paragraph shall cease to have effect on the making of an order under section 192(4) of the Consumer Credit Act 1974 bringing into operation the amendment contained in paragraph 17 of Schedule 4 to that Act.*

(2) *In Part I of this Act any reference to selling goods includes a reference to letting goods under a hire-purchase agreement as defined by section 1 of the Hire-Purchase Act 1965.*

(3) *In the application of Part I—*

　(a) *to Scotland, for the reference to a hire-purchase agreement as defined by section 1 of the Hire-Purchase Act 1965 substitute a reference to letting under a hire-purchase agreement as defined by section 1 of the Hire-Purchase (Scotland) Act 1965 or to an agreement to sell under a conditional sale agreement as defined by that section; and*

　(b) *to Northern Ireland, for the reference to section 1 of the Hire-Purchase Act 1965 substitute a reference to section 1 of the Hire-Purchase Act (Northern Ireland) 1966.*

NOTE
Para 1, which related to hire-purchase agreements before amendment by the Consumer Credit Act 1974, ceased to have effect on 19 May 1985

Hire-purchase agreements after amendment by the Consumer Credit Act 1974

2.—(1) This paragraph shall not have effect until the making of an order under section 192(4) of the Consumer Credit Act 1974 bringing into operation the amendment contained in paragraph 17 of Schedule 4 to that Act, and sub-paragraph (2) below (which is in the same terms as that paragraph) shall then give effect to that amendment.

(2) In Part I of this Act any reference to selling goods includes a reference to bailing or (in Scotland) hiring goods under a hire-purchase agreement or to agreeing to sell the goods under a conditional sale agreement.

In this sub-paragraph—

　"conditional sale agreement" means an agreement for the sale of goods under which the purchase price or part of it is payable by instalments, and the property in the goods is to remain in the seller (notwithstanding that the buyer is to be in possession of the goods) until such conditions as to the payment of instalments or otherwise as may be specified in the agreement are fulfilled; and

"hire-purchase agreement" means an agreement, other than a conditional sale agreement, under which—

(a) goods are bailed or (in Scotland) hired in return for periodical payments by the person to whom they are bailed or hired, and

(b) the property in the goods will pass to that person if the terms of the agreement are complied with and one or more of the following occurs—

(i) the exercise of an option to purchase by that person,

(ii) the doing of any other specified act by any party to the agreement,

(iii) the happening of any other specified event. **[225]**

SCHEDULE 2

Section 29

TRANSITIONAL PROVISIONS AND SAVINGS

General provisions

1.—(1) In so far as anything done under an enactment repealed by this Act could have been done under a corresponding provision of this Act it shall not be invalidated by the repeal but shall have effect as if done under that provision.

(2) Without prejudice to sub-paragraph (1) above, any express or implied reference in and in relation to this Act to a thing done or not done or to an event shall (subject to its context) include a reference to the corresponding thing or event in relation to the repealed enactments.

2. Where a document refers expressly or by implication to an enactment repealed by this Act the reference shall (subject to its context) be construed as a reference to the corresponding provision of this Act.

3. Where any period of time specified in an enactment repealed by this Act is current at the commencement of this Act, and there is a corresponding provision in this Act, this Act shall have effect as if that corresponding provision had been in force when that period began to run.

Proceedings of the Restrictive Practices Court under repealed enactments

4. Nothing in this Act affects the validity of the decisions and proceedings of the Restrictive Practices Court under any enactment repealed by this Act, and those decisions and proceedings shall have effect in relation to this Act accordingly. **[226]**

SCHEDULE 3

Section 29

REPEALS

(not reproduced in this work)

THE COMPETITION ACT 1980
(1980 c 21)

ARRANGEMENT OF SECTIONS

SCHEDULES:
    Schedule 1—*Supplementary provisions in connection with dissolution of Price
        Commission* (not reproduced in this work)
    Schedule 2—*Enactments repealed* (not reproduced in this work)

An Act to abolish the Price Commission; to make provision for the control of anti-competitive practices in the supply and acquisition of goods and the supply and securing of services; to provide for references of certain public bodies and other persons to the Monopolies and Mergers Commission; to provide for the investigation of prices and charges by the Director General of Fair Trading; to provide for the making of grants to certain bodies; to amend and provide for the amendment of the Fair Trading Act 1973; to make amendments with respect to the Restrictive Trade Practices Act 1976; to repeal the remaining provisions of the Counter-Inflation Act 1973; and for the purposes connected therewith [3 April 1980]

Abolition of Price Commission

1. Abolition of Price Commission . . . [227]
AMENDMENT
Section repealed by the SL(R) Act 1989.

Control of anti-competitive practices

2. Anti-competitive practices

(1) The provisions of sections 3 to 10 below have effect with a view to the control of anti-competitive practices, and for the purposes of this Act a person engages in an anti-competitive practice if, in the course of business, that person pursues a course of conduct which, of itself or when taken together with a course of conduct pursued by persons associated with him, has or is intended to have or is likely to have the effect of restricting, distorting or preventing competition in connection with the production, supply or acquisition of goods in the

United Kingdom or any part of it or the supply or securing of services in the United Kingdom or any part of it.

(2) To the extent that a course of conduct is required or envisaged by a material provision of, or a material recommendation in, an agreement which is registered or subject to registration under the Restrictive Trade Practices Act 1976, that course of conduct shall not be regarded as constituting an anti-competitive practice for the purposes of this Act; and for the purposes of this subsection —

   (*a*) a provision of an agreement is a material provision if, by virtue of the existence of the provision (taken alone or together with other provisions) the agreement is one to which that Act applies; and
   (*b*) a recommendation is a material recommendation in an agreement if it is one to which a term implied into the agreement by any provision of section 8 or section 16 of that Act (terms implied into trade association agreements and services supply association agreements) applies.

(3) For the purposes of this Act, a course of conduct does not constitute an anti-competitive practice if it is excluded for those purposes by an order made by the Secretary of State; and any such order may limit the exclusion conferred by it by reference to a particular class of persons or to particular circumstances.

(4) Without prejudice to the generality of subsection (3) above, an order under that subsection may exclude the conduct of any person by reference to the size of his business, whether expressed by reference to turnover, as defined in the order, or to his share of a market, as so defined, or in any other manner.

(5) For the purpose only of enabling the Director General of Fair Trading (in this Act referred to as "the Director") to establish whether any person's course of conduct is excluded by virtue of any such provision of an order under subsection (3) above as is referred to in subsection (4) above, the order may provide for the application, with appropriate modifications, of any provisions of sections 44 and 46 of the Fair Trading Act 1973 (power of Director to require information).

(6) For the purposes of this section any two persons are to be treated as associated —

   (*a*) if one is a body corporate of which the other directly or indirectly has control either alone or with other members of a group of interconnected bodies corporate of which he is a member, or
   (*b*) if both are bodies corporate of which one and the same person or group of persons directly or indirectly has control;

and for the purposes of this subsection a person or group of persons able directly or indirectly to control or materially to influence the policy of a body corporate, but without having a controlling interest in that body corporate, may be treated as having control of it.

(7) In this section "the supply or securing of services" includes providing a place or securing that a place is provided other than on a highway, or in Scotland a public right of way, for the parking of a motor vehicle (within the meaning of [the Road Traffic Act 1988][1].

(8) For the purposes of this Act any question whether, by pursuing any course of conduct in connection with the acquisition of goods or the securing of services by it, a local authority is engaging in an anti-competitive practice shall be determined as if the words "in the course of business" were omitted from subsection (1) above; and in this subsection "local authority" means—

(a) in England and Wales, a local authority within the meaning of the Local Government Act 1972, the Common Council of the City of London or the Council of the Isles of Scilly.

(b) (*applies to Scotland*), and

(c) in Northern Ireland, a district council established under the Local Government Act (Northern Ireland) 1972. **[228]**

NOTE
By the Telecommunications Act 1984, s 50(3), the functions of the Director General of Fair Trading under this section and ss 3–10 and 16 so far as relating to courses of conduct which have or are intended to have or are likely to have the effect of restricting, distorting or preventing competition in connection with the production, supply or acquisition of telecommunication apparatus or the supply or securing of telecommunication services (as defined in s 4(3) of the Act of 1984) are transferred to the Director General of Telecommunications (so as to be exercisable concurrently with the Director General of Fair Trading); and references in this section, ss 3–10, 16 and 19 of this Act to the Director are to be construed accordingly.

AMENDMENT
1 Sub-s (7) amended by the Road Traffic (Consequential Provisions) Act 1988, s 4, Sch 3, para 19.

ORDER UNDER THIS SECTION
The Anti-Competitive Practices (Exclusions) Order 1980, SI 1980 No 979, as amended by SI 1984 No 1919

3. Preliminary investigation by Director of possible anti-competitive practice

(1) If it appears to the Director that any person has been or is pursuing a course of conduct which may amount to an anti-competitive practice, the Director may in accordance with this section carry out an investigation with a view to establishing whether that person has been or is pursuing a course of conduct which does amount to such a practice.

(2) Before carrying out an investigation under this section, the Director shall—

(a) give to the Secretary of State and the person or persons whose conduct is to be investigated notice of the proposed investigation, together with an indication of the matters to be investigated, the person or persons concerned and the goods or services to which the investigation is to relate; and

(b) arrange for notice of the proposed investigation, together with an indication of the matters to be investigated, the person or persons concerned and the goods or services to which the investigation is to relate, to be published in such manner as the Director considers most suitable for bringing the proposed investigation to the attention of any other persons who, in the opinion of the Director, would be affected by or be likely to have an interest in the investigation.

(3) The Secretary of State may by regulations prescribe the manner in which

any notice is to be given under subsection (2) above, and the evidence which is to be sufficient evidence of its having been given, and of its contents and authenticity.

(4) Subject to the following provisions of this section, where notice of a proposed investigation has been given in accordance with paragraph (*a*) and published in accordance with paragraph (*b*) of subsection (2) above, the Director shall proceed with the investigation as expeditiously as possible.

(5) If, before the end of the period of two weeks beginning with the day on which the Secretary of State receives notice of a proposed investigation under paragraph (*a*) of subsection (2) above, the Secretary of State directs the Director not to proceed with the investigation the Director shall take no further action under this section with respect to the matters referred to in the notice; but nothing in this subsection shall prevent the Director from proceeding with a subsequent investigation, notwithstanding that it relates wholly or partly to the same matters.

(6) Where the Secretary of State gives a direction under subsection (5) above, he shall—

(*a*) give notice of the direction to the person or persons whose conduct was to be investigated; and

(*b*) arrange for the direction to be published in such manner as he considers most suitable for bringing it to the attention of any other person who, in his opinion, would have been affected by, or likely to have had an interest in, the direction.

(7) For the purposes of an investigation under this section the Director may, by notice in writing signed by him—

(*a*) require any person to produce, at a time and place specified in the notice, to the Director or to any person appointed by him for the purpose, any documents which are specified or described in the notice and which are documents in his custody or under his control and relating to any matter relevant to the investigation; or

(*b*) require any person carrying on any business to furnish to the Director such estimates, returns or other information as may be specified or described in the notice, and specify the time, the manner and the form in which any such estimates, returns or information are to be furnished;

but no person shall be compelled for the purpose of any such investigation to produce any document which he could not be compelled to produce in civil proceedings before the High Court or, in Scotland, the Court of Session or, in complying with any requirement for the furnishing of information, to give any information which he could not be compelled to give in evidence in such proceedings.

(8) Subsections [(6)]¹ to (8) of section 85 of the Fair Trading Act 1973 (enforcement provisions relating to notices under subsection (1) of that section requiring production of documents etc) shall apply in relation to a notice under subsection (7) above as they apply in relation to a notice under subsection (1) of that section [but as if, in subsection (7) of that section, for the words from "any one" to "the Commission" there were substituted "the Director"].¹

(9) At any time before the completion of an investigation under this section the Director may, with the consent of the Secretary of State, determine not to proceed with the investigation and, in that event, he shall —

(*a*) give notice of his determination to the person or persons whose conduct was being investigated; and

(*b*) arrange for the determination to be published in such manner as he considers most suitable for bringing it to the attention of any other person who, in his opinion, would have been affected by, or likely to have had an interest in, the investigation.

(10) As soon as practicable after the completion of an investigation under this section the Director shall, in such manner as he considers appropriate publish a report stating, with reasons, whether in his opinion any course of conduct described in the report constituted or constitutes an anti-competitive practice and, if so —

(*a*) specifying the person or persons concerned and the goods or services in question; and

(*b*) stating, with reasons, whether he considers that it is appropriate for him to make a reference under section 5 below.   **[229]**

AMENDMENT
'Sub-s (8) amended by the Companies Act 1989, s 153, Sch 20, para 21, as from 1 April 1990.

REGULATIONS UNDER THIS SECTION
The Competition (Notices) Regulations 1980, SI 1980 No 980 are partly made under sub-s (3) above.

4. Undertakings in consequence of Director's reports

(1) Where a report is published under section 3 above stating, in accordance with subsection (10)(*b*) of that section, that it is appropriate for the Director to make a reference under section 5 below, the Director shall consider any representations in writing which are made to him by a person specified in the report as a person who was or is engaged in an anti-competitive practice and which contain proposals as to what should be done in consequence of the conclusions of the report so far as they relate to that person.

(2) Any such representations may include an undertaking by which the person who makes the representations agrees to be bound, if the undertaking is accepted by the Director, for a period specified in the representations.

(3) At any time before the Director makes a reference under section 5 below in relation to a report under section 3 above, the Director may, by notice given to the person concerned, accept an undertaking which is offered by that person by reference to that report.

(4) It shall be the duty of the Director —

[(*a*) to arrange for —
(i) any undertaking accepted by him under this section, and
(ii) any variation or release of such an undertaking after the passing of the Companies Act 1989,

to be published in such manner as appears to him to be appropriate.]¹

(b)   to keep under review the carrying out of any such undertaking and from time to time to consider whether, by reason of any change of circumstances, the undertaking is no longer appropriate and either the person concerned can be released from the undertaking or the undertaking needs to be varied or superseded by a new undertaking, and

(c)   if it appears to him that the person by whom an undertaking was given has failed to carry it out, to give that person notice of that fact.

(5)   If at any time the Director concludes under subsection (4)(b) above—

(a)   that any person can be released from an undertaking, or

(b)   that an undertaking needs to be varied or superseded by a new undertaking,

he shall give notice to that person stating that he is so released, or specifying the variation or, as the case may be, the new undertaking which in his opinion is required.

(6)   Where a notice is served on any person under subsection (5) above specifying a variation or new undertaking, the notice shall state the change of circumstances by virtue of which the notice is served.

(7)   Subject to subsection (8) below, the Director may at any time, by notice given to the person concerned—

(a)   agree to the continuation of an undertaking in relation to which he has given notice under subsection (5) above specifying a variation or new undertaking, or

(b)   accept a new or varied undertaking which is offered by that person as a result of such a notice.

(8)   If the Director makes a reference under section 5 below in relation to a notice under subsection (5) above, he shall not, after the reference has been made, agree to the continuation of the undertaking in relation to which that notice was given or accept a new or varied undertaking which is offered as a result of that notice.

(9)   The Secretary of State may by regulations prescribe the manner in which any notice is to be given under this section, and the evidence which is to be sufficient evidence of its having been given, and of its contents and authenticity.

[230]

AMENDMENT
  1 Sub-s (4)(a) substituted by the Companies Act 1989, s 153, Sch 20, para 22, as from 16 November 1989.
REGULATIONS UNDER THIS SECTION
  The Competition (Notices) Regulations 1980, SI 1980 No 980 are partly made under Sub-s (9) above.

5. Competition references

(1)   In any case where—

(a)   a report has been published under section 3 above stating, in accordance with subsection (10)(b) of that section, that it is appropriate for the Director to make a reference under this section and the Director has not accepted from each of the persons specified in the relevant report such undertaking or undertakings as, in his opinion, covers or cover every course of conduct which is described in the report as constituting an anti-competitive practice, or

    (b) the Director has given notice to any person under section 4(4)(c) above with respect to an undertaking given by that person, or

    (c) the Director has given notice to any person under section 4(5) above specifying either a variation of an undertaking or a new undertaking which is required and has neither accepted a new or varied undertaking from that person nor agreed upon the continuation of the original undertaking,

then, subject to the following provisions of this section, the Director may make a reference under this section to the Monopolies and Mergers Commission (in the following provisions of this Act referred to as a "competition reference").

(2) In this section a competition reference is referred to —

    (a) as a "report reference" if it is made by virtue of subsection (1)(a) above; and

    (b) as a "notice reference" if it is made by virtue of subsection (1)(b) or subsection (1)(c) above.

(3) No competition reference may be made within the period of four weeks beginning with the relevant date nor, subject to subsection (4) below, may such a reference be made after the expiry of the period of eight weeks beginning on that date; and in this subsection "the relevant date" means —

    (a) in the case of a report reference, the date on which was first published, in accordance with section 3(10) above, the report of the Director to which the reference relates; and

    (b) in the case of a notice reference, the date on which notice was given as mentioned in subsection (1)(b) or, as the case may be, subsection (1)(c) above.

(4) If the Secretary of State so directs, subsection (3) above shall have effect in relation to a competition reference of a description specified in the direction as if for the period of eight weeks specified in that subsection there were substituted such longer period not exceeding twelve weeks as may be specified in the direction; but the Secretary of State shall not give a direction under this subsection unless, upon representations made to him by the Director, it appears to the Secretary of State that it would be appropriate in the case in question to allow the Director a longer period in which to negotiate one or more undertakings under section 4 above.

(5) In this section and section 6 below "the relevant report" means —

    (a) in the case of a report reference, the report referred to in subsection (1)(a) above;

    (b) in the case of a notice reference made by virtue of subsection (1)(b) above, the report by reference to which the person to whom the notice was given under section 4(4)(c) above gave the undertaking to which that notice refers; and

    (c) in the case of a notice reference made by virtue of subsection (1)(c) above, the report by reference to which the person to whom the notice was given

under section 4(5) above gave the undertaking which the Director
proposes should be varied or superseded.   **[231]**

6. Scope of competition references

(1) In a competition reference the Director shall specify —

   (*a*) the person or persons whose activities are to be investigated by the Commission (in this section referred to as the person or persons "subject
   to the reference"),

   (*b*) the goods or services to which the investigation is to extend, and

   (*c*) the course or courses of conduct to be investigated.

(2) The Director may not under subsection (1) above specify in a competition
reference any person who is not specified in the relevant report nor any goods
or services which are not so specified nor any course of conduct which is not
described in that report but, subject to that and subsection (3) below, the Director
may under subsection (1) above specify such person or persons, such goods or
services and such course or courses of conduct as he considers appropriate.

(3) To the extent that the Director is of the opinion that an undertaking
accepted by him under section 4 above covers the activities of any person specified in the relevant report, or any goods or services so specified, or any course
of conduct described in that report, the Director shall exclude that person, those
goods or services or, as the case may require, that course of conduct from the
reference.

(4) In subsection (3) above the reference to an undertaking accepted by the
Director under section 4 above does not include —

   (*a*) an undertaking in respect of which notice has been served under subsection (4)(*c*) of that section, or

   (*b*) an undertaking in respect of which the Director has given notice under
   subsection (5)(*b*) of that section specifying a new or varied undertaking, unless he has agreed upon its continuation with or without variation.

(5) Subject to subsection (6) below, on a competition reference the Commission shall investigate and report on the following questions, namely —

   (*a*) whether any person subject to the reference was at any time during the
   period of twelve months ending on the date of the reference pursuing,
   in relation to goods or services specified in the reference, a course of
   conduct so specified or any other course of conduct which appears to
   be similar in form and effect to the one so specified; and

   (*b*) whether, by pursuing any such course of conduct, a person subject to
   the reference was at any time during that period engaging in an anti-
   competitive practice; and

   (*c*) whether, if any person was so engaging in an anti-competitive practice,
   the practice operated or might be expected to operate against the public
   interest.

(6) The Director may at any time, by notice given to the Commission, restrict
the scope of a competition reference by excluding from the reference —

(a) some or all of the activities of any person subject to the reference,

(b) any goods or services specified in the reference, or

(c) any course of conduct so specified,

and, subject to section 7 below, on the receipt of such notice the Commission shall discontinue their investigation so far as it relates to any matter so excluded and shall make no reference to any such matter in their report.   **[232]**

7. Supplementary provisions as to competition references

(1) On making a competition reference or on varying such a reference under section 6(6) above the Director shall send a copy of the reference or, as the case may be, the variation to the Secretary of State.

(2) If, below the end of the period of two weeks beginning with the day on which the Secretary of State receives a copy of a competition reference under subsection (1) above, the Secretary of State directs the Commission not to proceed with the reference—

(a) the Commission shall not proceed with that reference, but

(b) nothing in paragraph (a) above shall prevent the Commission from proceeding with a subsequent competition reference, notwithstanding that it relates wholly or partly to the same matters.

(3) If, before the end of the period of two weeks beginning with the day on which the Secretary of State receives a copy of a variation of a competition reference under subsection (1) above, the Secretary of State directs the Commission not to give effect to the variation—

(a) the Commission shall proceed with the reference as if that variation had not been made, but

(b) nothing in paragraph (a) above shall prevent the Commission from giving effect to any subsequent variation, notwithstanding that it relates wholly or partly to the matters to which that variation related.

(4) On making a competition reference or on varying such a reference under section 6(6) above the Director shall arrange for the reference or, as the case may be, the variation to be published in such manner as he considers most suitable for bringing it to the attention of persons who, in his opinion, would be affected by it or be likely to have an interest in it.

(5) Where the Secretary of State gives a direction under subsection (2) or subsection (3) above, the Secretary of State shall arrange for the direction to be published in such manner as he considers most suitable for bringing it to the attention of persons who, in his opinion, would have been affected by, or likely to have had an interest in, the reference or variation to which the direction relates.

(6) Sections 70 (time limit for report on merger reference), 84 (public interest) and 85 (attendance of witnesses and production of documents) of the Fair Trading Act 1973 and Part II of Schedule 3 to that Act (performance of functions of Commission) shall apply in relation to competition references as if—

(a) the functions of the Commission in relation to those references were functions under that Act;

(*b*) the expression "merger reference" included a competition reference;
(*c*) in paragraph 11 of that Schedule the reference to section 71 of that Act
were a reference to section 6(6) above; and
(*d*) in paragraph 16(2) of that Schedule the reference to section 56 of that
Act were a reference to sections 9 and 10 below.   **[233]**

8. Conclusions and reports of the Commission

(1) A report of the Commission on a competition reference shall be made to
the Secretary of State.

(2) Subject to section 6(6) above and subsection (3) below, a report on a competition reference shall state, with reasons, the conclusions of the Commission
with respect to the following matters —

(*a*) whether any person whose activities were investigated was at any time
during the period of twelve months referred to in paragraph (*a*) of subsection (5) of section 6 above pursuing any such course of conduct as
is referred to in that paragraph; and
(*b*) if so, whether by pursuing such a course of conduct any such person
was at any time during that period engaging in an anti-competitive practice; and
(*c*) if so, whether that anti-competitive practice operated or might be
expected to operate against the public interest; and
(*d*) if so, what are, or are likely to be, the effects adverse to the public
interest.

(3) If, on a competition reference, the Commission conclude that any person
was pursuing such a course of conduct as is referred to in section 6(5)(*a*) above
but that, by virtue of section 2(2) above, that course of conduct does not, in
whole or in part, constitute an anti-competitive practice, the Commission shall
state their conclusion in their report and shall not make any recommendation
under subsection (4) below with respect to things done as mentioned in section
2(2) above.

(4) If, on a competition reference, the Commission conclude that any person
was at any time during the period of twelve months referred to in section 6(5)(*a*)
above engaging in an anti-competitive practice which operated or might be
expected to operate against the public interest, the Commission —

(*a*) shall, as part of their investigations, consider what action (if any) should
be taken for the purpose of remedying or preventing the adverse effects
of that practice; and
(*b*) may, if they think fit, include in their report recommendations as to
such action including, where appropriate, action by one or more
Ministers (including Northern Ireland departments) or other public
authorities.

(5) A copy of every report of the Commission on a competition reference shall
be transmitted by the Commission to the Director; and the Secretary of State
shall take account of any advice given to him by the Director with respect to
any such report.   **[234]**

9. Undertakings following report on competition reference

(1) In any case where—

(a) the report of the Commission on a competition reference concludes that any person specified in the report was engaging in an anti-competitive practice which operated or might be expected to operate against the public interest, and

(b) it appears to the Secretary of State that the effects of that practice which are adverse to the public interest might be remedied or prevented if that person or any other person specified in the report took or refrained from taking any action,

the Secretary of State may by notice in writing request the Director to seek to obtain from the person or, as the case may be, each of the persons specified in the notice an undertaking to take or refrain from taking any action with a view to remedying or preventing those adverse effects.

(2) Where the Secretary of State makes a request under subsection (1) above—

(a) he shall at the same time send a copy of the notice by which the request is made to the person or, as the case may be, each of the persons from whom an undertaking is to be sought; and

(b) it shall be the duty of the Director to seek to obtain an undertaking or undertakings of the description requested.

(3) In any case where—

(a) the Director is satisfied that a person from whom he has been requested to seek to obtain an undertaking is unlikely to give a suitable undertaking within a reasonable time, or

(b) having allowed such time as in his opinion is reasonable for the purpose, he is satisfied that a suitable undertaking has not been given by the person in question,

the Director shall give such advice to the Secretary of State as he may think proper in the circumstances.

(4) Where, following a request under subsection (1) above, an undertaking has been accepted by the Director, it shall be his duty—

(a) to give a copy of the undertaking [and of any variation of it after the passing of the Companies Act 1989][1] to the Secretary of State;

(b) to arrange for the undertaking [and any variation or release of it after that time][1] to be published in such manner as appears to him to be appropriate;

(c) to keep under review the carrying out of the undertaking and from time to time to consider whether, by reason of any change of circumstances, the undertaking is no longer appropriate and either the person concerned can be released from the undertaking or the undertaking needs to be varied or to be superseded by a new undertaking; and

(d) if it appears to him that any person can be so released or that an undertaking has not been or is not being fulfilled, or needs to be varied or superseded, to give such advice to the Secretary of State as he may think proper in the circumstances.

(5) If, following advice from the Director that a person can be released from an undertaking, the Secretary of State considers that it is appropriate for the Director to release him from it —

(a) the Secretary of State shall request the Director to do so, and

(b) the Director shall give the person concerned notice that he is released from the undertaking;

and regulations under subsection (9) of section 4 above shall apply in relation to such a notice as they apply to a notice under subsection (5) of that section.

(6) The Secretary of State shall take account of any advice given to him by the Director under this section (including advice as to the exercise by the Secretary of State of any of his powers under this Act).   [235]

AMENDMENT
1 Sub-s (4)(a),(b) amended by the Companies Act 1989, s 153, Sch 20, para 23, as from 16 November 1989.

10. Orders following report on competition reference

(1) If, in any case where the report of the Commission on a competition reference concludes that any person specified in the report was engaged in an anti-competitive practice which operated or might be expected to operate against the public interest —

(a) the Secretary of State has not under section 9(1) above requested the Director to seek to obtain undertakings from one or more of the persons so specified, or

(b) following a request under subsection (1) of section 9 above, the Director has informed the Secretary of State that he is satisfied as mentioned in paragraph (a) or paragraph (b) of subsection (3) of that section, or

(c) the Director has informed the Secretary of State that an undertaking accepted by him under section 9 above from a person specified in the report has not been or is not being fulfilled,

the Secretary of State may, if he thinks fit, make an order under this section.

(2) Subject to the following provisions of this section, an order under this section may do either or both of the following, that is to say —

(a) prohibit a person named in the order from engaging in any anti-competitive practice which was specified in the report or from pursuing any other course of conduct which is similar in form and effect to that practice; and

(b) for the purpose of remedying or preventing any adverse effects which are specified in the report as mentioned in section 8(2)(d) above, exercise one or more of the powers specified in Part I of Schedule 8 to the Fair Trading Act 1973 to such extent and in such manner as the Secretary of State considers necessary for that purpose.

(3) No order may be made by virtue of paragraph (a) of subsection (2) above

in respect of any person unless he is a person specified in the Commission's report and either —

(*a*) he has not given an undertaking which the Director sought to obtain from him in pursuance of a request under section 9(1) above; or

(*b*) the Director was not requested under section 9(1) above to seek to obtain an undertaking from him; or

(*c*) the Director has informed the Secretary of State that an undertaking given by him and accepted by the Director under section 9 above has not been or is not being fulfilled.

(4) In the Fair Trading Act 1973 —

(*a*) section 90 (general provisions as to orders under section 56 etc) except subsection (2),

(*b*) section 91(2) (publication of proposals to make an order),

(*c*) section 93 (enforcement of certain orders), and

(*d*) Part I of Schedule 8 (powers exercisable by orders under section 56 etc),

shall have effect as if any reference in those provisions to an order under section 56 of that Act included a reference to an order under this section.   **[236]**

ORDER UNDER THIS SECTION
   The Unichem Limited (Allotment of Shares) Order 1989, SI 1989 No 1061

Further references and investigations

11. References of public bodies and certain other persons to the Commission

(1) The Secretary of State may at any time refer to the Commission any question relating to —

(*a*) the efficiency and costs of,

(*b*) the service provided by, or

(*c*) possible abuse of a monopoly situation by,

a person falling within subsection (3) below and specified in the reference, including any question whether, in relation to a matter falling within paragraph (*a*), (*b*) or (*c*) above, the person is pursuing a course of conduct which operates against the public interest.

(2) For the purposes of subsection (1)(*c*) above "monopoly situation" includes a monopoly situation which is limited to a part of the United Kingdom and, accordingly, for those purposes references to the United Kingdom in sections 6 and 7 of the Fair Trading Act 1973 shall be taken to include references to a part of the United Kingdom.

(3) The persons referred to in subsection (1) above are —

(*a*)   any body corporate —

(i) which supplies goods or services by way of business,

(ii) the affairs of which are managed by its members, and

(iii) the members of which hold office as such by virtue of their appointment to that or another office by a Minister under any enactment; or

[(b)   any person (not falling within paragraph (a) above) who provides in Northern Ireland a bus service within the meaning of section 14 of the Finance Act (Northern Ireland) 1966];[1]

[(bb)   any person who provides a railway passenger service in pursuance of an agreement entered into by London Regional Transport by virtue of section 3(2) of the London Regional Transport Act 1984; or][2]

[(c)   the National Rivers Authority][3]; or

(d)   any board administering a scheme under the Agricultural Marketing Act 1958 [or the Agricultural Marketing (Northern Ireland) Order 1982]; or

(e)   any body corporate with a statutory duty to promote and assist the maintenance and development of the efficient supply of any goods or services by a body falling within paragraphs (a) to (d) above; or

(f)   any subsidiary, within the meaning of the [Companies Act 1985], of a body falling within paragraphs (a) to (e) above.

(4) The Secretary of State may by order exclude from subsection (3)(b) [or (bb)][1] above persons of such descriptions as may be specified in the order.

(5) No question concerning a person falling within subsection (3)(b) [or (bb)][1] above or a subsidiary of a body falling within [either of those paragraphs] may be referred to the Commission under this section unless it relates to the carriage of passengers by the person or, as the case may be, the subsidiary.

(6) The Secretary of State may at any time by notice given to the Commission vary a reference under this section.

(7) On making a reference under this section or on varying such a reference under subsection (6) above the Secretary of State shall arrange for the reference or, as the case may be, the variation to be published in such manner as he considers most suitable for bringing it to the attention of persons who in his opinion would be affected by it or be likely to have an interest in it.

(8) On a reference under this section the Commission shall investigate and report on any question referred to them but shall exclude from their investigation and report consideration of —

(a)   any question relating to the appropriateness of any financial obligations or guidance as to financial objectives (however expressed) imposed on or given to the person in question by or under any enactment, or otherwise by a Minister; and

(b)   the question whether any course of conduct required or envisaged as mentioned in section 2(2) above operates against the public interest.

(9) Sections 70 (time limit for report on merger reference), 84 (public interest) and 85 (attendance of witnesses and production of documents) of the Fair Trading Act 1973 and Part II of Schedule 3 to that Act (performance of functions of Commission) shall apply in relation to a reference under this section as if —

(a) the functions of the Commission under this section were functions under that Act;

(b) the expression "merger reference" included a reference to the Commission under this section;

(c) in paragraph 11 of that Schedule, the reference to section 71 of that Act were a reference to subsection (6) above; and

(d) in paragraph 16(2) of that Schedule, the reference to section 56 of that Act were a reference to section 12 below.

(10) A report of the Commission on a reference under this section shall be made to the Secretary of State and shall state, with reasons, the conclusions of the Commission with respect to any question referred to them and, where the Commission conclude that the person specified in the reference is pursuing a course of conduct which operates against the public interest, the report may include recommendations as to what action (if any) should be taken by the person for the purpose of remedying or preventing what the Commission consider are the adverse effects of that course of conduct.

(11) In this section "Minister" includes a Northern Ireland department and the head of such a department. **[237]**

AMENDMENTS
1 Sub-s (3)(b) substituted by the Transport Act 1985, s 114(1) with effect from 26 July 1986: the Transport Act 1985 (Commencement No 4) Order 1986, SI 1986 No 1088.
2 Sub-s (3)(bb) inserted together with the words in sub-ss (4) and (5) by the London Regional Transport Act 1984, s 71(3)(a), Sch 6, para 15 and amended by the Transport Act 1985, s 114(1).
3 Sub-s (3)(c) substituted by the Water Act 1989, s 190(1), Sch 25, para 59(1).

PROSPECTIVE AMENDMENT
In sub-s (3)(f), after the words "within the meaning of", the words "section 736 of" are inserted by the Companies Act 1989, s 144(4), Sch 18, para 22, as from a day to be appointed under s 215 of that Act.

ORDERS UNDER THIS SECTION
The Competition (Exclusion of Bus Operators) Order 1980, SI 1980 No 981 (made under sub-s (4) above) excluded from sub-s (3)(b) (as originally enacted) any person whose annual turnover from the provision of bus services, as defined by the order, is less than £1 million except where the aggregate of that annual turnover of that person and of any other person or persons associated with him, within the meaning of s (2)(6) is £1 million or more.

12. Orders following report under section 11

(1) This section applies where a report of the Commission on a reference under section 11 above concludes that the person specified in the reference is pursuing a course of conduct which operates against the public interest.

(2) If it appears to the Secretary of State that any other Minister has functions directly relating to the person specified in the reference or, in the case of a reference only concerning the activities of the person in a part of the United Kingdom, functions directly relating to the person in respect of his activities in that part, he shall send a copy of the report of the Commission on the reference to that Minister; and in subsection (3) below "the relevant Minister" means –

(a) in a case where it appears to the Secretary of State that any Minister (including himself) has such functions, that Minister, and

(b) in a case where it appears to the Secretary of State that no Minister has such functions, the Secretary of State.

(3) If—

(a) the relevant Minister considers it appropriate for the purpose of remedying or preventing what he considers are the adverse effects of the course of conduct specified in the report of the Commission as operating against the public interest, and
(b) the person specified in the reference does not fall within paragraph (d) of section 11(3) above and is not a subsidiary of a body falling within that paragraph,

he may by order direct the person to prepare within such time, if any, as may be specified in the order a plan for remedying or preventing such of those effects as are so specified; but where there is more than one relevant Minister no such order shall be made except by all the relevant Ministers acting jointly and where none of the relevant Ministers is the Secretary of State no such order shall be made except after consultation with him.

(4) It shall be the duty of a person to whom a direction is given under subsection (3) above to prepare such a plan as is mentioned in that subsection and to send a copy of that plan to the Minister or Ministers by whom the order containing the direction was made who shall lay it before Parliament; and, in a case where the plan involves the use by a body of its powers in relation to any subsidiary within the meaning of the [Companies Act 1985] the plan shall specify the manner in which the body proposes using those powers.

(5) Whether or not an order has been or may be made under subsection (3) above, the Secretary of State may, if he considers it appropriate for the purpose of remedying or preventing what he considers are the adverse effects of the course of conduct specified in the report of the Commission as operating against the public interest, by order exercise one or more of the powers specified in Part I, excluding paragraph 10, of Schedule 8 to the Fair Trading Act 1973, to such extent and in such manner as he considers appropriate.

(6) In the Fair Trading Act 1973—

(a) section 90 (general provisions as to orders under section 56 etc) except subsections (2) and (3),
(b) section 91(2) (publication of proposals to make an order),
(c) section 93 (enforcement of certain orders), and
(d) Part I (except paragraph 10) of Schedule 8 (powers exercisable by orders under section 56 etc),

shall have effect as if any reference in those provisions to an order under section 56 of that Act included a reference to an order under subsection (5) above.

[238]

PROSPECTIVE AMENDMENT
    In sub-s (4), after the words "within the meaning of", the words "section 736 of" are inserted by the Companies Act 1989, s 144(4), Sch 18, para 22, as from a day to be appointed under s 215 of that Act.

13. Investigations of prices directed by Secretary of State

(1) If so directed by the Secretary of State, the Director shall carry out an investigation into any price specified in the direction with a view to providing the Secretary of State with information of a description so specified relating to that price: but the giving of a direction under this section shall not affect the power of the Director to initiate an investigation under section 3 above (subject to subsection (5) of that section) into a course of conduct pursued by any person by or to whom the price specified in the direction is charged.

(2) The Secretary of State shall not give a direction under this section unless he is satisfied that the price in question is one of major public concern and, in this connection, he shall have regard to whether—

(*a*) the provision or acquisition of the goods or services in question is of general economic importance; or

(*b*) consumers are significantly affected, whether directly or indirectly, by the price.

(3) The Secretary of State may at any time vary or revoke a direction given under this section, but he shall not exercise his power to vary such a direction unless he is satisfied that the direction as proposed to be varied would be such as he could have given, having regard to subsection (2) above.

(4) On giving a direction under this section or on varying or revoking such a direction, the Secretary of State shall arrange for the direction, variation or revocation to be published in such manner as he considers most suitable for bringing it to the attention of persons who, in his opinion, would be affected by, or be likely to have an interest in, the investigation to which the direction, variation or revocation relates.

(5) A direction under this section shall specify a period within which the Director is to report on his investigation to the Secretary of State, and, before the expiry of the period specified in the direction (whether as originally given or as varied under subsection (3) above), the Director shall make a report on the investigation to the Secretary of State—

(*a*) stating his findings of fact which are material to the information which he is required to provide in accordance with the direction; and

(*b*) containing such additional observations (if any) as the Director considers should be brought to the attention of the Secretary of State as a result of the investigation.

(6) Subsections (7) and (8) of section 3 above shall have effect in relation to an investigation under this section as they have effect in relation to an investigation under that section. **[239]**

Patents and agricultural schemes

14. Applications by Crown concerning patents . . . [240]

AMENDMENT

Section repealed by the Copyright, Designs and Patents Act 1988, s 303(2), Sch 8.

15. Agricultural schemes: special provisions

(1) . . .¹

(2) The Secretary of State shall not—

(a) give a direction under subsection (5) of section 3 above or a consent under subsection (9) of that section in relation to an investigation under that section, or

(b) give a direction under section 7(2) or (3) above in relation to a competition reference, or

(c) make or vary a reference under section 11 above,

in a case where the person to whom or to whose conduct or activities the investigation or reference relates falls within section 11(3)(d) above unless he has first consulted the relevant Minister.

(3) Where the report of the Commission on a competition reference concludes that a board administering a scheme under the said Act of 1958 [or the Agricultural Marketing (Northern Ireland) Order 1982] was engaging in an anticompetitive practice which operated or might be expected to operate against the public interest, the Secretary of State shall not exercise any function under section 9 above except acting jointly with the relevant Minister and, in its application in such a case, section 9 above shall have effect as if the references in it to the Secretary of State (except the second reference in subsection (6)) were references to both the Secretary of State and the relevant Minister.

(4) Before carrying out an investigation under section 3 above into any course of conduct being pursued by a person falling within section 11(3)(d) above the Director shall give notice as required by section 3(2)(a) above also to the relevant Minister and on making any competition reference arising from that investigation or varying such a reference under section 6(6) above the Director shall send a copy of the reference or, as the case may be, the variation to the relevant Minister.

(5) In this section "the relevant Minister" means—

(a) in the case of a board administering a scheme under the said Act of 1958, the Minister who would have power to make an order under section 19 of that Act in relation to that board or the board administering that scheme, and

(b) in the case of a board administering a scheme under the said [Order of 1982] the Department of Agriculture for Northern Ireland.

[241]

NOTE

1 Sub-s (1): amending only.

General provisions about references and investigations

16. General provisions as to reports

(1) In making any report under this Act the Commission or the Director shall have regard to the need for excluding, so far as that is practicable —

(a) any matter which relates to the private affairs of an individual, where the publication of that matter would or might, in the opinion of the Commission or the Director, as the case may be, seriously and prejudicially affect the interests of that individual, and

(b) any matter which relates specifically to the affairs of a body of persons, whether corporate or unincorporate, where publication of that matter would or might, in the opinion of the Commission or the Director, as the case may be, seriously and prejudicially affect the interests of that body, unless in the opinion of the Commission or the Director, as the case may be, the inclusion of that matter relating specifically to that body is necessary for the purposes of the report.

(2) For the purposes of the law relating to defamation, absolute privilege shall attach to any report of the Commission or of the Director under this Act.

[242]

17. Laying before Parliament and publication of reports

(1) Subject to subsection (2) below, the Secretary of State shall lay a copy of any report made to him under section 8(1), 11(10) or 13(5) above before each House of Parliament and shall arrange for the report to be published in such manner as appears to him appropriate.

(2) The Secretary of State shall not lay a copy of a report made to him under section 8(1) or 11(10) above before either House of Parliament unless at least twenty-four hours before doing so he has transmitted to every person specified in the reference a copy of the report in the form in which it is laid (or by virtue of subsection (3) below is treated as being laid) before each House of Parliament.

(3) If a report made to him under section 8(1), 11(10) or 13(5) above is presented by command of Her Majesty to either House of Parliament otherwise than at or during the time of a sitting of that House, the presentation of the report shall for the purposes of this section be treated as the laying of a copy of it before that House by the Secretary of State.

(4) If it appears to the Secretary of State that the publication of any matter in a report made to him under section 8(1), 11(10) or 13(5) above would be against the public interest, he shall exclude that matter from the copies of the report as laid before Parliament and from the report as published under this section.

(5) Without prejudice to subsection (4) above, if the Secretary of State considers that it would not be in the public interest to disclose —

(a) any matter contained in a report made to him under section 8(1), 11(10) or 13(5) above relating to the private affairs of an individual whose interests would, in the opinion of the Secretary of State, be seriously and prejudicially affected by the publication of that matter, or

(b) any matter contained in such a report relating specifically to the affairs of a particular person whose interests would, in the opinion of the Secretary of State, be seriously and prejudicially affected by the publication of that matter,

the Secretary of State shall exclude that matter from the copies of the report as laid before Parliament and from the report as published by virtue of subsection (1) above.

(6) Any reference in sections 9, 10 or 12 above to a report of the Commission shall be construed as a reference to the report in the form in which copies of it are laid (or by virtue of subsection (3) of this section are treated as having been laid) before each House of Parliament under this section.   **[243]**

18. Information and advice about operation of Act

The Director shall arrange for the dissemination in such form and manner as he considers appropriate of such information and advice as it may appear to him expedient to give the public in the United Kingdom about the operation of this Act.   **[244]**

19. Restriction on disclosure of information

(1) Subject to subsection (2) below, no information obtained under or by virtue of the preceding provisions of this Act about any business shall, so long as the business continues to be carried on, be disclosed without the consent of the person for the time being carrying it on.

(2) Subsection (1) above does not apply to any disclosure of information made—

(a) for the purposes of facilitating the performance of any functions under this Act or any of the enactments [or subordinate legislation] specified in subsection (3) below of any Minister, any Northern Ireland department, the head of any such department, the Director, [the Director General of Telecommunications] [the Director General of Gas Supply], [the Civil Aviation Authority], [the Director General of Water Services], [the Director General of Electricity Supply] the Commission or a local weights and measures authority in Great Britain; or

(b) in connection with the investigation of any criminal offence or for the purposes of any criminal proceedings; or

(c) for the purposes of any civil proceedings brought under or by virtue of this Act or any of the enactments [or subordinate legislation] specified in subsection (3) below; or

(d) in pursuance of a Community obligation.

(3) The enactments [and subordinate legislation] referred to in subsection (2) above are—

(a) the Trade Descriptions Act 1968;

(b) the Fair Trading Act 1973;

(c) the Consumer Credit Act 1974;
(d) the Restrictive Trade Practices Act 1976;
(e) the Resale Prices Act 1976; . . .
(f) the Estate Agents Act 1979;
[(g) the Telecommunications Act 1984]¹
[(h) the Gas Act 1986]
[(h) Chapter XIV of Part I of the Financial Services Act 1986]
[(i) the Airports Act 1986]
[(j) the Consumer Protection Act 1987]
[(k) the Control of Misleading Advertisements Regulations 1988]
[(l) the Water Act 1989]
[(m) the Electricity Act 1989].

(4) . . .¹

(5) Nothing in subsection (1) above shall be construed —

(a) as limiting the matters which may be included in any report of the Director or of the Commission made under this Act; or
(b) as applying to any information which has been made public as part of such a report or as part of the register kept for the purposes of the Act of 1976.

(6) Any person who discloses information in contravention of this section shall be liable on summary conviction to a fine not exceeding the statutory maximum² and, on conviction on indictment, to imprisonment for a term not exceeding two years or to a fine or both.

(7) In subsection (6) above "the statutory maximum", in relation to a fine on summary conviction, means —

(a) in England and Wales . . . the prescribed sum within the meaning of [section 32 of the Magistrates' Courts Act 1980]² (at the passing of this Act £1,000); and
(b) in Scotland, the prescribed sum within the meaning of section 289B of the Criminal Procedure (Scotland) Act 1975 (at the passing of this Act £1,000²); and
[(c) in Northern Ireland, the prescribed sum within the meaning of Article 4 of the Fines and Penalties (Northern Ireland) Order 1984; . . .]

[245]

NOTE
1 Sub-s (4): amending only.
2 Statutory maximum: now £2,000 in England and Wales, Northern Ireland and Scotland.

AMENDMENTS
This section is set out as amended by the Magistrates' Courts Act 1980, s 154(1), Sch 7, para 206; the Agricultural Marketing (Northern Ireland) Order 1982; the Telecommunications Act 1984, s 109(1), (6), Sch 4, para 73, Sch 7, Pt I; the Fines and Penalties (Northern Ireland) Order 1984, SI 1984 No 703; the Gas Act 1986, s 67(1), Sch 7, para 28; the Financial Services Act 1986, s 182, Sch 13, para 5; (both latter Acts of 1986 purported to insert paragraphs (h)); the Airports Act 1986, s 83(1), Sch 4, para 7; the Consumer Protection Act 1987, s 48(1), Sch 4, para 7; the Control of Misleading Advertisements Regulations 1988, SI 1988 No 915; the Water Act 1989, s 190(1), Sch 25, para 59(2); and the Electricity Act 1989, s 112(1), Sch 16, para 25.

Grants

20. Power to make grants to certain bodies

If the Secretary of State is satisfied that —

(a) the general advice of any body on matters of interest to users of goods and services would be useful to him in the formulation of policy concerning those matters and

(b) the body disseminates information of such interest,

he may make a grant to the body on such terms as he thinks fit.   [246]

Amendments of Fair Trading Act 1973

21. Monopoly references by Secretary of State alone

It is hereby declared that where it appears to the Secretary of State that —

(a) a monopoly situation exists or may exist as mentioned in subsection (1) of section 51 of the Fair Trading Act 1973 (monopoly references by Ministers), and

(b) the goods or services in question are of a description mentioned in subsection (2) of that section, and

(c) none of the Ministers mentioned in subsection (3) of that section has such functions as are mentioned in subsection (2) of that section in relation to goods or services of that description,

the Secretary of State may make a monopoly reference with respect to the existence or possible existence of that situation acting alone; and accordingly any reference which has been made in such circumstances by the Secretary of State acting alone has been made in compliance with that section.   [247]

22. Disclosure of reports on monopoly references to persons named . . . [248]

NOTE

This section is amending only. See Fair Trading Act 1973, s 83.

23. Amendment of s 137(3) of Fair Trading Act 1973 . . .   [249]

NOTE

This section is amending only.

24. Modification of provisions about performance of Commission's functions

(1) The Secretary of State may by order make such modifications in Part II of Schedule 3 to the Fair Trading Act 1973 (performance of functions of Commission) as appear to him to be appropriate for improving the performance by the Commission of their functions.

(2) An order under this section may contain such transitional, incidental or supplementary provisions as the Secretary of State thinks fit. **[250]**

ORDER UNDER THIS SECTION
The Monopolies and Mergers Commission (Membership of Groups for Newspaper Merger References) Order 1982, SI 1982 No 1889.

Amendments of Restrictive Trade Practices Act 1976

25. Suspension of declarations under section 1(3) of Restrictive Trade Practices Act 1976 pending appeals

Where on an application under section 1(3) of the Restrictive Trade Practices Act 1976 the Court declares at any time after the coming into force of this section that any restrictions or information provisions are contrary to the public interest, that declaration shall not have effect —

(a) until the expiration of the period of 21 days beginning with the expiration of the period within which any party to that application may appeal against the declaration, and

(b) in a case where such an appeal is brought, until the expiration of the period of 21 days after the date on which the appeal has been finally determined or withdrawn. **[251]**

26. Suspension of declarations under section 1(3) of Restrictive Trade Practices Act 1976 pending revision of agreements

(1) Where the Court has declared under section 1(3) of the Restrictive Trade Practices Act 1976 that any restrictions or information provisions in an agreement are contrary to the public interest, any party to the agreement or to the proceedings in which the declaration was made may, at any time before the declaration comes into effect, submit a revised agreement or a draft of a revised agreement to the Court and the Court may declare that any restrictions or information provisions contained in the revised agreement by virtue of which the said Act of 1976 applies or would apply to that agreement are not contrary to the public interest.

(2) Variations of the agreement in relation to which the declaration under section 1(3) of the said Act of 1976 was made may not be submitted to the Court under subsection (1) above unless particulars of them have been furnished to the Director under section 24(2) of that Act and a new agreement may not be so submitted unless it has been registered under that Act and particulars of any variation of it have been so furnished.

(3) The duty of taking proceedings before the Court imposed on the Director by section 1(2)(c) of the said Act of 1976 shall not apply in respect of an agreement if the Court has declared under subsection (1) above that all the restrictions or information provisions by virtue of which that Act applies to the agreement are not contrary to the public interest.

(4) Where any person who may make an application under subsection (1) above

in relation to a declaration applies to the Court at any time before the declaration comes into effect for an extension of the period after which it will come into effect to enable an application to be made to the Court under subsection (1) above and it appears to the Court reasonable to do so, it may extend that period by such period (not exceeding six months on a first application under this subsection or three months on a second such application) as it thinks fit, but no more than two extensions may be made in respect of any declaration.

(5) Where, following a declaration under section 1(3) of the said Act of 1976, an application is made under subsection (1) or (4), above, the declaration shall not come into effect until the application has been determined.

(6) The Court may, if it thinks fit, grant an extension under subsection (4) above in relation to some but not all of the restrictions and information provisions in question and in that event—

  (a) the period within which an application under subsection (1) above or a second application under subsection (4) above may be made shall not expire until the declaration has come into effect in relation to all the restrictions or information provisions, and

  (b) subsection (5) above shall not prevent a declaration coming into effect in relation to any restriction or information provision in relation to which no extension was granted.

(7) Notice of an application made under subsection (1) or (4) above shall be served on the Director in accordance with rules of court and the Director shall be entitled in accordance with such rules to appear and to be heard on the application.

(8) Where a declaration is made under subsection (1) above the Director shall cause notice of it to be entered in the register kept by him under section 23 of the said Act of 1976—

  (a) in the case of a declaration in relation to restrictions or information provisions contained in an agreement registered under the Act, on the making of the declaration, and

  (b) in the case of a declaration in relation to restrictions or information provisions contained in a draft agreement, on the registration of an agreement in the form of the draft.

(9) Sections 10 and 19 of the said Act of 1976 (public interest) shall apply to proceedings under this section as they apply to proceedings under Part I of that Act.   **[252]**

NOTE
For rules of court in sub-s (7), see the Restrictive Practices Court Rules 1976, rr 57A – 57F, below, laying down the procedures to be followed when applications are made under sub-ss (1) and (4) of this section.

27. Recommendations by services supply associations

(1) An order under section 11 of the Restrictive Trade Practices Act 1976 (restrictive agreements as to services) may provide that section 16(3) of that Act (recommendations by services supply associations to members about services) shall not

apply to recommendations of such descriptions as may be specified in the order and an order under section 12 of that Act (information agreements as to services) may make similar provision in relation to section 16(5) of that Act (recommendations by services supply associations to members about furnishing information).

(2) Where—

(a) section 16 of that Act would (apart from this subsection) apply in relation to a recommendation by a services supply association, and

(b) if the sole term of the agreement for the constitution of the association were a term by which each member of it agreed to comply with that recommendation, the agreement would be excluded by the terms of the order from the operation of an order made, or having effect as if made, under section 11 of that Act which came into force after 21st March 1976 and before the coming into force of this section,

subsection (3) of the said section 16 shall not apply and shall be deemed never to have applied in relation to that recommendation during the continuance in force of the order.

(3) Subsection (2) above shall have effect in relation to a recommendation made before the repeal of section 112(3) of the Fair Trading Act 1973 as if each reference to section 16(3) of the 1976 Act included a reference to that section.

(4) . . .[1] **[253]**

NOTE
1 Sub-s (4): amending only. See Restrictive Trade Practices Act 1976, Sch 2, para 5.

28. Amendments to s 19 of Restrictive Trade Practices Act 1976 . . . [254]

NOTE
This section is amending only.

29. Exemption of certain undertakings from Restrictive Trade Practices Acts

(1) The Restrictive Trade Practices Act 1976 shall not apply in relation to any agreement by virtue only of restrictions being accepted or information provisions being made under it which are comprised in undertakings which have been—

(a) given pursuant to section [75G or][1] 88 of the Fair Trading Act 1973, or

(b) certified by the Secretary of State under paragraph 9 of Schedule 11 to the said Act of 1973, or

(c) accepted under section 4 or 9 above.

(2) The said Act of 1976 and Part I of the Restrictive Trade Practices Act 1956 shall be deemed never to have applied in relation to any agreement by virtue only of restrictions being accepted or information provisions being made under it which are comprised in undertakings falling within paragraph (a) or (b) of subsection (1) above. **[255]**

AMENDMENT
   1 Sub-s (1)(*a*) amended by the Companies Act 1989, s 153, Sch 20, para 24, as from 16 November 1989.

30. Exemption of copyright agreements from Restrictive Trade Practices Acts

(1) . . .[1]

(2) The said Act of 1976 and Part I of the Restrictive Trade Practices Act 1956 shall be deemed never to have applied in relation to—

   (*a*) a licence granted by the owner or a licensee of any copyright,

   (*b*) an assignment or assignation of any copyright, or

   (*c*) an agreement for such a licence, assignment or assignation,

by virtue only of restrictions being accepted or information provisions being made under it in respect of the work or other subject-matter in which the copyright subsists or will subsist.   [256]

NOTE
   1 Sub-s (1): amending only. See Restrictive Trade Practices Act 1976, Sch 3, para 5A.

Supplementary

31. Orders and regulations

(1) Any power of the Secretary of State to make orders or regulations under this Act shall be exercisable by statutory instrument.

(2) An order under section 2(3) above shall be laid before Parliament and shall cease to have effect (but without prejudice to the making of a new statutory instrument) unless, within forty days of the making of the order, it is approved by a resolution of each House of Parliament; and in reckoning any period of forty days for the purposes of this subsection, no account shall be taken of any period during which Parliament is dissolved or prorogued or during which both Houses are adjourned for more than four days.

(3) Any statutory instrument containing regulations under this Act or an order under section 10, 11(4) or 12(3) or (5) above shall be subject to annulment in pursuance of a resolution of either House of Parliament.

(4) No order shall be made under section 24(1) above unless a draft of the order has been laid before, and approved by a resolution of, each House of Parliament.   [257]

32. Financial provisions

(1) There shall be defrayed out of moneys provided by Parliament—

   (*a*) any expenses incurred by the Secretary of State in consequence of the provisions of this Act; and (*b*) any increase attributable to this Act in the sums payable out of moneys so provided under any other Act.

(2) In section 135(2)(*c*) of the Fair Trading Act 1973 (which provides for any expenses duly incurred by the Director or his staff in consequence of the provisions of that Act to be defrayed out of moneys provided by Parliament) for the words "of this Act" there shall be substituted the words "of this or any other Act". **[258]**

33. Short title, interpretation, repeals, commencement and extent

(1) This Act may be cited as the Competition Act 1980.

(2) Except in so far as any provision of this Act otherwise provides, section 137 of the Fair Trading Act 1973 (general interpretation provisions) shall have effect in relation to sections 2 to 24 above as if those sections were contained in that Act; and for ease of reference the expressions which are used in those sections and have meanings assigned to them by the said section 137 are—

"the Act of 1976"
"agreement"
"business"
"the Commission"
"consumer"
"the Director"
"enactment"
"goods"
"group"
"group of interconnected bodies corporate"
"interconnected bodies corporate"
"Minister"
"monopoly situation"
"practice"
"price"
"services"
"supply"
"the supply of services".

(3) Section 43 of the Restrictive Trade Practices Act 1976 (interpretation and construction) shall have effect in relation to sections 25 to 30 above as if those sections were contained in that Act; and for ease of reference the expressions which are used in those sections and have meanings assigned to them by the said section 43 are—

"agreement"
"the Court"
"the Director"
"goods"
"information provision"
"restriction"
"services supply association"
"supply".

(4) So much of the Counter-Inflation Act 1973 as remains in force immediately before the passing of this Act shall cease to have effect and, in consequence of that and of the preceding provisions of this Act, the enactments specified in Schedule 2 to this Act are hereby repealed to the extent specified in the third column of that Schedule.

(5) This Act shall come into operation on such day as the Secretary of State may by order appoint, and different days may be so appointed for different provisions and for different purposes.

(6) An order under this section appointing a day for the coming into operation of any provision of Schedule 2 to this Act may contain such savings with respect to the operation of that provision and such incidental and transitional provisions as appear to the Secretary of State to be appropriate.

(7) Any reference in any provision of this Act to the appointed day shall be construed as a reference to the day appointed or, as the case may require, first appointed under this section for the coming into operation of that provision.

(8) This Act extends to Northern Ireland. **[259]**

SCHEDULES

SCHEDULE 1

Section 1(3)

SUPPLEMENTARY PROVISIONS IN CONNECTION WITH DISSOLUTION OF PRICE COMMISSION

(repealed by the SC(R) Act 1989)

SCHEDULE 2

Section 33(4)

ENACTMENTS REPEALED

(not reproduced in this work)

FINANCIAL SERVICES ACT 1986
(1986 c 60)

ARRANGEMENT OF SECTIONS

PART I

REGULATION OF INVESTMENT BUSINESS

CHAPTER XIV

PREVENTION OF RESTRICTIVE PRACTICES

Examination of rules and practices

An Act to regulate the carrying on of investment business; to make related provision with respect to insurance business and business carried on by friendly societies; to make new provision with respect to the official listing of securities, offers of unlisted securities, takeover offers and insider dealing; to make provision as to the disclosure of information obtained under enactments relating to fair trading, banking, companies and insurance; to make provision for securing reciprocity with other countries in respect of facilities for the provision of financial services; and for connected purposes.

[7 November 1986]

PART I

REGULATION OF INVESTMENT BUSINESS

CHAPTER XIV

PREVENTION OF RESTRICTIVE PRACTICES

Examination of rules and practices

119. Recognised self-regulating organisations, investment exchanges and clearing houses

(1) The Secretary of State shall not make a recognition order in respect of a self-regulating organisation, investment exchange or clearing house unless he is satisfied that —

    [(*a*) in the case of a self-regulating organisation, the rules and any guidance of which copies are furnished with the application for the order, together

with any statements of principle, rules, regulations or codes of practice
to which members of the organisation would be subject by virtue of
Chapter V of this Part,

(*b*) in the case of an investment exchange, the rules and any guidance of
which copies are furnished with the application for the order, together
with any arrangements of which particulars are furnished with the
application,

(*c*) in the case of a clearing house, the rules and any guidance of which
copies are furnished with the application for the order,]

do not have, and are not intended or likely to have, to any significant extent
the effect of restricting, distorting or preventing competition or, if they have
or are intended or likely to have that effect to any significant extent, that the
effect is not greater than is necessary for the protection of investors.

(2) The powers conferred by subsection (3) below shall be exercisable by the
Secretary of State if at any time it appears to him that —

[(*a*) in the case of a self-regulating organisation,
  (i) any rules made or guidance issued by the organisation,
  (ii) any practices of the organisation, or
  (iii) any practices of persons who are members of, or otherwise subject
       to the rules made by, the organisation,

  together with any statements of principle, rules, regulations or codes
  of practice to which members of the organisation are subject by virtue
  of Chapter V of this Part,

(*b*) in the case of a recognised investment exchange —

  (i) any rules made or guidance issued by the exchange,
  (ii) any practices of the exchange, or
  (iii) any practices of persons who are members of, or otherwise subject
       to the rules made by, the exchange,

(*c*) in the case of a recognised clearing house —

  (i) any rules made or guidance issued by the clearing house,
  (ii) any practices of the the clearing house, or
  (iii) any practices of persons who are members of, or otherwise subject
       to the rules made by, the clearing house,

  or any clearing arrangements made by the clearing house,]

have, or are intended or likely to have, to a significant extent the effect of
restricting, distorting or preventing competition and that that effect is greater
than is necessary for the protection of investors.

(3) The powers exercisable under this subsection are —

(*a*) to revoke the recognition order of the organisation, exchange or clearing house;

(*b*) to direct it to take specified steps for the purpose of securing that [its
rules, or the] guidance, arrangements or practices in question do not
have the effect mentioned in subsection (2) above;

(*c*) to make alterations in [its rules] for that purpose;

and subsections (2) to (5), (7) and (9) of section 11 above shall have effect in relation to the revocation of a recognition order under this subsection as they have effect in relation to the revocation of such an order under subsection (1) of that section.

(4) Subsection (3)(*c*) above does not apply to an overseas investment exchange or overseas clearing house.

(5) The practices referred to in [paragraph (*a*)(ii), (*b*)(ii) and (*c*)(ii)] of subsection (2) above are practices of the organisation, exchange or clearing house in its capacity as such, being, in the case of a clearing house, practices in respect of its clearing arrangements; . . . **[260]**

[(6) The practices referred to in paragraph (*a*)(iii), (*b*)(iii) and (*c*)(iii) of subsection (2) above are—

(*a*) in relation to a recognized self-regulating organisation, practices in relation to business in respect of which the persons in question are subject to—

(i) the rules of the organisation, or
(ii) statements of principle, rules, regulations or codes of practice to which its members are subject by virtue of Chapter V of this Part,

and which are required or contemplated by the rules of the organisation or by those statements, rules, regulations or codes, or by guidance issued by the organisation,

(*b*) in relation to a recognised investment exchange or clearing house, practices in relation to business in respect of which the persons in question are subject to the rules of the exchange or clearing house, and which are required or contemplated by its rules or guidance,

or which are otherwise attributable to the conduct of the organisation, exchange or clearing house as such.]

AMENDMENTS
All amendments made by the Companies Act 1989, ss 206, 212, Sch 23, Pt I, para 14, Sch 24, as from 15 March 1990.

120. Modification of s 119 where recognition function is transferred

(1) This section applies instead of section 119 above where the function of making or revoking a recognition order in respect of a self-regulating organisation, investment exchange or clearing house is exercisable by a designated agency.

(2) The designated agency—

(*a*) shall send to the Secretary of State a copy of the rules and of any guidance or arrangements of which copies or particulars are furnished with any application made to the agency for a recognition order together with any other information supplied with or in connection with the application; and
(*b*) shall not make the recognition order without the leave of the Secretary of State;

and he shall not give leave in any case in which he would (apart from the delegation order) have been precluded by section 119(1) above from making the recognition order.

(3) A designated agency shall send the Secretary of State a copy of any notice
received by it under section 14(6) or 41(5) or (6) above.

(4) If at any time it appears to the Secretary of State in the case of a recognised self-regulating organisation, recognised investment exchange or recognised
clearing house that there are circumstances such that (apart from the delegation
order) he would have been able to exercise any of the powers conferred by subsection (3) of section 119 above he may, notwithstanding the delegation order,
himself exercise the power conferred by paragraph (*a*) of that subsection or direct
the designated agency to exercise the power conferred by paragraph (*b*) or (*c*)
of that subsection in such manner as he may specify.   [261]

121. Designated agencies

(1) The Secretary of State shall not make a delegation order transferring any
function to a designated agency unless he is satisfied that any [statements of
principle, rules, regulations, codes of practice] and guidance of which copies
are furnished to him under section 114(9) or (10) above do not have, and are
not intended or likely to have, to any significant extent the effect of restricting,
distorting or preventing competition or, if they have or are intended or likely
to have that effect to any significant extent, that the effect is not greater than
is necessary for the protection of investors.

(2) The powers conferred by subsection (3) below shall be exercisable by the
Secretary of State if at any time it appears to him that —

  (*a*) any [statements of principle, rules, regulations, or codes of practice
       issued or made] by a designated agency in the exercise of functions trans-
       ferred to it by a delegation order or any guidance issued by a designated
       agency;
  (*b*) any practices of a designated agency; or
  (*c*) any practices of persons who are subject to [statements of principle,
       rules, regulations, or codes of practice issued or made] made by it in
       the exercise of those functions,

have, or are intended or are likely to have, to any significant extent the effect
of restricting, distorting or preventing competition and that that effect is greater
than is necessary for the protection of investors.

(3) The powers exercisable under this subsection are —

  (*a*) to make an order in respect of the agency under section 115(2) above
       as if the circumstances were such as are there mentioned; or
  (*b*) to direct the agency to take specified steps for the purpose of securing
       that the [statements of principle, rules, regulations, codes of practice]
       guidance or practices in question do not have the effect mentioned in
       subsection (2) above.

(4) The practices referred to in paragraph (*b*) of subsection (2) above are
practices of the designated agency in its capacity as such; and the practices referred

to in paragraph (c) of that subsection are practices in relation to business in respect of which the persons in question are subject to any such [statements of principle, rules, regulations, or codes of practice] as are mentioned in paragraph (a) of that subsection and which are required or contemplated by those [statements of principle,rules, regulations or codes of practice] or by any such guidance as is there mentioned or are otherwise attributable to the conduct of the agency in its capacity as such. **[262]**

AMENDMENTS
All amendments made by the Companies Act 1989, s 206, Sch 23, Pt I, para 15, as from 15 March 1990.

Consultation with Director General of Fair Trading

122. Report by Director General of Fair Trading

(1) The Secretary of State shall before deciding —

    (a) whether to refuse to make, or to refuse leave for the making of, a recognition order in pursuance of section 119(1) or 120(2) above; or

    (b) whether he is precluded by section 121(1) above from making a delegation order,

send to the Director General of Fair Trading (in this Chapter referred to as "the Director") a copy of the rules [statements of principle, regulations and codes of practice] and of any guidance or arrangements which the Secretary of State is required to consider in making that decision together with such other information as the Secretary of State considers will assist the Director in discharging his functions under subsection (2) below.

(2) The Director shall report to the Secretary of State whether, in his opinion, the rules, [statements of principle, regulations, codes of practice,] guidance or arrangements of which copies are sent to him under subsection (1) above have, or are intended or likely to have, to any significant extent the effect of restricting, distorting, or preventing competition and, if so, what that effect is likely to be; and in making any such decision as is mentioned in that subsection the Secretary of State shall have regard to the Director's report.

(3) The Secretary of State shall send the Director copies of any notice received by him under section 14(6), 41(5) or (6) or 120(3) above or under paragraph 4 of Schedule 9 to this Act together with such other information as the Secretary of State considers will assist the Director in discharging his functions under subsections (4) and (5) below.

(4) The Director shall keep under review —

    (a) the [rules, statements of principle, regulations, codes of practice, guidance and arrangements] mentioned in sections 119(2) and 121(2) above; and

    (b) the matters specified in the notices of which copies are sent to him under subsection (3) above;

and if at any time he is of the opinion that any such [rules, statements of principle, regulations, codes of practice, guidance, arrangements] or matters, or any such [rules, statements of principle, regulations, codes of practice, guidance or arrangements] taken together with any such matters, have, or are intended or likely to have, to any significant extent the effect mentioned in subsection (2) above, he shall make a report to the Secretary of State stating his opinion and what that effect is or is likely to be.

(5) The Director may report to the Secretary of State his opinion that any such matter as is mentioned in subsection (4)(*b*) above does not in his opinion have, and is not intended or likely to have, to any significant extent the effect mentioned in subsection (2) above.

(6) The Director may from time to time consider whether any such practices as are mentioned in section 119(2) or 121(2) above have, or are intended or likely to have, to any significant extent the effect mentioned in subsection (2) above and, if so, what that effect is or is likely to be; and if he is of that opinion he shall make a report to the Secretary of State stating his opinion and what the effect is or is likely to be.

(7) The Secretary of State shall not exercise his powers under section 119(3), 120(4) or 121(3) above except after receiving and considering a report from the Director under subsection (4) or (6) above.

(8) The Director may, if he thinks fit, publish any report made by him under this section but shall exclude from a published report, so far as practicable, any matter which relates to the affairs of a particular person (other than the self-regulating organisation, investment exchange, clearing house or designated agency concerned) the publication of which would or might in his opinion seriously and prejudicially affect the interests of that person.   **[263]**

AMENDMENTS
    All amendments made by the Companies Act 1989, s 206, Sch 23, Pt I, para 16, as from 15 March 1990.

123. Investigations by Director General of Fair Trading

(1) For the purpose of investigating any matter with a view to its consideration under section 122 above the Director may by a notice in writing—

  (*a*) require any person to produce, at a time and place specified in the notice, to the Director or to any person appointed by him for the purpose, any documents which are specified or described in the notice and which are documents in his custody or under his control and relating to any matter relevant to the investigation; or

  (*b*) require any person carrying on any business to furnish to the Director such information as may be specified or described in the notice, and specify the time within which, and the manner and form in which, any such information is to be furnished.

(2) A person shall not under this section be required to produce any document or disclose any information which he would be entitled to refuse to produce or disclose on grounds of legal professional privilege in proceedings in the

High Court or on grounds of confidentiality as between client and professional legal adviser in proceedings in the Court of Session.

(3) Subsections [(16)][1] to (8) of section 85 of the Fair Trading Act 1973 (enforcement provisions) shall apply in relation to a notice under this section as they apply in relation to a notice under subsection (1) of that section [but as if, in subsection (7) of that section, for the words from "any one" to "the Commission" there were substituted "the Director"].[1]   **[264]**

AMENDMENTS
All amendments made by the Companies Act 1989, s 153, Sch 20, para 26, as from 1 April 1990.

Consequential exemptions from competition law

124. The Fair Trading Act 1973

(1) For the purpose of determining whether a monopoly situation within the meaning of the Fair Trading Act 1973 exists by reason of the circumstances mentioned in section 7(1)(c) of that Act, no account shall be taken of—

    (a) the rules made or guidance issued by a recognised self-regulating organisation, recognised investment exchange or recognised clearing house or any conduct constituting such a practice as is mentioned in section 119(2) above;

    (b) any clearing arrangements or any conduct required or contemplated by any such arrangements; or

    (c) the [statement of principle, rules, regulations, codes of practice or guidance issued or made] by a designated agency in the exercise of functions transferred to it by a delegation order or any conduct constituting such a practice as is mentioned in section 121(2) above.

(2) Where a recognition order is revoked there shall be disregarded for the purpose mentioned in subsection (1) above any such conduct as is mentioned in that subsection which occurred while the order was in force.

(3) Where on a monopoly reference under section 50 or 51 of the said Act of 1973 falling within section 49 of that Act the Monopolies and Mergers Commission find that a monopoly situation within the meaning of that Act exists and—

    (a) that the person (or, if more than one, any of the persons) in whose favour it exists is subject to the rules of a recognised self-regulating organisation, recognised investment exchange or recognised clearing house or to the [statements of principle, rules, regulations or codes of practice issued or made] by a designated agency in the exercise of functions transferred to it by a delegation order; or

    (b) that any such person's conduct in carrying on any business to which those [statements of principle, rules, regulations or codes of practice] relate is the subject of guidance issued by such an organisation, exchange, clearing house or agency; or

    (c) that any such person is a party to any clearing arrangements; or (*d*) that the person (or, if more than one, any of the persons) in whose favour the monopoly situation exists is such an organisation, exchange or clearing house as is mentioned in paragraph (*a*) above or a designated agency,

the Commission, in making their report on that reference, shall exclude from their consideration the question whether the [statements of principle, rules, regulations, codes of practice] guidance or clearing arrangements or any acts or omissions of such an organisation, exchange, clearing house or agency as is mentioned in paragraph (*d*) above in its capacity as such operate, or may be expected to operate, against the public interest; and section 54(3) of that Act shall have effect subject to the provisions of this subsection.   **[265]**

AMENDMENTS

All amendments made by the Companies Act 1989, s 206, Sch 23, Pt I, para 17, as from 15 March 1990.

125. The Restrictive Trade Practices Act 1976

(1) The Restrictive Trade Practices Act 1976 shall not apply to any agreement for the constitution of a recognised self-regulating organisation, recognised investment exchange or recognised clearing house, including any term deemed to be contained in it by virtue of section 8(2) or 16(3) of that Act.

(2) The said Act of 1976 shall not apply to any agreement the parties to which consist of or include —

(*a*) any such organisation, exchange or clearing house as is mentioned in subsection (1) above; or

(*b*) a person who is subject to the rules of any such organisation, exchange or clearing house or to the rules or regulations made by a designated agency in the exercise of functions transferred to it by a delegation order,

by reason of any term the inclusion of which in the agreement is required or contemplated by the rules, regulations or guidance of that organisation, exchange, clearing house or agency.

(3) The said Act of 1976 shall not apply to any clearing arrangements or to any agreement between a recognised investment exchange and a recognised clearing house by reason of any term the inclusion of which in the agreement is required or contemplated by any clearing arrangements.

(4) Where the recognition order in respect of a self-regulating organisation, investment exchange or clearing house is revoked the foregoing provisions shall have effect as if the organisation, exchange or clearing house had continued to be recognised until the end of the period of six months beginning with the day on which the revocation takes effect.

(5) Where an agreement ceases by virtue of this section to be subject to registration —

(*a*) the Director shall remove from the register maintained by him under the said Act of 1976 any particulars which are entered or filed in that register in respect of the agreement; and (*b*) any proceedings in respect of the agreement which are pending before the Restrictive Practices Court shall be discontinued.

(6) Where an agreement which has been exempt from registration by virtue of this section ceases to be exempt in consequence of the revocation of a recognition order, the time within which particulars of the agreement are to be furnished in accordance with section 24 of and Schedule 2 to the said Act of 1976 shall be the period of one month beginning with the day on which the agreement ceased to be exempt from registration.

(7) Where in the case of an agreement registered under the said Act of 1976 a term ceases to fall within subsection (2) or (3) above in consequence of the revocation of a recognition order and particulars of that term have not previously been furnished to the Director under section 24 of that Act, those particulars shall be furnished to him within the period of one month beginning with the day on which the term ceased to fall within that subsection.

(8) The Restrictive Trade Practices (Stock Exchange) Act 1984 shall cease to have effect. **[266]**

126. The Competition Act 1980

(1) No course of conduct constituting any such practice as is mentioned in section 119(2) or 121(2) above shall constitute an anti-competitive practice for the purposes of the Competition Act 1980.

(2) Where a recognition order or delegation order is revoked, there shall not be treated as an anti-competitive practice for the purposes of that Act any such course of conduct as is mentioned in subsection (1) above which occurred while the order was in force. **[267]**

Recognised professional bodies

127. Modification of Restrictive Trade Practices Act 1976 in relation to recognised professional bodies

(1) This section applies to—

(*a*) any agreement for the constitution of a recognised professional body, including any term deemed to be contained in it by virtue of section 16(3) of the Restrictive Trade Practices Act 1976; and

(*b*) any other agreement—

(i) the parties to which consist of or include such a body, a person certified by such a body or a member of such a body; and

(ii) to which that Act applies by virtue of any term the inclusion of which in the agreement is required or contemplated by rules or guidance of that body relating to the carrying on of investment business by persons certified by it.

(2) If it appears to the Secretary of State that the restrictions in an agreement to which this section applies—

(*a*) do not have, and are not intended or likely to have, to any significant extent the effect of restricting, distorting or preventing competition; or

(*b*) if all or any of them have, or are intended or likely to have, that effect to any significant extent, that the effect is not greater than is necessary for the protection of investors,

he may give a direction to the Director requiring him not to make an application to the Restrictive Practices Court under Part I of the said Act of 1976 in respect of the agreement.

(3) If it appears to the Secretary of State that one or more (but not all) of the restrictions in an agreement to which this section applies —

(*a*) do not have, and are not intended or likely to have, to any significant extent the effect mentioned in subsection (2) above; or

(*b*) if they have, or are intended or likely to have, that effect to any significant extent that the effect is not greater than is necessary for the protection of investors,

he may make a declaration to that effect and give notice of it to the Director and the Restrictive Practices Court.

(4) The Restrictive Practices Court shall not in any proceedings begun by an application made after notice has been given to it of a declaration under this section make any finding or exercise any power under Part I of the said Act of 1976 in relation to a restriction in respect of which the declaration has effect.

(5) The Director shall not make any application to the Restrictive Practices Court under Part I of the said Act of 1976 in respect of any agreement to which this section applies unless —

(*a*) he has notified the Secretary of State of his intention to do so; and

(*b*) the Secretary of State has either notified him that he does not intend to give a direction or make a declaration under this section or has given him notice of a declaration in respect of it;

and where the Director proposes to make any such application he shall furnish the Secretary of State with particulars of the agreement and the restrictions by virtue of which the said Act of 1976 applies to it and such other information as he considers will assist the Secretary of State in deciding whether to exercise his powers under this section or as the Secretary of State may request.

(6) The Secretary of State may —

(*a*) revoke a direction or declaration under this section;

(*b*) vary any such declaration; or

(*c*) give a direction or make a declaration notwithstanding a previous notification to the Director that he did not intend to give a direction or make a declaration,

if he is satisfied that there has been a material change of circumstances such that the grounds for the direction or declaration have ceased to exist, that there are grounds for a different declaration or that there are grounds for giving a direction or making a declaration, as the case may be.

(7) The Secretary of State shall give notice to the Director of the revocation of a direction and to the Director and the Restrictive Practices Court of the revocation or variation of a declaration; and no such variation shall have effect so as to restrict the powers of the Court in any proceedings begun by an application already made by the Director.

(8) A direction or declaration under this section shall cease to have effect if the agreement in question ceases to be one to which this section applies.

(9) This section applies to information provisions as it applies to restrictions.
[268]

Supplemental

128. Supplementary provisions

(1) Before the Secretary of State exercises a power under section 119(3)(*b*) or (*c*) above, his power to refuse leave under section 120(2) above or his power to give a direction under section 120(4) above in respect of a self-regulating organisation, investment exchange or clearing house, or his power under section 121(3)(*b*) above in respect of a designated agency, he shall—

    (*a*) give written notice of his intention to do so to the organisation, exchange, clearing house or agency and take such steps (whether by publication or otherwise) as he thinks appropriate for bringing the notice to the attention of any other person who in his opinion is likely to be affected by the exercise of the power; and

    (*b*) have regard to any representation made within such time as he considers reasonable by the organisation, exchange, clearing house or agency or by any such other person.

(2) A notice under subsection (1) above shall give particulars of the manner in which the Secretary of State proposes to exercise the power in question and state the reasons for which he proposes to act; and the statement of reasons may include matters contained in any report received by him under section 122 above.

(3) Any direction given under this Chapter shall, on the application of the person by whom it was given, be enforceable by mandamus or, in Scotland, by an order for specific performance under section 91 of the Court of Session Act 1868.

(4) The fact that any rules or regulations made by a recognised self-regulating organisation, investment exchange or clearing house or by a designated agency have been altered by or pursuant to a direction given by the Secretary of State under this Chapter shall not preclude their subsequent alteration or revocation by that organisation, exchange, clearing house or agency.

(5) In determining under this Chapter whether any guidance has, or is likely to have, any particular effect the Secretary of State and the Director may assume that the persons to whom it is addressed will act in conformity with it. **[269]**

COMPANIES ACT 1989
(1989 c40)

An Act to amend the law relating to company accounts; to make new provision with respect to the persons eligible for appointment as company auditors; to amend the Companies Act 1985 and certain other enactments with respect to investigations and powers to obtain information and to confer new powers exercisable to assist overseas regulatory authorities; to make new provision with respect to the registration of company charges and otherwise to amend the law relating to companies; to amend the Fair Trading Act 1973; to enable provision to be made for the payment of fees in connection with the exercise by the Secretary of State, the Director General of Fair Trading and the Monopolies and Mergers Commission of their functions under Part V of that Act; to make provision for safeguarding the operation of certain financial markets; to amend the Financial Services Act 1986; to enable provision to be made for the recording and transfer of title to securities without a written instrument; to amend the Company Directors Disqualification Act 1986, the Company Securities (Insider Dealing) Act 1985, the Policyholders Protection Act 1975 and the law relating to building societies; and for connected purposes   [16 November 1989]

46. Delegation of functions of Secretary of State

(1) The Secretary of State may by order (a "delegation order") establish a body corporate to exercise his functions under this Part.

(2) A delegation order has the effect of transferring to the body established by it, subject to such exceptions and reservations as may be specified in the order, all the functions of the Secretary of State under this Part except—

(*a*) such functions under Part I of Schedule 14 (prevention of restrictive practices) as are excepted by regulations under section 47, and

(*b*) his functions in relation to the body itself;

and the order may also confer on the body such other functions supplementary or incidental to those transferred as appear to the Secretary of State to be appropriate.

(3) Any transfer of the functions under the following provisions shall be subject to the reservation that they remain exercisable concurrently by the Secretary of State —

(*a*) section 38 (power to call for information), and

(*b*) section 40 (directions to comply with international obligations);

and any transfer of the function of refusing to approve an overseas qualification, or withdrawing such approval, on the grounds referred to in section 33(3) (lack of reciprocity) shall be subject to the reservation that the function is exercisable only with the consent of the Secretary of State.

(4) A delegation order may be amended or, if it appears to the Secretary of State that it is no longer in the public interest that the order should remain in force, revoked by a further order under this section.

(5) Where functions are transferred or resumed, the Secretary of State may by order confer or, as the case may be, take away such other functions supplementary or incidental to those transferred or resumed as appear to him to be appropriate.

(6) The provisions of Schedule 13 have effect with respect to the status, constitution and proceedings of a body established by a delegation order, the exercise by it of certain functions transferred to it and other supplementary matters.

(7) An order under this section shall be made by statutory instrument.

(8) An order which has the effect of transferring or resuming any functions shall not be made unless a draft of it has been laid before and approved by resolution of each House of Parliament; and any other description of order shall be subject to annulment in pursuance of a resolution of either House of Parliament.

[270]

_____

NOTE

Commencement: Not in force at time of going to press.

47. Restrictive practices

(1) The provisions of Schedule 14 have effect with respect to certain matters relating to restrictive practices and competition law.

(2) The Secretary of State may make provision by regulations as to the discharge of the functions under paragraphs 1 to 7 of that Schedule when a delegation order is in force.

(3) The regulations may —

(*a*) except any function from the effect of the delegation order,

(*b*) modify any of the provisions mentioned in subsection (2), and

(c) impose such duties on the body established by the delegation order, the Secretary of State and Director General of Fair Trading as appear to the Secretary of State to be appropriate.

(4) The regulations shall contain such provision as appears to the Secretary of State to be necessary or expedient for reserving to him the decision—

(a) to refuse recognition on the ground mentioned in paragraph 1(3) of that Schedule, or

(b) to exercise the powers conferred by paragraph 6 of that Schedule.

(5) For that purpose the regulations may—

(a) prohibit the body from granting a recognition order without the leave of the Secretary of State, and

(b) empower the Secretary of State to direct the body to exercise its powers in such manner as may be specified in the direction.

(6) Regulations under this section shall be made by statutory instrument which shall be subject to annulment in pursuance of a resolution of either House of Parliament. **[271]**

NOTE
Commencement: Sub-s (1) in force 1 March 1990 (SI 1990 No 142). Remainder not in force at time of going to press.

48. Exemption from liability for damages

(1) Neither a recognised supervisory body, nor any of its officers or employees or members of its governing body, shall be liable in damages for anything done or omitted in the discharge or purported discharge of functions to which this subsection applies, unless the act or omission is shown to have been in bad faith.

(2) Subsection (1) applies to the functions of the body so far as relating to, or to matters arising out of—

(a) such rules, practices, powers and arrangements of the body to which the requirements of Part II of Schedule 11 apply, or

(b) the obligations with which paragraph 16 of that Schedule requires the body to comply

(c) any guidance issued by the body, or

(d) the obligations to which the body is subject by virtue of this Part.

(3) Neither a body established by a delegation order, nor any of its members, officers or employees, shall be liable in damages for anything done or omitted in the discharge or purported discharge of the functions exercisable by virtue of an order under section 46, unless the act or omission is shown to have been in bad faith. **[272]**

NOTE
Commencement: Sub-ss (1),(2) in force 1 March 1990 (SI 1990 No 142). Sub-s (3) not in force at time of going to press.

49. Service of notices

(1) This section has effect in relation to any notice, direction or other document

required or authorised by or under this Part to be given to or served on any person other than the Secretary of State.

(2) Any such document may be given to or served on the person in question —

(a) by delivering it to him,
(b) by leaving it at his proper address, or
(c) by sending it by post to him at that address.

(3) Any such document may —

(a) in the case of a body corporate, be given to or served on the secretary or clerk of that body;
(b) in the case of a partnership, be given to or served on any partner;
(c) in the case of an unincorporated association other than a partnership, be given to or served on any member of the governing body of the association.

(4) For the purposes of this section and section 7 of the Interpretation Act 1978 (service of documents by post) in its application to this section, the proper address of any person is his last known address (whether of his residence or of a place where he carries on business or is employed) and also —

(a) in the case of a person who is eligible under the rules of a recognised supervisory body for appointment as company auditor and who does not have a place of business in the United Kingdom, the address of that body;
(b) in the case of a body corporate, its secretary or its clerk, the address of its registered or principal office in the United Kingdom;
(c) in the case of an unincorporated association (other than a partnership) or a member of its governing body, its principal office in the United Kingdom. **[273]**

NOTE
Commencement: 1 March 1990 for the purposes of ss 47(1), 48(1), (2), and Sch 14 of the Act (SI 1990 No 142). Not in force at time of going to press otherwise.

50. Fees

(1) The Secretary of State may by regulations made by statutory instrument require the payment to him or to the Director of such fees as may be prescribed by the regulations in connection with the exercise by the Secretary of State, the Director and the Commission of their functions under Part V of the Fair Trading Act 1973.

(2) The regulations may provide for fees to be payable —

(a) in respect of —

(i) an application for the consent of the Secretary of State under section 58(1) of the Fair Trading Act 1973 to the transfer of a newspaper or of newspaper assets, and
(ii) a notice under section 75A(1) of that Act, and

(b) on the occurrence of any event specified in the regulations.

(3) The events that may be specified in the regulations by virtue of subsection (2)(*b*) above include —

(*a*) the making by the Secretary of State of a merger reference to the Commission under section 64 or 75 of the Fair Trading Act 1973;

(*b*) the announcement by the Secretary of State of his decision not to make a merger reference in any case where, at the time the accouncement is made, he would under one of those sections have power to make such a reference.

(4) The regulations may also contain provision —

(*a*) for ascertaining the persons by whom fees are payable,

(*b*) specifying whether any fee is payable to the Secretary of State or to the Director,

(*c*) for the amount of any fee to be calculated by reference to matters which may include —

(i) in a case involving functions of the Secretary of State under sections 57 to 61 of the Fair Trading Act 1973, the number of newspapers concerned, the number of separate editions (determined in accordance with the regulations) of each newspaper and the average circulation per day of publication (within the meaning of Part V of that Act) of each newspaper, and

(ii) in any other case, the value (determined in accordance with the regulations) of any assets concerned,

(*d*) as to the time when any fee is to be paid, and

(*e*) for the repayment by the Secretary of State or the Director of the whole or part of any fee in specified circumstances.

(5) The regulations may make different provision for different cases.

(6) Subsections (2) to (5) above do not prejudice the generality of subsection (1) above.

(7) In determining the amount of any fees to be prescribed by the regulations, the Secretary of State may take into account all costs incurred by him and by the Director in respect of the exercise by him, by the Commission and by the Director of their respective functions —

(*a*) under Part V of the Fair Trading Act 1973, and

(*b*) under Parts I, VII and VIII of that Act in relation to merger references or other matters arising under Part V.

(8) A statutory instrument containing regulations under this section shall be subject to annulment in pursuance of a resolution of either House of Parliament.

(9) Fees paid to the Secretary of State or the Director under this section shall be paid into the Consolidated Fund.

(10) In this section —
"the Commission",
"the Director", and
"merger reference",

have the same meaning as in the Fair Trading Act 1973, and "newspaper" has the same meaning as in Part V of that Act.

(11) References in this section to Part V of the Fair Trading Act 1973 and to merger references under section 64 or 75 of that Act or under that Part include sections 29 and 30 of the Water Act 1989 and any reference under section 29 of that Act. **[274]**

NOTE
Commencement: 1 March 1990 (SI 1990 No 142).

REGULATIONS UNDER THIS SECTION.
At the time of going to press no regulations had been made under this section.

SCHEDULE 14
Section 47(1)
SUPERVISORY AND QUALIFYING BODIES: RESTRICTIVE PRACTICES

PART I
PREVENTION OF RESTRICTIVE PRACTICES

Refusal of recognition on grounds related to competition

1. – (1) The Secretary of State shall before deciding whether to make a recognition order in respect of a supervisory body or professional qualification send to the Director General of Fair Trading (in this Schedule referred to as "the Director") a copy of the rules and of any guidance which the Secretary of State is required to consider in making that decision together with such other information as the Secretary of State considers will assist the Director.

(2) The Director shall consider whether the rules or guidance have, or are intended or likely to have, to any significant extent the effect of restricting, distorting or preventing competition, and shall report to the Secretary of State; and the Secretary of State shall have regard to his report in deciding whether to make a recognition order.

(3) The Secretary of State shall not make a recognition order if it appears to him that the rules and any guidance of which copies are furnished with the application have, or are intended or likely to have, to any significant extent the effect of restricting, distorting or preventing competition, unless it appears to him that the effect is reasonably justifiable having regard to the purposes of this Part of this Act.

Notification of changes to rules or guidance

2. – (1) Where a recognised supervisory or qualifying body amends, revokes or adds to its rules or guidance in a manner which may reasonably be regarded as likely –

(a) to restrict, distort or prevent competition to any significant extent, or
(b) otherwise to affect the question whether the recognition order granted to the body should continue in force,

it shall within seven days give the Secretary of State written notice of the amendment, revocation or addition.

(2) Notice need not be given under sub-paragraph (1) of the revocation of guidance not intended to have continuing effect or issued otherwise than in writing or other legible form, or of any amendment or addition to guidance which does not result in or consist of guidance which is intended to have continuing effect and is issued in writing or other legible form.

Continuing scrutiny by the Director General of Fair Trading

3. – (1) The Director shall keep under review the rules made or guidance issued by a recognised supervisory or qualifying body, and if he is of the opinion that any rules or guidance of such a body have, or are intended or likely to have, to any significant extent the effect of restricting, distorting or preventing competition, he shall report his opinion to the Secretary of State, stating what in his opinion the effect is or is likely to be.

(2) The Secretary of State shall send to the Director copies of any notice received by him under paragraph 2, together with such other information as he considers will assist the Director.

(3) The Director may report to the Secretary of State his opinion that any matter mentioned in such a notice does not have, and is not intended or likely to have, to any significant extent the effect of restricting, distorting or preventing competition.

(4) The Director may from time to time consider whether –

    (*a*) any practices of a recognised supervisory or qualifying body in its capacity as such, or

    (*b*) any relevant practices required or contemplated by the rules or guidance of such a body or otherwise attributable to its conduct in its capacity as such,

have, or are intended or likely to have, to any significant extent the effect of restricting, distorting or preventing competition and, if so, what that effect is or is likely to be; and if he is of that opinion he shall make a report to the Secretary of State stating his opinion and what the effect is or is likely to be.

(5) The practices relevant for the purposes of sub-paragraph (4)(*b*) in the case of a recognised supervisory body are practices engaged in for the purposes of, or in connection with, appointment as a company auditor or the conduct of company audit work by persons who –

    (*a*) are eligible under its rules for appointment as a company auditor, or

    (*b*) hold an appropriate qualification and are directors or other officers of bodies corporate which are so eligible or partners in, or employees of, partnerships which are so eligible.

(6) The practices relevant for the purposes of sub-paragraph (4)(*b*) in the case of a recognised qualifying body are –

    (*a*) practices engaged in by persons in the course of seeking to obtain a recognised professional qualification from that body, and

    (*b*) practices engaged in by persons approved by the body for the purposes of giving practical training to persons seeking such a qualification and which relate to such training.

Investigatory powers of the Director

4. – (1) The following powers are exercisable by the Director for the purpose of investigating any matter in connection with his functions under paragraph 1 or 3.

(2) The Director may by a notice in writing require any person to produce, at a time and place specified in the notice, to the Director or to any person appointed by him for the purpose, any documents which are specified or described in the notice and which are documents in his custody or under his control and relating to any matter relevant to the investigation.

(3) The Director may by a notice in writing require any person to furnish to the Director such information as may be specified or described in the notice, and specify the time within

which and the manner and form in which any such information is to be furnished.

(4) A person shall not under this paragraph be required to produce any document or disclose any information which he would be entitled to refuse to produce or disclose on grounds of legal professional privilege in proceedings in the High Court or on the grounds of confidentiality as between client and professional legal adviser in proceedings in the Court of Session.

(5) Subsections (6) to (8) of section 85 of the Fair Trading Act 1973 (enforcement provisions) apply in relation to a notice under this paragraph as they apply in relation to a notice under subsection (1) of that section but as if, in subsection (7) of that section, for the words from "any one" to "the Commission" there were substituted "the Director".

Publication of Director's reports

5.—(1) The Director may, if he thinks fit, publish any report made by him under paragraph 1 or 3.

(2) He shall exclude from a published report, so far as practicable, any matter which relates to the affairs of a particular person (other than the supervisory or qualifying body concerned) the publication of which would or might in his opinion seriously and prejudicially affect the interests of that person.

Powers exercisable by the Secretary of State in consequence of report.

6.—(1) The powers conferred by this section are exercisable by the Secretary of State if, having received and considered a report from the Director under paragraph 3(1) or (4), it appears to him that—

(a) any rules made or guidance issued by a recognised supervisory or qualifying body, or

(b) any such practices as are mentioned in paragraph 3(4).

have, or are intended or likely to have, to any significant extent the effect of restricting, distorting or preventing competition and that that effect is greater than is reasonably justifiable having regard to the purposes of this Part of this Act.

(2) The powers are—

(a) to revoke the recognition order granted to the body concerned,

(b) to direct it to take specified steps for the purpose of securing that the rules, guidance or practices in question do not have the effect mentioned in sub-paragraph (1), and

(c) to make alterations in the rules of the body for that purpose.

(3) The provisions of paragraph 3(2) to (5), (7) and (9) of Schedule 11 or, as the case may be, Schedule 12 have effect in relation to the revocation of a recognition order under sub-paragraph (2)(a) above as they have effect in relation to the revocation of such an order under that Schedule.

(4) Before the Secretary of State exercises the power conferred by sub-paragraph (2)(b) or (c) above he shall—

(a) give written notice of his intention to do so to the body concerned and take such steps (whether by publication or otherwise) as he thinks appropriate for bringing the notice to the attention of any other person who in his opinion is likely to be affected by the exercise of the power, and (*b*)   have regard to any representation made within such time as he considers reasonable by the body or any such other person.

(5)   A notice under sub-paragraph (4) shall give particulars of the manner in which the Secretary of State proposes to exercise the power in question and state the reasons for which he proposes to act; and the statement of reasons may include matters contained in any report received by him under paragraph 4.

Supplementary provisions

7. – (1)   A direction under paragraph 6 is, on the application of the Secretary of State, enforceable by injunction or, in Scotland, by an order under section 45 of the Court of Session Act 1988.

(2)   The fact that any rules made by a recognised supervisory or qualifying body have been altered by the Secretary of State, or pursuant to a direction of the Secretary of State, under paragraph 6 does not preclude their subsequent alteration or revocation by that body.

(3)   In determining for the purposes of this Part of this Schedule whether any guidance has, or is likely to have, any particular effect the Secretary of State and the Director may assume that the persons to whom it is addressed will act in conformity with it.   **[275]**

NOTE
   Commencement: 1 March 1990 (SI 1990 No 142).

PART II
CONSEQUENTIAL EXEMTIONS FROM COMPETITION LAW
Fair Trading Act 1973 (c 41)

8. – (1)   For the purpose of determining whether a monopoly situation within the meaning of the Fair Trading Act 1973 exists by reason of the circumstances mentioned in section 7(1)(*c*) of that Act (supply of services by or for group of two or more persons), no account shall be taken of –

   (*a*)   the rules of or guidance issued by a recognised supervisory or qualifying body, or
   (*b*)   conduct constituting such a practice as is mentioned in paragraph 3(4) above.

(2)   Where a recognition order is revoked there shall be disregarded for the purpose mentioned in sub-paragraph (1) any such conduct as is mentioned in that sub-paragraph which occurred while the order was in force.

(3)   Where on a monopoly reference under section 50 or 51 of the Fair Trading Act 1973 falling within section 49 of that Act (monopoly reference not limited to the facts) the Monopolies and Mergers Commission find that a monopoly situation within the meaning of that Act exists and –

   (*a*)   that the person (or, if more than one, any of the persons) in whose favour it exists is –

      (i)   a recognised supervisory or qualifying body, or
      (ii)   a person of a description mentioned in paragraph 3(5) or (6) above, or

   (*b*)   that any such person's conduct in doing anything to which the rules of such a body relate is subject to guidance issued by the body,

the Commission in making their report on that reference shall exclude from their consideration the question whether the rules or guidance of the body concerned, or the acts or omissions of that body in its capacity as such, operate or may be expected to operate against the public interest.

Restrictive Trade Practices Act 1976 (c 34)

9. – (1) The Restrictive Trade Practices Act 1976 does not apply to an agreement for the constitution of a recognised supervisory or qualifying body in so far as it relates to rules of or guidance issued by the body, and incidental matters connected therewith, including any term deemed to be contained in it by virtue of section 8(2) or 16(3) of that Act.

(2) Nor does that Act apply to an agreement the parties to which consist of or include –

(*a*) a recognised supervisory or qualifying body, or

(*b*) any such person as is mentioned in paragraph 3(5) or (6) above,

by reason that it includes any terms the inclusion of which is required or contemplated by the rules or guidance of that body.

(3) Where an agreement ceases by virtue of this paragraph to be subject to registration –

(*a*) the Director shall remove from the register maintained by him under the Act of 1976 any particulars which are entered or filed in that register in respect of the agreement, and

(*b*) any proceedings in respect of the agreement which are pending before the Restrictive Practices Court shall be discontinued.

(4) Where a recognition order is revoked, sub-paragraphs (1) and (2) above shall continue to apply for a period of six months beginning with the day on which the revocation takes effect, as if the order were still in force.

(5) Where an agreement which has been exempt from registration by virtue of this paragraph ceases to be exempt in consequence of the revocation of a recognition order, the time within which particulars of the agreement are to be furnished in accordance with section 24 of and Schedule 2 to the Act of 1976 shall be the period of one month beginning with the day on which the agreement ceased to be exempt from registration.

(6) Where in the case of an agreement registered under the 1976 Act a term ceases to fall within sub-paragraph (2) above in consequence of the revocation of a recognition order and particulars of that term have not previously been furnished to the Director under section 24 of that Act, those particulars shall be furnished to him within the period of one month beginning with the day on which the term ceased to fall within that sub-paragraph.

Competition Act 1980 (c 21)

10. – (1) No course of conduct constituting any such practice as is mentioned in paragraph 3(4) above shall constitute an anti-competitive practice for the purposes of the Competition Act 1980.

(2) Where a recognition order is revoked there shall not be treated as an anti-competitive practice for the purposes of that Act any such course of conduct as is mentioned in sub-paragraph (1) which occurred while the order was in force. **[276–499]**

NOTE

Commencement: 1 March 1990 (SI 1990 No 142).

PART I

UK LEGISLATION

B   SELECTED STATUTORY INSTRUMENTS

THE RESTRICTIVE TRADE PRACTICES (INFORMATION AGREEMENTS) ORDER 1969
(SI 1969 No 1842)

1. This Order may be cited as the Restrictive Trade Practices (Information Agreements) Order 1969 and shall come into operation on 1st February 1970.
[500]

2. (1) In this Order "the Act of 1956" and "the Act of 1968" mean, respectively, the Restrictive Trade Practices Act 1956 and the Restrictive Trade Practices Act 1968.

(2) The Interpretation Act 1889 shall apply for the interpretation of this Order as it applies for the interpretation of an Act of Parliament. **[501]**

NOTE
In the context of this order references to the RTPA 1956 and to the RTPA 1968 are to be construed as references to the RTPA 1976, by virtue of para 2 of Sch 4 to that Act.
The Interpretation Act 1889 has been repealed and replaced by the Interpretation Act 1978.

3. (1) It is directed that the provisions of Part I of the Act of 1956 (including sections 7 and 8 thereof) shall apply in relation to the following class of information agreements, that is to say, agreements (other than agreements described in Part I of the Schedule hereto) which relate to any of the matters specified in paragraph (2) of this Article, whether or not they relate to any other matters.

(2) The matters referred to in paragraph (1) are as follows:—

(a) the prices charged or quoted or to be charged or quoted otherwise than to any of the parties to the relevant agreement for goods which have been or are to be supplied or offered or for the application of any process of manufacture to goods;

(b) the terms or conditions on or subject to which goods have been or are to be supplied otherwise than to any such party or any such process has been or is to be applied to goods otherwise than for any such party.
[502]

NOTE
For the meaning of "information agreement" (as to goods), see RTPA 1976, s 7.

[4. (1) In this Article "financing terms" means provisions for any of the following, that is to say—

(a) the making or continuation of a loan;

(b) the granting or continuation of any form of credit or of facilities for credit;

(c) the supply of any property by way of lease or hire (with or without the option to acquire the ownership of the property);

(d) the assumption of any liability in the event of a person's default; and

(e) the granting of any right to resort to any property in the event of a person's default.

(2) Where an agreement contains financing terms the following provisions apply for the purpose of determining whether the agreement is one to which Part I of the Restrictive Trade Practices Act 1956 applies by virtue of this order.

(3) No account shall be taken of any provision for or in relation to the furnishing of information if the sole purpose of the provision is to enable either or both of the following to be assessed —

(*a*) the ability of any person who has incurred or may incur a liability under or in connection with the financing terms to discharge that liability; and

(*b*) the observance by such a person of any terms of the agreement.

(4) If the financing terms relate to the doing of anything outside the United Kingdom by a person who neither resides nor carries on a business within the United Kingdom, no account shall be taken of any provision requiring information to be furnished only —

(*a*) by him; or

(*b*) by one or more other such persons; or

(*c*) by him and one or more other such persons.]¹ **[503]**

AMENDMENT
1 Article 4 was added by the RTPA 1977.

SCHEDULE

Article 3(1)

PART I

AGREEMENTS TO WHICH THE ORDER DOES NOT APPLY

1. An agreement particulars of which would, but for the provisions of this paragraph, be required to be furnished to the Secretary of State by virtue of section 31 (provisions relating to export agreements) of the Act of 1956.

2. An agreement which, in so far as it contains provisions for or in relation to the furnishing of information with respect to the matters mentioned in Article 3(2), contains only provisions of one or more of the following kinds, that is to say, —

(*a*) provision for or in relation to the furnishing of such information by parties to the agreement whereby each such party is to furnish such information separately and directly to a specified authority;

(*b*) provision for or in relation to the furnishing of such information by parties to the agreement whereby each such party is to furnish such information separately and directly to a person who does not carry on such a business as is mentioned in section 6(1) of the Act of 1956 or, where the parties are members of an unincorporated trade association, to a person employed by them solely for the purposes of the association, and under which neither that information nor information based thereon is to be furnished directly or indirectly by that person to any party to the agreement except —

(i) information which does not relate to any party other than the party to whom it is furnished; or

(ii) information which has been furnished to a specified authority at the written request of the authority, and then only in a form that prevents any information being identified, except by the party to whom the information relates, as being information relating to any particular party;

(c) provision for or in relation to the furnishing of such information which at the time it is to be furnished is information which has already been published in such manner that it is readily available to persons who are or may be purchasing goods or who are or may be requiring the application of processes of manufacture to goods, being goods or processes of descriptions to which the information relates; including but without prejudice to the generality of the foregoing, the furnishing of particulars of prices charged for goods at any market or other place at which such goods are regularly offered for sale by a substantial number of sellers;

(d) provision for or in relation to the furnishing of such information by parties to the agreement whereby each such party is to furnish such information separately and directly to a person who does not carry on such a business as is mentioned in section 6(1) of the Act of 1956 or, where the parties are members of an unincorporated trade association, to a person employed by them solely for the purposes of the association, and under which neither that information nor information based thereon is to be furnished directly or indirectly by that person to any party before the information or, as the case may be, the information based thereon has been published in the manner described in head (c) of this paragraph.

3. An agreement —

(a) of which the terms, by virtue of which it is an information agreement to which Part I of the Act of 1956 would but for this paragraph apply by virtue of this Order, are incidental to other terms of the agreement, and

(b) of which those other terms are terms by virtue of which, apart from this Order, the said Part I would apply to the agreement but for the provisions of section 7 or section 8 of the said Part I.

4. (1) An agreement, made before the date on which this Order comes into operation, in respect of which the Minister certifies before that date that it is an agreement in relation to which the provisions of section 45(2) of the Agriculture (Miscellaneous Provisions) Act 1968 would have applied if this Order, apart from this paragraph, had been in force at all relevant times, and that had notice of the proposed terms thereof been served on him he would not have objected to those terms.

(2) An agreement, whenever made, of a kind mentioned in paragraph (a) or paragraph (b) of subsection (5) of the said section 45 and which is made as the result of the making of an agreement, between a board and a trade association, which is excluded from the operation of this Order by virtue of sub-paragraph (1) of this paragraph.

(3) In this paragraph "Minister" and "board" have the meanings respectively assigned to them in subsection (7) of the said section 45.

5. (1) An agreement to which the only parties are bodies carrying on the business of the production and supply of gas under national ownership.

(2) An agreement to which the only parties are bodies carrying on the business of generation and supply of electricity under national ownership.

6. In this Part "specified authority" means any of the bodies mentioned in Part II of this Schedule.   **[504]**

NOTE

Sections 6(1), 7 and 8 of the RTPA 1956 are now replaced by provisions in ss 6(1) and 9 of, and Sch 3 to, the RTPA 1976. Section 31 of the 1956 Act was repealed by the Fair Trading Act 1973.

PART II

NOTE

This Part lists the following bodies referred to in para 6 of Part I of this Schedule: — (1) Any Government Department (including any Department of the Government of Northern Ireland) and any Committee established by any such Department; (2) The National Economic Development Council and any of its Economic Development Committees; (3) The National Board for the Review of Government Contracts (now the Review Board for Government Contracts); (4) The National Board for Prices and Incomes (now defunct); (5) The Industrial Reorganisation Corporation (dissolved; see SI 1971 No 665 (lapsed)); (6) The Monopolies Commission (now called the Monopolies and Mergers Commission); (7) Any local authority as defined in s 66 (repealed) of the Finance Act 1965 (see now s 519 of the Income and Corporation Taxes Act 1988); (8) The White Fish Authority and the Herring Industry Board (the functions of both of which are now exercised by the Sea Fish Industry Authority); (9) The Home-Grown Cereals Authority; (10) The Meat and Livestock Commission; (11) The Northern Ireland Livestock Marketing Commission; (12) The Central Council for Agricultural and Horticultural Co-operation (the functions of which are now exercised by Food from Britain); (13) The National Seed Development Organisation; (14) The Sugar Board (now dissolved); (15) The Shipbuilding Industry Board (now dissolved); (16) The National Research Development Corporation; (17) The Metrication Board; (18) Any development council established under the Industrial Organisation and Development Act 1947; (19) Any Royal Commission; (20) Any consultative council or committee or consumers' council established by Act of Parliament in relation to an industry carried on under national ownership. **[505]**

THE REGISTRATION OF RESTRICTIVE TRADING AGREEMENTS (EEC DOCUMENTS) REGULATIONS 1973
(SI 1973 No 950)

The Registrar of Restrictive Trading Agreements[1] (in these regulations referred to as "the Registrar") in exercise of the powers conferred upon him by sections 11 and 19 of the Restrictive Trade Practices Act 1956[2] (hereinafter referred to as "the Act of 1956") and subsection (2) of section 10 of the European Communities Act 1972 hereby orders that the following regulations shall have effect: —

NOTES

1 The functions of the Registrar were transferred to the Director General of Fair Trading and the former office was abolished as from 1 November 1973 by FTA 1973, s 94.

2 The enabling powers referred to were repealed by the RTPA 1976 but by virtue of para 1 of Sch 4 to that Act these regulations continue to have effect as if made under ss 23 and 27 thereof.

1. (1) These regulations may be cited as the Registration of Restrictive Trading Agreements (EEC Documents) Regulations 1973 and shall come into operation on the 25th June 1973.

(2) The Interpretation Act 1889 shall apply to the interpretation of these regulations as it applies to the interpretation of an Act of Parliament. **[506]**

2. (1) Where in relation to any agreement which is subject to registration under the Act of 1956[1] any such step or any such decision as is specified in paragraph (2) hereof is or has been taken or given under or for the purposes of any directly applicable Community provision affecting that agreement, there shall be delivered or sent to the Registrar by or on behalf of the parties to that agreement the information so specified in respect of that step or decision within 30 days of the taking or giving thereof or within 30 days of the coming into operation of these regulations, whichever is the later.

(2) The steps, decisions and information referred to are the following: —

(*a*) applying for negative clearance for or notifying the agreement to the Commission of the European Communities — a copy of the application or notification submitted to the Commission;

(*b*) notification by the Commission to the parties to the agreement of the opportunity to be heard in relation to objections raised against them — a memorandum to that effect specifying the date of the notification;

(*c*) a decision of the Commission giving negative clearance in respect of the agreement — four copies of such part of the decision as sets out the effects thereof;

(*d*) a decision of the Commission pursuant to article 85(3) of the EEC Treaty given in respect of the agreement — four copies of such part of the decision as sets out the effects thereof;

(*e*) a decision of the Commission finding infringement of article 85 of the EEC Treaty by the agreement — four copies of such part of the decision as sets out the effects thereof;

(*f*) a decision of the European Court relating to any decision of the Commission hereinbefore described — four copies of such part of the decision as sets out the effects thereof.   **[507]**

NOTE

1 "The Act of 1956" must now be construed as referring to the RTPA 1976.

3. The particulars of an agreement subject to registration under the Act of 1956 to be entered or filed in the register shall include a copy of any such part of a decision of the Commission of the European Communities or the European Court affecting that agreement furnished in pursuance of regulation 2 hereof.

                                                              [508]

4. Anything required by these regulations to be delivered or sent to the Registrar shall be addressed to: —

The Registrar of Restrictive Trading Agreements (Branch R)[1]
    Chancery House
        Chancery Lane
            London WC2A 1SP.   **[509]**

NOTE

1 Now the Director General of Fair Trading, whose address is the Office of Fair Trading, Field House, Bream's Buildings, London EC4A 1PR

EXPLANATORY NOTE

(*This Note is not part of the Regulations.*)

Section 10 of the European Communities Act 1972 enables the Registrar to refrain from taking proceedings before the Restrictive Practices Court in respect of an agreement where appropriate having regard to the operation of Community provisions, and by regulations to require information as to any steps taken or decisions given under or for the purpose of a Community provision affecting an agreement.

These Regulations require parties to agreements to inform the Registrar when notifying an agreement to the Commission or seeking negative clearance therefor and when proceedings are instituted and decisions given in respect of an agreement. Decisions are to be entered on the register with other particulars of the agreement and accordingly four copies are required. **[510]**

THE RESTRICTIVE TRADE PRACTICES (SERVICES) ORDER 1976
(SI 1976 No 98)

Whereas a notice has been published by the Secretary of State complying with the terms of section 111(2) of the Fair Trading Act 1973 (hereinafter referred to as "the Act of 1973") and all the representations made with respect thereto have been taken into consideration:

And whereas a draft of this Order has been laid before Parliament and approved by resolution of each House of Parliament:

Now, therefore, the Secretary of State in exercise of powers conferred on her by sections 107 and 110 of the Act of 1973 hereby makes the following Order: —

1. (1) This Order may be cited as the Restrictive Trade Practices (Services) Order 1976 and shall come into operation on 22nd March 1976.

(2) The Interpretation Act 1889 shall apply for the interpretation of this Order as it applies for the interpretation of an Act of Parliament. **[511]**

2. (1) The services brought under control by this Order are all services without exception.

(2) The services described in this Order as designated services are all services except those described in Schedule 4 to the Act of 1973. **[512]**

3. (1) It is directed that, subject to the provisions of Part X of the Act of 1973, the agreements to which Part I of the Restrictive Trade Practices Act 1956 applies shall include agreements (whether made before or after the passing of the Act of 1973 and whether before or after the making of this Order) which —

(a) are agreements between two or more persons carrying on business within the United Kingdom in the supply of services brought under control by this Order, or between two or more such persons together with one or more other parties, and

(b) are agreements under which restrictions, in respect of the matters specified in paragraph (2) below for the purposes of section 107(1)(b) of the Act of 1973, are accepted by two or more parties, and

(c) are not agreements described in the Schedule hereto.

(2) The matters specified for the purposes of the said section 107(1)(*b*) are the following, that is to say —

   (*a*) the charges to be made, quoted or paid for designated services supplied, offered or obtained;

   (*b*) the terms or conditions on or subject to which designated services are to be supplied or obtained;

   (*c*) the extent (if any) to which, or the scale (if any) on which, designated services are to be made available, supplied or obtained;

   (*d*) the form or manner in which designated services are to be made available, supplied or obtained;

   (*e*) the persons or classes of persons for whom or from whom, or the areas or places in or from which, designated services are to be made available or supplied or are to be obtained.   **[513]**

[**4.** (1) In this Article "financing terms" means provisions for any of the following, that is to say: —

   (*a*) the making or continuation of a loan;

   (*b*) the granting or continuation of any form of credit or of facilities for credit;

   (*c*) the supply of any property by way of lease or hire (with or without the option to acquire the ownership of the property);

   (*d*) the assumption of any liability in the event of a person's default; and

   (*e*) the granting of any right to resort to any property in the event of a person's default.

(2) Where an agreement contains financing terms the following provisions apply for the purpose of determining whether the agreement is one to which Part I of the Restrictive Trade Practices Act 1956 applies by virtue of this order.

(3) No account shall be taken of any restriction the sole purpose of which is either or both of the following: —

   (*a*) to maintain a person's ability to discharge any liability incurred by him under or in connection with the financing terms; and

   (*b*) to protect a person against the consequences of another person's default in discharging such a liability.

(4) If the financing terms relate to the doing of anything outside the United Kingdom by a person who neither resides nor carries on a business within the United Kingdom, no account shall be taken of any restriction which is accepted only: —

   (*a*) by him; or

   (*b*) by one or more other such persons; or

   (*c*) by him and one or more other such persons.][1]   **[514]**

AMENDMENT
1 Article 4 inserted by RTPA 1977, s 1(3) with retrospective effect.

5. (1) This article applies to an agreement made on or after the date on which the Restrictive Trade Practices (Services) (Amendment) Order 1989 came into force—

(a) the parties to which include a person (the "vendor") who agrees to transfer shares in a company or the whole of his interest in a business to a purchaser;

(b) under which, in the case of an agreement for the transfer of shares in a company, more than 50 per cent in nominal value of the issued share capital of that company is transferred or agreed to be transferred to one purchaser or to more than one purchaser each of which is a member of the same group;

(c) under which no relevant restriction in respect of any of the matters specified in article 3(2)(a) of this Order is accepted by a person; and

(d) under which no relevant restriction in respect of any of the matters specified in article 3(2)(b) to (e) of this Order is accepted by a person other than such a person as is described in paragraph (2) below.

(2) Persons by whom a relevant restriction may be accepted for the purpose of paragraph (1)(d) above are—

(a) any vendor;

(b) any member of the same group as any vendor; and

(c) any individual;

other than a body corporate or unincorporate which is also a purchaser under the agreement in question, or a member of the same group as such a body.

[515]

[6. (1) In determining whether an agreement to which article 5 applies is an agreement to which the Act of 1976 applies by virtue of this Order, no account shall be taken of any relevant restriction—

(a) which is accepted for a period not exceeding that permitted under paragraph (2) below; and

(b) which limits the extent to which the person accepting the restriction may compete with the acquired enterprise, or may be engaged or interested in, disclose information to, or otherwise assist any business which so competes.

(2) For the purpose of paragraph (1)(a) above, a permitted period is:—

(a) a period of 5 years beginning with the date of the agreement; or

(b) in the case of restrictions accepted by an individual who is to have a contract of employment with or a contract for the supply of services to the acquired enterprise, the purchaser, or a member of the same group as the purchaser, a period beginning with the date of the agreement and ending 2 years after the date of expiry or termination of the contract,

whichever ends the later. **[516]**

7. This article applies to an agreement made on or after the date on which the Restrictive Trade Practices (Services) (Amendment) Order 1989 came into force—

(*a*) which provides for a person (the "subscriber") to subscribe (whether or not in cash) for shares in a company (the "issuing company");

(*b*) under which no relevant restriction in respect of any of the matters specified in article 3(2)(*a*) of this Order is accepted by a person; and

(*c*) under which no relevant restriction in respect of any of the matters specified in article 3(2)(*b*) to (*e*) of this Order is accepted by a body corporate or unincorporate.   **[517]**

8.—(1) In determining whether an agreement to which article 7 applies is an agreement to which the Act of 1976 applies by virtue of this Order, no account shall be taken of any relevant restriction—

(*a*) which is accepted for a period not exceeding that permitted under paragraph (2) below; and

(*b*) which limits the extent to which the person accepting the restriction may compete with the issuing company, or may be engaged or interested in, disclose information to, or otherwise assist any business which so competes.

(2) For the purpose of paragraph (1)(*a*) above, a permitted period is:—

(*a*) a period of 5 years beginning with the date of the agreement; or

(*b*) in the case of restrictions accepted—

  (i) by a member of the issuing company, a period beginning with the date of the agreement and ending 2 years after the date on which that person ceases to be a member; or

  (ii) by an individual who is to have a contract of employment with or a contract for the supply of services to the issuing company, a period beginning with the date of the agreement and ending 2 years after the expiry or termination of the contract,

whichever ends the later.   **[518]**

9. In articles 5 to 8 above—

"the Act of 1976" means the Restrictive Trade Practices Act 1976;
"acquired enterprise" means a company in which shares are acquired or a business an interest in which is acquired;
"business" means any undertaking which is, or any part of an undertaking which part is—

(*a*) carried on as a going concern for gain or reward; or

(*b*) carried on as a going concern in the course of which goods or services are supplied otherwise than free of charge;

"company" means a company as defined in section 735 of the Companies Act 1985 and an oversea company as defined in section 744 of that Act;
"contract of employment" means a contract of service whether it is express or implied and (if it is express) whether it is oral or in writing;
"goods" has the same meaning as in section 43(1) of the Act of 1976;
"group" means a group of interconnected bodies corporate within the meaning of section 43(1) of the Act of 1976;
"member of the issuing company" is to be construed in accordance with section 22 of the Companies Act 1985;

"purchaser" means a person acquiring shares in a company, or acquiring
an interest in a business, whether for cash or otherwise;
"relevant restriction" means a restriction in respect of the matters specified
in article 3(2) of this Order;
"services" has the same meaning as in section 20 of the Act of 1976.][1]

[519]

AMENDMENT
1 Articles 5 – 9 inserted by the Restrictive Trade Practices (Services) (Amendment) Order 1989,
SI 1989 No 1082, which came into force on 30 June 1989.

SCHEDULE

1. For the purposes of determining whether any agreement to which such an association
as is mentioned in section 112 of the Act of 1973 is a party falls within a paragraph of
this Schedule —

  (a) if the association does not carry on business in the supply of the relevant service
       or belong to the relevant class of persons, but represents persons who do, it shall
       be deemed to carry on such a business or belong to that class; and
  (b) there shall be disregarded any person who does not carry on the relevant business
       or belong to the relevant class and who is a party to the agreement by virtue
       only of the operation of that section.

2. (1) An agreement to which the only parties are operators of international sea transport
services and the only restrictions accepted thereunder are in respect of such services.

(2) An agreement to which the only parties are such operators and persons for whom
such services are being supplied and the only restrictions accepted thereunder are in respect
of such services so far as those services relate to goods.

(3) An agreement to which the only parties are operators of international sea transport
services and one other person carrying on business in the supply of another service
and the only restrictions accepted under the agreement relate to the supply or acquisition of that other service in connection with the operation of international sea transport
services.

(4) In this paragraph "international sea transport services" means the international
carriage of passengers or goods wholly or partly by sea; and where the carriage is not
wholly by sea, the carriage by sea and the carriage otherwise than by sea form part of
the same service.

3. (1) An agreement to which the only parties are air transport undertakings and the
only restrictions accepted thereunder are in respect of carriage by air.

(2) An agreement entered into between an air transport undertaking and its agent and
the only restrictions accepted thereunder are accepted in pursuance of such an agreement
as is described in (1) above.

(3) In this paragraph "air transport undertaking" shall have the same meaning as in
the Air Navigation Order 1974.

4. (1) An agreement to which the only parties are road passenger transport operators,
and the only restrictions accepted thereunder relate to the provision [in Northern Ireland,
or in Northern Ireland and the Republic of Ireland, of services, using one or more public

service vehicles (within the meaning of the Public Passenger Vehicle Act 1981), for the carriage of passengers by road at separate fares.][1]

(2) . . .[1]

5. *(1) An agreement entered into between the Treasury or both the Treasury and the Secretary of State and building societies and the only restrictions accepted thereunder relate to the raising of funds or the making of loans.*

(2) An agreement to which the only parties are building societies and the only restrictions accepted thereunder are accepted in pursuance of such an agreement as is described in (1) above.

(3) An agreement to which the only parties are building societies, and the only restrictions accepted thereunder relate to the rates of interest charged or to be charged for loans, or to the rates of interest paid or to be paid to shareholders or depositors.

(4) In this paragraph a "building society" means a society incorporated under the Building Societies Act 1962 or any enactment repealed by that Act (and includes a Northern Ireland society defined in section 134 of that Act).

6. An agreement to which the Bank of England or the Treasury or both are parties and which relates exclusively to the exercise of control by the Bank of England and the Treasury or one of them, as the case may be, over financial institutions or over the monetary system generally, or to the conduct of markets in money, in public sector debt instruments or in foreign currencies.

7. *An agreement to which the only parties carry on business in the supply of banking services and the only restrictions accepted thereunder relate to the supply of such services in Northern Ireland, or in Northern Ireland and the Republic of Ireland.*[3]

8. An agreement to which the only parties are persons permitted by or under Part I of the Insurance Companies Act 1974, or Part II of the Insurance Companies Act (Northern Ireland) 1968 to carry on insurance business and the only restrictions accepted thereunder relate to the provision of insurance services.

9. An agreement to which the only parties are trustees or managers of unit trust schemes authorised under the provisions of the Prevention of Fraud (Investments) Act 1958 or of the Prevention of Fraud (Investments) Act (Northern Ireland) 1940, and the only restrictions accepted thereunder relate to the management of, or the sale and purchase of units of, unit trust schemes authorised as aforesaid.

10. An agreement arising by virtue of a recommendation made by an association such as is described in section 112(1) of the Act of 1973 and which is either represented on the body known as the Panel on Take-overs and Mergers or is a member of such an association represented thereon, being a recommendation to comply with the provisions of the City Code on Take-overs and Mergers or a recommendation made for the purpose of implementing a decision of the Panel.   **[520]**

AMENDMENTS

1 Para 4(2) revoked by the Transport Act 1985, s 139(5) with effect from 6 January 1986: Transport Act 1985 (Commencement No 1) Order 1985, SI 1985 No 1887. Para 4(1) amended and para 4(2)

revoked by s 115(1) of the 1985 Act with effect from 26 July 1986: Transport Act 1985 (Commencement No 4) Order 1986, SI 1986 No 1088.

2 Para 5 ceased to have effect on 1 January 1987 by the operation of the Restrictive Trade Practices (Services) (Amendment) Order 1986, SI 1986 No 2204.

3 Para 7 ceased to have effect on 21 December 1985 by the operation of the Restrictive Trade Practices (Services) (Amendment) Order 1985, SI 1985 No 2044.

EXPLANATORY NOTE

(This Note is not part of the Order.)

This Order applies Part I of the Restrictive Trade Practices Act 1956 (which relates to the registration and judicial investigation of agreements about goods) to restrictive agreements in the supply and acquisition of services.

All services are brought under control by the Order, and all services are designated services with the exception of those listed in Schedule 4 to the Fair Trading Act 1973. As a consequence agreements between two or more persons carrying on business in the supply of any services under which restrictions in respect of the matters specified in Article 3(2) of the Order are accepted in relation to those or other services (other than those listed in Schedule 4) will in general be brought within Part I of the 1956 Act.

Part I will not however apply to agreements of the particular descriptions specified in the Schedule to this Order. These, subject to the conditions laid down in the Schedule, relate to —

(*a*) international sea transport services;
(*b*) carriage by air;
(*c*) road passenger transport;
(*d*) the raising of funds and making of loans by building societies;
(*e*) the exercise of financial control by the Treasury or the Bank of England;
(*f*) banking services in Northern Ireland;
(*g*) the provision of insurance services;
(*h*) Unit Trust schemes;
(*i*) the implementation of decisions of the Panel on Take-overs and Mergers.

Particulars of agreements existing at the date of operation of this Order must be furnished for registration within three months from that date, unless the agreement is terminated within that time, and particulars of other agreements must be furnished before the relevant restrictions become effective and in any event within three months of their making. **[521]**

THE RESTRICTIVE PRACTICES COURT RULES 1976
(SI 1976 No 1897)

The Lord Chancellor, in exercise of the powers conferred on him by section 9(1) and (2) of the Restrictive Practices Court Act 1976 and section 22(1) of the Restrictive Trade Practices Act 1976, hereby makes the following Rules: —

Introductory

1. These Rules may be cited as the Restrictive Practices Court Rules 1976 and shall come into operation on 15th December 1976.   **[522]**

2. (1) The Interpretation Act 1889 shall apply to the interpretation of these Rules as it applies to the interpretation of an Act of Parliament.

(2) In these Rules, unless the context otherwise requires: —

"the Act" means the Restrictive Trade Practices Act 1976;
["the Act of 1980" means the Competition Act 1980];¹
"association" means a services supply association or, as the case may be, a trade association as defined in section 43 of the Act;
"final hearing" includes a hearing under rule 43(3);
"judge" means a judge of the Court sitting in the part of the United Kingdom in which the proceedings were instituted or, as the case may be, to which they have been transferred;
"the proper officer of the Court" means the Clerk of the Court or other proper officer at the central office of the Court or at the office of the Court in Scotland or Northern Ireland, as the case may be;
references to a party to an agreement include references to any person deemed to be a party for the purposes of the Act;
[expressions used in these Rules which are used in the Act or the Act of 1980 have the same meaning in these Rules as in the Act or the Act of 1980].¹   **[523]**

AMENDMENT
 1 Words in r 2(2) inserted or substituted by The Restrictive Practices Court (Amendment) Rules 1982, SI 1982 No 871.

Institution of proceedings

3. (1) Subject to paragraph (7), proceedings under the Act shall be instituted by a notice of reference stating that the agreements to which the notice applies are referred to the Court.

(2) A notice of reference may apply to one agreement or to a number of agreements appearing to the Director to be related in such a way as to make it desirable that they should be considered in the same proceedings.

(3) A notice of reference shall sufficiently identify the agreement or agreements to which it applies.

(4) A notice of reference shall specify the part of the United Kingdom in which the proceedings are to take place and shall be issued out of the central office of the Court or the office of the Court in Scotland or Northern Ireland, as the case may be.

(5) A notice of reference shall be issued by being sealed with the Court's seal by the proper officer of the Court; and when issued the notice shall be

returned to the Director who shall leave a copy to be filed by the proper officer.

(6) Subject to rules 5 and 6, the Director shall cause a copy of the notice of reference to be served on all parties to the agreement or agreements to which the notice applies, and all such parties shall be respondents to the notice.

(7) This rule does not apply to applications under sections 3, 4, 26, 35, 37 and 40 of the Act, or to such an application as is mentioned in rule 51.

[524]

4. (1) Where the Director intends to apply for an order under section 2(2) of the Act against an association or any person acting on behalf of an association, he shall serve on the association a copy of the notice of reference and the association, though not itself a party to any relevant agreement, shall be made a respondent to the notice.

(2) The Director may, if he thinks fit, serve a copy of the notice of reference on any association whose members or any of them are parties to any relevant agreement and the association, though not itself a party to any such agreement, shall in that event be made a respondent to the notice. **[525]**

Representative respondents

5. (1) Where, in the case of proceedings to which rule 3 applies, several persons have a common interest in the proceedings by reason that they are all parties to the same agreement or have entered into substantially similar agreements, the Director may, in accordance with paragraph (2), nominate any of those persons (or any association of which any of those persons is a member, whether or not it is itself a party to any such agreement) to represent all or some of them and, subject to rules 6 and 9, those persons shall, for the purpose of the proceedings, be treated as being represented by the person so nominated (hereinafter called a "representative respondent").

(2) In any case such as is mentioned in paragraph (1), the Director shall, after issue but before service of the notice of reference—

(*a*) give to each person nominated as a representative respondent notice in writing that he is so nominated, including short particulars of the notice of reference and identifying the persons, or classes of persons, whom it is proposed he shall represent, together with a copy of any statement the Director may propose to have published in pursuance of sub-paragraph (*c*) below; and

(*b*) in so far as may be practicable, give to all, or to all other, parties to the agreement written notice of the action taken under sub-paragraph (*a*) above; and

(*c*) unless he is satisfied that such notice has been given to all such parties, cause a statement containing the particulars referred to in sub-paragraph (*a*) above (including the name and address of each representative respondent) and setting out the effect of rule 6, to be published in—

(i) the London, Edinburgh and Belfast Gazettes, and

(ii) at least one daily newspaper circulating throughout the United Kingdom, and

(iii) if there is in circulation an appropriate trade journal which is published at intervals not exceeding one month, in such a trade journal; and

(*d*) file with the proper officer of the Court an affidavit setting out the names of the persons to whom, and the dates on which, he has given written notice in accordance with sub-paragraphs (*a*) and (*b*), together with an extract containing any publication made in accordance with sub-paragraph (*c*) above. 				[526]

6. (1) Any person or association who objects to being made a representative respondent, or to being represented by the representative respondent nominated for that purpose by the Director, may, within 28 days of being given notice in writing under sub-paragraph (*a*) or (*b*) of rule 5(2) (or, in the case of a person who has not been given such notice, of the latest publication referred to in sub-paragraph (*c*) of that rule) apply by notice in writing to the Court for an order revoking or modifying the nomination and containing such other directions as may be specified in the notice.

(2) A person applying under paragraph (1) above shall file his notice of application with the proper officer of the Court, together with an affidavit setting out the facts and matters on which he relies, and shall at the same time serve copies of the notice and affidavit on the Director and (if the applicant is not a person nominated as a representative respondent) on the person nominated to represent him.

(3) On the hearing of an application under this rule, the Court may make such order and give such consequential directions as it may think fit.

(4) Where the Director has nominated a representative respondent, he shall not serve a copy of the notice of reference upon the person so nominated until either —

(*a*) the time limited for making an application under paragraph (1) has expired without any such application having been made; or

(*b*) if such an application has been made, it has been disposed of by the Court. 				[527]

Entry of appearance

7. Every respondent who wishes to be heard in the proceedings shall, within 14 days of the service upon him of the copy of the notice of reference, enter an appearance in the office of the Court out of which the notice issued by delivering to the proper officer of the Court two copies of a memorandum stating that the respondent wishes to be heard in the proceedings and containing the name of his solicitor (if any) and an address in the United Kingdom at which documents may be served on him; and the proper officer shall thereupon send one copy of the memorandum, sealed with the seal of the Court, to the Director.

				[528]

Alteration of scope of proceedings, parties and venue

8. Where a notice of reference applies to a number of agreements, any respondent may, within 14 days of entering an appearance to the notice, apply to the Court to exclude from the notice any agreement to which he is a party on the ground that the agreement is not related to the other agreements to which the notice applies, or is not related to some of those agreements, in such a way as to make it desirable that they should all be considered in the same proceedings; and the Court may, on the hearing of the application, amend the notice by excluding any agreement or agreements therefrom, and shall give all such consequential directions as it considers necessary, including a direction that any respondent who is a party to the agreement in question be treated as if he had not entered an appearance. **[529]**

9. Without prejudice to the operation of rule 6, the Director, or any person or association who falls to be treated as being, or as being represented by, a representative respondent, may at any time apply to the Court for an order such as is mentioned in rule 6(1). **[530]**

10. The Director, any respondent, and any person or association represented by a representative respondent, may apply to the Court for the transfer of the proceedings to another part of the United Kingdom named in the application; and on the hearing of the application the Court may order that all further proceedings shall take place in the part of the United Kingdom named in the order. **[531]**

Statement of case, answer, reply, etc

11. (1) Every respondent who has entered an appearance shall, within three months of his entry of appearance, deliver to the Director, and file with the proper officer of the Court, a statement of his case, which shall include—

    (*a*) particulars of the provisions of section 10(1) or 19(1) of the Act on which he intends to rely;

    (*b*) particulars of the facts and matters alleged by him to entitle him to rely on those provisions;

and shall be accompanied by a list of all the documents relevant to the proceedings which are or have been in his possession or power, indicating for which (if any) of those documents he claims privilege and the grounds of the claim.

(2) Without prejudice to the provisions of these Rules relating to discovery, every respondent shall, within seven days after receiving notice in that behalf from the Director, produce for the Director's inspection the documents specified in his list or such of them as may be specified in the notice, and shall permit the Director to make copies thereof:

Provided that nothing in this paragraph shall affect the right of a respondent to claim privilege for any document. **[532]**

12. (1) Where a statement of case is delivered, the Director shall deliver an answer within three months after the expiry of the time limited for the delivery of a statement of case by every respondent who has entered an appearance.

(2) Where there is more than one respondent, the Director may deliver a joint answer, or separate answers to each or to some only of the respondents, with or without a joint answer to the remainder.

(3) A copy of every answer shall be delivered to the respondent or respondents to whose statement it is directed and shall be filed with the proper officer of the Court. [533]

13. In proceedings in England and Wales or in Northern Ireland where a respondent intends to rely on facts or matters which, if not raised, would be likely to take the Director by surprise or would raise issues of fact not arising out of the statement of case or answer, he shall, within six weeks of the delivery of the answer, deliver a reply to the Director and file a copy thereof with the proper officer of the Court. [534]

14. (1) Every allegation of fact in a statement of case shall be deemed to be admitted unless in the answer it is denied specifically or by necessary implication, or is stated not to be admitted.

(2) Subject to paragraph (3), in proceedings in England and Wales or in Northern Ireland, where a reply is delivered, every allegation of fact in the answer shall be deemed to be admitted unless in the reply it is denied specifically or by necessary implication or is stated not to be admitted.

(3) A respondent in his reply may join issue on the answer and in that case he shall be deemed to deny every material allegation of fact in the answer except any which he specifically admits. [535]

15. If a respondent fails to deliver a statement of his case or to comply with any order of the Court within the time limited for doing so, the Court may, on the application of the Director, direct that the respondent be debarred from taking any further part in the proceedings (save for the purpose of being heard on any application by the Director for discovery, or the answering of interrogatories or a statement of facts by that respondent, or for a final order under rule 45 or 46) or make such other order as the Court may think just. [536]

16. In proceedings in England and Wales or in Northern Ireland, any party may apply to any opposite party for further and better particulars of the notice of reference, or of any statement of case, answer or reply, as the case may be, and, if such particulars are not supplied within 14 days or such further time as may be agreed, he may apply to the Court, which may order the delivery of such further and better particulars as it considers necessary. [537]

17. In proceedings in England and Wales or in Northern Ireland, the Court may, on the application of any party, strike out the whole or any part of a statement of case, answer or reply which appears to the Court to be frivolous, vexatious

or irrelevant and may in that event allow further time for the delivery of a fresh
or amended statement of case, answer or reply. **[538]**

18. In proceedings in England and Wales or in Northern Ireland, a notice of
reference, statement of case, answer or reply may be amended—

(a) at any time by leave of the Court;

(b) without leave at any time before the hearing of the application for
directions, if—

(i) in the case of a notice of reference or answer, the Director and all
respondents who have entered an appearance or, as the case may
be, to whose statement of case the answer is directed, agree; or

(ii) in the case of a statement of case or reply, the Director and all
respondents seeking to amend agree;

and a copy of the notice or other document as amended shall be delivered to
all opposite parties and filed with the proper officer of the Court within such
time as may be allowed by the Court or agreed between the parties concerned.
[539]

19. In proceedings in Scotland—

(a) the Director shall, within seven days after the expiration of the time
limited for filing answers, make up an open record consisting of the
notice of reference, the statement or statements of case and the answer
or answers, and file two copies thereof with the proper officer of the
Court, at the same time delivering a copy thereof to each of the
respondents; and thereafter the parties shall forthwith proceed to adjust
their pleadings;

(b) upon the expiration of 28 days from the filing of the open record, or
of such period of continuation as may be allowed by the Court on cause
shown, the record shall be deemed to be closed, and thereafter no amendment of the pleadings shall be made except by leave of the Court; and

(c) within 14 days after the closing of the record the Director shall file
two copies of the closed record with the proper officer of the Court,
and shall at the same time deliver 15 copies thereof to each of the
respondents. **[540]**

Joinder of parties and consolidation

20. (1) The Director, and any respondent who has entered an appearance, may
at any time apply to the Court for an order that any person not already a party
be added as a respondent to the proceedings, and shall give notice of the application to all other parties and to the person sought to be added.

(2) Any person who is not a party to the proceedings may apply to the Court
for an order adding him as a respondent and shall give notice of the application
to all parties to the proceedings.

(3) A copy of the notice of reference and, in Scotland, a copy of the closed
record or, as the case may be, of the open record as adjusted to date shall within

14 days after the making of the order be served by the Director on every person
added as a respondent under paragraph (1) or (2), and these Rules shall thereafter apply to such person as if he had been made a respondent under rule 3(6).
                                                                         [541]

21. (1) The Director, and any respondent who has entered an appearance, may
at any time apply to the Court for an order that any proceedings pending before
the Court in the same part of the United Kingdom be consolidated and heard
together.

(2) On making an order adding a respondent or an order for the consolidation of any proceedings, the Court shall give all such consequential directions
as it considers necessary.   **[542]**

Application for directions

22. As soon as practicable after every respondent to whom the Director has
delivered an answer has delivered his reply or after the time for his doing so has
expired, or in Scotland as soon as practicable after the closing of the record,
the Director shall make an application to the Court for directions, with a view
to providing an occasion for the consideration of the preparations for the final
hearing so that —

    (*a*) all matters which can be dealt with on interlocutory application and
        have not already been dealt with (including, in Scotland, any prelim-
        inary question of relevance or sufficiency of specification arising on
        the pleadings) may, so far as possible, be dealt with; and

    (*b*) such directions may be given as to the future course of the proceedings
        as appear best adapted to secure the just, expeditious and economical
        disposal thereof;

and the Court shall fix a date for the hearing of the application.   **[543]**

23. (1) Not less than 21 days before the application for directions is due to be
heard, the Director shall serve notice of the application on every respondent who
has entered an appearance (with the exception of any respondent who has been
debarred under rule 15 from taking any further part in the proceedings) and shall
set out in his notice full particulars of the directions for which he intends to apply,
and a copy of the notice shall at the same time be filed with the proper officer
of the Court.

(2) Every respondent on whom notice is served under paragraph (1) shall,
within 14 days of service of the notice, serve on the Director a notice specifying
any directions which he may desire in so far as they differ from those applied
for by the Director, and shall at the same time file a copy of the notice with the
proper officer of the Court.

(3) On the hearing of the application the Court shall give such directions as
it considers necessary to secure the purposes mentioned in rule 22 and, without
prejudice to the generality of the foregoing, may give such directions as it may
think fit as to —

(a) the amendment of the notice of reference or any statement of case, answer or reply;

(b) the delivery of further and better particulars or, in Scotland, the further specification, of the notice of reference or of any statement of case, answer or reply;

(c) the delivery of interrogatories or, in Scotland, the answering of any statement of facts;

(d) the admission of any facts or documents;

(e) the discovery or further discovery of any documents;

(f) the admission in evidence of any documents;

(g) the mode in which evidence is to be given at the final hearing;

(h) the taking and recording of any evidence before the final hearing, including the appointment of an examiner or, in Scotland, a commissioner for that purpose;

(i) the reference to the Court for determination in a summary way of any issue arising in relation to any agreement to which the notice of reference applies;

(j) the disposal of a preliminary point of law (including, in Scotland, any preliminary question of relevancy or sufficiency of specification arising on the pleadings);

(k) an investigation of the cost incurred by any respondent (or, as the case may be, any person or association represented by a representative respondent) in producing or supplying any goods or in applying any process of manufacture to goods, or in supplying any services, and the manner in which the result of such investigation is to be brought before the Court at the final hearing;

(l) the consolidation of the proceedings with any other proceedings pending before the Court in the same part of the United Kingdom;

(m) the place and date of the final hearing.   **[544]**

24. Any application subsequent to the application for directions and before the final hearing as to any matter capable of being dealt with on an interlocutory application shall be made under the application for directions by two clear days' notice to the opposite party stating the grounds on which it is made.   **[545]**

Notice to produce documents and to admit documents and facts

25. Any party may give to any opposite party notice to produce at the final hearing any relevant documents specified in the notice which are in the possession or power of the opposite party and, if such notice is not complied with, secondary evidence of the contents of the documents may be given by the party who gave the notice.   **[546]**

26. Any party may, not less than 21 days before the date fixed for the final hearing, serve notice on any opposite party requiring him to admit (saving all just exceptions) the authenticity of any document specified in the notice and, unless the opposite party within seven days of service of the notice upon him gives notice requiring the document to be proved at the hearing or unless the

Court otherwise directs, he shall be deemed to have admitted its authenticity.
[547]

27. Any party may, not less than 21 days before the date fixed for the final hearing, give to any opposite party notice to admit, for the purpose of the proceedings, any facts specified in the notice, and the Court shall, in exercising its discretion as to making an order for costs under rule 58(1), take into consideration any unreasonable failure to admit, or delay in admitting, such facts.
[548]

Discovery of documents and interrogatories

28. (1) In proceedings in England and Wales or in Northern Ireland any party may apply to the Court for an order directing any opposite party to make discovery, or further discovery, either on oath or otherwise, of the documents relating to the proceedings which are or have been in his possession or power, and on the hearing of the application the Court may make such order, either generally or limited to certain classes of documents or to particular documents, as it thinks fit, including an order for the production or inspection of any documents.

(2) In proceedings in Scotland any party may apply to the Court for a commission and diligence for the recovery of documents, and for this purpose the provisions of rules 95 to 99 of the Rules of the Court of Session shall apply with the necessary modifications; and any reference in these Rules to discovery, or further discovery, of documents shall be construed as a reference to the recovery of documents under a commission and diligence granted under this paragraph.
[549]

29. If it appears to the Court on the application of the Director (which may be made at any time after a respondent has delivered a statement of his case or after the time for doing so has expired) that the cost incurred by the respondent in producing or supplying any goods, or in applying any process of manufacture to goods, or in supplying any services is a material fact in the proceedings, the Court may authorise the Director to investigate such cost and may require the respondent concerned to afford to the Director all such facilities as may be necessary for the investigation, and may give directions as to the manner in which the result of the investigation is to be brought before the Court at the final hearing.
[550]

30. (1) Subject to paragraph (2), in proceedings in England and Wales or in Northern Ireland any party may apply to the Court for an order requiring any opposite party to answer interrogatories on oath within such time as the Court may direct, and in proceedings in Scotland any party may apply to the Court for an order requiring any opposite party to answer a statement of facts; and copies of the interrogatories or statement of facts shall, unless the Court otherwise directs, be delivered to the opposite party and filed with the proper officer of the Court not less than two days before the day fixed for the hearing of the application.

(2) An application by any party for an order requiring a respondent to answer interrogatories or a statement of facts may be made only after that respondent has delivered a statement of his case or after the time for his doing so has expired; and a respondent may apply for an order to answer interrogatories or a statement of facts only after he has delivered a statement of his case.

(3) The Director may answer any interrogatories or statement of facts by himself or by any officer nominated by him for that purpose, and a body corporate or an association shall answer by a director, manager, secretary or other officer.   **[551]**

31. An application may be made by the Director under rules 28 to 30 against any person or association represented by a representative respondent as if that person or association were a respondent to the proceedings and had delivered a statement of his case at or within such time as the representative respondent did or might have done so.   **[552]**

Interlocutory applications

32. (1) Except where these Rules otherwise provide or the Court otherwise directs, every interlocutory application shall be made on not less than seven days' notice to the Director or, as the case may be, to every respondent concerned in the subject matter of the application, and the notice shall include particulars of the directions or order sought.

(2) Except where the President of the Court or a judge, whether generally or in any particular case, otherwise directs, every interlocutory application (including an application under rules 33(4) and (49) shall be made to a judge, who may—

  (*a*) dispose of it himself; or
  (*b*) refer it in whole or in part to a Court consisting of a presiding judge and at least two other members; or
  (*c*) (except in the case of an application under rules 33(4) and (49) refer it in whole or in part to the Clerk of the Court, or officer acting as Clerk of the Court in Scotland or Northern Ireland, as the case may be;

and references in these Rules to the Court shall be construed accordingly.

(3) Where an application is made or referred to the Clerk of the Court or officer acting as Clerk of the Court in Scotland or Northern Ireland, as the case may be, any party aggrieved by his decision may appeal to a judge within seven days of the decision on giving notice to all parties concerned and to the proper officer of the Court; and in that case the judge may dispose of the appeal himself, or refer it in whole or in part to a Court consisting of a presiding judge and at least two other members.

(4) For the hearing of any interlocutory application or appeal, the Court or judge may sit either in private or in public.   **[553]**

Application for interim order

33. (1) At any time after the issue of a notice of reference, and notwithstanding that it has not been served, the Director may apply to the Court for an interim order under section 3 of the Act by a notice of application issued out of the office of the Court out of which the notice of reference was issued.

(2) In addition to the matters required by section 3(2) of the Act to be specified in the application the notice shall specify the persons (including any association, whether or not it is itself a party to the agreement to which the notice applies) against whom an interim order is sought.

(3) The notice of application shall be issued by being sealed with the Court's seal by the proper officer of the Court, and when issued shall be returned to the applicant who shall—

(a) leave a copy to be filed by the proper officer; and
(b) at the same time file with the proper officer an affidavit setting out the facts and matters on which he relies in support of the application.

(4) Where the case is one of urgency the application may be made *ex parte*, but in any other case the Director shall serve a copy of the notice of application and of the affidavit on the persons (including any association) against whom an interim order is sought and those persons shall be made respondents to the notice.

(5) Where the application is made *ex parte*, the Court may make such interim order, and give such directions as to the service of notice of the application, the joinder of parties, or the further hearing of the application as the Court thinks fit.

(6) Any respondent who wishes to oppose the application shall within seven days of service upon him of notice of the application file with the proper officer of the Court an affidavit setting out the grounds of his objection and the facts and matters on which he relies and shall at the same time serve a copy thereof on the Director.

(7) Not later than seven days after every respondent has filed an affidavit or the time for doing so has expired the Director shall apply to the Court for directions.

(8) The provisions of these Rules relating to a reference to the Court by the Director (other than rule 23(1) and (2)) shall apply with the necessary modifications to directions under paragraph (5) and paragraph (7) and to all further proceedings on the application.

(9) An application under section 3(5) of the Act for a fresh interim order in substitution for an earlier one may be made by notice of application specifying the interim order to which the application relates, and paragraph (3) shall apply to a notice under this paragraph as it applies to the original application.

(10) A notice under paragraph (9) shall be served on all those persons who were parties to the proceedings relating to the previous interim order, and such persons shall be respondents to the notice.

(11) Paragraphs (6), (7) and (except for the words "paragraph (5) and") (8)

shall apply to an application under paragraph (9) as they apply to an application
by the Director under paragraph (1).   **[554]**

Evidence

34. Subject to these Rules, and to any enactment relating to evidence, any fact
required to be proved at the hearing of the reference shall be proved by the oral
examination of the witnesses.   **[555]**

35. The Court may, on the hearing or adjourned hearing of the application for
directions or at the final hearing, order that all or any of the evidence at the
final hearing shall be given by affidavit, and may make such order on such terms
as to the filing and giving of copies of the affidavits or proposed affidavits and
as to the production of the deponents for cross-examination as the Court may
think fit.   **[556]**

36. Without prejudice to rule 35, the Court may order that evidence of any
particular fact shall be given at the final hearing in such manner as may be
specified in the order and in particular—

    (*a*) by statement on oath of information or belief;
    (*b*) by the production of documents or entries in books;
    (*c*) by copies of documents or entries in books;
    (*d*) in the case of scientific, technical or statistical information relevant to
        the proceedings, by the production of specified scientific, technical,
        economic or trade publications or works of reference containing such
        information.   **[557]**

37. Where it appears to the Court, on the hearing or adjourned hearing of the
application for directions or at the final hearing, that the Court would be assisted
in determining any issue in the proceedings by the admission of evidence (whether
oral or documentary) which would not otherwise be admissible under the law
relating to evidence, the Court may make an order allowing the admission of
such evidence.   **[558]**

38. Any order under rules 35 to 37 made before the final hearing may be revoked
or varied by a subsequent order made at or before the final hearing.
                                                                        [559]

39. The Court may, on the application of any party, make an order for the
examination on oath of any witness before such examiner as the Court may direct,
and may give such directions as the Court may think fit as to the taking and
recording of such evidence and its reception at the final hearing, and at the
examination of the witness the same practice shall be followed as on the examination of a witness before an examiner of the Supreme Court or, in proceedings
in Scotland, before a commissioner appointed by the Court of Session to take
evidence.   **[560]**

40. Where a witness is required to attend before the Court to give oral evidence or to produce any document in his possession or power, the proper officer of the Court shall issue a summons ordering the attendance of the witness, which shall be served personally on him a reasonable time before he is required to attend, and there shall at the same time be paid or tendered to the witness a sum sufficient to cover his reasonable expenses for travelling to and from, and his attendance at, the Court.   **[561]**

Final hearing

41. Subject to the provisions of section 7(1) of the Restrictive Practices Court Act 1976, the final hearing of any proceedings shall take place before such members of the Court as the President thereof may nominate for the purpose.
                                                                        [562]

42. The final hearing shall take place in public:

Provided that if the Court is satisfied that it is in the public interest that the hearing or part thereof should not take place in public or that evidence may be given as to a secret process of manufacture or as to the presence, absence or situation of any mineral or other deposits or as to any similar matter the publication of which would substantially damage the legitimate business interests of any person, it shall, and may in any other case in which it appears proper to the Court to do so, order that the hearing, or such part thereof as the Court may direct, shall take place in private.   **[563]**

Summary determination of issues and preliminary points of law

43. (1) In the Director's application for directions and in any notice given by a respondent under rule 23(2) there may be included an application for the determination in a summary way of any issue arising in relation to any agreement to which the notice of reference applies, and any such application shall state the issue to be determined and shall include particulars of any relevant matters considered in previous proceedings before the Court, and of the judgment or order given or made in those proceedings.

(2) If, on the hearing of the application, it appears to the Court that the relevant provisions of the agreement and the circumstances of the case are substantially similar to those considered in previous proceedings before the Court, it may direct that the issue be referred for determination in a summary way.

(3) Where a direction has been given under paragraph (2), the Court may at the hearing, unless it is satisfied that the relevant provisions of the agreement or the circumstances of the case differ in some material respect from the provisions and circumstances considered in the previous proceedings—

(a) determine the issue in a summary way without hearing evidence, or on such evidence, whether oral or documentary, as it may think fit; and

(b) make any declaration or order which the Court could have made under section 1(3) or 2 of the Act if the issue had been determined after a final hearing in the ordinary way, or defer the making of any such declaration or order until all other issues in the proceedings have been disposed of. **[564]**

44. The Director, and any respondent who has entered an appearance, may apply to the Court at any time for an order that a point of law arising on the notice of reference, or on any statement of case, answer or reply, be determined before the final hearing of the proceedings and the Court may, if it thinks fit, dispose of the point of law on the hearing of the application or at any later stage in the proceedings. **[565]**

Procedure on summary application for final order

45. If at any time before the final hearing every respondent who has entered an appearance (with the exception of any respondent who has been debarred under rule 15 from taking any further part in the proceedings) notifies the Director that he is willing to submit to a declaration that the restrictions in the agreement to which the notice of reference applies are contrary to the public interest or, as the case may be, to such a declaration and to an order under section 1(3) or 2 of the Act, the Director shall apply to the Court for such a declaration and, where appropriate, for such an order within 28 days after being so notified by every such respondent. **[566]**

46. Where no appearance has been entered or where, after entry of an appearance, no statement of case has been delivered, the Director may apply to the Court for a declaration that the restrictions in the agreement to which the notice of reference applies are contrary to the public interest and, where appropriate, for an order under section 1(3) or 2 of the Act; and any such application may be made—

(a) where no appearance has been entered, not earlier than 28 days after the expiration of the time limited for entry of appearance by the respondent on whom the notice of reference was last served;

(b) where no statement of case has been delivered, not earlier than 28 days after the expiration of the time limited for delivery of a statement of case by the respondent who last entered an appearance. **[567]**

47. Not later than 21 days before an application under rule 45 or 46 is due to be heard the Director shall file with the proper officer of the Court a draft of the declaration and of any order for which he intends to apply and shall at the same time serve a copy of the draft on every respondent, whether he has entered an appearance or not, together with notice of the time and place appointed for the hearing of the application. **[568]**

48. Every respondent shall be entitled to be heard on the application as to whether the restrictions set out in the draft declaration are restrictions accepted by the parties to the agreement to which the notice of reference applies and as to any other matters which the Court considers can properly be raised on the hearing

of the application, not being matters which, in the opinion of the Court, ought
to have been raised in a statement of case.   [569]

Applications under section 4 of the Act

49. (1) An application for leave to apply under section 4 of the Act for the discharge of any declaration made by the Court in any proceedings, and of any
order made in pursuance thereof, shall be made to the Court in the part of the
United Kingdom in which the previous proceedings took place and shall
be supported by evidence on affidavit of the matters on which the applicant
relies.

(2) Unless the Court otherwise directs, notice of the application for leave,
together with copies of the affidavits in support thereof, shall be served on every
party who appeared on the hearing of the previous proceedings and every such
party shall be entitled to be heard on the application.   [570]

50. If leave is granted under rule 49, the Court shall give such directions as it
thinks fit as to the delivery by the applicant of a statement of his case and by
the Director (if he is not the applicant) and by any other party of an answer,
and, subject to any directions so given, the provisions of these Rules relating
to a reference to the Court by the Director shall apply with the necessary modifications to all further proceedings on the application.   [571]

Applications to discharge orders made by other courts or for declarations under section 40 of the Act

51. Any person who wishes to apply to the Court for the discharge of an order
made under section 18(2) of the Restrictive Trade Practices Act 1956 by the High
Court, the Court of Session or the High Court in Northern Ireland may do so
by a notice of application which shall—

(*a*) be issued out of the office of the Court situate in that part of the United
Kingdom in which the order was made; and

(*b*) contain—

  (i) particulars of the order which the applicant seeks to have discharged
  and of the grounds on which he alleges that the order ought to be
  discharged;

  (ii) particulars of the provisions of section 10(1) or 19(1) of the Act
  on which he intends to rely;

  (iii) particulars of the facts and matters alleged by him to entitle him
  to rely on those provisions; and

(*c*) be accompanied by a list of all the documents relevant to the application which are or have been in the possession or power of the applicant,
indicating for which (if any) of those documents he claims privilege and
the grounds of the claim.   [572]

52. (1) Any person who wishes to apply to the Court for a declaration under section 40(1) of the Act may do so by a notice of application issued out of the central office of the Court, or the office of the Court in Scotland or Northern Ireland.

(2) A notice of application under paragraph (1) shall—

(*a*) contain—

(i) particulars of the agreement which the applicant desires to make and of the order in force under section 56 of the Fair Trading Act 1973 or having effect as if made under that section, by virtue of which the making of the agreement is unlawful, or of any relevant undertaking or assurance given to the appropriate Minister within the meaning of the said section 56;

(ii) particulars of the provisions of section 10(1) or 19(1) of the Act on which the applicant intends to rely; and

(iii) particulars of the facts and matters alleged by him to entitle him to rely on those provisions; and

(*b*) be accompanied by a list of all the documents relevant to the application which are or have been in the possession or power of the applicant, indicating for which (if any) of those documents he claims privilege and the grounds of the claim. **[573]**

53. (1) A notice of application under rule 51 or 52 shall be issued by being sealed with the Court's seal by the proper officer of the Court; and when issued the notice shall be returned to the applicant who shall leave a copy to be filed by the proper officer and shall serve a copy on the Director, who shall be the respondent to the notice.

(2) Without prejudice to the provisions of these Rules relating to discovery, the applicant shall within seven days after receiving notice in that behalf from the Director produce for his inspection the documents specified in the applicant's list of documents, or such of them as may be specified in the notice, and shall permit the Director to make copies thereof:

Provided that nothing in this paragraph shall affect the applicant's right to claim privilege for any document.

(3) If the Director wishes to oppose the application, he shall, within six weeks of the service upon him of the copy of the notice of application, deliver an answer to the applicant and file a copy thereof with the proper officer of the Court.

(4) The provisions of these Rules relating to a reference to the Court by the Director shall apply with the necessary modifications to all further proceedings on the application.

(5) Where an order is made for the discharge of an order made under section 18(2) of the Restrictive Trade Practices Act 1956, the proper officer of the Court shall send a copy of the first-mentioned order to the Chief Registrar of the Chancery Division of the High Court, the Principal Clerk of Session in Scotland or the Registrar of the Supreme Court of Northern Ireland, as the case may be.

[574]

Applications under section 26 or 35 of the Act

54. (1) An application to the Court under section 26 or 35 of the Act shall be made by notice in writing issued out of the central office of the Court, or the office of the Court in Scotland or Northern Ireland, as the case may be, specifying the part of the United Kingdom in which the hearing is to take place and containing particulars of any order or declaration sought and identifying the agreement to which the application relates.

(2) A notice under paragraph (1) shall be issued by being sealed with the Court's seal by the proper officer of the Court and when issued shall be returned to the applicant who shall —

(*a*) leave a copy to be filed by the proper officer; and

(*b*) at the same time file with the proper officer an affidavit setting out the facts and matters on which he relies in support of the application.

[575]

55. (1) Where an application under section 26 of the Act is made by a person other than the Director, the applicant shall serve a copy of the notice and affidavit on the Director, who shall be made a respondent to the application.

(2) Where an application is made by the Director under section 26 or 35 of the Act, the Director —

(*a*) shall, unless all the parties to the agreement are treated under subparagraph (*c*) as represented by an association, serve copies of the notice and affidavit on one or more parties to the agreement, who shall be made respondents to the application and (subject to any directions of the Court) be treated as representing such other parties, if any, to the agreement as the Director may specify; and

(*b*) shall, in any case where he intends to apply for an order under section 35(3) of the Act against an association or any person acting on behalf of an association, serve such copies on the association, which shall be made a respondent to the application; and

(*c*) may, if he thinks fit, serve such copies on any association whose members include parties to the agreement (notwithstanding that the association is not itself a party thereto), and that association shall thereupon be made a respondent to the application and be treated as representing such other parties, if any, to the agreement as the Director may specify.

(3) Where, by virtue of paragraph (2), any parties to an agreement fall to be treated as being represented by a respondent to the application —

(*a*) the Director shall —

(i) inform them of the proceedings by notice in writing and, unless he is satisfied that such notice has been given to all of them, by advertisement in the manner described in rule 5(2)(*c*); and

(ii) file with the proper officer of the Court an affidavit such as is referred to in rule 5(2)(*d*); and

(*b*) the provisions of rule 6 (except paragraph (4) thereof) shall apply with the necessary modifications.   **[576]**

56. (1) Any respondent who wishes to oppose an application made under section 26 or 35 of the Act shall, within six weeks of service upon him of notice of the application (or, if his representing, or being represented by, any other person has been the subject of an objection, within such further time as the Court may direct) file with the proper officer of the Court an affidavit setting out the grounds of his objection and the facts and matters on which he relies and shall at the same time serve a copy thereof on the applicant.

(2) Not later than 21 days after every respondent has filed an affidavit in accordance with paragraph (1), or after the time for doing so has expired, the Director shall apply to the Court for directions and the provisions of these Rules relating to a reference to the Court by the Director shall apply with the necessary modifications to such directions and to all further proceedings on the application. **[577]**

Applications under section 37 of the Act

57. (1) An application by the Director to the Court under section 37 of the Act shall be made *ex parte* by notice in writing issued out of the central office of the Court, or the office of the Court in Scotland or Northern Ireland, as the case may be, specifying the persons against whom the order is sought.

(2) A notice under paragraph (1) shall be issued by being sealed with the Court's seal by the proper officer of the Court and, when issued, shall be returned to the Director, who shall —

(a) leave a copy to be filed with the proper officer; and

(b) at the same time file with the proper officer an affidavit setting out the information the Director requires, the steps he has taken under section 36 of the Act to obtain that information from the persons specified in the notice and the facts and matters relied on in support of the application.

(3) If the Director is seeking an order against any person in his capacity as an officer of, or person employed by, a body corporate or an unincorporated association, the affidavit referred to in paragraph (2) shall state the office or post held by that person.

(4) The notes of the examination of any person taken in pursuance of an order under section 37 of the Act shall be filed with the proper officer of the Court. **[578]**

[Applications under section 26(4) of the Act of 1980

57A. (1) Any application to the Court under section 26(4) of the Act of 1980 shall be made by a notice in writing issued out of the office of the Court in the part of the United Kingdom in which the relevant proceedings under section 1(3) of the Act took place containing particulars of those parts of the declaration made in those proceedings the operation of which it is sought to suspend.

(2) A notice under paragraph (1) shall be issued by being sealed with the Court's seal by the proper officer of the Court and when issued shall be returned to the applicant who shall—

   (*a*) leave a copy to be filed by the proper officer; and

   (*b*) at the same time file with the proper officer an affidavit setting out the facts and matters on which he relies in support of the application; and

   (*c*) at the same time serve a copy of the notice and affidavit on the Director, who shall be made a respondent to the application.   **[579]**

57B. (1) If the Director wishes to oppose any application made under section 26(4) of the Act of 1980 he shall, within 21 days in the case of a first application made thereunder, or within 14 days in the case of a second and final application made thereunder, of the service upon him of the applicant's notice and affidavit, file with the proper officer of the court an affidavit in reply setting out the grounds for his opposition and the facts and matters on which he relies and shall at the same time serve a copy thereof on the applicant.

(2) The applicant shall, no later than 7 days after the Director has served upon him an affidavit in accordance with paragraph (1), or after the period for doing so has expired, or after the Director has indicated that no such affidavit will be served, whichever period is the shortest, apply to the Court for the fixing of a date for the hearing of the application and the Court shall fix such a date.

(3) The Director shall, if no application is made under paragraph (2) within the period specified, apply to the Court for the fixing of a date for the hearing and the Court shall fix such a date.   **[580]**

57C. Except where the President of the Court or a judge, whether generally or in any particular case, otherwise directs every application under section 26(4) of the Act of 1980 shall be made to a judge who may—

   (*a*) dispose of it himself; or

   (*b*) refer it in whole or in part to a Court consisting of a presiding judge and at least two other members; or

   (*c*) refer it in whole or in part to the Clerk of the Court, or officer acting as Clerk of the Court in Scotland and Northern Ireland, as the case may be;

and references in these Rules to the Court shall be construed accordingly.

[581]

Applications under section 26(1) of the Act of 1980

57D. (1) An application to the Court under section 26(1) of the Act of 1980 shall be made by a notice in writing issued out of the office of the Court in the part of the United Kingdom in which the relevant proceedings under section 1(3) of the Act took place identifying the declaration made in those proceedings to which the application relates and containing particulars of the revised agreement, or a draft of the revised agreement, for which approval is sought.

(2) A notice under paragraph (1) shall be issued by being sealed with the Court's seal by the proper officer of the Court and when issued shall be returned to the applicant who shall—

(a) leave a copy to be filed by the proper officer; and

   (b) at the same time file with the proper officer an affidavit setting out the facts and matters on which he relies in support of the application; and

(c) at the same time serve a copy of the notice and of the affidavit on the Director and on all other parties to the agreement in relation to which the declaration under section 1(3) of the Act was made or to the proceedings in which that declaration was made.   **[582]**

57E. The Court may, on the application either of the Director or of the applicant at any time before the service of the notice and affidavit referred to in rule 57D(2)(c) above, order that the requirements as to such service may be varied or dispensed with altogether.   **[583]**

57F. (1) If the Director wishes to oppose an application made under section 26(1) of the Act of 1980 he shall, within 28 days of the service upon him of the applicant's notice and affidavit, file with the proper officer of the Court an affidavit in reply setting out the grounds for his opposition and the facts and matters on which he relies and shall at the same time serve a copy thereof on the applicant.

(2) Not later than 7 days after the Director has filed an affidavit in reply in accordance with paragraph (1), or after the time for doing so has expired, or after the Director has indicated that no such affidavit will be served, whichever period is the shortest, the applicant shall apply to the Court for directions and the provisions of these Rules relating to a reference to the Court by the Director shall apply with the necessary modifications to such directions and to all further proceedings on the application.

(3) If no application is made under paragraph (2) within the time specified, the Director shall himself apply to the Court for directions and the provisions of these Rules relating to a reference to the Court by the Director shall apply with the necessary modifications to such directions and to all further proceedings on the application.]¹   **[584]**

AMENDMENT
1 Additional rules inserted by the Restrictive Practices Court (Amendment) Rules 1982, SI 1982 No 871.

Costs

58. (1) Where it appears to the Court that any party has been guilty of unreasonable delay, or of improper, vexatious, prolix or unnecessary steps in any proceedings under section 1, 2 or 4 of the Act or of other unreasonable conduct (including, but without prejudice to the generality of the foregoing, a refusal to make any admission or agreement as to the conduct of the proceedings which he ought reasonably to have made), the Court may make an order for costs against him.

(2) Where an order is made under paragraph (1) or under the powers conferred on the Court by section 22(2)(*b*) of the Act (which enables the Court to make an order for costs in proceedings under section 26, 35 or 37 of the Act) the Court may direct that the party against whom the order is made shall pay to any party—

  (*a*) a lump sum by way of costs; or
  (*b*) such costs or such proportion of the costs as may be just.

(3) Where the Court gives a direction under paragraph (2)(*b*) it may—

  (*a*) itself assess the sum to be paid; or
  (*b*) direct that it be assessed by the proper officer of the Court; or
  (*c*) direct that the proper officer of the Court refer the costs to be taxed or assessed by a Master of the Supreme Court (Taxing Office) or by the Auditor of the Court of Session in Scotland or by the Taxing Master of the Supreme Court of Northern Ireland.

(4) Where a direction is given under paragraph (3)(*b*) or (*c*), any party aggrieved by the taxation or assessment may appeal to a judge within seven days of the taxation or assessment on giving notice to all parties concerned and to the officer who made the taxation or assessment; and the judge may dispose of the appeal himself, or refer it in whole or in part to a Court consisting of a presiding judge and at least two other members, and, in either event, rule 32(4) shall apply to the hearing of the appeal.   **[585]**

Drawing up and enforcement of orders

59. The proper officer of the Court shall deliver or send to the Director a copy, sealed with the seal of the Court, of every declaration or order made by the Court as soon as may be after it has been drawn up.   **[586]**

60. Any clerical mistake in any declaration or order of the Court, or error therein arising from any accidental slip or omission, may at any time be corrected by the Court on the application of any party.   **[587]**

61. Every order of the Court may be enforced in the same way as an order of the High Court, the Court of Session or the High Court in Northern Ireland is enforceable in England and Wales, Scotland or Northern Ireland respectively, and the practice of those Courts in regard to the enforcement of their orders shall apply to the enforcement of orders of the Court.   **[588]**

62. (1) The judgment of the Court shall, in so far as facts are stated therein, be deemed to be a case stated for the purpose of any appeal on a question of law to which those facts give rise, so, however, that any party may, at or before the conclusion of the hearing, request the Court to find in its judgment the facts giving rise to any specific question of law.

(2) Any party to such proceedings who wishes to appeal shall, within 21 days after the judgment has been delivered, apply in writing to the proper officer of the Court for a copy of the judgment and the proper officer shall thereupon send him a copy of the judgment signed by the presiding judge.

(3) If such party considers that the facts found in the judgment are not sufficient to enable the question of law to be fully argued, he may, within seven days after receiving the copy of the judgment, apply to the Court for it to be amplified or amended. **[589]**

Service of documents

63. (1) Every notice or other document required by these Rules to be served on or delivered to any person may be sent to that person by prepaid post at his address for service or, where no address for service has been given, at his registered office, principal place of business or last known address in the United Kingdom, and every notice or other document required to be delivered to or filed with the proper officer of the Court may be sent by prepaid post to the Clerk of the Court at the Royal Courts of Justice, Strand, London, WC2A 2LL, or to the officer acting as Clerk of the Court at 2, Parliament Square, Edinburgh, EH1 1RF, or at the Royal Courts of Justice (Ulster), Chichester Street, Belfast, BT1 3JF, as the case may require.

(2) Any notice or other document required to be served on or delivered to an association may, if the association is not a body corporate, be sent to its secretary, manager or other similar officer. **[590]**

64. The Court may on the application of the Director, which may be made *ex parte*, give leave for the service of a notice of reference outside the United Kingdom and may in that event give directions as to the mode of service and as to the extension of the time within which the respondent may enter an appearance and deliver a statement of his case. **[591]**

65. The Court may on the application of any party, which may be made *ex parte*, direct that service of any document be dispensed with or effected otherwise than in the manner provided by these Rules, including (without prejudice to the generality of the foregoing) the publication of notice thereof in such trade journal or other newspaper as the Court may direct. **[592]**

Miscellaneous

66. The time prescribed by these Rules or by order of the Court for doing any act may be extended (whether it has already expired or not) or abridged by the Court or, except where the Court otherwise directs, by consent in writing. **[593]**

67. Unless the Court otherwise directs, the months of August and September

shall be excluded in calculating time under these Rules for the delivery of any
statement of case, answer or reply, or for the making of any application to the
Court. [594]

68. The central office of the Court shall be open at such times as the President
of the Court may direct, and the offices of the Court in Scotland and Northern
Ireland shall be open at such times as may be directed by the judge of the Court
in Scotland or Northern Ireland, as the case may be. [595]

69. Where the last day for the doing of any act falls on a day on which the appropriate office of the Court is closed and by reason thereof the act cannot be done
on that day, it may be done on the next day on which the office is open.
[596]

70. Failure to comply with any requirement of these Rules shall not invalidate
any proceedings unless the Court so directs and, subject to the provisions of the
Act, of the Restrictive Practices Court Act 1976 and of these Rules, the Court
shall have power to regulate its own procedure. [597]

Revocation of Rules

71. The Restrictive Practices Court Rules 1957, the Restrictive Practices Court
(Amendment) Rules 1962, the Restrictive Practices Court (Amendment) Rules
1965, the Restrictive Practices Court (Amendment) Rules 1968, and the Restrictive
Practices Court (Amendment) Rules 1973 are hereby revoked. [598]

EXPLANATORY NOTE

(*This Note is not part of the Rules.*)

These Rules, which come into operation on the same day as the Restrictive
Practices Court Act 1976 and the Restrictive Trade Practices Act 1976, consolidate
and replace the Restrictive Practices Court Rules 1957 and the amending Rules
of 1962, 1965, 1968 and 1973, with changes consequential upon the consolidation
of the enactments relating to restrictive trade practices. [599]

THE RESTRICTIVE PRACTICES COURT (PROTECTION OF CONSUMERS) RULES 1976
(SI 1976 No 1898)

The Lord Chancellor, in exercise of the powers conferred on him by section 9(1)
and (2) of the Restrictive Practices Court Act 1976, hereby makes the following
Rules: —

Introductory

1. These Rules may be cited as the Restrictive Practices Court (Protection of

Consumers) Rules 1976 and shall come into operation on 15th December 1976.
[600]

2. (1) The Interpretation Act 1889 shall apply to the interpretation of these Rules as it applies to the interpretation of an Act of Parliament.

(2) In these Rules, unless the context otherwise requires —

"the Act" means the Fair Trading Act 1973;
"the Court" means the Restrictive Practices Court;
"judge" means a judge of the Court sitting in the part of the United Kingdom in which the proceedings were instituted or, as the case may be, to which they have been transferred;
"the principal Rules" means the Restrictive Practices Court Rules 1976 and any rules amending or replacing those Rules;
"the proper officer of the Court" means the Clerk of the Court or other proper officer at the central office of the Court or at the office of the Court in Scotland or Northern Ireland, as the case may be;
expressions used in these Rules which are used in the Act have the same meaning in these Rules as in the Act. **[601]**

Notice of application under section 35 or 38 of the Act

3. (1) Proceedings before the Court under section 35 or 38 of the Act shall be instituted by a notice of application issued out of the central office of the Court, or the office of the Court in Scotland or Northern Ireland, as the case may be, specifying the part of the United Kingdom in which the hearing is to take place and the persons against whom an order is sought, and containing the particulars and other information required by this rule.

(2) Every notice of application shall contain particulars of —

(*a*) the person carrying on a business;
(*b*) the course of conduct complained of;
(*c*) the ground or grounds upon which it is alleged that the course of conduct is —

(i) detrimental to the interests of consumers in the United Kingdom, and
(ii) to be regarded as unfair to consumers;

(*d*) the facts and matters on which the Director intends to rely in order to show that the person carrying on a business —

(i) has persisted in the course of conduct, and
(ii) has so persisted in the course of that business.

(3) A notice of application under section 35 of the Act shall further state —

(*a*) that the Director is unable, despite his best endeavours (of which particulars shall be given), to obtain a satisfactory written assurance from the person carrying on a business that he will refrain from continuing the course of conduct complained of and from carrying on any similar course of conduct in the course of that business; or

(b) the facts and matters from which it appears to the Director that the person who has given such an assurance has failed to observe it.

(4) A notice of application under section 38 of the Act shall further state—

(a) the name and address of each alleged accessory;

(b) (except where the same notice of application relates to proceedings under section 35 as well as under section 38), whether or not proceedings have been commenced under section 35 against the body corporate, and if so where and when they were commenced and what stage they have reached;

(c) the facts and matters from which it appears to the Director that each alleged accessory—

(i) consented to or connived at the course of conduct, and

(ii) fulfilled at a material time, which shall also be stated, the relevant conditions in relation to the body corporate;

(d) in relation to each alleged accessory, the particulars corresponding to those required by paragraph (3) of this rule in relation to a person carrying on a business.

(5) If the Director, in reliance on section 11 of the Civil Evidence Act 1968, section 10 of the Law Reform (Miscellaneous Provisions) (Scotland) Act 1968, section 7 of the Civil Evidence Act (Northern Ireland) 1971 or section 36(2) of the Act, intends to adduce evidence of a conviction or a finding of breach of contract or breach of duty in civil proceedings he must include in the notice of application under this rule a statement of his intention with particulars of—

(a) the conviction or finding and the date thereof;

(b) the court which made the conviction or finding and, in the case of a finding, the proceedings in which it was made;

(c) the person or persons convicted or, as the case may be, against whom the finding was made; and

(d) the issue in the proceedings to which the conviction or finding is relevant.

(6) A notice of application shall be accompanied by a list of all documents relevant to the application which are or have been in the Director's possession or power.   **[602]**

4. A notice of application shall be issued by being sealed with the Court's seal by the proper officer of the Court with whom a copy of the notice shall be left to be filed by him.   **[603]**

5. The Director shall serve a copy of the notice of application and of the list referred to in rule 3(6) on all persons or bodies against whom an order is sought, and those persons or bodies shall be respondents to the proceedings.   **[604]**

Entry of appearance

6. Every respondent who wishes to be heard in the proceedings shall within 14

days of service upon him of a copy of the notice of application enter an appearance in accordance with rule 7 of the principal Rules. **[605]**

Delivery of answer

7. Every respondent who has entered an appearance shall, within 28 days of his entry of appearance, deliver to the Director and file with the proper officer of the Court an answer which shall be accompanied by a list of all the documents relevant to the proceedings which are or have been in his possession or power, indicating for which (if any) of those documents he claims privilege and the grounds of the claim. **[606]**

8. Every allegation of fact in a notice of application shall be deemed to be admitted unless in the answer it is denied specifically or by necessary implication, or is stated not to be admitted, and any respondent who wishes to allege that a conviction or finding referred to in the notice was erroneous or is irrelevant must do so in his answer. **[607]**

9. No reply or further pleading may be filed without leave. **[608]**

Inspection of documents

10. Without prejudice to the provisions of these Rules relating to discovery, the Director and any respondent shall within seven days after receiving notice in that behalf from any opposite party, provide for his inspection the documents specified in the list referred to in rule 3(6) or 7 or such of them as may be specified in the notice, and shall permit that party to take copies thereof:

Provided that nothing in this rule shall affect the right of a respondent to claim privilege for any document. **[609]**

Particulars

11. (1) In proceedings in England and Wales or in Northern Ireland, any party may apply to any opposite party for further and better particulars of the notice of application, answer or reply and, if such particulars are not supplied within 14 days or such further time as may be agreed, he may apply to the Court which may order the delivery of such further and better particulars as it considers necessary.

(2) In proceedings in Scotland—

　(*a*) the Director shall, within seven days after the expiration of the time limited for filing an answer, make up an open record consisting of the notice of application and the answer and file two copies thereof with the proper officer of the Court, at the same time delivering a copy thereof to each of the respondents, and thereafter the parties shall forthwith proceed to adjust their pleadings;

　(*b*) upon expiration of 28 days from the filing of the open record, or of such period of continuation as may be allowed by the Court on cause shown, the record shall be deemed to be closed, and thereafter no amendment of the pleadings shall be made except by leave of the Court; and

(c) within 14 days after the closing of the record the Director shall file two copies of the closed record with the proper officer of the Court, and shall at the same time deliver 15 copies thereof to each of the respondents.   **[610]**

Amendment of pleadings

12. In proceedings in England and Wales or in Northern Ireland a notice of application, answer or reply may be amended—

(a) at any time by leave of the Court;

(b) at any time before the hearing of the application for directions without leave, if—

    (i) in the case of a notice of application or reply, the Director and all respondents who have entered an appearance or, as the case may be, to whose answer the reply is directed, agree; or

    (ii) in the case of an answer, the Director and all respondents seeking to amend agree;

and a copy of the pleading as amended shall be delivered to all opposite parties and filed with the proper officer of the Court within such time as may be allowed by the Court or agreed between the parties concerned.   **[611]**

Application for directions

13. (1) With a view to providing an occasion for the consideration of the preparations for the final hearing, so that—

(a) all matters which can be dealt with on interlocutory applications and have not already been dealt with (including, in Scotland, any preliminary question of relevancy or sufficiency of specification arising on the pleadings) may, so far as possible, be dealt with; and

(b) such directions may be given as to the future course of the proceedings as appear best adapted to secure the just, expeditious and economical disposal thereof,

the Director shall, as soon as practicable after every respondent has delivered an answer or after the time for doing so has expired (or in Scotland as soon as practicable after the closing of the record), make an application to the Court for directions and shall serve notice of the application on every respondent who has entered an appearance.

(2) The proper officer of the Court shall fix a date for the hearing of the application for directions and serve notice of the time and place of the hearing on every respondent who has entered an appearance, and rule 23(3) of the principal Rules (except sub-paragraph (k)) shall apply, with the necessary

modifications, to the application for directions as if —

(*a*) references to the notice of reference or to any statement of case were references to the notice of application; and

(*b*) for the word "agreement" in sub-paragraph (*i*) there were substituted the words "course of conduct". **[612]**

Application of principal Rules

14. Rules 10, 20 and 21, 24 to 28, 30 and 32, 34 to 40 and 44 of the principal Rules shall apply, with the necessary modifications, to proceedings instituted by a notice of application under these Rules as they apply to proceedings instituted by a notice of reference under the principal Rules. **[613]**

Final hearing

15. Subject to the provisions of section 7(1) of the Restrictive Practices Court Act 1976 the final hearing shall take place in public before such members of the Court as the President thereof may nominate for the purpose. **[614]**

Interconnected bodies corporate

16. (1) Where in any proceedings under section 35 or 38 of the Act the Director intends to apply for a direction under section 40 thereof that any order made against a body corporate which is a member of a group of interconnected bodies corporate shall be binding on all members of the group, he shall serve a notice to that effect on each of them and shall file a copy thereof with the proper officer of the Court.

(2) As soon as a date and place have been fixed for the final hearing of the proceedings or for any hearing under rule 20(4), the Director shall give notice thereof to each of the bodies corporate other than the respondent on which notice under paragraph (1) was served.

(3) Every body corporate on which notice is served under paragraph (1) may appear at the final hearing or at any hearing under rule 20(4) notwithstanding that it is not a respondent to the proceedings and may be heard on the question whether any order made under section 37 or 39 of the Act should be directed to be binding on each member of the group.

(4) If at any time the respondent wishes the application for a direction under section 40 of the Act to extend to an interconnected body corporate not mentioned in the notice served under paragraph (1), it shall serve on that body and on the Director, and file with the proper officer of the Court, a notice containing particulars of that body; and paragraphs (2) and (3) shall thereupon apply to that body as if it had been served with notice under paragraph (1).

(5) With a view to deciding whether or on whom to serve notice under paragraph (1) the Director may, at any time before applying for directions under

rule 14 or 20(2), serve on the respondent a notice requiring it to give to the Director within 14 days after service of the notice particulars of any interconnected bodies corporate which are members of a group of which the respondent is a member and shall file a copy of any such notice with the proper officer of the Court.

(6) The respondent shall comply with any notice served under paragraph (5) by delivering to the Director and filing with the proper officer of the Court the particulars required by the notice within the time thereby prescribed.   **[615]**

17. Any directions given by the Court under section 40(2) of the Act shall be contained in an order of the Court which shall be drawn up in accordance with rule 21.   **[616]**

Applications under section 40(3) of the Act

18. (1) An application by the Director for a direction under section 40(3) of the Act may be made by notice in writing issued out of the central office of the Court, or the office of the Court in Scotland or Northern Ireland, as the case may be, specifying the bodies corporate against which the order was made and the bodies corporate in respect of which a direction is sought.

(2) The notice of application shall be issued by being sealed with the Court's seal by the proper officer of the Court with whom a copy of the notice shall be left to be filed by him.

(3) The Director shall serve a copy of the notice on every body corporate specified therein and those bodies shall be respondents to the notice.

(4) The provisions of these Rules shall apply, with the necessary modifications, to all further proceedings on an application under this rule as they apply to an application under rule 3.   **[617]**

Costs

19. (1) In exercising its discretion as to costs the Court shall, subject to paragraph (2), have regard to the practice observed in civil proceedings in the High Court, the Court of Session or the High Court in Northern Ireland, as the case may be, and, without prejudice to the generality of the foregoing, may order the payment by any party of costs incurred by any person entitled under these Rules to be heard in the proceedings.

(2) Where the Court makes an order for the payment of costs by any party it may direct that the proper officer of the Court refer the costs to be taxed or assessed by a Master of the Supreme Court (Taxing Office) or by the Auditor of the Court of Session in Scotland or by the Taxing Master of the Supreme Court of Northern Ireland.

(3) Where the Court gives a direction under paragraph (2) in proceedings in England and Wales, the provisions of Order 62 of the Rules of the Supreme Court 1965 shall apply, with the necessary modifications, to the taxation of the costs

as if the proceedings in the Court were a cause or matter in the Supreme Court.

(4) Where the Court gives a direction under paragraph (2) in proceedings in Scotland, the provisions of rules 348 and 349 of the Rules of the Court of Session shall apply, with the necessary modifications, to the taxation of the costs as if the proceedings in the Court were a cause or matter in the Court of Session.

(5) Where the Court gives a direction under paragraph (2) in proceedings in Northern Ireland, the provisions of Order 65 of the Rules of the Supreme Court (Northern Ireland) 1936 shall apply, with the necessary modifications, to the taxation of the costs as if the proceedings in the Court were a cause or matter in the High Court in Northern Ireland.   **[618]**

Discontinuance and summary application for final order

20. (1) The Director may at any time discontinue the proceedings against any or all of the respondents without the leave of the Court, on giving notice to every respondent who has entered an appearance and on his undertaking to pay the costs incurred by any respondent against whom the proceedings are discontinued.

(2) If at any time before the final hearing any respondent informs the Director that he is willing to submit to an order under section 37 or 39 of the Act or to give an undertaking under either of those sections, the Director shall apply to the Court for directions and shall serve notice on every other party that he has done so.

(3) On receipt of an application under paragraph (2) the proper officer of the Court shall fix a date for the hearing of the application and serve notice of the time and place of the hearing on the Director and on all respondents who have entered an appearance.

(4) On the hearing of the application the Court may take such steps as it thinks fit for disposing of the proceedings against any respondent who is willing to submit to an order or to give such an undertaking as aforesaid and for continuing the proceedings against any other respondent, and, without prejudice to the generality of the foregoing, may—

  (*a*) make and record any finding against any respondent if he consents;
  (*b*) make an order that the proceedings against any respondent be stayed, except for the purpose of carrying into effect the agreed terms on which the proceedings are stayed; and
  (*c*) make such order as to costs as it thinks fit.   **[619]**

Drawing up and enforcement of orders

21. The proper officer of the Court shall deliver or send to the Director a copy, sealed with the seal of the Court, of every order made under section 37 or 39 of the Act or containing directions given under section 40 thereof as well as of any order made under rule 20(4) as soon as may be after the order has been drawn up.   **[620]**

Supplementary

22. Rules 60 to 70 (except rule 62) of the principal Rules shall apply, with the necessary modifications, to proceedings instituted by a notice of application under these Rules as they apply to proceedings instituted by a notice of reference under the principal Rules.   **[621]**

Revocation of Rules

23. The Restrictive Practices Court (Protection of Consumers) Rules 1973 are hereby revoked.   **[622]**

EXPLANATORY NOTE

(This Note is not part of the Rules.)

These Rules, which come into operation on the same day as the Restrictive Practices Court Act 1976 and the Restrictive Practices Court Rules 1976, replace the Restrictive Practices Court (Protection of Consumers) Rules 1973. The amendments are consequential upon the consolidation of the enactments and rules of procedure relating to restrictive trade practices.   **[623]**

THE RESTRICTIVE PRACTICES COURT (RESALE PRICES) RULES 1976
(SI 1976 No 1899)

The Lord Chancellor, in exercise of the powers conferred on him by section 9(1) and (2) of the Restrictive Practices Court Act 1976 and section 21(1) and (2) of the Resale Prices Act 1976, hereby makes the following Rules: —

Introductory

1. These Rules may be cited as the Restrictive Practices Court (Resale Prices) Rules 1976 and shall come into operation on 15th December 1976.   **[624]**

2. (1) The Interpretation Act 1889 shall apply to the interpretation of these Rules as it applies to the interpretation of an Act of Parliament.

(2) In these Rules, unless the context otherwise requires —

"the Act" means the Resale Prices Act 1976;
"final hearing" includes a hearing under rule 43(3) of the principal Rules;
"judge" means a judge of the Court sitting in the part of the United Kingdom in which the proceedings were instituted or, as the case may be, to which they have been transferred;

"the principal Rules" means the Restrictive Practices Court Rules 1976 and any rules amending or replacing those Rules;

"the proper officer of the Court" means the Clerk of the Court or other proper officer at the central office of the Court or at the office of the Court in Scotland or Northern Ireland, as the case may be;

"representation order" means an order made under rule 9(*b*) or having effect as if made under that rule;

"supplier" and "retailer", in relation to any class of goods, include trade associations consisting of or including suppliers and retailers respectively of that class of goods;

expressions used in these Rules which are used in the Act have the same meaning in these Rules as in the Act.   **[625]**

Applications under section 16(1)

3. An applicant who wishes to obtain leave to apply under section 16(1) of the Act for an order in respect of goods of any class must apply for leave by notice issued out of the central office of the Court, or the office of the Court in Scotland or Northern Ireland.   **[626]**

4. A notice under rule 3 shall be accompanied by a copy of the intended application, which shall state the class of goods to which it relates and the provisions of section 14(2) of the Act on which the applicant intends to rely, and shall be supported by evidence on affidavit of the facts alleged by the applicant to justify the making of an order under section 16(1) of the Act; and copies of the notice, the intended application, and every affidavit shall be served on the Director not less than six weeks before the date fixed by the Court for the hearing of the application for leave, and the Director shall be entitled to be heard thereon.
                                                                      [627]

5. If leave is granted, the applicant shall, not later than 14 days thereafter, cause to be published in the London Gazette, the Edinburgh Gazette and the Belfast Gazette, and in at least one daily newspaper circulating throughout the United Kingdom, a notice of the application, which shall include a statement setting out the effect of rule 6.   **[628]**

6. Any supplier or retailer of goods of a class to which the application relates, and any trade association representing employees in the distributive trades, who wishes to be represented before the Court on the hearing of the application must notify the applicant and the Director in writing within 28 days after the publication of the notice—

(*a*) stating the nature of his interest;

(*b*) stating whether he supports or opposes the maintenance of minimum resale prices in respect of all or any of the goods to which the application relates;

(*c*) giving the name of his solicitor (if any); and

(*d*) giving an address in the United Kingdom at which documents may be served on him. **[629]**

Preliminary application for directions

7. Not later than 28 days after the expiration of the time limited for notifying an interest under rule 6, the applicant shall—

(*a*) apply to the Court to fix a date for the hearing of a preliminary application for directions;

(*b*) give not less than 28 days' notice of the date so fixed to the Director as well as to every supplier, retailer and trade association who has notified an interest;

(*c*) include with his notice a list containing the names and addresses of the persons to whom the notice is given and particulars of the interest notified and other information supplied by each person other than the Director; and

(*d*) file a copy of the list with the proper officer of the Court. **[630]**

8. Any person to whom notice of the preliminary application for directions is given who intends to apply for a representation order or for any directions under rule 9 shall give to the Director and to all other persons to whom notice of the preliminary application was given not less than 14 days' notice of his intention, specifying the directions for which he intends to ask, together with a copy of any affidavit on which he intends to rely, and shall file a copy of the notice and of any such affidavit with the proper officer of the Court. **[631]**

9. On the hearing of the preliminary application for directions the Court—

(*a*) shall determine which (if any) of the suppliers, retailers and trade associations from whom notification has been received under rule 6 have such an interest as to entitle them to be represented before the Court in the proceedings;

(*b*) may order that some or all of the suppliers, retailers or trade associations who are before the Court be represented by such representative respondent as the Court may direct;

(*c*) may order that the application be amended by including therein or excluding therefrom any goods, or be divided into and treated as two or more separate applications each relating to such classes of goods as the Court may direct;

(*d*) may give directions as to the delivery of a statement of case by the applicant and by any supplier, retailer or trade association; and

(*e*) may give such consequential directions as it thinks fit. **[632]**

Service of application

10. Subject to rule 11, the applicant shall serve a copy of the application on the Director and on every supplier, retailer and trade association entitled to take part in the proceedings by virtue of directions given under rule 9(*a*); and the Director and every supplier, retailer and trade association on whom a copy of the application is served shall be a respondent to the application.   **[633]**

11. Where on the hearing of the preliminary application for directions the Court makes a representation order, then, unless the Court otherwise directs —

(*a*) a copy of the application and of the representation order shall be served on the Director and on each representative respondent;

(*b*) a copy of the application shall also be served on any supplier, retailer and trade association entitled to take part in the proceedings by virtue of directions given under rule 9(*a*) to whom the representation order does not extend; and

(*c*) the applicant shall cause to be published in such trade journal or other newspaper as the Court may direct short particulars of the application and of the representation order;

but (subject to rule 14) no other supplier, retailer or trade association shall be served with the application or made a respondent.   **[634]**

Entry of appearance

12. Every respondent who wishes to be heard in the proceedings shall, within 14 days after service on him of a copy of the application, enter an appearance in the office of the Court out of which notice of the application was issued by delivering to the proper officer of the Court two copies of a memorandum stating that the respondent wishes to be heard in the proceedings and containing the name of his solicitor (if any) and an address in the United Kingdom at which documents may be served on him; and the proper officer shall thereupon send one copy of the memorandum, sealed with the seal of the Court, to the Director.
          [635]

Subsequent proceedings on application

13. Rules 10 to 44 (except rule 33) of the principal Rules shall apply to all subsequent proceedings on the application as they apply to proceedings instituted by a notice of reference under the principal Rules, with the necessary modifications, and in particular as if —

(*a*) references to an agreement were references to the class of goods to which the application relates; and

(*b*) references to section 10(1) or 19(1) of the Restrictive Trade Practices Act 1976 were references to section 14 of the Act.   **[636]**

14. An application for the making of a representation order (where no such order was made on the hearing of the preliminary application for directions) or for the revocation or modification of a representation order (whenever made) may be made at any time before the final hearing —

(*a*) by the applicant under section 16(1) of the Act; or
(*b*) by the Director; or
(*c*) by any respondent or any member of a class represented by a representative respondent,

and on the hearing of the application the Court may make any order which it could have made under rule 9(*b*) or, as the case may require, may revoke or modify the representation order, and shall give all such consequential directions as it considers necessary.   **[637]**

15. (1) Where the applicant or a respondent is a trade association consisting of or including suppliers or retailers, as the case may be, the Director may apply for an order for discovery under rule 28(1) of the principal Rules or for an order for an investigation under rule 29 of those Rules against any member of the association who supplies or retails any goods to which the application relates under arrangements for maintaining minimum prices on resale; and on the hearing of the application for directions mentioned in rule 22 of the principal Rules the Court may give directions for discovery of documents by any such member or for an investigation of the cost incurred by him in producing, supplying or retailing any goods or in applying any process of manufacture to goods.

(2) In the application of this rule to proceedings in Scotland, for the reference to rule 28(1) of the principal Rules there shall be substituted a reference to rule 28(2) of those Rules, and for any reference to discovery of documents there shall be substituted a reference to recovery of documents under a commission and diligence.   **[638]**

Settlement of issues

16. On the hearing of the application for directions mentioned in rule 22 of the principal Rules or at any time thereafter, the Court may, either on the application of any party or of its own motion, give such directions as it thinks fit as to the formulation by the parties of the issues of fact and law which fall to be determined by the Court at the final hearing.   **[639]**

17. The Court shall settle the issues formulated by the parties in accordance with the directions given under rule 16 and the issues so settled (or as amended in pursuance of rule 18) shall, unless the Court otherwise directs, be those to be determined at the final hearing.   **[640]**

18. Any party may apply to the Court for amendment of the issues as settled by the Court and shall, except where the application is made at the final hearing, give all other parties not less than seven days' notice of the date fixed for the hearing of the application and of the amendments for which he asks, and the Court may on such application make such amendment of the issues as it thinks just.   **[641]**

Applications under section 17(1)

19. An applicant who wishes to obtain leave to apply for an order under section 17(1)(*a*) or (*b*) of the Act must apply for leave by notice issued out of the office of the Court in that part of the United Kingdom in which the previous proceedings relating to the class of goods which are the subject of the application took place.   **[642]**

20. (1) A notice under rule 19 shall be accompanied by a copy of the intended application and be supported by evidence on affidavit of the material change in the relevant circumstances on which the applicant relies.

(2) Unless the Court otherwise directs, a copy of the notice and of every affidavit shall be served on every party who appeared on the hearing of the previous proceedings not less than six weeks before the date fixed by the Court for the hearing of the application for leave.

(3) Every person on whom notice of the application for leave is served shall be entitled to be heard on that application.   **[643]**

21. If leave is granted, the Court shall give such directions as it thinks fit as to—

(*a*) the delivery of a statement of case by the applicant and of an answer by the parties to the previous proceedings on whom notice was served under rule 20; and

(*b*) the inclusion in or exclusion from the application of any goods;

and, subject to any such direction, the provisions of these Rules relating to an application under section 16(1) of the Act shall apply with the necessary modifications to all further proceedings on the application as if the Court had given any directions which it has power to give under rule 9.   **[644]**

Costs

22. (1) Where it appears to the Court that any party has been guilty of unreasonable delay, or of improper, vexatious, prolix or unnecessary steps in any proceedings under Part II of the Act or of other unreasonable conduct (including, but without prejudice to the generality of the foregoing, a refusal to make any admission or agreement as to the conduct of the proceedings which he ought reasonably to have made), the Court may make an order for costs against him.

(2) Where an order is made under paragraph (1) the Court may direct that the party against whom the order is made shall pay to any other party—

(*a*) a lump sum by way of costs; or

(*b*) such costs or such proportion of the costs as may be just.

(3) Where the Court gives a direction under paragraph (2)(*b*) it may—

(*a*) itself assess the sum to be paid; or

(*b*) direct that it be assessed by the proper officer of the Court; or

(*c*) direct that the proper officer of the Court refer the costs to be taxed or assessed by a Master of the Supreme Court (Taxing Office) or by the Auditor of the Court of Session in Scotland or by the Taxing Master of the Supreme Court of Northern Ireland.

(4) Where a direction is given under paragraph (3)(*b*) or (*c*), any party aggrieved by the taxation or assessment may appeal to a judge within seven days of the taxation or assessment on giving notice to all parties concerned and to the officer who made the taxation or assessment; and the judge may dispose of the appeal himself, or refer it in whole or in part to a Court consisting of a presiding judge and at least two other members, and, in either event, rule 32(4) of the principal Rules shall apply to the hearing of the appeal.   **[645]**

23. Where the Court makes an order for the payment of costs by the Director under the powers conferred on it by section 21(4) of the Act, the provisions of rule 22(3) and (4) shall apply with the necessary modifications.   **[646]**

Supplementary

24. Rules 59 to 70 of the principal Rules shall apply with the necessary modifications to proceedings under Part II of the Act as they apply to proceedings instituted by a notice of reference under the principal Rules.   **[647]**

Revocation of Rules

25. The Restrictive Practices Court (Resale Prices) Rules 1965, and the Restrictive Practices Court (Resale Prices) (Amendment) Rules 1966 are hereby revoked.   **[648]**

EXPLANATORY NOTE

(*This Note is not part of the Rules.*)

These Rules, which come into operation on the same day as the Restrictive Practices Court Act 1976 and the Resale Prices Act 1976, consolidate and replace the Restrictive Practices Court (Resale Prices) Rules 1965 and the amending Rules of 1966, with changes consequential upon the consolidation of the enactments relating to resale price maintenance.   **[649]**

THE ANTI-COMPETITIVE PRACTICES (EXCLUSIONS) ORDER 1980
(SI 1980 No 979)

1. (1) This Order may be cited as the Anti-Competitive Practices (Exclusions) Order 1980 and shall come into operation on 12th August 1980.

(2) In this Order, "the Act" means the Competition Act 1980.   **[650]**

2. For the purposes of the Act, a course of conduct is excluded from constituting an anti-competitive practice if it is—

(*a*) a course of conduct described in Schedule 1 to this Order, or

(*b*) the course of conduct of a person (not being a local authority within the meaning of section 2(8) of the Act)—

(i) whose relevant annual turnover in the United Kingdom is less than £5 million, and

(ii) who enjoys less than one quarter of a relevant market, and

(iii) who is not a member of a group of interconnected bodies corporate which has an aggregate annual turnover in the United Kingdom of £5 million or more or which enjoys one quarter or more of a relevant market;

and the provisions of Schedule 2 to this Order shall have effect for the purpose of determining whether a person is such a person as is described in sub-paragraph (*b*) above. **[651]**

3. For the purposes of enabling the Director General of Fair Trading to establish whether any person's course of conduct is excluded by Article 2(*b*) above from constituting an anti-competitive practice, sections 44(2) and 46 of the Fair Trading Act 1973 (power of the Director to require information) shall apply, subject to the modifications that—

(*a*) the Director may exercise the power in section 44(2) in the circumstances mentioned in section 3(1) of the Act and for the purpose mentioned above instead of in the circumstances and for the purpose mentioned in section 44(1);

(*b*) where the Director exercises the said power for the purpose of establishing whether a person is one whose relevant annual turnover in the United Kingdom is less than £5 million, as mentioned in Article 2(*b*)(i) above, references in section 44(2) to any person shall be treated as references to that person and references in the said section to goods or services of a particular description shall be treated as references to any goods or services;

(*c*) where the Director exercises the said power for the purpose of establishing whether a person enjoys less than one quarter of a relevant market, as mentioned in Article 2(*b*)(ii) above, references in section 44(2) to goods or services of a particular description shall be treated as references to goods or services of a description in relation to which a person was or is pursuing a course of conduct in respect of which the question arises whether it is excluded by Article 2(*b*) above from being an anti-competitive practice;

(*d*) paragraphs (*b*) and (*c*) of section 44(2) shall not apply; and

(*e*) section 46(1) shall apply as if it related to the power conferred on the Director by section 44(2) as modified by this Article:

Provided that those sections shall not apply to enable the Director to establish whether a person is a member of such a group of interconnected bodies corporate as is described in Article 2(*b*)(iii) above, or whether a group is such a group as is so described. **[652]**

SCHEDULE 1

Article 2(*a*)

EXCLUDED COURSES OF CONDUCT

1. Any course of conduct which consists of—

   (*a*) the inclusion in contracts for the supply of goods of conditions relating solely to the supply of those goods outside the United Kingdom, or
   (*b*) the refusal to supply goods except upon such conditions.

2. Any course of conduct required or envisaged by any provision of an agreement or arrangement made under section 24 of the Transport Act 1968 or section 1 or 3 of the Transport Act 1978, being a provision the inclusion of which in the agreement or arrangement was pursuant to a duty imposed by the provision of those Acts under which the agreement or arrangement was made.

3. (1) Any course of conduct pursued by an operator of international sea transport services in respect of such services or in respect of the acquisition of any goods or the securing of any other services in connection with the operation of such services.

   (2) Any course of conduct pursued by any person solely in respect of the securing by him of international sea transport services.

   (3) In this paragraph, "international sea transport services" means the international carriage of passengers or goods wholly by sea or (where the carriage is not wholly by sea and the carriage by sea and the carriage otherwise than by sea form part of the same service) partly by sea, and includes carriage by hovercraft.

4. (1) Any course of conduct pursued by an air transport undertaking solely in respect of international carriage by air [otherwise than on a charter flight].[1]

   (2) Any course of conduct required or envisaged by a restriction accepted under an agreement described in paragraph 3(2) of the Schedule to the Restrictive Trade Practices (Services) Order 1976, being a course of conduct pursued solely in respect of international carriage by air [otherwise than on a charter flight].[1]

   (3) [In this paragraph, "air transport undertaking" has the same meaning as in the Air Navigation Order 1980 and "charter flight" means a flight on which the whole capacity of the aircraft is available for purchase by one or more charterers for his or their own use or for resale.][1]

5. (1) Any course of conduct required or envisaged by any agreement entered into between the Treasury (or the Treasury and the Secretary of State) and building societies which relates solely to the raising of funds or the making of loans.

   (2) In this paragraph, a "building society" means a society incorporated under the Building Societies Act 1962 or any enactment repealed by that Act (and includes a Northern Ireland society as defined in section 134 of that Act).

6. Any course of conduct required or envisaged by an agreement described in paragraph 6 of the Schedule to the said Order of 1976.

7. (1) Any course of product pursued by a member of an association to which section 33 of the Restrictive Trade Practices Act 1976 applies, being a course of conduct required

or envisaged by an agreement to which, by virtue of that section, the said Act does not apply.

(2) Any course of conduct pursued by such an association which is required or envisaged by such an agreement, not being an agreement made between the association and a person who is a member neither of the association nor of a constituent association.

8. Any course of conduct pursued by a parish or community council within the meaning of the Local Government Act 1972 or a community council established under Part IV of the Local Government (Scotland) Act 1973.   **[653]**

AMENDMENT
1 Words in para 4 added or substituted by the Anti-Competitive Practices (Exclusions) (Amendment) Order 1984, SI 1984 No 1919 with effect from 1 January 1985.

SCHEDULE 2

Article 2

PROVISIONS FOR DETERMINING WHETHER A PERSON IS SUCH A PERSON AS IS DESCRIBED IN ARTICLE 2(*b*) OF THIS ORDER

1. In this Schedule —

"relevant date" means —

(*a*) in a case in which notice has been given under section 3(2)(*a*) of the Act to the person in respect of whose course of conduct the question arises whether it is excluded by Article 2(*b*) above from constituting an anti-competitive practice —

(i) the first day of April last preceding the day on which notice was so given if that day was not the first day of April in any year, or

(ii) the day on which notice was so given if that day was the first day of April in any year, and

(*b*) in a case in which no notice has been given to the said person under the said section —

(i) the first day of April last preceding the day on which the said question arises if that day is not the first day of April in any year, or

(ii) the day on which the said question arises if that day is the first day of April in any year;

"relevant goods or services" means, in any particular case, goods or services of the description in relation to which the person in respect of whose course of conduct the question arises whether it is excluded by Article 2(*b*) above from constituting an anti-competitive practice was or is pursuing that course of conduct;

"relevant period" means, in relation to any particular person —

(*a*) where that person has, within the two years ending immediately before the relevant date, completed an accounting period of more than six months, the last such period so to be completed, or

(*b*) where that person has not so completed such a period but has, within the six months ending immediately before the relevant date, completed an accounting period of six months or less, so much of the period of twelve months ending on the last day of the last such period so to be completed as during which that person was carrying on a business of supplying goods or services in the United Kingdom or otherwise carrying on business in the United Kingdom, or

(*c*) in any other case, so much of the period of twelve months ending immediately before the relevant date as during which that person was carrying on a business of supplying goods or services in the United Kingdom or otherwise carrying on business in the United Kingdom; and

"turnover in the United Kingdom" during any particular period means the total amount charged for the supply of goods and services in the United Kingdom during that period in the ordinary course of a person's business, after deduction —

(a) of trade discounts, rebates and other allowances;
(b) of Value Added Tax and other taxes directly related to turnover; and
(c) of any amount charged for any such supply where both the person supplying the goods or services and the person to whom they were supplied were members of one and the same group of interconnected bodies corporate at the time of supply:

Provided that in a case in which the total amount of revenue receivable by a person during any particular period in the ordinary course of his business in the United Kingdom, after deduction —

(i) of amounts receivable in respect of the supply by him of goods or services;
(ii) of trade discounts, rebates and other allowances;
(iii) of Value Added Tax and other taxes directly related to turnover; and
(iv) of any amount receivable from any other person where both he and that other person were members of one and the same group of interconnected bodies corporate when payment fell due,

equals one third or more of the total amount charged for the supply of goods and services in the United Kingdom during the said period in the ordinary course of his business, after the deductions mentioned in sub-paragraphs (a), (b) and (c) above, "turnover in the United Kingdom" during that period means the aggregate of the two said total amounts after the aforementioned respective deductions.

2. For the purposes of Article 2(b)(i) above, the relevant annual turnover in the United Kingdom of a person in any particular case is —

(a) where the relevant period equals twelve months, the turnover in the United Kingdom of that person during that period, and
(b) where the relevant period does not equal twelve months, the amount which bears the same proportion to the turnover in the United Kingdom of that person during that period as twelve months does to that period.

3. For the purposes of Article 2(b)(ii) above, a person enjoys less than one quarter of a relevant market unless, during the relevant period, he supplied, or there were supplied to him, at least one quarter (whether determined by value, by cost, by price or by quantity) of all the relevant goods or services supplied in the United Kingdom or any part of it during that period, no account being taken of any goods or services supplied when both the person supplying the goods or services and the person to whom they were supplied were members of one and the same group of interconnected bodies corporate at the time of supply.

4. For the purposes of Article 2(b)(iii) above, a person is a member of a group of inter-connected bodies corporate if he is a member of the group on the relevant date.

5. For the purposes of Article 2(b)(iii) above, the aggregate annual turnover in the United Kingdom of a group of interconnected bodies corporate in any particular case is the aggregate of the relevant annual turnover in the United Kingdom (within the meaning of paragraph 2 above) of each person who is a member of the group on the relevant date.

6. For the purposes of Article 2(*b*)(iii) above, a group of interconnected bodies corporate enjoys one quarter or more of a relevant market if, during the relevant period, the persons who are members of the group on the relevant date supplied in total, or there were supplied to such persons in total, at least one quarter (whether determined by value, by cost, by price or by quantity) of all the relevant goods or services supplied in the United Kingdom or any part of it during that period, no account being taken of any goods or services supplied when both the person supplying the goods or services and the person to whom they were supplied were members of one and the same group of interconnected bodies corporate at the time of supply.   [654]

THE RESTRICTION ON AGREEMENTS (MANUFACTURERS AND IMPORTERS OF MOTOR CARS) ORDER 1982

(SI 1982 No 1146)

Whereas the Secretary of State, in accordance with section 91(2) of the Fair Trading Act 1973, published on 14 June 1982 a notice stating his intention to make this Order, indicating the nature of the provisions to be embodied in it and stating that any person whose interests were likely to be affected by it and who was desirous of making representations in respect of it should do so in writing before 14 July 1982:

And whereas the Secretary of State has considered the representations made to him in accordance with that notice:

Now, therefore, the Secretary of State, being the appropriate Minister within the meaning of section 56 of the said Act, in exercise of the powers conferred by sections 56(2) and 90(2) and (4) of, and paragraphs 1 and 2 of Part I of Schedule 8 to, the said Act and for the purpose of remedying or preventing adverse effects specified in a report of the Monopolies and Mergers Commission entitled "A Report on the matter of the existence or the possible existence of a complex monopoly situation in relation to the wholesale supply of motor car parts in the United Kingdom" as laid before Parliament and ordered by the House of Commons to be printed on 26 May 1982, hereby makes the following Order: —

1. This Order may be cited as the Restriction on Agreements (Manufacturers and Importers of Motor Cars) Order 1982 and all articles thereof shall come into operation on 1st November 1982 except 3(*b*) and 4 which shall come into operation on 1st April 1983.   [655]

2. In this Order: —

"car parts" means replacements for parts which are fitted to a motor car as standard equipment when sold new, excluding equipment for in-car entertainment and liquids;

"franchisee" means any person who is or has been appointed by a manufacturer or importer of motor cars to deal in motor cars or car parts supplied to that person by the manufacturer or importer; and

"recall campaign" means the steps taken by a manufacturer or importer of motor cars to ensure that motor cars or car parts which in the opinion of the manufacturer or importer are likely to contain defects or to be defective, in circumstances in which they would not normally be expected, as a result of ordinary use, to contain defects or to be defective are taken to a franchisee for the purpose of inspection and, if necessary, rectification or replacement.   **[656]**

3. Subject to article 5 below, it shall be unlawful for any manufacturer or importer of motor cars—

(*a*) to make an agreement; or

(*b*) to carry out an agreement, whenever made

with a franchisee to the extent that the agreement contains a provision under or by virtue of which the franchisee is required to acquire all or any car parts exclusively from that manufacturer or importer, or exclusively from sources approved or specified by that manufacturer or importer.   **[657]**

4. Subject to article 5 below, any manufacturer or importer of motor cars or franchisee who is a party to an agreement containing a provision under or by virtue of which the franchisee is required to acquire all or any car parts exclusively from that manufacturer or importer, or exclusively from sources approved or specified by that manufacturer or importer, shall, to the extent that it contains such a provision, terminate it before 1st August 1983.   **[658]**

5. Neither article 3 nor article 4 above shall apply in relation to a provision in an agreement between a manufacturer or an importer of motor cars on the one hand and a franchisee on the other hand under or by virtue of which the franchisee is required to acquire a car part exclusively from that manufacturer or importer, or exclusively from sources approved or specified by that manufacturer or importer, for the purpose of

(*a*) fitting a car part to a motor car in pursuance of the manufacturer's or importer's warranty to which the motor car is subject; or

(*b*) supplying a car part in pursuance of a recall campaign.   **[659]**

EXPLANATORY NOTE

(This Note is not part of the Order.)

This Order makes it unlawful, subject to the exceptions mentioned below, for a manufacturer or importer of motor cars to make or carry out an agreement with a franchisee to the extent that the agreement contains an "exclusive buying" provision relating to replacement car parts. It also requires manufacturers and importers of motor cars and their franchisees to terminate any such agreement to the extent that it contains such a provision.

The Order does not apply in relation to "exclusive buying" provisions which operate when a replacement car part—

(*a*) is to be fitted to a motor car in pursuance of the manufacturer's or importer's warranty; or (*b*) is to be supplied by the franchisee as a result of a recall campaign conducted by the manufacturer or importer.

Copies of the report of the Monopolies and Mergers Commission upon which the Order is based (HC 318 Session 1981/82) may be obtained from Her Majesty's Stationery Office. **[660]**

THE REGISTRATION OF RESTRICTIVE TRADING AGREEMENTS REGULATIONS 1984
(SI 1984 No 392)

The Director General of Fair Trading (in these regulations referred to as "the Director") in exercise of the powers conferred on him by sections 23 and 27 of the Restrictive Trade Practices Act 1976 (in these regulations referred to as the "the Act"), hereby makes the following regulations: —

Citation, commencement, revocation and interpretation

1. (1) These regulations may be cited as the Registration of Restrictive Trading Agreements Regulations 1984 and shall come into operation on 18th April 1984.

(2) The Registration of Restrictive Trading Agreements Regulations 1976 are hereby revoked.

(3) In these regulations —

"agreement", except in regulation 3, means an agreement subject to registration under the Act and includes an agreement so subject by virtue of the application of the Act by or under any other enactment; and

"association" means an association as defined in section 16(1) of the Act or a trade association within the meaning of section 43(1) of the Act.

[661]

Furnishing of particulars of agreements

2. (1) Subject to the following provisions of these regulations, a person furnishing particulars of an agreement to the Director pursuant to section 24 of the Act shall send or deliver to him within the time specified in Schedule 2 to the Act for furnishing those particulars the documents mentioned in paragraph (2) below.

(2) The documents to be sent or delivered pursuant to paragraph (1) are —

(*a*) two copies of any document setting out the terms of the agreement so far as they are in writing;

(*b*) where the agreement or part of it is not in writing, two copies of a memorandum in writing signed by the person furnishing particulars and setting out the terms thereof or such of the terms thereof as are not in writing, as the case may be.

(3) Where the documents sent or delivered pursuant to paragraph (1) above do not disclose the name and the address of any person party to the agreement, there shall also be sent or delivered therewith two copies of a document indicating that person's name and address:

Provided that this paragraph shall not require the name or address of any of them to be provided if their number exceeds 100 and there is sent or delivered with the documents sent or delivered pursuant to the said paragraph (1) two copies of a document indicating their number or their approximate number.

(4) At least one of the copies of any document mentioned in paragraph (2)(*a*) or (3) above shall be signed by, or identified by the signature of, the person furnishing particulars.

(5) In relation to an agreement in which a term is to be implied by virtue of section 8(2) and (3), section 8(4) and (5) or section 16(2) and (3) of the Act (specific recommendations to members of associations) references in this regulation to the terms of an agreement include references to the terms of any relevant recommendations.   [662]

Newly registrable agreements varied before registration

3. In the case of an agreement becoming subject to registration by virtue of an order made under section 7 of the Act (information agreements relating to goods) or Part III of the Act (agreements relating to services) which was made before the commencement of the relevant order and is varied not later than three months after such commencement but before particulars of the agreement are furnished to the Director, regulation 2(2) above shall have effect—

   (*a*) in a case where the original agreement was in writing, as if it referred to two copies of the original agreement incorporating the variations; or

   (*b*) in a case where the original agreement was not in writing, as if it referred to two copies of a memorandum signed by the person furnishing particulars and setting out the agreement as varied.   [663]

Common form agreements

4. (1) Where particulars of an agreement are being or have been furnished to the Director pursuant to section 24 of the Act and a person party thereto is also party to other agreements differing therefrom only as respects the other party thereto or the date of making, it shall be a sufficient compliance with regulation 2 in relation to those other agreements to send or deliver to the Director two copies of a memorandum which—

   (*a*) refers to the agreement of which the particulars are being or have been furnished;

   (*b*) indicates the dates of the other agreements and the names and addresses of the parties thereto; and

(*c*) states that those agreements are otherwise identical to the agreement
of which particulars are being or have been furnished.

(2) At least one of the copies of a memorandum sent or delivered pursuant
to paragraph (1) above shall be signed by the person furnishing particulars.

(3) The proviso to regulation 2(3) above shall apply in relation to paragraph
(1)(*b*) above as it applies in relation to the said regulation 2(3).   **[664]**

Extent of the obligation to furnish particulars of variations of agreements

5. The obligation to furnish particulars of any variation of an agreement to the
Director pursuant to section 24 of the Act shall apply only to variations whereby—

(*a*) a further restriction is accepted by one or more of the parties; or
(*b*) a restriction ceases to have effect; or
(*c*) the application of an existing restriction is extended or reduced as regards
the areas or places or the classes of persons, goods, processes of manufacture or services to which it relates; or
(*d*) so far as restrictions are accepted as to the terms or conditions on which
goods are to be supplied or acquired or any process of manufacture
is to be applied to goods or any designated service is to be supplied or
obtained, the terms or conditions are varied.   **[665]**

Furnishing of particulars of the variation or determination of an agreement

6. (1) A person furnishing particulars of the variation or determination of an
agreement to the Director pursuant to section 24 of the Act shall send or deliver
to him within the time specified in Schedule 2 to the Act for furnishing those
particulars the documents hereinafter specified.

(2) The documents to be sent or delivered pursuant to paragraph (1) above
are—

(*a*) in a case where the variation or determination is effected by an instrument in writing, two copies of the instrument;
(*b*) in a case where the variation or determination is not effected by an instrument in writing, two copies of a memorandum in writing signed by the
person furnishing particulars and setting out complete particulars of
the variation or determination.

(3) At least one of the copies of any document mentioned in paragraph (2)(*a*)
above shall be signed by, or identified by the signature of, the person furnishing
particulars.   **[666]**

Certificate of particulars

7. A person sending or delivering documents to the Director in accordance with
these regulations shall send or deliver therewith a certificate signed by him or

on his behalf in the form set out in the Schedule hereto and completed as therein
indicated.   [667]

Contents of the register

8. (1) The particulars of agreements which shall be entered or filed in the register
shall be—

   (*a*) copies of the documents duly sent or delivered to the Director pursuant
        to these regulations;
   (*b*) any documents or information obtained by him under sections 36 or
        37 of the Act; and
   (*c*) any other particulars which any party to an agreement may furnish to
        him and which the Director thinks it appropriate to include in the
        register.

(2) Nothing in paragraph (1) above shall apply to any details as to parties or
other persons, prices, terms or other matters as are material for the purpose only
of defining the particular application from time to time of a continuing restriction accepted under an agreement of which particulars are entered or filed in
the register, being details which the Director considers it unnecessary to enter
or file therein.   [668]

The special section of the register

9. (1) There shall be maintained a special section of the register which shall not
be open to public inspection.

(2) There shall be entered or filed in the special section such particulars
described in section 23(3) of the Act (information the publication of which may
be contrary to the public interest or information of a specified nature the.
publication of which may substantially damage legitimate business interests) as
the Secretary of State may by virtue of that subsection direct.

(3) Where particulars are being furnished to the Director by a person who
considers that any of them should be included in the special section of the register
he shall send or deliver therewith a signed memorandum indicating the particulars
in question and the grounds on which he considers that they should be included
in that section.   [669]

Public inspection of the register

10. The public section of the register shall be open to public inspection between
10.00 am and 4.30 pm except on Saturdays, Sundays and official holidays on
which the Office of Fair Trading is closed.   [670]

Addressing of documents

11. Any documents to be sent or delivered to the Director pursuant to these regulations shall be addressed to —

The Office of Fair Trading
(RTP Registration)
Field House
Bream's Buildings
London EC4A 1PR   **[671]**

Application for extension of time for furnishing particulars

12. (1) Any application to the Director for further time for furnishing any particulars in relation to any agreement beyond the time specified in Schedule 2 to the Act shall be made in writing within the time so specified.

(2) Any such application shall —

(*a*) identify the agreement to which it relates;
(*b*) indicate the further time requested; and
(*c*) state why it is impracticable to furnish particulars within the time so specified.   **[672]**

SCHEDULE   Regulation 7
FORM OF CERTIFICATE

Form RTP (C)

Restrictive Trade
Practices Act 1976

Certificate
---

to accompany documents
for registration

IMPORTANT

If you do not submit the details of agreements to
the Director General of Fair Trading within the
time limits laid down by the Act the restrictions
in them will become void. If you are in any
doubt about timing you should consult your legal
adviser before entering into an agreement which
might be registrable under the Act.

Notes for guidance

1 The Registration of Restrictive Trading Agreement Regulations 1984 set out more fully how to give the details of agreements for registration.

2 All the parties to a registrable agreement are responsible for giving details of the agreement to the Office of Fair Trading. But it is enough if one of the parties – or someone on their behalf – does so. The person giving details must complete and sign the Certificate (opposite).

3 Two copies of all the documents which together make up the agreement should accompany the Certificate.

4 If the agreement is not in writing you should provide two copies of a memorandum setting out all the terms of the agreement. If part of the agreement is not in writing you should provide two copies of a memorandum setting out the unwritten terms of the agreement together with two copies of the written part of the agreement.

5 You should provide a list of names and addresses of all parties to the agreement. But there is an exception for agreements to which trade associations or service supply associations with more than 100 members are parties. In these cases you can omit names and addresses and list only the number or approximate number of members of the association.

6 Common form agreements are a series of almost identical agreements where one party remains the same. The only differences between the agreements are in the other parties and the dates on which the agreements were made. You need only provide full details of one agreement. For the rest you should provide memoranda giving the dates of other agreements as they are entered into and the names and addresses of the parties to them and stating that otherwise they are the same as the first agreement.

7 Where an agreement is altered or ended you should provide two copies of the document altering or ending the agreement. If the agreement is not altered or ended in writing, you should provide two copies of a memorandum setting out the changes..

8 Please list all the documents provided, including memoranda, on the back of the Certificate.

9 One copy of each documents provided, including any memorandum, should be signed by the person who signs the Certificate.

10 When you have completed and signed the Certificate please detach it and send it with your documents to:

**Office of Fair Trading
(RTP Registration)
Field House
Bream's Buildings
London EC4 1PR**

Form RTP (C)

Restrictive Trade
Practices Act 1976

Certificate

I certify that to the best of my knowledge the
documents I enclose with this form give:

★ All the terms of an agreement subject to
registration under the Restrictive Trade
Practices Act 1976

tick box(es)

☐

★ Full details of the changes to the agreement(s)

☐

Office of Fair Trading reference(s):

_____

☐

★ full details of the ending of the agreement(s)

Office of Fair Trading reference(s):

_____

The documents are listed on the other side of this form.
I have signed one copy of each document and/or memorandum.

Signed

_____

Name in BLOCK CAPITALS

_____

on behalf of

_____

_____

_____

_____

(a party to the above agreement)

Status and address of person signing

_____

_____

_____

_____

Dated

Please turn over

List of documents and/or memoranda

Please enclose **two** copies of each document and/or memorandum, **one** of which should be signed.

EXPLANATORY NOTE

(This Note is not part of the Regulations.)

These Regulations relate to the furnishing of restrictive trading agreements to the Director General of Fair Trading in accordance with the Restrictive Trade Practices Act 1976 and to the keeping by him under that Act of a register of such agreements.

The regulations replace the Registration of Restrictive Trading Agreements Regulations 1976, which are revoked.

The changes introduced by these Regulations are: —

(a) subject as indicated below the 1976 Regulations are re-enacted under the Restrictive Trade Practices Act 1976 with minor textual amendments;

(b) the number of copies of any document, memorandum, agreement or instrument to be furnished is reduced from three to two;

(c) one form to cover all the circumstances in which the documents are required to be furnished to the Director General of Fair Trading is introduced in place of the four separate forms covering different sets of circumstances as appropriate previously required;

(d) the address for the delivery of particulars is altered.   **[674]**

THE RESTRICTIVE TRADE PRACTICES (SALE AND PURCHASE AND SHARE SUBSCRIPTION AGREEMENTS) (GOODS) ORDER 1989

(SI 1989 No 1081)

Whereas a draft of this Order has been approved by resolution of each House of Parliament pursuant to section 2(5) of the Restrictive Trade Practices Act 1977;

Now, therefore, the Secretary of State, in exercise of the powers conferred on him by section 2(3) of the said Act of 1977, hereby makes the following Order: —

Citation and Commencement

1. (1) This Order may be cited as the Restrictive Trade Practices (Sale and Purchase and Share Subscription Agreements) (Goods) Order 1989 and shall come into force on the day after the day on which it is made.   **[675]**

Interpretation

2. In this Order —

"the Act of 1976" means the Restrictive Trade Practices Act 1976;

"acquired enterprise" means a company in which shares are acquired or a business an interest in which is acquired;

"business" means any undertaking which is, or any part of an undertaking which part is —

(a) carried on as a going concern for gain or reward; or

(b) carried on as a going concern in the course of which goods or services are supplied otherwise than free of charge;

"company" means a company as defined in section 735 of the Companies Act 1985 and an oversea company as defined in section 744 of that Act;

"contract of employment" means a contract of service whether it is express or implied and (if it is express) whether it is oral or in writing;

"goods" has the same meaning as in section 43(1) of the Act of 1976;

"group" means a group of interconnected bodies corporate within the meaning of section 43(1) of the Act of 1976;

"member of the issuing company" is to be construed in accordance with section 22 of the Companies Act 1985;

"purchaser" means a person acquiring shares in a company, or acquiring an interest in a business, whether for cash or otherwise;

"relevant restriction" means a restriction described in section 6(1) of the Act of 1976;

"services" has the same meaning as in section 20 of the Act of 1976.

[676]

Sale and Purchase Agreements

3. (1) This article applies to an agreement made on or after the date on which this Order comes into force—

(a) the parties to which include a person (the "vendor") who agrees to transfer shares in a company or the whole of his interest in a business to a purchaser;

(b) under which, in the case of an agreement for the transfer of shares in a company, more than 50 per cent in nominal value of the issued share capital of that company is transferred or agreed to be transferred to one purchaser or to more than one purchaser each of which is a member of the same group;

(c) under which no relevant restriction in respect of any of the matters described in section 6(1)(a) or (b) of the Act of 1976 is accepted by a person; and

(d) under which no relevant restriction in respect of any of the matters described in section 6(1)(c) to (f) of that Act is accepted by a person other than such a person as is described in paragraph (2) below.

(2) Persons by whom a relevant restriction may be accepted for the purpose of paragraph (1)(d) above are—

(a) any vendor;

(b) any member of the same group as any vendor; and

(c) any individual;

other than a body corporate or unincorporate which is also a purchaser under the agreement in question, or a member of the same group as such a body.

[677]

4. (1) In determining whether an agreement to which article 3 applies is an agreement to which the Act of 1976 applies by virtue of section 6 of that Act, no account shall be taken of any relevant restriction —

(a) which is accepted for a period not exceeding that permitted under paragraph (2) below; and

(b) which limits the extent to which the person accepting the restriction may compete with the acquired enterprise, or may be engaged or interested in, disclose information to, or otherwise assist any business which so competes.

(2) For the purpose of paragraph (1)(a) above, a permitted period is: —

(a) a period of 5 years beginning with the date of the agreement; or

(b) in the case of restrictions accepted by an individual who is to have a contract of employment with or a contract for the supply of services to the acquired enterprise, the purchaser, or a member of the same group as the purchaser, a period beginning with the date of the agreement and ending 2 years after the date of expiry or termination of the contract,

whichever ends the later.   **[678]**

Share Subscription Agreements

5. This article applies to an agreement made on or after the date on which this Order comes into force —

(a) which provides for a person (the "subscriber") to subscribe (whether or not in cash) for shares in a company (the "issuing company");

(b) under which no relevant restriction in respect of any of the matters described in section 6(1)(a) or (b) of the Act of 1976 is accepted by a person; and

(c) under which no relevant restriction in respect of any of the matters described in section 6(1)(c) to (f) of that Act is accepted by a body corporate or unincorporate.   **[679]**

6. (1) In determining whether an agreement to which article 5 applies is an agreement to which the Act of 1976 applies by virtue of section 6 of that Act, no account shall be taken of any relevant restriction —

(a) which is accepted for a period not exceeding that permitted under paragraph (2) below; and

(b) which limits the extent to which the person accepting the restriction may compete with the issuing company, or may be engaged or interested in, disclose information to, or otherwise assist any business which so competes.

(2) For the purpose of paragraph (1)(a) above, a permitted period is: —

(a) a period of 5 years beginning with the date of the agreement; or

(b) in the case of restrictions accepted —

  (i) by a member of the issuing company, a period beginning with the
      date of the agreement and ending 2 years after the date on which
      that person ceases to be a member; or
 (ii) by an individual who is to have a contract of employment with or
      a contract for the supply of services to the issuing company, a period
      beginning with the date of the agreement and ending 2 years after
      the date of expiry or termination of the contract,   **[680]**

whichever ends the later.

EXPLANATORY NOTE

(This note is not part of the Order)

The Restrictive Trade Practices Act 1976 requires that restrictive agreements
between two or more persons carrying on business in the United Kingdom in
the supply of goods be furnished to the Director General of Fair Trading for
registration.

This Order exempts from the registration requirements of the 1976 Act agreements for the sale and purchase of shares in a company or of a business ("sale
and purchase agreements") and agreements for the subscription of shares in a
company ("share subscription agreements") provided that the agreements satisfy
certain conditions.

In the case of sale and purchase agreements the main conditions are (articles
3 and 4) —

  (a) that more than 50 per cent in nominal value of the issued share capital
      of the company be transferred to one purchaser or to more than one
      where they are all members of the same group of companies, or (as the
      case may be) that the whole of the vendor's interest in a business be
      transferred to one or more purchasers;
  (b) that the agreements only contain registrable restrictions of the type
      described in section 6(1)(c) to (f) of the 1976 Act;
  (c) that such restrictions only be accepted by vendors, their associated
      companies, or by individuals (save that bodies corporate or unincor-
      porate cannot accept such restrictions where they are also purchasers
      under the agreement in question);
  (d) that the restrictions to be disregarded only limit the extent to which the
      persons accepting them may compete with the company or business
      which is the subject of the sale, or be involved in or assist any business
      which so competes; and
  (e) that the restrictions to be disregarded only be operative for a period
      not exceeding 5 years beginning with the date of the agreement or a
      period beginning with the date of the agreement and ending 2 years after
      the date of expiry or termination of the relevant employment or services
      contract, whichever is the later.

In the case of share subscription agreements the main conditions are (articles
5 and 6) —

(a) that the agreements only contain registrable restrictions of the type described in section 6(1)(c) to (f) of the 1976 Act;
(b) that such restrictions only be accepted by individuals;
(c) that the restrictions to be disregarded only limit the extent to which the persons accepting them may compete with the issuing company or be involved in or assist any business which so competes; and
(d) that the restrictions to be disregarded only be operative for a period not exceeding 5 years beginning with the date of the agreement or a period beginning with the date of the agreement and ending 2 years after the relevant person ceases to be a member of the issuing company or after the date of expiry or termination of the relevant employment or services contract, whichever is the later.   [681]

THE SUPPLY OF BEER (LOAN TIES, LICENSED PREMISES AND WHOLESALE PRICES) ORDER 1989
(SI 1989 No 2258)

Whereas the Secretary of State, in accordance with section 91(2) of the Fair Trading Act 1973, published on 22nd, 25th and 26th August 1989 a notice stating his intention to make this Order, indicating the nature of the provisions to be embodied in it and stating that any person whose interests were likely to be affected by it and who was desirous of making representations in respect of it should do so in writing before 10th October 1989;

And whereas the Secretary of State has considered the representations made to him in accordance with that notice:

Now, therefore, the Secretary of State, being the appropriate Minister within the meaning of section 56 of the said Act, in exercise of the powers conferred by sections 56(2) and 90(2), (3) and (4) of, and paragraphs 1, 2, 4, 8 and 9 of Schedule 8 to, the said Act, and for the purpose of remedying or preventing adverse effects specified in a report of the Monopolies and Mergers Commission entitled "The Supply of Beer—a report on the supply of beer for retail sale in the United Kingdom", hereby makes the following Order:—

1. (1) This Order may be cited as the Supply of Beer (Loan Ties, Licensed Premises and Wholesale Prices) Order 1989 and shall come into force—

(a) for the purposes of articles 2(2)(a) and 3(2)(a) below, on 1st January 1990, and
(b) for all other purposes, on 1st May 1990.

(2) In this Order—

"beer" includes any beverage of an alcoholic strength (within the meaning of the Alcoholic Liquor Duties Act 1979) exceeding 1.2 per cent which is made with beer;

"brewer" means a person who carries on business in the manufacture of beer which is supplied by retail in the United Kingdom;

"brewery group" means a group which is

(a) a group of interconnected bodies corporate, or

(b) a group consisting of a body corporate, or a group of inter-connected bodies corporate, all other bodies corporate in which it, or any of them, has a substantial minority holding, and all subsidiaries of those other bodies corporate,

and at least one member of which is a brewer;
"licensed premises" means—

(a) in England and Wales, premises for which a justices' on-licence (within the meaning of the Licensing Act 1964), other than a Part IV licence (within the meaning of that Act), is in force, or in respect of which a club is registered within the meaning of that Act;

(b) in Scotland, premises in respect of which a public house licence, a hotel licence or a refreshment licence (within the meaning of the Licensing (Scotland) Act 1976) is in force or which are occupied by a registered club within the meaning of that Act;

(c) in Northern Ireland, premises in which the sale of intoxicating liquor is authorised by a licence granted under the Licensing Act (Northern Ireland) 1971, being premises of a kind mentioned in paragraph (a) or (f) of section 3(1) of that Act, or in respect of which a club is registered within the meaning of the Registration of Clubs (Northern Ireland) Order 1987;

"relevant purchase", in the context of an agreement to which a brewer or a member of a brewery group is a party, means purchase by any other person who is not a member of the same group, for retail sale on licensed premises, of beer or other drink manufactured or supplied by any person not a party to the agreement;
"subsidiary" has the same meaning as in section 736 of the Companies Act 1985;
"substantial minority holding" means a holding by a body corporate of fifteen per cent or more, or an interest in shares conferring fifteen per cent or more, of the voting rights in another body corporate, other than its subsidiary; and for that purpose—

(a) an "interest in shares" includes an entitlement, by a person who is not the registered holder, to exercise any right conferred by the holding of the shares in question or an entitlement to control the exercise of any such right, and

(b) "voting rights" means rights conferred on shareholders in respect of their shares, either at all times or for the time being, to vote at general meetings of the body corporate in question on all, or substantially all, matters.

(3) For the purpose of determining whether a body corporate has a substantial minority holding in another body corporate—

(a) it is immaterial whether a holding is direct or through a nominee or trustee,

(b) the holdings of the subsidiaries of a body corporate shall be treated as its own,

(c) where one body corporate has a holding in a second body corporate

(not being its subsidiary) and the second body corporate has a holding
in a third body corporate (not being its subsidiary), the first body
corporate shall be treated as having a holding in the third equivalent
to the product of the two actual holdings expressed as percentages, and

(*d*) where a body corporate has, in consequence of the application of
subparagraphs (*a*), (*b*) and (*c*) above, more than one holding in another
body corporate, the holdings shall be aggregated and treated as a single
holding.

(4) In the case of a body corporate which is both a brewer and a member of
a brewery group, the provisions of this Order shall apply in relation to that body
corporate both as a brewer and as a member of a brewery group.

(5) For the purpose of determining whether an agreement is an agreement to
which article 2 or 3 below applies, a person shall be regarded as a brewer or a
member of a brewery group if he is for the time being a brewer or a member
of a brewery group, and it is immaterial that he may not have been such a person
when the agreement was made.

(6) For the purposes of this Order —

(*a*) a person shall not be treated as carrying out an agreement by reason
only that he refrains from doing something the doing of which is the
subject of a prohibition or restriction imposed by the agreement; and

(*b*) an agreement precludes or restricts a relevant purchase whether it does
so wholly or only in part, whether that is the object or merely the effect
of the agreement, and whether the provisions in question are expressed
as negative or positive obligations.

(7) This Order shall extend so as to prohibit the carrying out of agreements
already in existence on the date on which this Order is made as it prohibits the
carrying out of agreements made subsequently.

(8) In the case of a person falling within paragraph (*a*), (*b*) or (*c*) of section
90(3) of the Fair Trading Act 1973, this Order (except for article 5 below) shall
extend to his acts and omissions outside the United Kingdom.   **[682]**

2. (1) This article applies to —

(*a*) any agreement under which a brewer or a member of a brewery group
makes a loan or gives any other financial assistance to another person
(except a member of the same group), and

(*b*) any agreement relating to any such agreement as is mentioned in
subparagraph (*a*) above,

if (in either case) it precludes or restricts relevant purchases.

(2) Subject to paragraph (4) and article 6 below —

(*a*) the parties to any agreement to which this article applies shall terminate
it before 1st May 1990 to the extent that it is not consistent with
paragraph (3) below, and

(*b*) it shall be unlawful for any person to make or carry out an agreement
to which this article applies except to the extent that it is consistent with
paragraph (3) below.

(3) An agreement is consistent with this paragraph only if —

(*a*) the person to whom the loan is made or other financial assistance is given may at any time repay the loan or make such payment as may be due in respect of the financial assistance, having given not more than three months' notice of the repayment or payment, and

(*b*) relevant purchases are no longer precluded or restricted once the loan is repaid or payment made, including payment of all interest due;

but it shall not be inconsistent with this paragraph for an agreement to provide that if interest is payable at one rate for an initial period of one year or less and a higher rate for a subsequent period and the loan is repaid or payment made before the end of the initial period, interest at the higher rate is due in respect of all or part of the initial period.

(4) Nothing in paragraph (2) above shall be taken either to advance the time at which any payment under the agreement is due from the person to whom the loan is made or other financial assistance is given, or to relieve that person from any obligation to make payments under the agreement as they fall due. **[683]**

3. (1) This article applies to any agreement under which —

(*a*) a brewer or a member of a brewery group ceases to hold an interest in licensed premises or in premises which have been licensed premises at any time since 1st January 1990, or

(*b*) a member of a brewery group one or more members of which hold interests in licensed premises ceases to be a member of the group,

and to any agreement relating to any such agreement.

(2) Subject to article 6 below —

(*a*) the parties to any agreement to which this article applies made on or after 1st January 1990 and before 1st May 1990 shall terminate it before the latter date to the extent that it imposes any prohibition or restriction on the use as licensed premises of any such premises as are mentioned in paragraph (1)(*a*) above, and

(*b*) it shall be unlawful for any person to make an agreement to which this article applies, or to carry out such an agreement if it was made on or after 1st January 1990, except (in either case) to the extent that it does not impose any such prohibition or restriction. **[684]**

4. (1) Every brewer and every member of a brewery group who (in either case) sells beer for resale on licensed premises shall publish a list of the prices charged by him therefor, together with information about any discount allowed where the beer is delivered to the purchaser at a place of business of the seller or an agent of his.

(2) Where a brewer or a member of a brewery group charges prices for sales to tied tenants or tied customers which differ from those charged to purchasers who are not tied tenants or tied customers, the list of prices provided for in paragraph (1) above shall indicate the prices charged to each such class of purchaser.

(3) It shall be unlawful for any brewer or member of a brewery group to charge prices for the sale of beer for resale on licensed premises which differ, except

to the extent of any discount which he may allow, from those in the list published by him in accordance with paragraph (1) above.

(4) For the purposes of this article —

(*a*) a "tied tenant" is a person who, not being a member of the group in question (if any), occupies licensed premises pursuant to an agreement which is, or has the effect of, a lease or a licence granted by the brewer in question or a member of the group in question, as the case may be, and is precluded or restricted, under that agreement or another agreement made with the brewer or a member of the group, as the case may be, from making relevant purchases;

(*b*) a "tied customer" is a person who, not being a tied tenant or a member of the group in question (if any), is precluded or restricted, under an agreement made with the brewer in question or a member of the group in question, as the case may be, from making relevant purchases; and

(*c*) beer is sold for resale on licensed premises whether such resale is by the purchaser or by a subsequent acquirer of the beer.		**[685]**

5. (1) It shall be unlawful, except to the extent provided in paragraph (2) below, for any brewer or member of a brewery group to withhold any supplies of beer for resale from any other person (except a member of the same group).

(2) It shall not be unlawful so to withhold such supplies where the person withholding the supplies has reasonable cause to believe —

(*a*) that the price for the supplies may not be duly paid, or

(*b*) that any containers of his, or of which he is bailee, in which the supplies would be made may not be duly returned to him or to such other person as might be appropriate, or

(*c*) that any beer which would be supplied may not be handled or kept properly.		**[686]**

6. (1) This Order shall not apply in respect of an agreement —

(*a*) so far as it is or, if made, would be an agreement to which the Restrictive Trade Practices Act 1976 applies or, as the case may be, would apply, or

(*b*) so long as none of the parties to it is a brewer and every member of a brewery group party to it —

(i) is a body corporate, or a subsidiary of a body corporate, in which another member of the group has a substantial minority holding, and

(ii) would not be a member of a brewery group if the holding did not exist.

(2) Articles 4 and 5 above shall impose no obligation on any member of a brewery group which

(*a*) is not a brewer,

(*b*) is a body corporate, or a subsidiary of a body corporate, in which another member of the group has a substantial minority holding, and

(*c*) would not be a member of a brewery group if the holding did not exist.		**[687]**

EXPLANATORY NOTE
(This note is not part of the Order)

This Order provides that where a brewer makes a loan or gives other financial assistance in return for a tie to his products, the recipient of the loan or assistance must be able to repay it or make whatever other payment may be due upon giving not more than three months' notice, and the tie must then cease. If interest is due at a lower rate during an initial period of up to one year and the loan is repaid during that period, the subsequent higher rate may be charged.

The Order also provides that brewers may not impose any prohibition on the use of premises as licensed premises when they dispose of them.

The Order requires brewers to publish wholesale price lists for beer and not charge higher prices. Discounts for collection must be shown. Prices may differ for tied tenants, other tied purchasers and purchasers who are not tied.

Brewers may not withhold wholesale beer supplies except where there are reasonable doubts about credit-worthiness, the return of containers or the handling or keeping of the beer.

The Order does not apply in respect of agreements so far as they are agreements to which the Restrictive Trade Practices Act 1976 applies.

Copies of the report of the Monopolies and Mergers Commission on which the Order is based (Cm 651) may be obtained from Her Majesty's Stationery Office.   **[688]**

THE SUPPLY OF BEER (TIED ESTATE) ORDER 1989
(SI 1989 No 2390)

Whereas the Secretary of State, in accordance with section 91(1) of and Schedule 9 to the Fair Trading Act 1973, caused notice of his intention to lay a draft of this Order to be published in the London Gazette and the Edinburgh Gazette on 22nd August 1989, the Belfast Gazette, the Daily Telegraph and the Financial Times on 25th August 1989 and the Morning Advertiser on 26th August 1989, stating that it was proposed to lay a draft of this Order before Parliament, indicating the nature of the provisions to be embodied in it, stating that a copy of the draft would be available to be seen at all reasonable times in the offices of the Department of Trade and Industry at 1 Victoria Street (Room 020), London SW1 and stating that any person whose interests were likely to be affected by this Order and who was desirous of making representations in respect of it should do so in writing before 10th October 1989;

And whereas the Secretary of State considered the representations duly made to him with respect to the draft of this Order and not withdrawn;

And whereas on 4th December 1989 the Secretary of State laid the draft of this Order before Parliament;

And whereas the said draft as so laid has been approved by resolution of each House of Parliament:

Now, therefore, the Secretary of State, being the appropriate Minister within the meaning of section 56 of the said Act, in exercise of the powers conferred by sections 56(2) and 90(2), (3) and (4) of, and paragraphs 1, 2 and 14 of Schedule 8 to, the said Act, and for the purpose of remedying or preventing adverse effects specified in a report of the Monopolies and Mergers Commission entitled "The Supply of Beer — a report on the supply of beer for retail sale in the United Kingdom", hereby makes the following Order: —

1. (1) This Order may be cited as the Supply of Beer (Tied Estate) Order 1989.

(2) In this Order —

"alcoholic strength" has the same meaning as in the Alcoholic Liquor Duties Act 1979;
"beer" includes any beverage of an alcoholic strength exceeding 1.2 per cent which is made with beer;
"brewer" means a person who carries on business in the manufacture of beer which is supplied by retail in the United Kingdom;
"brewery group" means a group which is —

(a) a group of interconnected bodies corporate, or
(b) a group consisting of a body corporate, or a group of interconnected bodies corporate, all other bodies corporate in which it, or any of them, has a substantial minority holding, and all subsidiaries of those other bodies corporate,

and at least one member of which is a brewer; and a brewery group is a "large brewery group" if one or more of its members holds interests in licensed premises, and the total number of licensed premises in which members of the group hold interests exceeds two thousand;
"interest in shares" includes an entitlement, by a person who is not the registered holder, to exercise any right conferred by the holding of the shares in question or an entitlement to control the exercise of any such right;
"licensed premises" means —

(a) in England and Wales, premises for which a justices' on-licence (within the meaning of the Licensing Act 1964), other than a Part IV licence (within the meaning of that Act), is in force, or in respect of which a club is registered within the meaning of that Act;
(b) in Scotland, premises in respect of which a public house licence, a hotel licence or a refreshment licence (within the meaning of the Licensing (Scotland) Act 1976) is in force or which are occupied by a registered club within the meaning of that Act;
(c) in Northern Ireland, premises in which the sale of intoxicating liquor is authorised by a licence granted under the Licensing Act (Northern Ireland) 1971, being premises of a kind mentioned in paragraph (a) or (f) of section 3(1) of that Act, or in respect of which a club is registered within the meaning of the Registration of Clubs (Northern Ireland) Order 1987;

"notified tied house" means licensed premises of which the name (if any) and address have been notified to the Director General of Fair Trading as premises to be treated as a notified tied house; and for that purpose —

(a) notification may be made or withdrawn at any time, and

(*b*) the making or withdrawal of notification may be effected only
by or on behalf of the brewer, or a member of the group, in respect
of which the notification is, or is no longer, required for the
purposes of the Schedule to this Order;

"relevant purchase", in the context of an agreement to which a brewer or
a member of a brewery group is a party, means purchase by any person
who is not a member of the same group, for retail sale on licensed premises,
of beer or other drink manufactured or supplied by any person not a party
to the agreement;

"subsidiary" has the same meaning as in section 736 of the Companies Act
1985;

"substantial minority holding" means a holding by a body corporate of
fifteen per cent or more, or an interest in shares conferring fifteen per cent
or more, of the voting rights in another body corporate, other than its
subsidiary;

"voting rights" means rights conferred on shareholders in respect of their
shares, either at all times or for the time being, to vote at general meetings
of the body corporate in question on all, or substantially all, matters.

(3) For the purpose of determining whether a body corporate has a substantial minority holding in another body corporate —

(*a*) it is immaterial whether a holding is direct or through a nominee or
trustee,

(*b*) the holdings of the subsidiaries of a body corporate shall be treated as
its own,

(*c*) where one body corporate has a holding in a second body corporate
(not being its subsidiary) and the second body corporate has a holding
in a third body corporate (not being its subsidiary), the first body
corporate shall be treated as having a holding in the third equivalent
to the product of the two actual holdings expressed as percentages, and

(*d*) where a body corporate has, in consequence of the application of sub-
paragraphs (*a*), (*b*) and (*c*) above, more than one holding in another
body corporate, the holdings shall be aggregated and treated as a single
holding.

(4) In the case of a body corporate which is both a brewer and a member of
a brewery group, the provisions of this Order shall apply in relation to that body
corporate both as a brewer and as a member of a brewery group.

(5) For the purpose of determining whether an agreement is an agreement to
which article 5, 6 or 7 below applies, a person shall be regarded as a brewer who
holds interests in more than two thousand licensed premises or a member of a
large brewery group if he is for the time being such a brewer or a member of
such a group, and it is immaterial that he may not have been such a person when
the agreement was made.

(6) For the purposes of this Order —

(*a*) in England and Wales and Northern Ireland, an interest is an interest
in licensed premises if it is —

(i) a right of occupation, or

    (ii) a legal or equitable estate or interest conferring an actual or prospective right of possession,

except for any such interest which is merely by way of mortgage, charge or other security or an equitable interest created by a contract to convey, transfer or assign an existing legal estate;

   (*b*) in Scotland, an interest is an interest in licensed premises if it is—

    (i) any right of ownership in such premises (other than in the superiority of them), or

    (ii) any right or interest of a tenant or sub-tenant of such premises, or

    (iii) any other right to occupy such premises,

but not including any right or interest which arises under any heritable security or floating charge or other security;

   (*c*) a person shall not be treated as carrying out an agreement by reason only that he refrains from doing something the doing of which is the subject of a prohibition or restriction imposed by the agreement; and

   (*d*) an agreement precludes or restricts a relevant purchase whether it does so wholly or only in part, whether that is the object or merely the effect of the agreement, and whether the provisions in question are expressed as negative or positive obligations.

    (7) Except as provided in article 6(2)(*b*) below, this Order shall extend so as to prohibit the carrying out of agreements already in existence on the date on which this Order is made as it prohibits the carrying out of agreements made subsequently.

    (8) In the case of a person falling within paragraph (*a*), (*b*) or (*c*) of section 90(3) of the Fair Trading Act 1973, this Order shall extend to his acts and omissions outside the United Kingdom.   **[689]**

2. (1) Every brewer who before 1st November 1992 holds interests in more than two thousand licensed premises shall do all such things as may be necessary to secure that on that date either—

   (*a*) he is no longer a brewer, or

   (*b*) he no longer holds interests in more than two thousand licensed premises, or

   (*c*) the provisions of the Schedule to this Order are satisfied with respect to him.

    (2) Every body corporate which before 1st November 1992 is a member of a large brewery group shall, subject to paragraphs (3), (4) and (5) below, do all such things as may be necessary to secure that on that date either—

   (*a*) it is no longer a member of such a group, or

   (*b*) the provisions of the Schedule to this Order are satisfied with respect to the group.

    (3) The obligations under this article of a member of a brewery group which is a body corporate, or a subsidiary of a body corporate, in which another member of the group has a substantial minority holding shall be determined as if the holding did not exist.

    (4) Paragraph (2) above shall impose no obligation on any body corporate which—

(a) neither is a brewer nor holds any interest in any licensed premises, and

(b) would not be a member of a brewery group or of a group one or more members of which hold interests in licensed premises were it not that it was a subsidiary of another body corporate.

(5) In any case in which both paragraph (2) above and article 4 below apply, the extent of the obligation imposed by paragraph (2) above shall be no greater than it would have been if the acquisition which caused article 4 below to apply had not been made. **[690]**

3. (1) Subject to paragraph (2) and article 8 below, it shall be unlawful on and after 1st November 1992 for any person to make or carry out an agreement if the carrying out of the agreement would result in any person becoming either —

(a) a brewer who holds interests in more than two thousand licensed premises and with respect to whom the provisions of the Schedule to this Order are not satisfied, or

(b) a member of a large brewery group with respect to which the provisions of the Schedule to this Order are not satisfied.

(2) This article shall not apply in respect of any agreement by which a body corporate, by acquiring shares in another body corporate or any interest in such shares, would become a member of a large brewery group or cause the other body corporate to become a member of such a group. **[691]**

4. Where a body corporate, by acquiring shares in another body corporate or any interest in such shares, becomes after 1st May 1992 a member of a large brewery group or causes the other body corporate to become a member of such a group and as a result (in either case) the provisions of the Schedule to this Order are not satisfied with respect to the group, it shall do all such things as may be necessary to secure that at the end of the period of six months beginning on the day of the acquisition in question, either —

(a) the group is no longer a large brewery group, or

(b) the provisions of the Schedule are satisfied with respect to the group. **[692]**

5. — (1) This article applies, except as provided in paragraph (4) below, to any agreement which is, or has the effect of, a lease or a licence and under which a brewer who holds interests in more than two thousand licensed premises or a member of a large brewery group permits another person not a member of the same group to occupy licensed premises other than a notified tied house, and to any agreement relating to any such agreement.

(2) Subject to article 8 below —

(a) the parties to any agreement to which this article applies made before 1st November 1992 shall terminate it before that date to the extent that it precludes or restricts relevant purchases; and

(b) it shall be unlawful on and after 1st November 1992 for any person to make or carry out an agreement to which this article applies except to the extent that it does not preclude or restrict any relevant purchase.

(3) For the purposes of this article, an agreement under which one person

permits another to occupy premises and which does not preclude use of those premises as licensed premises shall be regarded as an agreement under which one person permits another to occupy licensed premises.

(4) This article does not apply to an agreement made before 1st November 1992 if immediately before that date no party to it is any longer a brewer who holds interests in more than two thousand licensed premises or a member of large brewery group unless subsequently a party to it becomes or, as the case may be, becomes again such a brewer or a member of such a group. **[693]**

6. (1) This article applies to any agreement which is, or has the effect of, a lease or a licence and to which article 5 above applies, except an agreement—

(*a*) which does not impose upon the brewer or any member of the group, as the case may be, any obligation on or after 1st November 1992 to put or keep all or any part of the premises in repair at any time when the premises are licensed premises, and

(*b*) under which the rent or other consideration for occupation on or after 1st November 1992 is an amount which, at the time when the agreement is (or was) made, might reasonably be (or might have reasonably been) sought and obtained on the open market by a lessor or licensor who was not a brewer or a member of a brewery group.

(2) Subject to article 8 below—

(*a*) the parties to any agreement to which this article applies made after the date on which this Order is made and before 1st November 1992 shall terminate it before the latter date; and

(*b*) it shall be unlawful on and after 1st November 1992 for any person to make an agreement to which this article applies or to carry out such an agreement if it was made after the date on which this Order was made. **[694]**

7. (1) This article applies, except as provided in paragraph (4) below, to any agreement to which one of the parties is—

(*a*) a brewer who holds interests in more than two thousand licensed premises, or

(*b*) a member of a large brewery group,

and which precludes or restricts relevant purchases.

(2) Subject to article 8 below—

(*a*) the parties to any agreement to which this article applies made before 1st May 1990 shall terminate it before that date—

(i) so far as it relates to beer of an alcoholic strength exceeding 1.2 per cent, to the extent that the person who is precluded or restricted from making relevant purchases is prevented by the agreement from purchasing from whomsoever he may choose at least one brand of draught cask-conditioned beer selected by him, and

(ii) so far as it relates to beer of an alcoholic strength not exceeding 1.2 per cent or any drink other than beer, to the extent of every provision which precludes or restricts relevant purchases, and (*b*) it shall be unlawful on and after 1st May 1990 for any person to make or carry out an agreement to which this article applies except to the extent that subparagraph (*a*) above would not require it to be terminated if made before that date.

(3) In this article, "cask-conditioned beer" means beer which undergoes fermentation in the container from which it is served for consumption; and a person is prevented by an agreement from purchasing from whomsoever he may choose at least one brand of draught cask-conditioned beer selected by him if the agreement imposes any prohibition or restriction on his so doing or if it subjects him to any disadvantage should he do so (including liability to pay as rent, interest or the price of goods or services an amount greater than he would otherwise pay).

(4) This article does not apply to an agreement made before 1st May 1990 if immediately before that date no party to it is any longer a brewer who holds interests in more than two thousand licensed premises or a member of a large brewery group unless subsequently a party to it becomes or, as the case may be, becomes again such a brewer or a member of such a group. **[695]**

8. (1) This Order shall not apply in respect of an agreement so far as it is or, if made, would be an agreement to which the Restrictive Trade Practices Act 1976 applies or, as the case may be, would apply.

(2) Articles 5, 6 and 7 above shall not apply in respect of an agreement so long as none of the parties to it is a brewer who holds interests in more than two thousand licensed premises and every member of a large brewery group party to it—

(*a*) is a body corporate, or a subsidiary of a body corporate, in which another member of the group has a substantial minority holding, and
(*b*) would not be a member of a large brewery group if the holding did not exist. **[696]**

SCHEDULE Articles 2(1) and (2),
3(1) and 4

PROVISIONS GOVERNING LARGE BREWERS AND LARGE BREWERY GROUPS

1. The provisions of this Schedule are satisfied with respect to a brewer only if each of the licensed premises—

(*a*) on which he carries on business in the supply of beer by retail, or
(*b*) which he permits another person not a member of the same group to occupy under an agreement precluding or restricting relevant purchases,

is a notified tied house and if the total number of the notified tied houses falling within subparagraph (*a*) or (*b*) above does not exceed the permitted maximum determined in accordance with paragraph 3 below.

2. The provisions of this Schedule are satisfied with respect to a group only if each of the licensed premises—

(*a*) on which any member of the group carries on business in the supply of beer by retail, or (*b*) which a member of the group permits another person not a member of the group to occupy under an agreement precluding or restricting relevant purchases,

is a notified tied house and if the total number of the notified tied houses falling within subparagraph (*a*) or (*b*) above does not exceed the permitted maximum determined in accordance with paragraph 3 below.

3.—(1) In respect of each brewer and each group, the permitted maximum referred to in paragraphs 1 and 2 above is the sum of—

(*a*) two thousand, and
(*b*) subject to the following provisions of this paragraph, one half of the total number of licensed premises in excess of two thousand in which the brewer in question or one or more members of the group in question hold, or at any time on or after 10th July 1989 have held, interests.

(2) No licensed premises may be taken into account in determining the permitted maximum in respect of more than one brewer or group; and if, apart from this subparagraph, any licensed premises would fall to be taken into account in respect of more than one brewer or group—

(*a*) they shall be taken into account in respect of that one of those brewers or groups in respect of which they first fall to be taken into account (or would first have fallen to be taken into account during the period beginning on 10th July 1989 and ending immediately before the making of this Order if this Order had then been in force), and
(*b*) where subparagraph (*a*) above fails to determine the matter in a case in which one of the brewers in question, or a member of one of the groups in question, holds an interest in the premises which is superior to that held by another of the brewers in question or by a member of another of the groups in question, they shall be taken into account in respect of the holder of the first-mentioned interest or (as the case may be) the group of which the holder of that interest is a member,

unless (in either case) that brewer or a member of that group, with the agreement of another of the brewers in question or of a member of another of the groups in question, gives notice to the Director General of Fair Trading that they should be taken into account in respect of that other brewer or group.

(3) No licensed premises may be taken into account in determining the permitted maximum in respect of a brewer or a group in any case in which the brewer does not hold, or (as the case may be) no member of the group holds, any interest in them for the time being if the brewer or a member of the group is party to an agreement in respect of the premises the carrying out of which is unlawful by virtue of article 7 above, or would be so unlawful but for article 8 above.

(4) No licensed premises which are not a notified tied house may be taken into account in determining the permitted maximum in respect of a brewer or a group if the brewer or (as the case may be) a member of the group is party to an agreement in respect of the premises the carrying out of which is not unlawful by virtue of article 7 above but would be so unlawful but for article 8 above.

(4) No licensed premises may be taken into account in determining the permitted maximum in respect of a group if a member of the group is party to an agreement in respect of the premises the carrying out of which is not unlawful by virtue of article 7 above but would be so unlawful but for article 8 above.

(5) Premises which are not licensed premises shall be deemed to be licensed premises

for the purpose of taking them into account in determining the permitted maximum in respect of a brewer or a group if —

(*a*) the brewer does not hold, or (as the case may be) no member of the group holds, any interest in them for the time being, and

(*b*) they were licensed premises immediately after —

(i) the brewer ceased to hold an interest in them, or

(ii) the member of the group last to hold an interest in them ceased to do so.

(6) In determining the permitted maximum in respect of a brewer or a group, no account shall be taken of any number of premises in excess of the greatest number of licensed premises in which the brewer or members of the group in question actually held interests at one and the same time on or after 10th July 1989. **[697]**

EXPLANATORY NOTE

(This note is not part of the Order)

This Order provides that brewers, and groups of companies including brewers, which own more than two thousand licensed premises have until 31st October 1992 to dispose of either their brewery business or the excess of licensed premises or to release their ties on half the excess. (A "group" for this purpose is defined as companies related by holdings of or interests in fifteen per cent or more of voting rights.) Any person who finds himself in the position of owning a prohibited interest by the acquisition of shares after 1st May 1992 has six months to get out of that position.

The half-excess on which ties must be released must be sold or let at a market rent without an obligation on the brewer, or on a member of the group, to put or keep the premises in repair.

From 1st May 1990, brewers and brewery groups owning more than two thousand licensed premises must allow their 'tied' premises to sell a draught cask-conditioned beer supplied by someone else and may not impose any ties relating to non-alcohol beers, low alcohol beers and non-beer drinks.

The Order does not apply in respect of agreements so far as they are agreements to which the Restrictive Trade Practices Act 1976 applies, and imposes no obligations on companies which are members of a brewery group because of a minority holding by another member of the group.

Copies of the report of the Monopolies and Mergers Commission on which the Order is based (Cm 651) may be obtained from Her Majesty's Stationery Office. **[698]**

THE MERGER (PRENOTIFICATION) REGULATIONS 1990

(SI 1990 No 501)

The Secretary of State for Trade and Industry, in exercise of the powers conferred upon him by sections 75A(1), 75C(1)(*c*), 75D(1), (2)(*b*), (*c*), (*d*), (*e*), (*f*), (*g*) and (*h*), (3) and (4) and 75E of the Fair Trading Act 1973 hereby makes the following Regulations: —

- Citation, commencement and interpretation

1. (1) These Regulations may be cited as the Merger (Prenotification) Regulations 1990 and shall come into force on 1st April 1990.

(2) In these Regulations —

"the Act" means the Fair Trading Act 1973;
"the Director" means the Director General of Fair Trading;
"working day" means any day which is not —

(a) Saturday, Sunday, Good Friday or Christmas Day, or
(b) a bank holiday in England and Wales.

(3) A reference in these Regulations to a person who does anything on behalf of a person who is authorised to give a merger notice or who has given such notice shall be construed as limited to a reference to a person who does so having been authorised so to act in accordance with regulation 13 of these Regulations.

[699]

Person authorised to give merger notice

2. A merger notice may be given under section 75A(1) of the Act by any person carrying on an enterprise to which the notified arrangements relate.   **[700]**

Time limit for disclosure of material information

3. The time specified for the purpose of section 75C(1)(c) of the Act (the time before the end of the period for considering a merger notice within which material information must be disclosed) is —

(a) where there has been no extension of that period, or only one such extension, five working days; and
(b) where there have been two such extensions, ten working days. **[701]**

Time and manner of the giving of a merger notice

4. (1) A merger notice shall be given by being delivered in writing to the office of the Director by hand or by post.

(2) Subject to paragraph (3) below, a merger notice shall be treated as having been received at the office of the Director on the day on which it is in fact delivered to that office.

(3) Where a merger notice is delivered to the office of the Director on any day which is not a working day or after 5.00 p.m. on any working day, it shall be treated as having been received on the next working day.

(4) Section 7 of the Interpretation Act 1978 shall not apply to the giving of a merger notice in accordance with this regulation.   **[702]**

Rejection of a merger notice

5. A rejection of a merger notice under section 75B(7) of the Act shall be given in writing (including by facsimile or other form of electronic transmission) and such a notice shall be treated as having been rejected at the time when the rejection is sent to the person who gave the merger notice or a person acting on his behalf.

[703]

Withdrawal of a merger notice

6. A merger notice may be withdrawn by or on behalf of the person who gave the notice by a notice in writing delivered to the office of the Director (including a notice delivered by facsimile or other form of electronic transmission).

[704]

Provision of information to the Director

7. (1) Any information which —

  (*a*) is, or ought to be, known to the person who gave the merger notice or any connected person, and

  (*b*) is material to the notified arrangements,

or any information requested by the Director under section 75B(4) of the Act shall be provided or disclosed in writing (including by facsimile or other form of electronic transmission).

(2) Subject to paragraph (3) below, any information provided or disclosed to the Director under this regulation shall be treated as having been so provided or disclosed on the day on which it is in fact delivered to the office of the Director.

(3) Where information is delivered to the office of the Director on any day, which is not a working day or after 5.00 p.m. on any working day, it shall be treated as having been provided or disclosed to the Director on the next working day.

(4) Section 7 of the Interpretation Act 1978 shall not apply to the provision or disclosure of any information under this regulation.   **[705]**

Notice to extend period for consideration of merger notice

8. A notice to extend the period mentioned in section 75B(2) of the Act (period for consideration of merger notice) may be given orally or in writing (including by facsimile or other form of electronic transmission).   **[706]**

Notice requesting further information

9. Any notice under section 75B(4) of the Act requesting information from the

person who gave a merger notice may be given in writing (including by facsimile
or other form of electronic transmission).   **[707]**

Time at which notices relating to undertakings are to be treated as received

10. A notice given to the Director under section 75B(5)(*a*) of the Act shall be
treated as having been received by him —   **[708]**

   (*a*) subject to paragraph (*b*) below, on the day on which it is in fact delivered
          to his office (including by facsimile or other form of electronic
          transmission);
   (*b*) where it is delivered to his office on any day which is not a working
          day or after 5.00 p.m. on any working day, on the next working day,

and section 7 of the Interpretation Act 1978 shall not apply.

Address to be treated as a person's proper address

11. (1) For the purposes of section 75B(6) and of these Regulations, the address
provided or disclosed in writing to the Director as a person's proper address by
or on behalf of the person giving a merger notice shall, subject to paragraph
(2) below, be treated as that person's proper address.

   (2) Where an address is provided or disclosed in writing to the Director as
a person's proper address by or on behalf of a person in respect of whom a
different address has previously been provided or disclosed in accordance with
paragraph (1) above, the new address shall be treated as that person's proper
address with effect from 9.00 a.m. on the working day following the day on which
it is delivered to the office of the Director.   **[709]**

Time at which fees are to be treated as paid

12. (1) Subject to paragraphs (2) and (3) below, any fee payable in accordance
with a merger notice shall be treated as having been paid on the day on which
a valid cheque or other instrument for the correct amount is received at the office
of the Director.

   (2) Where a cheque or other instrument received as payment for a fee referred
to in paragraph (1) above is dishonoured on presentation, the fee shall, subject
to paragraph (3) below, nevertheless be treated as having been paid on the day
on which that cheque or other instrument is received if the condition specified
in paragraph (4) below is subsequently satisfied.

   (3) Where a cheque or other instrument in respect of a fee referred to in
paragraph (1) above is delivered to the office of the Director on any day which
is not a working day or after 5.00 p.m. on any working day, it shall be treated
as having been received on the next working day.

   (4) The condition referred to in paragraph (2) above is that, within the period
of 20 days determined in accordance with section 75B(9) of the Act and beginning

with the first day after the merger notice is, in accordance with regulation 4 of these Regulations, treated as having been received at the office of the Director, the correct amount of the fee has been properly paid by a valid cheque or other instrument.

(5) Section 7 of the Interpretation Act 1978 shall not apply to the giving or sending of a cheque or other instrument in respect of a fee referred to in paragraph (1) above. **[710]**

Circumstances in which a person is or is not to be treated as acting on behalf of the giver of a merger notice

13. (1) A person shall be treated as acting on behalf of a person who is authorised to give a merger notice or who has given such a notice only if the person on whose behalf he is to be treated as acting has authorised him so to act in accordance with paragraph (2) below.

(2) An authorisation to act on behalf of another person for the purposes of paragraph (1) above shall be given to the Director in writing and an authorisation to act on behalf of a company shall be signed by a director or other officer of that company.

(3) A person who has given an authorisation in accordance with paragraph (1) above may revoke it by a notice in writing given to the Director and, where that person is a company, the notice shall be signed by a director or other officer of that company. **[711]**

EXPLANATORY NOTE

(This note is not part of the Regulations)

These Regulations are made under the Fair Trading Act 1973 ("the 1973 Act") as amended by the Companies Act 1989. The 1973 Act as amended includes provisions in sections 75A to 75E to enable a prospective merger to be prenotified to the Director General of Fair Trading by means of a merger notice. Unless the merger is referred to the Monopolies and Mergers Commission within the period for considering the notice, no reference may be made.

The Regulations provide for the person by whom a merger notice is to be given; the time at which notices (including merger notices) are treated as received or rejected; the manner in which they are to be given, rejected or withdrawn; which address is to be treated as a person's proper address; the time at which fees are to be treated as paid and the circumstances in which a person is to be treated as acting on behalf of a person entitled to give a merger notice. **[712]**

THE MERGER (FEES) REGULATIONS 1990
(SI 1990 No 1660)

The Secretary of State for Trade and Industry, in exercise of the powers conferred on him by section 152 of the Companies Act 1989, hereby makes the following Regulations:

Citation, commencement and interpretation

1. (1) These Regulations may be cited as the Merger (Fees) Regulations 1990 and shall come into force on 1st October 1990.

(2) In these Regulations —

(a) "the Act" means the Fair Trading Act 1973;

(b) a reference to a numbered Regulation shall be construed as a reference to the Regulation bearing that number in these Regulations.

(3) These Regulations shall be construed as one with Part V of the Act and as if sections 67 and 77 of the Act applied for the purpose of construing these Regulations.   **[713]**

Matters in respect of which fees are payable

2. A fee of the amount specified in Regulation 4 shall be payable in respect of —

(a) subject to Regulation 3(1), an application for the consent of the Secretary of State under section 58(1) of the Act to the transfer of a newspaper or of newspaper assets;

(b) the giving of a merger notice under section 75A(1) of the Act;

(c) the making by the Secretary of State of a merger reference to the Commission under section 29(1) of the Water Act 1989;

(d) subject to Regulation 3(2), the making by the Secretary of State of a merger reference to the Commission under section 64 or 75 of the Act;

(e) subject to Regulation 3(2), the announcement by the Secretary of State of his decision not to make a merger reference in any case where, at the time the announcement is made, he would, under section 64 or 75 of the Act, have the power to make such a reference.   **[714]**

Circumstances in which certain fees are not payable

3. (1) A fee shall not be payable under Regulation 2(a) in respect of an application for the consent of the Secretary of State under section 58(1) of the Act to the transfer of a newspaper or of newspaper assets —

(a) where an application has been made by the same person within the previous six months in relation to the transfer to the same person of the same newspaper or the same newspaper assets and that application was expressed to depend on the operation of section 58(3) or (4) of the Act; or

(b) the value of the newspaper or newspaper assets transferred is less than £100,000.

(2) A fee shall not be payable under Regulation 2(*d*) in respect of a merger reference or under Regulation 2(*e*) in respect of the announcement by the Secretary of State of his decision not to make a merger reference —

(a) where a fee has been paid under Regulation 2(*b*) in respect of a merger notice given in relation to proposed arrangements and either —

(i) the merger reference or, as the case may be, the Secretary of State's decision not to make a merger reference is made in relation to those arrangements, or

(ii) if the fee under Regulation 2(*b*) became due within the previous six months, the result of carrying those arrangements into effect is the creation or possible creation of the merger situation qualifying for investigation which is the subject of the merger reference or, as the case may be, the Secretary of State's decision not to make a merger reference;

(b) where the creation or possible creation of the merger situation depends or would depend on the operation of section 65(3) or (4)(*b*) of the Act.

[715]

Amount of fees

4. The amount of the fee payable under Regulation 2 shall be —

(a) in a case falling within paragraph (*a*) of that Regulation —

(i) where the average circulation per day of publication of any of the newspapers concerned in the transfer is more than 25,000, £10,000, and

(ii) where sub-paragraph (i) above does not apply, £5,000;

(b) in a case falling within paragraph (*b*), (*c*), (*d*) or (*e*) of that Regulation —

(i) where the value of the assets which have been taken over, or, as the case may be, which it is proposed or contemplated should be taken over, does not exceed £30 million, £5,000,

(ii) where the value of such assets exceeds £30 million but does not exceed £100 million, £10,000,

(iii) where the value of such assets exceeds £100 million, £15,000.

[716]

Person by whom fees are payable

5. (1) In a case falling within Regulation 2(*a*), the fee shall be payable by the person who makes the application for the consent of the Secretary of State under section 58(1) of the Act.

(2) In a case falling within Regulation 2(*b*), the fee shall be payable by the person who gives the merger notice.

(3) Subject to paragraph (5) below, in a case falling within Regulation 2(*c*), (*d*) or (*e*), the fee shall be payable—

    (*a*) where it appears to the Secretary of State that it is or may be the fact that—

        (i) there is a merger situation to which section 65(1)(*a*) of the Act applies, or

        (ii) arrangements are in progress or in contemplation which if carried into effect would result in the creation of a merger situation to which that provision of the Act would apply, or

        (iii) there is a situation to which either paragraph (*a*) or (*b*) of subsection (1) of section 29 of the Water Act 1989 applies,

    by the person, or group of persons, who has or have acquired or will, if those arrangements are carried into effect, acquire either—

        (iv) a controlling interest in one of the enterprises which was or is involved in the merger or prospective merger and in which he or they did not previously have such an interest, or

        (v) in the case of such an enterprise carried on by a body corporate in which he or they did not previously have a controlling interest, a controlling interest in that body corporate; or

    (*b*) where it appears to the Secretary of State that it is or may be the fact that—

        (i) there is a merger situation to which section 65(1)(*b*) of the Act applies, or

        (ii) arrangements are in progress or in contemplation which if carried into effect would result in the creation of a merger situation to which that provision of the Act would apply,

    by the person or group of persons who—

        (iii) carried on or are carrying on the enterprise involved in the merger or prospective merger which did not cease or will not, if those arrangements are carried into effect, cease to be carried on at all, or

        (iv) had or have a controlling interest in that enterprise, or

        (v) in the case where that enterprise was or is carried on by a body corporate, had or have a controlling interest in that body corporate.

(4) In a case where paragraph (3) above applies to more than one person, whether by virtue of them being treated as one by the operation of section 77 of the Act or otherwise, the persons to whom it applies shall be jointly and severally liable for the fee in that case.

(5) Where a fee is payable under Regulation 2(*c*) in respect of a merger reference under section 29(1) of the Water Act 1989, under Regulation 2(*d*) in respect of a merger reference under section 64 or 75 of the Act or under Regulation 2(*e*) in respect of the announcement by the Secretary of State of his decision not to make such a merger reference but the person specified in subparagraph (3) above is not—

(*a*) a British citizen, a British Dependent Territories citizen, a British Overseas citizen or a British National (Overseas); or

(*b*) a body corporate incorporated under the law of the United Kingdom or of a part of the United Kingdom; or

(*c*) a person carrying on business in the United Kingdom, either alone or in partnership with one or more persons;

he shall not be liable to pay the fee unless the merger situation or, as the case may be, the arrangements in progress or in contemplation result, wholly or partially, from anything done by him within the United Kingdom.   **[717]**

Person to whom fees are payable

6. (1) In a case falling within Regulation 2(*a*), the fee shall be payable to the Secretary of State.

(2) In a case falling within Regulation 2(*b*), (*c*), (*d*) or (*e*), the fee shall be payable to the Director.   **[718]**

Time when fees are payable

7. (1) In a case falling within Regulation 2(*b*), the fee shall be payable at the time when the application for the consent of the Secretary of State under section 58(1) of the Act is made.

(2) In a case falling within Regulation 2(*b*), the fee shall be payable at the time when the merger notice is given.

(3) In a case falling within Regulation 2(*c*), (*d*) or (*e*), the fee shall be payable when the Secretary of State publishes the merger reference or, as the case may be, announces his decision not to make a merger reference.   **[719]**

Repayment of fees

8. In a case falling within Regulation 2(*b*) —

(*a*) the Director may repay the whole of the fee where the notified arrangements would not, if they were carried into effect, result in the creation of a merger situation qualifying for investigation; and

(*b*) the Director shall repay the whole of the fee where he rejects the merger notice under section 75B(7)(*d*) of the Act (rejection of merger notice where the notified arrangements are or would result in a concentration with a Community dimension).   **[720]**

EXPLANATORY NOTE

(This note is not part of the Regulations)

These Regulations provide for fees to be payable in connection with the exercise by the Secretary of State, the Director General of Fair Trading and the Monopolies and Mergers Commission of their functions under Part V of the Fair Trading Act 1973 ("the Act") relating to the supervision of actual and prospective mergers.

Regulation 2 provides that fees are to be payable in five cases: in respect of an application for the Secretary of State's consent to the transfer of a newspaper or of newspaper assets; in respect of a prenotification of a merger under section 75A(1) of the Act; in respect of a decision to make a merger reference under section 29(1) of the Water Act 1989; in respect of a merger reference under section 64 or 75 of the Act; and in respect of the announcement by the Secretary of State of his decision not to make a merger reference.

Regulation 3 specifies certain cases in which fees are not payable in respect of applications for the Secretary of State's consent to the transfer of a newspaper or of newspaper assets; merger references under section 64 or 75 of the Act and announcements of decisions by the Secretary of State not to make such references. Regulation 4 specifies the amount of the fee payable in each case. Provision is also made as to the persons by whom the fee is to be payable (Regulation 5) and to whom fees are payable (Regulation 6), and the time when fees are payable (Regulation 7). Provision is also made for the refund of fees payable in respect of merger prenotifications where the notice is rejected because the notified arrangements are or would result in a concentration with a Community dimension (within the meaning of Council Regulation (EEC) No 4064/89) or where the notified arrangements would not, if carried into effect, result in a merger situation qualifying for investigation (Regulation 8). [721]

THE EEC MERGER CONTROL (DISTINCT MARKET INVESTIGATIONS) REGULATIONS 1990
(SI 1990 No 1715)

The Secretary of State being designated for the purposes of section 2(2) of the European Communities Act 1972 in relation to measures relating to the control of concentrations between undertakings, in exercise of the powers conferred on him by the said section 2(2) hereby makes the following Regulations:

1. (1) These Regulations may be cited as the EEC Merger Control (Distinct Market Investigations) Regulations 1990 and shall come into force on 21 September 1990.

(2) In these Regulations, "the Merger Control Regulation" means Council Regulation (EEC) No. 4064/89 on the control of concentrations between undertakings, and expressions used in that Regulation shall bear the same meaning in these Regulations. [722]

2. At any time after the Commission has transmitted to the competent authorities of the United Kingdom a copy of the notification to the Commission of a concentration with a Community dimension, the Director General of Fair Trading ("the Director") may, for the purpose of furnishing information to the Commission under the second sentence of Article 19(2) of the Merger Control Regulation, and by notice in writing signed by him—

(*a*) require any person to produce, at a time and place specified in the notice, to the Director or to any person appointed by him for the purpose, any documents which are specified or described in the notice and which are documents in his custody or under his control and relating to any matter relevant to the furnishing of information as aforesaid, or

(*b*) require any person carrying on any business to furnish to the Director such estimates, returns or other information as may be specified or described in the notice, and specify the time, the manner and the form in which such estimates, returns or information are to be furnished;

but no person shall be compelled by virtue of this regulation to produce any documents which he could not be compelled to produce in civil proceedings before the High Court or, in Scotland, the Court of Session or, in complying with any requirement for the furnishing of information, to give any information which he could not be compelled to give in evidence in such proceedings.   **[723]**

3. (1) Subsections (6) to (8) of section 85 of the Fair Trading Act 1973 (enforcement provisions relating to notices under subsection (1) of that section requiring production of documents etc) shall, subject to paragraph (2) below, apply in relation to a notice under regulation 2 above as they apply in relation to a notice under subsection (1) of that section, but as if—

(*a*) the reference in subsection (6) of that section to a fine not exceeding the prescribed sum were a reference to a fine not exceeding an amount equal to level 5 on the standard scale, and

(*b*) in subsection (7) of that section, for the words from "any one" to "the Commission" there were substituted "the Director".

(2) In punishing a defaulter under subsection (7A) of the said section 85, the court shall not impose any penalty which could not be imposed on summary conviction for an offence created in exercise of the powers conferred by section 2(2) of the European Communities Act 1972.   **[724]**

4. Sections 93B (furnishing false or misleading information to the Director) and 133 (restrictions on disclosure of information) of the Fair Trading Act 1973 shall apply as if these Regulations were contained in Part V of that Act and the references in—

(*a*) subsection (3)(*a*) of the said section 93B to a fine not exceeding the statutory maximum, and

(*b*) subsection (5)(*a*) of the said section 133 to a fine not exceeding the prescribed sum were references to a fine not exceeding an amount equal to level 5 on the standard scale.   **[725]**

EXPLANATORY NOTE

(This note is not part of the Regulations)

These Regulations confer investigative powers (based on section 3(7) of the Competition Act 1980) upon the Director General of Fair Trading for the purpose of furnishing information to the European Commission under Council Regulation (EEC) No. 4064/89 (on the control of concentrations between undertakings) when a concentration with a Community dimension (as defined in that Regulation) may impede competition in a distinct market within the United Kingdom. The enforcement provisions of section 85(6) to (8) of the Fair Trading Act 1973 apply. Sections 93B and 133 of that Act also apply.   **[726 – 999]**

PART II
EEC LEGISLATION

TREATY ESTABLISHING THE EUROPEAN COMMUNITY (TREATY OF ROME)
[25 March 1957]

PART THREE
POLICY OF THE COMMUNITY
TITLE 1 — COMMON RULES
CHAPTER 1 — RULES ON COMPETITION
SECTION 1 — RULES APPLYING TO UNDERTAKINGS

Article 85

1. The following shall be prohibited as incompatible with the common market: all agreements between undertakings, decisions by associations of undertakings and concerted practices which may affect trade between Member States and which have as their object or effect the prevention, restriction or distortion of competition within the common market, and in particular those which:

   (a) directly or indirectly fix purchase or selling prices or any other trading conditions;
   (b) limit or control production, markets, technical development, or investment;
   (c) share markets or sources of supply;
   (d) apply dissimilar conditions to equivalent transactions with other trading parties, thereby placing them at a competitive disadvantage;
   (e) make the conclusion of contracts subject to acceptance by the other parties of supplementary obligations which, by their nature or according to commercial usage, have no connection with the subject of such contracts.

2. Any agreements or decisions prohibited pursuant to this Article shall be automatically void.

3. The provisions of paragraph 1 may, however, be declared inapplicable in the case of:

   — any agreement or category of agreements between undertakings;
   — any decision or category of decisions by associations of undertakings;
   — any concerted practice or category of concerted practices;

which contributes to improving the production or distribution of goods or to promoting technical or economic progress, while allowing consumers a fair share of the resulting benefit, and which does not:

   (a) impose on the undertakings concerned restrictions which are not indispensable to the attainment of these objectives;
   (b) afford such undertakings the possibility of eliminating competition in respect of a substantial part of the products in question. **[1000]**

Article 86

Any abuse by one or more undertakings of a dominant position within the common market or in a substantial part of it shall be prohibited as incompatible with the common market in so far as it may affect trade between Member States. Such abuse may, in particular, consist in:

   (a) directly or indirectly imposing unfair purchase or selling prices or other unfair trading conditions;

(*b*) limiting production, markets or technical development to the prejudice of consumers;

(*c*) applying dissimilar conditions to equivalent transactions with other trading parties, thereby placing them at a competitive disadvantage;

(*d*) making the conclusion of contracts subject to acceptance by the other parties of supplementary obligations which, by their nature or according to commercial usage, have no connection with the subject of such contracts. **[1001]**

Article 87

1. Within three years of the entry into force of this Treaty the Council shall, acting unanimously on a proposal from the Commission and after consulting the Assembly, adopt any appropriate regulations or directives to give effect to the principles set out in Articles 85 and 86.

If such provisions have not been adopted within the period mentioned, they shall be laid down by the Council, acting by a qualified majority on a proposal from the Commission and after consulting the Assembly.

2. The regulations or directives referred to in paragraph 1 shall be designed, in particular:

(*a*) to ensure compliance with the prohibitions laid down in Article 85(1) and in Article 86 by making provision for fines and periodic penalty payments;

(*b*) to lay down detailed rules for the application of Article 85(3), taking into account the need to ensure effective supervision on the one hand, and to simplify administration to the greatest possible extent on the other;

(*c*) to define, if need be, in the various branches of the economy, the scope of the provisions of Articles 85 and 86;

(*d*) to define the respective functions of the Commission and of the Court of Justice in applying the provisions laid down in this paragraph;

(*e*) to determine the relationship between national laws and the provisions contained in this Section or adopted pursuant to this Article. **[1002]**

Article 88

Until the entry into force of the provisions adopted in pursuance of Article 87, the authorities in Member States shall rule on the admissibility of agreements, decisions and concerted practices and on abuse of a dominant position in the common market in accordance with the law of their country and with the provisions of Article 85, in particular paragraph 3, and of Article 86. **[1003]**

Article 89

1. Without prejudice to Article 88, the Commission shall, as soon as it takes up its duties, ensure the application of the principles laid down in Articles 85 and 86. On application by a Member State or on its own initiative, and in cooperation with the competent authorities in the Member States, who shall give it their assistance, the Commission shall investigate cases of suspected infringement of these principles. If it finds that there has been an infringement, it shall propose appropriate measures to bring it to an end.

2. If the infringement is not brought to an end, the Commission shall record such infringement of the principles in a reasoned decision. The Commission may publish its decision and authorise Member States to take the measures, the conditions and details of which it shall determine, needed to remedy the situation. **[1004]**

Article 90

1. In the case of public undertakings and undertakings to which Member States grant special or exclusive rights, Member States shall neither enact nor maintain in force any measure contrary to the rules contained in this Treaty, in particular to those rules provided for in Article 7 and Articles 85 to 94.

2. Undertakings entrusted with the operation of services of general economic interest or having the character of a revenue-producing monopoly shall be subject to the rules contained in this Treaty, in particular to the rules on competition, in so far as the application of such rules does not obstruct the performance, in law or in fact, of the particular tasks assigned to them. The development of trade must not be affected to such an extent as would be contrary to the interests of the Community.

3. The Commission shall ensure the application of the provisions of this Article and shall, where necessary, address appropriate directives or decisions to Member States.

[1005]

SECTION 2 – DUMPING

Article 91

1. If, during the transitional period, the Commission, on application by a Member State or by any other interested party, finds that dumping is being practised within the common market, it shall address recommendations to the person or persons with whom such practices originate for the purpose of putting an end to them.

Should the practices continue, the Commission shall authorise the injured Member State to take protective measures, the conditions and details of which the Commission shall determine.

2. As soon as this Treaty enters into force, products which originate in or are in free circulation in one Member State and which have been exported to another Member State shall, on re-importation, be admitted into the territory of the first-mentioned State free of all customs duties, quantitative restrictions or measures having equivalent effect. The Commission shall lay down appropriate rules for the application of this paragraph.

[1006]

SECTION 3 – AIDS GRANTED BY STATES

Article 92

1. Save as otherwise provided in this Treaty, any aid granted by a Member State or through State resources in any form whatsoever which distorts or threatens to distort competition by favouring certain undertakings or the production of certain goods shall, in so far as it affects trade between Member States, be incompatible with the common market.

2. The following shall be compatible with the common market:

    (*a*) aid having a social character, granted to individual consumers, provided that such aid is granted without discrimination related to the origin of the products concerned;

    (*b*) aid to make good the damage caused by natural disasters or other exceptional occurrences;

    (*c*) aid granted to the economy of certain areas of the Federal Republic of Germany affected by the division of Germany, in so far as such aid is required in order to compensate for the economic disadvantages caused by that division.

3. The following may be considered to be compatible with the common market:

(a) aid to promote the economic development of areas where the standard of living is abnormally low or where there is serious underemployment;

(b) aid to promote the execution of an important project of common European interest or to remedy a serious disturbance in the economy of a Member State;

(c) aid to facilitate the development of certain economic activities or of certain economic areas, where such aid does not adversely affect trading conditions to an extent contrary to the common interest. However, the aids granted to ship-building as of 1 January 1957 shall, in so far as they serve only to compensate for the absence of customs protection, be progressively reduced under the same conditions as apply to the elimination of customs duties, subject to the provisions of this Treaty concerning common commercial policy towards third countries;

(d) such other categories of aid as may be specified by decision of the Council acting by a qualified majority on a proposal from the Commission.   **[1007]**

Article 93

1. The Commission shall, in cooperation with Member States, keep under constant review all systems of aid existing in those States. It shall propose to the latter any appropriate measures required by the progressive development or by the functioning of the common market.

2. If, after giving notice to the parties concerned to submit their comments, the Commission finds that aid granted by a State or through State resources is not compatible with the common market having regard to Article 92, or that such aid is being misused, it shall decide that the State concerned shall abolish or alter such aid within a period of time to be determined by the Commission.

If the State concerned does not comply with this decision within the prescribed time, the Commission or any other interested State may, in derogation from the provisions of Articles 169 and 170, refer the matter to the Court of Justice direct.

On application by a Member State, the Council may, acting unanimously, decide that aid which that State is granting or intends to grant shall be considered to be compatible with the common market, in derogation from the provisions of Article 92 or from the regulations provided for in Article 94, if such a decision is justified by exceptional circumstances. If, as regards the aid in question, the Commission has already initiated the procedure provided for in the first subparagraph of this paragraph, the fact that the State concerned has made its application to the Council shall have the effect of suspending that procedure until the Council has made its attitude known.

If, however, the Council has not made its attitude known within three months of the said application being made, the Commission shall give its decision on the case.

3. The Commission shall be informed, in sufficient time to enable it to submit its comments, of any plans to grant or alter aid. If it considers that any such plan is not compatible with the common market having regard to Article 92, it shall without delay initiate the procedure provided for in paragraph 2. The Member State concerned shall not put its proposed measures into effect until this procedure has resulted in a final decision.

[1008]

Article 94

The Council may, acting by a qualified majority on a proposal from the Commission, make any appropriate regulations for the application of Articles 92 and 93 and may in particular determine the conditions in which Article 93(3) shall apply and the categories of aid exempted from this procedure. **[1009]**

REGULATION (EEC) No 17/62 OF THE COUNCIL

First Regulation implementing Articles 85 and 86 of the Treaty

THE COUNCIL OF THE EUROPEAN ECONOMIC COMMUNITY,
  Having regard to the Treaty establishing the European Economic Community, and in particular Article 87 thereof;
  Having regard to the proposal from the Commission;
  Having regard to the Opinion of the Economic and Social Committee;
  Having regard to the Opinion of the European Parliament;
  Whereas, in order to establish a system ensuring that competition shall not be distorted in the common market, it is necessary to provide for balanced application of Articles 85 and 86 in a uniform manner in the Member States;
  Whereas in establishing the rules for applying Article 85(3) account must be taken of the need to ensure effective supervision and to simplify administration to the greatest possible extent;
  Whereas it is accordingly necessary to make it obligatory, as a general principle, for undertakings which seek application of Article 85(3) to notify to the Commission their agreements, decisions and concerted practices;
  Whereas, on the one hand, such agreements, decisions and concerted practices are probably very numerous and cannot therefore all be examined at the same time and, on the other hand, some of them have special features which may make them less prejudicial to the development of the common market;
  Whereas there is consequently a need to make more flexible arrangements for the time being in respect of certain categories of agreement, decision and concerted practice without prejudging their validity under Article 85;
  Whereas it may be in the interest of undertakings to know whether any agreements, decisions or practices to which they are party, or propose to become party, may lead to action on the part of the Commission pursuant to Article 85(1) or Article 86;
  Whereas, in order to secure uniform application of Articles 85 and 86 in the common market, rules must be made under which the Commission, acting in close and constant liaison with the competent authorities of the Member States, may take the requisite measures for applying those Articles;
  Whereas for this purpose the Commission must have the co-operation of the competent authorities of the Member States and be empowered, throughout the common market, to require such information to be supplied and to undertake such investigations as are necessary to bring to light any agreement, decision or concerted practice prohibited by Article 85(1) or any abuse of a dominant position prohibited by Article 86;
  Whereas, in order to carry out its duty of ensuring that the provisions of the Treaty are applied, the Commission must be empowered to address to undertakings or associations of undertakings recommendations and decisions for the purpose of bringing to an end infringements of Articles 85 and 86;
  Whereas compliance with Articles 85 and 86 and the fulfilment of obligations imposed on undertakings and associations of undertakings under this Regulation must be enforceable by means of fines and periodic penalty payments;
  Whereas undertakings concerned must be accorded the right to be heard by the Commission, third parties whose interests may be affected by a decision must be given the opportunity of submitting their comments beforehand, and it must be ensured that wide publicity is given to decisions taken;
  Whereas all decisions taken by the Commission under this Regulation are subject to review by the Court of Justice under the conditions specified in the Treaty; whereas it is moreover desirable to confer upon the Court of Justice, pursuant to Article 172, unlimited jurisdiction in respect of decisions under which the Commission imposes fines or periodic penalty payments;
  Whereas this Regulation may enter into force without prejudice to any other provisions that may hereafter be adopted pursuant to Article 87;
  HAS ADOPTED THIS REGULATION:

Article 1 – Basic provision

Without prejudice to Articles 6, 7 and 23 of this Regulation, agreements, decisions and concerted practices of the kind described in Article 85(1) of the Treaty and the abuse of a dominant position in the market, within the meaning of Article 86 of the Treaty, shall be prohibited, no prior decision to that effect being required.   **[1010]**

Article 2 – Negative clearance

Upon application by the undertakings or associations of undertakings concerned, the Commission may certify that, on the basis of the facts in its possession, there are no grounds under Article 85(1) or Article 86 of the Treaty for action on its part in respect of an agreement, decision or practice.   **[1011]**

Article 3 – Termination of infringements

1. Where the Commission, upon application or upon its own initiative, finds that there is infringement of Article 85 or Article 86 of the Treaty, it may by decision require the undertakings or associations of undertakings concerned to bring such infringement to an end.

2. Those entitled to make application are:

   (*a*) Member States;

   (*b*) natural or legal persons who claim a legitimate interest.

3. Without prejudice to the other provisions of this Regulation, the Commission may, before taking a decision under paragraph 1, address to the undertakings or associations of undertakings concerned recommendations for termination of the infringement.

                    [1012]

Article 4 – Notification of new agreements, decisions and practices

1. Agreements, decisions and concerted practices of the kind described in Article 85(1) of the Treaty which come into existence after the entry into force of this Regulation and in respect of which the parties seek application of Article 85(3) must be notified to the Commission. Until they have been notified, no decision in application of Article 85(3) may be taken.

2. Paragraph 1 shall not apply to agreements, decisions or concerted practices where:

   (1) the only parties thereto are undertakings from one Member State and the agreements, decisions or practices do not relate either to imports or to exports between Member States;

   (2) not more than two undertakings are party thereto, and the agreements only:

   (*a*) restrict the freedom of one party to the contract in determining the prices or conditions of business upon which the goods which he has obtained from the other party to the contract may be resold; or

   (*b*) impose restrictions on the exercise of the rights of the assignee or user of industrial property rights – in particular patents, utility models, designs or trade marks – or of the person entitled under a contract to the assignment, or grant, of the right to use a method of manufacture or knowledge relating to the use and to the application of industrial processes;

   (3) they have as their sole object:

   (*a*) the development or uniform application of standards or types; or

[(*b*) joint research and development;
(*c*) specialisation in the manufacture of products, including agreements necessary for the achievement thereof;

—where the products which are the object of specialisation do not, in a
substantial part of the common market, represent more than 15 per cent
of the volume of business done in identical products or those considered
by the consumers to be similar by reason of their characteristics, price
and use, and
—where the total annual turnover of the participating undertakings does
not exceed 200 million units of account.

These agreements decisions and concerted practices may be notified to the Commission].[1]
[1013]

AMENDMENT
   1 Sub-para (*b*) amended and sub-para (*c*) and the remaining words added by EEC Council Regulation No 2822/71.

Article 5 — Notification of existing agreements, decisions and practices

1. Agreements, decisions and concerted practices of the kind described in Article 85(1)
of the Treaty which are in existence at the date of entry into force of this Regulation
and in respect of which the parties seek application of Article 85(3) shall be notified to
the Commission before [1 November 1962].[1] [However, notwithstanding the foregoing
provisions, any agreements, decisions and concerted practices to which not more than
two undertakings are party shall be notified before 1 February 1963].[2]

2. Paragraph 1 shall not apply to agreements, decisions or concerted practices falling
within Article 4(2); these may be notified to the Commission.   **[1014]**

AMENDMENTS
   1 Words substituted by EEC Council Regulation No 59/62, Art 1(1).
   2 Words added by EEC Council Regulation No 59/62, Art 1(2).

Article 6 — Decisions pursuant to Article 85(3)

1. Whenever the Commission takes a decision pursuant to Article 85(3) of the Treaty,
it shall specify therein the date from which the decision shall take effect. Such date shall
not be earlier than the date of notification.

2. The second sentence of paragraph 1 shall not apply to agreements, decisions or
concerted practices falling within Article 4(2) and Article 5(2), nor to those falling within
Article 5(1) which have been notified within the time limit specified in Article 5(1).
[1015]

Article 7 — Special provisions for existing agreements, decisions and practices

1. Where agreements, decisions and concerted practices in existence at the date of entry
into force of this Regulation and notified [within the limits specified in Article 5(1)][1]
do not satisfy the requirements of Article 85(3) of the Treaty and the undertakings or
associations of undertakings concerned cease to give effect to them or modify them in
such manner that they no longer fall within the prohibition contained in Article 85(1)
or that they satisfy the requirements of Article 85(3), the prohibition contained in Article
85(1) shall apply only for a period fixed by the Commission. A decision by the Commission pursuant to the foregoing sentence shall not apply as against undertakings and associations of undertakings which did not expressly consent to the notification.

2. Paragraph 1 shall apply to agreements, decisions and concerted practices falling within Article 4(2) which are in existence at the date of entry into force of this Regulation if they are notified [before 1 January 1967].[2]   **[1016]**

AMENDMENTS

1 Words substituted by EEC Council Regulation No 59/62, Art 1(3).

2 Words substituted by EEC Council Regulation No 118/63, Art 1.

Article 8 – Duration and revocation of decisions under Article 85(3)

1. A decision in application of Article 85(3) of the Treaty shall be issued for a specified period and conditions and obligations may be attached thereto.

2. A decision may on application be renewed if the requirements of Article 85(3) of the Treaty continue to be satisfied.

3. The Commission may revoke or amend its decision or prohibit specified acts by the parties:

    (a) where there has been a change in any of the facts which were basic to the making of the decision;

    (b) where the parties commit a breach of any obligation attached to the decision;

    (c) where the decision is based on incorrect information or was induced by deceit;

    (d) where the parties abuse the exemption from the provisions of Article 85(1) of the Treaty granted to them by the decision.

In cases to which subparagraphs (b), (c) or (d) apply, the decision may be revoked with retroactive effect.   **[1017]**

Article 9 – Powers

1. Subject to review of its decision by the Court of Justice, the Commission shall have sole power to declare Article 85(1) inapplicable pursuant to Article 85(3) of the Treaty.

2. The Commission shall have power to apply Article 85(1) and Article 86 of the Treaty; this power may be exercised notwithstanding that the time limits specified in Article 5(1) and in Article 7(2) relating to notification have not expired.

3. As long as the Commission has not initiated any procedure under Articles 2, 3 or 6, the authorities of the Member States shall remain competent to apply Article 85(1) and Article 86 in accordance with Article 88 of the Treaty; they shall remain competent in this respect notwithstanding that the time limits specified in Article 5(1) and in Article 7(2) relating to notification have not expired.   **[1018]**

Article 10 – Liaison with the authorities of the Member States

1. The Commission shall forthwith transmit to the competent authorities of the Member States a copy of the applications and notifications together with copies of the most important documents lodged with the Commission for the purpose of establishing the existence of infringements of Articles 85 or 86 of the Treaty or of obtaining negative clearance or a decision in application of Article 85(3).

2. The Commission shall carry out the procedure set out in paragraph 1 in close and constant liaison with the competent authorities of the Member States; such authorities shall have the right to express their views upon that procedure.

3. An Advisory Committee on Restrictive Practices and Monopolies shall be consulted prior to the taking of any decision following upon a procedure under paragraph 1, and

of any decision concerning the renewal, amendment or revocation of a decision pursuant to Article 85(3) of the Treaty.

4. The Advisory Committee shall be composed of officials competent in the matter of restrictive practices and monopolies. Each Member State shall appoint an official to represent it who, if prevented from attending, may be replaced by another official.

5. The consultation shall take place at a joint meeting convened by the Commission; such meeting shall be held not earlier than fourteen days after dispatch of the notice convening it. The notice shall, in respect of each case to be examined, be accompanied by a summary of the case together with an indication of the most important documents, and a preliminary draft decision.

6. The Advisory Committee may deliver an opinion notwithstanding that some of its members or their alternates are not present. A report of the outcome of the consultative proceedings shall be annexed to the draft decision. It shall not be made public.

[1019]

Article 11 — Requests for information

1. In carrying out the duties assigned to it by Article 89 and by provisions adopted under Article 87 of the Treaty, the Commission may obtain all necessary information from the Governments and competent authorities of the Member States and from undertakings and associations of undertakings.

2. When sending a request for information to an undertaking or association of undertakings, the Commission shall at the same time forward a copy of the request to the competent authority of the Member State in whose territory the seat of the undertaking or association of undertakings is situated.

3. In its request the Commission shall state the legal basis and the purpose of the request and also the penalties provided for in Article 15(1)(*b*) for supplying incorrect information.

4. The owners of the undertakings or their representatives and, in the case of legal persons, companies or firms, or of associations having no legal personality, the persons authorised to represent them by law or by their constitution shall supply the information requested.

5. Where an undertaking or association of undertakings does not supply the information requested within the time limit fixed by the Commission, or supplies incomplete information, the Commission shall by decision require the information to be supplied. The decision shall specify what information is required, fix an appropriate time limit within which it is to be supplied and indicate the penalties provided for in Article 15(1)(*b*) and Article 16(1)(*c*) and the right to have the decision reviewed by the Court of Justice.

6. The Commission shall at the same time forward a copy of its decision to the competent authority of the Member State in whose territory the seat of the undertaking or association of undertakings is situated.   **[1020]**

Article 12 — Inquiry into sectors of the economy

1. If in any sector of the economy the trend of trade between Member States, price movements, inflexibility of prices or other circumstances suggest that in the economic sector concerned competition is being restricted or distorted within the common market, the Commission may decide to conduct a general inquiry into that economic sector and in the course thereof may request undertakings in the sector concerned to supply the information necessary for giving effect to the principles formulated in Articles 85 and 86 of the Treaty and for carrying out the duties entrusted to the Commission.

2. The Commission may in particular request every undertaking or association of undertakings in the economic sector concerned to communicate to it all agreements, decisions and concerted practices which are exempt from notification by virtue of Article 4(2) and Article 5(2).

3. When making inquiries pursuant to paragraph 2, the Commission shall also request undertakings or groups of undertakings whose size suggests that they occupy a dominant position within the common market or a substantial part thereof to supply to the Commission such particulars of the structure of the undertakings and of their behaviour as are requisite to an appraisal of their position in the light of Article 86 of the Treaty.

4. Article 10(3) to (6) and Articles 11, 13 and 14 shall apply correspondingly.

[1021]

Article 13 – Investigations by the authorities of the Member States

1. At the request of the Commission, the competent authorities of the Member States shall undertake the investigations which the Commission considers to be necessary under Article 14(1), or which it has ordered by decision pursuant to Article 14(3). The officials of the competent authorities of the Member States responsible for conducting these investigations shall exercise their powers upon production of an authorisation in writing issued by the competent authority of the Member State in whose territory the investigation is to be made. Such authorisation shall specify the subject matter and purpose of the investigation.

2. If so requested by the Commission or by the competent authority of the Member State in whose territory the investigation is to be made, the officials of the Commission may assist the officials of such authorities in carrying out their duties.   **[1022]**

Article 14 – Investigating powers of the Commission

1. In carrying out the duties assigned to it by Article 89 and by provisions adopted under Article 87 of the Treaty, the Commission may undertake all necessary investigations into undertakings and associations of undertakings. To this end the officials authorised by the Commission are empowered:

   (a) to examine the books and other business records;
   (b) to take copies of or extracts from the books and business records;
   (c) to ask for oral explanations on the spot;
   (d) to enter any premises, land and means of transport of undertakings.

2. The officials of the Commission authorised for the purpose of these investigations shall exercise their powers upon production of an authorisation in writing specifying the subject matter and purpose of the investigation and the penalties provided for in Article 15(1)(c) in cases where production of the required books or other business records is incomplete. In good time before the investigation, the Commission shall inform the competent authority of the Member State in whose territory the same is to be made of the investigation and of the identity of the authorised officials.

3. Undertakings and associations of undertakings shall submit to investigations ordered by decision of the Commission. The decision shall specify the subject matter and purpose of the investigation, appoint the date on which it is to begin and indicate the penalties provided for in Article 15(1)(c) and Article 16(1)(d) and the right to have the decision reviewed by the Court of Justice.

4. The Commission shall take decisions referred to in paragraph 3 after consultation with the competent authority of the Member State in whose territory the investigation is to be made.

5. Officials of the competent authority of the Member State in whose territory the investigation is to be made may, at the request of such authority or of the Commission, assist the officials of the Commission in carrying out their duties.

6. Where an undertaking opposes an investigation ordered pursuant to this Article, the Member State concerned shall afford the necessary assistance to the officials authorised by the Commission to enable them to make their investigation. Member States shall, after consultation with the Commission, take the necessary measures to this end before 1 October 1962.			**[1023]**

Article 15 – Fines

1. The Commission may by decision impose on undertakings or associations of undertakings fines of from 100 to 5000 units of account where, intentionally or negligently:

(a) they supply incorrect or misleading information in an application pursuant to Article 2 or in a notification pursuant to Articles 4 or 5; or

(b) they supply incorrect information in response to a request made pursuant to Article 11(3) or (5) or to Article 12, or do not supply information within the time limit fixed by a decision taken under Article 11(5); or

(c) they produce the required books or other business records in incomplete form during investigations under Article 13 or 14, or refuse to submit to an investigation ordered by decision issued in implementation of Article 14(3).

2. The Commission may by decision impose on undertakings or associations of undertakings fines of from 1000 to 1 000 000 units of account, or a sum in excess thereof but not exceeding 10% of the turnover in the preceding business year of each of the undertakings participating in the infringement where, either intentionally or negligently:

(a) they infringe Article 85(1) or Article 86 of the Treaty; or

(b) they commit a breach of any obligation imposed pursuant to Article 8(1).

In fixing the amount of the fine, regard shall be had both to the gravity and to the duration of the infringement.

3. Article 10(3) to (6) shall apply.

4. Decisions taken pursuant to paragraphs 1 and 2 shall not be of a criminal law nature.

5. The fines provided for in paragraph 2(a) shall not be imposed in respect of acts taking place:

(a) after notification to the Commission and before its decision in application of Article 85(3) of the Treaty, provided they fall within the limits of the activity described in the notification;

(b) before notification and in the course of agreements, decisions or concerted practices in existence at the date of entry into force of this Regulation, provided that notification was effected within the time limits specified in Article 5(1) and Article 7(2).

6. Paragraph 5 shall not have effect where the Commission has informed the undertakings concerned that after preliminary examination it is of opinion that Article 85(1) of the Treaty applies and that application of Article 85(3) is not justified.			**[1024]**

Article 16 – Periodic penalty payments

1. The Commission may by decision impose on undertakings or associations of undertakings periodic penalty payments of from 50 to 1000 units of account per day, calculated from the date appointed by the decision, in order to compel them:

(a) to put an end to an infringement of Article 85 or 86 of the Treaty, in accordance with a decision taken pursuant to Article 3 of this Regulation;

(b) to refrain from any act prohibited under Article 8(3);

(c) to supply complete and correct information which it has requested by decision taken pursuant to Article 11(5);

(d) to submit to an investigation which it has ordered by decision taken pursuant to Article 14(3).

2. Where the undertakings or associations of undertakings have satisfied the obligation which it was the purpose of the periodic penalty payment to enforce, the Commission may fix the total amount of the periodic penalty payment at a lower figure than that which would arise under the original decision.

3. Article 10(3) to (6) shall apply. **[1025]**

Article 17 — Review by the Court of Justice

The Court of Justice shall have unlimited jurisdiction within the meaning of Article 172 of the Treaty to review decisions whereby the Commission has fixed a fine or periodic penalty payment; it may cancel, reduce or increase the fine or periodic penalty payment imposed. **[1026]**

Article 18 — Unit of account

For the purposes of applying Articles 15 to 17 the unit of account shall be that adopted in drawing up the budget of the Community in accordance with Articles 207 and 209 of the Treaty. **[1027]**

Article 19 — Hearing of the parties and of third persons

1. Before taking decisions as provided for in Articles 2, 3, 6, 7, 8, 15 and 16, the Commission shall give the undertakings or associations of undertakings concerned the opportunity of being heard on the matters to which the Commission has taken objection.

2. If the Commission or the competent authorities of the Member States consider it necessary, they may also hear other natural or legal persons. Applications to be heard on the part of such persons shall, where they show a sufficient interest, be granted.

3. Where the Commission intends to give negative clearance pursuant to Article 2 or take a decision in application of Article 85(3) of the Treaty, it shall publish a summary of the relevant application or notification and invite all interested third parties to submit their observations within a time limit which it shall fix being not less than one month. Publication shall have regard to the legitimate interest of undertakings in the protection of their business secrets. **[1028]**

Article 20 — Professional secrecy

1. Information acquired as a result of the application of Articles 11, 12, 13 and 14 shall be used only for the purpose of the relevant request or investigation.

2. Without prejudice to the provisions of Articles 19 and 21, the Commission and the competent authorities of the Member States, their officials and other servants shall not disclose information acquired by them as a result of the application of this Regulation and of the kind covered by the obligation of professional secrecy.

3. The provisions of paragraphs 1 and 2 shall not prevent publication of general information or surveys which do not contain information relating to particular undertakings or associations of undertakings.   **[1029]**

Article 21 — Publication of decisions

1. The Commission shall publish the decisions which it takes pursuant to Articles 2, 3, 6, 7 and 8.

2. The publication shall state the names of the parties and the main content of the decision; it shall have regard to the legitimate interest of undertakings in the protection of their business secrets.   **[1030]**

Article 22 — Special provisions

1. The Commission shall submit to the Council proposals for making certain categories of agreement, decision and concerted practice falling within Article 4(2) or Article 5(2) compulsorily notifiable under Article 4 or 5.

2. Within one year from the date of entry into force of this Regulation, the Council shall examine, on a proposal from the Commission, what special provisions might be made for exempting from the provisions of this Regulation agreements, decisions and concerted practices falling within Article 4(2) or Article 5(2).   **[1031]**

Article 23 — Transitional provisions applicable to decisions of authorities of the Member States

1. Agreements, decisions and concerted practices of the kind described in Article 85(1) of the Treaty to which, before the entry into force of this Regulation, the competent authority of a Member State has declared Article 85(1) to be inapplicable pursuant to Article 85(3) shall not be subject to compulsory notification under Article 5. The decision of the competent authority of the Member State shall be deemed to be a decision within the meaning of Article 6; it shall cease to be valid upon expiration of the period fixed by such authority but in any event not more than three years after the entry into force of this Regulation. Article 8(3) shall apply.

2. Applications for renewal of decisions of the kind described in paragraph 1 shall be decided upon by the Commission in accordance with Article 8(2).   **[1032]**

Article 24 — Implementing provisions

The Commission shall have power to adopt implementing provisions concerning the form, content and other details of applications pursuant to Articles 2 and 3 and of notifications pursuant to Articles 4 and 5, and concerning hearings pursuant to Article 19(1) and (2).
                                                                                  [1033]

[Article 25

1. As regards agreements, decisions and concerted practices to which Article 85 of the Treaty applies by virtue of accession, the date of accession shall be substituted for the date of entry into force of this regulation in every place where reference is made in this Regulation to this latter date.

2. Agreements, decisions and concerted practices existing at the date of accession to which Article 85 of the Treaty applies by virtue of accession shall be notified pursuant to Article 5(1) or Article 7(1) and (2) within six months from the date of accession.

3. Fines under Article 15(2)(a) shall not be imposed in respect of any act prior to notification of the agreements, decisions and practices to which paragraph 2 applies and which have been notified within the period therein specified.

4. New Member States shall take the measures referred to in Article 14(6) within six months from the date of accession after consulting the Commission.

5. The provisions of paragraphs (1) to (4) above still apply in the same way in the case of accession of the Hellenic Republic, the Kingdom of Spain and of the Portuguese Republic.]   **[1034]**

AMENDMENT
Art 25, paras 1 to 4 were added by the Act of 1972 concerning the conditions of accession and the adjustments to the Treaty of Rome, Annex I(V)(1); and para 5 was added by the 1979 Act of Accession of the Hellenic Republic, Annex I(V)(1) and subsequently replaced by the Act of Accession of the Kingdom of Spain and the Portuguese Republic, Annex I(IV)(5).

This Regulation shall be binding in its entirety and directly applicable in all Member States.

Done at Brussels, 6 February 1962.

REGULATION (EEC) No 26/62 OF THE COUNCIL

applying certain rules of competition to production of and trade in agricultural products

THE COUNCIL OF THE EUROPEAN ECONOMIC COMMUNITY,
Having regard to the Treaty establishing the European Economic Community, and in particular Articles 42 and 43 thereof;
Having regard to the proposal from the Commission;
Having regard to the Opinion of the European Parliament;
Whereas by virtue of Article 42 of the Treaty one of the matters to be decided under the common agricultural policy is whether the rules on competition laid down in the Treaty are to apply to production of and trade in agricultural products, and accordingly the provisions hereinafter contained will have to be supplemented in the light of developments in that policy;
Whereas the proposals submitted by the Commission for the formulation and implementation of the common agricultural policy show that certain rules on competition must forthwith be made applicable to production of and trade in agricultural products in order to eliminate practices contrary to the principles of the common market and prejudicial to attainment of the objectives set out in Article 39 of the Treaty and in order to provide a basis for the future establishment of a system of competition adapted to the development of the common agricultural policy;
Whereas the rules on competition relating to the agreements, decisions and practices referred to in Article 85 of the Treaty and to the abuse of dominant positions must be applied to production of and trade in agricultural products, in so far as their application does not impede the functioning of national organisations of agricultural markets or jeopardise attainment of the objectives of the common agricultural policy;
Whereas special attention is warranted in the case of farmers' organisations which are particularly concerned with the joint production or marketing of agricultural products or the use of joint facilities, unless such joint action excludes competition or jeopardises attainment of the objectives of Article 39 of the Treaty;
Whereas, in order both to avoid compromising the development of a common agricultural policy and to ensure certainty in the law and non-discriminatory treatment of the undertakings concerned, the Commission must have sole power, subject to review by the Court of Justice, to determine whether the conditions provided for in the two preceding recitals are fulfilled as regards the agreements, decisions and practices referred to in Article 85 of the Treaty;
Whereas, in order to enable the specific provisions of the Treaty regarding agriculture, and in particular those of Article 39 thereof, to be taken into consideration, the Commission must, in

questions of dumping, assess all the causes of the practices complained of and in particular the price level at which products from other sources are imported into the market in question; whereas it must, in the light of its assessment, make recommendations and authorise protective measures as provided in Article 91(1) of the Treaty;

Whereas, in order to implement, as part of the development of the common agricultural policy, the rules on aids for production of or trade in agricultural products, the Commission should be in a position to draw up a list of existing, new or proposed aids, to make appropriate observations to the Member States and to propose suitable measures to them;

HAS ADOPTED THIS REGULATION:

Article 1

From the entry into force of this Regulation, Articles 85 to 90 of the Treaty and provisions made in implementation thereof shall, subject to Article 2 below, apply to all agreements, decisions and practices referred to in Articles 85(1) and 86 of the Treaty which relate to production of or trade in the products listed in Annex II to the Treaty.

[1035]

Article 2

1. Article 85(1) of the Treaty shall not apply to such of the agreements, decisions and practices referred to in the preceding Article as form an integral part of a national market organisation or are necessary for attainment of the objectives set out in Article 39 of the Treaty. In particular, it shall not apply to agreements, decisions and practices of farmers, farmers' associations, or associations of such associations belonging to a single Member State which concern the production or sale of agricultural products or the use of joint facilities for the storage, treatment or processing of agricultural products, and under which there is no obligation to charge identical prices, unless the Commission finds that competition is thereby excluded or that the objectives of Article 39 of the Treaty are jeopardised.

2. After consulting the Member States and hearing the undertakings or associations of undertakings conerned and any other natural or legal person that it considers appropriate, the Commission shall have sole power, subject to review by the Court of Justice, to determine, by decision which shall be published, which agreements, decisions and practices fulfil the conditions specified in paragraph 1.

3. The Commission shall undertake such determination either on its own initiative or at the request of a competent authority of a Member State or of an interested undertaking or association of undertakings.

4. The publication shall state the names of the parties and the main content of the decision; it shall have regard to the legitimate interest of undertakings in the protection of their business secrets.   **[1036]**

Article 3

1. Without prejudice to Article 46 of the Treaty, Article 91(1) thereof shall apply to trade in the products listed in Annex II to the Treaty.

2. With due regard for the provisions of the Treaty relating to agriculture, and in particular those of Article 39, the Commission shall assess all the causes of the practices complained of, in particular the price level at which products from other sources are imported into the market in question.

In the light of its assessment, it shall make recommendations and authorise protective measures as provided in Article 91(1) of the Treaty.   **[1037]**

Article 4

The provisions of Article 93(1) and of the first sentence of Article 93(3) of the Treaty shall apply to aids granted for production of or trade in the products listed in Annex II to the Treaty. **[1038]**

Article 5

This Regulation shall enter into force on the day following its publication in the *Official Journal of the European Communities*, with the exception of Articles 1 to 3, which shall enter into force on 1 July 1962. **[1039]**

This Regulation shall be binding in its entirety and directly applicable in all Member States.

Done at Brussels, 4 April 1962.

REGULATION (EEC) No 27/62 OF THE COMMISSION

First Regulation implementing Council Regulation No 17 of 6 February 1962 (Form, content and other details concerning applications and notifications)

THE COMMISSION OF THE EUROPEAN ECONOMIC COMMUNITY,

Having regard to the provisions of the Treaty establishing the European Economic Community, and in particular Articles 87 and 155 thereof;

Having regard to Article 24 of Council Regulation No 17 of 6 February 1962 (First Regulation implementing Articles 85 and 86 of the Treaty);

Whereas under Article 24 of Council Regulation No 17 the Commission is authorised to adopt implementing provisions concerning the form, content and other details of applications under Articles 2 and 3 and of notifications under Articles 4 and 5 of that Regulation;

Whereas the submission of such applications and notifications may have important legal consequences for each of the undertakings which is party to an agreement, decision or concerted practice; whereas every undertaking should accordingly have the right to submit an application or a notification to the Commission; whereas, furthermore, an undertaking exercising this right must inform the other undertakings which are parties to the agreement, decision or concerted practice in order to enable them to protect their interests;

Whereas it is for the undertakings and associations of undertakings to transmit to the Commission information as to facts and circumstances in support of applications under Article 2 and of notifications under Articles 4 and 5;

Whereas it is desirable to prescribe forms for use in applications for negative clearance relating to implementation of Article 85(1) and for notifications relating to implementation of Article 85(3) of the Treaty, in order to simplify and accelerate consideration by the competent departments, in the interests of all concerned;

HAS ADOPTED THIS REGULATION:

Article 1 — Persons entitled to submit applications and notifications

1. Any undertaking which is party to agreements, decisions or practices of the kind described in Articles 85 and 86 of the Treaty may submit an application under Article 2 or a notification under Articles 4 and 5 of Regulation No 17. Where the application or notification is submitted by some, but not all, of the undertakings concerned, they shall give notice to the others.

2. Where applications and notifications under Articles 2, 3(1), 3(2)(*b*), 4 and 5 of Regulation No 17 are signed by representatives of undertakings, associations of undertakings, or natural or legal persons, such representatives shall produce written proof that they are authorised to act.

3. Where a joint application or notification is submitted, a joint representative should be appointed.   **[1040]**

Article 2 – Submission of applications and notifications

[1. [Thirteen][1] copies of each application and notification . . .[2] shall be summited to the Commission].[3]

2. The supporting documents shall be either originals or copies. Copies must be certified as true copies of the original.

3. Applications and notifications shall be in one of the official languages of the Community. Supporting documents shall be submitted in their original language. Where the original language is not one of the official languages, a translation in one of the official languages shall be attached.   **[1041]**

AMENDMENTS
  1 Word in para (1) substituted by the Act of Accession of the Hellenic Republic, 1979, and subsequently by the Act of Accession of the Kingdom of Spain and the Portuguese Republic, 1985, Annex I(IV)(6).
  2 Words omitted as indicated by dots deleted by EEC Commission Regulation No 2526/85.
  3 Para 1 substituted by EEC Commission Regulation No 1699/75.

Article 3 – Effective date of submission of applications and registrations

The date of submission of an application or notification shall be the date on which it is received by the Commission. Where, however, the application or notification is sent by registered post, it shall be deemed to have been received on the date shown on the postmark of the place of posting.   **[1042]**

Article 4 – Content of applications and notifications

[1. Applications under Article 2 of Regulation 17 relating to the applicability of Article 85(1) of the Treaty and notifications under Article 4 or Article 5(2) of Regulation 17 shall be submitted on Form A/B in the manner prescribed on the Form and in the Complementary Note thereto, as shown in the Annex to this Regulation.

2. Applications and notifications shall contain the information asked for in Form A/B and the Complementary Note.

3. Several participating undertakings may submit an application or notification on a single form.

4. Applications under Article 2 of Regulation 17 relating to the applicability of Article 86 of the Treaty shall contain a full statement of the facts, specifying, in particular, the practice concerned and the position of the undertaking or undertakings within the common market or a substantial part thereof in regard to products or services to which the practice relates. Form A/B may be used.]   **[1043]**

AMENDMENT
  Art 4 replaced by EEC Commission Regulation No 2526/85.

Article 5 – Transitional provisions

1. Applications and notifications submitted prior to the date of entry into force of this Regulation otherwise than on the prescribed forms shall be deemed to comply with Article 4 of this Regulation.

2. The Commission may require a duly completed form to be submitted to it within such time as it shall appoint. In that event, applications and notifications shall be treated

as properly made only if the forms are submitted within the prescribed period and in accordance with the provisions of this Regulation. **[1044]**

Article 6

This Regulation shall enter into force on the day following its publication in the *Official Journal of the European Communities*. **[1045]**

This Regulation shall be binding in its entirety and directly applicable in all Member States.

Done at Brussels, 3 May 1962.

ANNEX[1]

Note. This form must be accompanied by an Annex containing the information specified in the attached Complementary Note.

The form and Annex must be supplied in 13 copies (one for the Commission and one for each Member State). Supply three copies of any relevant agreement and one copy of other supporting documents.

FORM A/B

Please do not forget to complete the Acknowledgement of Receipt annexed.

If space is insufficient, please use extra pages, specifying to which item on the form they relate.

TO THE COMMISSION OF THE EUROPEAN COMMUNITIES

Directorate-General for Competition,
Rue de la Loi, 200,
B-1049 Brussels.

A. Application for negative clearance pursuant to Article 2 of Council Regulation No 17 of 6 February 1962 relating to implementation of Article 85(1) or of Article 86 of the Treaty establishing the European Economic Community.

B. Notification of an agreement, decision or concerted practice under Article 4 (or 5) of Council Regulation No 17 of 6 February 1962 with a view to obtaining exemption under Article 85(3) of the Treaty establishing the European Economic Community, including notifications claiming benefit of an opposition procedure.

Identity of the parties

1. *Identity of applicant/notifier*

Full name and address, telephone, telex and facsimile numbers, and brief description([1]) of the undertaking(s) or association(s) of undertakings submitting the application or notification.

For partnerships, sole traders or any other unincorporated body trading under a business name, give, also, the name, forename(s) and address of the proprietor(s) or partner(s).

Where an application or notification is submitted on behalf of some other person (or is submitted by more than one person) the name, address and position of the representative (or joint representative) must be given, together with proof of his authority to act. Where an application or notification is submitted by or on behalf of more than one person they should appoint a joint representative (Article 1(2) and (3) of Commission Regulation No 27).

(1) Eg "Motor vehicle manufacturer", "Computer service bureau", "Conglomerate".

2. *Identity of any other parties*

Full name and address and brief description of any other parties to the agreement, decision or concerted practice (hereinafter referred to as "the arrangements").

State what steps have been taken to inform these other parties of this application or notification.

(This information is not necessary in respect of standard contracts which an undertaking submitting the application or notification has concluded or intends to conclude with a number of parties (eg a contract appointing dealers).)

Purpose of this application/notification (see Complementary Note)

(Please answer yes or no to the questions)

Are you asking for negative clearance alone? (See Complementary Note – Section IV, end of first paragraph – for the consequence of such a request.)

Are you applying for negative clearance, and also notifying the arrangements to obtain an exemption in case the Commission does not grant negative clearance?

Are you only notifying the arrangements in order to obtain an exemption?

Do you claim that this application may benefit from an opposition procedure? (See Complementary Note—Sections III, IV, VI and VII and Annex 2.) If you answer "yes", please specify the Regulation and Article number on which you are relying.

Would you be satisfied with a comfort letter? (See the end of Section VII of the Complementary Note.)

The undersigned declare that the information given above and in the . . . pages annexed hereto is correct to the best of their knowledge and belief, that all estimates are identified as such and are their best estimates of the underlying facts and that all the opinions expressed are sincere.

They are aware of the provisions of Article 15(1)(*a*) of Regulation No 17 (see attached Complementary Note).

Place and date: ....

    Signatures: ....

            ....

            ....

COMMISSION   Brussels ....
OF THE
EUROPEAN COMMUNITIES
———

Directorate-General for Competition

To

ACKNOWLEDGEMENT OF RECEIPT

(This form will be returned to the address inserted above if the top half is completed in a single copy by the person lodging it)

Your application for negative clearance dated: ....

Your notification dated: ....

concerning: ....

Your reference: ....

Parties:

1. ....

2. .... and others

(There is no need to name the other undertakings party to the arrangement)

(To be completed by the Commission.)

was received on: ....

and registered under No IV/: ....

Please quote the above number in all correspondence

Provisional address: *Telephone:*   *Telex:*   *Telegraphic address:*
Rue de la Loi 200   Direct line: 235....   COMEU B 21877   COMEUR Brussels
B-1049 Brussels   Telephone exchange: 235 11 11

COMPLEMENTARY NOTE

CONTENTS

I.   Purpose of Community rules on competiton

II.   Negative clearance

III.   Exemption under Article 85(3)

IV.   Purpose of the form

V.   Nature of the form

VI.   The need for complete and accurate information

VII. Subsequent procedure

VIII. Secrecy

IX.   Further information and headings to be used in Annex to Form A/B

Annex 1: Text of Articles 85 and 86 of the EEC Treaty

Annex 2: List of relevant Acts

Annex 3: List of Member States and Commission Press and Information Offices within the Community

Additions or alterations to the information given in these Annexes will be published by the Commission from time to time.

Nota bene: Any undertaking uncertain about how to complete a notification or wishing further explanation may contact the Directorate-General for Competition (DG IV) in Brussels. Alternatively, any Commission Information Office (those in the Community are listed in Annex 3) will be able to obtain guidance or indicate an official in Brussels who speaks the preferred official Community language.

I. Purpose of Community rules on competition

The purpose of these rules is to prevent the distortion of competition in the common market by monopolies or restrictive practices; they apply to any enterprise trading directly or indirectly in the common market, wherever established. Article 85(1) of the Treaty establishing the European Economic Community (the text of Articles 85 and 86 is reproduced in Annex 1 to this note) prohibits restrictive agreements or concerted practices which may affect trade between Member States, and Article 85(2) declares contracts or other otherwise legally binding arrangements containing such restrictions void (although the European Court of Justice has held that if restrictive terms of contracts are severable, only those terms are void); Article 85(3), however, gives the Commission power to exempt practices with beneficial effects. Article 86 prohibits the abuse of a dominant position. The original procedures for implementing these Articles, which provide for "negative clearance" and exemption under Article 85(3), were laid down in Council Regulation No 17 (the references to this and all other acts mentioned in this note or relevant to applications made on Form A/B are listed in Annex 2 to this note).

II. Negative clearance

The purpose of the negative clearance procedure is to allow businesses ("undertakings") to ascertain whether or not the Commission considers that any of their arrangements or behaviour are prohibited under Articles 85(1) or 86 of the Treaty. (It is governed by Article 2 of Regulation No 17.) Clearance takes the form of a decision by the Commission certifying that, on the basis of the facts in its possession, there are no grounds under Article 85(1) or 86 of the Treaty for action on its part in respect of the arrangements or behaviour.

Any party may apply for negative clearance, even without the consent (but not without the knowledge) of other parties to arrangements. There would be little point in applying, however, where arrangements or behaviour clearly do not fall within the scope of Article 85(1) or Article 86. (In this connection, your attention is drawn to the last paragraph of IV below and to Annex 2.) Nor is the Commission obliged to give negative clearance — Article 2 of Regulation No 17 states that ". . . the Commission *may* certify . . .". The Commission does not usually issue negative clearance decisions in cases which, in its opinion, so clearly do not fall within the scope of the prohibition of Article 85(1) that there is no reasonable doubt for it to resolve by such a decision.

III. Exemption under Article 85(3)

The purpose of the procedure for exemption under Article 85(3) is to allow undertakings to enter into arrangements which, in fact, offer economic advantages but which, without an exemption, would be prohibited under Article 85(1). (It is governed by Articles 4, 6 and 8 of Regulation No 17 and, for new Member States, by Articles 5, 7 and 25.) It takes the form of a decision by the Commission declaring Article 85(1) to be inapplicable to the arrangements described in the decision. Article 8 requires the Commission to specify the period of validity of any such decision, allows the Commission to attach conditions and obligations and provides for decisions to be amended or revoked or specified acts by the parties to be prohibited in certain circumstances, notably if the decisions were based on incorrect information or if there is any material change in the facts.

Any party may notify arrangements, even without the consent (but not without the knowledge) of other parties.

The Commission has adopted a number of Regulations granting exemption to categories of agreements. Some of these Regulations (see Annex 2 for the latest list) provide that some agreements may benefit by such an exemption only if they are notified to the Commission under Article 4 (or 5) of Regulation No 17 with a view to obtaining exemption under Article 85(3) of the Treaty and the benefit of an opposition procedure is claimed in the notification.

A decision granting exemption under Article 85(3) may have retroactive effect but, with certain exceptions, cannot be made effective earlier than the date of notification (Article 6 of Regulation No 17). Should the Commission find that notified arrangements are indeed prohibited by Article 85(1) and cannot be exempted under Article 85(3) and, therefore, take a decision condemning them, the parties are nevertheless protected, from the date of notification, against fines for any infringement described in the notification (Articles 3 and 15(5) and (6)).

IV. Purpose of the form

The purpose of Form A/B is to allow undertakings, or associations of undertakings, wherever situated, to apply to the Commission for negative clearance for arrangements or behaviour, or to notify such arrangements and apply to have them exempted from the prohibition of Article 85(1) of the Treaty by virtue of Article 85(3). The form allows undertakings applying for negative clearance to notify, at the same time, in order to obtain an exemption. It should be noted that only a notification in order to obtain exemption affords immunity from fines (Article 15(5)).

To be valid, applications for negative clearance in respect of Article 85, notifications to obtain an exemption and notifications claiming the benefit of an opposition procedure must be made on Form A/B (by virtue of Article 4 of Commission Regulation No 27). (Undertakings applying for negative clearance for their behaviour in relation to a possible dominant position — Article 86 — need not use Form A/B (see Article 4(4) of Regulation No 27), but they are strongly recommended to give all the information requested at IX below in order to ensure that their application gives a full statement of the facts.)

Before completing a form, your attention is particularly drawn to the Regulations granting block exemption and the notices listed in Annex 2 — these were published to allow undertakings to judge for themselves, in many cases, whether there was any doubt about their arrangements. This would allow them to avoid the considerable bother and expense, both for themselves and for the Commission, of submitting and examining an application or notification where there is clearly no doubt.

V. Nature of the form

The form consists of a single sheet calling for the identity of the applicant(s) or notifier(s) and of any other parties. This must be supplemented by further information given under the headings and references detailed below (see IX). For preference the paper used should be A4 (21 × 29.7 cm — the same size as the form) but must not be bigger. Leave a margin of at least 25 mm or one inch on the left-hand side of the page and, if you use both sides, on the right-hand side of the reverse.

VI. The need for complete and accurate information

It is important that applicants give all the relevant facts. Although the Commission has the right to seek further information from applicants or third parties, and is obliged to publish a summary of the application before granting negative clearance or exemption under Article 85(3), it will usually base its decision on the information provided by the applicant. Any decision taken on the basis of incomplete information could be without effect in the case of a negative clearance, or voidable in that of an exemption. For the same reason, it is also important to inform the Commission of any material changes to your arrangements made after your application or notification.

Complete information is of particular importance if you are claiming the benefit of a block exemption through an opposition procedure. Such exemption is dependent on the information supplied being ". . . complete and in accordance with the facts". If the Commission does not oppose a claim to benefit under this procedure on the basis of the facts in a notification and, subsequently, additional or different facts come to light that could and should have been in the notification, then the benefit of the exemption will be lost, and with retroactive effect. Similarly, there would be little point in claiming the benefit of an opposition procedure with clearly incomplete information; the Commission would be bound either to reject such a notification or oppose exemption in order to allow time for further information to be provided.

Moreover, you should be aware of the provisions of Article 15(1)(*a*) of Regulation No 17 which reads:

> "The Commission may by decision impose on undertakings or associations of undertakings fines of from 100 to 5 000 units of account(^{1}) where, intentionally or negligently, they supply incorrect or misleading information in an application pursuant to Article 2 or in a notification pursuant to Articles 4 or 5."

(1) The value of the European Currency Unit, which has replaced the unit of account, is published daily in the "C" series of the *Official Journal of the European Communities*.

The key words here are "incorrect or misleading information". However, it often remains a matter of judgement how much detail is relevant; the Commission accepts estimates where accurate information is not readily available in order to facilitate notifications; and the Commission calls for opinions as well as facts.

You should therefore note that the Commission will use these powers only where applicants or notifiers have, intentionally or negligently, provided false information or grossly inaccurate estimates or suppressed readily available information or estimates, or have deliberately expressed false opinions in order to obtain negative clearance or exemption.

VII. Subsequent procedure

The application or notification is registered in the Registry of the Directorate-General for Competition (DG IV). The date of receipt by the Commission (or the date of posting if sent by registered post) is the effective date of the submission. The application or notification might be considered invalid if obviously incomplete or not on the obligatory form.

Further information might be sought from the applicants or from third parties (Article 11 or 14 of Regulation No 17) and suggestions might be made as to amendments to the arrangements that might make them acceptable.

A notification claiming the benefit of an opposition procedure may be opposed by the Commission either because the Commission does not agree that the arrangements should benefit from a block exemption or to allow for more information to be sought. If the Commission opposes a claim, and unless the Commission subsequently withdraws its opposition, that notification will then be treated as an application for an individual exemption decision.

If, after examination, the Commission intends to grant the application, it is obliged (by Article 19(3) of Regulation No 17) to publish a summary and invite comments from third parties.

Subsequently, a preliminary draft decision has to be submitted to and discussed with the Advisory Committee on Restrictive Practices and Dominant Positions composed of officials of the Member States competent in the matter of restrictive practices and monopolies (Article 10 of Regulation No 17) – they will already have received a copy of the application or notification. Only then, and providing nothing has happened to change the Commission's intention, can it adopt a decision.

Sometimes files are closed without any formal decision being taken, for example, because it is found that the arrangements are already covered by a block exemption, or because the applicants are satisfied by a less formal letter from the Commission's departments (sometimes called a "comfort letter") indicating that the arrangements do not call for any action by the Commission, at least in present circumstances. Although not a Commission decision, a comfort letter indicates how the Commission's departments view the case on the facts currently in their possession which means that the Commission could if necessary – if, for example, it were to be asserted that a contract was void under Article 85(2) – take an appropriate decision.

VIII. Secrecy

Article 214 of the Treaty and Articles 20 and 21 of Regulation No 17 require the Commission and Member States not to disclose information of the kind covered by the obligation of professional secrecy. On the other hand, Article 19 of the Regulation requires the Commission to publish a summary of your application, should it intend to grant it, before taking the relevant decision. In this publication, the Commission ". . . shall have regard to the legitimate interest of undertakings in the protection of their business secrets" (Article 19(3)). In this connection, if you believe that your interests would be harmed if any of the information you are asked to supply were to be published or otherwise divulged to other parties, please put all such information in a second annex, with each page clearly marked "Business Secrets"; in the principal annex, under any affected heading state "see second annex" or "also see second annex"; in the second annex repeat the affected heading(s) and reference(s) and give the information you do not wish to have published, together with your reasons for this. Do not overlook the fact that the Commission may have to publish a summary of your application.

Before publishing an Article 19(3) notice, the Commission will show the undertakings concerned a copy of the proposed text.

IX. Further information and headings to be used in Annex to Form A/B

The further information is to be given under the following headings and reference numbers. Wherever possible give exact information. If this is not readily available, give your best estimate, and identify what you give as an estimate. If you believe any detail asked for to be unavailable or irrelevant, please explain why. This may, in particular, be the case if one party is notifying arrangements alone without the cooperation of other parties. Do not overlook the fact that Commission officials are ready to discuss what detail is relevant (see the *nota bene* at the beginning of this Complementary Note). An example that might help you is available on request.

1. *Brief description*

    Give a brief description of the arrangements or behaviour (nature, purpose, date(s) and duration) – (full details are requested below).

2. *Market*

    The nature of the goods or services affected by the arrangements or behaviour (include the customs tariff heading number according to the CCC Nomenclature or the Community's Common Customs Tariff or the *Nimexe* code if you know it – specify which). A brief description of the structure of the market (or markets) for these goods or services – eg who sells in it, who buys in it, its geographical extent, the turnover in it, how competitive it is, whether it is easy for new suppliers to enter the market, whether there are substitute products. If you are notifying a standard contract (eg a contract appointing dealers), say how many you expect to conclude. If you know of any studies of the market, it would be helpful to refer to them.

3. *Fuller details of the party or parties*

3.1. Do any of the parties form part of a group of companies? A group relationship is deemed to exist where a firm:

— owns more than half the capital or business assets, or

— has the power to exercise more than half the voting rights, or

— has the power to appoint more than half the members of the supervisory board, board of directors or bodies legally representing the undertaking, or

— has the right to manage the affairs of another.

If the answer is yes, give:

— the name and address of the ultimate parent company,

— a brief description of the business of the group() (and, if possible, one copy of the last set of group accounts),

— the name and address of any other company in the group competing in a market affected by the arrangements or in any related market, that is to say any other company competing directly or indirectly with the parties ("relevant associated company").

3.2. The most recently available total turnover of each of the parties and, as the case may be, of the group of which it forms part (it could be helpful also if you could provide one copy of the last set of accounts).

3.3. The sales or turnover of each party in the goods or services affected by the arrangements in the Community and worldwide. If the turnover in the Community is material (say more than a 5% market share), please also give figures for each Member State(^{2}), and for previous years (in order to show any significant trends), and give each party's sales targets for the future. Provide the same figures for any relevant associated company. (Under this heading, in particular, your best estimate might be all that you can readily supply.)

(1) Eg "Motor vehicle manufacturer", "Computer service bureau", "Conglomerate".
(2) See list in Annex 3.

3.4. In relation to the market (or markets) for the goods or services described at 2 above, give, for each of the sales or turnover figures in 3.3, your estimate of the market share it represents.

3.5. If you have a substantial interest falling short of control (more than 25% but less than 50%) in some other company competing in a market affected by the arrangements, or if some other such company has a substantial interest in yours, give its name and address and brief details.

4. *Full details of the arrangements*

4.1. If the contents are reduced to writing give a brief description of the purpose of the arrangements and attach three copies of the text (except that the technical descriptions often contained in know-how agreements may be omitted; in such cases, however, indicate parts omitted).

If the contents are not, or are only partially, reduced to writing, give a full description.

4.2. Detail any provisions contained in the arrangements which may restrict the parties in their freedom to take independent commercial decisions, for example regarding:

  —buying or selling prices, discounts or other trading conditions;

  —the quantities of goods to be manufactured or distributed or services to be offered;

  —technical development or investment;

  —the choice of markets or sources of supply;

  —purchases from or sales to third parties;

  —whether to apply similar terms for the supply of equivalent goods or services;

  —whether to offer different goods or services separately or together.

  (If you are claiming the benefit of an opposition procedure, identify particularly in this list the restrictions that exceed those automatically exempted by the relevant regulation.)

4.3. State between which Member States[1] trade may be affected by the arrangements, and whether trade between the Community and any third countries is affected.

NOTE
1 See list in Annex 3.

5. *Reasons for negative clearance*

  If you are applying for negative clearance state, under the reference:

5.1. why, ie state which provision or effects of the arrangements or behaviour might, in your view, raise questions of compatibility with the Community's rules on competition. The object of this subheading is to give the Commission the clearest possible idea of the doubts you have about your arrangements or behaviour that you wish to have resolved by a negative clearance decision.

  Then, under the following two references, give a statement of the relevant facts and reasons as to why you consider Articles 85(1) or 86 to be inapplicable, ie:

5.2. why the arrangements do not have the object or effect of preventing, restricting or distorting competition within the common market to any appreciable extent, or why your undertaking does not have or its behaviour does not abuse a dominant position; and/or

5.3. why the arrangements or behaviour are not such as may affect trade between Member States to any appreciable extent.

6. *Reasons for exemption under Article 85(3)*

  If you are notifying the arrangements, even if only as a precaution, in order to obtain an exemption under Article 85(3), explain how:

6.1. the arrangements contribute to improving production or distribution, and/or promoting technical or economic progress;

6.2. a proper share of the benefits arising from such improvement or progress accrues to consumers;

6.3. all restrictive provisions of the arrangements are indispensable to the attainment of the aims set out under 6.1 above (if you are claiming the benefit of an opposition procedure, it is particularly important that you should identify and justify restrictions that exceed those automatically exempted by the relevant Regulation); and

6.4. the arrangements do not eliminate competition in respect of a substantial part of the goods or services concerned.

7. *Other information*

7.1. Mention any earlier proceedings or informal contacts, of which you are aware, with the Commission and any earlier proceedings with any national authorities or courts concerning these or any related arrangements.

7.2. Give any other information presently available that you think might be helpful in allowing the Commission to appreciate whether there are any restrictions contained in the agreement, or any benefits that might justify them.

7.3. State whether you intend to produce further supporting facts or arguments not yet available and, if so, on which points.

7.4. State, with reasons, the urgency of your application or notification.

Annex 1

TEXT OF ARTICLES 85 AND 86 OF THE EEC TREATY

ARTICLE 85

1. The following shall be prohibited as incompatible with the common market: all agreements between undertakings, decisions by associations of undertakings and concerted practices which may affect trade between Member States and which have as their object or effect the prevention, restriction or distortion of competition within the common market, and in particular those which:

(*a*) directly or indirectly fix purchase or selling prices or any other trading conditions;
(*b*) limit or control production, markets, technical development, or investment;
(*c*) share markets or sources of supply;
(*d*) apply dissimilar conditions to equivalent transactions with other trading parties, thereby placing them at a competitive disadvantage;
(*e*) make the conclusion of contracts subject to acceptance by the other parties of supplementary obligations which, by their nature or according to commercial usage, have no connection with the subject of such contracts.

2. Any agreements or decisions prohibited pursuant to this Article shall be automatically void.

3. The provisions of paragraph 1 may, however, be declared inapplicable in the case of:

— any agreement or category of agreements between undertakings,
— any decision or category of decisions by associations of undertakings,
— any concerted practice or category of concerted practices,

which contributes to improving the production or distribution of goods or to promoting technical or economic progress, while allowing consumers a fair share of the resulting benefit, and which does not:

(a) impose on the undertakings concerned restrictions which are not indispensable to the attainment of these objectives;
(b) afford such undertakings the possibility of eliminating competition in respect of a substantial part of the products in question.

ARTICLE 86

Any abuse by one or more undertakings of a dominant position within the common market or in a substantial part of it shall be prohibited as incompatible with the common market in so far as it may affect trade between Member States.

Such abuse may, in particular, consist in:

(a) directly or indirectly imposing unfair purchase or selling prices or other unfair trading conditions;
(b) limiting production, markets or technical development to the prejudice of consumers;
(c) applying dissimilar conditions to equivalent transactions with other trading parties, thereby placing them at a competitive disadvantage;
(d) making the conclusion of contracts subject to acceptance by the other parties of supplementary obligations which, by their nature or according to commercial usage, have no connection with the subject of such contracts.

Annex 2

LIST OF RELEVANT ACTS

(as of 5 August 1985)

(If you think it possible that your arrangements do not need to be notified by virtue of any of these Regulations or notices it may be worth your while to obtain a copy.)

IMPLEMENTING REGULATIONS

Council Regulation No 17 of 6 February 1962 implementing Articles 85 and 86 of the Treaty (OJ No 13, 21. 2. 1962, p 204/62, English Special Edition 1959 – 62, November 1972, p 87) as amended (OJ No 58, 10. 7. 1962, p 1655/62; OJ No 162, 7. 11. 1963, p 2696/63; OJ No L 285, 29. 12. 1971, p 49; OJ No L 73, 27. 3. 1972, p 92; OJ No L 291, 19. 11. 1979, p 94).

Commission Regulation No 27 of 3 May 1962 implementing Council Regulation No 17 (OJ No 35, 10. 5. 1962, p 1118/62, English Special Edition 1959 – 62, November 1972, p 87) as amended (OJ No L 189, 1. 8. 1968, p 1; OJ No L 172, 3. 7. 1975, p 11; OJ No L 291, 19. 11. 1979, p 94).

REGULATIONS GRANTING BLOCK EXEMPTION IN RESPECT OF A WIDE RANGE OF AGREEMENTS

Commission Regulation (EEC) No 1983/83 of 22 June 1983 on the application of Article 85(3) of the Treaty to categories of exclusive distribution agreements (OJ No L 173, 30. 6. 1983, p 1, as corrected in OJ No L 281, 13. 10. 1983, p 24).

Commission Regulation (EEC) No 1984/83 of 22 June 1983 on the application of Article 85(3) of the Treaty to categories of exclusive purchasing agreements (OJ No L 173, 30. 6. 1983, p 5, as corrected in OJ No L 281, 13. 10. 1983, p 24).

See also the Commission notice concerning Commission Regulations (EEC) No 1983/83 and (EEC) No 1984/83 of 22 June 1983 on the application of Article 85(3) of the Treaty to categories of exclusive distribution and exclusive purchasing agreements (OJ No C 101, 13. 4. 1984, p 2).

Commission Regulation (EEC) No 2349/84 of 23 July 1984 on the application of Article 85(3) of the Treaty to certain categories of patent licensing agreements (OJ No L 219, 16. 8. 1984, p 15, as corrected in OJ No L 113, 26. 4. 1985, p 34). Article 4 of this Regulation provides for an opposition procedure.

Commission Regulation (EEC) No 123/85 of 12 December 1984 on the application of Article 85(3) of the Treaty to certain categories of motor vehicle distribution and servicing agreements (OJ No L 15, 18. 1. 1985, p 16). See also the Commission notice concerning this Regulation (OJ No C 17, 18. 1. 1985, p 4).

Commission Regulation (EEC) No 417/85 of 19 December 1984 on the application of Article 85(3) of the Treaty to categories of specialization agreements (OJ No L 53, 22. 2. 1985, p 1). Article 4 of this Regulation provides for an opposition procedure.

Commission Regulation (EEC) No 418/85 of 19 December 1984 on the application of Article 85(3) of the Treaty to categories of research and development cooperation agreements (OJ No L 53, 22. 2. 1985, p 5). Article 7 of this Regulation provides for an opposition procedure.

COMMISSION NOTICES OF A GENERAL NATURE

Commission notice on exclusive dealing contracts with commercial agents (OJ No 139, 24. 12. 1962, p 2921/62). This states that the Commission does not consider most such agreements to fall under the prohibition of Article 85(1).

Commission notice concerning agreements, decisions and concerted practices in the field of cooperation between enterprises (OJ No C 75, 29. 7. 1968, p 3, as corrected in OJ No C 84, 28. 8. 1968, p 14). This defines the sorts of cooperation on market studies, accounting, R & D, joint use of production, storage or transport, *ad hoc* consortia, selling or after-sales service, advertising or quality labelling that the Commission considers not to fall under the prohibition of Article 85(1).

Commission notice on agreements, decisions and concerted practices of minor importance which do not fall under Article 85(1) of the Treaty (OJ No C 313, 29. 12. 1977, p 3) – in the main, those where the parties have less than 5% of the market between them, and a combined annual turnover of less than 50 million ECU.

Commission notice concerning its assessment of certain subcontracting agreements in relation to Article 85(1) of the Treaty (OJ No C 1, 3. 1. 1979, p 2).

A collection of these texts (as at 30 June 1981) was published by the Office for Official Publications of the European Communities (Refs. ISBN 92-825-2389-6, Catalogue No CB 30-80-576-EN-C). This is now in short supply in some languages and out of stock in others. An updated collection is in preparation.[1]

NOTE

1 The updated collection of these texts (as at 31 December 1985) is now available.

Annex 3

LIST OF MEMBER STATES AND COMMISSION PRESS AND INFORMATION OFFICES WITHIN THE COMMUNITY

(as of 1 January 1986)

The Member States as at the date of this Annex are: Belgium, Denmark, France, Germany, Greece, Ireland, Italy, Luxembourg, the Netherlands, Portugal, Spain and the United Kingdom.

The address of the Commission's Press and Information Offices in the Community are:

BELGIUM

Rue Archimède 73,
B-1040 Bruxelles
Tel. 235 11 11

DENMARK

Højbrohus
Østergade 61
Postbox 144
DK-1004 København K
Tel. 14 41 40

FRANCE

61, rue des Belles-Feuilles
F-75782 Paris, Cedex 16
Tel. 501 58 85

CMCI/Bureau 320
2, rue Henri Barbusse
F-13241 Marseille, Cedex 01
Tel. 08 62 00

FEDERAL REPUBLIC OF GERMANY

Zitelmannstrasse 22
D-5300 Bonn
Tel. 23 80 41
Kurfürstendamm 102
D-1000 Berlin 31
Tel. 892 40 28

Erhardtstrasse 27
D-8000 München
Tel. 23 99 29 00

GREECE

2 Vassilissis Sofias
TK 1602
GR-Athina 134
Tel. 724 39 82/724 39 83/724 39 84

IRELAND

39 Molesworth Street
IRL-Dublin 2
Tel. 712244

ITALY

Via Poli 29
I-00187 Roma
Tel. 678 97 22

Corso Magenta 61
I-20123 Milano
Tel. 80 15 05/6/7/8

LUXEMBOURG

Bâtiment Jean Monnet
Rue Alcide de Gasperi
L-2920 Luxembourg
Tel. 430 11

NETHERLANDS

Lange Voorhout 29
NL-Den Haag
Tel. 46 93 26

PORTUGAL

Rua do Sacremento à Lapa 35
P-1200 Lisboa
Tel. 60 21 99

SPAIN

Calle de Serrano 41
5a Planta
E-1 Madrid
Tel. 435 17 00

UNITED KINGDOM

8 Storey's Gate
UK-London SW1P 3AT
Tel. 222 8122

Windsor House
9/15 Bedford Street
UK-Belfast BT2 7EG
Tel. 40708

4 Cathedral Road
UK-Cardiff CF1 9SG
Tel. 37 16 31

7 Alva Street
UK-Edinburgh EH2 4PH
Tel. 225 2058   **[1046]**

AMENDMENT

1 This annex to EEC Commission Regulation No 27/62 substituted by EEC Commission Regulation 2526/85.

REGULATION (EEC) No 141/62 OF THE COUNCIL

exempting transport from the application of Council Regulation No 17

THE COUNCIL OF THE EUROPEAN ECONOMIC COMMUNITY,

Having regard to the Treaty establishing the European Economic Community, and in particular Article 67 thereof;

Having regard to the first Regulation made in implementation of Articles 85 and 86 of the Treaty (Regulation No 17) of 6 February 1962, as amended by Regulation No 59 of 3 July 1962;

Having regard to the proposal from the Commission;

Having regard to the Opinion of the Economic and Social Committee;

Having regard to the Opinion of the Assembly;

Whereas, in pursuance of the common transport policy, account being taken of the distinctive features of the transport sector, it may prove necessary to lay down rules governing competition different from those laid down or to be laid down for other sectors of the economy, and whereas Regulation No 17 should not therefore apply to transport;

Whereas, in the light of work in hand on the formulation of a common transport policy, it is possible, as regards transport by rail, road and inland waterway, to envisage the introduction within a foreseeable period of rules of competition; whereas, on the other hand, as regards sea and air transport it is impossible to foresee whether and at what date the Council will adopt appropriate provisions; whereas accordingly a limit to the period during which Regulation No 17 shall not apply can be set only for transport by rail, road and inland waterway;

Whereas the distinctive features of transport make it justifiable to exempt from the application of Regulation No 17 only agreements, decisions and concerted practices directly relating to the provision of transport services;

HAS ADOPTED THIS REGULATION:

Article 1

Regulation No 17 shall not apply to agreements, decisions or concerted practices in the transport sector which have as their object or effect the fixing of transport rates and conditions, the limitation or control of the supply of transport or the sharing of transport markets; nor shall it apply to the abuse of a dominant position, within the meaning of Article 86 of the Treaty, within the transport market.   **[1047]**

Article 2

The Council, taking account of any measures that may be taken in pursuance of the common transport policy, shall adopt appropriate provisions in order to apply rules of competition to transport by rail, road and inland waterway. To this end, the Commission shall, before 30 June 1964, submit proposals to the Council.   **[1048]**

Article 3

Article 1 of this Regulation shall remain in force, as regards transport by rail, road and inland waterway, until 31 December 1965.   **[1049]**

Article 4

This Regulation shall enter into force on 13 March 1962. These provisions shall not be invoked against undertakings or associations of undertakings which, before the day following the date of publication of this Regulation in the *Official Journal of the European Communities*, shall have terminated any agreement, decision or concerted practice covered by Article 1.   **[1050]**

This Regulation shall be binding in its entirety and directly applicable in all Member States.

Done at Paris, 26 November 1962.

REGULATION (EEC) No 99/63 OF THE COMMISSION
of 25 July 1963

on the hearings provided for in Article 19(1) and (2) of Council Regulation No 17

THE COMMISSION OF THE EUROPEAN ECONOMIC COMMUNITY,

Having regard to the Treaty establishing the European Economic Community, and in particular Articles 87 and 155 thereof;

Having regard to Article 24 of Council Regulation No 17 of 6 February 1962 (First Regulation implementing Articles 85 and 86 of the Treaty);

Whereas the Commission has power under Article 24 of Council Regulation No 17 to lay down implementing provisions concerning the hearings provided for in Article 19(1) and (2) of that Regulation;

Whereas in most cases the Commission will in the course of its inquiries already be in close touch with the undertakings or associations of undertakings which are the subject thereof and they will accordingly have the opportunity of making known their views regarding the objections raised against them;

Whereas, however, in accordance with Article 19(1) of Regulation No 17 and with the rights of defence, the undertakings and associations of undertakings concerned must have the right on conclusion of the inquiry to submit their comments on the whole of the objections raised against them which the Commission proposes to deal with in its decisions;

Whereas persons other than the undertakings or associations of undertakings which are the subject of the inquiry may have an interest in being heard; whereas, by the second sentence of Article 19(2) of Regulation No 17, such persons must have the opportunity of being heard if they apply and show that they have a sufficient interest;

Whereas it is desirable to enable persons who, pursuant to Article 3(2) of Regulation No 17, have applied for an infringement to be terminated to submit their comments where the Commission considers that on the basis of the information in its possession there are insufficient grounds for granting the application;

Whereas the various persons entitled to submit comments must do so in writing, both in their own interest and in the interests of good administration, without prejudice to oral procedure where appropriate to supplement the written evidence; .

Whereas it is necessary to define the rights of persons who are to be heard, and in particular the conditions upon which they may be represented or assisted and the setting and calculation of time limits;

Whereas the Advisory Committee on Restrictive Practices and Monopolies delivers its Opinion on the basis of a preliminary draft decision; whereas it must therefore be consulted concerning a case after the inquiry in respect thereof has been completed; whereas such consultation does not prevent the Commission from re-opening an inquiry if need be;

HAS ADOPTED THIS REGULATION:

Article 1

Before consulting the Advisory Committee on Restrictive Practices and Monopolies, the Commission shall hold a hearing pursuant to Article 19(1) of Regulation No 17.

[1051]

Article 2

1. The Commission shall inform undertakings and associations of undertakings in writing of the objections raised against them. The communication shall be addressed to each of them or to a joint agent appointed by them.

2. The Commission may inform the parties by giving notice in the *Official Journal of the European Communities*, if from the circumstances of the case this appears appropriate, in particular where notice is to be given to a number of undertakings but no joint

agent has been appointed. The notice shall have regard to the legitimate interest of the undertakings in the protection of their business secrets.

3. A fine or a periodic penalty payment may be imposed on an undertaking or association of undertakings only if the objections were notified in the manner provided for in paragraph 1.

4. The Commission shall when giving notice of objections fix a time limit up to which the undertakings and associations of undertakings may inform the Commission of their views. **[1052]**

Article 3

1. Undertakings and associations of undertakings shall, within the appointed time limit, make known in writing their views concerning the objections raised against them.

2. They may in their written comments set out all matters relevant to their defence.

3. They may attach any relevant documents in proof of the facts set out. They may also propose that the Commission hear persons who may corroborate those facts. **[1053]**

Article 4

The Commission shall in its decisions deal only with those objections raised against undertakings and associations of undertakings in respect of which they have been afforded the opportunity of making known their views. **[1054]**

Article 5

If natural or legal persons showing a sufficient interest apply to be heard pursuant to Article 19(2) of Regulation No 17, the Commission shall afford them the opportunity of making known their views in writing within such time limit as it shall fix. **[1055]**

Article 6

Where the Commission, having received an application pursuant to Article 3(2) of Regulation No 17, considers that on the basis of the information in its possession there are insufficient grounds for granting the application, it shall inform the applicants of its reasons and fix a time limit for them to submit any further comments in writing. **[1056]**

Article 7

1. The Commission shall afford to persons who have so requested in their written comments the opportunity to put forward their arguments orally, if those persons show a sufficient interest or if the Commission proposes to impose on them a fine or periodic penalty payment.

2. The Commission may likewise afford to any other person the opportunity of orally expressing his views. **[1057]**

Article 8

1. The Commission shall summon the persons to be heard to attend on such date as it shall appoint.

2. It shall forthwith transmit a copy of the summons to the competent authorities of the Member States, who may appoint an official to take part in the hearing.   **[1058]**

Article 9

1. Hearings shall be conducted by the persons appointed by the Commission for that purpose.

2. Persons summoned to attend shall appear either in person or be represented by legal representatives or by representatives authorised by their constitution. Undertakings and associations of undertakings may moreover be represented by a duly authorised agent appointed from among their permanent staff.

Persons heard by the Commission may be assisted by lawyers or university teachers who are entitled to plead before the Court of Justice of the European Communities in accordance with Article 17 of the Protocol on the Statute of the Court, or by other qualified persons.

3. Hearings shall not be public. Persons shall be heard separately or in the presence of other persons summoned to attend. In the latter case, regard shall be had to the legitimate interest of the undertakings in the protection of their business secrets.

4. The essential content of the statements made by each person heard shall be recorded in minutes which shall be read and approved by him.   **[1059]**

Article 10

Without prejudice to Article 2(2), information and summonses from the Commission shall be sent to the addressees by registered letter with acknowledgement of receipt, or shall be delivered by hand against receipt.   **[1060]**

Article 11

1. In fixing the time limits provided for in Articles 2, 5 and 6, the Commission shall have regard both to the time required for preparation of comments and to the urgency of the case. The time limit shall be not less than two weeks; it may be extended.

2. Time limits shall run from the day following receipt of a communication or delivery thereof by hand.

3. Written comments must reach the Commission or be dispatched by registered letter before expiry of the time limit. Where the time limit would expire on a Sunday or public holiday, it shall be extended up to the end of the next following working day. For the purpose of calculating this extension, public holidays shall, in cases where the relevant date is the date of receipt of written comments, be those set out in the Annex to this Regulation, and in cases where the relevant date is the date of dispatch, those appointed by law in the country of dispatch.   **[1061]**

This Regulation shall be binding in its entirety and directly applicable in all Member States.

Done at Brussels, 25 July 1963.

ANNEX

referred to in the third sentence of Article 11(3)

(List of public holidays)

New Year	1 Jan
Good Friday	
Easter Saturday	
Easter Monday	
Labour Day	1 May
Schuman Plan Day	9 May
Ascension Day	
Whit Monday	
Belgian National Day	21 July
Assumption	15 Aug
All Saints	1 Nov
All Souls	2 Nov
Christmas Eve	24 Dec
Christmas Day	25 Dec
The day following Christmas Day	26 Dec
New Year's Eve	31 Dec **[1062]**

REGULATION (EEC) No 19/65 OF THE COUNCIL
of 2 March 1965

on application of Article 85(3) of the Treaty to certain categories of agreements and concerted practices

THE COUNCIL OF THE EUROPEAN ECONOMIC COMMUNITY,

Having regard to the Treaty establishing the European Economic Community, and in particular Article 87 thereof;

Having regard to the proposal from the Commission;

Having regard to the Opinion of the European Parliament;

Having regard to the Opinion of the Economic and Social Committee;

Whereas Article 85(1) of the Treaty may in accordance with Article 85(3) be declared inapplicable to certain categories of agreements, decisions and concerted practices which fulfil the conditions contained in Article 85(3);

Whereas the provisions for implementation of Article 85(3) must be adopted by way of regulation pursuant to Article 87;

Whereas in view of the large number of notifications submitted in pursuance of Regulation No 17 it is desirable that in order to facilitate the task of the Commission it should be enabled to declare by way of regulation that the provisions of Article 85(1) do not apply to certain categories of agreements and concerted practices;

Whereas it should be laid down under what conditions the Commission, in close and constant liaison with the competent authorities of the Member States, may exercise such powers after sufficient experience has been gained in the light of individual decisions and it becomes possible to define categories of agreements and concerted practices in respect of which the conditions of Article 85(3) may be considered as being fulfilled;

Whereas the Commission has indicated by the action it has taken, in particular by Regulation No 153, that there can be no easing of the procedures prescribed by Regulation No 17 in respect of certain types of agreements and concerted practices that are particularly liable to distort competition in the common market;

Whereas under Article 6 of Regulation No 17 the Commission may provide that a decision taken pursuant to Article 85(3) of the Treaty shall apply with retroactive effect; whereas it is desirable that the Commission be also empowered to adopt, by regulation, provisions to the like effect;

Whereas under Article 7 of Regulation No 17 agreements, decisions and concerted practices may, by decision of the Commission, be exempted from prohibition in particular if they are modified in such manner that they satisfy the requirements of Article 85(3); whereas it is desirable that the Commission be enabled to grant like exemption by regulation to such agreements and concerted practices if they are modified in such manner as to fall within a category defined in an exempting regulation;

Whereas, since there can be no exemption if the conditions set out in Article 85(3) are not satisfied, the Commission must have power to lay down by decision the conditions that must be satisfied by an agreement or concerted practice which owing to special circumstances has certain effects incompatible with Article 85(3);

HAS ADOPTED THIS REGULATION:

Article 1

1. Without prejudice to the application of Council Regulation No 17 and in accordance with Article 85(3) of the Treaty the Commission may by regulation declare that Article 85(1) shall not apply to categories of agreements to which only two undertakings are party and:

(a) — whereby one party agrees with the other to supply only to that other certain goods for resale within a defined area of the common market; or
— whereby one party agrees with the other to purchase only from that other certain goods for resale; or
— whereby the two undertakings have entered into obligations, as in the two preceding subparagraphs, with each other in respect of exclusive supply and purchase for resale;

(b) which include restrictions imposed in relation to the acquisition or use of industrial property rights — in particular of patents, utility models, designs or trade marks — or to the rights arising out of contracts for assignment of, or the right to use, a method of manufacture or knowledge relating to the use or to the application of industrial processes.

2. The regulation shall define the categories of agreements to which it applies and shall specify in particular:

(a) the restrictions or clauses which must not be contained in the agreements;
(b) the clauses which must be contained in the agreements, or the other conditions which must be satisfied.

3. Paragraphs 1 and 2 shall apply by analogy to categories of concerted practices to which only two undertakings are party.   **[1063]**

Article 2

1. A regulation pursuant to Article 1 shall be made for a specified period.

2. It may be repealed or amended where circumstances have changed with respect to any factor which was basic to its being made; in such case, a period shall be fixed for modification of the agreements and concerted practices to which the earlier regulation applies.   **[1064]**

Article 3

A regulation pursuant to Article 1 may stipulate that it shall apply with retroactive effect to agreements and concerted practices to which, at the date of entry into force of that regulation, a decision issued with retroactive effect in pursuance of Article 6 of Regulation No 17 would have applied.   **[1065]**

Article 4

1. A regulation pursuant to Article 1 may stipulate that the prohibition contained in Article 85(1) of the Treaty shall not apply, for such period as shall be fixed by that regulation, to agreements and concerted practices already in existence on 13 March 1962 which do not satisfy the conditions of Article 85(3), where:
[A regulation pursuant to Article 1 may stipulate that the prohibition contained in Article 85(1) of the Treaty shall not apply, for such period as shall be fixed by that regulation, to agreements and concerted practices already in existence at the date of accession to which Article 85 applies by virtue of accession and which do not satisfy the conditions of Article 85(3), where:]¹

- within three months from the entry into force of the regulation, they are so modified as to satisfy the said conditions in accordance with the provisions of the regulation; and
- the modifications are brought to the notice of the Commission within the time limit fixed by the regulation.

[The provisions of the preceding subparagraph shall apply in the same way in the case of the accession of the Hellenic Republic, the Kingdom of Spain and of the Portuguese Republic.]²

2. Paragraph 1 shall apply to agreements and concerted practices which had to be notified before 1 February 1963, in accordance with Article 5 of Regulation No 17, only where they have been so notified before that date.
[Paragraph 1 shall not apply to agreements and concerted practices to which Article 85(1) of the Treaty applies by virtue of accession and which must be notified before 1 July 1973, in accordance with Articles 5 and 25 of Regulation No 17, unless they have been so notified before that date.]³
[Paragraph 1 shall not apply to agreements and concerted practices to which Article 85(1) of the Treaty applies by virtue of the accession of the Hellenic Republic and which must be notified before 1 July 1981, in accordance with Articles 5 and 25 of Regulation No 17, unless they have been so notified before that date.]⁴
[Paragraph 2 shall not apply to agreements and concerted practices to which Article 85(1) of the Treaty applies by virtue of the accession of the Kingdom of Spain and of the Portuguese Republic and which must be notified before 1 July 1986, in accordance with Articles 5 and 25 of Regulation No 17, unless they have been so notified before that date.]⁵

3. The benefit of the provisions laid down pursuant to paragraph 1 may not be claimed in actions pending at the date of entry into force of a regulation adopted pursuant to Article 1; neither may it be relied on as grounds for claims for damages against third parties.

[1066]

AMENDMENTS
    1 This sub-paragraph inserted by the Act of Accession of Denmark, Ireland and the United Kingdom, 1972.
    2 This sub-paragraph added by the Act of Accession of the Hellenic Republic, 1979, and subsequently replaced by the Act of Accession of the Kingdom of Spain and the Portuguese Republic, 1985.
    3 This sub-paragraph inserted by the Act of Accession of Denmark, Ireland and the United Kingdom, 1972.
    4 This sub-paragraph inserted by the Act of Accession of the Hellenic Republic, 1979.
    5 This sub-paragraph added by the Act of Accession of the Kingdom of Spain and the Portuguese Republic, 1985.

Article 5

Before adopting a regulation, the Commission shall publish a draft thereof and invite all persons concerned to submit their comments within such time limit, being not less than one month, as the Commission shall fix.   [1067]

Article 6

1. The Commission shall consult the Advisory Committee on Restrictive Practices and Monopolies:

   (*a*) before publishing a draft regulation;
   (*b*) before adopting a regulation.

   2. Article 10(5) and (6) of Regulation No 17, relating to consultation with the Advisory Committee, shall apply by analogy, it being understood that joint meetings with the Commission shall take place not earlier than one month after dispatch of the notice convening them.   [1068]

Article 7

Where the Commission, either on its own initiative or at the request of a Member State or of natural or legal persons claiming a legitimate interest, finds that in any particular case agreements or concerted practices to which a regulation adopted pursuant to Article 1 of this Regulation applies have nevertheless certain effects which are incompatible with the conditions laid down in Article 85(3) of the Treaty, it may withdraw the benefit of application of that regulation and issue a decision in accordance with Articles 6 and 8 of Regulation No 17, without any notification under Article 4(1) of Regulation No 17 being required.   [1069]

Article 8

The Commission shall, before 1 January 1970, submit to the Council a proposal for a Regulation for such amendment of this Regulation as may prove necessary in the light of experience.   [1070]

This Regulation shall be binding in its entirety and directly applicable in all Member States.

Done at Brussels, 2 March 1965.

REGULATION (EEC) No 1017/68 OF THE COUNCIL
of 19 July 1968

applying rules of competition to transport by rail, road and inland waterway

THE COUNCIL OF THE EUROPEAN COMMUNITIES,
   Having regard to the Treaty establishing the European Economic Community, and in particular Articles 75 and 87 thereof;
   Having regard to the proposal from the Commission;
   Having regard to the Opinion of the European Parliament;
   Having regard to the Opinion of the Economic and Social Committee;
   Whereas Council Regulation No 141 exempting transport from the application of Regulation No 17 provides that the said Regulation No 17 shall not apply to agreements, decisions and concerted practices in the transport sector the effect of which is to fix transport rates and conditions, to limit or control the supply of transport or to share transport markets, nor to dominant positions, within the meaning of Article 86 of the Treaty, on the transport market;
   Whereas, for transport by rail, road and inland waterway, Regulation No 1002/67/CEE provides that such exemption shall not extend beyond 30 June 1968;

Whereas the establishing of rules of competition for transport by rail, road and inland waterway is part of the common transport policy and of general economic policy;

Whereas, when rules of competition for these sectors are being settled, account must be taken of the distinctive features of transport;

Whereas, since the rules of competition for transport derogate from the general rules of competition, it must be made possible for undertakings to ascertain what rules apply in any particular case;

Whereas, with the introduction of a system of rules on competition for transport, it is desirable that such rules should apply equally to the joint financing or acquisition of transport equipment for the joint operation of services by certain groupings of undertakings, and also to certain operations in connection with transport by rail, road or inland waterway of providers of services ancillary to transport;

Whereas, in order to ensure that trade between Member States is not affected or competition within the common market distorted, it is necessary to prohibit in principle for the three modes of transport specified above all agreements between undertakings, decisions of associations of undertakings and concerted practices between undertakings and all instances of abuse of a dominant position within the common market which could have such effects;

Whereas certain types of agreement, decision and concerted practice in the transport sector the object and effect of which is merely to apply technical improvements or to achieve technical co-operation may be exempted from the prohibition on restrictive agreements since they contribute to improving productivity; whereas, in the light of experience following application of this Regulation, the Council may, on a proposal from the Commission, amend the list of such types of agreement;

Whereas, in order that an improvement may be fostered in the sometimes too dispersed structure of the industry in the road and inland waterway sectors, there should also be exempted from the prohibition on restrictive agreements those agreements, decisions and concerted practices providing for the creation and operation of groupings of undertakings in these two transport sectors whose object is the carrying on of transport operations, including the joint financing or acquisition of transport equipment for the joint operation of services; whereas such overall exemption can be granted only on condition that the total carrying capacity of a grouping does not exceed a fixed maximum, and that the individual capacity of undertakings belonging to the grouping does not exceed certain limits so fixed as to ensure that no one undertaking can hold a dominant position within the grouping; whereas the Commission must, however, have power to intervene if, in specific cases, such agreements should have effects incompatible with the conditions under which a restrictive agreement may be recognised as lawful, and should constitute an abuse of the exemption; whereas, nevertheless, the fact that a grouping has a total carrying capacity greater than the fixed maximum, or cannot claim the overall exemption because of the individual capacity of the undertakings belonging to the grouping, does not in itself prevent such a grouping from constituting a lawful agreement, decision or concerted practice if it satisfies the conditions therefor laid down in this Regulation;

Whereas, where an agreement, decision or concerted practice contributes towards improving the quality of transport services, or towards promoting greater continuity and stability in the satisfaction of transport needs on markets where supply and demand may be subject to considerable temporal fluctuation, or towards increasing the productivity of undertakings, or towards furthering technical or economic progress, it must be made possible for the prohibition to be declared not to apply, always provided, however, that the agreement, decision or concerted practice takes fair account of the interests of transport users, and neither imposes on the undertakings concerned any restriction not indispensable to the attainment of the above objectives nor makes it possible for such undertakings to eliminate competition in respect of a substantial part of the transport market concerned, having regard to competition from alternative modes of transport;

Whereas it is desirable until such time as the Council, acting in pursuance of the common transport policy, introduces appropriate measures to ensure a stable transport market, and subject to the condition that the Council shall have found that a state of crisis exists, to authorise, for the market in question, such agreements as are needed in order to reduce disturbance resulting from the structure of the transport market;

Whereas, in respect of transport by rail, road and inland waterway, it is desirable that Member States should neither enact nor maintain in force measures contrary to this Regulation concerning public undertakings or undertakings to which they grant special or exclusive rights; whereas it is also desirable that undertakings entrusted with the operation of services of general economic importance should be subject to the provisions of this Regulation in so far as the application thereof does not obstruct, in law or in fact, the accomplishment of the particular tasks assigned to them, always provided that the development of trade is not thereby affected to such an extent as would be contrary to the interests of the Community; whereas the Commission must have power to see that these principles are applied and to address the appropriate directives or decisions for this purpose to Member States;

Whereas the detailed rules for application of the basic principles of this Regulation must be so drawn that they not only ensure effective supervision while simplifying administration as far as possible but also meet the needs of undertakings for certainty in the law;

Whereas it is for the undertakings themselves, in the first instance, to judge whether the predominant effects of their agreements, decisions or concerted practices are the restriction of competition or the economic benefits acceptable as justification for such restriction and to decide accordingly, on their own responsibility, as to the illegality or legality of such agreements, decisions or concerted practices;

Whereas, therefore, undertakings should be allowed to conclude or operate agreements without declaring them; whereas this exposes such agreements to the risk of being declared void with retroactive effect should they be examined following a complaint or on the Commission's own initiative, but does not prevent their being retroactively declared lawful in the event of such subsequent examination;

Whereas, however, undertakings may, in certain cases, desire the assistance of the competent authorities to ensure that their agreements, decisions or concerted practices are in conformity with the rules applicable; whereas for this purpose there should be made available to undertakings a procedure whereby they may submit applications to the Commission and a summary of each such application is published in the *Official Journal of the European Communities*, enabling any interested third parties to submit their comments on the agreement in question; whereas, in the absence of any complaint from Member States or interested third parties and unless the Commission notifies applicants within a fixed time limit, that there are serious doubts as to the legality of the agreement in question, that agreement should be deemed exempt from the prohibition for the time already elapsed and for a further period of three years;

Whereas, in view of the exceptional nature of agreements needed in order to reduce disturbances resulting from the structure of the transport market, once the Council has found that a state of crisis exists undertakings wishing to obtain authorisation for such an agreement should be required to notify it to the Commission; whereas authorisation by the Commission should have effect only from the date when it is decided to grant it; whereas the period of validity of such authorisation should not exceed three years from the finding of a state of crisis by the Council; whereas renewal of the decision should depend upon renewal of the finding of a state of crisis by the Council; whereas, in any event, the authorisation should cease to be valid not later than six months from the bringing into operation by the Council of appropriate measures to ensure the stability of the transport market to which the agreement relates;

Whereas, in order to secure uniform application within the common market of the rules of competition for transport, rules must be made under which the Commission, acting in close and constant liaison with the competent authorities of the Member States, may take the measures required for the application of such rules of competition;

Whereas for this purpose the Commission must have the co-operation of the competent authorities of the Member States and be empowered throughout the common market to request such information and to carry out such investigations as are necessary to bring to light any agreement, decision or concerted practice prohibited under this Regulation, or any abuse of a dominant position prohibited under this Regulation;

Whereas, if, on the application of the Regulation to a specific case, a Member State is of the opinion that a question of principle concerning the common transport policy is involved, it should be possible for such questions of principle to be examined by the Council; whereas it should be possible for any general questions raised by the implementation of the competition policy in the transport sector to be referred to the Council; whereas a procedure must be provided for which ensures that any decision to apply the Regulation in a specific case will be taken by the Commission only after the questions of principle have been examined by the Council, and in the light of the policy guidelines that emerge from that examination;

Whereas, in order to carry out its duty of ensuring that the provisions of this Regulation are applied, the Commission must be empowered to address to undertakings or associations of undertakings recommendations and decisions for the purpose of bringing to an end infringements of the provisions of this Regulation prohibiting certain agreements, decisions or practices;

Whereas compliance with the prohibitions laid down in this Regulation and the fulfilment of obligations imposed on undertakings and associations of undertakings under this Regulation must be enforceable by means of fines and periodic penalty payments;

Whereas undertakings concerned must be accorded the right to be heard by the Commission, third parties whose interests may be affected by a decision must be given the opportunity of submitting their comments beforehand, and it must be ensured that wide publicity is given to decisions taken;

Whereas it is desirable to confer upon the Court of Justice, pursuant to Article 172, unlimited jurisdiction in respect of decisions under which the Commission imposes fines or periodic penalty payments;

Whereas it is expedient to postpone for six months, as regards agreements, decisions and concerted practices in existence at the date of publication of this Regulation in the *Official Journal of the European Communities*, the entry into force of the prohibition laid down in the Regulation, in order to make it easier for undertakings to adjust their operations so as to conform to its provisions;

Whereas, following discussions with the third countries signatories to the Revised Convention for the Navigation of the Rhine, and within an appropriate period of time from the conclusion of those discussions, this Regulation as a whole should be amended as necessary in the light of the obligations arising out of the Revised Convention for the Navigation of the Rhine;

Whereas the Regulation should be amended as necessary in the light of the experience gained over a three-year period; whereas it will in particular be desirable to consider whether, in the light of the development of the common transport policy over that period, the scope of the Regulation should be extended to agreements, decisions and concerted practices, and to instances of abuse of a dominant position, not affecting trade between Member States;

HAS ADOPTED THIS REGULATION:

Article 1 — Basic provision

The provisions of this Regulation shall, in the field of transport by rail, road and inland waterway, apply both to all agreements, decisions and concerted practices which have as their object or effect the fixing of transport rates and conditions, the limitation or control of the supply of transport, the sharing of transport markets, the application of technical improvements or technical co-operation, or the joint financing or acquisition of transport equipment or supplies where such operations are directly related to the provision of transport services and are necessary for the joint operation of services by a grouping within the meaning of Article 4 of road or inland waterway transport undertakings, and to the abuse of a dominant position on the transport market. These provisions shall apply also to operations of providers of services ancillary to transport which have any of the objects or effects listed above. **[1071]**

Article 2 — Prohibition of restrictive practices

Subject to the provisions of Articles 3 to 6, the following shall be prohibited as incompatible with the common market, no prior decision to that effect being required: all agreements between undertakings, decisions by associations of undertakings and concerted practices liable to affect trade between Member States which have as their object or effect the prevention, restriction or distortion of competition within the common market, and in particular those which:

(a) directly or indirectly fix transport rates and conditions or any other trading conditions;

(b) limit or control the supply of transport, markets, technical development or investment;

(c) share transport markets;

(d) apply dissimilar conditions to equivalent transactions with other trading parties, thereby placing them at a competitive disadvantage;

(e) make the conclusion of contracts subject to acceptance by the other parties of additional obligations which, by their nature or according to commercial usage, have no connection with the provision of transport services. **[1072]**

Article 3 – Exception for technical agreements

1. The prohibition laid down in Article 2 shall not apply to agreements, decisions or concerted practices the object and effect of which is to apply technical improvements or to achieve technical co-operation by means of:

(a) the standardisation of equipment, transport supplies, vehicles or fixed installations;

(b) the exchange or pooling, for the purpose of operating transport services, of staff, equipment, vehicles or fixed installations;

(c) the organisation and execution of successive, complementary, substitute or combined transport operations, and the fixing and application of inclusive rates and conditions for such operations, including special competitive rates;

(d) the use, for journeys by a single mode of transport, of the routes which are most rational from the operational point of view;

(e) the co-ordination of transport timetables for connecting routes;

(f) the grouping of single consignments;

(g) the establishment of uniform rules as to the structure of tariffs and their conditions of application, provided such rules do not lay down transport rates and conditions.

2. The Commission shall, where appropriate, submit proposals to the Council with a view to extending or reducing the list in paragraph 1.   **[1073]**

Article 4 – Exemption for groups of small and medium-sized undertakings

1. The agreements, decisions and concerted practices referred to in Article 2 shall be exempt from the prohibition in that Article where their purpose is:

– the constitution and operation of groupings of road or inland waterway transport undertakings with a view to carrying on transport activities;

– the joint financing or acquisition of transport equipment or supplies, where these operations are directly related to the provision of transport services and are necessary for the joint operations of the aforesaid groupings;

always provided that the total carrying capacity of any grouping does not exceed:

– 10 000 metric tons in the case of road transport,

– 500 000 metric tons in the case of transport by inland waterway.

The individual capacity of each undertaking belonging to a grouping shall not exceed 1 000 metric tons in the case of road transport or 50 000 metric tons in the case of transport by inland waterway.

2. If the implementation of any agreement, decision or concerted practice covered by paragraph 1 has, in a given case, effects which are incompatible with the requirements of Article 5 and which constitute an abuse of the exemption from the provisions of Article 2, undertakings or associations of undertakings may be required to make such effects cease.

        [1074]

Article 5 – Non-applicability of the prohibition

The prohibition in Article 2 may be declared inapplicable with retroactive effect to:

– any agreement or category of agreement between undertakings,

– any decision or category of decision of an association of undertakings, or

– any concerted practice or category of concerted practice which contributes towards:

– improving the quality of transport services; or

– promoting greater continuity and stability in the satisfaction of transport needs on markets where supply and demand are subject to considerable temporal fluctuation; or
– increasing the productivity of undertakings; or
– furthering technical or economic progress;

and at the same time takes fair account of the interests of transport users and neither:

(a) imposes on the transport undertakings concerned any restriction not essential to the attainment of the above objectives; nor
(b) makes it possible for such undertakings to eliminate competition in respect of a substantial part of the transport market concerned. **[1075]**

Article 6 – Agreements intended to reduce disturbances resulting from the structure of the transport market

1. Until such time as the Council, acting in pursuance of the common transport policy, introduces appropriate measures to ensure a stable transport market, the prohibition laid down in Article 2 may be declared inapplicable to any agreement, decision or concerted practice which tends to reduce disturbances on the market in question.

2. A decision not to apply the prohibition laid down in Article 2, made in accordance with the procedure laid down in Article 14, may not be taken until the Council, either acting by a qualified majority or, where any Member State considers that the conditions set out in Article 75(3) of the Treaty are satisfied, acting unanimously, has found, on the basis of a report by the Commission, that a state of crisis exists in all or part of a transport market.

3. Without prejudice to the provisions of paragraph 2, the prohibition in Article 2 may be declared inapplicable only where:

(a) the agreement, decision or concerted practice in question does not impose upon the undertakings concerned any restriction not indispensable to the reduction of disturbances; and
(b) does not make it possible for such undertakings to eliminate competition in respect of a substantial part of the transport market concerned. **[1076]**

Article 7 – Invalidity of agreements and decisions

Any agreement or decision prohibited under the foregoing provisions shall be automatically void. **[1077]**

Article 8 – Prohibition of abuse of dominant positions

Any abuse by one or more undertakings of a dominant position within the common market or in a substantial part of it shall be prohibited as incompatible with the common market in so far as trade between Member States may be affected thereby.
Such abuse may, in particular, consist in:

(a) directly or indirectly imposing unfair transport rates or conditions;
(b) limiting the supply of transport, markets or technical development to the prejudice of consumers;
(c) applying dissimilar conditions to equivalent transactions with other trading parties, thereby placing them at a competitive disadvantage;
(d) making the conclusion of contracts subject to acceptance by the other parties of supplementary obligations which, by their nature or according to commercial usage, have no connection with the provision of transport services. **[1078]**

Article 9 – Public undertakings

1. In the case of public undertakings and undertakings to which Member States grant special or exclusive rights, Member States shall neither enact nor maintain in force any measure contrary to the provisions of the foregoing Articles.

2. Undertakings entrusted with the operation of services of general economic importance shall be subject to the provisions of the foregoing Articles, in so far as the application thereof does not obstruct, in law or in fact, the accomplishment of the particular tasks assigned to them. The development of trade must not be affected to such an extent as would be contrary to the interests of the Community.

3. The Commission shall see that the provisions of this Article are applied and shall, where necessary, address appropriate directives or decisions to Member States.

[1079]

Article 10 – Procedures on complaint or on the Commission's own initiative

Acting on receipt of a complaint or on its own initiative, the Commission shall initiate procedures to terminate any infringement of the provisions of Article 2 or of Article 8 or to enforce Article 4(2).

Complaints may be submitted by:

(*a*) Member States;

(*b*) natural or legal persons who claim a legitimate interest.			[1080]

Article 11 – Result of procedures on complaint or on the Commission's own initiative

1. Where the Commission finds that there has been an infringement of Article 2 or Article 8, it may by decision require the undertakings or associations of undertakings concerned to bring such infringement to an end.

Without prejudice to the other provisions of this Regulation, the Commission may, before taking a decision under the preceding subparagraph, address to the undertakings or associations of undertakings concerned recommendations for termination of the infringement.

2. Paragraph 1 shall apply also to cases falling within Article 4(2).

3. If the Commission, acting on a complaint received, concludes that on the evidence before it there are no grounds for intervention under Article 2, Article 4(2) or Article 8 in respect of any agreement, decision or practice, it shall issue a decision rejecting the complaint as unfounded.

4. If the Commission, whether acting on a complaint received or on its own initiative, concludes that an agreement, decision or concerted practice satisfies the provisions both of Article 2 and of Article 5, it shall issue a decision applying Article 5. Such decision shall indicate the date from which it is to take effect. This date may be prior to that of the decision.			[1081]

Article 12 – Application of Article 5 – objections

1. Undertakings and associations of undertakings which seek application of Article 5 in respect of agreements, decisions and concerted practices falling within the provisions of Article 2 to which they are parties may submit applications to the Commission.

2. If the Commission judges an application admissible and is in possession of all the available evidence, and no action under Article 10 has been taken against the agreement,

decision or concerted practice in question, then it shall publish as soon as possible in the *Official Journal of the European Communities* a summary of the application and invite all interested third parties to submit their comments to the Commission within thirty days. Such publication shall have regard to the legitimate interest of undertakings in the protection of their business secrets.

3. Unless the Commission notifies applicants, within ninety days from the date of such publication in the *Official Journal of the European Communities*, that there are serious doubts as to the applicability of Article 5, the agreement, decision or concerted practice shall be deemed exempt, in so far as it conforms with the description given in the application, from the prohibition for the time already elapsed and for a maximum of three years from the date of publication in the *Official Journal of the European Communities*.

If the Commission finds, after expiry of the ninety-day time limit, but before expiry of the three-year period, that the conditions for applying Article 5 are not satisfied, it shall issue a decision declaring that the prohibition in Article 2 is applicable. Such decision may be retroactive where the parties concerned have given inaccurate information or where they abuse the exemption from the provisions of Article 2.

4. If, within the ninety-day time limit, the Commission notifies applicants as referred to in the first subparagraph of paragraph 3, it shall examine whether the provisions of Article 2 and of Article 5 are satisfied.

If it finds that the provisions of Article 2 and of Article 5 are satisfied it shall issue a decision applying Article 5. The decision shall indicate the date from which it is to take effect. This date may be prior to that of the application. **[1082]**

Article 13 – Duration and revocation of decisions applying Article 5

1. Any decision applying Article 5 taken under Article 11(4) or under the second subparagraph of Article 12(4) shall indicate the period for which it is to be valid; normally such period shall not be less than six years. Conditions and obligations may be attached to the decision.

2. The decision may be renewed if the conditions for applying Article 5 continue to be satisfied.

3. The Commission may revoke or amend its decision or prohibit specified acts by the parties:

 (a) where there has been a change in any of the facts which were basic to the making of the decision;

 (b) where the parties commit a breach of any obligation attached to the decision;

 (c) where the decision is based on incorrect information or was induced by deceit;

 (d) where the parties abuse the exemption from the provisions of Article 2 granted to them by the decision.

In cases falling within (b), (c) or (d), the decision may be revoked with retroactive effect. **[1083]**

Article 14 – Decisions applying Article 6

1. Any agreement, decision or concerted practice covered by Article 2 in respect of which the parties seek application of Article 6 shall be notified to the Commission.

2. Any decision by the Commission to apply Article 6 shall have effect only from the date of its adoption. It shall state the period for which it is to be valid. Such period shall not exceed three years from the finding of a state of crisis by the Council provided for in Article 6(2).

3. Such decision may be renewed by the Commission if the Council again finds, acting under the procedure provided for in Article 6(2), that there is a state of crisis and if the other conditions laid down in Article 6 continue to be satisfied.

4. Conditions and obligations may be attached to the decision.

5. The decision of the Commission shall cease to have effect not later than six months from the coming into operation of the measures referred to in Article 6(1).

6. The provisions of Article 13(3) shall apply.   **[1084]**

Article 15 – Powers

Subject to review of its decision by the Court of Justice, the Commission shall have sole power:

– to impose obligations pursuant to Article 4(2);
– to issue decisions pursuant to Articles 5 and 6.

The authorities of the Member States shall retain the power to decide whether any case falls within the provisions of Article 2 or Article 8, until such time as the Commission has initiated a procedure with a view to formulating a decision in the case in question or has sent notification as provided for in the first subparagraph of Article 12(3).

[1085]

Article 16 – Liaison with the authorities of the Member States

1. The Commission shall carry out the procedures provided for in this Regulation in close and constant liaison with the competent authorities of the Member States; these authorities shall have the right to express their views on such procedures.

2. The Commission shall immediately forward to the competent authorities of the Member States copies of the complaints and applications and of the most important documents sent to it or which it sends out in the course of such procedures.

3. An Advisory Committee on Restrictive Practices and Monopolies in the Transport Industry shall be consulted prior to the taking of any decision following upon a procedure under Article 10 or of any decision under the second subparagraph of Article 12(3), or under the second subparagraph of paragraph 4 of the same Article, or under paragraph 2 or paragraph 3 of Article 14. The Advisory Committee shall also be consulted prior to adoption of the implementing provisions provided for in Article 29.

4. The Advisory Committee shall be composed of officials competent in the matter of restrictive practices and monopolies in transport. Each Member State shall appoint two officials to represent it, each of whom, if prevented from attending, may be replaced by some other official.

5. Consultation shall take place at a joint meeting convened by the Commission; such meeting shall be held not earlier than fourteen days after dispatch of the notice convening it. This notice shall, in respect of each case to be examined, be accompanied by a summary of the case together with an indication of the most important documents, and a preliminary draft decision.

6. The Advisory Committee may deliver an opinion notwithstanding that some of its members or their alternates are not present. A report of the outcome of the consultative proceedings shall be annexed to the draft decision. It shall not be made public.

[1086]

Article 17—Consideration by the Council of questions of principle concerning the common transport policy raised in connection with specific cases

1. The Commission shall not give a decision in respect of which consultation as laid down in Article 16 is compulsory until after the expiry of twenty days from the date on which the Advisory Committee has delivered its Opinion.

2. Before the expiry of the period specified in paragraph 1, any Member State may request that the Council be convened to examine with the Commission any question of principle concerning the common transport policy which such Member State considers to be involved in the particular case for decision.

The Council shall meet within thirty days from the request by the Member State concerned for the sole purpose of considering such questions of principle.

The Commission shall not give its decision until after the Council meeting.

3. Further, the Council may at any time, at the request of a Member State or of the Commission, consider general questions raised by the implementation of the competition policy in the transport sector.

4. In all cases where the Council is asked to meet to consider under paragraph 2 questions of principle or under paragraph 3 general questions, the Commission shall, for the purposes of this Regulation, take into account the policy guidelines which emerge from that meeting. **[1087]**

Article 18—Inquiries into transport sectors

1. If trends in transport, fluctuations in or inflexibility of transport rates, or other circumstances, suggest that competition in transport is being restricted or distorted within the common market in a specific geographical area, or over one or more transport links, or in respect of the carriage of passengers or goods belonging to one or more specific categories, the Commission may decide to conduct a general inquiry into the sector concerned, in the course of which it may request transport undertakings in that sector to supply the information and documentation necessary for giving effect to the principles formulated in Articles 2 to 8.

2. When making inquiries pursuant to paragraph 1, the Commission shall also request undertakings or groups of undertakings whose size suggests that they occupy a dominant position within the common market or a substantial part thereof to supply such particulars of the structure of the undertakings and of their behaviour as are requisite to an appraisal of their position in the light of the provisions of Article 8.

3. Article 16(2) to (6) and Articles 17, 19, 20 and 21 shall apply. **[1088]**

Article 19—Requests for information

1. In carrying out the duties assigned to it by this Regulation, the Commission may obtain all necessary information from the Governments and competent authorities of the Member States and from undertakings and associations of undertakings.

2. When sending a request for information to an undertaking or association of undertakings, the Commission shall at the same time forward a copy of the request to the competent authority of the Member State in whose territory the seat of the undertakings is situated.

3. In its request, the Commission shall state the legal basis and the purpose of the request, and also the penalties provided for in Article 22(1)(*b*) for supplying incorrect information.

4. The owners of the undertakings or their representatives and, in the case of legal persons, companies or firms, or of associations having no legal personality, the person authorised to represent them by law or by their constitution, shall be bound to supply the information requested.

5. Where an undertaking or association of undertakings does not supply the information requested within the time limit fixed by the Commission, or supplies incomplete information, the Commission shall by decision require the information to be supplied. The decision shall specify what information is required, fix an appropriate time limit within which it is to be supplied and indicate the penalties provided for in Article 22(1)(b) and Article 23(1)(c), and the right to have the decision reviewed by the Court of Justice.

6. The Commission shall at the same time forward a copy of its decision to the competent authority of the Member State in whose territory the seat of the undertaking or association of undertakings is situated.   **[1089]**

Article 20 – Investigations by the authorities of the Member States

1. At the request of the Commission, the competent authorities of the Member States shall undertake the investigations which the Commission considers to be necessary under Article 21(1), or which it has ordered by decision pursuant to Article 21(3). The officials of the competent authorities of the Member States responsible for conducting these investigations shall exercise their powers upon production of an authorisation in writing issued by the competent authority of the Member State in whose territory the investigation is to be made. Such authorisation shall specify the subject matter and purpose of the investigation.

2. If so requested by the Commission or by the competent authority of the Member State in whose territory the investigation is to be made, the officials of the Commission may assist the officials of such authority in carrying out their duties.   **[1090]**

Article 21 – Investigating powers of the Commission

1. In carrying out the duties assigned to it by this Regulation, the Commission may undertake all necessary investigations into undertakings and associations of undertakings. To this end the officials authorised by the Commission are empowered:

(a) to examine the books and other business records;
(b) to take copies of or extracts from the books and business records;
(c) to ask for oral explanations on the spot;
(d) to enter any premises, land and vehicles of undertakings.

2. The officials of the Commission authorised for the purpose of these investigations shall exercise their powers upon production of an authorisation in writing specifying the subject matter and purpose of the investigation and the penalties provided for in Article 22(1)(c) in cases where production of the required books or other business records is incomplete.

In good time before the investigation, the Commission shall inform the competent authority of the Member State in whose territory the same is to be made of the investigation and of the identity of the authorised officials.

3. Undertakings and associations of undertakings shall submit to investigations ordered by decision of the Commission. The decision shall specify the subject matter and purpose of the investigation, appoint the date on which it is to begin and indicate the penalties provided for in Article 22(1)(c) and Article 23(1)(d) and the right to have the decision reviewed by the Court of Justice.

4. The Commission shall take decisions referred to in paragraph 3 after consultation with the competent authority of the Member State in whose territory the investigation is to be made.

5. Officials of the competent authority of the Member State in whose territory the investigation is to be made, may at the request of such authority or of the Commission, assist the officials of the Commission in carrying out their duties.

6. Where an undertaking opposes an investigation ordered pursuant to this Article, the Member State concerned shall afford the necessary assistance to the officials authorised by the Commission to enable them to make their investigation. Member States shall, after consultation with the Commission, take the necessary measures to this end before 1 January 1970. **[1091]**

Article 22 – Fines

1. The Commission may by decision impose on undertakings or associations of undertakings fines of from one hundred to five thousand units of account where, intentionally or negligently:

   (a) they supply incorrect or misleading information in an application pursuant to Article 12 or in a notification pursuant to Article 14; or

   (b) they supply incorrect information in response to a request made pursuant to Article 18 or to Article 19(3) or (5), or do not supply information within the time limit fixed by a decision taken under Article 19(5); or

   (c) they produce the required books or other business records in incomplete form during investigations under Article 20 or Article 21, or refuse to submit to an investigation ordered by decision issued in implementation of Article 21(3).

2. The Commission may by decision impose on undertakings or associations of undertakings fines of from one thousand to one million units of account, or a sum in excess thereof but not exceeding 10% of the turnover in the preceding business year of each of the undertakings participating in the infringement, where either intentionally or negligently:

   (a) they infringe Article 2 or Article 8; or

   (b) they commit a breach of any obligation imposed pursuant to Article 13(1) or Article 14(4).

In fixing the amount of the fine, regard shall be had both to the gravity and to the duration of the infringement.

3. Article 16(3) to (6) and Article 17 shall apply.

4. Decisions taken pursuant to paragraphs 1 and 2 shall not be of a criminal law nature. **[1092]**

Article 23 – Periodic penalty payments

1. The Commission may by decision impose on undertakings or associations of undertakings periodic penalty payments of from fifty to one thousand units of account per day, calculated from the date appointed by the decision, in order to compel them:

   (a) to put an end to an infringement of Article 2 or Article 8 of this Regulation the termination of which it has ordered pursuant to Article 11 or to comply with an obligation imposed pursuant to Article 4(2);

   (b) to refrain from any act prohibited under Article 13(3);

(c) to supply complete and correct information which it has requested by decision taken pursuant to Article 19(5);

(d) to submit to an investigation which it has ordered by decision taken pursuant to Article 21(3).

2. Where the undertakings or associations of undertakings have satisfied the obligation which it was the purpose of the periodic penalty payment to enforce, the Commission may fix the total amount of the periodic penalty payment at a lower figure than that which would arise under the original decision.

3. Article 16(3) to (6) and Article 17 shall apply. **[1093]**

Article 24 — Review by the Court of Justice

The Court of Justice shall have unlimited jurisdiction within the meaning of Article 172 of the Treaty to review decisions whereby the Commission has fixed a fine or periodic penalty payment; it may cancel, reduce or increase the fine or periodic penalty payment imposed. **[1094]**

Article 25 — Unit of account

For the purpose of applying Articles 23 to 24 the unit of account shall be that adopted in drawing up the budget of the Community in accordance with Articles 207 and 209 of the Treaty. **[1095]**

Article 26 — Hearing of the parties and of third persons

1. Before taking decisions as provided for in Articles 11, 12(3), second subparagraph, and 12(4), 13(3), 14(2) and (3), 22 and 23, the Commission shall give the undertakings or associations of undertakings concerned the opportunity of being heard on the matters to which the Commission has taken objection.

2. If the Commission or the competent authorities of the Member States consider it necessary, they may also hear other natural or legal persons. Applications to be heard on the part of such persons where they show a sufficient interest shall be granted.

3. Where the Commission intends to give negative clearance pursuant to Article 5 or Article 6, it shall publish a summary of the relevant agreement, decision or concerted practice and invite all interested third parties to submit their observations within a time limit which it shall fix being not less than one month. Publication shall have regard to the legitimate interest of undertakings in the protection of their business secrets. **[1096]**

Article 27 — Professional secrecy

1. Information acquired as a result of the application of Articles 18, 19, 20 and 21 shall be used only for the purpose of the relevant request or investigation.

2. Without prejudice to the provisions of Articles 26 and 28, the Commission and the competent authorities of the Member States, their officials and other servants shall not disclose information acquired by them as a result of the application of this Regulation and of the kind covered by the obligation of professional secrecy.

3. The provisions of paragraphs 1 and 2 shall not prevent publication of general information or surveys which do not contain information relating to particular undertakings or associations of undertakings. **[1097]**

Article 28 – Publication of decisions

1. The Commission shall publish the decisions which it takes pursuant to Articles 11, 12(3), second subparagraph, 12(4), 13(3) and 14(2) and (3).

2. The publication shall state the names of the parties and the main content of the decision; it shall have regard to the legitimate interest of undertakings in the protection of their business secrets. **[1098]**

Article 29 – Implementing provisions

The Commission shall have power to adopt implementing provisions concerning the form, content and other details of complaints pursuant to Article 10, applications pursuant to Article 12, notifications pursuant to Article 14(1) and the hearings provided for in Article 26(1) and (2). **[1099]**

Article 30 – Entry into force, existing agreements

1. This Regulation shall enter into force on 1 July 1968.

2. Notwithstanding the provisions of paragraph 1, Article 8 shall enter into force on the day following the publication of this Regulation in the *Official Journal of the European Communities*.

3. The prohibition in Article 2 shall apply from 1 January 1969 to all agreements, decisions and concerted practices falling within Article 2 which were in existence at the date of entry into force of this Regulation or which came into being between that date and the date of publication of this Regulation in the *Official Journal of the European Communities*.

4. Paragraph 3 shall not be invoked against undertakings or associations of undertakings which, before the day following publication of this Regulation in the *Official Journal of the European Communities*, shall have terminated any agreements, decisions or concerted practices to which they are party. **[1100]**

Article 31 – Review of the Regulation

1. Within six months of the conclusion of discussions with the third countries signatories to the Revised Convention for the Navigation of the Rhine, the Council, on a proposal from the Commission, shall make any amendments to this Regulation which may prove necessary in the light of the obligations arising out of the Revised Convention for the Navigation of the Rhine.

2. The Commission shall submit to the Council, before 1 January 1971, a general report on the operation of this Regulation and, before 1 July 1971, a proposal for a Regulation to make the necessary amendments to this Regulation. **[1101]**

This Regulation shall be binding in its entirety and directly applicable in all Member States.

Done at Brussels, 19 July 1968.

375 *Commission Regulation 1629/69* **[1103]**

REGULATION (EEC) No 1629/69 OF THE COMMISSION
of 8 August 1969

on the form, content and other details of complaints pursuant to Article 10, applications pursuant to Article 12 and notifications pursuant to Article 14(1) of Council Regulation (EEC) No 1017/68 of 19 July 1968

THE COMMISSION OF THE EUROPEAN COMMUNITIES,
    Having regard to the Treaty establishing the European Economic Community, and in particular Articles 75, 87 and 155 thereof;
    Having regard to Article 29 of Regulation (EEC) No 1017/68 of 19 July 1968 applying rules of competition to transport by rail, road and inland waterway;
    Having regard to the Opinion of the Advisory Committee on Restrictive Practices and Monopolies in the field of transport;
    Whereas, pursuant to Article 29 of Regulation (EEC) No 1017/68, the Commission is authorised to adopt implementing provisions concerning the form, content and other details of complaints pursuant to Article 10, applications pursuant to Article 12 and notifications pursuant to Article 14(1) of that Regulation;
    Whereas the complaints may make it easier for the Commission to take action for infringement of the provisions of Regulation (EEC) No 1017/68; whereas it would consequently seem appropriate to make the procedure for submitting complaints as simple as possible; whereas it is appropriate, therefore, to provide for complaints to be submitted in one written copy, the use of forms being left to the discretion of the complainants;
    Whereas the submission of the applications and notifications may have important legal consequences for each undertaking which is a party to an agreement, decision or concerted practice; whereas each undertaking should, therefore, have the right to submit such applications or notifications to the Commission; whereas, on the other hand, if an undertaking makes use of that right, it must so inform the other undertakings which are parties to the agreement, decision or concerted practice, in order that they may protect their interests;
    Whereas it is for the undertakings and associations of undertakings to inform the Commission of the facts and circumstances in support of the applications submitted in accordance with Article 12 and the notifications provided for in Article 14(1);
    Whereas it is desirable to prescribe that forms be used for applications and notifications in order, in the interest of all concerned, to simplify and speed-up examination thereof by the competent departments;
    HAS ADOPTED THIS REGULATION:

Article 1 – Complaints

1. Complaints pursuant to Article 10 of Regulation (EEC) No 1017/68 shall be submitted in writing in one of the official languages of the Community; they may be submitted on Form I shown in the Annex.

    2. When representatives of undertakings, of associations of undertakings, or of natural or legal persons sign such complaints, they shall produce written proof that they are authorised to act.   **[1102]**

Article 2 – Persons entitled to submit applications and notifications

1. Any undertaking which is party to agreements, decisions or practices of the kind described in Article 2 of Regulation (EEC) No 1017/68 may submit an application under Article 12 or a notification under Article 14(1) of Regulation (EEC) No 1017/68. Where the application or notification is submitted by some, but not all, of the undertakings concerned, they shall give notice to the others.

    2. Where applications or notifications under Articles 12 and 14(1) of Regulation (EEC) No 1017/68 are signed by representatives of undertakings, of associations of undertakings,

or of natural or legal persons, such representatives shall produce written proof that they are authorised to act.

3. Where a joint application or notification is submitted, a joint representative shall be appointed.   **[1103]**

Article 3 — Submission of applications and notifications

1. Applications pursuant to Article 12 of Regulation (EEC) No 1017/68 shall be submitted on Form III shown in the Annex.

2. Notifications pursuant to Article 14(1) of Regulation (EEC) No 1017/68 shall be submitted on Form III shown in the Annex.

3. Several participating undertakings may submit an application or notification on a single form.

4. Applications and notifications shall contain the information requested in the forms.

5. Eight copies of each application or notification and of the supporting documents shall be submitted to the Commission.

6. The supporting documents shall be either originals or copies. Copies must be certified as true copies of the original.

7. Applications and notifications shall be in one of the official languages of the Community. Supporting documents shall be submitted in their original language. Where the original language is not one of the official languages, a translation in one of the official languages shall be attached.   **[1104]**

Article 4 — Entry into force

This Regulation shall enter into force on the day following its publication in the *Official Journal of the European Communities*.   **[1105]**

This Regulation shall be binding in its entirety and directly applicable in all Member States.

Done at Brussels, 8 August 1969.

ANNEX

FORM I

This form and the supporting documents should be forwarded in eight copies together with proof in a single copy of the representative's authority to act.

If the space opposite each question is insufficient, please use extra pages, specifying to which item on the form they relate.

To the Commission of the European Communities

Directorate General for Competition

170 rue de la Loi, Brussels 4

Complaint submitted by natural or legal persons pursuant to Article 10 of Council Regulation (EEC) No 1017/68 of 19 July 1968 and having as its object the opening of proceedings for the verification of infringements of Article 2 or Article 8, or the application of Article 4(2), of that Regulation

I. *Information regarding parties*

    1. Name, forenames and address of person submitting the complaint. If such person is acting as representative, state also the name and address of his principal; for undertakings, and associations of undertakings or persons, state the name, forenames and address of the proprietors or partners or, in the case of legal persons, of their legal representatives.

    Proof of representative's authority to act must be supplied.

    If the complaint is submitted by a number of persons or on behalf of a number of persons, the information must be given in respect of each complainant and each principal.

    2. Name and address of persons about whom the complaint is made.

II. *Object of the complaint*

    A. Description of the alleged infringement of Article 2 or Article 8

    Attach a detailed statement of the facts which, in your opinion, constitute an infringement of Article 2 or Article 8:

    State in particular:

    1. which practices by undertakings or associations of undertakings, referred to in the complaint, have the object or effect of preventing, restricting or distorting competition or constitute an improper exploitation of a dominant position in the common market, and

    2. to what extent trade between Member States may be affected thereby.

    B. Description of the alleged abuse of exemption for groups of small or medium-sized undertakings (Article 4(2))

Attach a detailed statement of the facts which, in your opinion, justify the application of Article 4(2):

State in particular:

1. against which of the agreements, decisions or concerted practices referred to in Article 4(1) the complaint is made;

2. to what extent implementation of the agreement, decision or concerted practice leads to results incompatible with the conditions laid down in Article 5;

3. to what extent this fact constitutes an abuse of exemption from the prohibition under Article 2.

III. *Existence of legitimate interest*

Describe — if necessary in an annex — the reasons for which you consider that you have a legitimate interest in the Commission's initiating the procedure laid down in Article 10.

IV. *Evidence*

1. State the name, forenames and address of persons in a position to give evidence as to the facts disclosed, in particular of the persons affected by the alleged infringement or abuse.

2. Submit all documents concerning the facts disclosed or directly connected with them (for example, the texts of agreements, minutes of negotiations or meetings, conditions of transport or dealing, documents relating to costs of transport, business letters, circulars).

3. Submit statistics or other data relating to the facts disclosed (concerning, for example, price trends, price determination, alterations in supply or demand with regard to transport services, conditions of transport or dealing, boycotting or discrimination).

4. Specify, where appropriate, any special technical features or name experts who can do so.

5. Indicate any other evidence available to establish that there has been an infringement or abuse as alleged.

V. State all the steps taken and measures adopted, before the complaint, by you or by any other person to whom the disclosed practice is prejudicial, with the object of putting a stop to the alleged infringement or abuse (proceedings before national courts or public authorities specifying in particular the reference number of the case and the results of such proceedings).

The undersigned declare that the information in this form and in its annexes has been given in all good faith.

.... dated ....

Signatures: ....

....

....

THE EUROPEAN COMMUNITIES
COMMISSION
Directorate General for Competition

Brussels, (date) ....

170 rue de la Loi

To ....

Acknowledgment of receipt

(This form will be returned to the address inserted above if completed in a single copy
by the complainant)

Your complaint dated ....

with regard to the opening of proceedings for

—verification of an infringement of Article 2 or Article 8
—application of Article 4(2)

of Regulation (EEC) No 1017/68

(*a*) Complainant: ....

....

(*b*) Author of the infringement or abuse: ....

....

was received on ....

and registered under No IV/TR ....

Please quote the above number in all correspondence   **[1106]**

R.T.C. LIBRARY, LETTERKENNY

FORM II

This form and the supporting documents should be forwarded in eight copies together with proof in a single copy of the representative's authority to act.

If the space opposite each question is insufficient, please use extra pages, specifying to which item on the form they relate.

To the Commission of the European Communities

Directorate General for Competition

170 rue de la Loi, Brussels 4

Application pursuant to Article 12 of Council Regulation (EEC) No 1017/68 of 19 July 1968 with a view to obtaining a declaration of non-applicability of the prohibition in Article 2 to agreements, decisions and concerted practices, in accordance with Article 5 of that Regulation

I. *Information regarding parties*

1. Name, forenames and address of person submitting the application. If such person is acting as representative, state also the name and address of the undertaking or association of undertakings represented and the name, forenames and address of the proprietors or partners or, in the case of legal persons, of their legal representatives.

   Proof of representative's authority to act must be supplied.

   If the application is submitted by a number of persons or on behalf of a number of undertakings, the information must be given in respect of each person or undertaking.

2. Name and address of the undertakings which are parties to the agreement, decision or concerted practice and name, forenames and address of the proprietors or partners or, in the case of legal persons, of their legal representatives (unless this information has been given under I(1)).

   If the undertakings which are parties are not all associated in submitting the application, state what steps have been taken to inform the other undertakings.

   This information is not necessary in respect of standard contracts (see Section II(2)(*b*) below).

3. If a firm or joint agency has been formed in pursuance of the agreement, decision or concerted practice, state the name and address of such firm or agency and the names, forenames and addresses of its legal or other representatives.

4. If a firm or joint agency is responsible for operating the agreement, decision or concerted practice state the name and address of such firm or agency and the names, forenames and addresses of its legal or other representatives.

   Attach a copy of the statutes.

5. In the case of a decision of an association of undertakings, state the name and address of the association and the names, forenames and addresses of its legal representatives.

   Attach a copy of the statutes.

6. If the undertakings are established or have their seat outside the territory of the Community (Article 227(1) and (2) of the Treaty), state the name and address of a representative or branch established in the territory of the Community.

II. *Information regarding contents of agreement, decision or concerted practice*

1. Does the agreement, decision or concerted practice concern transport:

   —by rail
   —by road
   —by inland waterway

   or operations of providers of services ancillary to transport?

2. If the contents were reduced to writing, attach a copy of the full text unless (*a*) or (*b*) below provides otherwise.

   (*a*) Is there only an outline agreement or outline decision?
         If so, attach also copy of the full text of the individual agreements and implementing provisions.
   (*b*) Is there a standard contract, i.e. a contract which the undertaking submitting the application regularly concludes with particular persons or groups of persons?
         If so, only the text of the standard contract need be attached.

3. If the contents were not, or were only partially, reduced to writing, state the contents in the space opposite.

4. In all cases give the following additional information:

   (*a*) Date of agreement, decision or concerted practice;
   (*b*) Date when it came into force and, where applicable, proposed period of validity;
   (*c*) Subject: exact description of the transport service or services involved, or of any other subject to which the agreement, decision or concerted practice relates;
   (*d*) Aims of the agreement, decision or concerted practice;
   (*e*) Terms of adherence, termination or withdrawal;
   (*f*) Sanctions which may be taken against participating undertakings (penalty clause, exclusion, etc.).

III. *Means of achieving the aims of the agreement, decision or concerted practice*

1. State whether and how far the agreement, decision or concerted practice relates to:

   —adherence to certain rates and conditions of transport or other operating conditions
   —restriction or control of the supply of transport, technical development or investment
   —sharing of transport markets
   —restrictions on freedom to conclude transport contracts with third parties (exclusive contracts)
   —application of different terms for supply of equivalent services.

2. Is the agreement, decision or concerted practice concerned with transport services:

   (*a*) within one Member State only?

(*b*) between Member States?

(*c*) between a Member State and third countries?

(*d*) between third countries in transit through one or more Member States?

IV. *Description of the conditions to be fulfilled by the agreement, decision or concerted practice so as to be exempt from the prohibition in Article 2*

Describe to what extent:

1. the agreement, decision or concerted practice contributes towards:

   —improving the quality of transport services; or

   —promoting, in markets subject to considerable temporal fluctuations of supply and demand, greater continuity and stability in the satisfaction of transport needs; or

   —increasing the productivity of undertakings; or

   —promoting technical or economic progress;

2. takes fair account of the interests of transport users;

3. the agreement, decision or concerted practice is essential for realising the aims set out under 1 above; and

4. the agreement, decision or concerted practice does not eliminate competition in respect of a substantial part of the transport market concerned.

V. State whether you intend to produce further supporting arguments and, if so, on which points.

The undersigned declare that the information given above and in the annexes attached hereto is correct. They are aware of the provisions of Article 22(1)(*a*) of Council Regulation (EEC) No 1017/68.

.... (date) ....

Signatures:

....

....

EUROPEAN COMMUNITIES   Brussels, (date) ....
COMMISSION   170, rue de la Loi
Directorate General for Competition

To

Acknowledgment of receipt

(This form will be returned to the address inserted above if completed in a single copy
by the person lodging it)

Your application dated ....

(*a*) Parties:

1. ....

2. .... and others

(There is no need to name the other undertakings party to the arrangement)

(*b*) Subject: ....

....

....

(brief description of the restriction on competition)

was received on ....

and registered under No IV/TR ....

Please quote the above number in all correspondence   **[1107]**

FORM III

This form and the supporting documents should be forwarded in eight copies together with proof in a single copy of the representative's authority to act.

If the space opposite each question is insufficient, please use extra pages, specifying to which item on the form they relate.

To the Commission of the European Communities

Directorate General for Competition

170, rue de la Loi, Brussels 4

Notification of an agreement, decision or concerted practice under Article 14(1) of Council Regulation (EEC) No 1017/68 of 19 July 1968 with a view to obtaining a declaration of non-applicability of the prohibition in Article 2, available in states of crisis, under Article 6 of that Regulation

I. *Information regarding parties*

1. Name, forenames and address of person submitting the notification. If such person is acting as representative, state also the name and address of the undertaking or association of undertakings represented and the name, forenames and address of the proprietors or partners or, in the case of legal persons, of their legal representatives.

   Proof of representative's authority to act must be supplied.

   If the notification is submitted by a number of persons or on behalf of a number of undertakings, the information must be given in respect of each person or undertaking.

2. Name and address of the undertakings which are parties to the agreement, decision or concerted practice and name, forenames and address of the proprietors or partners or, in the case of legal persons, name, forenames and address of their legal representatives (unless this information has been given under I(1)).

   If the undertakings which are parties are not all associated in submitting the notification, state what steps have been taken to inform the other undertakings.

   This information is not necessary in respect of standard contracts (see Section II(2)(*b*) below).

3. If a firm or joint agency has been formed in pursuance of the agreement, decision or concerted practice, state the name and address of such firm or agency and the names, forenames and addresses of its legal or other representatives.

4. If a firm or joint agency is responsible for operating the agreement, decision or concerted practice, state the name and address of such firm or agency and the names, forenames and addresses of its legal or other representatives.

   Attach a copy of the statutes.

5. In the case of a decision of an association of undertakings, state the name and address of the association and the names, forenames and addresses of its legal representatives.

   Attach a copy of the statutes.

6. If the undertakings are established or have their seat outside the territory of the Community (Article 227(1) and (2) of the EEC Treaty), state the name and address of a representative or branch established in the territory of the Community.

II. *Information regarding contents of agreement, decision or concerted practice*

1. Does the agreement, decision or concerted practice concern transport:

 — by rail
 — by road
 — by inland waterway

 or operations of providers of services ancillary to transport?

2. If the contents were reduced to writing, attach a copy of the full text unless (*a*) or (*b*) below provides otherwise.

 (*a*) Is there only an outline agreement or outline decision?
 If so, attach also copy of the full text of the individual agreements and implementing provisions.
 (*b*) Is there a standard contract, i.e. a contract which the undertaking submitting the notification regularly concludes with particular persons or groups of persons?
 If so, only the text of the standard contract need be attached.

3. If the contents were not, or were only partially, reduced to writing, state the contents in the space opposite.

4. In all cases give the following additional information:

 (*a*) Date of agreement, decision or concerted practice;
 (*b*) Date when it came into force and, where applicable, proposed period of validity;
 (*c*) Subject; exact description of the transport service or services involved, or of any other subject to which the agreement, decision or concerted practice relates;
 (*d*) Aims of the agreement, decision or concerted practice;
 (*e*) Terms of adherence, termination or withdrawal;
 (*f*) Sanctions which may be taken against participating undertakings (penalty clause, expulsion, etc.).

III. *Means of achieving the aims of the agreement, decision or concerted practice:*

1. State whether and how far the agreement, decision or concerted practice relates to:

 — adherence to certain rates and conditions of transport or other operating conditions
 — restriction or control of the supply of transport, technical development or investment
 — sharing of transport markets
 — restrictions on freedom to conclude transport contracts with third parties (exclusive contracts)
 — application of different terms for supply of equivalent services.

2. Is the agreement, decision or concerted practice concerned with transport services:

    (*a*) within one Member State only?

    (*b*) between Member States?

    (*c*) between a Member State and third countries?

    (*d*) between third countries in transit through one or more Member States?

IV. *Description of the conditions to be fulfilled by the agreement, decision or concerted practice so as to be exempt from the prohibition in Article 2*

Describe to what extent:

1. the transport market is disturbed,

2. the agreement, decision or concerted practice is essential for reducing that disturbance,

3. the agreement, decision or concerted practice does not eliminate competition in respect of a substantial part of the transport market concerned.

V. State whether you intend to produce further supporting arguments and, if so, on which points.

The undersigned declare that the information given above and in the annexes attached hereto is correct. They are aware of the provisions of Article 22(1)(*a*) of Council Regulation (EEC) No 1017/68.

                  .... (date) ....

Signatures:

....

....

....

EUROPEAN COMMUNITIES
COMMISSION
Directorate General for Competition

Brussels, (date) ....
170, rue de la Loi

To

Acknowledgment of receipt

(This form will be returned to the address inserted above if completed in a single copy by the person lodging it)

Your notification dated ....

(*a*) Parties:

1. ....

2. .... and others

(There is no need to name the other undertakings party to the arrangement)

(*b*) Subject: ....

....

....

(brief description of the restriction on competition)

was received on ....

and registered under No IV/TR ....

Please quote the above number in all correspondence **[1108]**

REGULATION (EEC) No 1630/69 OF THE COMMISSION
of 8 August 1969

on the hearings provided for in Article 26(1) and (2) of Council Regulation (EEC) No 1017/68 of 19 July 1968

THE COMMISSION OF THE EUROPEAN COMMUNITIES,

Having regard to the Treaty establishing the European Economic Community, and in particular Articles 75, 87 and 155 thereof;

Having regard to Article 29 of Council Regulation (EEC) No 1017/68 of 19 July 1968 applying rules of competition to transport by rail, road and inland waterways;

Having regard to the Opinion of the Advisory Committee on Restrictive Practices and Monopolies in the field of transport;

Whereas, pursuant to Article 29 of Regulation (EEC) No 1017/68, the Commission is empowered to adopt implementing provisions concerning the hearings provided for in Article 26(1) and (2) of that Regulation;

Whereas in most cases the Commission will in the course of the procedure already be in close touch with the participating undertakings or associations of undertakings and they will accordingly have the opportunity of making known their views regarding the objections raised against them;

Whereas, however, in accordance with Article 26(1) of Regulation No 1017/68 and with the rights of defence, the undertakings and associations of undertakings concerned must have the right on conclusion of the procedure to submit their comments on the whole of the objections raised against them which the Commission proposes to deal with in its decisions;

Whereas persons other than the undertakings or associations of undertakings which are involved in the procedure may have an interest in being heard; whereas, by the second sentence of Article 26(2) of Regulation No 1017/68, such persons must have the opportunity of being heard if they apply and show that they have a sufficient interest;

Whereas it is desirable to enable persons who pursuant to Article 10(2) of Regulation No 1017/68 have lodged a complaint to submit their comments where the Commission considers that on the basis of the information in its possession there are insufficient grounds for action;

Whereas the various persons entitled to submit comments must do so in writing, both in their own interest and in the interests of good administration, without prejudice to oral procedure where appropriate to supplement the written procedure;

Whereas it is necessary to define the rights of persons who are to be heard, and in particular the conditions upon which they may be represented or assisted and the setting and calculation of time limits;

Whereas the Advisory Committee on Restrictive Practices and Monopolies delivers its Opinion on the basis of a preliminary draft decision; whereas it must therefore be consulted concerning a case after the inquiry in respect thereof has been completed; whereas such consultation does not prevent the Commission from re-opening an inquiry if need be;

HAS ADOPTED THIS REGULATION:

Article 1

Before consulting the Advisory Committee on Restrictive Practices and Monopolies, the Commission shall hold a hearing pursuant to Article 26(1) of Regulation No 1017/68.

[1109]

Article 2

1. The Commission shall inform undertakings and associations of undertakings in writing of the objections raised against them. The communication shall be addressed to each of them or to a joint agent appointed by them.

2. The Commission may inform the parties by giving notice in the *Official Journal of the European Communities*, if from the circumstances of the case this appears appropriate, in particular where notice is to be given to a number of undertakings but no joint agent has been appointed. The notice shall have regard to the legitimate interest of the undertakings in the protection of their business secrets.

3. A fine or a periodic penalty payment may be imposed on an undertaking or association of undertakings only if the obligations were notified in the manner provided for in paragraph 1.

4. The Commission shall when giving notice of objections fix a time limit up to which the undertakings and associations of undertakings may inform the Commission of their views.

[1110]

Article 3

1. Undertakings and associations of undertakings shall, within the appointed time limit, make known in writing their views concerning the objections raised against them.

2. They may in their written comments set out all matters relevant to their defence.

3. They may attach any relevant documents in proof of the facts set out. They may also propose that the Commission hear persons who may corroborate those facts.

[1111]

Article 4

The Commission shall in its decision deal only with those objections raised against undertakings and associations of undertakings in respect of which they have been afforded the opportunity of making known their views. **[1112]**

Article 5

If natural or legal persons showing a sufficient interest apply to be heard pursuant to Article 26(2) of Regulation No 1017/68, the Commission shall afford them the opportunity of making known their views in writing within such time limits as it shall fix.

[1113]

Article 6

Where the Commission, having received an application pursuant to Article 10(2) of Regulation No 1017/68, considers that on the basis of the information in its possession there are insufficient grounds for granting the application, it shall inform the applicants of its reasons and fix a time limit for them to submit any further comments in writing.

[1114]

Article 7

1. The Commission shall afford to persons who have so requested in their written comments the opportunity to put forward their arguments orally, if those persons show a sufficient interest or if the Commission proposes to impose on them a fine or periodic penalty payment.

2. The Commission may likewise afford to any other person the opportunity of orally expressing his views. **[1115]**

Article 8

1. The Commission shall summon the persons to be heard to attend on such date as it shall appoint.

2. It shall forthwith transmit a copy of the summons to the competent authorities of the Member States, who may appoint an official to take part in the hearing. **[1116]**

Article 9

1. Hearings shall be conducted by the persons appointed by the Commission for that purpose.

2. Persons summoned to attend shall appear either in person or be represented by legal representatives or by representatives authorised by their constitution. Undertakings and associations of undertakings may moreover be represented by a duly authorised agent appointed from among their permanent staff.

Persons heard by the Commission may be assisted by lawyers or university teachers who are entitled to plead before the Court of Justice of the European Communities in accordance with Article 17 of the Protocol on the Statute of the Court, or by other qualified persons.

3. Hearings shall not be public. Persons shall be heard separately or in the presence of other persons summoned to attend. In the latter case, regard shall be had to the legitimate interest of the undertakings in the protection of their business secrets.

4. The essential content of the statements made by each person heard shall be recorded in minutes which shall be read and approved by him. **[1117]**

Article 10

Without prejudice to Article 2(2), information and summonses from the Commission shall be sent to the addressees by registered letter with acknowledgement of receipt, or shall be delivered by hand against receipt. **[1118]**

Article 11

1. In fixing the time limits provided for in Articles 2, 5 and 6, the Commission shall have regard both to the time required for preparation of comments and to the urgency of the case. The time limit shall be not less than two weeks; it may be extended.

2. Time limits shall run from the day following receipt of a communication or delivery thereof by hand.

3. Written comments must reach the Commission or be dispatched by registered letter before expiry of the time limit. Where the time limit would expire on a Sunday or public holiday, it shall be extended up to the end of the next following working day. For the purpose of calculating the extension, public holidays shall, in cases where the relevant date is the date of receipt of written comments, be those set out in the Annex to this Regulation, and in cases where the relevant date is the date of dispatch, those appointed by law in the country of dispatch.

This Regulation shall enter into force on the day following its publication in the *Official Journal of the European Communities*. **[1119]**

This Regulation shall be binding in its entirety and directly applicable in all Member States.

Done at Brussels, 8 August 1969.

ANNEX

referred to in the third sentence of Article 11(3) (List of public holidays)

New Year	1 Jan
Good Friday	
Easter Saturday	
Easter Monday	
Labour Day	1 May
Schuman Plan Day	9 May
Ascension Day	
Whit Monday	
Belgian National Day	21 July
Assumption	15 Aug
All Saints	1 Nov
All Souls	2 Nov

Christmas Eve	24 Dec
Christmas Day	25 Dec
The day following Christmas Day	26 Dec
New Year's Eve	31 Dec **[1120]**

REGULATION (EEC) No 2821/71 OF THE COUNCIL
of 20 December 1971

on application of Article 85(3) of the Treaty to categories of agreements, decisions and concerted practices

THE COUNCIL OF THE EUROPEAN COMMUNITIES,

Having regard to the Treaty establishing the European Economic Community, and in particular Article 87 thereof;

Having regard to the proposal from the Commission;

Having regard to the Opinion of the European Parliament;

Having regard to the Opinion of the Economic and Social Committee;

Whereas Article 85(1) of the Treaty may in accordance with Article 85(3) be declared inapplicable to categories of agreements, decisions and concerted practices which fulfil the conditions contained in Article 85(3);

Whereas the provisions for implementation of Article 85(3) must be adopted by way of regulation pursuant to Article 87;

Whereas the creation of a common market requires that undertakings be adapted to the conditions of the enlarged market and whereas co-operation between undertakings can be a suitable means of achieving this;

Whereas agreements, decisions and concerted practices for co-operation between undertakings which enable the undertakings to work more rationally and adapt their productivity and competitiveness to the enlarged market may, in so far as they fall within the prohibition contained in Article 85(1), be exempted therefrom under certain conditions; whereas this measure is necessary in particular as regards agreements, decisions and concerted practices relating to the application of standards and types, research and development of products or processes up to the stage of industrial application, exploitation of the results thereof and specialisation;

Whereas it is desirable that the Commission be enabled to declare by way of regulation that the provisions of Article 85(1) do not apply to those categories of agreements, decisions and concerted practices, in order to make it easier for undertakings to co-operate in ways which are economically desirable and without adverse effect from the point of view of competition policy;

Whereas it should be laid down under what conditions the Commission, in close and constant liaison with the competent authorities of the Member States, may exercise such powers;

Whereas under Article 6 of Regulation No 17 the Commission may provide that a decision taken in accordance with Article 85(3) of the Treaty shall apply with retroactive effect; whereas it is desirable that the Commission be empowered to issue regulations whose provisions are to the like effect;

Whereas under Article 7 of Regulation No 17 agreements, decisions and concerted practices may by decision of the Commission be exempted from prohibition, in particular if they are modified in such manner that Article 85(3) applies to them; whereas it is desirable that the Commission be enabled to grant by regulation like exemption to such agreements, decisions and concerted practices if they are modified in such manner as to fall within a category defined in an exempting regulation;

Whereas the possibility cannot be excluded that, in a specific case, the conditions set out in Article 85(3) may not be fulfilled; whereas the Commission must have power to regulate such a case in pursuance of Regulation No 17 by way of decision having effect for the future;

HAS ADOPTED THIS REGULATION:

Article 1

1. Without prejudice to the application of Regulation No 17 the Commission may, by regulation and in accordance with Article 85(3) of the Treaty, declare that Article 85(1)

shall not apply to categories of agreements between undertakings, decisions of associations of undertakings and concerted practices which have as their object:

(a) the application of standards or types;
(b) the research and development of products or processes up to the stage of industrial application, and exploitation of the results, including provisions regarding industrial property rights and confidential technical knowledge;
(c) specialisation, including agreements necessary for achieving it.

2. Such regulation shall define the categories of agreements, decisions and concerted practices to which it applies and shall specify in particular:

(a) the restrictions or clauses which may, or may not, appear in the agreements, decisions and concerted practices;
(b) the clauses which must be contained in the agreements, decisions and concerted practices or the other conditions which must be satisfied. **[1121]**

Article 2

1. Any regulation pursuant to Article 1 shall be made for a specified period.

2. It may be repealed or amended where circumstances have changed with respect to any of the facts which were basic to its being made; in such case, a period shall be fixed for modification of the agreements, decisions and concerted practices to which the earlier regulation applies. **[1122]**

Article 3

A regulation pursuant to Article 1 may provide that it shall apply with retroactive effect to agreements, decisions and concerted practices to which, at the date of entry into force of that regulation, a decision issued with retroactive effect in pursuance of Article 6 of Regulation No 17 would have applied. **[1123]**

Article 4

1. A regulation pursuant to Article 1 may provide that the prohibition contained in Article 85(1) of the Treaty shall not apply, for such period as shall be fixed by that regulation, to agreements, decisions and concerted practices already in existence on 13 March 1962 which do not satisfy the conditions of Article 85(3), where:

— within six months from the entry into force of the regulation, they are so modified as to satisfy the said conditions in accordance with the provisions of the regulation; and
— the modifications are brought to the notice of the Commission within the time limit fixed by the regulation.

[A regulation adopted pursuant to Article 1 may lay down that the prohibition referred to in Article 85(1) of the Treaty shall not apply, for the period fixed in the same regulation, to agreements and concerted practices which existed at the date of accession and which, by virtue of accession, come within the scope of Article 85 and do not fulfil the conditions set out in Article 85(3).][1]

[The provisions of the preceding sub-paragraph shall apply in the same way in the case of the accession of the Hellenic Republic, the Kingdom of Spain and of the Portuguese Republic.][2]

2. Paragraph 1 shall apply to agreements, decisions and concerted practices which had to be notified before 1 February 1963, in accordance with Article 5 of Regulation No 17, only where they have been so notified before that date.

[Paragraph 1 shall be applicable to those agreements and concerted practices which, by virtue of the accession, come within the scope of Article 85(1) of the Treaty and for which notification before 1 July 1973 is mandatory, in accordance with Articles 5 and 25 of Regulation 17, only if notification was given before that date.][3]

[Paragraph 1 shall not apply to agreements and concerted practices to which Article 85(1) of the Treaty applies by virtue of the accession of the Hellenic Republic and which must be notified before 1 July 1981, in accordance with Articles 5 and 25 of Regulation 17, unless they have been so notified before that date.][4]

[Paragraph 1 shall not apply to agreements and concerted practices to which Article 85(1) of the Treaty applies by virtue of the accession of the Kingdom of Spain and the Portuguese Republic and which must be notified before 1 July 1986, in accordance with Articles 5 and 25 of Regulation 17, unless they have been so notified before that date.][5]

3. The benefit of the provisions laid down pursuant to paragraph 1 may not be claimed in actions pending at the date of entry into force of a regulation adopted pursuant to Article 1; neither may it be relied on as grounds for claims for damages against third parties.

[1124]

AMENDMENTS
1 This sub-paragraph added by EEC Council Regulation No 2743/72, Art 1.
2 This sub-paragraph added by the Act of Accession of the Hellenic Republic, Annex I(V)(5) and subsequently replaced by the Act of Accession of the Kingdom of Spain and the Portuguese Republic, Annex I(IV)(9).
3 This sub-paragraph added by EEC Council Regulation No 2743/72.
4 This sub-paragraph added by the Act of Accession of the Hellenic Republic.
5 This sub-paragraph added by the Act of Accession of the Kingdom of Spain and the Portuguese Republic.

Article 5

Before making a regulation, the Commission shall publish a draft thereof to enable all persons and organisations concerned to submit their comments within such time limit, being not less than one month, as the Commission shall fix. [1125]

Article 6

1. The Commission shall consult the Advisory Committee on Restrictive Practices and Monopolies:

   (*a*) before publishing a draft regulation;
   (*b*) before making a regulation.

2. Paragraphs 5 and 6 of Article 10 of Regulation No 17, relating to consultation with the Advisory Committee, shall apply by analogy, it being understood that joint meetings with the Commission shall take place not earlier than one month after dispatch of the notice convening them. [1126]

Article 7

Where the Commission, either on its own initiative or at the request of a Member State or of natural or legal persons claiming a legitimate interest, finds that in any particular case agreements, decisions or concerted practices to which a regulation made pursuant to Article 1 of this Regulation applies have nevertheless certain effects which are incompatible with the conditions laid down in Article 85(3) of the Treaty, it may withdraw the benefit of application of that regulation and take a decision in accordance with Articles

6 and 8 of Regulation No 17, without any notification under Article 4(1) of Regulation
No 17 being required.   [1127]

This Regulation shall be binding in its entirety and directly applicable in all Member States.

Done at Brussels, 20 December 1971.

REGULATION (EEC) No 2988/74 OF THE COUNCIL
of 26 November 1974

**concerning limitation periods in proceedings and the enforcement of sanctions
under the rules of the European Economic Community relating to transport and
competition**

THE COUNCIL OF THE EUROPEAN COMMUNITIES,

Having regard to the Treaty establishing the European Economic Community, and in particular
Articles 75, 79 and 87 thereof;

Having regard to the proposal from the Commission;

Having regard to the Opinion of the European Parliament;

Having regard to the Opinion of the Economic and Social Committee;

Whereas under the rules of the European Economic Community relating to transport and competition the Commission has the power to impose fines, penalties and periodic penalty payments
on undertakings or associations of undertakings which infringe Community law relating to information or investigation, or to the prohibition on discrimination, restrictive practices and abuse of
dominant position; whereas those rules make no provision for any limitation period;

Whereas it is necessary in the interests of legal certainty that the principle of limitation be introduced and that implementing rules be laid down; whereas, for the matter to be covered fully, it
is necessary that provision for limitation be made not only as regards the power to impose fines
or penalties, but also as regards the power to enforce decisions, imposing fines, penalties or periodic
penalty payments; whereas such provisions should specify the length of limitation periods, the date
on which time starts to run and the events which have the effect of interrupting or suspending the
limitation period; whereas in this respect the interests of undertakings and associations of undertakings on the one hand, and the requirements imposed by administrative practice, on the other hand,
should be taken into account;

Whereas this Regulation must apply to the relevant provisions of Regulation No 11 concerning
the abolition of discrimination in transport rates and conditions, in implementation of Article 79(3)
of the Treaty establishing the European Economic Community, of Regulation No 17: first Regulation implementing Articles 85 and 86 of the Treaty, and of Council Regulation (EEC) No 1017/68
of 19 July 1968 applying rules of competition to transport by rail, road and inland waterway; whereas
it must also apply to the relevant provisions of future regulations in the fields of European Economic
Community law relating to transport and competition,

HAS ADOPTED THIS REGULATION:

Article 1 – Limitation periods in proceedings

1. The power of the Commission to impose fines or penalties for infringements of the
rules of the European Economic Community relating to transport or competition shall
be subject to the following limitation periods:

   (a) three years in the case of infringements of provisions concerning applications
       or notifications of undertakings or associations of undertakings, requests for
       information, or the carrying out of investigations;

   (b) five years in the case of all other infringements.

2. Time shall begin to run upon the day on which the infringement is committed. However, in the case of continuing or repeated infringements, time shall begin to run on the day on which the infringement ceases.				**[1128]**

Article 2 – Interruption of the limitation period in proceedings

1. Any action taken by the Commission, or by any Member State, acting at the request of the Commission, for the purpose of the preliminary investigation or proceedings in respect of an infringement shall interrupt the limitation period in proceedings. The limitation period shall be interrupted with effect from the date on which the action is notified to at least one undertaking or association of undertakings which have participated in the infringement.

Actions which interrupt the running of the period shall include in particular the following:

    (*a*) written requests for information by the Commission, or by the competent authority of a Member State acting at the request of the Commission; or a Commission decision requiring the requested information;

    (*b*) written authorisations to carry out investigations issued to their officials by the Commission or by the competent authority of any Member State at the request of the Commission; or a Commission decision ordering an investigation;

    (*c*) the commencement of proceedings by the Commission;

    (*d*) notification of the Commission's statement of objections.

2. The interruption of the limitation period shall apply for all the undertakings or associations of undertakings which have participated in the infringement.

3. Each interruption shall start time running afresh. However, the limitation period shall expire at the latest on the day on which a period equal to twice the limitation period has elapsed without the Commission having imposed a fine or a penalty; that period shall be extended by the time during which limitation is suspended pursuant to Article 3.

                                                      [1129]

Article 3 – Suspension of the limitation period in proceedings

The limitation period in proceedings shall be suspended for as long as the decision of the Commission is the subject of proceedings pending before the Court of Justice of the European Communities.				**[1130]**

Article 4 – Limitation period for the enforcement of sanctions

1. The power of the Commission to enforce decisions imposing fines, penalties or periodic payments for infringements of the rules of the European Economic Community relating to transport or competition shall be subject to a limitation period of five years.

2. Time shall begin to run on the day on which the decision becomes final. **[1131]**

Article 5 – Interruption of the limitation period for the enforcement of sanctions

1. The limitation period for the enforcement of sanctions shall be interrupted:

    (*a*) by notification of a decision varying the original amount of the fine, penalty or periodic penalty payments or refusing an application for variation;

    (*b*) by any action of the Commission, or of a Member State at the request of the Commission, for the purpose of enforcing payment of a fine, penalty or periodic penalty payment.

2. Each interruption shall start time running afresh. **[1132]**

Article 6 – Suspension of the limitation period for the enforcement of sanctions

The limitation period for the enforcement of sanctions shall be suspended for so long as:

(*a*) time to pay is allowed; or
(*b*) enforcement of payment is suspended pursuant to a decision of the Court of Justice of the European Communities. **[1133]**

Article 7 – Application to transitional cases

This Regulation shall also apply in respect of infringements committed before it enters into force. **[1134]**

Article 8 – Entry into force

This Regulation shall enter into force on 1 January 1975. **[1135]**

This Regulation shall be binding in its entirety and directly applicable in all Member States.

Done at Brussels, 26 November 1974.

REGULATION (EEC) No 1983/83 OF THE COMMISSION
of 22 June 1983[1]

on the application of Article 85(3) of the Treaty to categories of exclusive distribution agreements

NOTE
1 This text of the Regulation incorporates the corrigenda published by the Commission in OJ 1983 No L 281/24–25. See, post, Commission Notice of 22 June 1983 concerning this Regulation.

THE COMMISSION OF THE EUROPEAN COMMUNITIES,
   Having regard to the Treaty establishing the European Economic Community,
   Having regard to Council Regulation No 19/65/EEC of 2 March 1965 on the application of Article 85(3) of the Treaty to certain categories of agreements and concerted practices, as last amended by the Act of Accession of Greece, and in particular Article 1 thereof,
   Having published a draft of this Regulation,
   Having consulted the Advisory Committee on Restrictive Practices and Dominant Positions,

(1) Whereas Regulation No 19/65/EEC empowers the Commission to apply Article 85(3) of the Treaty by regulation to certain categories of bilateral exclusive distribution agreements and analogous concerted practices falling within Article 85(1);
(2) Whereas experience to date makes it possible to define a category of agreements and concerted practices which can be regarded as normally satisfying the conditions laid down in Article 85(3);
(3) Whereas exclusive distribution agreements of the category defined in Article 1 of this Regulation may fall within the prohibition contained in Article 85(1) of the Treaty; whereas this will apply only in exceptional cases to exclusive agreements of this kind to which only undertakings from one Member State are party and which concern the resale of goods within that Member State; whereas, however, to the extent that such agreements may affect trade between Member States and also satisfy all the requirements set out in this Regulation there is no reason to withhold from them the benefit of the exemption by category;

(4) Whereas it is not necessary expressly to exclude from the defined category those agreements which do not fulfil the conditions of Article 85(1) of the Treaty;

(5) Whereas exclusive distribution agreements lead in general to an improvement in distribution because the undertaking is able to concentrate its sales activities, does not need to maintain numerous business relations with a larger number of dealers and is able, by dealing with only one dealer, to overcome more easily distribution difficulties in international trade resulting from linguistic, legal and other differences;

(6) Whereas exclusive distribution agreements facilitate the promotion of sales of a product and lead to intensive marketing and to continuity of supplies while at the same time rationalizing distribution; whereas they stimulate competition between the products of different manufacturers; whereas the appointment of an exclusive distributor who will take over sales promotion, customer services and carrying of stocks is often the most effective way, and sometimes indeed the only way, for the manufacturer to enter a market and compete with other manufacturers already present; whereas this is particularly so in the case of small and medium-sized undertakings; whereas it must be left to the contracting parties to decide whether and to what extent they consider it desirable to incorporate in the agreements terms providing for the promotion of sales;

(7) Whereas, as a rule, such exclusive distribution agreements also allow consumers a fair share of the resulting benefit as they gain directly from the improvement in distribution, and their economic and supply position is improved as they can obtain products manufactured in particular in other countries more quickly and more easily;

(8) Whereas this Regulation must define the obligations restricting competition which may be included in exclusive distribution agreements; whereas the other restrictions on competition allowed under this Regulation in addition to the exclusive supply obligation produce a clear division of functions between the parties and compel the exclusive distributor to concentrate his sales efforts on the contract goods and the contract territory; whereas they are, where they are agreed only for the duration of the agreement, generally necessary in order to attain the improvement in the distribution of goods sought through exclusive distribution; whereas it may be left to the contracting parties to decide which of these obligations they include in their agreements; whereas further restrictive obligations and in particular those which limit the exclusive distributor's choice of customers or his freedom to determine his prices and conditions of sale cannot be exempted under this Regulation;

(9) Whereas the exemption by category should be reserved for agreements for which it can be assumed with sufficient certainty that they satisfy the conditions of Article 85(3) of the Treaty;

(10) Whereas it is not possible, in the absence of a case-by-case examination, to consider that adequate improvements in distribution occur where a manufacturer entrusts the distribution of his goods to another manufacturer with whom he is in competition; whereas such agreements should, therefore, be excluded from the exemption by category; whereas certain derogations from this rule in favour of small and medium-sized undertakings can be allowed;

(11) Whereas consumers will be assured of a fair share of the benefits resulting from exclusive distribution only if parallel imports remain possible; whereas agreements relating to goods which the user can obtain only from the exclusive distributor should therefore be excluded from the exemption by category; whereas the parties cannot be allowed to abuse industrial property rights or other rights in order to create absolute territorial protection; whereas this does not prejudice the relationship between competition law and industrial property rights, since the sole object here is to determine the conditions for exemption by category;

(12) Whereas, since competition at the distribution stage is ensured by the possibility of parallel imports, the exclusive distribution agreements covered by this Regulation will not normally afford any possibility of eliminating competition in respect of a substantial part of the products in question; whereas this is also true of agreements that allot to the exclusive distributor a contract territory covering the whole of the common market;

(13) Whereas, in particular cases in which agreements or concerted practices satisfying the requirements of this Regulation nevertheless have effects incompatible with Article 85(3) of the Treaty, the Commission may withdraw the benefit of the exemption by category from the undertakings party to them;

(14) Whereas agreements and concerted practices which satisfy the conditions set out in this Regulation need not be notified; whereas an undertaking may nonetheless in a particular case where real doubt exists, request the Commission to declare whether its agreements comply with this Regulation;

(15) Whereas this Regulation does not affect the applicability of Commission Regulation (EEC) No 3604/82 of 23 December 1982 on the application of Article 85(3) of the Treaty to categories of specialization agreements; whereas it does not exclude the application of Article 86 of the Treaty,

HAS ADOPTED THIS REGULATION:

Article 1

Pursuant to Article 85(3) of the Treaty and subject to the provisions of this Regulation, it is hereby declared that Article 85(1) of the Treaty shall not apply to agreements to which only two undertakings are party and whereby one party agrees with the other to supply certain goods for resale within the whole or a defined area of the common market only to that other. **[1136]**

Article 2

1. Apart from the obligation referred to in Article 1 no restriction on competition shall be imposed on the supplier other than the obligation not to supply the contract goods to users in the contract territory.

2. No restriction on competition shall be imposed on the exclusive distributor other than:

  (a) the obligation not to manufacture or distribute goods which compete with the contract goods;

  (b) the obligation to obtain the contract goods for resale only from the other party;

  (c) the obligation to refrain, outside the contract territory and in relation to the contract goods, from seeking customers, from establishing any branch and from maintaining any distribution depot.

3. Article 1 shall apply notwithstanding that the exclusive distributor undertakes all or any of the following obligations:

  (a) to purchase complete ranges of goods or minimum quantities;

  (b) to sell the contract goods under trade marks or packed and presented as specified by the other party;

  (c) to take measures for promotion of sales, in particular:

  — to advertise,
  — to maintain a sales network or stock of goods,
  — to provide customer and guarantee services,
  — to employ staff having specialized or technical training. **[1137]**

Article 3

Article 1 shall not apply where:

  (a) manufacturers of identical goods or of goods which are considered by users as equivalent in view of their characteristics, price and intended use enter into reciprocal exclusive distribution agreements between themselves in respect of such goods;

  (b) manufacturers of identical goods or of goods which are considered by users as equivalent in view of their characteristics, price and intended use enter into a non-reciprocal exclusive distribution agreements between themselves in respect of such goods unless at least one of them has a total annual turnover of no more than 100 million ECU;

  (c) users can obtain the contract goods in the contract territory only from the exclusive distributor and have no alternative source of supply outside the contract territory;

(*d*) one or both of the parties makes it difficult for intermediaries or users to obtain the contract goods from other dealers inside the common market or, in so far as no alternative source of supply is available there, from outside the common market, in particular where one or both of them:

1. exercises industrial property rights so as to prevent dealers or users from obtaining outside, or from selling in, the contract territory properly marked or otherwise properly marketed contract goods;
2. exercises other rights or takes other measures so as to prevent dealers or users from obtaining outside, or from selling in, the contract territory contract goods.   **[1138]**

Article 4

1. Article 3(*a*) and (*b*) shall also apply where the goods there referred to are manufactured by an undertaking connected with a party to the agreement.

2. Connected undertakings are:

(*a*) undertakings in which a party to the agreement, directly or indirectly:

— owns more than half the capital or business assets, or
— has the power to exercise more than half the voting rights, or
— has the power to appoint more than half the members of the supervisory board, board of directors or bodies legally representing the undertaking, or
— has the right to manage the affairs;

(*b*) undertakings which directly or indirectly have in or over a party to the agreement the rights or powers listed in (*a*);

(*c*) undertakings in which an undertaking referred to in (*b*) directly or indirectly has the rights or powers listed in (*a*).

3. Undertakings in which the parties to the agreement or undertakings connected with them jointly have the rights or powers set out in paragraph 2(*a*) shall be considered to be connected with each of the parties to the agreement.   **[1139]**

Article 5

1. For the purpose of Article 3(*b*), the ECU is the unit of account used for drawing up the budget of the Community pursuant to Articles 207 and 209 of the Treaty.

2. Article 1 shall remain applicable where during any period of two consecutive financial years the total turnover referred to in Article 3(*b*) is exceeded by no more than 10%.

3. For the purpose of calculating total turnover within the meaning of Article 3(*b*), the turnovers achieved during the last financial year by the party to the agreement and connected undertakings in respect of all goods and services, excluding all taxes and other duties, shall be added together. For this purpose, no account shall be taken of dealings between the party to the agreement and its connected undertakings or between its connected undertakings.   **[1140]**

Article 6

The Commission may withdraw the benefit of this Regulation, pursuant to Article 7 of Regulation No 19/65/EEC, when it finds in a particular case that an agreement which is exempted by this Regulation nevertheless has certain effects which are incompatible with the conditions set out in Article 85(3) of the Treaty, and in particular where:

(a) the contract goods are not subject, in the contract territory, to effective competition from identical goods or goods considered by users as equivalent in view of their characteristics, price and intended use;

(b) access by other suppliers to the different stages of distribution within the contract territory is made difficult to a significant extent;

(c) for reasons other than those referred to in Article 3(c) and (d) it is not possible for intermediaries or users to obtain supplies of the contract goods from dealers outside the contract territory on the terms there customary;

(d) the exclusive distributor:

1. without any objectively justified reason refuses to supply in the contract territory categories of purchasers who cannot obtain contract goods elsewhere on suitable terms or applies to them differing prices or conditions of sale;
2. sells the contract goods at excessively high prices. **[1141]**

Article 7

In the period 1 July 1983 to 31 December 1986, the prohibition in Article 85(1) of the Treaty shall not apply to agreements which were in force on 1 July 1983 or entered into force between 1 July and 31 December 1983 and which satisfy the exemption conditions of Regulation No 67/67/EEC.

[The provisions of the preceding paragraph shall apply in the same way to agreements which were in force on the date of accession of the Kingdom of Spain and of the Portuguese Republic and which, as a result of accession, fall within the scope of Article 85(1) of the Treaty.]⁵ **[1142]**

Article 8

This Regulation shall not apply to agreements entered into for the resale of drinks in premises used for the sale and consumption of drinks or for the resale of petroleum products in service stations. **[1143]**

Article 9

This Regulation shall apply *mutatis mutandis* to concerted practices of the type defined in Article 1. **[1144]**

Article 10

This Regulation shall enter into force on 1 July 1983.
It shall expire on 31 December 1997. **[1145]**

NOTE
5 Paragraph added by the Act of Accession of the Kingdom of Spain and the Portuguese Republic, Annex I(IV)(10).

This Regulation shall be binding in its entirety and directly applicable in all Member States.

Done at Brussels, 22 June 1983.

REGULATION (EEC) No 1984/83 OF THE COMMISSION
of 22 June 1983[1]

on the application of Article 85(3) of the Treaty to categories of exclusive purchasing agreements

NOTE
1 This text of the Regulation incorporates the corrigenda published by the Commission in OJ 1983 No L 281/24–25. See, post, Commission Notice of 22 June 1983 concerning this Regulation.

THE COMMISSION OF THE EUROPEAN COMMUNITIES,
Having regard to the Treaty establishing the European Economic Community,
Having regard to Council Regulation No 19/65/EEC of 2 March 1965 on the application of Article 85(3) of the Treaty to certain categories of agreements and concerted practices, as last amended by the Act of Accession of Greece, and in particular Article 1 thereof,
Having published a draft of this Regulation,
Having consulted the Advisory Committee on Restrictive Practices and Dominant Positions,

(1) Whereas Regulation No 19/65/EEC empowers the Commission to apply Article 85(3) of the Treaty by regulation to certain categories of bilateral exclusive purchasing agreements entered into for the purpose of the resale of goods and corresponding concerted practices falling within Article 85(1);

(2) Whereas experience to date makes it possible to define three categories of agreements and concerted practices which can be regarded as normally satisfying the conditions laid down in Article 85(3); whereas the first category comprises exclusive purchasing agreements of short and medium duration in all sectors of the economy; whereas the other two categories comprise long-term exclusive purchasing agreements entered into for the resale of beer in premises used for the sale and consumption of drinks (beer supply agreements) and of petroleum products in service stations (service-station agreements);

(3) Whereas exclusive purchasing agreements of the categories defined in this Regulation may fall within the prohibition contained in Article 85(1) of the Treaty; whereas this will often be the case with agreements concluded between undertakings from different Member States; whereas an exclusive purchasing agreement to which undertakings from only one Member State are party and which concerns the resale of goods within that Member State may also be caught by the prohibition; whereas this is in particular the case where it is one of a number of similar agreements which together may affect trade between Member States;

(4) Whereas it is not necessary expressly to exclude from the defined categories those agreements which do not fulfil the conditions of Article 85(1) of the Treaty;

(5) Whereas the exclusive purchasing agreements defined in this Regulation lead in general to an improvement in distribution; whereas they enable the supplier to plan the sales of his goods with greater precision and for a longer period and ensure that the reseller's requirements will be met on a regular basis for the duration of the agreement; whereas this allows the parties to limit the risk to them of variations in market conditions and to lower distribution costs;

(6) Whereas such agreements also facilitate the promotion of the sales of a product and lead to intensive marketing because the supplier, in consideration for the exclusive purchasing obligation, is as a rule under an obligation to contribute to the improvement of the structure of the distribution network, the quality of the promotional effort or the sales success; whereas, at the same time, they stimulate competition between the products of different manufacturers; whereas the appointment of several resellers, who are bound to purchase exclusively from the manufacturer and who take over sales promotion, customer services and carrying of stock, is often the most effective way, and sometimes the only way, for the manufacturer to penetrate a market and compete with other manufacturers already present; whereas this is particularly so in the case of small and medium-size undertakings; whereas it must be left to the contracting parties to decide whether and to what extent they consider it desirable to incorporate in their agreements terms concerning the promotion of sales;

(7) Whereas, as a rule, exclusive purchasing agreements between suppliers and resellers also allow consumers a fair share of the resulting benefit as they gain the advantages of regular supply and are able to obtain the contract goods more quickly and more easily;

(8) Whereas this Regulation must define the obligations restricting competition which may be included in an exclusive purchasing agreement; whereas the other restrictions of competition allowed under this Regulation in addition to the exclusive purchasing obligation lead to a clear division of functions between the parties and compel the reseller to concentrate his sales efforts on the contract goods; whereas they are, where they are agreed only for the duration of the agreement, generally necessary in order to attain the improvement in the distribution of goods sought through exclusive purchasing; whereas further restrictive obligations and in particular those which limit the reseller's choice of customers or his freedom to determine his prices and conditions of sale cannot be exempted under this Regulation;

(9) Whereas the exemption by categories should be reserved for agreements for which it can be assumed with sufficient certainty that they satisfy the conditions of Article 85(3) of the Treaty;

(10) Whereas it is not possible, in the absence of a case-by-case examination, to consider that adequate improvements in distribution occur where a manufacturer imposes an exclusive purchasing obligation with respect to his goods on a manufacturer with whom he is in competition; whereas such agreements should, therefore, be excluded from the exemption by categories; whereas certain derogations from this rule in favour of small and medium-sized undertakings can be allowed;

(11) Whereas certain conditions must be attached to the exemption by categories so that access by other undertakings to the different stages of distribution can be ensured; whereas, to this end, limits must be set to the scope and to the duration of the exclusive purchasing obligation; whereas it appears appropriate as a general rule to grant the benefit of a general exemption from the prohibition on restrictive agreements only to exclusive purchasing agreements which are concluded for a specified product or range of products and for not more than five years;

(12) Whereas, in the case of beer supply agreements and service-station agreements, different rules should be laid down which take account of the particularities of the markets in question;

(13) Whereas these agreements are generally distinguished by the fact that, on the one hand, the supplier confers on the reseller special commercial or financial advantages by contributing to his financing, granting him or obtaining for him a loan on favourable terms, equipping him with a site or premises for conducting his business, providing him with equipment or fittings, or undertaking other investments for his benefit and that, on the other hand, the reseller enters into a long-term exclusive purchasing obligation which in most cases is accompanied by a ban on dealing in competing products;

(14) Whereas beer supply and service-station agreements, like the other exclusive purchasing agreements dealt with in this Regulation, normally produce an appreciable improvement in distribution in which consumers are allowed a fair share of the resulting benefit;

(15) Whereas the commercial and financial advantages conferred by the supplier on the reseller make it significantly easier to establish, modernize, maintain and operate premises used for the sale and consumption of drinks and service stations; whereas the exclusive purchasing obligation and the ban on dealing in competing products imposed on the reseller incite the reseller to devote all the resources at his disposal to the sale of the contract goods; whereas such agreements lead to durable cooperation between the parties allowing them to improve or maintain the quality of the contract goods and of the services to the customer and sales efforts of the reseller; whereas they allow long-term planning of sales and consequently a cost effective organization of production and distribution; whereas the pressure of competition between products of different makes obliges the undertakings involved to determine the number and character of premises used for the sale and consumption of drinks and service stations, in accordance with the wishes of customers;

(16) Whereas consumers benefit from the improvements described, in particular because they are ensured supplies of goods of satisfactory quality at fair prices and conditions while being able to choose between the products of different manufacturers;

(17) Whereas the advantages produced by beer supply agreements and service-station agreements cannot otherwise be secured to the same extent and with the same degree of certainty; whereas the exclusive purchasing obligation on the reseller and the non-competition clause imposed on him are essential components of such agreements and thus usually indispensable for the attainment of these advantages; whereas, however, this is true only as long as the reseller's obligation to purchase from the supplier is confined in the case of premises used for the sale and consumption of drinks to beers and other drinks of the types offered by the supplier, and in the case of service stations to petroleum-based fuel for motor vehicles and other petroleum-

based fuels; whereas the exclusive purchasing obligation for lubricants and related petroleum-based products can be accepted only on condition that the supplier provides for the reseller or finances the procurement of specific equipment for the carrying out of lubrication work; whereas this obligation should only relate to products intended for use within the service station;

(18) Whereas, in order to maintain the reseller's commercial freedom and to ensure access to the retail level of distribution on the part of other suppliers, not only the scope but also the duration of the exclusive purchasing obligation must be limited; whereas it appears appropriate to allow drinks suppliers a choice between a medium-term exclusive purchasing agreement covering a range of drinks and a long-term exclusive purchasing agreement for beer; whereas it is necessary to provide special rules for those premises used for the sale and consumption of drinks which the supplier lets to the reseller; whereas, in this case, the reseller must have the right to obtain from other undertakings, under the conditions specified in this Regulation, other drinks, except beer, supplied under the agreement or of the same type but bearing a different trademark; whereas a uniform maximum duration should be provided for service-station agreements, with the exception of tenancy agreements between the supplier and the reseller, which takes account of the long-term character of the relationship between the parties;

(19) Whereas to the extent that Member States provide, by law or administrative measures, for the same upper limit of duration for the exclusive purchasing obligation upon the reseller in service-station agreements as laid down in this Regulation but provide for a permissible duration which varies in proportion to the consideration provided by the supplier or generally provide for a shorter duration than that permitted by this Regulation, such laws or measures are not contrary to the objectives of this Regulation which, in this respect, merely sets an upper limit to the duration of service-station agreements; whereas the application and enforcement of such national laws or measures must therefore be regarded as compatible with the provisions of this Regulation;

(20) Whereas the limitations and conditions provided for in this Regulation are such as to guarantee effective competition on the markets in question; whereas, therefore, the agreements to which the exemption by category applies do not normally enable the participating undertakings to eliminate competition for a substantial part of the products in question;

(21) Whereas, in particular cases in which agreements or concerted practices satisfying the conditions of this Regulation nevertheless have effects incompatible with Article 85(3) of the Treaty, the Commission may withdraw the benefit of the exemption by category from the undertakings party thereto;

(22) Whereas agreements and concerted practices which satisfy the conditions set out in this Regulation need not be notified; whereas an undertaking may nonetheless, in a particular case where real doubt exists, request the Commission to declare whether its agreements comply with this Regulation;

(23) Whereas this Regulation does not affect the applicability of Commission Regulation (EEC) No 3604/82 of 23 December 1982 on the application of Article 85(3) of the Treaty to categories of specialization agreements; whereas it does not exclude the application of Article 86 of the Treaty,

HAS ADOPTED THIS REGULATION:

TITLE I – GENERAL PROVISIONS

Article 1

Pursuant to Article 85(3) of the Treaty, and subject to the conditions set out in Articles 2 to 5 of this Regulation, it is hereby declared that Article 85(1) of the Treaty shall not apply to agreements to which only two undertakings are party and whereby one party, the reseller, agrees with the other, the supplier, to purchase certain goods specified in the agreement for resale only from the supplier or from a connected undertaking or from another undertaking which the supplier has entrusted with the sale of his goods.

[1146]

Article 2

1. No other restriction of competition shall be imposed on the supplier than the obligation not to distribute the contract goods or goods which compete with the contract goods in the reseller's principal sales area and at the reseller's level of distribution.

2. Apart from the obligation described in Article 1, no other restriction of competition shall be imposed on the reseller than the obligation not to manufacture or distribute goods which compete with the contract goods.

3. Article 1 shall apply notwithstanding that the reseller undertakes any or all of the following obligations;

(a) to purchase complete ranges of goods;
(b) to purchase minimum quantities of goods which are subject to the exclusive purchasing obligation;
(c) to sell the contract goods under trademarks, or packed and presented as specified by the supplier;
(d) to take measures for the promotion of sales, in particular:

  – to advertise,
  – to maintain a sales network or stock of goods,
  – to provide customer and guarantee services,
  – to employ staff having specialized or technical training. **[1147]**

Article 3

Article 1 shall not apply where:

(a) manufacturers of identical goods or of goods which are considered by users as equivalent in view of their characteristics, price and intended use enter into reciprocal exclusive purchasing agreements between themselves in respect of such goods;
(b) manufacturers of identical goods or of goods which are considered by users as equivalent in view of their characteristics, price and intended use enter into a non-reciprocal exclusive purchasing agreement between themselves in respect of such goods, unless at least one of them has a total annual turnover of no more than 100 million ECU;
(c) the exclusive purchasing obligation is agreed for more than one type of goods where these are neither by their nature nor according to commercial usage connected to each other;
(d) the agreement is concluded for an indefinite duration or for a period of more than five years. **[1148]**

Article 4

1. Article 3(a) and (b) shall also apply where the goods there referred to are manufactured by an undertaking connected with a party to the agreement.

2. Connected undertakings are:

(a) undertakings in which a party to the agreement, directly or indirectly:

  – owns more than half the capital or business assets, or
  – has the power to exercise more than half the voting rights, or
  – has the power to appoint more than half the members of the supervisory board, board of directors or bodies legally representing the undertaking, or
  – has the right to manage the affairs;

(*b*) undertakings which directly or indirectly have in or over a party to the agreement the rights or powers listed in (*a*);

(*c*) undertakings in which an undertaking referred to in (*b*) directly or indirectly has the rights or powers listed in (*a*).

3. Undertakings in which the parties to the agreement or undertakings connected with them jointly have the rights or powers set out in paragraph 2(*a*) shall be considered to be connected with each of the parties to the agreement. **[1149]**

Article 5

1. For the purpose of Article 3(*b*), the ECU is the unit of account used for drawing up the budget of the Community pursuant to Articles 207 and 209 of the Treaty.

2. Article 1 shall remain applicable where during any period of two consecutive financial years the total turnover referred to in Article 3(*b*) is exceeded by no more than 10%.

3. For the purpose of calculating total turnover within the meaning of Article 3(*b*), the turnovers achieved during the last financial year by the party to the agreement and connected undertakings in respect of all goods and services, excluding all taxes and other duties, shall be added together. For this purpose, no account shall be taken of dealings between the party to the agreement and its connected undertakings or between its connected undertakings. **[1150]**

TITLE II – SPECIAL PROVISIONS FOR BEER SUPPLY AGREEMENTS

Article 6

1. Pursuant to Article 85(3) of the Treaty, and subject to Articles 7 to 9 of this Regulation, it is hereby declared that Article 85(1) of the Treaty shall not apply to agreements to which only two undertakings are party and whereby one party, the reseller, agrees with the other, the supplier, in consideration for the according of special commercial or financial advantages, to purchase only from the supplier, an undertaking connected with the supplier or another undertaking entrusted by the supplier with the distribution of his goods, certain beers, or certain beers and certain other drinks, specified in the agreement for resale in premises used for the sale and consumption of drinks and designated in the agreement.

2. The declaration in paragraph 1 shall also apply where exclusive purchasing obligations of the kind described in paragraph 1 are imposed on the reseller in favour of the supplier by another undertaking which is itself not a supplier. **[1151]**

Article 7

1. Apart from the obligation referred to in Article 6, no restriction on competition shall be imposed on the reseller other than:

(*a*) the obligation not to sell beers and other drinks which are supplied by other undertakings and which are of the same type as the beers or other drinks supplied under the agreement in the premises designated in the agreement;

(*b*) the obligation, in the event that the reseller sells in the premises designated in the agreement beers which are supplied by other undertakings and which are of a different type from the beers supplied under the agreement, to sell such beers only in bottles, cans or other small packages, unless the sale of such beers in draught form is customary or is necessary to satisfy a sufficient demand from consumers;

(c) the obligation to advertise goods supplied by other undertakings within or outside the premises designated in the agreement only in proportion to the share of these goods in the total turnover realized in the premises.

2. Beers or other drinks are of different types where they are clearly distinguishable by their composition, appearance or taste. **[1152]**

Article 8

1. Article 6 shall not apply where:

(a) the supplier or a connected undertaking imposes on the reseller exclusive purchasing obligations for goods other than drinks or for services;

(b) the supplier restricts the freedom of the reseller to obtain from an undertaking of his choice either services or goods for which neither an exclusive purchasing obligation nor a ban on dealing in competing products may be imposed;

(c) the agreement is concluded for an indefinite duration or for a period of more than five years and the exclusive purchasing obligation relates to specified beers and other drinks;

(d) the agreement is concluded for an indefinite duration or for a period of more than 10 years and the exclusive purchasing obligation relates only to specified beers;

(e) the supplier obliges the reseller to impose the exclusive purchasing obligation on his successor for a longer period than the reseller would himself remain tied to the supplier.

2. Where the agreement relates to premises which the supplier lets to the reseller or allows the reseller to occupy on some other basis in law or in fact, the following provisions shall also apply:

(a) notwithstanding paragraphs (1)(c) and (d), the exclusive purchasing obligations and bans on dealing in competing products specified in this Title may be imposed on the reseller for the whole period for which the reseller in fact operates the premises;

(b) the agreement must provide for the reseller to have the right to obtain:

— drinks, except beer, supplied under the agreement from other undertakings where these undertakings offer them on more favourable conditions which the supplier does not meet,

— drinks, except beer, which are of the same type as those supplied under the agreement but which bear different trade marks, from other undertakings where the supplier does not offer them. **[1153]**

Article 9

Articles 2(1) and (3), 3(a) and (b), 4 and 5 shall apply *mutatis mutandis*. **[1154]**

TITLE III — SPECIAL PROVISIONS FOR SERVICE-STATION AGREEMENTS

Article 10

Pursuant to Article 85(3) of the Treaty and subject to Articles 11 to 13 of this Regulation, it is hereby declared that Article 85(1) of the Treaty shall not apply to agreements to which only two undertakings are party and whereby one party, the reseller, agrees with the other, the supplier, in consideration for the according of special commercial or financial advantages, to purchase only from the supplier, an undertaking connected with the supplier or another undertaking entrusted by the supplier with the distribution of his goods, certain petroleum-based motor-vehicle fuels or certain petroleum-based motor-vehicle and other fuels specified in the agreement for resale in a service station designated in the agreement.

[1155]

Article 11

Apart from the obligation referred to in Article 10, no restriction on competition shall be imposed on the reseller other than:

(a) the obligation not to sell motor-vehicle fuel and other fuels which are supplied by other undertakings in the service station designated in the agreement;

(b) the obligation not to use lubricants or related petroleum-based products which are supplied by other undertakings within the service station designated in the agreement where the supplier or a connected undertaking has made available to the reseller, or financed, a lubrication bay or other motor-vehicle lubrication equipment;

(c) the obligation to advertise goods supplied by other undertakings within or outside the service station designated in the agreement only in proportion to the share of these goods in the total turnover realized in the service station;

(d) the obligation to have equipment owned by the supplier or a connected undertaking or financed by the supplier or a connected undertaking serviced by the supplier or an undertaking designated by him.   **[1156]**

Article 12

1. Article 10 shall not apply where:

(a) the supplier or a connected undertaking imposes on the reseller exclusive purchasing obligations for goods other than motor-vehicle and other fuels or for services, except in the case of the obligations referred to in Article 11(b) and (d);

(b) the supplier restricts the freedom of the reseller to obtain from an undertaking of his choice goods or services for which under the provisions of this Title neither an exclusive purchasing obligation nor a ban on dealing in competing products may be imposed;

(c) the agreement is concluded for an indefinite duration or for a period of more than 10 years;

(d) the supplier obliges the reseller to impose the exclusive purchasing obligation on his successor for a longer period than the reseller would himself remain tied to the supplier.

2. Where the agreement relates to a service station which the supplier lets to the reseller, or allows the reseller to occupy on some other basis, in law or in fact, exclusive purchasing obligations or bans on dealing in competing products specified in this Title may, notwithstanding paragraph 1(c), be imposed on the reseller for the whole period for which the reseller in fact operates the premises.   **[1157]**

Article 13

Articles 2(1) and (3), 3(a) and (b), 4 and 5 of this Regulation shall apply *mutatis mutandis*.

[1158]

TITLE IV — MISCELLANEOUS PROVISIONS

Article 14

The Commission may withdraw the benefit of this Regulation, pursuant to Article 7 of Regulation No 19/65/EEC, when it finds in a particular case that an agreement which is exempted by this Regulation nevertheless has certain effects which are incompatible with the conditions set out in Article 85(3) of the Treaty, and in particular where:

    (*a*) the contract goods are not subject, in a substantial part of the common market, to effective competition from identical goods or goods considered by users as equivalent in view of their characteristics, price and intended use;

    (*b*) access by other suppliers to the different stages of distribution in a substantial part of the common market is made difficult to a significant extent;

    (*c*) the supplier without any objectively justified reason:

        1. refuses to supply categories of resellers who cannot obtain the contract goods elsewhere on suitable terms or applies to them differing prices or conditions of sale;

        2. applies less favourable prices or conditions of sale to resellers bound by an exclusive purchasing obligation as compared with other resellers at the same level of distribution.   **[1159]**

Article 15

1. In the period 1 July 1983 to 31 December 1986, the prohibition in Article 85(1) of the Treaty shall not apply to agreements of the kind described in Article 1 which either were in force on 1 July 1983 or entered into force between 1 July and 31 December 1983 and which satisfy the exemption conditions of Regulation No 67/67/EEC.

2. In the period 1 July 1983 to 31 December 1988, the prohibition in Article 85(1) of the Treaty shall not apply to agreements of the kinds described in Articles 6 and 10 which either were in force on 1 July 1983 or entered into force between 1 July and 31 December 1983 and which satisfy the exemption conditions of Regulation No 67/67/EEC.

3. In the case of agreements of the kinds described in Articles 6 and 10, which were in force on 1 July 1983 and which expire after 31 December 1988, the prohibition in Article 85(1) of the Treaty shall not apply in the period from 1 January 1989 to the expiry of the agreement but at the latest to the expiry of this Regulation to the extent that the supplier releases the reseller, before 1 January 1989, from all obligations which would prevent the application of the exemption under Titles II and III.

4. The provisions of the preceding paragraphs shall apply in the same way to the agreements referred to respectively in those paragraphs, which were in force on the date of accession of the Kingdom of Spain and of the Portuguese Republic and which, as a result of accession, fall within the scope of Article 85(1) of the Treaty.[1]   **[1160]**

AMENDMENT

   1 Paragraph added by the Act of Accession of the Kingdom of Spain and the Portuguese Republic, Annex I(IV)(11).

Article 16

This Regulation shall not apply to agreements by which the supplier undertakes with the reseller to supply only to the reseller certain goods for resale, in the whole or in a defined part of the Community, and the reseller undertakes with the supplier to purchase these goods only from the supplier.   **[1161]**

Article 17

This Regulation shall not apply where the parties or connected undertakings, for the purpose of resale in one and the same premises used for the sale and consumption of drinks or service station, enter into agreements both of the kind referred to in Title I and of a kind referred to in Title II or III.					**[1162]**

Article 18

This Regulation shall apply *mutatis mutandis* to the categories of concerted practices defined in Articles 1, 6 and 10.					**[1163]**

Article 19

This Regulation shall enter into force on 1 July 1983.
It shall expire on 31 December 1997.					**[1164]**

This Regulation shall be binding in its entirety and directly applicable in all Member States.

Done at Brussels, 22 June 1983.

COMMISSION NOTICE
of 22 June 1983

Concerning Commission Regulations (EEC) No 1983/83 and (EEC) No 1984/83 of 22 June 1983 on the application of Article 85(3) of the Treaty to categories of exclusive distribution and exclusive purchasing agreements

I. Introduction

1. Commission Regulation No 67/67/EEC of 22 March 1967 on the application of Article 85(3) of the Treaty to certain categories of exclusive dealing agreements expired on 30 June 1983 after being in force for over 15 years. With Regulations (EEC) No 1983/83 and (EEC) No 1984/83, the Commission has adapted the block exemption of exclusive distribution agreements and exclusive purchasing agreements to the intervening developments in the common market and in Community law. Several of the provisions in the new Regulations are new. A certain amount of interpretative guidance is therefore called for. This will assist undertakings in bringing their agreements into line with the new legal requirements and will also help ensure that the Regulations are applied uniformly in all the Member States.

2. In determining how a given provision is to be applied, one must take into account, in addition to the ordinary meaning of the words used, the intention of the provision, as this emerges from the preamble. For further guidance, reference should be made to the principles that have been involved in the case law of the Court of Justice of the European Communities and in the Commission's decisions on individual cases.

3. This notice sets out the main considerations which will determine the Commission's view of whether or not an exclusive distribution or purchasing agreement is covered by the block exemption. The notice is without prejudice to the jurisdiction of national courts to apply the Regulations, although it may well be of persuasive authority in proceedings before such courts. Nor does the notice necessarily indicate the interpretation which might be given to the provisions by the Court of Justice.					**[1165]**

II. Exclusive distribution and exclusive purchasing agreements (Regulations (EEC) No 1983/83 and (EEC) No 1984/83)

1. *Similarities and differences*

4. Regulations (EEC) No 1983/83 and (EEC) No 1984/83 are both concerned with exclusive agreements between two undertakings for the purpose of the resale of goods. Each deals with a particular type of such agreements. Regulation (EEC) No 1983/83 applies to exclusive distribution agreements, Regulation (EEC) No 1984/83 to exclusive purchasing agreements. The distinguishing feature of exclusive distribution agreements is that one party, the supplier, allots to the other, the reseller, a defined territory (the contract territory) on which the reseller has to concentrate his sales effort, and in return undertakes not to supply any other reseller in that territory. In exclusive purchasing agreements, the reseller agrees to purchase the contract goods only from the other party and not from any other supplier. The supplier is entitled to supply other resellers in the same sales area and at the same level of distribution. Unlike an exclusive distributor, the tied reseller is not protected against competition from other resellers who, like himself, receive the contract goods direct from the supplier. On the other hand, he is free of restrictions as to the area over which he may make his sales effort.

5. In keeping with their common starting point, the Regulations have many provisions that are the same or similar in both Regulations. This is true of the basic provision in Article 1, in which the respective subject-matters of the block exemption, the exclusive supply or purchasing obligation, are defined, and of the exhaustive list of restrictions of competition which may be agreed in addition to the exclusive supply or purchasing obligation (Article 2(1) and (2)), the nonexhaustive enumeration of other obligations which do not prejudice the block exemption (Article 2(3)), the inapplicability of the block exemption in principle to exclusive agreements between competing manufacturers (Article 3(a) and (b), 4 and 5), the withdrawal of the block exemption in individual cases (Article 6 of Regulation (EEC) No 1983/83 and Article 14 of Regulation (EEC) No 1984/83), the transitional provisions (Article 7 of Regulation (EEC) No 1983/83 and Article 15(1) of Regulation (EEC) No 1984/83), and the inclusion of concerted practices within the scope of the Regulations (Article 9 of Regulation (EEC) No 1983/83 and Article 18 of Regulation (EEC) No 1984/83). In so far as their wording permits, these parallel provisions are to be interpreted in the same way.

6. Different rules are laid down in the Regulations wherever they need to take account of matters which are peculiar to the exclusive distribution agreements or exclusive purchasing agreements respectively. This applies in Regulation (EEC) No 1983/83, to the provisions regarding the obligation on the exclusive distributor not actively to promote sales outside the contract territory (Article 2(2)(c)) and the inapplicability of the block exemption to agreements which give the exclusive distributor absolute territorial protection (Article 3(c) and (d)) and, in Regulation (EEC) No 1984/83, to the provisions limiting the scope and duration of the block exemption for exclusive purchasing agreements in general (Article 3(c) and (d) and for beer-supply and service-station agreements in particular (Titles II and III).

7. The scope of the two Regulations has been defined so as to avoid any overlap (Article 16 of Regulation (EEC) No 1984/83).

2. *Basic provision*

(Article 1)

8. Both Regulations apply only to agreements entered into for the purpose of the resale of goods to which not more than two undertakings are party.

(a) "For resale"

9. The notion of resale requires that the goods concerned be disposed of by the purchasing party to others in return for consideration. Agreements on the supply or purchase of goods which the purchasing party transforms or processes into other goods or uses or consumes in manufacturing other goods are not agreements for resale. The same applies to the supply of components which are combined with other components into a different product. The criterion is that the goods distributed by the reseller are the same as those the other party has supplied to him for that purpose. The economic identity of the goods is not affected if the reseller merely breaks up and packages the goods in smaller quantities, or repackages them, before resale.

10. Where the reseller performs additional operations to improve the quality, durability, appearance or taste of the goods (such as rust-proofing of metals, sterilization of food or the addition of colouring matter or flavourings to drugs), the position will mainly depend on how much value the operation adds to the goods. Only a slight addition in value can be taken not to change the economic identity of the goods. In determining the precise dividing line in individual cases, trade usage in particular must be considered. The Commission applies the same principles to agreements under which the reseller is supplied with a concentrated extract for a drink which he has to dilute with water, pure alcohol or another liquid and to bottle before reselling.

(b) "Goods"

11. Exclusive agreements for the supply of services rather than the resale of goods are not covered by the Regulations. The block exemption still applies, however, where the reseller provides customer or after-sales services incidentally to the resale of the goods. Nevertheless, a case where the charge for the service is higher than the price of the goods would fall outside the scope of the Regulations.

12. The hiring out of goods in return for payment comes closer, economically speaking, to a resale of goods than to provision of services. The Commission therefore regards exclusive agreements under which the purchasing party hires out or leases to others the goods supplied to him as covered by the Regulations.

(c) "Only two undertakings party"

13. To be covered by the block exemption, the exclusive distribution or purchasing agreement must be between only one supplier and one reseller in each case. Several undertakings forming one economic unit count as one undertaking.

14. This limitation on the number of undertakings that may be party relates solely to the individual agreement. A supplier does not lose the benefit of the block exemption if he enters into exclusive distribution or purchasing agreements covering the same goods with several resellers.

15. The supplier may delegate the performance of his contractual obligations to a connected or independent undertaking which he has entrusted with the distribution of his goods, so that the reseller has to purchase the contract goods from the latter undertaking. This principle is expressly mentioned only in Regulation (EEC) No 1984/83 (Article 1, 6, and 10), because the question of delegation arises mainly in connection with exclusive purchasing agreements. It also applies, however, to exclusive distribution agreements under Regulation (EEC) No 1983/83.

16. The involvement of undertakings other than the contracting parties must be confined to the execution of deliveries. The parties may accept exclusive supply or purchase obligations only for themselves, and not impose them on third parties, since otherwise more than two undertakings would be party to the agreement. The obligation of the parties to ensure that the obligations they have accepted are respected by connected undertakings is, however, covered by the block exemption.

3. *Other restrictions on competition that are exempted*

(Article 2(1) and (2))

17. Apart from the exclusive supply obligation (Regulation (EEC) No 1983/83) or exclusive purchase obligation (Regulation (EEC) No 1984/83), obligations defined in Article 1 which must be present if the block exemption is to apply, the only other restrictions of competition that may be agreed by the parties are those set out in Article 2(1) and (2). If they agree on further obligations restrictive of competition, the agreement as a whole is no longer covered by the block exemption and requires individual exemption. For example, an agreement will exceed the bounds of the Regulations if the parties relinquish the possibility of independently determining their prices or conditions of business or undertake to refrain from, or even prevent, cross-border trade, which the Regulations expressly state must not be impeded. Among other clauses which in general are not permissible under the Regulations are those which impede the reseller in his free choice of customers.

18. The obligations restrictive of competition that are exempted may be agreed only for the duration of the agreement. This also applies to restrictions accepted by the supplier or reseller on competing with the other party.

4. *Obligations upon the reseller which do not prejudice the block exemption*

(Article 2(3))

19. The obligations cited in this provision are examples of clauses which generally do not restrict competition. Undertakings are therefore free to include one, several or all of these obligations in their agreements. However, the obligations may not be formulated or applied in such a way as to take on the character of restrictions of competition that are not permitted. To forestall this danger, Article 2(3)(b) of Regulation (EEC) No 1984/83 expressly allows minimum purchase obligations only for goods that are subject to an exclusive purchasing obligation.

20. As part of the obligation to take measures for promotion of sales and in particular to maintain a distribution network (Article 2(3)(c) of Regulation (EEC) No 1983/83 and Article 2(3)(d) of Regulation (EEC) No 1984/83), the reseller may be forbidden to supply the contract goods to unsuitable dealers. Such clauses are unobjectionable if admission to the distribution network is based on objective criteria of a qualitative nature relating to the professional qualifications of the owner of the business or his staff or the suitability of his business premises, if the criteria are the same for all potential dealers, and if the criteria are actually applied in a nondiscriminatory manner. Distribution systems which do not fulfil these conditions are not covered by the block exemption.

5. *Inapplicability of the block exemption to exclusive agreements between competing manufacturers*

(Articles 3(a) and (b), 4 and 5)

21. The block exemption does not apply if either the parties themselves or undertakings connected with them are manufacturers, manufacture goods belonging to the same product market, and enter into exclusive distribution or purchasing agreements with one another in respect of those goods. Only identical or equivalent goods are regarded as belonging to the same product market. The goods in question must be interchangeable. Whether or not this is the case must be judged from the vantage point of the user, normally taking the characteristics, price and intended use of the goods together. In certain cases, however, goods can form a separate market on the basis of their characteristics, their price or their intended use alone. This is true especially where consumer preferences have developed. The above provisions are applicable regardless of whether or not the parties or the undertakings connected with them are based in the Community and whether or not they are

already actually in competition with one another in the relevant goods inside or outside the Community.

22. In principle, both reciprocal and non-reciprocal exclusive agreements between competing manufacturers are not covered by the block exemption and are therefore subject to individual scrutiny of their compatibility with Article 85 of the Treaty, but there is an exception for non-reciprocal agreements of the abovementioned kind where one or both of the parties are undertakings with a total annual turnover of no more than 100 million ECU (Article 3(*b*)). Annual turnover is used as a measure of the economic strength of the undertakings involved. Therefore, the aggregate turnover from goods and services of all types, and not only from the contract goods, is to be taken. Turnover taxes and other turnover-related levies are not included in turnover. Where a party belongs to a group of connected undertakings, the world-wide turnover of the group, excluding intra-group sales (Article 5(3)), is to be used.

23. The total turnover limit can be exceeded during any period of two successive financial years by up to 10% without loss of the block exemption. The block exemption is lost if, at the end of the second financial year, the total turnover over the preceding two years has been over 220 million ECU (Article 5(2)).

6. *Withdrawal of the block exemption in individual cases*

(Article 6 of Regulation (EEC) No 1983/83 and Article 14 of Regulation (EEC) No 1984/83)

24. The situations described are meant as illustrations of the sort of situations in which the Commission can exercise its powers under Article 7 of Council Regulation No 19/65/EEC to withdraw a block exemption. The benefit of the block exemption can only be withdrawn by a decision in an individual case following proceedings under Regulation No 17. Such a decision cannot have retroactive effect. It may be coupled with an individual exemption subject to conditions or obligations or, in an extreme case, with the finding of an infringement and an order to bring it to an end.

7. *Transitional provisions*

(Article 7 of Regulation (EEC) No 1983/83 and Article 15(1) of Regulation (EEC) No 1984/83)

25. Exclusive distribution or exclusive purchasing agreements which were concluded and entered into force before 1 January 1984 continue to be exempted under the provisions of Regulation No 67/67/EEC until 31 December 1986. Should the parties wish to apply such agreements beyond 1 January 1987, they will either have to bring them into line with the provisions of the new Regulations or to notify them to the Commission. Special rules apply in the case of beer-supply and service-station agreements (see paragraphs 64 and 65 below).

8. *Concerted practices*

(Article 9 of Regulation (EEC) No 1983/83 and Article 18 of Regulation (EEC) No 1984/83)

26. These provisions bring within the scope of the Regulations exclusive distribution and purchasing arrangements which are operated by undertakings but are not the subject of a legally-binding agreement.   **[1166]**

III. Exclusive distribution agreements (Regulation (EEC) No 1983/83)

1. *Exclusive supply obligation*

(Article 1)

27. The exclusive supply obligation does not prevent the supplier from providing the contract goods to other resellers who afterwards sell them in the exclusive distributor's territory. It makes no difference whether the other dealers concerned are established outside or inside the territory. The supplier is not in breach of his obligation to the exclusive distributor provided that he supplies the resellers who wish to sell the contract goods in the territory only at their request and that the goods are handed over outside the territory. It does not matter whether the reseller takes delivery of the goods himself or through an intermediary, such as a freight forwarder. However, supplies of this nature are only permissible if the reseller and not the supplier pays the transport costs of the goods into the contract territory.

28. The goods supplied to the exclusive distributor must be intended for resale in the contract territory. This basic requirement does not, however, mean that the exclusive distributor cannot sell the contract goods to customers outside his contract territory should he receive orders from them. Under Article 2(2)(*c*), the supplier can prohibit him only from seeking customers in other areas, but not from supplying them.

29. It would also be incompatible with the Regulation for the exclusive distributor to be restricted to supplying only certain categories of customers (e.g. specialist retailers) in his contract territory and prohibited from supplying other categories (e.g. department stores), which are supplied by other resellers appointed by the supplier for that purpose.

2. *Restriction on competition by the supplier*

(Article 2(1))

30. The restriction on the supplier himself supplying the contract goods to final users in the exclusive distributor's contract territory need not be absolute. Clauses permitting the supplier to supply certain customers in the territory—with or without payment of compensation to the exclusive distributor—are compatible with the block exemption provided the customers in question are not resellers. The supplier remains free to supply the contract goods outside the contract territory to final users based in the territory. In this case the position is the same as for dealers (see paragraph 27 above).

3. *Inapplicability of the block exemption in cases of absolute territorial protection*

(Articles 3(*c*) and (*d*)).

31. The block exemption cannot be claimed for agreements that give the exclusive distributor absolute territorial protection. If the situation described in Article 3(*c*) obtains, the parties must ensure either that the contract goods can be sold in the contract territory by parallel importers or that users have a real possibility of obtaining them from undertakings outside the contract territory, if necessary outside the Community, at the prices and on the terms there prevailing. The supplier can represent an alternative source of supply for the purposes of this provision if he is prepared to supply the contract goods on request to final users located in the contract territory.

32. Article 3(*d*) is chiefly intended to safeguard the freedom of dealers and users to obtain the contract goods in other Member States. Action to impede imports into the Community from third countries will only lead to loss of the block exemption if there are no alternative sources of supply in the Community. This situation can arise especially

where the exclusive distributor's contract territory covers the whole or the major part of the Community.

33. The block exemption ceases to apply as from the moment that either of the parties takes measures to impede parallel imports into the contract territory. Agreements in which the supplier undertakes with the exclusive distributor to prevent his other customers from supplying into the contract territory are ineligible for the block exemption from the outset. This is true even if the parties agree only to prevent imports into the Community from third countries. In this case it is immaterial whether or not there are alternative sources of supply in the Community. The inapplicability of the block exemption follows from the mere fact that the agreement contains restrictions on competition which are not covered by Article 2(1).   **[1167]**

IV Exclusive purchasing agreements (Regulation (EEC) No 1984/83)

1. Structure of the Regulation

34. Title I of the Regulation contains general provisions for exclusive purchasing agreements and Titles II and III special provisions for beer-supply and service-station agreements. The latter types of agreement are governed exclusively by the special provisions, some of which (Articles 9 and 13), however, refer to some of the general provisions, Article 17 also excludes the combination of agreements of the kind referred to in Title I with those of the kind referred to in Titles II or III to which the same undertakings or undertakings connected with them are party. To prevent any avoidance of the special provisions for beer-supply-and service-station agreements, it is also made clear that the provisions governing the exclusive distribution of goods do not apply to agreements entered into for the resale of drinks on premises used for the sale or consumption of beer or for the resale of petroleum products in service stations (Article 8 of Regulation (EEC) No 1983/83).

2. *Exclusive purchasing obligation*

(Article 1)

35. The Regulation only covers agreements whereby the reseller agrees to purchase all his requirements for the contract goods from the other party. If the purchasing obligation relates to only part of such requirements, the block exemption does not apply. Clauses which allow the reseller to obtain the contract goods from other suppliers, should these sell them more cheaply or on more favourable terms than the other party are still covered by the block exemption. The same applies to clauses releasing the reseller from his exclusive purchasing obligation should the other party be unable to supply.

36. The contract goods must be specified by brand or denomination in the agreement. Only if this is done will it be possible to determine the precise scope of the reseller's exclusive purchasing obligation (Article 1) and of the ban on dealing in competing products (Article 2(2)).

3. *Restriction on competition by the supplier*

(Article 2(1))

37. This provision allows the reseller to protect himself against direct competition from the supplier in his principal sales area. The reseller's principal sales area is determined by his normal business activity. It may be more closely defined in the agreement. However, the supplier cannot be forbidden to supply dealers who obtain the contract goods outside this area and afterwards resell them to customers inside it or to appoint other resellers in the area.

4. *Limits of the block exemption*

(Article 3(c) and (d))

38. Article 3(c) provides that the exclusive purchasing obligation can be agreed for one or more products, but in the latter case the products must be so related as to be thought of as belonging to the same range of goods. The relationship can be founded on technical (e.g., a machine, accessories and spare parts for it) or commercial grounds (e.g. several products used for the same purpose) or on usage in the trade (different goods that are customarily offered for sale together). In the latter case, regard must be had to the usual practice at the reseller's level of distribution on the relevant market, taking into account all relevant dealers and not only particular forms of distribution. Exclusive purchasing agreements covering goods which do not belong together can only be exempted from the competition rules by an individual decision.

39. Under Article 3(d), exclusive purchasing agreements concluded for an indefinite period are not covered by the block exemption. Agreements which specify a fixed term but are automatically renewable unless one of the parties gives notice to terminate are to be considered to have been concluded for an indefinite period.   **[1168]**

V. Beer-supply agreements (Title II of Regulation (EEC) No 1984/83)

1. *Exclusive purchasing obligation*

(Article 6)

40. The beers and other drinks covered by the exclusive purchasing obligation must be specified by brand or denomination in the agreement. An exclusive purchasing obligation can only be imposed on the reseller for drinks which the supplier carries at the time the contract takes effect and provided that they are supplied in the quantities required, at sufficiently regular intervals and at prices and on conditions allowing normal sales to the consumer. Any extension of the exclusive purchasing obligation to drinks not specified in the agreement requires an additional agreement, which must likewise satisfy the requirements of Title II of the Regulation. A change in the brand or denomination of a drink which in other respects remains unchanged does not constitute such an extension of the exclusive purchasing obligation.

41. The exclusive purchasing obligation can be agreed in respect of one or more premises used for the sale and consumption of drinks which the reseller runs at the time the contract takes effect. The name and location of the premises must be stated in the agreement. Any extension of the exclusive purchasing obligation to other such premises requires an additional agreement, which must likewise satisfy the provisions of Title II of the Regulation.

42. The concept of "premises used for the sale and consumption of drinks" covers any licensed premises used for this purpose. Private clubs are also included. Exclusive purchasing agreements between the supplier and the operator of an off-licence shop are governed by the provisions of Title I of the Regulation.

43. Special commercial or financial advantages are those going beyond what the reseller could normally expect under an agreement. The explanations given in the 13th recital are illustrations. Whether or not the supplier is affording the reseller special advantages depends on the nature, extent and duration of the obligations undertaken by the parties. In doubtful cases usage in the trade is the decisive element.

44. The reseller can enter into exclusive purchasing obligations both with a brewery in respect of beers of a certain type and with a drinks wholesaler in respect of beers of another type and/or other drinks. The two agreements can be combined into one document.

Article 6 also covers cases where the drinks wholesaler performs several functions at once, signing the first agreement on the brewery's and the second on his own behalf and also undertaking delivery of all the drinks. The provision of Title II do not apply to the contractual relations between the brewery and the drinks wholesaler.

45. Article 6(2) makes the block exemption also applicable to cases in which the supplier affords the owner of premises financial or other help in equipping them as a public house, restaurant, etc., and in return the owner imposes on the buyer or tenant of the premises an exclusive purchasing obligation in favour of the supplier. A similar situation, economically speaking, is the transmission of an exclusive purchasing obligation from the owner of a public house to his successor. Under Article 8(1)(e) this is also, in principle, permissible.

2. *Other restrictions of competition that are exempted*

(Article 7)

46. The list of permitted obligations given in Article 7 is exhaustive. If any further obligations restricting competition are imposed on the reseller, the exclusive purchasing agreement as a whole is no longer covered by the block exemption.

47. The obligation referred to in paragraph 1(a) applies only so long as the supplier is able to supply the beers or other drinks specified in the agreement and subject to the exclusive purchasing obligation in sufficient quantities to cover the demand the reseller anticipates for the products from his customers.

48. Under paragraph 1(b), the reseller is entitled to sell beer of other types in draught form if the other party has tolerated this in the past. If this is not the case, the reseller must indicate that there is sufficient demand from his customers to warrant the sale of other draught beers. The demand must be deemed sufficient if it can be satisfied without a simultaneous drop in sales of the beers specified in the exclusive purchasing agreement. It is definitely not sufficient if sales of the additional draught beer turn out to be so slow that there is a danger of its quality deteriorating. It is for the reseller to assess the potential demand of his customers for other types of beer; after all, be bears the risk if his forecasts are wrong.

49. The provision in paragraph 1(c) is not only intended to ensure the possibility of advertising products supplied by other undertakings to the minimum extent necessary in any given circumstances. The advertising of such products should also reflect their relative importance *vis-à-vis* the competing products of the supplier who is party to the exclusive purchasing agreement. Advertising for products which the public house has just begun to sell may not be excluded or unduly impeded.

50. The Commission believes that the designations of types customary in inter-State trade and within the individual Member States may afford useful pointers to the interpretation of Article 7(2). Nevertheless the alternative criteria stated in the provision itself are decisive. In doubtful cases, whether or not two beers are clearly distinguishable by their composition, appearance or taste depends on custom at the place where the public house is situated. The parties may, if they wish, jointly appoint an expert to decide the matter.

3. *Agreements excluded from the block exemption*

(Article 8)

51. The reseller's right to purchase drinks from third parties may be restricted only to the extent allowed by Articles 6 and 7. In his purchases of goods other than drinks and in his procurement of services which are not directly connected with the supply of drinks by the other party, the reseller must remain free to choose his supplier. Under Article 8(1)(a) and (b), any action by the other party or by an undertaking connected with or

appointed by him or acting at his instigation or with his agreement to prevent the reseller exercising his rights in this regard will entail the loss of the block exemption. For the purposes of these provisions it makes no difference whether the reseller's freedom is restricted by contract, informal understanding, economic pressures or other practical measures.

52. The installation of amusement machines in tenanted public houses may by agreement be made subject to the owner's permission. The owner may refuse permission on the ground that this would impair the character of the premises or he may restrict the tenant to particular types of machines. However, the practice of some owners of tenanted public houses to allow the tenant to conclude contracts for the installation of such machines only with certain undertakings which the owner recommends is, as a rule, incompatible with this Regulation, unless the undertakings are selected on the basis of objective criteria of a qualitative nature that are the same for all potential providers of such equipment and are applied in a non-discriminatory manner. Such criteria may refer to the reliability of the undertaking and its staff and the quality of the services it provides. The supplier may not prevent a public house tenant from purchasing amusement machines rather than renting them.

53. The limitation of the duration of the agreement in Article 8(1)(c) and (d) does not affect the parties' right to renew their agreement in accordance with the provisions of Title 11 of the Regulation.

54. Article 8(2)(b) must be interpreted in the light both of the aims of the Community competition rules and of the general legal principle whereby contracting parties must exercise their rights in good faith.

55. Whether or not a third undertaking offers certain drinks covered by the exclusive purchasing obligation on more favourable terms than the other party for the purposes of the first indent of Article 8(2)(b) is to be judged in the first instance on the basis of a comparison of prices. This should take into account the various factors that go to determine the prices. If a more favourable offer is available and the tenant wishes to accept it, he must inform the other party of his intentions without delay so that the other party has an opportunity of matching the terms offered by the third undertaking. If the other party refuses to do so or fails to let the tenant have his decision within a short period, the tenant is entitled to purchase the drinks from the other undertaking. The Commission will ensure that exercise of the brewery's or drinks wholesaler's right to match the prices quoted by another supplier does not make it significantly harder for other suppliers to enter the market.

56. The tenant's right provided for in the second indent of Article 8(2)(b) to purchase drinks of another brand or denomination from third undertakings obtains in cases where the other party does not offer them. Here the tenant is not under a duty to inform the other party of his intentions.

57. The tenant's rights arising from Article 8(2)(b) override any obligation to purchase minimum quantities imposed upon him under Article 9 in conjunction with Article 2(3)(b) to the extent that this is necessary to allow the tenant full exercise of those rights.

[1169]

VI. Service-station agreements (Title III of Regulation (EEC) No 1984/83)

1. *Exclusive purchasing obligation*

(Article 10)

58. The exclusive purchasing obligation can cover either motor vehicle fuels (e.g., petrol, diesel fuel, LPG, kerosene) alone or motor vehicle fuels and other fuels (e.g., heating oil, bottled gas, paraffin). All the goods concerned must be petroleum-based products.

59. The motor vehicle fuels covered by the exclusive purchasing obligations must be for use in motor-powered land or water vehicles or aircraft. The term 'service station' is to be interpreted in a correspondingly wide sense.

60. The Regulation applies to petrol stations adjoining public roads and fuelling installations on private property not open to public traffic.

2. *Other restrictions on competition that are exempted*

(Article 11)

61. Under Article 11(*b*) only the use of lubricants and related petroleum-based products supplied by other undertakings can be prohibited. This provision refers to the servicing and maintenance of motor vehicles, i.e., to the reseller's activity in the field of provision of services. It does not affect the reseller's freedom to purchase the said products from other undertakings for resale in the service station. The petroleum-based products related to lubricants referred to in paragraph(*b*) are additives and brake fluids.

62. For the interpretation of Article 11(*c*), the considerations stated in paragraph 49 above apply by analogy.

3. *Agreements excluded from the block exemption*

(Article 12)

63. These provisions are analogous to those of Article 8(1)(*a*),(*b*),(*d*) and (*e*) and 8(2)(*a*). Reference is therefore made to paragraphs 51 and 53 above.   **[1170]**

VII. Transitional provisions for beer-supply and service-station agreements (Article 15(2) and (3))

64. Under Article 15(2), all beer-supply and service-station agreements which were concluded and entered into force before 1 January 1984 remain covered by the provisions of Regulation No 67/67/EEC until 31 December 1988. From 1 January 1989 they must comply with the provisions of Titles II and III of Regulation (EEC) No 1984/83. Under Article 15(3), in the case of agreements which were in force on 1 July 1983, the same principle applies except that the 10-year maximum duration for such agreements laid down in Article 8(1)(*d*) and Article 12(1)(*c*) may be exceeded.

65. The sole requirement for the eligible beer-supply and service-station agreements to continue to enjoy the block exemption beyond 1 January 1989 is that they be brought into line with the new provisions. It is left to the undertakings concerned how they do so. One way is for the parties to agree to amend the original agreement, another for the supplier unilaterally to release the reseller from all obligations that would prevent the application of the block exemption after 1 January 1989. The latter method is only mentioned in Article 15(3) in relation to agreements in force on 1 July 1983. However, there is no reason why this possibility should not also be open to parties to agreements entered into between 1 July 1983 and 1 January 1984.

66. Parties lose the benefit of application of the transitional provisions if they extend the scope of their agreement as regards persons, places or subject matter, or incorporate into it additional obligations restrictive of competition. The agreement then counts as a new agreement. The same applies if the parties substantially change the nature or extent of their obligations to one another. A substantial change in this sense includes a revision of the purchase price of the goods supplied to the reseller or of the rent for a public house or service station which goes beyond mere adjustment to the changing economic environment.   **[1171]**

REGULATION (EEC) No 2349/84 OF THE COMMISSION
of 23 July 1984

on the application of Article 85(3) of the Treaty to certain categories of patent licensing agreements[1]

NOTE
1 This text of the Regulation incorporates the corrigenda published by the Commission in OJ No L 113 26.4.85 p 34.

THE COMMISSION OF THE EUROPEAN COMMUNITIES,
Having regard to the Treaty establishing the European Economic Community,
Having regard to Council Regulation No 19/65/EEC of 2 March 1965 on the application of Article 85(3) of the Treaty to certain categories of agreements and concerted practices, as last amended by the Act of Accession of Greece, and in particular Article 1 thereof,
Having published a draft of this Regulation,
After consulting the Advisory Committee on Restrictive Practices and Dominant Positions,
Whereas:

(1) Regulation No 19/65/EEC empowers the Commission to apply Article 85(3) of the Treaty by Regulation to certain categories of agreements and concerted practices falling within the scope of Article 85(1) to which only two undertakings are party and which include restrictions imposed in relation to the acquisition or use of industrial property rights, in particular patents, utility models, designs or trade marks, or to the rights arising out of contracts for assignment of, or the right to use, a method of manufacture or knowledge relating to the use or application of industrial processes.

(2) Patent licensing agreements are agreements whereby one undertaking, the holder of a patent (the licensor), permits another undertaking (the licensee) to exploit the patented invention by one or more of the means of exploitation afforded by patent law, in particular manufacture, use or putting on the market.

(3) In the light of experience acquired so far, it is possible to define a category of patent licensing agreements which are capable of falling within the scope of Article 85(1), but which can normally be regarded as satisfying the conditions laid down in Article 85(3). To the extent that patent licensing agreements to which undertakings in only one Member State are party and which concern only one or more patents for that Member State are capable of affecting trade between Member States, it is appropriate to include them in the exempted category.

(4) The present Regulation applies to licences issued in respect of national patents of the Member States, Community patents, or European patents granted for Member States, licences in respect of utility models or "certificats d'utilité" issued in the Member States, and licences in respect of inventions for which a patent application is made within one year. Where such patent licensing agreements contain obligations relating not only to territories within the common market but also obligations relating to non-member countries, the presence of the latter does not prevent the present Regulation from applying to the obligations relating to territories within the common market.

(5) However, where licensing agreements for non-member countries or for territories which extend beyond the frontiers of the Community have effects within the common market which may fall within the scope of Article 85(1), such agreements should be covered by the Regulation to the same extent as would agreements for territories within the common market.

(6) The Regulation should also apply to agreements concerning the assignment and acquisition of the rights referred to in point 4 above where the risk associated with exploitation remains with the assignor, patent licensing agreements in which the licensor is not the patentee but is authorized by the patentee to grant the licence (as in the case of sub-licences) and patent licensing agreements in which the parties' rights or obligations are assumed by connected undertakings.

(7) The Regulation does not apply to agreements concerning sales alone, which are governed by the provisions of Commission Regulation (EEC) No 1983/83 of 22 June 1983 concerning the application of Article 85(3) of the Treaty to categories of exclusive distribution agreements.

(8) Since the experience so far acquired is inadequate, it is not appropriate to include within the scope of the Regulation patent pools, licensing agreements entered into in connection with joint ventures, reciprocal licensing or licensing agreements in respect of plant breeder's rights. Reciprocal agreements which do not involve any territorial restrictions within the common market should, however, be so included.

(9) On the other hand, it is appropriate to extend the scope of the Regulation to patent licensing agreements which also contain provisions assigning, or granting the right to use, non-patented technical knowledge, since such mixed agreements are commonly concluded in order to allow the transfer of a complex technology containing both patented and non-patented elements. Such agreements can only be regarded as fulfilling the conditions of Article 85(3) for the purposes of this Regulation where the communicated technical knowledge is secret and permits a better exploitation of the licensed patents (know-how). Provisions concerning know-how are covered by the Regulation only in so far as the licensed patents are necessary for achieving the objects of the licensed technology and as long as at least one of the licensed patents remains in force.

(10) It is also appropriate to extend the scope of the Regulation to patent licensing agreements containing ancillary provisions relating to trade marks, subject to ensuring that the trade-mark licence is not used to extend the effects of the patent licence beyond the life of the patents. For this purpose it is necessary to allow the licensee to identify himself within the "licensed territory", i.e. the territory covering all or part of the common market where the licensor holds patents which the licensee is authorized to exploit, as the manufacturer of the "licensed product", i.e. the product which is the subject matter of the licensed patent or which has been obtained directly from the process which is the subject matter of the licensed patent, to avoid his having to enter into a new trade-mark agreement with the licensor when the licensed patents expire in order not to lose the goodwill attaching to the licensed product.

(11) Exclusive licensing agreements, i.e. agreements in which the licensor undertakes not to exploit the "licensed invention", i.e. the licensed patented invention and any know-how communicated to the licensee, in the licensed territory himself and not to grant further licences there, are not in themselves incompatible with Article 85(1) where they are concerned with the introduction and protection of a new technology in the licensed territory, by reason of the scale of the research which has been undertaken and of the risk that is involved in manufacturing and marketing a product which is unfamiliar to users in the licensed territory at the time the agreement is made. This may also be the case where the agreements are concerned with the introduction and protection of a new process for manufacturing a product which is already known. In so far as in other cases agreements of this kind may fall within the scope of Article 85(1), it is useful for the purposes of legal certainty to include them in Article 1, in order that they may also benefit from the exemption. However, the exemption of exclusive licensing agreements and certain export bans imposed on the licensor and his licensees is without prejudice to subsequent developments in the case law of the Court of Justice regarding the status of such agreements under Article 85(1).

(12) The obligations listed in Article 1 generally contribute to improving the production of goods and to promoting technical progress; they make patentees more willing to grant licences and licensees more inclined to undertake the investment required to manufacture, use and put on the market a new product or to use a new process, so that undertakings other than the patentee acquire the possibility of manufacturing their products with the aid of the latest techniques and of developing those techniques further. The result is that the number of production facilities and the quantity and quality of goods produced in the common market are increased. This is true, in particular, of obligations on the licensor and on the licensee not to exploit the licensed invention in, and in particular not to export the licensed product into, the licensed territory in the case of the licensor and the "territories reserved for the licensor", that is to say, territories within the common market in which the licensor has patent protection and has not granted any licences, in the case of the licensee. This is also true both of the obligation of the licensee not to conduct an active policy of putting the product on the market (i.e. a prohibition of active competition as defined in Article 1(1)(5)) in the territories of other licensees for a period which may equal the duration of the licence and also the obligation of the licensee not to put the licensed product on the market in the territories of other licensees for a limited period of a few years (i.e. a prohibition not only of active competition but also of "passive competition" whereby the licensee of a territory simply responds to requests which he has not solicited from users or resellers established in the territories of other licensees – Article 1(1)(6)). However,

such obligations may be permitted under the Regulation only in respect of territories in which the licensed product is protected by "parallel patents", that is to say, patents covering the same invention, within the meaning of the case law of the Court of Justice, and as long as the patents remain in force.

(13) Consumers will as a rule be allowed a fair share of the benefit resulting from this improvement in the supply of goods on the market. To safeguard this effect, however, it is right to exclude from the application of Article 1 cases where the parties agree to refuse to meet demand from users or resellers within their respective territories who would resell for export, or to take other steps to impede parallel imports, or where the licensee is obliged to refuse to meet unsolicited demand from the territory of other licensees (passive sales). The same applies where such action is the result of a concerted practice between the licensor and the licensee.

(14) The obligations referred to above thus do not impose restrictions which are not indispensable to the attainment of the abovementioned objectives.

(15) Competition at the distribution stage is safeguarded by the possibility of parallel imports and passive sales. The exclusivity obligations covered by the Regulation thus do not normally entail the possibility of eliminating competition in respect of a substantial part of the products in question. This is so even in the case of agreements which grant exclusive licences for a territory covering the whole of the common market.

(16) To the extent that in their agreements the parties undertake obligations of the type referred to in Articles 1 and 2 but which are of more limited scope and thus less restrictive of competition than is permitted by those Articles, it is appropriate that these obligations should also benefit under the exemptions provided for in the Regulation.

(17) If in a particular case an agreement covered by this Regulation is found to have effects which are incompatible with the provisions of Article 85(3) of the Treaty, the Commission may withdraw the benefit of the block exemption from the undertakings concerned, in accordance with Article 7 of Regulation No 19/65/EEC.

(18) It is not necessary expressly to exclude from the category defined in the Regulation agreements which do not fulfil the conditions of Article 85(1). Nevertheless it is advisable, in the interests of legal certainty for the undertakings concerned, to list in Article 2 a number of obligations which are not normally restrictive of competition, so that these also may benefit from the exemption in the event that, because of particular economic or legal circumstances, they should exceptionally fall within the scope of Article 85(1). The list of such obligations given in Article 2 is not exhaustive.

(19) The Regulation must also specify what restrictions or provisions may not be included in patent licensing agreements if these are to benefit from the block exemption. The restrictions listed in Article 3 may fall under the prohibition of Article 85(1); in these cases there can be no general presumption that they will lead to the positive effects required by Article 85(3), as would be necessary for the granting of a block exemption.

(20) Such restrictions include those which deny the licensee the right enjoyed by any third party to challenge the validity of the patent or which automatically prolong the agreement by the life of any new patent granted during the life of the licensed patents which are in existence at the time the agreement is entered into. Nevertheless, the parties are free to extend their contractual relationship by entering into new agreements concerning such new patents, or to agree the payment of royalties for as long as the licensee continues to use know-how communicated by the licensor which has not entered into the public domain, regardless of the duration of the original patents and of any new patents that are licensed.

(21) They also include restrictions on the freedom of one party to compete with the other and in particular to involve himself in techniques other than those licensed, since such restrictions impede technical and economic progress. The prohibition of such restrictions should however be reconciled with the legitimate interest of the licensor in having his patented invention exploited to the full and to this end to require the licensee to use his best endeavours to manufacture and market the licensed product.

(22) Such restrictions include, further, an obligation on the licensee to continue to pay royalties after all the licensed patents have ceased to be in force and the communicated know-how has entered into the public domain, since such an obligation would place the licensee at a disadvantage by comparison with his competitors, unless it is established that this obligation results from arrangements for spreading payments in respect of previous use of the licensed invention.

(23) They also include restrictions imposed on the parties regarding prices, customers or marketing of the licensed products or regarding the quantities to be manufactured or sold, especially since restrictions of the latter type may have the same effect as export bans.

(24) Finally, they include restrictions to which the licensee submits at the time the agreement is made because he wishes to obtain the licence, but which give the licensor an unjustified competitive advantage, such as an obligation to assign to the licensor any improvements the licensee may make to the invention, or to accept other licences or goods and services that the licensee does not want from the licensor.

(25) It is appropriate to offer to parties to patent licensing agreements containing obligations which do not come within the terms of Articles 1 and 2 and yet do not entail any of the effects restrictive of competition referred to in Article 3 a simplified means of benefiting, upon notification, from the legal certainty provided by the block exemption (Article 4). This procedure should at the same time allow the Commission to ensure effective supervision as well as simplifying the administrative control of agreements.

(26) The Regulation should apply with retroactive effect to patent licensing agreements in existence when the Regulation comes into force where such agreements already fulfil the conditions for application of the Regulation or are modified to do so (Articles 6 to 8). Under Article 4(3) of Regulation No 19/65/EEC, the benefit of these provisions may not be claimed in actions pending at the date of entry into force of this Regulation, nor may it be relied on as grounds for claims for damages against third parties.

(27) Agreements which come within the terms of Articles 1 and 2 and which have neither the object nor the effect of restricting competition in any other way need no longer be notified. Nevertheless, undertakings will still have the right to apply in individual cases for negative clearance under Article 2 of Council Regulation No 17 or for exemption under Article 85(3).

HAS ADOPTED THIS REGULATION:

Article 1

1. Pursuant to Article 85(3) of the Treaty and subject to the provisions of this Regulation, it is hereby declared that Article 85(1) of the Treaty shall not apply to patent licensing agreements, and agreements combining the licensing of patents and the communication of know-how, to which only two undertakings are party and which include one or more of the following obligations:

1. an obligation on the licensor not to license other undertakings to exploit the licensed invention in the licensed territory, covering all or part of the common market, in so far and as long as one of the licensed patents remains in force;
2. an obligation on the licensor not to exploit the licensed invention in the licensed territory himself in so far and as long as one of the licensed patents remains in force;
3. an obligation on the licensee not to exploit the licensed invention in territories within the common market which are reserved for the licensor, in so far and as long as the patented product is protected in those territories by parallel patents;
4. an obligation on the licensee not to manufacture or use the licensed product, or use the patented process or the communicated know-how, in territories within the common market which are licensed to other licensees, in so far and as long as the licensed product is protected in those territories by parallel patents;
5. an obligation on the licensee not to pursue an active policy of putting the licensed product on the market in the territories within the common market which are licensed to other licensees, and in particular not to engage in advertising specifically aimed at those territories or to establish any branch or maintain any distribution depot there, in so far and as long as the licensed product is protected in those territories by parallel patents;
6. an obligation on the licensee not to put the licensed product on the market in the territories licensed to other licensees within the common market for a period not exceeding five years from the date when the product is first put on the market within the common market by the licensor or one of his licensees, in so far as and for as long as the product is protected in these territories by parallel patents;
7. an obligation on the licensee to use only the licensor's trade mark or the get-up determined by the licensor to distinguish the licensed product, provided that the licensee is not prevented from identifying himself as the manufacturer of the licensed product.

2. The exemption of restrictions on putting the licensed product on the market resulting from the obligations referred to in paragraph 1(2), (3), (5) and (6) shall apply only if the licensee manufactures the licensed product himself or has it manufactured by a connected undertaking or by a subcontractor.

3. The exemption provided for in paragraph 1 shall also apply where in a particular agreement the parties undertake obligations of the types referred to in that paragraph but with a more limited scope than is permitted by the paragraph.   **[1172]**

Article 2

1. Article 1 shall apply notwithstanding the presence in particular of any of the following obligations, which are generally not restrictive of competition:

1. an obligation on the licensee to procure goods or services from the licensor or from an undertaking designated by the licensor, in so far as such products or services are necessary for a technically satisfactory exploitation of the licensed invention;
2. an obligation on the licensee to pay a minimum royalty or to produce a minimum quantity of the licensed product or to carry out a minimum number of operations exploiting the licensed invention;
3. an obligation on the licensee to restrict his exploitation of the licensed invention to one or more technical fields of application covered by the licensed patent;
4. an obligation on the licensee not to exploit the patent after termination of the agreement in so far as the patent is still in force;
5. an obligation on the licensee not to grant sub-licences or assign the licence;
6. an obligation on the licensee to mark the licensed product with an indication of the patentee's name, the licensed patent or the patent licensing agreement;
7. an obligation on the licensee not to divulge know-how communicated by the licensor; the licensee may be held to this obligation even after the agreement has expired;
8. obligations:

    (a) to inform the licensor of infringements of the patent,
    (b) to take legal action against an infringer,
    (c) to assist the licensor in any legal action against an infringer,

    provided that these obligations are without prejudice to the licensee's right to challenge the validity of the licensed patent;
9. an obligation on the licensee to observe specifications concerning the minimum quality of the licensed product, provided that such specifications are necessary for a technically satisfactory exploitation of the licensed invention, and to allow the licensor to carry out related checks;
10. an obligation on the parties to communicate to one another any experience gained in exploiting the licensed invention and to grant one another a licence in respect of inventions relating to improvements and new applications, provided that such communication or licence is non-exclusive;
11. an obligation on the licensor to grant the licensee any more favourable terms than the licensor may grant to another undertaking after the agreement is entered into.

2. In the event that, because of particular circumstances, the obligations referred to in paragraph 1 fall within the scope of Article 85(1), they shall also be exempted even if they are not accompanied by any of the obligations exempted by Article 1.

The exemption provided for in this paragraph shall also apply where in an agreement the parties undertake obligations of the types referred to in paragraph 1 but with a more limited scope than is permitted by that paragraph.   **[1173]**

Article 3

Articles 1 and 2(2) shall not apply where:

1. the licensee is prohibited from challenging the validity of licensed patents or other industrial or commercial property rights within the common market belonging to the licensor or undertakings connected with him, without prejudice to the right of the licensor to terminate the licensing agreement in the event of such a challenge;
2. the duration of the licensing agreement is automatically prolonged beyond the expiry of the licensed patents existing at the time the agreement was entered into by the inclusion in it of any new patent obtained by the licensor, unless the agreement provides each party with the right to terminate the agreement at least annually after the expiry of the licensed patents existing at the time the agreement was entered into, without prejudice to the right of the licensor to charge royalties for the full period during which the licensee continues to use know-how communicated by the licensor which has not entered into the public domain, even if that period exceeds the life of the patents;
3. one party is restricted from competing with the other party, with undertakings connected with the other party or with other undertakings within the common market in respect of research and development, manufacture, use or sales, save as provided in Article 1 and without prejudice to an obligation on the licensee to use his best endeavours to exploit the licensed invention;
4. the licensee is charged royalties on products which are not entirely or partially patented or manufactured by means of a patented process, or for the use of know-how which has entered into the public domain otherwise than by the fault of the licensee or an undertaking connected with him, without prejudice to arrangements whereby, in order to facilitate payment, the royalty payments for the use of a licensed invention are spread over a period extending beyond the life of the licensed patents or the entry of the know-how into the public domain;
5. the quantity of licensed products one party may manufacture or sell or the number of operations exploiting the licensed invention he may carry out are subject to limitations;
6. one party is restricted in the determination of prices, components of prices or discounts for the licensed products;
7. one party is restricted as to the customers he may serve, in particular by being prohibited from supplying certain classes of user, employing certain forms of distribution or, with the aim of sharing customers, using certain types of packaging for the products, save as provided in Article 1(1)(7) and Article 2(1)(3);
8. the licensee is obliged to assign wholly or in part to the licensor rights in or to patents for improvements or for new applications of the licensed patents;
9. the licensee is induced at the time the agreement is entered into to accept further licences which he does not want or to agree to use patents, goods or services which he does not want, unless such patents, products or services are necessary for a technically satisfactory exploitation of the licensed invention;
10. without prejudice to Article 1(1)(5), the licensee is required, for a period exceeding that permitted under Article 1(1)(6), not to put the licensed product on the market in territories licensed to other licensees within the common market or does not do so as a result of a concerted practice between the parties;
11. one or both of the parties are required:

    (*a*) to refuse without any objectively justified reason to meet demand from users or resellers in their respective territories who would market products in other territories within the common market;
    (*b*) to make it difficult for users or resellers to obtain the products from other resellers within the common market, and in particular to exercise industrial or commercial property rights or take measures so as to prevent users or resellers from

obtaining outside, or from putting on the market in, the licensed territory products which have been lawfully put on the market within the common market by the patentee or with his consent;

or do so as a result of a concerted practice between them. **[1174]**

Article 4

1. The exemption provided for in Articles 1 and 2 shall also apply to agreements containing obligations restrictive of competition which are not covered by those Articles and do not fall within the scope of Article 3, on condition that the agreements in question are notified to the Commission in accordance with the provisions of Commission Regulation No 27, as last amended by Regulation (EEC) No 1699/75, and that the Commission does not oppose such exemption within a period of six months.

2. The period of six months shall run from the date on which the notification is received by the Commission. Where, however, the notification is made by registered post, the period shall run from the date shown on the postmark of the place of posting.

3. Paragraph 1 shall apply only if:

   (*a*) express reference is made to this Article in the notification or in a communication accompanying it; and
   (*b*) the information furnished with the notification is complete and in accordance with the facts.

4. The benefit of paragraph 1 may be claimed for agreements notified before the entry into force of this Regulation by submitting a communication to the Commission referring expressly to this Article and to the notification. Paragraphs 2 and 3(*b*) shall apply *mutatis mutandis*.

5. The Commission may oppose the exemption. It shall oppose exemption if it receives a request to do so from a Member State within three months of the transmission to the Member State of the notification referred to in paragraph 1 or of the communication referred to in paragraph 4. This request must be justified on the basis of considerations relating to the competition rules of the Treaty.

6. The Commission may withdraw the opposition to the exemption at any time. However, where the opposition was raised at the request of a Member State and this request is maintained, it may be withdrawn only after consultation of the Advisory Committee on Restrictive Practices and Dominant Positions.

7. If the opposition is withdrawn because the undertakings concerned have shown that the conditions of Article 85(3) are fulfilled, the exemption shall apply from the date of notification.

8. If the opposition is withdrawn because the undertakings concerned have amended the agreement so that the conditions of Article 85(3) are fulfilled, the exemption shall apply from the date on which the amendments take effect.

9. If the Commission opposes exemption and the opposition is not withdrawn, the effects of the notification shall be governed by the provisions of Regulation No 17.
[1175]

Article 5

1. This Regulation shall not apply:

1. to agreements between members of a patent pool which relate to the pooled patents;
2. to patent licensing agreements between competitors who hold interests in a joint venture

or between one of them and the joint venture, if the licensing agreements relate to the activities of the joint venture;

3. to agreements under which one party grants to the other party a patent licence and that other party, albeit in separate agreements or through connected undertakings, grants to the first party a licence under patents or trade-marks or reciprocal sales rights for unprotected products or communicates to him know-how, where the parties are competitors in relation to the products covered by those agreements;

4. to licensing agreements in respect of plant breeder's rights.

2. However, this Regulation shall apply to reciprocal licences of the types referred to in paragraph 1(3) where the parties are not subject to any territorial restriction within the common market on the manufacture, use or putting on the market of the products covered by these agreements or on the use of the licensed processes. **[1176]**

Article 6

1. As regards agreements existing on 13 March 1962 and notified before 1 February 1963 and agreements, whether notified or not, to which Article 4(2)(2)(*b*) of Regulation No 17 applies, the declaration of inapplicability of Article 85(1) of the Treaty contained in this Regulation shall have retroactive effect from the time at which the conditions for application of this Regulation were fulfilled.

2. As regards all other agreements notified before this Regulation entered into force, the declaration of inapplicability of Article 85(1) of the Treaty contained in this Regulation shall have retroactive effect from the time at which the conditions for application of this Regulation were fulfilled, or from the date of notification, whichever is the later.

[1177]

Article 7

If agreements existing on 13 March 1962 and notified before 1 February 1963 or agreements to which Article 4(2)(2)(*b*) of Regulation No 17 applies and notified before 1 January 1967 are amended before 1 April 1985 so as to fulfil the conditions for application of this Regulation, and if the amendment is communicated to the Commission before 1 July 1985 the prohibition in Article 85(1) of the Treaty shall not apply in respect of the period prior to the amendment. The communication shall take effect from the time of its receipt by the Commission. Where the communication is sent by registered post, it shall take effect from the date shown on the postmark of the place of posting.

[1178]

Article 8

1. As regards agreements to which Article 85 of the Treaty applies as a result of the accession of the United Kingdom, Ireland and Denmark, Articles 6 and 7 shall apply except that the relevant dates shall be 1 January 1973 instead of 13 March 1962 and 1 July 1973 instead of 1 February 1963 and 1 January 1967.

2. As regards agreements to which Article 85 of the Treaty applies as a result of the accession of Greece, Articles 6 and 7 shall apply except that the relevant dates shall be 1 January 1981 instead of 13 March 1962 and 1 July 1981 instead of 1 February 1963 and 1 January 1967.

3. As regards agreements to which Article 85 of the Treaty applies as a result of the accession of the Kingdom of Spain and of the Portuguese Republic, Articles 6 and 7 shall apply except that the relevant dates shall be 1 January 1986 instead of 13 March 1962 and 1 July 1986 instead of 1 February 1963, 1 January 1967 and 1 April 1985. The

amendment made to these agreements in accordance with Article 7 need not be notified to the Commission.[1]   **[1179]**

AMENDMENT
1 Para 3 added by the Act of Accession of the Kingdom of Spain and the Portuguese Republic, 1985.

Article 9

The Commission may withdraw the benefit of this Regulation, pursuant to Article 7 of Regulation No 19/65/EEC, where it finds in a particular case that an agreement exempted by this Regulation nevertheless has certain effects which are incompatible with the conditions laid down in Article 85(3) of the Treaty, and in particular where:

1. such effects arise from an arbitration award;
2. the licensed products or the services provided using a licensed process are not exposed to effective competition in the licensed territory from identical products or services or products or services considered by users as equivalent in view of their characteristics, price and intended use;
3. the licensor does not have the right to terminate the exclusivity granted to the licensee at the latest five years from the date the agreement was entered into and at least annually thereafter if, without legitimate reason, the licensee fails to exploit the patent or to do so adequately;
4. without prejudice to Article 1(1)(6), the licensee refuses, without objectively valid reason, to meet unsolicited demand from users or resellers in the territory of other licensees;
5. one or both of the parties:

   (*a*) without any objectively justified reason, refuse to meet demand from users or resellers in their respective territories who would market the products in other territories within the common market; or

   (*b*) make it difficult for users or resellers to obtain the products from other resellers within the common market, and in particular where they exercise industrial or commercial property rights or take measures so as to prevent resellers or users from obtaining outside, or from putting on the market in, the licensed territory products which have been lawfully put on the market within the common market by the patentee or with his consent.   **[1180]**

Article 10

1. This Regulation shall apply to:

   (*a*) patent applications;
   (*b*) utility models;
   (*c*) applications for registration of utility models;
   (*d*) "certificats d'utilité" and "certificats d'addition" under French law; and
   (*e*) applications for "certificats d'utilité" and "certificats d'addition" under French law;

equally as it applies to patents.

2. This Regulation shall also apply to agreements relating to the exploitation of an invention if an application within the meaning of paragraph 1 is made in respect of the invention for the licensed territory within one year from the date when the agreement was entered into.   **[1181]**

Article 11

This Regulation shall also apply to:

1. patent licensing agreements where the licensor is not the patentee but is authorized by the patentee to grant a licence or a sub-licence;
2. assignments of a patent or of a right to a patent where the sum payable in consideration of the assignment is dependent upon the turnover attained by the assignee in respect of the patented products, the quantity of such products manufactured or the number of operations carried out employing the patented invention;
3. patent licensing agreements in which rights or obligations of the licensor or the licensee are assumed by undertakings connected with them.   [1182]

Article 12

1. "Connected undertakings" for the purposes of this Regulation means:

   (a) undertakings in which a party to the agreement, directly or indirectly:

   – owns more than half the capital or business assets, or
   – has the power to exercise more than half the voting rights, or
   – has the power to appoint more than half the members of the supervisory board, board of directors or bodies legally representing the undertaking, or
   – has the right to manage the affairs of the undertaking;

   (b) undertakings which directly or indirectly have in or over a party to the agreement the rights or powers listed in (a);
   (c) undertakings in which an undertaking referred to in (b) directly or indirectly has the rights or powers listed in (a).

2. Undertakings in which the parties to the agreement or undertakings connected with them jointly have the rights or powers set out in paragraph 1(a) shall be considered to be connected with each of the parties to the agreement.   [1183]

Article 13

1. Information acquired pursuant to Article 4 shall be used only for the purposes of this Regulation.

2. The Commission and the authorities of the Member States, their officials and other servants shall not disclose information acquired by them pursuant to this Regulation of the kind covered by the obligation of professional secrecy.

3. The provisions of paragraphs 1 and 2 shall not prevent publication of general information or surveys which do not contain information relating to particular undertakings or associations of undertakings.   [1184]

Article 14

This Regulation shall enter into force on 1 January 1985.
It shall apply until 31 December 1994.   [1185]

This Regulation shall be binding in its entirety and directly applicable in all Member States.

Done at Brussels, 23 July 1984.

REGULATION (EEC) No 123/85 OF THE COMMISSION
of 12 December 1984[1]

on the application of Article 85(3) of the Treaty to certain categories of motor vehicle distribution and servicing agreements

NOTE
1 See, post, Commission Notice of 12 December 1984 concerning this Regulation

THE COMMISSION OF THE EUROPEAN COMMUNITIES,
Having regard to the Treaty establishing the European Economic Community,
Having regard to Council Regulation No 19/65/EEC of 2 March 1965 on the application of Article 85(3) of the Treaty to certain categories of agreements and concerted practices, as last amended by the Act of Accession of Greece,
Having published a draft of this Regulation,
Having consulted the Advisory Committee on Restrictive Practices and Dominant Positions,
Whereas:

(1) Under Article 1(1)(*a*) of Regulation No 19/65/EEC the Commission is empowered to declare by means of a Regulation that Article 85(3) of the Treaty applies to certain categories of agreements falling within Article 85(1) to which only two undertakings are party and by which one party agrees with the other to supply only to that undertaking other certain goods for resale within a defined territory of the common market. In the light of experience since Commission Decision 75/73/EEC and of the many motor vehicle distribution and servicing agreements which have been notified to the Commission pursuant to Articles 4 and 5 of Council Regulation No 17, as last amended by Regulation (EEC) No 2821/71, a category of agreements can be defined as satisfying the conditions laid down in Regulation No 19/65/EEC. They are agreements, for a definite or an indefinite period, by which the supplying party entrusts to the reselling party the task of promoting the distribution and servicing of certain products of the motor vehicle industry in a defined area and by which the supplier undertakes to supply contract goods for resale only to the dealer, or only to a limited number of undertakings within the distribution network besides the dealer, within the contract territory.
A list of definitions for the purpose of this Regulation is set out in Article 13.

(2) Notwithstanding that the obligations imposed by distribution and servicing agreements which are listed in Articles 1, 2 and 3 of this Regulation normally have as their object or effect the prevention, restriction or distortion of competition within the common market and are normally apt to affect trade between Member States, the prohibition in Article 85(1) of the Treaty may nevertheless be declared inapplicable to these agreements by virtue of Article 85(3), albeit only under certain restrictive conditions.

(3) The applicability of Article 85(1) of the Treaty to distribution and servicing agreements in the motor vehicle industry stems in particular from the fact that restrictions on competition and the obligations connected with the distribution system listed in Articles 1 to 4 of this Regulation are regularly imposed in the same or similar form throughout the common market for the products supplied within the distribution system of a particular manufacturer. The motor vehicle manufacturers cover the whole common market or substantial parts of it by means of a cluster of agreements involving similar restrictions on competition and affect in this way not only distribution and servicing within Member States but also trade between them.

(4) The exclusive and selective distribution clauses can be regarded as indispensable measures of rationalization in the motor vehicle industry because motor vehicles are consumer durables which at both regular and irregular intervals require expert maintenance and repair, not always in the same place. Motor vehicle manufacturers cooperate with the selected dealers and repairers in order to provide specialized servicing for the product. On grounds of capacity and efficiency alone, such a form of cooperation cannot be extended to an unlimited number of dealers and repairers. The linking of servicing and distribution must be regarded as more efficient than a separation between a distribution organization for new vehicles on the one hand and a servicing organization which would also distribute spare parts on the other, particularly as, before a new vehicle is delivered to the final consumer, the undertaking within the distribution system must give it a technical inspection according to the manufacturer's specification.

(5)   However, obligatory recourse to the authorized network is not in all respects indispensable for efficient distribution. The exceptions to the block exemption provide that the supply of contract goods to resellers may not be prohibited where they:

— belong to the same distribution system (Article 3, point 10(*a*)),
or
— purchase spare parts for their own use in effecting repairs or maintenance (Article 3, point 10(*b*)).

Measures taken by a manufacturer or by undertakings within the distribution system with the object of protecting the selective distribution system are compatible with the exemption under this Regulation. This applies in particular to a dealer's obligation to sell vehicles to a final consumer using the services of an intermediary only where that consumer has authorized that intermediary to act as his agent (Article 3, point 11).

(6)   It should be possible to bar wholesalers not belonging to the distribution system from reselling parts originating from motor vehicle manufacturers. It may be supposed that the system of rapid availability of spare parts across the whole contract programme, including those with a low turnover, which is beneficial to the consumer, could not be maintained without obligatory recourse to the authorized network.

(7)   The ban on dealing in competing products and that on dealing in other vehicles at stated premises may in principle be exempted, because they contribute to concentration by the undertakings in the distribution network of their efforts on the products supplied by the manufacturer or with his consent, and thus ensure distribution and servicing appropriate for the vehicles (Article 3, point 3). Such obligations provide an incentive for the dealer to develop sales and servicing of contract goods and thus promote competition in the supply of those products as well as between those products and competing products.

(8)   However, bans on dealing in competing products cannot be regarded as indispensable in all circumstances to efficient distribution. Dealers must be free to obtain from third parties supplies of parts which match the quality of those offered by the manufacturer, for example where the parts are produced by a sub-contract manufacturer who also supplies the motor vehicle manufacturer, and to use and sell them. They must also keep their freedom to choose parts which are usable in motor vehicles within the contract programme and which not only match but exceed the quality standard. Such a limit on the ban on dealing in competing products takes account of the importance of vehicle safety and of the maintenance of effective competition (Article 3, point 4 and Article 4(1), points 6 and 7).

(9)   The restrictions imposed on the dealer's activities outside the allotted area lead to more intensive distribution and servicing efforts in an easily supervised contract territory, to knowledge of the market based on closer contact with consumers, and to more demand-orientated supply (Article 3, points 8 and 9). However, demand for contract goods must remain flexible and should not be limited on a regional basis. Dealers must not be confined to satisfying the demand for contract goods within their contract territories, but must also be able to meet demand from persons and undertakings in other areas of the common market. Dealers' advertising in a medium which is directed to customers in the contract territory but also covers a wider area should not be prevented, because it does not run counter to the obligation to promote sales within the contract territory.

(10) The obligations listed in Article 4(1) are directly related to the obligations in Articles 1, 2 and 3, and influence their restrictive effect. These obligations, which might in individual cases be caught by the prohibition in Article 85(1) of the Treaty, may also be exempted because of their direct relationship with one or more of the obligations exempted by Articles 1, 2 and 3 (Article 4(2)).

(11) According to Article 1(2)(*b*) of Regulation No 19/65/EEC, conditions which must be satisfied if the declaration of inapplicability is to take effect must be specified.

(12) Under Article 5(1), points 1(*a*) and (*b*) it is a condition of exemption that the undertaking should honour the minimum guarantee and provide the minimum free servicing and vehicle recall work laid down by the manufacturer, irrespective of where in the common market the vehicle was purchased. These provisions are intended to prevent the consumer's freedom to buy anywhere in the common market from being limited.

(13) Article 5(1), point 2(*a*) is intended to allow the manufacturer to build up a coordinated distribution system, but without hindering the relationship of confidence between dealers and sub-dealers. Accordingly, if the supplier reserves the right to approve appointments of sub-dealers by the dealer, he must not be allowed to withhold approval arbitrarily.

(14) Article 5(1), point 2(*b*) obliges the supplier not to impose on a dealer within the distribution system requirements, as defined in Article 4(1), which are discriminatory or inequitable.

(15) Article 5(1), point 2(*c*) is intended to counter the concentration of the dealer's demand on the supplier which might follow from cumulation of discounts. The purpose of this provision is to allow spare-parts suppliers which do not offer as wide a range of goods as the manufacturer to compete on equal terms.

(16) Article 5(1), point 2(*d*) makes exemption subject to the conditions that the dealer must be able to purchase for customers in the common market volume-produced passenger cars with the specifications appropriate for their place of residence or where the vehicle is to be registered, in so far as the corresponding model is also supplied by the manufacturer through undertakings within the distribution system in that place (Article 13, point 10). This provision obviates the danger that the manufacturer and undertakings within the distribution network might make use of product differentiation as between parts of the common market to partition the market.

(17) Article 5(2) makes the exemption of the no-competition clause and of the ban on dealing in other makes of vehicle subject to further threshold conditions. This is to prevent the dealer from becoming economically over-dependent on the supplier because of such obligations, and abandoning the competitive activity which is nominally open to him, because to pursue it would be against the interests of the manufacturer or other undertakings within the distribution network.

(18) Under Article 5(2), point 1(*a*), the dealer may, where there are exceptional reasons, oppose application of excessive obligations covered by Article 3, point 3 or 5.

(19) The supplier may reserve the right to appoint further distribution and servicing undertakings in the contract territory or to alter the territory, but only if he can show that there are exceptional reasons for doing so (Article 5(2), point 1(*b*) and Article 5(3)). This is, for example, the case where there would otherwise be reason to apprehend a serious deterioration in the distribution or servicing of contract goods.

(20) Article 5(2), points 2 and 3 lay down minimum requirements for exemption which concern the duration and termination of the distribution and servicing agreement; the combined effect of a no-competition clause or a ban on dealing in other makes of vehicle, the investments the dealer makes in order to improve the distribution and servicing of contract goods and a short-term agreement or one terminable at short notice is greatly to increase the dealer's dependence on the supplier.

(21) In accordance with Article 1(2)(*a*) of Regulation No 19/65/EEC, restrictions or provisions which must not be contained in the agreements, if the declaration of inapplicability of Article 85(1) by this Regulation is to take effect, are to be specified.

(22) Agreements under which one motor vehicle manufacturer entrusts the distribution of its products to another must be excluded from the block exemption under this Regulation because of their far-reaching impact on competition (Article 6, point 1).

(23) An obligation to apply minimum resale prices or maximum trade discounts precludes exemption under this Regulation (Article 6, point 2).

(24) The exemption does not apply where the parties agree between themselves obligations concerning goods covered by this Regulation which would be acceptable in the combination of obligations which is exempted by Commission Regulations (EEC) No 1983/83 or (EEC) No 1984/83 on the application of Article 85(3) of the Treaty to categories of exclusive distribution agreements and exclusive purchasing agreements respectively, but which go beyond the scope of the obligations exempted by this Regulation (Article 6, point 3).

(25) Distribution and servicing agreements can be exempted, subject to the conditions laid down in Articles 5 and 6, so long as the application of obligations covered by Articles 1 to 4 of this Regulation brings about an improvement in distribution and servicing to the benefit of the consumer and effective competition exists, not only between manufacturers' distribution systems but also to a certain extent within each system within the common market. As regards the categories of products set out in Article 1 of this Regulation, the conditions necessary for effective competition, including competition in trade between Member States, may be taken to exist at present, so that European consumers may be considered in general to take an equitable share in the benefit from the operation of such competition.

(26) Articles 7, 8 and 9, concerning the retroactive effect of the exemption, are based on Articles 3 and 4 of Regulation No 19/65/EEC and Articles 4 to 7 of Regulation No 17. Article 10 embodies the Commission's powers under Article 7 of Regulation No 19/65/EEC to withdraw the benefit of its exemption or to alter its scope in individual cases, and lists several important examples of such cases.

(27) In view of the extensive effect of this Regulation on the persons it concerns, it is appropriate that it should not enter into force until 1 July 1985. In accordance with Article 2(1) of Regulation No 19/65/EEC, the exemption may be made applicable for a definite period. A period extending until 30 June 1995 is appropriate, because overall distribution schemes in the motor vehicle sector must be planned several years in advance.

(28) Agreements which fulfil the conditions set out in this Regulation need not be notified.

(29) This Regulation does not affect the application of Regulations (EEC) No 1983/83 or (EEC) No 1984/83 or of Commission Regulation (EEC) No 3604/82 of 23 December 1982 on the application of Article 85(3) of the Treaty to categories of specialization agreements, or the right to request a Commission decision in an individual case pursuant to Council Regulation No 17. It is without prejudice to laws and administrative measures of the Member States by which the latter, having regard to particular circumstances, prohibit or declare unenforceable particular restrictive obligations contained in an agreement exempted under this Regulation; the foregoing cannot, however, affect the primacy of Community law,

HAS ADOPTED THIS REGULATION:

Article 1

Pursuant to Article 85(3) of the Treaty it is hereby declared that subject to the conditions laid down in this Regulation Article 85(1) shall not apply to agreements to which only two undertakings are party and in which one contracting party agrees to supply within a defined territory of the common market

— only to the other party, or
— only to the other party and to a specified number of other undertakings within the distribution system,

for the purpose of resale certain motor vehicles intended for use on public roads and having three or more road wheels, together with spare parts therefor.   **[1186]**

Article 2

The exemption under Article 85(3) of the Treaty shall also apply where the obligation referred to in Article 1 is combined with an obligation on the supplier neither to sell contract goods to final consumers nor to provide them with servicing for contract goods in the contract territory.   **[1187]**

Article 3

The exemption under Article 85(3) of the Treaty shall also apply where the obligation referred to in Article 1 is combined with an obligation on the dealer:

1. not, without the supplier's consent, to modify contract goods or corresponding goods, unless such modification is the subject of a contract with a final consumer and concerns a particular motor vehicle within the contract programme purchased by that final consumer;
2. not to manufacture products which compete with contract goods;
3. neither to sell new motor vehicles which compete with contract goods nor to sell, at the premises used for the distribution of contract goods, new motor vehicles other than those offered for supply by the manufacturer;
4. neither to sell spare parts which compete with contract goods and do not match the quality of contract goods nor to use them for repair or maintenance of contract goods or corresponding goods;
5. not to conclude with third parties distribution or servicing agreements for goods which compete with contract goods;
6. without the supplier's consent, neither to conclude distribution or servicing agreements with undertakings operating in the contract territory for contract goods or corresponding goods nor to alter or terminate such agreements;

7. to impose upon undertakings with which the dealer has concluded agreements in accordance with point 6 obligations corresponding to those which the dealer has accepted in relation to the supplier and which are covered by Articles 1 to 4 and are in conformity with Articles 5 and 6;

8. outside the contract territory:

  (a) not to maintain branches or depots for the distribution of contract goods or corresponding goods,
  (b) not to seek customers for contract goods or corresponding goods;

9. not to entrust third parties with the distribution or servicing of contract goods or corresponding goods outside the contract territory;

10. to supply to a reseller:

  (a) contract goods or corresponding goods only where the reseller is an undertaking within the distribution system, or
  (b) spare parts within the contract programme only where they are for the purposes of repair or maintenance of a motor vehicle by the reseller;

11. to sell motor vehicles within the contract programme or corresponding goods to final consumers using the services of an intermediary only if that intermediary has prior written authority to purchase a specified motor vehicle and, as the case may be, to accept delivery thereof on their behalf;

12. to observe the obligations referred to in points 1 and 6 to 11 for a maximum period of one year after termination or expiry of the agreement. **[1188]**

Article 4

1. Articles 1, 2 and 3 shall apply notwithstanding any obligation imposed on the dealer to:

  (1) observe, for distribution and servicing, minimum standards which relate in particular to:

    (a) the equipment of the business premises and of the technical facilities for servicing;
    (b) the specialized and technical training of staff;
    (c) advertising;
    (d) the collection, storage and delivery to customers of contract goods or corresponding goods and servicing relating to them;
    (e) the repair and maintenance of contract goods and corresponding goods, particularly as concerns the safe and reliable functioning of motor vehicles;

  (2) order contract goods from the supplier only at certain times or within certain periods, provided that the interval between ordering dates does not exceed three months;

  (3) endeavour to sell, within the contract territory and within a specified period, such minimum quantity of contract goods as may be determined by agreement between the parties or, in the absence of such agreement, by the supplier on the basis of estimates of the dealer's potential sales;

  (4) keep in stock such quantity of contract goods as may be determined by agreement between the parties or, in the absence of such agreement, by the supplier on the basis of estimates of the dealer's potential sales of contract goods within the contract territory and within a specified period;

  (5) keep such demonstration vehicles within the contract programme, or such number thereof, as may be determined by agreement between the parties or, in the absence of such agreement, by the supplier on the basis of estimates of the dealer's potential sales of motor vehicles within the contract programme;

(6) perform guarantee work, free servicing and vehicle recall work for contract goods and corresponding goods;

(7) use only spare parts within the contract programme or corresponding goods for guarantee work, free servicing and vehicle recall work in respect of contract goods or corresponding goods;

(8) inform customers, in a general manner, of the extent to which spare parts from other sources might be used for the repair or maintenance of contract goods or corresponding goods;

(9) inform customers whenever spare parts from other sources have been used for the repair or maintenance of contract goods or corresponding goods for which spare parts within the contract programme or corresponding goods, bearing a mark of the manufacturer, were also available.

2. The exemption under Article 85(3) of the Treaty shall also apply where the obligation referred to in Article 1 is combined with obligations referred to in paragraph 1 above and such obligations fall in individual cases under the prohibition contained in Article 85(1).

[1189]

Article 5

1. Articles 1, 2 and 3 and Article 4(2) shall apply provided that:

(1) the dealer undertakes

(a) in respect of motor vehicles within the contract programme or corresponding thereto which have been supplied in the common market by another undertaking within the distribution network, to honour guarantees and to perform free servicing and vehicle recall work to an extent which corresponds to the dealer's obligation covered by point 6 of Article 4(1) but which need not exceed that imposed upon the undertaking within the distribution system or accepted by the manufacturer when supplying such motor vehicles;

(b) to impose upon the undertakings operating within the contract territory with which the dealer has concluded distribution and servicing agreements as provided for in point 6 of Article 3 an obligation to honour guarantees and to perform free servicing and vehicle recall work at least to the extent to which the dealer himself is so obliged;

(2) the supplier

(a) shall not without objectively valid reasons withhold consent to conclude, alter or terminate sub-agreements referred to in Article 3, point 6;

(b) shall not apply, in relation to the dealer's obligations referred to in Article 4(1), minimum requirements or criteria for estimates such that the dealer is subject to discrimination without objectively valid reasons or is treated inequitably;

(c) shall, in any scheme for aggregating quantities or values of goods obtained by the dealer from the supplier and from connected undertakings within a specified period for the purpose of calculating discounts, at least distinguish between supplies of

— motor vehicles within the contract programme.

— spare parts within the contract programme, for supplies of which the dealer is dependent on undertakings within the distribution network, and

— other goods;

(d) shall also supply to the dealer, for the purpose of performance of a contract of sale concluded between the dealer and a final customer in the common market, any passenger car which corresponds to a model within the contract programme and which is marketed by the manufacturer or with the manufacturer's consent in the Member State in which the vehicle is to be registered.

2. In so far as the dealer has, in accordance with Article 5(1), assumed obligations for the improvement of distribution and servicing structures, the exemption referred to in Article 3, points 3 and 5 shall apply to the obligation not to sell new motor vehicles other than those within the contract programme or not to make such vehicles the subject of a distribution and servicing agreement, provided that

(1) the parties

    (*a*) agree that the supplier shall release the dealer from the obligations referred to in Article 3, points 3 and 5 where the dealer shows that there are objectively valid reasons for doing so;

    (*b*) agree that the supplier reserves the right to conclude distribution and servicing agreements for contract goods with specified further undertakings operating within the contract territory or to alter the contract territory only where the supplier shows that there are objectively valid reasons for doing so;

(2) the agreement is for a period of at least four years or, if for an indefinite period, the period of notice for regular termination of the agreement is at least one year for both parties, unless

    — the supplier is obliged by law or by special agreement to pay appropriate compensation on termination of the agreement, or

    — the dealer is a new entrant to the distribution system and the period of the agreement, or the period of notice for regular termination of the agreement, is the first agreed by that dealer.

(3) each party undertakes to give the other at least six months' prior notice of intention not to renew an agreement concluded for a definite period.

3. A party may only invoke particular objectively valid grounds within the meaning of this Article which have been exemplified in the agreement if such grounds are applied without discrimination to undertakings within the distribution system in comparable cases.

4. The conditions for exemption laid down in this Article shall not affect the right of a party to terminate the agreement for cause. **[1190]**

Article 6

Articles 1, 2 and 3 and Article 4(2) shall not apply where:

1. both parties to the agreement or their connected undertakings are motor vehicle manufacturers; or
2. the manufacturer, the supplier or another undertaking within the distribution system obliges the dealer not to resell contract goods or corresponding goods below stated prices or not to exceed stated rates of trade discount; or
3. the parties make agreements or engage in concerted practices concerning motor vehicles having three or more road wheels or spare parts therefor which are exempted from the prohibition in Article 85(1) of the Treaty under Regulations (EEC) No 1983/83, or (EEC) No 1984/83 to an extent exceeding the scope of this Regulation. **[1191]**

Article 7

1. As regards agreements existing on 13 March 1962 and notified before 1 February 1963 and agreements, whether notified or not, falling under Article 4(2), point 1 of Regulation No 17, the declaration of inapplicability of Article 85(1) of the Treaty contained in this

Regulation shall apply with retroactive effect from the time at which the conditions of this Regulation were fulfilled.

2. As regards all other agreements notified before this Regulation entered into force, the declaration of inapplicability of Article 85(1) of the Treaty contained in this Regulation shall apply from the time at which the conditions of this Regulation were fulfilled, or from the date of notification, whichever is the later.   **[1192]**

Article 8

If agreements existing on 13 March 1962 and notified before 1 February 1963 or agreements to which Article 4(2), point 1 of Regulation No 17 applies and which were notified before 1 January 1967 are amended before 1 October 1985 so as to fulfil the conditions for application of this Regulation, and if the amendment is communicated to the Commission before 31 December 1985, the prohibition in Article 85(1) of the Treaty shall not apply in respect of the period prior to the amendment. The communication shall take effect from the time of its receipt by the Commission. Where the communication is sent by registered post, it shall take effect from the date shown on the postmark of the place of posting.   **[1193]**

Article 9

1. As regards agreements to which Article 85 of the Treaty applies as a result of the accession of the United Kingdom, Ireland and Denmark, Articles 7 and 8 shall apply except that the relevant dates shall be 1 January 1973 instead of 13 March 1962 and 1 July 1973 instead of 1 February 1963 and 1 January 1967.

2. As regards agreements to which Article 85 of the Treaty applies as a result of the accession of Greece, Articles 7 and 8 shall apply except that the relevant dates shall be 1 January 1981 instead of 13 March 1962 and 1 July 1981 instead of 1 February 1963 and 1 January 1967.

3. As regards agreements to which Article 85 of the Treaty applies as a result of the accession of the Kingdom of Spain and of the Portuguese Republic, Articles 7 and 8 shall apply except that the relevant dates shall be 1 January 1986 instead of 13 March 1962 and 1 July 1986 instead of 1 February 1963, 1 January 1967 and 1 October 1985. The amendment made to the agreements in accordance with Article 8 need not be notified to the Commission.[1]   **[1194]**

AMENDMENT
1 Paragraph added by the Act of Accession of the Kingdom of Spain and the Portuguese Republic, Annex I(IV)(13).

Article 10

The Commission may withdraw the benefit of the application of this Regulation, pursuant to Article 7 of Regulation No 19/65/EEC, where it finds that in an individual case an agreement which falls within the scope of this Regulation nevertheless has effects which are incompatible with the provisions of Article 85(3) of the Treaty, and in particular:

1. where, in the common market or a substantial part thereof, contract goods or corresponding goods are not subject to competition from products considered by consumers as similar by reason of their characteristics, price and intended use;
2. where the manufacturer or an undertaking within the distribution system continuously or systematically, and by means not exempted by this Regulation, makes it difficult for final consumers or other undertakings within the distribution system to obtain

contract goods or corresponding goods, or to obtain servicing for such goods, within the common market;

3. where, over a considerable period, prices or conditions of supply for contract goods or for corresponding goods are applied which differ substantially as between Member States, and such substantial differences are chiefly due to obligations exempted by this Regulation;

4. where, in agreements concerning the supply to the dealer of passenger cars which correspond to a model within the contract programme, prices or conditions which are not objectively justifiable are applied, with the object or the effect of partitioning the common market. **[1195]**

Article 11

The provisions of this Regulation shall also apply in so far as the obligations referred to in Articles 1 to 4 apply to undertakings which are connected with a party to an agreement.
[1196]

Article 12

This Regulation shall apply *mutatis mutandis* to concerted practices of the types defined in Articles 1 to 4. **[1197]**

Article 13

For the purposes of this Regulation the following terms shall have the following meanings.

1. "Distribution and servicing agreements" are framework agreements between two undertakings, for a definite or indefinite period, whereby the party supplying goods entrusts to the other the distribution and servicing of those goods.

2. "Parties" are the undertakings which are party to an agreement within the meaning of Article 1: "the supplier" being the undertaking which supplies the contract goods, and "the dealer", the undertaking entrusted by the supplier with the distribution and servicing of contract goods.

3. The "contract territory" is the defined territory of the common market to which the obligation of exclusive supply in the meaning of Article 1 applies.

4. "Contract goods" are motor vehicles intended for use on public roads and having three or more road wheels, and spare parts therefor, which are the subject of an agreement within the meaning of Article 1.

5. The "contract programme" refers to the totality of the contract goods.

6. "Spare parts" are parts which are to be installed in or upon a motor vehicle so as to replace components of that vehicle. They are to be distinguished from other parts and accessories according to customary usage in the trade.

7. The "manufacturer" is the undertaking

   (*a*) which manufacturers or procures the manufacture of the motor vehicles in the contract programme, or

   (*b*) which is connected with an undertaking described at (*a*).

8. "Connected undertakings" are:

   (*a*) undertakings one of which directly or indirectly

   — holds more than half of the capital or business assets of the other, or
   — has the power to exercise more than half the voting rights in the other, or
   — has the power to appoint more than half the members of the supervisory board, board of directors or bodies legally representing the other, or
   — has the right to manage the affairs of the other;

(b) undertakings in relation to which a third undertaking is able directly or indirectly to exercise such rights or powers as are mentioned in (a) above.

9. "Undertakings within the distribution system" are, besides the parties to the agreement, the manufacturer and undertakings which are entrusted by the manufacturer or with the manufacturer's consent with the distribution or servicing of contract goods or corresponding goods.

10. A "passenger car which corresponds to a model within the contract programme" is a passenger car

— manufactured or assembled in volume by the manufacturer, and
— identical as to body style, drive-line, chassis, and type of motor with a passenger car within the contract programme.

11. "Corresponding goods", "corresponding motor vehicles" and "corresponding parts" are those which are similar in kind to those in the contract programme, are distributed by the manufacturer or with the manufacturer's consent, and are the subject of a distribution or servicing agreement with an undertaking within the distribution system.

12. "Distribute" and "sell" include other forms of supply such as leasing.   **[1198]**

Article 14

This Regulation shall enter into force on 1 July 1985.
It shall remain in force until 30 June 1995.   **[1199]**

This Regulation shall be binding in its entirety and directly applicable in all Member States.

Done at Brussels, 12 December 1984.

COMMISSION NOTICE
of 12 December 1984

concerning Regulation (EEC) No 123/85 of 12 December 1984 on the application of Article 85(3) of the Treaty to certain categories of motor vehicle distribution and servicing agreements

In Regulation (EEC) No 123/85 on the block exemption of motor vehicle distribution agreements the Commission recognizes that exclusive and selective distribution in this industry is in principle compatible with Article 85(3) of the Treaty. This assessment is subject to a number of conditions. At the request of some of the commercial sectors involved, this notice sets out some of those conditions and lays down certain administrative principles for the procedures which the Commission might initiate under Article 7 of Council Regulation No 19/65/EEC in combination with Article 10, points 3 and 4 of Regulation (EEC) No 123/85, taking account of the present stage of integration of the European Community.

I

1. Freedom of movement of European consumers and limited availability of vehicle models

The Commission starts from the position that the common market affords advantages to European consumers, and that this is especially so where there is effective competition. Accordingly, Regulation (EEC) No 123/85 presupposes that in the motor vehicles sector effective competition exists between manufacturers and between their distribution networks. The European consumer must derive a fair share of the benefits which flow from the distribution and servicing agreements. Admittedly, the consumer may benefit from the fact that servicing is carried out by specialists (Article 3, points 3 and 5) and that such service can be obtained throughout the network from dealers and repairers who are obliged to observe minimum requirements (Article 4(1)).

However, the European consumer's basic rights include above all the right to buy a motor vehicle and to have it maintained or repaired wherever prices and quality are most advantageous to him.

(a) This right to buy relates to new vehicles from a manufacturer each of whose dealers offers them in a form and specification mainly required by final consumers in the dealer's contract territory (contract goods).

(b) In the interests of competition at the various stages of distribution in the common market and in those of European consumers, a certain limited availability of other vehicles within the distribution system is also considered indispensable. Any dealer within the distribution system must be able to order from a supplier within the distribution system any volume-produced passenger car which a final consumer has ordered from him and intends to register in another Member State, in the form and specification marketed by the manufacturer or with his consent in that Member State (passenger cars corresponding to those in the contract programme, Article 5(1), point 2(d) and Article 13, point 10 of Regulation (EEC) No 123/85).

This provision does not oblige the manufacturer to produce vehicles which he would not otherwise offer within the common market. Nor does it oblige the manufacturer to sell particular vehicle models in any particular part of the common market where he does not, or does not yet, wish to market them. He is only obliged to supply to a dealer within his distribution system a new passenger car required by that dealer to fulfil a contract with a final consumer and intended for another Member State where that dealer's contract programme includes cars of a corresponding kind.

2. Abusive hindrance

The European consumer must not be subject to abusive hindrance either in the exporting country, where he wishes to buy a vehicle, or in the country of destination, where he seeks to register it. The restrictions inherent in an exempted exclusive and selective distribution system do not represent abuses. However, further agreements or concerted practices between undertakings in the distribution system that limit the European consumer's final freedom to purchase do jeopardize the exemption given by the Regulation, as do unilateral measures on the part of a manufacturer or his importers or dealers which have a widespread effect against consumers' interests (Article 10, point 2). Examples are: dealers refuse to perform guarantee work on vehicles which they have not sold and which have been imported from other Member States; manufacturers or their importers withhold their cooperation in the registration of vehicles which European consumers have imported from other Member States; abnormally long delivery periods.

3. Intermediaries

The European consumer must be able to make use of the services of individuals or undertakings to assist in purchasing a new vehicle in another Member State (Article 3, points 10 and 11). However, except as regards contracts between dealers within the distribution system for the sale of contract goods, undertakings within the distribution system can be obliged not to supply new motor vehicles within the contract programme or corresponding vehicles to or through a third party who represents himself as an authorized reseller of new vehicles within the contract programme or corresponding vehicles or carries on an activity equivalent to that of a reseller. It is for the intermediary or the consumer to give the dealer within the distribution system documentary evidence that the intermediary, in buying and accepting delivery of a vehicle, is acting on behalf and for account of the consumer. **[1200]**

II

The Commission may withdraw the benefit of the application of Regulation (EEC) No 123/85, pursuant to Article 7 of Regulation No 19/65/EEC, where it finds that in an individual case an agreement which falls within the scope of Regulation (EEC) No 123/85 nevertheless has effects which are incompatible with the provisions of Article 85(3) of the Treaty, and in particular

— where, over a considerable period, prices or conditions of supply for contract goods or for corresponding goods are applied which differ substantially as between Member States, and such substantial differences are chiefly due to obligations exempted by Regulation (EEC) No 123/85 (Article 10, point 3);
— where, in agreements concerning the supply to the dealer of passenger cars which correspond to a model within the contract programme, prices or conditions which are not objectively justifiable are applied, with the object or effect of partitioning the common market (Article 10, point 4).

The Commission may pursue such proceedings in individual cases, upon application (particularly on the basis of complaints from consumers) or on its own initiative, in accordance with the procedural rules laid down in Council Regulation No 17 and Commission Regulation No 99/63/EEC, under which the parties concerned must be informed of the objections raised and given an opportunity to respond to them before the Commission adopts a decision. Whether the Commission initiates such proceedings depends chiefly on the results of preliminary inquiries, the circumstances of the case and the degree of prejudice to the public interest.

Price differentials for motor vehicles as between Member States are to a certain extent a reflection of the particular play of supply and demand in the areas concerned. Substantial price differences generally give reason to suspect that national measures or private restrictive practices are behind them.

In view of the present stage of integration of the common market, for the time being certain circumstances will not of themselves justify an investigation of whether an agreement exempted by Regulation (EEC) No 123/85 is incompatible with the conditions of Article 85(3) of the Treaty. For the time being, the Commission does not propose to carry out investigations into private practices under Article 10, point 3 or 4 of Regulation (EEC) No 123/85 where the following circumstances obtain (this does not exclude intervention by the Commission in particular cases):

1. Price differentials between Member States (Article 10, point 3 in association with Article 13, point 11)

Recommended net prices for resale to final consumers (list prices) of a motor vehicle within the contract programme in one Member State and of the same or a corresponding motor vehicle in another Member State differ, and

(*a*) the difference expressed in ECU does not exceed 12% of the lower price, or, over a period of less than one year, exceeds that percentage either

— by not more than a further 6% of the list price, or
— only in respect of an insignificant portion of the motor vehicles within the contract programme, or

(*b*) the difference is to be attributed, following analysis of the objective datas, to the fact that

— the purchaser of the vehicle in one of those Member States must pay taxes, charges or fees amounting in total to more than 100% of the net price, or
— the freedom to set the price or margin for the resale of the vehicle is directly

or indirectly subject in one of those Member States to restriction by national measures lasting longer than one year;

and that such measures do not represent infringements of the Treaty.

Insofar as they are public knowledge, prices net of discounts shall replace recommended net prices. Particular account will be taken, for an appropriate period, of alterations of the parities within the European Monetary System or fluctuations in exchange rates in a Member State.

2. **Price differentials between passenger cars within the contract programme and corresponding cars (Article 10, point 4 in association with Article 5(1), point 2(*d*) and Article 13, point 10)**

When selling to a dealer a passenger car corresponding to a model within the contract programme, the supplier charges an objectively justifiable supplement on account of special distribution costs and any differences in equipment and specification.

In a Member State where pricing is affected in the manner described at II 1(*b*) above, the supplier charges a further supplement; however, he does not exceed the price which would be charged in similar cases in that Member State not subject to such effects in which the lowest price net of tax is recommended for the sale to a final consumer of that vehicle within the contract programme (or, as the case may be, of a corresponding vehicle).

3. Where the limits indicated above are exceeded, the Commission may open a procedure on its own initiative under Article 10, points 3 and 4 of Regulation (EEC) No 123/85; whether it does so or not will depend mainly on the results of investigations that may be made as to whether the exempted agreement is in fact the principal cause of actual price differences in the meaning of Article 10, point 3 or 4 or, as the case may be, has led to a partitioning of the common market or is, in the light of experience, liable to do so. Price comparisons made in this connection will take account of differences in equipment and specification and in ancillary items such as the extent of the guarantee, delivery services or registration formalities.   **[1201]**

III

1. The rights of Member States, persons and associations of persons to make applications to the Commission under Article 3 of Council Regulation No 17 (i.e. complaints) are unaffected. The Commission will examine such complaints with all due diligence.
2. This notice is without prejudice to any finding of the Court of Justice of the European Communities or of courts of the Member States.
3. Any withdrawal of or amendment to this notice will be effected by publication in the *Official Journal of the European Communities.*   **[1202]**

REGULATION (EEC) No 417/85 OF THE COMMISSION
of 19 December 1984

on the application of Article 85(3) of the Treaty to categories of specialization agreements

THE COMMISSION OF THE EUROPEAN COMMUNITIES,

Having regard to the Treaty establishing the European Economic Community,

Having regard to Council Regulation (EEC) No 2821/71 of 20 December 1971 on the application of Article 85(3) of the Treaty to categories of agreements, decisions and concerted practices, as last amended by the Act of Accession of Greece, and in particular Article 1 thereof,

Having published a draft of this Regulation,

Having consulted the Advisory Committee on Restrictive Practices and Dominant Positions,

Whereas:

(1) Regulation (EEC) No 2821/71 empowers the Commission to apply Article 85(3) of the Treaty by Regulation to certain categories of agreements, decisions and concerted practices falling within the scope of Article 85(1) which relate to specialization, including agreements necessary for achieving it.

(2) Agreements on specialization in present or future production may fall within the scope of Article 85(1).

(3) Agreements on specialization in production generally contribute to improving the production or distribution of goods, because undertakings concerned can concentrate on the manufacture of certain products and thus operate more efficiently and supply the products more cheaply. It is likely that, given effective competition, consumers will receive a fair share of the resulting benefit.

(4) Such advantages can arise equally from agreements whereby each participant gives up the manufacture of certain products in favour of another participant and from agreements whereby the participants undertake to manufacture certain products or have them manufactured only jointly.

(5) The Regulation must specify what restrictions of competition may be included in specialization agreements. The restrictions of competition that are permitted in the Regulation in addition to reciprocal obligations to give up manufacture are normally essential for the making and implementation of such agreements. These restrictions are therefore, in general, indispensable for the attainment of the desired advantages for the participating undertakings and consumers. It may be left to the parties to decide which of these provisions they include in their agreements.

(6) The exemption must be limited to agreements which do not give rise to the possibility of eliminating competition in respect of a substantial part of the products in question. The Regulation must therefore apply only as long as the market share and turnover of the participating undertakings do not exceed a certain limit.

(7) It is, however, appropriate to offer undertakings which exceed the turnover limit set in the Regulation a simplified means of obtaining the legal certainty provided by the block exemption. This must allow the Commission to exercise effective supervision as well as simplifying its administration of such agreements.

(8) In order to facilitate the conclusion of long-term specialization agreements, which can have a bearing on the structure of the participating undertakings, it is appropriate to fix the period of validity of the Regulation at 13 years. If the circumstances on the basis of which the Regulation was adopted should change significantly within this period, the Commission will make the necessary amendments.

(9) Agreements, decisions and concerted practices which are automatically exempted pursuant to this Regulation need not be notified. Undertakings may none the less in an individual case request a decision pursuant to Council Regulation No 17, as last amended by the Act of Accession of Greece.

HAS ADOPTED THIS REGULATION:

Article 1

Pursuant to Article 85(3) of the Treaty and subject to the provisions of this Regulation, it is hereby declared that Article 85(1) of the Treaty shall not apply to agreements on specialization whereby, for the duration of the agreement, undertakings accept reciprocal obligations:

    (*a*) not to manufacture certain products or to have them manufactured, but to leave it to other parties to manufacture the products or have them manufactured; or

    (*b*) to manufacture certain products or have them manufactured only jointly.

Article 2

1. Apart from the obligations referred to in Article 1, no restrictions of competition may be imposed on the parties other than:

   (*a*) an obligation not to conclude with third parties specialization agreements relating to identical products or to products considered by users to be equivalent in view of their characteristics, price and intended use;

   (*b*) an obligation to procure products which are the subject of the specialization exclusively from another party, a joint undertaking or an undertaking jointly charged with their manufacture, except where they are obtainable on more favourable terms elsewhere and the other party, the joint undertaking or the undertaking charged with manufacture is not prepared to offer the same terms;

   (*c*) an obligation to grant other parties the exclusive right to distribute products which are the subject of the specialization provided that intermediaries and users can also obtain the products from other suppliers and the parties do not render it difficult for intermediaries or users thus to obtain the products.

2. Article 1 shall also apply where the parties undertake obligations of the types referred to in paragraph 1 but with a more limited scope than is permitted by that paragraph.

3. Article 1 shall apply notwithstanding that any of the following obligations, in particular, are imposed:

   (*a*) an obligation to supply other parties with products which are the subject of the specialization and in so doing to observe minimum standards of quality;

   (*b*) an obligation to maintain minimum stocks of products which are the subject of the specialization and of replacement parts for them;

   (*c*) an obligation to provide customer and guarantee services for products which are the subject of the specialization. **[1204]**

Article 3

1. Article 1 shall apply only if:

   (*a*) the products which are the subject of the specialization together with the participating undertakings' other products which are considered by users to be equivalent in view of their characteristics, price and intended use do not represent more than 20% of the market for such products in the common market or a substantial part thereof;

   (*b*) the aggregate annual turnover of all the participating undertakings does not exceed 500 million ECU.

2. Article 1 shall continue to apply if the market share referred to in paragraph 1(*a*) or the turnover referred to in paragraph 1(*b*) is exceeded during any period of two consecutive financial years by not more than one-tenth.

3. Where one of the limits laid down in paragraphs 1 and 2 is exceeded, Article 1 shall continue to apply for a period of six months following the end of the financial year during which it was exceeded. **[1205]**

Article 4

1. The exemption provided for in Article 1 shall also apply to agreements involving participating undertakings whose aggregate turnover exceeds the limits laid down in Article 3(1)(*b*) and (2), on condition that the agreements in question are notified to the Commission in accordance with the provisions of Commission Regulation No 27, and that the Commission does not oppose such exemption within a period of six months.

2. The period of six months shall run from the date on which the notification is received by the Commission. Where, however, the notification is made by registered post, the period shall run from the date shown on the postmark of the place of posting.

3. Paragraph 1 shall apply only if:

(a) express reference is made to this Article in the notification or in a communication accompanying it; and

(b) the information furnished with the notification is complete and in accordance with the facts.

4. The benefit of paragraph 1 may be claimed for agreements notified before the entry into force of this Regulation by submitting a communication to the Commission referring expressly to this Article and to the notification. Paragraphs 2 and 3(b) shall apply *mutatis mutandis*.

5. The Commission may oppose the exemption. It shall oppose exemption if it receives a request to do so from a Member State within three months of the forwarding to the Member State of the notification referred to in paragraph 1 or of the communication referred to in paragraph 4. This request must be justified on the basis of considerations relating to the competition rules of the Treaty.

6. The Commission may withdraw the opposition to the exemption at any time. However, where the opposition was raised at the request of a Member State and this request is maintained, it may be withdrawn only after consultation of the Advisory Committee on Restrictive Practices and Dominant Positions.

7. If the opposition is withdrawn because the undertakings concerned have shown that the conditions of Article 85(3) are fulfilled, the exemption shall apply from the date of notification.

8. If the opposition is withdrawn because the undertakings concerned have amended the agreement so that the conditions of Article 85(3) are fulfilled, the exemption shall apply from the date on which the amendments take effect.

9. If the Commission opposes exemption and the opposition is not withdrawn, the effects of the notification shall be governed by the provisions of Regulation No 17.

[1206]

Article 5

1. Information acquired pursuant to Article 4 shall be used only for the purposes of this Regulation.

2. The Commission and the authorities of the Member States, their officials and other servants shall not disclose information acquired by them pursuant to this Regulation of a kind that is covered by the obligation of professional secrecy.

3. Paragraphs 1 and 2 shall not prevent publication of general information or surveys which do not contain information relating to particular undertakings or associations of undertakings.   **[1207]**

Article 6

For the purpose of calculating total annual turnover within the meaning of Article 3(1)(b), the turnovers achieved during the last financial year by the participating undertakings in respect of all goods and services excluding tax shall be added together. For this purpose, no account shall be taken of dealings between the participating undertakings or between these undertakings and a third undertaking jointly charged with manufacture.

[1208]

Article 7

1. For the purposes of Article 3(1)(*a*) and (*b*) and Article 6, participating undertakings are:

   (*a*) undertakings party to the agreement;
   (*b*) undertakings in which a party to the agreement, directly or indirectly:

   — owns more than half the capital or business assets,
   — has the power to exercise more than half the voting rights,
   — has the power to appoint at least half the members of the supervisory board, board of management or bodies legally representing the undertakings, or
   — has the right to manage the affairs;

   (*c*) undertakings which directly or indirectly have in or over a party to the agreement the rights or powers listed in (*b*);
   (*d*) undertakings in or over which an undertaking referred to in (*c*) directly or indirectly has the rights or powers listed in (*b*).

2. Undertakings in which the undertakings referred to in paragraph 1(*a*) to (*d*) directly or indirectly jointly have the rights or powers set out in paragraph 1(*b*) shall also be considered to be participating undertakings.   **[1209]**

Article 8

The Commission may withdraw the benefit of this Regulation, pursuant to Article 7 of Regulation (EEC) No 2821/71, where it finds in a particular case that an agreement exempted by this Regulation nevertheless has effects which are incompatible with the conditions set out in Article 85(3) of the Treaty, and in particular where:

   (*a*) the agreement is not yielding significant results in terms of rationalization or consumers are not receiving a fair share of the resulting benefit; or
   (*b*) the products which are the subject of the specialization are not subject in the common market or a substantial part thereof to effective competition from identical products or products considered by users to be equivalent in view of their characteristics, price and intended use.   **[1210]**

Article 9

This Regulation shall apply *mutatis mutandis* to decisions of associations of undertakings and concerted practices.

[Article 9A

The prohibition in Article 85(1) of the Treaty shall not apply to the specialization agreements which were in existence at the date of the accession of the Kingdom of Spain and of the Portuguese Republic and which, by reason of this accession, fall within the scope of Article 85(1), if, before 1 July 1986, they are so amended that they comply with the conditions laid down in this Regulation.][1]   **[1211]**

AMENDMENT
   1 Article 9A inserted by the Act of Accession of the Kingdom of Spain and the Portuguese Republic, Anex I(IV)(14).

Article 10

1. This Regulation shall enter into force on 1 March 1985. It shall apply until 31 December 1997.

2. Commission Regulation (EEC) No 3604/82 is hereby repealed.   **[1212]**

This Regulation shall be binding in its entirety and directly applicable in all Member States.
Done at Brussels, 19 December 1984.

REGULATION (EEC) No 418/85 OF THE COMMISSION
of 19 December 1984

on the application of Article 85(3) of the Treaty to categories of research and development agreements

THE COMMISSION OF THE EUROPEAN COMMUNITIES,
Having regard to the Treaty establishing the European Economic Community,
Having regard to Council Regulation (EEC) No 2821/71 of 20 December 1971 on the application of Article 85(3) of the Treaty to categories of agreements, decisions and concerted practices, as last amended by the Act of Accession of Greece, and in particular Article 1 thereof,
Having published a draft of this Regulation,
Having consulted the Advisory Committee on Restrictive Practices and Dominant Positions,
Whereas:

(1) Regulation (EEC) No 2821/71 empowers the Commission to apply Article 85(3) of the Treaty by Regulation to certain categories of agreements, decisions and concerted practices falling within the scope of Article 85(1) which have as their object the research and development of products or processes up to the stage of industrial application, and exploitation of the results, including provisions regarding industrial property rights and confidential technical knowledge.

(2) As stated in the Commission's 1968 notice concerning agreements, decisions and concerted practices in the field of cooperation between enterprises, agreements on the joint execution of research work or the joint development of the results of the research, up to but not including the stage of industrial application, generally do not fall within the scope of Article 85(1) of the Treaty. In certain circumstances, however, such as where the parties agree not to carry out other research and development in the same field, thereby forgoing the opportunity of gaining competitive advantages over the other parties, such agreements may fall within Article 85(1) and should therefore not be excluded from this Regulation.

(3) Agreements providing for both joint research and development and joint exploitation of the results may fall within Article 85(1) because the parties jointly determine how the products developed are manufactured or the processes developed are applied or how related intellectual property rights or know-how are exploited.

(4) Cooperation in research and development and in the exploitation of the results generally promotes technical and economic progress by increasing the dissemination of technical knowledge between the parties and avoiding duplication of research and development work, by stimulating new advances through the exchange of complementary technical knowledge, and by rationalizing the manufacture of the products or application of the processes arising out of the research and development. These aims can be achieved only where the research and development programme and its objectives are clearly defined and each of the parties is given the opportunity of exploiting any of the results of the programme that interest it; where universities or research institutes participate and are not interested in the industrial exploitation of the results, however, it may be agreed that they may use the said results solely for the purpose of further research.

(5) Consumers can generally be expected to benefit from the increased volume and effectiveness of research and development through the introduction of new or improved products or services or the reduction of prices brought about by new or improved processes.

(6) This Regulation must specify the restrictions of competition which may be included in the exempted agreements. The purpose of the permitted restrictions is to concentrate the research activities of the parties in order to improve their chances of success, and to facilitate the introduction of new products and services onto the market. These restrictions are generally necessary to secure the desired benefits for the parties and consumers.

(7) The joint exploitation of results can be considered as the natural consequence of joint research and development. It can take different forms ranging from manufacture to the exploitation of intellectual property rights or know-how that substantially contributes to technical or economic progress. In order to attain the benefits and objectives described above and to justify the restrictions of competition which are exempted, the joint exploitation must relate to products or processes for which the use of the results of the research and development is decisive. Joint exploitation is not therefore justified where it relates to improvements which were not made within the framework of a joint research and development programme but under an agreement having some other principal objective, such as the licensing of intellectual property rights, joint manufacture or specialization, and merely containing ancillary provisions on joint research and development.

(8) The exemption granted under the Regulation must be limited to agreements which do not afford the undertakings the possibility of eliminating competition in respect of a substantial part of the products in question. In order to guarantee that several independent poles of research can exist in the common market in any economic sector, it is necessary to exclude from the block exemption agreements between competitors whose combined share of the market for products capable of being improved or replaced by the results of the research and development exceeds a certain level at the time the agreement is entered into.

(9) In order to guarantee the maintenance of effective competition during joint exploitation of the results, it is necessary to provide that the block exemption will cease to apply if the parties' combined shares of the market for the products arising out of the joint research and development become too great. However, it should be provided that the exemption will continue to apply, irrespective of the parties' market shares, for a certain period after the commencement of joint exploitation, so as to await stabilization of their market shares, particularly after the introduction of an entirely new product, and to guarantee a minimum period of return on the generally substantial investments involved.

(10) Agreements between undertakings which do not fulfil the market share conditions laid down in the Regulation may, in appropriate cases, be granted an exemption by individual decision, which will in particular take account of world competition and the particular circumstances prevailing in the manufacture of high technology products.

(11) It is desirable to list in the Regulation a number of obligations that are commonly found in research and development agreements but that are normally not restrictive of competition and to provide that, in the event that, because of the particular economic or legal circumstances, they should fall within Article 85(1), they also would be covered by the exemption. This list is not exhaustive.

(12) The Regulation must specify what provisions may not be included in agreements if these are to benefit from the block exemption by virtue of the fact that such provisions are restrictions falling within Article 85(1) for which there can be no general presumption that they will lead to the positive effects required by Article 85(3).

(13) Agreements which are not automatically covered by the exemption because they include provisions that are not expressly exempted by the Regulation and are not expressly excluded from exemption are none the less capable of benefiting from the general presumption of compatibility with Article 85(3) on which the block exemption is based. It will be possible for the Commission rapidly to establish whether this is the case for a particular agreement. Such an agreement should therefore be deemed to be covered by the exemption provided for in this Regulation where it is notified to the Commission and the Commission does not oppose the application of the exemption within a specified period of time.

(14) Agreements covered by this Regulation may also take advantage of provisions contained in other block exemption Regulations of the Commission, and in particular Regulation (EEC) No 417/85 on specialization agreements, Regulation (EEC) No 1983/83 on exclusive distribution agreements, Regulation (EEC) No 1984/83, on exclusive purchasing agreements and Regulation (EEC) No 2349/84 on patent licensing agreements, if they fulfil the conditions set out in these Regulations. The provisions of the aforementioned Regulations are, however, not applicable in so far as this Regulation contains specific rules.

(15) If individual agreements exempted by this Regulation nevertheless have effects which are incompatible with Article 85(3), the Commission may withdraw the benefit of the block exemption.

(16) The Regulation should apply with retroactive effect to agreements in existence when the Regulation comes into force where such agreements already fulfil its conditions or are modified to do so. The benefit of these provisions may not be claimed in actions pending at the

date of entry into force of this Regulation, nor may it be relied on as grounds for claims for damages against third parties.

(17) Since research and development cooperation agreements are often of a long-term nature, especially where the cooperation extends to the exploitation of the results, it is appropriate to fix the period of validity of the Regulation at 13 years. If the circumstances on the basis of which the Regulation was adopted should change significantly within this period, the Commission will make the necessary amendments.

(18) Agreements which are automatically exempted pursuant to this Regulation need not be notified. Undertakings may nevertheless in a particular case request a decision pursuant to Council Regulation No 17, as last amended by the Act of Accession of Greece,

HAS ADOPTED THIS REGULATION:

Article 1

1. Pursuant to Article 85(3) of the Treaty and subject to the provisions of this Regulation, it is hereby declared that Article 85(1) of the Treaty shall not apply to agreements entered into between undertakings for the purpose of:

(a) joint research and development of products or processes and joint exploitation of the results of that research and development;

(b) joint exploitation of the results of research and development of products or processes jointly carried out pursuant to a prior agreement between the same undertakings; or

(c) joint research and development of products or processes excluding joint exploitation of the results, in so far as such agreements fall within the scope of Article 85(1).

2. For the purposes of this Regulation:

(a) *research and development of products or processes* means the acquisition of technical knowledge and the carrying out of theoretical analysis, systematic study or experimentation, including experimental production, technical testing of products or processes, the establishment of the necessary facilities and the obtaining of intellectual property rights for the results;

(b) *contract processes* means processes arising out of the research and development;

(c) *contract products* means products or services arising out of the research and development or manufactured or provided applying the contract processes;

(d) *exploitation of the results* means the manufacture of the contract products or the application of the contract processes or the assignment or licensing of intellectual property rights or the communication of know-how required for such manufacture or application;

(e) *technical knowledge* means technical knowledge which is either protected by an intellectual property right or is secret (know-how).

3. Research and development of the exploitation of the results are carried out *jointly* where:

(a) the work involved is:

— carried out by a joint team, organization or undertaking,
— jointly entrusted to a third party, or
— allocated between the parties by way of specialization in research, development or production;

(b) the parties collaborate in any way in the assignment or the licensing of intellectual property rights or the communication of know-how, within the meaning of paragraph 2(d), to third parties. **[1213]**

Article 2

The exemption provided for in Article 1 shall apply on condition that:

(a) the joint research and development work is carried out within the framework of a programme defining the objectives of the work and the field in which it is to be carried out;

(b) all the parties have access to the results of the work;

(c) where the agreement provides only for joint research and development, each party is free to exploit the results of the joint research and development and any pre-existing technical knowledge necessary therefor independently;

(d) the joint exploitation relates only to results which are protected by intellectual property rights or constitute know-how which substantially contributes to technical or economic progress and that the results are decisive for the manufacture of the contract products or the application of the contract processes;

(e) any joint undertaking or third party charged with manufacture of the contract products is required to supply them only to the parties;

(f) undertakings charged with manufacture by way of specialization in production are required to fulfil orders for supplies from all the parties.   **[1214]**

Article 3

1. Where the parties are not competing manufacturers of products capable of being improved or replaced by the contract products, the exemption provided for in Article 1 shall apply for the duration of the research and development programme and, where the results are jointly exploited, for five years from the time the contract products are first put on the market within the common market.

2. Where two or more of the parties are competing manufacturers within the meaning of paragraph 1, the exemption provided for in Article 1 shall apply for the period specified in paragraph 1 only if, at the time the agreement is entered into, the parties' combined production of the products capable of being improved or replaced by the contract products does not exceed 20% of the market for such products in the common market or a substantial part thereof.

3. After the end of the period referred to in paragraph 1, the exemption provided for in Article 1 shall continue to apply as long as the production of the contract products together with the parties' combined production of other products which are considered by users to be equivalent in view of their characteristics, price and intended use does not exceed 20% of the total market for such products in the common market or a substantial part thereof. Where contract products are components used by the parties for the manufacture of other products, reference shall be made to the markets for such of those latter products for which the components represent a significant part.

4. The exemption provided for in Article 1 shall continue to apply where the market share referred to in paragraph 3 is exceeded during any period of two consecutive financial years by not more than one-tenth.

5. Where market shares referred to in paragraphs 3 and 4 are exceeded, the exemption provided for in Article 1 shall continue to apply for a period of six months following the end of the financial year during which it was exceeded.   **[1215]**

Article 4

1. The exemption provided for in Article 1 shall also apply to the following restrictions of competition imposed on the parties:

(a) an obligation not to carry out independently research and development in the field to which the programme relates or in a closely connected field during the execution of the programme;

(b) an obligation not to enter into agreements with third parties on research and development in the field to which the programme relates or in a closely connected field during the execution of the programme;

(c) an obligation to procure the contract products exclusively from parties, joint organizations or undertakings or third parties, jointly charged with their manufacture;

(d) an obligation not to manufacture the contract products or apply the contract processes in territories reserved for other parties;

(e) an obligation to restrict the manufacture of the contract products or application of the contract processes to one or more technical fields of application, except where two or more of the parties are competitors within the meaning of Article 3 at the time the agreement is entered into;

(f) an obligation not to pursue, for a period of five years from the time the contract products are first put on the market within the common market, an active policy of putting the products on the market in territories reserved for other parties, and in particular not to engage in advertising specifically aimed at such territories or to establish any branch or maintain any distribution depot there for the distribution of the products, provided that users and intermediaries can obtain the contract products from other suppliers and the parties do not render it difficult for intermediaries and users to thus obtain the products;

(g) an obligation on the parties to communicate to each other any experience they may gain in exploiting the results and to grant each other non-exclusive licences for inventions relating to improvements or new applications.

2. The exemption provided for in Article 1 shall also apply where in a particular agreement the parties undertake obligations of the types referred to in paragraph 1 but with a more limited scope than is permitted by that paragraph. **[1216]**

Article 5

1. Article 1 shall apply notwithstanding that any of the following obligations, in particular, are imposed on the parties during the currency of the agreement:

(a) an obligation to communicate patented or non-patented technical knowledge necessary for the carrying out of the research and development programme for the exploitation of its results;

(b) an obligation not to use any know-how received from another party for purposes other than carrying out the research and development programme and the exploitation of its results;

(c) an obligation to obtain and maintain in force intellectual property rights for the contract products or processes;

(d) an obligation to preserve the confidentiality of any know-how received or jointly developed under the research and development programme; this obligation may be imposed even after the expiry of the agreement;

(e) an obligation:

(i) to inform other parties of infringements of their intellectual property rights,
(ii) to take legal action against infringers, and
(iii) to assist in any such legal action or share with the other parties in the cost thereof;

(f) an obligation to pay royalties or render services to other parties to compensate for unequal contributions to the joint research and development or unequal exploitation of its results;

(g) an obligation to share royalties received from third parties with other parties;
(h) an obligation to supply other parties with minimum quantities of contract
      products and to observe minimum standards of quality.

2. In the event that, because of particular circumstances, the obligations referred to
in paragraph 1 fall within the scope of Article 85(1), they also shall be covered by the
exemption. The exemption provided for in this paragraph shall also apply where in a
particular agreement the parties undertake obligations of the types referred to in paragraph
1 but with a more limited scope than is permitted by that paragraph.   **[1217]**

Article 6

The exemption provided for in Article 1 shall not apply where the parties, by agreement,
decision or concerted practice:

(a) are restricted in their freedom to carry out research and development
      independently or in cooperation with third parties in a field unconnected with
      that to which the programme relates or, after its completion, in the field to
      which the programme relates or in a connected field;
(b) are prohibited after completion of the research and development programme
      from challenging the validity of intellectual property rights which the parties
      hold in the common market and which are relevant to the programme or, after
      the expiry of the agreement, from challenging the validity of intellectual property
      rights which the parties hold in the common market and which protect the results
      of the research and development;
(c) are restricted as to the quantity of the contract products they may manufacture
      or sell or as to the number of operations employing the contract process they
      may carry out;
(d) are restricted in their determination of prices, components of prices or discounts
      when selling the contract products to third parties;
(e) are restricted as to the customers they may serve, without prejudice to
      Article 4(1)(e);
(f) are prohibited from putting the contract products on the market or pursuing
      an active sales policy for them in territories within the common market that
      are reserved for other parties after the end of the period referred to in
      Article 4(1)(f);
(g) are prohibited from allowing third parties to manufacture the contract products
      or apply the contract processes in the absence of joint manufacture;
(h) are required:

— to refuse without any objectively justified reason to meet demand from users
      or dealers established in their respective territories who would market the
      contract products in other territories within the common market, or
— to make it difficult for users or dealers to obtain the contract products from
      other dealers within the common market, and in particular to exercise intellec-
      tual property rights or take measures so as to prevent users or dealers from
      obtaining, or from putting on the market within the common market, products
      which have been lawfully put on the market within the common market by
      another party or with its consent.   **[1218]**

Article 7

1. The exemption provided for in this Regulation shall also apply to agreements of the
kinds described in Article 1 which fulfil the conditions laid down in Articles 2 and 3 and
which contain obligations restrictive of competition which are not covered by Articles
4 and 5 and do not fall within the scope of Article 6, on condition that the agreements

in question are notified to the Commission in accordance with the provisions of Commission Regulation No 27, and that the Commission does not oppose such exemption within a period of six months.

2. The period of six months shall run from the date on which the notification is received by the Commission. Where, however, the notification is made by registered post, the period shall run from the date shown on the postmark of the place of posting.

3. Paragraph 1 shall apply only if:

    (*a*) express reference is made to this Article in the notification or in a communication accompanying it, and

    (*b*) the information furnished with the notification is complete and in accordance with the facts.

4. The benefit of paragraph 1 may be claimed for agreements notified before the entry into force of this Regulation by submitting a communication to the Commission referring expressly to this Article and to the notification. Paragraphs 2 and 3(*b*) shall apply *mutatis mutandis*.

5. The Commission may oppose the exemption. It shall oppose exemption if it receives a request to do so from a Member State within three months of the forwarding to the Member State of the notification referred to in paragraph 1 or of the communication referred to in paragraph 4. This request must be justified on the basis of considerations relating to the competition rules of the Treaty.

6. The Commission may withdraw the opposition to the exemption at any time. However, where the opposition was raised at the request of a Member State and this request is maintained, it may be withdrawn only after consultation of the Advisory Committee on Restrictive Practices and Dominant Positions.

7. If the opposition is withdrawn because the undertakings concerned have shown that the conditions of Article 85(3) are fulfilled, the exemption shall apply from the date of notification.

8. If the opposition is withdrawn because the undertakings concerned have amended the agreement so that the conditions of Article 85(3) are fulfilled, the exemption shall apply from the date on which the amendments take effect.

9. If the Commission opposes exemption and the opposition is not withdrawn, the effects of the notification shall be governed by the provisions of Regulation No 17.

[1219]

Article 8

1. Information acquired pursuant to Article 7 shall be used only for the purposes of this Regulation.

2. The Commission and the authorities of the Member States, their officials and other servants shall not disclose information acquired by them pursuant to this Regulation of a kind that is covered by the obligation of professional secrecy.

3. Paragraphs 1 and 2 shall not prevent publication of general information or surveys which do not contain information relating to particular undertakings or associations of undertakings.

[1220]

Article 9

1. The provisions of this Regulation shall also apply to rights and obligations which the parties create for undertakings connected with them. The market shares held and the actions

and measures taken by connected undertakings shall be treated as those of the parties themselves.

2. Connected undertakings for the purposes of this Regulation are:

(a) undertakings in which a party to the agreement, directly or indirectly:
  – owns more than half the capital or business assets,
  – has the power to exercise more than half the voting rights,
  – has the power to appoint more than half the members of the supervisory board, board of directors or bodies legally representing the undertakings, or
  – has the right to manage the affairs;

(b) undertakings which directly have in or over a party to the agreement the rights or powers listed in (a);

(c) undertakings in or over which an undertaking referred to in (b) directly or indirectly has the rights or powers listed in (a);

3. Undertakings in which the parties to the agreement or undertakings connected with them jointly have, directly or indirectly, the rights or powers set out in paragraph 2(a) shall be considered to be connected with each of the parties to the agreement. **[1221]**

Article 10

The Commission may withdraw the benefit of this Regulation, pursuant to Article 7 of Regulation (EEC) No 2821/71, where it finds in a particular case that an agreement exempted by this Regulation nevertheless has certain effects which are incompatible with the conditions laid down in Article 85(3) of the Treaty, and in particular where:

(a) the existence of the agreement substantially restricts the scope for third parties to carry out research and development in the relevant field because of the limited research capacity available elsewhere;

(b) because of the particular structure of supply, the existence of the agreement substantially restricts the access of third parties to the market for the contract products;

(c) without any objectively valid reason, the parties do not exploit the results of the joint research and development;

(d) the contract products are not subject in the whole or a substantial part of the common market to effective competition from identical products or products considered by users as equivalent in view of their characteristics, price and intended use. **[1222]**

Article 11

1. In the case of agreements notified to the Commission before 1 March 1985, the exemption provided for in Article 1 shall have retroactive effect from the time at which the conditions for application of this Regulation were fulfilled or, where the agreement does not fall within Article 4(2)(3)(b) of Regulation No 17, not earlier than the date of notification.

2. In the case of agreements existing on 13 March 1962 and notified to the Commission before 1 February 1963, the exemption shall have retroactive effect from the time at which the conditions for application of this Regulation were fulfilled.

3. Where agreements which were in existence on 13 March 1962 and which were notified to the Commission before 1 February 1963, or which are covered by Article 4(2)(3)(b) of Regulation No 17 and were notified to the Commission before 1 January 1967, are amended before 1 September 1985 so as to fulfil the conditions for application of this Regulation, such amendment being communicated to the Commission before 1 October

1985, the prohibition laid down in Article 85(1) of the Treaty shall not apply in respect of the period prior to the amendment. The communication of amendments shall take effect from the date of their receipt by the Commission. Where the communication is sent by registered post, it shall take effect from the date shown on the postmark of the place of posting.

4. In the case of agreements to which Article 85 of the Treaty applies as a result of the accession of the United Kingdom, Ireland and Denmark, paragraphs 1 to 3 shall apply except that the relevant dates shall be 1 January 1973 instead of 13 March 1962 and 1 July 1973 instead of 1 February 1963 and 1 January 1967.

5. In the case of agreements to which Article 85 of the Treaty applies as a result of the accession of Greece, paragraphs 1 to 3 shall apply except that the relevant dates shall be 1 January 1981 instead of 13 March 1962 and 1 July 1981 instead of 1 February 1963 and 1 January 1967.

[6. As regards agreements to which Article 83 of the Treaty applies as a result of the accession of the Kingdom of Spain and of the Portuguese Republic, paragraphs 1 to 3 shall apply except that the relevant dates should be 1 January 1986 instead of 13 March 1962 and 1 July 1986 instead of 1 February 1963, I January 1967, 1 March 1985 and 1 September 1985. The amendment made of the agreements in accordance with the provisions of paragraph 3 need not be notified to the Commission.][1]   **[1223]**

AMENDMENTS
1 Paragraph added by the Act of Accession of the Kingdom of Spain and the Portuguese Republic, Annex I(IV)(15).

Article 12

This Regulation shall apply *mutatis mutandis* to decisions of associations of undertakings.
           [1224]

Article 13

This Regulation shall enter into force on 1 March 1985.
It shall apply until 31 December 1997.   **[1225]**

This Regulation shall be binding in its entirety and directly applicable in all Member States.

Done at Brussels, 19 December 1984.

REGULATION (EEC) No 4056/86 OF THE COUNCIL
of 22 December 1986

laying down detailed rules for the application of Articles 85 and 86 of the Treaty to maritime transport

THE COUNCIL OF THE EUROPEAN COMMUNITIES,
    Having regard to the Treaty establishing the European Economic Community, and in particular Articles 84(2) and 87 thereof,
    Having regard to the proposal from the Commission,
    Having regard to the opinion of the European Parliament,
    Having regard to the opinion of the Economic and Social Committee,
    Whereas the rules on competition form part of the Treaty's general provisions which also apply to maritime transport; whereas detailed rules for applying those provisions are set out in the Chapter of the Treaty dealing with the rules on competition or are to be determined by the procedures laid down therein;

Whereas according to Council Regulation No 141, Council Regulation No 17 does not apply to transport; whereas Council Regulation (EEC) No 1017/68 applies to inland transport only; whereas, consequently, the Commission has no means at present of investigating directly cases of suspected infringement of Articles 85(1) and 86 in maritime transport; whereas, moreover, the Commission lacks such powers of its own to take decisions or impose penalties as are necessary for it to bring to an end infringements established by it;

Whereas this situation necessitates the adoption of a Regulation applying the rules of competition to maritime transport; whereas Council Regulation (EEC) No 954/79 of 15 May 1979 concerning the ratification by Member States of, or their accession to, the United Nations Convention on a Code of Conduct for Liner Conferences will result in the application of the Code of Conduct to a considerable number of conferences serving the Community; whereas the Regulation applying the rules of competition to maritime transport foreseen in the last recital of Regulation (EEC) No 954/79 should take account of the adoption of the Code;

Whereas, as far as conferences subject to the Code of Conduct are concerned, the Regulation should supplement the Code or make it more precise;

Whereas it appears preferable to exclude tramp vessel services from the scope of this Regulation, rates for these services being freely negotiated on a case-by-case basis in accordance with supply and demand conditions;

Whereas this Regulation should take account of the necessity, on the one hand to provide for implementing rules that enable the Commission to ensure that competition is not unduly distorted within the common market, and on the other hand to avoid excessive regulation of the sector;

Whereas this Regulation should define the scope of the provisions of Articles 85 and 86 of the Treaty, taking into account the distinctive characteristics of maritime transport; whereas trade between Member States may be affected where restrictive practices or abuses concern international maritime transport, including intra-Community transport, from or to Community ports; whereas such restrictive practices or abuses may influence competition, firstly, between ports in different Member States by altering their respective catchment areas, and secondly, between activities in those catchment areas, and disturb trade patterns within the common market;

Whereas certain types of technical agreement, decisions and concerted practices may be excluded from the prohibition on restrictive practices on the ground that they do not, as a general rule, restrict competition;

Whereas provision should be made for block exemption of liner conferences; whereas liner conferences have a stabilizing effect, assuring shippers of reliable services; whereas they contribute generally to providing adequate efficient scheduled maritime transport services and give fair consideration to the interests of users; whereas such results cannot be obtained without the cooperation that shipping companies promote within conferences in relation to rates and, where appropriate, availability of capacity or allocation of cargo for shipment, and income; whereas in most cases conferences continue to be subject to effective competition from both non-conference scheduled services and, in certain circumstances, from tramp services and from other modes of transport; whereas the mobility of fleets, which is a characteristic feature of the structure of availability in the shipping field, subjects conferences to constant competition which they are unable as a rule to eliminate as far as a substantial proportion of the shipping services in question is concerned;

Whereas, however, in order to prevent conferences from engaging in practices which are incompatible with Article 85(3) of the Treaty, certain conditions and obligations should be attached to the exemption;

Whereas the aim of the conditions should be to prevent conferences from imposing restrictions on competition which are not indispensable to the attainment of the objectives on the basis of which exemption is granted; whereas, to this end, conferences should not, in respect of a given route, apply rates and conditions of carriage which are differentiated solely by reference to the country of origin or destination of the goods carried and thus cause within the Community deflections of trade that are harmful to certain ports, shippers, carriers or providers of services ancillary to transport; whereas, furthermore, loyalty arrangements should be permitted only in accordance with rules which do not restrict unilaterally the freedom of users and consequently competition in the shipping industry, without prejudice, however, to the right of a conference to impose penalties on users who seek by improper means to evade the obligation of loyalty required in exchange for the rebates, reduced freight rates or commission granted to them by the conference; whereas users must be free to determine the undertakings to which they have recourse in respect of inland transport or quayside services not covered by the freight charge or by other charges agreed with the shipping line;

Whereas certain obligations should also be attached to the exemption; whereas in this respect users must at all times be in a position to acquaint themselves with the rates and conditions of carriage applied by members of the conference, since in the case of inland transports organized by shippers, the latter continue to be subject to Regulation (EEC) No 1017/68; whereas provision should be made that awards given at arbitration and recommendations made by conciliators and accepted by the parties be notified forthwith to the Commission in order to enable it to verify that conferences are not thereby exempted from the conditions provided for in the Regulation and thus do not infringe the provisions of Articles 85 and 86;

Whereas consultations between users or associations of users and conferences are liable to secure a more efficient operation of maritime transport services which takes better account of users' requirements; whereas, consequently, certain restrictive practices which could ensue from such consultations should be exempted;

Whereas there can be no exemption if the conditions set out in Article 85(3) are not satisfied; whereas the Commission must therefore have power to take the appropriate measures where an agreement or concerted practice owing to special circumstances proves to have certain effects incompatible with Article 85(3); whereas, in view of the specific role fulfilled by the conferences in the sector of the liner services, the reaction of the Commission should be progressive and proportionate; whereas the Commission should consequently have the power first to address recommendations, then to take decisions;

Whereas the automatic nullity provided for in Article 85(2) in respect of agreements or decisions which have not been granted exemption pursuant to Article 85(3) owing to their discriminatory or other features applies only to the elements of the agreement covered by the prohibition of Article 85(1) and applies to the agreement in its entirety only if those elements do not appear to be severable from the whole of the agreement; whereas the Commission should therefore, if it finds an infringement of the block exemption, either specify what elements of the agreement are covered by the prohibition and consequently automatically void, or indicate the reasons why those elements are not severable from the rest of the agreement and why the agreement is therefore void in its entirety;

Whereas, in view of the characteristics of international maritime transport, account should be taken of the fact that the application of this Regulation to certain restrictive practices or abuses may result in conflicts with the laws and rules of certain third countries and prove harmful to important Community trading and shipping interests; whereas consultations and, where appropriate, negotiations authorized by the Council should be undertaken by the Commission with those countries in pursuance of the maritime transport policy of the Community;

Whereas this Regulation should make provision for the procedures, decision-making powers and penalties that are necessary to ensure compliance with the prohibitions laid down in Article 85(1) and Article 86, as well as the conditions governing the application of Article 85(3);

Whereas account should be taken in this respect of the procedural provisions of Regulation (EEC) No 1017/68 applicable to inland transport operations which takes account of certain distinctive features of transport operations viewed as a whole;

Whereas, in particular, in view of the special characteristics of maritime transport, it is primarily the responsibility of undertakings to see to it that their agreements, decisions and concerted practices conform to the rules on competition, and consequently their notification to the Commission need not be made compulsory;

Whereas in certain circumstances undertakings may, however, wish to apply to the Commission for confirmation that their agreements, decisions and concerted practices are in conformity with the provisions in force; whereas a simplified procedure should be laid down for such cases,

HAS ADOPTED THIS REGULATION:

SECTION I

Article 1 – Subject-matter and scope of the Regulation

1. This Regulation lays down detailed rules for the application of Articles 85 and 86 of the Treaty to maritime transport services.

2. It shall apply only to international maritime transport services from or to one or more Community ports, other than tramp vessel services.

3. For the purposes of this Regulation:

    (a) 'tramp vessel services' means the transport of goods in bulk or in break-bulk in a vessel chartered wholly or partly to one or more shippers on the basis of a voyage or time charter or any other form of contract for non-regularly scheduled or non-advertised sailings where the freight rates are freely negotiated case by case in accordance with the conditions of supply and demand;

(b) 'liner conference' means a group of two or more vessel-operating carriers which provides international liner services for the carriage of cargo on a particular route or routes within specified geographical limits and which has an agreement or arrangement, whatever its nature, within the framework of which they operate under uniform or common freight rates and any other agreed conditions with respect to the provision of liner services;

(c) 'transport user' means an undertaking (e.g. shippers, consignees, forwarders, etc.) provided it has entered into, or demonstrates an intention to enter into, a contractual or other arrangement with a conference or shipping line for the shipment of goods, or any association of shippers. **[1226]**

Article 2 – Technical agreements

1. The prohibition laid down in Article 85(1) of the Treaty shall not apply to agreements, decisions and concerted practices whose sole object and effect is to achieve technical improvements or cooperation by means of:

(a) the introduction or uniform application of standards or types in respect of vessels and other means of transport, equipment, supplies or fixed installations;

(b) the exchange or pooling for the purpose of operating transport services, of vessels, space on vessels or slots and other means of transport, staff, equipment or fixed installations;

(c) the organization and execution of successive or supplementary maritime transport operations and the establishment or application of inclusive rates and conditions for such operations;

(d) the co-ordination of transport timetables for connecting routes;

(e) the consolidation of individual consignments;

concerning the structure and the conditions governing the application of transport tariffs.

2. The Commission shall, if necessary, submit to the Council proposals for the amendment of the list contained in paragraph 1. **[1227]**

Article 3 – Exemption for agreements between carriers concerning the operation of scheduled maritime transport services

Agreements, decisions and concerted practices of all or part of the members of one or more liner conferences are hereby exempted from the prohibition in Article 85(1) of the Treaty, subject to the condition imposed by Article 4 of this Regulation, when they have as their objective the fixing of rates and conditions of carriage, and, as the case may be, one or more of the following objectives:

(a) the co-ordination of shipping timetables, sailing dates or dates of calls;

(b) the determination of the frequency of sailings or calls;

(c) the co-ordination or allocation of sailings or calls among members of the conference;

(d) the regulation of the carrying capacity offered by each member;

(e) the allocation of cargo or revenue among members. **[1228]**

Article 4 – Condition attaching to exemption

The exemption provided for in Article 3 and 6 shall be granted subject to the condition that the agreement, decision or concerted practice shall not, within the common market, cause detriment to certain ports, transport users or carriers by applying for the carriage of the same goods and in the area covered by the agreement, decision or concerted practice, rates and conditions of carriage which differ according to the country of origin or destination or port of loading or discharge, unless such rates or conditions can be economically justified.

Any agreement or decision or, if it is severable, any part of such an agreement or decision not complying with the preceding paragraph shall automatically be void pursuant to Article 85(2) of the Treaty.   **[1229]**

Article 5 – Obligations attaching to exemption

The following obligations shall be attached to the exemption provided for in Article 3:

1. *Consultations*
There shall be consultations for the purpose of seeking solutions on general issues of principle between transport users on the one hand and conferences on the other concerning the rates, conditions and quality of scheduled maritime transport services.

These consultations shall take place whenever requested by any of the abovementioned parties.

2. *Loyalty arrangements*
The shipping lines' members of a conference shall be entitled to institute and maintain loyalty arrangements with transport users, the form and terms of which shall be matters for consultation between the conference and transport users' organizations. These loyalty arrangements shall provide safeguards making explicit the rights of transport users and conference members. These arrangements shall be based on the contract system or any other system which is also lawful.

Loyalty arrangements must comply with the following conditions:

(a) Each conference shall offer transport users a system of immediate rebates or the choice between such a system and a system of deferred rebates:

   – under the system of immediate rebates each of the parties shall be entitled to terminate the loyalty arrangement at any time without penalty and subject to a period of notice of not more than six months; this period shall be reduced to three months when the conference rate is the subject of a dispute;

   – under the system of deferred rebates neither the loyalty period on the basis of which the rebate is calculated nor the subsequent loyalty period required before payment of the rebate may exceed six months; this period shall be reduced to three months where the conference rate is the subject of a dispute.

(b). The conference shall, after consulting the transport users concerned, set out:

   (i) a list of cargo and any portion of cargo agreed with transport users which is specifically excluded from the scope of the loyalty arrangement; 100% loyalty arrangements may be offered but may not be unilaterally imposed;

   (ii) a list of circumstances in which transport users are released from their obligation of loyalty; these shall include:

   – circumstances in which consignments are dispatched from or to a port in the area covered by the conference but not advertised and where the request for a waiver can be justified, and

   – those in which waiting time at a port exceeds a period to be determined for each port and for each commodity or class of commodities following consultation of the transport users directly concerned with the proper servicing of the port.

The conference must, however, be informed in advance by the transport user, within a specified period, of his intention to dispatch the consignment from a port not advertised by the conference or to make use of a non-conference vessel at a port served by the conference as soon as he has been able to establish from the published schedule of sailings that the maximum waiting period will be exceeded.

3. *Services not covered by the freight charges*
Transport users shall be entitled to approach the undertakings of their choice in respect of inland transport operations and quayside services not covered by the freight charge or charges on which the shipping line and the transport user have agreed.

4. *Availability of tariffs*
Tariffs, related conditions, regulations and any amendments thereto shall be made available on request to transport users at reasonable cost, or they shall be available for examination at offices of shipping lines and their agents. They shall set out all the conditions concerning loading and discharge, the exact extent of the services covered by the freight charge in proportion to the sea transport and the land transport or by any other charge levied by the shipping line and customary practice in such matters.

5. *Notification to the Commission of awards at arbitration and recommendations*
Awards given at arbitration and recommendations made by conciliators that are accepted by the parties shall be notified forthwith to the Commission when they resolve disputes relating to the practices of conferences referred to in Article 4 and in points 2 and 3 above.
[1230]

Article 6 – Exemption for agreements between transport users and conferences concerning the use of scheduled maritime transport services

Agreements, decisions and concerted practices between transport users, on the one hand, and conferences, on the other hand, and agreements between transport users which may be necessary to that end, concerning the rates, conditions and quality of liner services, as long as they are provided for in Article 5(1) and (2) are hereby exempted from the prohibition laid down in Article 85(1) of the Treaty. **[1231]**

Article 7 – Monitoring of exempted agreements

1. *Breach of an obligation*
Where the persons concerned are in breach of an obligation which, pursuant to Article 5, attaches to the exemption provided for in Article 3, the Commission may, in order to put an end to such breach and under the conditions laid down in Section 11:

— address recommendations to the persons concerned;
— in the event of failure by such persons to observe those recommendations and depending upon the gravity of the breach concerned, adopt a decision that either prohibits them from carrying out or requires them to perform specific acts or, while withdrawing the benefit of the block exemption which they enjoyed, grants them an individual exemption according to Article 11(4) or withdraws the benefit of the block exemption which they enjoyed.

2. *Effects incompatible with Article 85(3)*
   (a) Where, owing to special circumstances as described below, agreements, decisions and concerted practices which qualify for the exemption provided for in Articles 3 and 6 have nevertheless effects which are incompatible with the conditions

laid down in Article 85(3) of the Treaty, the Commission, on receipt of a complaint or on its own initiative, under the conditions laid down in Section 11, shall take the measures described in (c) below. The severity of these measures must be in proportion to the gravity of the situation.

(b) Special circumstances are, inter alia, created by:

    (i) acts of conferences or a change of market conditions in a given trade resulting in the absence or elimination of actual or potential competition such as restrictive practices whereby the trade is not available to competition; or

    (ii) acts of conference which may prevent technical or economic progress or user participation in the benefits;

    (iii) acts of third countries which:

        — prevent the operation of outsiders in a trade,

        — impose unfair tariffs on conference members,

        — impose arrangements which otherwise impede technical or economic progress (cargo-sharing, limitations on types of vessels).

(c)   (i) If actual or potential competition is absent or may be eliminated as a result of action by a third country, the Commission shall enter into consultations with the competent authorities of the third country concerned, followed if necessary by negotiations under directives to be given by the Council, in order to remedy the situation.

        If the special circumstances result in the absence or elimination of actual or potential competition contrary to Article 85(3)(b) of the Treaty the Commission shall withdraw the benefit of the block exemption. At the same time it shall rule on whether and, if so, under what additional conditions and obligations an individual exemption should be granted to the relevant conference agreement with a view, inter alia, to obtaining access to the market for non-conference lines;

    (ii) If, as a result of special circumstances as set out in (b), there are effects other than those referred to in (i) hereof, the Commission shall take one or more of the measures described in paragraph 1.   **[1232]**

Article 8 — Effects incompatible with Article 86 of the Treaty

1. The abuse of a dominant position within the meaning of Article 86 of the Treaty shall be prohibited, no prior decision to that effect being required.

2. Where the Commission, either on its own initiative or at the request of a Member State or of natural or legal persons claiming a legitimate interest, finds that in any particular case the conduct of conferences benefiting from the exemption laid down in Article 3 nevertheless has effects which are incompatible with Article 86 of the Treaty, it may withdraw the benefit of the block exemption and take, pursuant to Article 10, all appropriate measures for the purpose of bringing to an end infringements of Article 86 of the Treaty.

3. Before taking a decision under paragraph 2, the Commission may address to the conference concerned recommendations for termination of the infringement.   **[1233]**

Article 9 — Conflicts of international law

1. Where the application of this Regulation to certain restrictive practices or clauses is liable to enter into conflict with the provisions laid down by law, regulation or administrative action of certain third countries which would compromise important Community

trading and shipping interests, the Commission shall, at the earliest opportunity, undertake with the competent authorities of the third countries concerned, consultations aimed at reconciling as far as possible the abovementioned interest with the respect of Community law. The Commission shall inform the Advisory Committee referred to in Article 15 of the outcome of these consultations.

2. Where agreements with third countries need to be negotiated, the Commission shall make recommendations to the Council, which shall authorize the Commission to open the necessary negotiations.

The Commission shall conduct these negotiations in consultation with an Advisory Committee as referred to in Article 15 and within the framework of such directives as the Council may issue to it.

3. In exercising the powers conferred on it by this Article, the Council shall act in accordance with the decision-making procedure laid down in Article 84(2) of the Treaty.

[1234]

SECTION II

RULES OF PROCEDURE

Article 10 — Procedures on complaint or on the Commission's own initiative

Acting on receipt of a complaint or on its own initiative, the Commission shall initiate procedures to terminate any infringement of the provisions of Articles 85(1) or 86 of the Treaty or to enforce Article 7 of this Regulation.

Complaints may be submitted by:

(a) Member States;

(b) natural or legal persons who claim a legitimate interest. **[1235]**

Article 11 — Result of procedures on complaint or on the Commission's own initiative

1. Where the Commission finds that there has been an infringement of Articles 85(1) or 86 of the Treaty, it may by decision require the undertakings or associations of undertakings concerned to bring such infringement to an end.

Without prejudice to the other provisions of this Regulation, the Commission may, before taking a decision under the preceding subparagraph, address to the undertakings or associations of undertakings concerned recommendations for termination of the infringement.

2. Paragraph 1 shall apply also to cases falling within Article 7 of this Regulation.

3. If the Commission, acting on a complaint received, concludes that on the evidence before it there are no grounds for intervention under Articles 85(1) or 86 of the Treaty or Article 7 of this Regulation, in respect of any agreement, decision or practice, it shall issue a decision rejecting the complaint as unfounded.

4. If the Commission, whether acting on a complaint received or on its own initiative, concludes that an agreement, decision or concerted practice satisfies the provisions both of Article 85(1) and of Article 85(3) of the Treaty, it shall issue a decision applying Article 85(3). Such decision shall indicate the date from which it is to take effect. This date may be prior to that of the decision. **[1236]**

Article 12 — Application of Article 85(3) — objections

1. Undertakings and associations of undertakings which seek application of Article 85(3) of the Treaty in respect of agreements, decisions and concerted practices falling within

the provisions of Article 85(1) to which they are parties shall submit applications to the Commission.

2. If the Commission judges an application admissible and is in possession of all the available evidence, and no action under Article 10 has been taken against the agreement, decision or concerted practice in question, then it shall publish as soon as possible in the *Official Journal of the European Communities* a summary of the application and invite all interested third parties and the Member States to submit their comments to the Commission within 30 days. Such publications shall have regard to the legitimate interest of undertakings in the protection of their business secrets.

3. Unless the Commission notifies applicants, within 90 days from the date of such publication in the *Official Journal of the European Communities*, that there are serious doubts as to the applicability of Article 85(3), the agreement, decision or concerted practice shall be deemed exempt, insofar as it conforms with the description given in the application, from the prohibition for the time already elapsed and for a maximum of six years from the date of publication in the *Official Journal of the European Communities*.

If the Commission finds, after expiry of the 90-day time limit, but before expiry of the six year period, that the conditions for applying Article 85(3) are not satisfied, it shall issue a decision declaring that the prohibition in Article 85(1) is applicable. Such decision may be retroactive where the parties concerned have given inaccurate information or where they abuse the exemption from the provisions of Article 85(1).

4. The Commission may notify applicants as referred to in the first subparagraph of paragraph 3 and shall do so if requested by a Member State within 45 days of the forwarding to the Member State of the application in accordance with Article 15(2). This request must be justified on the basis of considerations relating to the competition rules of the Treaty.

If it finds that the conditions of Article 85(1) and of Article 85(3) are satisfied, the Commission shall issue a decision applying Article 85(3). The decision shall indicate the date from which it is to take effect. This date may be prior to that of the application.

[1237]

Article 13 — Duration and revocation of decisions applying Article 85(3)

1. Any decision applying Article 85(3) taken under Article 11(4) or under the second subparagraph of Article 12(4) shall indicate the period for which it is to be valid; normally such period shall not be less than six years. Conditions and obligations may be attached to the decision.

2. The decision may be renewed if the conditions for applying Article 85(3) continue to be satisfied.

3. The Commission may revoke or amend its decision or prohibit specified acts by the parties:

(a) where there has been a change in any of the facts which were basic to the making of the decision;

(b) where the parties commit a breach of any obligation attached to the decision;

(c) where the decision is based on incorrect information or was induced by deceit, or

(d) where the parties abuse the exemption from the provisions of Article 85(1) granted to them by the decision.

In cases falling within (b), (c) or (d), the decision may be revoked with retroactive effect.

[1238]

Article 14 — Powers

Subject to review of its decision by the Court of Justice, the Commission shall have sole power:

- to impose obligations pursuant to Article 7;
- to issue decisions pursuant to Article 85(3).

The authorities of the Member States shall retain the power to decide whether any case falls within the provisions of Article 85(1) or Article 86, until such time as the Commission has initiated a procedure with a view to formulating a decision in the case in question or has sent notification as provided for in the first subparagraph of Article 12(3).

[1239]

Article 15 — Liaison with the authorities of the Member States

1. The Commission shall carry out the procedures provided for in this Regulation in close and constant liaison with the competent authorities of the Member States; these authorities shall have the right to express their views on such procedures.

2. The Commission shall immediately forward to the competent authorities of the Member States copies of the complaints and applications, and of the most important documents sent to it or which it sends out in the course of such procedures.

3. An Advisory Committee on agreements and dominant positions in maritime transport shall be consulted prior to the taking of any decision following upon a procedure under Article 10 or of any decision issued under the second subparagraph of Article 12(3), or under the second subparagraph of paragraph 4 of the same Article. The Advisory Committee shall also be consulted prior to the adoption of the implementing provisions provided for in Article 26.

4. The Advisory Committee shall be composed of officials competent in the sphere of maritime transport and agreements and dominant positions. Each Member State shall nominate two officials to represent it, each of whom may be replaced, in the event of his being prevented from attending, by another official.

5. Consultation shall take place at a joint meeting convened by the Commission; such meeting shall be held not earlier than fourteen days after dispatch of the notice convening it. This notice shall, in respect of each case to be examined, be accompanied by a summary of the case together with an indication of the most important documents, and a preliminary draft decision.

6. The Advisory Committee may deliver an opinion notwithstanding that some of its members or their alternates are not present. A report of the outcome of the consultative proceedings shall be annexed to the draft decision. It shall not be made public.

[1240]

Article 16 — Requests for information

1. In carrying out the duties assigned to it by this Regulation, the Commission may obtain all necessary information from the Governments and competent authorities of the Member States and from undertakings and associations of undertakings.

2. When sending a request for information to an undertaking or association of undertakings, the Commission shall at the same time forward a copy of the request to the competent authority of the Member State in whose territory the seat of the undertaking or association of undertakings is situated.

3. In its request, the Commission shall state the legal basis and the purpose of the

request, and also the penalties provided for in Article 19(1)(*b*) for supplying incorrect information.

4. The owners of the undertakings or their representatives and, in the case of legal persons, companies or firms, or of associations having no legal personality, the person authorized to represent them by law or by their constitution, shall be bound to supply the information requested.

5. Where an undertaking or association of undertakings does not supply the information requested within the time limit fixed by the Commission, or supplies incomplete information, the Commission shall by decision require the information to be supplied. The decision shall specify what information is required, fix an appropriate time limit within which it is to be supplied and indicate the penalties provided for in Article 19(1)(*b*) and Article 20(1)(*c*) and the right to have the decision reviewed by the Court of Justice.

6. The Commission shall at the same time forward a copy of its decision to the competent authority of the Member State in whose territory the seat of the undertaking or association of undertakings is situated. **[1241]**

Article 17 – Investigations by the authorities of the Member States

1. At the request of the Commission, the competent authorities of the Member States shall undertake the investigations which the Commission considers to be necessary under Article 18(1), or which it has ordered by decision pursuant to Article 18(3). The officials of the competent authorities of the Member States responsible for conducting these investigations shall exercise their powers upon production of an authorization in writing issued by the competent authority of the Member State in whose territory the investigation is to be made. Such authorization shall specify the subject matter and purpose of the investigation.

2. If so requested by the Commission or by the competent authority of the Member State in whose territory the investigation is to be made, Commission officials may assist the officials of such authority in carrying out their duties.
The officials of the Commission authorized for the purpose of these investigations shall exercise their powers upon production of an authorization in writing specifying the subject matter and purpose of the investigation and the penalties provided for in Article 19(1)(*c*) in cases where production of the required books or other business records is incomplete. In good time before the investigation, the Commission shall inform the competent authority of the Member State in whose territory the same is to be made of the investigation and of the identity of the authorized officials.

3. Undertakings and associations of undertakings shall submit to investigations ordered by decision of the Commission. The decision shall specify the subject matter and purpose of the investigation, appoint the date on which it is to begin and indicate the penalties provided for in Article 19(1)(*c*) and Article 20(1)(*d*) and the right to have the decision reviewed by the Court of Justice.

4. The Commission shall take decisions referred to in paragraph 3 after consultation with the competent authority of the Member State in whose territory the investigation is to be made.

5. Officials of the competent authority of the Member State in whose territory the investigation is to be made, may at the request of such authority or of the Commission, assist the officials of the Commission in carrying out their duties.

6. Where an undertaking opposes an investigation ordered pursuant to this Article, the Member State concerned shall afford the necessary assistance to the officials authorized by the Commission to enable them to make their investigation. To this end, Member

States shall take the necessary measures, after consulting the Commission, before 1 January 1989. **[1242]**

Article 18 – Investigating powers of the Commission

1. In carrying out the duties assigned to it by this Regulation, the Commission may undertake all necessary investigations into undertakings and associations of undertakings.
To this end the officials authorized by the Commission are empowered:

    (a)   to examine the books and other business records;
    (b)   to take copies of or extracts from the books and business records:
    (c)   to ask for oral explanations on the spot;
    (d)   to enter any premises, land and vehicles of undertakings. **[1243]**

Article 19 – Fines

1. The Commission may by decision impose on undertakings or associations of undertakings fines of from 100 to 5 000 ECU where, intentionally or negligently:

    (a)   they supply incorrect or misleading information, either in a communication pursuant to Article 5(5) or in an application pursuant to Article 12; or
    (b)   they supply incorrect information in response to a request made pursuant to Article 16(3) or (5), or do not supply information within the time limit fixed by a decision taken under Article 16(5); or
    (c)   they produce the required books or other business records in incomplete form during investigations under Article 17 or Article 18, or refuse to submit to an investigation ordered by decision issued in implementation of Article 18(3).

2. The Commission may by decision impose on undertakings or associations of undertakings fines of from 1 000 to one million ECU, or a sum in excess thereof but not exceeding 10% of the turnover in the preceding business year of each of the undertakings participating in the infringement, where either intentionally or negligently:

    (a)   they infringe Article 85(1) or Article 86 of the Treaty, or do not comply with an obligation imposed under Article 7 of this Regulation;
    (b)   they commit a breach of any obligation imposed pursuant to Article 5 or to Article 13(1).

In fixing the amount of the fine, regard shall be had both to the gravity and to the duration of the infringement.

3. Article 15(3) and (4) shall apply.

4. Decisions taken pursuant to paragraphs 1 and 2 shall not be of criminal law nature.
The fines provided for in paragraph 2(a) shall not be imposed in respect of acts taking place after notification to the Commission and before its Decision in application of Article 85(3) of the Treaty, provided they fall within the limits of the activity described in the notification.
However, this provision shall not have effect where the Commission has informed the undertakings concerned that after preliminary examination it is of the opinion that Article 85(1) of the Treaty applies and that application of Article 85(3) is not justified.

[1244]

Article 20 – Periodic penalty payments

1. The Commission may by decision impose on undertakings or associations of undertakings periodic penalty payments of from 50 to 1 000 ECU per day, calculated from the date appointed by the decision, in order to compel them:

(a) to put an end to an infringement of Article 85(1) or Article 86 of the Treaty the termination of which it has ordered pursuant to Article 11, or to comply with an obligation imposed pursuant to Article 7;

(b) to refrain from any act prohibited under Article 13(3);

(c) to supply complete and correct information which it has requested by decision taken pursuant to Article 16(5);

(d) to submit to an investigation which it has ordered by decision taken pursuant to Article 18(3).

2. Where the undertakings or associations of undertakings have satisfied the obligation which it was the purpose of the periodic penalty payment to enforce, the Commission may fix the total amount of the periodic penalty payment at a lower figure than that which would arise under the original decision.

3. Article 15(3) and (4) shall apply.   **[1245]**

Article 21 — Review by the Court of Justice

The Court of Justice shall have unlimited jurisdiction within the meaning of Article 172 of the Treaty to review decisions whereby the Commission has fixed a fine or periodic penalty payment; it may cancel, reduce or increase the fine or periodic penalty payment imposed.   **[1246]**

Article 22 — Unit of account

For the purpose of applying Articles 19 to 21 the ECU shall be that adopted in drawing up the budget of the Community in accordance with Articles 207 and 209 of the Treaty.   **[1247]**

Article 23 — Hearing of the parties and of third persons

1. Before taking decisions as provided for in Articles 11, 12(3) second subparagraph, and 12(4), 13(3), 19 and 20, the Commission shall give the undertakings or associations of undertakings concerned the opportunity of being heard on the matters to which the Commission has taken objection.

2. If the Commission or the competent authorities of the Member States consider it necessary, they may also hear other natural or legal persons. Applications to be heard on the part of such persons where they show a sufficient interest shall be granted.

3. Where the Commission intends to give negative clearance pursuant to Article 85(3) of the Treaty, it shall publish a summary of the relevant agreement, decision or concerted practice and invite all interested third parties to submit their observations within a time limit which it shall fix being not less than one month. Publication shall have regard to the legitimate interest of undertakings in the protection of their business secrets.   **[1248]**

Article 24 — Professional secrecy

1. Information acquired as a result of the application of Articles 17 and 18 shall be used only for the purpose of the relevant request or investigation.

2. Without prejudice to the provisions of Articles 23 and 25, the Commission and the competent authorities of the Member States, their officials and other servants shall not disclose information acquired by them as a result of the application of this Regulation and of the kind covered by the obligation of professional secrecy.

3. The provisions of paragraphs 1 and 2 shall not prevent publication of general information or surveys which do not contain information relating to particular undertakings or associations of undertakings. **[1249]**

Article 25 – Publication of decisions

1. The Commission shall publish the decisions which it takes pursuant to Articles 11, 12(3), second paragraph, 12(4) and 13(3).

2. The publication shall state the names of the parties and the main content of the decision; it shall have regard to the legitimate interest of undertakings in the protection of their business secrets. **[1250]**

Article 26 – Implementing provisions

The Commission shall have power to adopt implementing provisions concerning the scope of the obligation of communication pursuant to Article 5(5), the form, content and other details of complaints pursuant to Article 10, applications pursuant to Article 12 and the hearings provided for in Article 23(1) and (2). **[1251]**

Article 27 – Entry into force

This Regulation shall enter into force on 1 July 1987. **[1252]**

This Regulation shall be binding in its entirety and directly applicable in all Member States.

Done at Brussels, 22 December 1986.

REGULATION (EEC) No 4057/86 OF THE COUNCIL
of 12 December 1986

on unfair pricing practices in maritime transport

THE COUNCIL OF THE EUROPEAN COMMUNITIES,

Having regard to the Treaty establishing the European Economic Community, and in particular Article 84(2) thereof,

Having regard to the draft Regulation submitted by the Commission,

Having regard to the opinion of the European Parliament,

Having regard to the opinion of the Economic and Social Committee,

Whereas there is reason to believe, inter alia on the basis of the information system set up by Council Decision 78/774/EEC, that the competitive participation of Community shipowners in international liner shipping is adversely affected by certain unfair practices of shipping lines of third countries;

Whereas the structure of the Community shipping industry is such as to make it appropriate that the provisions of this Regulation should also apply to nationals of Member States established outside the Community or cargo shipping companies established outside the Community and controlled by nationals of Member States, if their ships are registered in a Member State in accordance with its legislation;

Whereas such unfair practices consist of continuous charging of freight rates for the transport of selected commodities which are lower than the lowest freight rates charged for the same commodities by established and representative shipowners;

Whereas such pricing practices are made possible by non-commercial advantages granted by a State which is not a member of the Community;

Whereas the Community should be able to take redressive action against such pricing practices;

Whereas there are no internationally agreed rules as to what constitutes an unfair price in the maritime transport field;

Whereas, in order to determine the existence of unfair pricing practices, provision should therefore be made for an appropriate method of calculation; whereas when calculating the 'normal freight rate' account should be taken of the comparable rate actually charged by established and representative companies operating within or outside conferences or otherwise of a constructed rate based on the costs of comparable companies plus a reasonable margin of profit;

Whereas appropriate factors relevant for the determination of injury should be laid down;

Whereas it is necessary to lay down the procedures for those acting on behalf of the Community shipping industry who consider themselves injured or threatened by unfair pricing practices to lodge a complaint; whereas it seems appropriate to make it clear that in the case of withdrawal of a complaint, proceedings may, but need not necessarily, be terminated;

Whereas there should be cooperation between the Member States and the Commission both as regards information about the existence of unfair pricing practices and injury resulting therefrom, and as regards the subsequent examination of the matter at Community level; whereas, to this end, consultations should take place within an Advisory Committee;

Whereas it is appropriate to lay down clearly the rules of procedure to be followed during the investigation, in particular the rights and obligations of the Community authorities and the parties involved, and the conditions under which interested parties may have access to information and may ask to be informed of the principal facts and considerations on the basis of which it is intended to propose the introduction of a redressive duty;

Whereas, in order to discourage unfair pricing practices, but without preventing, restricting or distorting price competition by non-conference lines, providing that they are working on a fair and commercial basis, it is appropriate to provide, in cases where the facts as finally established show that there is an unfair pricing practice and injury, for the possibility of imposing redressive duties on particular grounds;

Whereas it is essential, in order to ensure that redressive duties are levied in a correct and uniform manner, that common rules for the application of such duties be laid down; whereas, by reason of the nature of the said duties, such rules may differ from the rules for the levying of normal import duties;

Whereas open and fair procedures should be provided for the review of measures taken and for the investigation to be reopened when circumstances so require;

Whereas appropriate procedures should be established for examining applications for refund of redressive duties,

HAS ADOPTED THIS REGULATION:

Article 1 – Objective

This Regulation lays down the procedure to be followed in order to respond to unfair pricing practices by certain third country shipowners engaged in international cargo liner shipping, which cause serious disruption of the freight pattern on a particular route to, from or within the Community and cause or threaten to cause major injury to Community shipowners operating on that route and to Community interests.   **[1253]**

Article 2

In response to unfair pricing practices as described in Article I which cause major injury, a redressive duty may be applied by the Community. A threat of major injury may only give rise to an examination within the meaning of Article 4.   **[1254]**

Article 3

For the purposes of this Regulation:

    (*a*) 'third country shipowner' means cargo liner shipping companies other than those mentioned under (*d*);

    (*b*) 'unfair pricing practices' means the continuous charging on a particular shipping route to, from or within the Community of freight rates for selected or all commodities which are lower than the normal freight rates charged during a period of at least six months, when such lower freight rates are made possible by the fact that the shipowner concerned enjoys non-commercial advantages which are granted by a State which is not a member of the Community;

(c) the 'normal freight rate' shall be determined taking into account:

  (i) the comparable rate actually charged in the ordinary course of shipping business for the like service on the same or comparable route by established and representative companies not enjoying the advantages in (b);

  (ii) or otherwise the constructed rate which is determined by taking the costs of comparable companies not enjoying the advantages in (b) plus a reasonable margin of profit. This cost shall be computed on the basis of all costs incurred in the ordinary course of shipping business, both fixed and variable, plus a reasonable amount for overhead expenses.

(d) 'Community shipowners' means:

  – all cargo shipping companies established under the Treaty in a Member State of the Community;

  – nationals of Member States established outside the Community or cargo shipping companies established outside the Community and controlled by nationals of Member States, if their ships are registered in a Member State in accordance with its legislation. **[1255]**

Article 4 – Examination of injury

1. Examination of injury shall cover the following factors:

(a) the freight rates offered by Community shipowners' competitors on the route in question, in particular in order to determine whether they have been significantly lower than the normal freight rate offered by Community shipowners, taking into account the level of service offered by all the Companies concerned;

(b) the effect of the above factor on Community shipowners as indicated by trends in a number of economic indicators such as:

  – sailings,
  – utilization of capacity,
  – cargo bookings,
  – market share,
  – freight rates (that is depression of freight rates or prevention of freight rate increases which would normally have occurred),
  – profits,
  – return of capital,
  – investment,
  – employment.

2. Where a threat of injury is alleged, the Commission may also examine whether it is clearly foreseeable that a particular situation is likely to develop into actual injury. In this regard, account may also be taken of factors such as:

(a) the increase in tonnage deployed on the shipping route where the competition with Community shipowners is taking place;

(b) the capacity which is already available or is to become available in the foreseeable future in the country of the foreign shipowners and the extent to which the tonnage resulting from that capcity is likely to be used on the shipping route referred to in (a).

3. Injury caused by other factors which, either individually or in combination, are

also adversely affecting Community shipowners must not be attributed to the practices in question.				**[1256]**

Article 5 – Complaint

1. Any natural or legal person, or any association not having legal personality, acting on behalf of the Community shipping industry who consider themselves injured or threatened by unfair pricing practices may lodge a written complaint.

2. The complaint shall contain sufficient evidence of the existence of the unfair pricing practice and injury resulting therefrom.

3. The complaint may be submitted to the Commission, or a Member State, which shall forward it to the Commission. The Commission shall send Member States a copy of any complaint it receives.

4. The complaint may be withdrawn, in which case proceedings may be terminated unless such termination would not be in the interest of the Community.

5. Where it becomes apparent after consultation that the complaint does not provide sufficient evidence to justify initiating an investigation, then the complainant shall be so informed.

6. Where, in the absence of any complaint, a Member State is in possession of sufficient evidence both of unfair pricing practices and of injury resulting therefrom for Community shipowners, it shall immediately communicate such evidence to the Commission.
				[1257]

Article 6 – Consultations

1. Any consultations provided for in this Regulation shall take place within an Advisory Committee, which shall consist of representatives of each Member State, with a representative of the Commission as Chairman. Consultations shall be held immediately on request by a Member State or on the initiative of the Commission.

2. The Committee shall meet when convened by its Chairman. He shall provide the Member States, as promptly as possible, with all relevant information.

3. Where necessary, consultation may be in writing only; in such case the Commission shall notify the Member States and shall specify a period within which they shall be entitled to express their opinions or to request an oral consultation.

4. Consultation shall in particular cover:

   (a) the existence of unfair pricing practices and the amount thereof;
   (b) the existence and extent of injury;
   (c) the causal link between the unfair pricing practices and injury;
   (d) the measures which, in the circumstances, are appropriate to prevent or remedy the injury caused by unfair pricing practices and the ways and means for putting such measures into effect.				**[1258]**

Article 7 – Initiation and subsequent investigation

1. Where, after consultation, it is apparent that there is sufficient evidence to justify initiating a proceeding the Commission shall immediately:

   (a) announce the initiation of a proceeding in the Official Journal of the European Communities; such announcements shall indicate the foreign shipowner concerned and his country of origin, give a summary of the information received, and provide that all relevant information is to be communicated to the Commission; it shall state the period within which interested parties may make known their views in writing and may apply to be heard orally by the Commission in accordance with paragraph 5;

(b) so advise the shipowners, shippers and freight forwarders known to the Commission to be concerned and the complainants;

(c) commence the investigation at Community level, acting in cooperation with the Member States; such investigation shall cover both unfair pricing practices and injury resulting therefrom and shall be carried out in accordance with paragraphs 2 to 8; the investigation of unfair pricing practices shall normally cover a period of not less than six months immediately prior to the initiation of the proceeding.

2. (a) Where appropriate the Commission shall seek all the information it deems necessary and attempt to check this information with the shipowners, agents, shippers, freight forwarders, conferences, associations and other organizations, provided that the undertakings or organizations concerned give their consent.

(b) Where necessary the Commission shall, after consultation, carry out investigations in third countries, provided that the firms concerned give their consent and the government of the country in question has been officially notified and raises no objection. The Commission shall be assisted by officials of those Member States which so request.

3. (a) The Commission may request Member States:

– to supply information,
– to carry out all necessary checks and inspections, particularly amongst shippers, freight forwarders, Community shipowners and their agents,
– to carry out investigations in third countries, provided the firms concerned give their consent and the government of the country in question has been officially notified and raises no objection.

(b) Member States shall take whatever steps are necessary in order to give effect to requests from the Commission. They shall send to the Commission the information requested together with the results of all inspections, checks or investigations carried out.

(c) Where this information is of general interest or where its transmission has been requested by a Member State, the Commission shall forward it to the Member States provided it is not confidential, in which case a non-confidential summary shall be forwarded.

(d) Officials of the Commission shall be authorized, if the Commission or a Member State so requests, to assist the officials of Member States in carrying out their duties.

4. (a) The complainant and the shippers and shipowners known to be concerned may inspect all information made available to the Commission by any party to an investigation as distinct from internal documents prepared by the authorities of the Community or its Member States provided that it is relevant to the defence of their interests and not confidential within the meaning of Article 8 and that it is used by the Commission in the investigation. To this end, they shall address a written request to the Commission, indicating the information required.

(b) Shipowners subject to investigation and the complainant may request to be informed of the essential facts and considerations on the basis of which it is intended to recommend the imposition of redressive duties.

(c) (i) Requests for information pursuant to (b) shall:

     – be addressed to the Commission in writing,
     – specify the particular issues on which information is sought.

  (ii) The information may be given either orally or in writing, as considered appropriate by the Commission. It shall not prejudice any subsequent decision which may be taken by the Council. Confidential information shall be treated in accordance with Article 8.

 (iii) Information shall normally be given no later than 15 days prior to the submission by the Commission of any proposal for action pursuant to Article 11. Representations made after the information is given may be taken into consideration only if received within a period to be set by the Commission in each case, which shall be at least 10 days, due consideration being given to the urgency of the matter.

5. The Commission may hear the interested parties. It shall so hear them if they have, within the periods prescribed in the notice published in the Official Journal of the European Communities, made a written request for a hearing showing that they are an interested party likely to be affected by the result of the proceeding and that there are particular reasons why they should be given a hearing.

6. Furthermore, the Commission shall, on request, give the parties directly concerned an opportunity to meet, so that opposing views may be presented and any argument put forward by way of rebuttal. In providing this opportunity the Commission shall take account of the need to preserve confidentiality and of the convenience of the parties. There shall be no obligation on any party to attend a meeting and failure to do so shall not be prejudicial to that party's case.

7. (a) This Article shall not preclude the Council from reaching preliminary determinations or from applying measures expeditiously.

  (b) In cases in which any interested party refuses access to, or otherwise does not provide, necessary information within a reasonable period, or significantly impedes the investigation, findings, affirmative or negative, may be made on the basis of the facts available.

8. Proceedings on unfair pricing practices shall not constitute a bar to customs clearance of the goods to which the freight rates concerned apply.

9. (a) An investigation shall be concluded either by its termination or by action pursuant to Article 11. Conclusion should normally take place within one year of the initiation of the proceeding.

  (b) A proceeding shall be concluded either by the termination of the investigation without the imposition of duties and without the acceptance of undertakings or by the expiry or repeal of such duties or by the lapse of undertakings in accordance with Articles 14 or 15. **[1259]**

Article 8 – Confidentiality

1. Information received in pursuance of this Regulation shall be used only for the purpose for which it was requested.

2. (a) Neither the Council, nor the Commission, nor Member States, nor the officials

of any of these, shall reveal any information received in pursuance of this Regulation of which confidential treatment has been requested by its supplier, without specific permission from the supplier.

(*b*) Each request for confidential treatment shall indicate why the information is confidential and shall be accompanied by a non-confidential summary of the information, or a statement of the reasons why the information is not susceptible of such summary.

3. Information will ordinarily be considered to be confidential if its disclosure is likely to have a significantly adverse effect upon the supplier or the source of such information.

4. However, if it appears that a request for confidentiality is not warranted and if the supplier is either unwilling to make the information public or to authorize its disclosure in generalized or summary form, the information in question may be disregarded.

The information may also be disregarded where such request is warranted and where the supplier is unwilling to submit a non-confidential summary, provided that the information is susceptible of such summary.

5. This Article shall not preclude the disclosure of general information by the Community authorities and in particular of the reasons on which decisions taken in pursuance of this Regulation are based, or disclosure of the evidence relied on by the Community authorities in so far as necessary to explain those reasons in court proceedings. Such disclosure must take into account the legitimate interest of the parties concerned that their business secrets should not be divulged. **[1260]**

Article 9 – Termination of proceedings where protective measures are unnecessary

1. If it becomes apparent after consultation that protective measures are unnecessary, then, where no objection is raised within the Advisory Committee referred to in Article 6(1), the proceeding shall be terminated. In all other cases the Commission shall submit to the Council forthwith a report on the results of the consultation, together with a proposal that the proceeding be terminated. The proceeding shall stand terminated if, within one month, the Council, acting by a qualified majority, has not decided otherwise.

2. The Commission shall inform the parties known to be concerned and shall announce the termination in the Official Journal of the European Communities setting forth its basic conclusions and a summary of the reasons therefor. **[1261]**

Article 10 – Undertakings

1. Where, during the course of investigation, undertakings are offered which the Commission, after consultation, considers acceptable, the investigation may be terminated without the imposition of redressive duties.

Save in exceptional circumstances, undertakings may not be offered later than the end of the period during which representations may be made under Article 7(4)(*c*)(iii). The termination shall be decided in conformity with the procedure laid down in Article 9(1) and information shall be given and notice published in accordance with Article 9(2).

2. The undertakings referred to under paragraph 1 are those under which rates are revised to an extent such that the Commission is satisfied that the unfair pricing practice, or the injurious effects thereof, are eliminated.

3. Undertakings may be suggested by the Commission, but the fact that such undertakings are not offered or an invitation to do so is not accepted, shall not prejudice consideration of the case. However, the continuation of unfair pricing practices may be taken as evidence that a threat of injury is more likely to be realized.

4. If the undertakings are accepted, the investigation of injury shall nevertheless be completed if the Commission, after consultation, so decides or if request is made by the Community shipowners concerned. In such a case, if the Commission, after consultation, makes a determination of no injury, the undertaking shall automatically lapse. However, where a determination of no threat of injury is due mainly to the existence of an undertaking, the Commission may require that the undertaking be maintained.

5. The Commission may require any party from whom an undertaking has been accepted to provide periodically information relevant to the fufilment of such undertakings, and to permit verification of pertinent data. Non-compliance with such requirements shall be construed as a violation of the undertaking. **[1262]**

Article 11 — Redressive duties

Where investigation shows that there is an unfair pricing practice, that injury is caused by it and that the interests of the Community make Community intervention necessary, the Commission shall propose to the Council, after the consultations provided for in Article 6, that it introduce a redressive duty. The Council, acting by a qualified majority, shall take a Decision within two months. **[1263]**

Article 12

In deciding on the redressive duties, the Council shall also take due account of the external trade policy considerations as well as the port interests and the shipping policy considerations of the Member States concerned. **[1264]**

Article 13 — General provisions on duties

1. Redressive duties shall be imposed on the foreign shipowners concerned by regulation.

2. Such regulation shall indicate in particular the amount and type of duty imposed, the commodity or commodities transported, the name and the country of origin of the foreign shipowner concerned and the reasons on which the Regulation is based.

3. The amount of the duties shall not exceed the difference between the freight rate charged and the normal freight rate referred to in Article 3(c). It shall be less if such lesser duty would be adequate to remove the injury.

4. (a) Duties shall be neither imposed nor increased with retroactive effect and shall apply to the transport of commodities which, after entry into force of such duties, are loaded or discharged in a Community port.

   (b) However, where the Council determines that an undertaking has been violated or withdrawn, the redressive duties may be imposed, on a proposal from the Commission, on the transport of commodities which were loaded or discharged in a Community port not more than 90 days prior to the date of application of these duties, except that in the case of violation or withdrawal of an undertaking such retroactive assessment shall not apply to the transport of commodities which were loaded or discharged in a Community port before the violation or withdrawal. These duties may be calculated on the basis of the facts established before the acceptance of the undertaking.

5. Duties shall be collected by Member States in the form, at the rate and according to the other criteria laid down when the duties were imposed, and independently of the customs duties, taxes and other charges normally imposed on imports of goods transported.

6. Permission to load or discharge cargo in a Community port may be made conditional upon the provision of security for the amount of the duties.   **[1265]**

Article 14 — Review

1. Regulations imposing redressive duties and decisions to accept undertakings shall be subject to review in whole or in part, where warranted. Such review may be held either at the request of a Member State or on the initiative of the Commission. A review shall also be held where an interested party so requests and submits evidence of changed circumstances sufficient to justify the need for such review, provided that at least one year has elapsed since the conclusion of the investigation. Such requests shall be addressed to the Commission, which shall inform the Member States.

2. Where, after consultation, it becomes apparent that review is warranted, the investigation shall be re-opened in accordance with Article 7, where the circumstances so require. Such reopening shall not per se affect the measures in operation.

3. Where warranted by the review, carried out either with or without reopening of the investigation, the measures shall be amended, repealed or annulled by the Community institution competent for their adoption.   **[1266]**

Article 15

1. Subject to paragraph 2, redressive duties and undertakings shall lapse after five years from the date on which they entered into force or were last amended or confirmed.

2. The Commission shall normally, after consultation and within six months prior to the expiry of the five year period, publish in the Official Journal of the European Communities a notice of the impending expiry of the measure in question and inform Community shipowners known to be concerned. This notice shall state the period within which interested parties may make known their views in writing and may apply to be given a hearing by the Commission in accordance with Article 7(5).

Where an interested party shows that the expiry of the measure would again lead to injury or threat of injury, the Commission shall carry out a review of the measure. The measure shall remain in force pending the outcome of this review.

Where redressive duties and undertakings lapse under this Article the Commission shall publish a notice to that effect in the Official Journal of the European Communities.   **[1267]**

Article 16 — Refund

1. Where the shipowner concerned can show that the duty collected exceeds the difference between the freight rate charged and the normal freight rate referred to in Article 3(c) the excess amount shall be reimbursed.

2. In order to request the reimbursement referred to in paragraph 1, the foreign shipowner may submit an application to the Commission. The application shall be submitted via the Member State within the territory of which the commodities transported were loaded or discharged and within three months of the date on which the amount of the redressive duties to be levied was duly determined by the competent authorities.

The Member State shall forward the application to the Commission as soon as possible, either with or without an opinion as to its merits.

The Commission shall inform the other Member States forthwith and give its opinion on the matter. If the Member States agree with the opinion given by the Commission or do not object to it within one month of being informed, the Commission may decide in accordance with the said opinion. In all other cases, the Commission shall, after consultation, decide whether and to what extent the application should be granted.

[1268]

Article 17 — Final provisions

This Regulation shall not preclude the application of any special rules laid down in agreements concluded between the Community and third countries. **[1269]**

Article 18 — Entry into force

This Regulation shall enter into force on 1 July 1987. **[1270]**

This regulation shall be binding in its entirety and directly applicable in all Member States.

Done at Brussels, 22 December 1986.

DIRECTIVE No 87/167 OF THE COUNCIL
of 26 January 1987

on aid to shipbuilding

THE COUNCIL OF THE EUROPEAN COMMUNITIES,

Having regard to the Treaty establishing the European Economic Community, and in particular Articles 92(3)(*d*) and 113 thereof,

Having regard to the proposal from the Commission,

Having regard to the opinion of the European Parliament

Having regard to the opinion of the Economic and Social Committee

Whereas Council Directive 81/363/EEC of 28 April 1981 on aid to shipbuilding, as last amended by Directive 85/2/EEC, will expire on 31 December 1986;

Whereas, although progress had been made in the structural adaptation of the Community's shipbuilding industry since the adoption of Directive 81/363/EEC (the Fifth Directive), the world crisis in shipbuilding continues to deepen together with the imbalance between shipbuilding capacity and demand, causing prices to fall to a level which is often below the fixed cost of European shipyards; whereas the price problem has been aggravated by the development of very cost-competitive capacity in third countries particularly in the production of standardized vessels in series;

Whereas the recovery in demand envisaged in the Fifth Directive has not taken place, given that the demand outlook for shipbuilding is not encouraging and in view of the fact that any resumption in demand is likely to lead immediately to an expansion of production facilities in certain third countries;

Whereas a competitive shipbuilding industry is of vital interest to the Community and contributes to its economic and social development by providing a substantial market for a range of industries, including those using advanced technology; whereas it contributes also to the maintenance of employment in a number of regions, including some which are already suffering a high rate of unemployment; whereas this is also true of ship conversion and ship repair;

Whereas it is now clear that the sector is suffering from a fundamental structural crisis, rather than a cyclical problem of demand, in which it would be short-sighted to continue to respond to the aggravation of the crisis by multiplying the volume of operating aids which tend to increase the segregation of the internal market and constitute a continuing drain on the scarce budgetary resources of the Member States without inducing any lasting improvement in the competitiveness of the Community's shipbuilding industry;

Whereas, in view in particular of the cost differences which exist for most categories of ship in comparison to shipyards in some third countries, the immediate abolition of aid to the sector may not be possible in view of the need to encourage restructuring in many yards; whereas a tighter and more selective aid policy is nevertheless necessary in order to support the present trend in production towards more technologically advanced ships and in order to ensure fair and uniform conditions for intra-Community competition; whereas such a policy constitutes the most appropriate approach in terms of ensuring the maintenance of a sufficient level of activity in European shipyards and thereby the survival of an efficient and competitive European shipbuilding industry;

Whereas these considerations call for a differentiated approach with regard to the various types of aid at present granted by Member States; whereas a level of production aid which is geared towards supporting production where the Community's cost disadvantage is lowest and where there is a real possibility of restoring long-term competitiveness seems to offer the most appropriate approach in response to the abovementioned objectives of improving competitiveness and reducing intra-Community distortions in trade; whereas this level of aid should be attained by means of a common maximum ceiling to be revised periodically after consultation with the Member States and on the basis of an independent expert study which takes due account of the expected long-term development of the shipbuilding industry so as to ensure both the optimal activity levels justifiable on economic grounds and the continuation of structural adjustment; whereas, since increased efficiency is a principal objective pursued by the premises of this Directive, the yearly review of the production aid ceiling should always aim at its progressive reduction; whereas it is necessary, in order to avoid discrimination, to make all forms of operating aid subject to the common maximum ceiling, including loss compensation and such aid as is granted indirectly through third persons; whereas, in order to permit all Member States to compete equally and in view of the persistent structural disparities of yards in the different Member States, it may be necessary to authorize restructuring aid to enable desirable structural changes to be carried out provided that they do not lead to increases in capacity; whereas, although it is proposed to treat ship conversion in the same way as shipbuilding, it is not appropriate to permit aid to the ship-repair sector in view of the continuing overcapacity in this sector, except for closure and research and development aid;

Whereas the restructuring process in Spain and Portugal is less advanced than in the other Member States and the immediate application of the common maximum ceiling for production aid may cause some difficulties in these two Member States, particular arrangements should be allowed to enable them gradually, after a further period of restructuring, to comply with the aid regime applicable to the Community as a whole;

Whereas, in order to ensure full transparency, which is a vital element in assuring the proper functioning of a Community aid system both in respect of operational aids and burden-sharing with regard to restructuring efforts, it will be necessary to strengthen the notification rules, including notification of aid to shipowners for the building or conversion of ships, together with the *a posteriori* reporting obligations of Member States as regards actual aid payments and the achievement of restructuring objectives;

Whereas the reductions in world shipping capacities should be made in such a way as to cause the least possible damage and to be as fair as possible;

Whereas additional measures should be adopted in order to alleviate the social and regional consequences of the restructuring of the shipbuilding sector;

Whereas Community measures should also be adopted in order to improve demand for new ships from Community shipyards,

HAS ADOPTED THIS DIRECTIVE:

CHAPTER I

GENERAL

Article 1

For the purpose of this Directive the following definitions shall apply:

(*a*) 'shipbuilding':
means the building in the Community of the following metal-hulled sea-going vessels:

— merchant ships for the carriage of passengers and/or cargo, of not less than 100 grt,
— fishing vessels of not less than 100 grt,
— dredgers or ships for other work at sea of not less than 100 grt excluding drilling platforms,
— tugs of not less than 365 kW;

(*b*) 'ship conversion':
means the conversion in the Community of metal-hulled sea-going vessels, as defined

in (*a*), of not less than 1 000 grt, on condition that conversion operations entail radical alterations to the cargo plan, the hull or the propulsion system or the passenger accommodation;

(*c*) 'ship repair':
means the repair of the vessels referred to in (*a*);

(*d*) 'aid'.
means State aid within the meaning of Articles 92 and 93 of the Treaty, including not only aid granted by the State itself but also that granted by regional or local authorities and any aid elements contained in the financing measures taken by Member States in respect of the shipbuilding or ship repair undertakings which they directly or indirectly control and which do not count as the provision of risk capital according to standard company practice in a market economy.

Such aid may be considered compatible with the common market provided that it complies with the criteria for derogation contained in this Directive;

(*e*) 'contract value before aid':
means the price laid down in the contract plus any aid granted directly to the shipyard.
[1271]

Article 2

No aid granted pursuant to this Directive may be conditional upon discriminatory practices as to products originating in other Member States.   **[1272]**

Article 3 — Aid to shipowners

1. All forms of aid to shipowners or to third parties which are available as aid for the building or conversion of ships shall be subject to the notification rules in Article 10.

These aids shall include credit facilities, guarantees and tax concessions granted to shipowners or third parties for the purposes referred to in the first subparagraph.

2. The grant equivalent of these aids shall be subject in full to the rules set forth in Article 4 and the monitoring procedures laid down in Article 11, where these aids are actually used for the building or conversion of ships in Community shipyards.

3. Aid granted by a Member State to its shipowners or to third parties in that State for the building or conversion of ships may not lead to distortions of competition between national shipyards and shipyards in other Member States in the placing of orders.

4. These provisions shall be entirely without prejudice to any future Community rules on aid to shipowners.   **[1273]**

CHAPTER II

OPERATING AID

Article 4 — Contract-related production aid

1. Production aid in favour of shipbuilding and ship conversion may be considered compatible with the common market provided that the total amount of aid granted in support of any individual contract does not exceed, in grant equivalent, a common maximum ceiling expressed as a percentage of the contract value before aid, hereinafter referred to as the ceiling.

2. The ceiling shall be fixed by the Commission with reference to the prevailing difference between the cost structures of the most competitive Community yards and the

prices charged by their main international competitors with particular regard to the market segments in which the Community yards remain relatively most competitive.

However, the Commission shall pay particular regard to ensure that the aid for the building of small specialized vessels, a market segment normally served by small yards, in particular small ships costing less than 6 million ECU, and for which the competition is mainly inter-European, is kept at the lowest possible level, nevertheless allowing for the particular situation in Greece.

3. The ceiling shall be reviewed every 12 months, or sooner if warranted by exceptional circumstances, with the aim of progressively reducing the ceiling. In its review of the ceiling, the Commission shall also ensure that there are no undue concentrations of shipbuilding activities in specific market segments to an extent contrary to Community interests.

4. The ceiling shall apply not only to all forms of production aid—whether under sectoral, general or regional aid schemes—granted directly to the yards but also to the aid covered by Article 3(2).

5. The combined effect of aid under the various aid schemes applied must in no case exceed the ceiling fixed according to paragraph 2; the granting of aid in individual cases shall not necessitate prior notification to, or authorization from, the Commission.

However, where there is competition between yards in different Member States for a particular contract, the Commission shall require prior notification of the relevant aid proposals at the request of any Member State. In such cases, the Commission shall adopt a position within 30 days of notification; such proposals may not be implemented before the Commission has given its authorization. By its decision in such cases the Commission shall ensure that the planned aid does not affect trading conditions to an extent contrary to the common interest.

6. Aid in the form of credit facilities for the building or conversion of vessels complying with the OECD Council resolution of 3 August 1981 (Understanding on Export Credits for Ships) or with any agreement replacing the Resolution shall not be counted within the ceiling. Such aid may be considered compatible with the common market provided that it complies with the abovementioned Resolution or any agreements which replace it.

7. Aid related to shipbuilding and ship conversion granted as development assistance to a developing country shall not be subject to the ceiling. It may be deemed compatible with the common market if it complies with the terms laid down for that purpose by OECD Working Party No 6 in its agreement concerning the interpretation of Articles 6 to 8 of the Understanding referred to in paragraph 6 of this Article or with any later addendum or corrigendum to the said Agreement.

Prior notification of any such individual aid proposal must be given to the Commission. The Commission shall verify the particular development content of the proposed aid and satisfy itself that it falls within the scope of the agreement referred to in the preceding subparagraph. **[1274]**

Article 5—Other operating aid

1. Aids to facilitate the continued operation of shipbuilding and ship conversion companies, including loss compensation, rescue aid and all other types of operating aid not directly supporting particular restructuring measures covered in Chapter III, may be deemed compatible with the common market provided that such aid together with production aid allocated directly to individual shipbuilding and ship conversion contracts in accordance with Article 4(4) does not exceed the ceiling expressed as a percentage of the aid recipient's annual turnover in shipbuilding and ship conversion.

2. It shall be incumbent on the Member States to furnish evidence of the extent to which the turnover and losses of the recipient of the aid result, on the one hand, from shipbuilding and ship conversion and, on the other, from its other activities, if any, and, if some of the aid is intended to offset losses or expenditure arising from the restructuring measures referred to in Chapter III, to identify and specify those measures.

[1275]

CHAPTER III

RESTRUCTURING AID

Article 6 – Investment aid

1. Investment aid, whether specific or non-specific, may not be granted for the creation of new shipyards or for investment in existing yards if such aid would be likely to increase the Member States' shipbuilding capacity.

Such aid may not be granted for ship repair unless linked to a restructuring plan which results in an overall reduction in the ship repair capacity of the Member State concerned. In this context the Commission may take into account capacity reductions carried out in the immediately preceding years.

2. Paragraph 1 shall not apply to the opening of a new shipyard in a Member State which otherwise would have no shipbuilding facilities or to investments in a Member State's only existing yard, provided that the effect of the yard in question on the Community market is minimal.

3. In accordance with paragraph 1, investment aid may be deemed compatible with the common market provided that:

- the amount and intensity of such aid are justified by the extent of the restructuring involved,
- it is limited to supporting expenditure directly related to the investment.

4. In examining the aid referred to in paragraphs 1 and 3, the Commission shall take account of the extent of the contribution of the investment programme concerned to such Community objectives for the sector as innovation, specialization, working conditions, health, safety and environment. **[1276]**

Article 7 – Aid for closures

1. Aid to defray the normal costs resulting from the partial or total closure of shipbuilding or ship repair yards may be considered compatible with the common market provided that the capacity reduction resulting from such aid is of a genuine and irreversible nature.

2. The costs eligible for such aid are, in particular:

- payments to workers made redundant or retired before legal retirement age,
- counselling services to workers made or to be made redundant or retired before legal retirement age including payments made by yards to facilitate the creation of small undertakings,
- payments to workers for vocational retraining,
- expenditure incurred for the redevelopment of the yard, its buildings, installations and infrastructure for use other than that specified in Article 1(a), (b), and (c),
- in the event of total closure of a yard, the residual book value of its installations (ignoring that portion of any revaluation since 1 January 1982 which exceeds the national inflation rate).

3. The amount and intensity of aid must be justified by the extent of the restructuring involved, account being taken of the structural problems of the region concerned and, in the case of conversion to other industrial activities, of the Community legislation and rules applicable to the new sector concerned. **[1277]**

Article 8 – Aid for research and development

1. Aid to defray expenditure by shipbuilding and ship repair undertakings for research and development projects may be considered compatible with the common market.

2. For the purpose of this Directive, the eligible costs shall be only those relating to fundamental research, basic industrial research and applied research and development, all as defined by the Commission in Annex I to the Community framework for State aids for research and development[1], excluding those related to industrial application and commercial exploitation of the results. **[1278]**

CHAPTER IV

SPAIN AND PORTUGAL

Article 9

1. Chapter II of this Directive shall be applicable neither in Spain nor, subject to paragraph 3 of this Article, in Portugal.

2. Operating aid for shipbuilding and ship conversion in Spain may be considered compatible with the common market provided that:

- Spain's shipbuilding industry has undertaken a systematic and specific restructuring programme, including capacity reductions, which can be considered capable of allowing it, within four years, to operate competitively,
- the aid is being progressively reduced.

3. The Portuguese Republic will be subject to all the provisions of this Directive. However, Portugal may, at any time before 31 December 1987 with immediate effect, or at the latest by 29 February 1988, with effect from 1 January 1988, opt for being exempted from the rules laid down in Chapter II either generally or as regards certain yards. Should Portugal choose this option, operating aid for shipbuilding and ship conversion may be considered compatible with the common market provided that:

- the shipbuilding industry or – should only certain yards be involved, those yards – has undertaken a systematic and specific restructuring programme, aiming at capacity reductions, which can be considered capable of allowing it, within four years, to operate competitively,
- the aid is progressively reduced. **[1279]**

CHAPTER V

MONITORING PROCEDURE

Article 10

1. In addition to the provisions of Articles 92 and 93 of the Treaty, aid to shipbuilding, ship conversion and ship repair undertakings covered by this Directive shall be subject to the special notification rules provided for in paragraph 2.

2. The following shall be notified to the Commission in advance by the Member States and authorized by the Commission before they are put into effect:

(a) any aid scheme – new or existing – or any amendment of an existing scheme covered by this;

(b) any decision to apply any general or regional aid scheme to the undertakings covered by this Directive;

(c) any individual application of aid schemes in the cases referred to in the second subparagraph of Article 4(5) and in Article 4(7) or when specifically provided for by the Commission in its approval of the aid scheme concerned.

[1280]

Article 11

1. For the Commission's monitoring of the implementation of the aid rules contained in Chapters II and III, Member States shall supply the Commission for its exclusive use with:

— current reports on each shipbuilding and ship conversion contract at the time of ordering and completion containing details of the financial contract support, in accordance with the form set out in the annexed schedule 1,

— six-monthly reports – to be provided by 1 October and 1 April in respect of the preceding half calendar years – on aid granted to shipowners, in accordance with the form set out in the annexed schedule 2,

— yearly reports giving details of the annual results of, and total financial support granted to, each individual national shipyard which has received aid, in accordance with the form set out in the attached schedule 3,

— yearly reports on the attainment of the restructuring objectives as regards the undertakings which have received aid according to Article 6, 7 and 9, in accordance with the form set out in the annexed schedule 4.

2. On the basis of the information communicated to it in accordance with Article 10 and paragraph 1 of this Article, the Commission shall draw up an annual overall report to serve as a basis for discussion with national experts. This report shall state inter alia the level of contract-related aid and other operating aid granted in each Member State during the period in question, and both the total volume of restructuring aid awarded and the progress made towards the attainment of the restructuring objectives in each Member State during the same period. **[1281]**

CHAPTER VI

FINAL PROVISIONS

Article 12

1. This Directive shall replace Council Directive 81/363/EEC.

The provisions of the aforementioned Directive shall, however, remain applicable to aid projects notified before 1 January 1987 which relate to activities initiated before that date and on which, by the date on which this Directive enters into force, no Commission decision has been taken.

2. Two years after notification of this Directive[2] the Commission shall report to the European Parliament and the Council on its application and propose any necessary adjustments. **[1282]**

Article 13

This Directive shall apply from 1 January 1987 to 31 December 1990.　　**[1283]**

Article 14

This Directive is addressed to the Member States.　　**[1284]**

Done at Brussels, 26 January 1987.

NOTES
　1　OJ No C 83, 11.4. 1986, p. 2.
　2　This Directive was notified to the Member States on 5 February 1987.

ANNEX
Schedule 1

EUROPEAN ECONOMIC COMMUNITY

REPORT OF MERCHANT SHIP ORDERS AND COMPLETIONS

1. New building/conversion	
2. Company	3. Yard 4. Yard No
5. Registered owner	
6. Holding owner	
7. Vessel's country of registration	
8. Date contract signed	9. Completion/delivery date

Section 2: Ship details

10. Type of vessel

11. Deadweight ....   13. Compensated gross tonnage (CGT)

12. Gross tonnage (GT) ....

	Currency	ECU (Prevailing rate)	% of contract price
14. Contract price			
15. Estimated contract loss (if any)			
16. Contract support			
A. Granted to yard:			
(a) grants			
(b) credit facilities			
(c) specific fiscal concession			
(d) other support			
B. Granted to customer or ultimate owners:			
(a) grants			
(b) credit facilities			
(c) fiscal concession			
(d) other support			

Contact for inquiries............   Date ....
....

Position:............   Signature:............

Schedule 2

EUROPEAN ECONOMIC COMMUNITY

REPORT ON AID TO SHIPOWNERS FOR ACQUISITION OR CONVERSION OF SHIPS

1	2	3			4	5			
		Aid granted				Acquisition or conversion contract concerned			
								Performing yard	
Case	Identification	Form	Volume	Details	Month of aid granting	Ship type	Tonnage (CGT)	Country	Name
1									
2									
3									
4									
5									
6									
7									
8									
9									
10									

Contact for inquiries: ....

Position: ....

Date: ....

Signature: ....

EUROPEAN ECONOMIC COMMUNITY

Schedule 3

REPORT OF COMPANY FINANCIAL SUPPORT

Name of company ....

Section 1: Public aid

Operating aid	Contract value (¹) Costs/loss (²)	Direct aid received	Indirect aid support (of sched.1)
1. Contract Support			
(a) related to contracts concluded before 1. 1. 1987			
(b) related to contracts concluded after 1. 1. 1987			
(c) hereof related to development assistance to developing countries			
2. Payment of other operation costs, inclusive loss compensation and rescue aid (cf. Article 5)			

Restructuring aid	Costs	Aid received
3. Investments		
4. Redundancy payments		
5. Other cash closure costs		
6. Asset disposal costs/receipts		
7. Conversion costs		
8. Research and development costs		
9. Other restructuring costs		

Contact for inquiries: ....   Date: ....

....

Position: ....   Signature: ....

Section 2: Turnover and profit/(loss) (to be filled in for all companies having received direct production aid)

	Most recent year	Previous
10. Turnover		
11. Hereof related to merchant shipbuilding and ship conversion		
(a) related to contracts concluded before 1 January 1987		
(b) related to contracts concluded after 1 January 1987		
(c) hereof related to development assistance to developing countries		
12. Losses (if any)		
13. Hereof related to merchant shipbuilding and ship conversion		
(a) related to profit/(loss) on contracts		
(b) related to movement in provisions		
(c) related to restructuring expenditures		

Section 3: **Cash flow** (to be filled in for all companies which have registered losses under 12 and have received funding from any public sources)

	Most recent year	Previous
Expenditures		
14. Trading losses before depreciation		
15. Capital expenditure		
16. Other expenditures		
17. Other change in working capital		
Source of Funds		
18. Equity receipts		
(a) from public shareholders		
(b) from private shareholders		
19. Loans and overdrafts		
(a) from public sources		
(a') hereof contract support		
(b) from private sources		
(b') hereof with state guarantee		
20. Government grants		
(a) hereof contract support		

[1287]

Schedule 4

EUROPEAN ECONOMIC COMMUNITY

REPORT OF MERCHANT SHIPYARD FACILITIES AND EMPLOYMENT

Section 1: **Facilities**   Date: . . . .   Company: . . . .

1. Berth/dock/pad	2. Current use	3. Size	4. Capacity

Section 2: **Merchant Orderbook**   Date: . . . .

5. Berth No	6. Ship No	7. Ship type	8. CGT	9. Completion date

10. Total new orders . . . . 19. . . . . Number. . . . . CGT. . . . .

11. Total completions. . . . . 19. . . . . Number. . . . . CGT. . . . .

Section 3: **Shipbuilding employment**   Date: . . . .

12. *By activity*	19. *By occupation*
13. Merchant	20. Manual
14. Offshore	21. Staff
15. Naval	22. Total merchant
16. Repair	23. Subcontractors
17. Other	24. Net change in employment
18. Total	
25. Total man-hours for the shipyard	
26. Hereof for merchant shipbuilding and conversion	

Contact for enquiries: . . . . Date: . . . .

Position: . . . . Signature: . . . .

REGULATION (EEC) No 3975/87 OF THE COUNCIL
of 14 December 1987

laying down the procedure for the application of the rules on competition to undertakings in the air transport sector

NOTE
1 This text of the Regulation incorporates the corrigenda published in OJ No L30, 2.2.88, p. 40, and OJ No L43, 15.2.89, p. 56.

THE COUNCIL OF THE EUROPEAN COMMUNITIES,
Having regard to the Treaty establishing the European Economic Community, and in particular Article 87 thereof,
Having regard to the proposal from the Commission,
Having regard to the opinions of the European Parliament
Having regard to the opinion of the Economic and Social Committee,
Whereas the rules on competition form part of the Treaty's general provisions which also apply to air transport; whereas the rules for applying these provisions are either specified in the Chapter on competition or fall to be determined by the procedures laid down therein;
Whereas, according to Council Regulation No 141, Council Regulation No 17 does not apply to transport services; whereas Council Regulation (EEC) No 1017/68 applies only to inland transport; whereas Council Regulation (EEC) No 4056/86 applies only to maritime transport; whereas consequently the Commission has no means at present of investigating directly cases of suspected infringement of Articles 85 and 86 of the Treaty in air transport; whereas moreover the Commission lacks such powers of its own to take decisions or impose penalties as are necessary for it to bring to an end infringements established by it;
Whereas air transport is characterized by features which are specific to this sector; whereas, furthermore, international air transport is regulated by a network of bilateral agreements between States which define the conditions under which air carriers designated by the parties to the agreements may operate routes between their territories;
Whereas practices which affect competition relating to air transport between Member States may have a substantial effect on trade between Member States; whereas it is therefore desirable that rules should be laid down under which the Commission, acting in close and constant liaison with the competent authorities of the Member States, may take the requisite measures for the application of Articles 85 and 86 of the Treaty to international air transport between Community airports;
Whereas such a regulation should provide for appropriate procedures, decision-making powers and penalties to ensure compliance with the prohibitions laid down in Articles 85 (1) and 86 of the Treaty; whereas account should be taken in this respect of the procedural provisions of Regulation (EEC) No 1017/68 applicable to inland transport operations, which takes account of certain distinctive features of transport operations viewed as a whole;
Whereas undertakings concerned must be accorded the right to be heard by the Commission, third parties whose interests may be affected by a decision must be given the opportunity of submitting their comments beforehand and it must be ensured that wide publicity is given to decisions taken;
Whereas all decisions taken by the Commission under this Regulation are subject to review by the Court of Justice under the conditions specified in the Treaty; whereas it is moreover desirable, pursuant to Article 172 of the Treaty, to confer upon the Court of Justice unlimited jurisdiction in respect of decisions under which the Commission imposes fines or periodic penalty payments;
Whereas it is appropriate to except certain agreements, decisions and concerted practices from the prohibition laid down in Article 85(1) of the Treaty, insofar as their sole object and effect is to achieve technical improvements or cooperation;
Whereas, given the specific features of air transport, it will in the first instance be for undertakings themselves to see that their agreements, decisions and concerted practices conform to the competition rules, and notification to the Commission need not be compulsory;
Whereas undertakings may wish to apply to the Commission in certain cases for confirmation that their agreements, decisions and concerted practices conform to the law, and a simplified procedure should be laid down for such cases;
Whereas this Regulation does not prejudice the application of Article 90 of the Treaty,
HAS ADOPTED THIS REGULATION:

Article 1 – Scope

1. This Regulation lays down detailed rules for the application of Articles 85 and 86 of the Treaty to air transport services.

2. This Regulation shall apply only to international air transport between Community airports. **[1289]**

Article 2 – Exceptions for certain technical agreements

1. The prohibition laid down in Article 85(1) of the Treaty shall not apply to the agreements, decisions and concerted practices listed in the Annex, in so far as their sole object and effect is to achieve technical improvements or cooperation. This list is not exhaustive.

2. If necessary, the Commission shall submit proposals to the Council for the amendment of the list in the Annex. **[1290]**

Article 3 – Procedures on complaint or on the Commission's own initiative

1. Acting on receipt of a complaint or on its own initiative, the Commission shall initiate procedures to terminate any infringement of the provisions of Articles 85(1) or 86 of the Treaty.
Complaints may be submitted by:

   (*a*) Member States;
   (*b*) natural or legal persons who claim a legitimate interest.

2. Upon application by the undertakings or associations of undertakings concerned, the Commission may certify that, on the basis of the facts in its possession, there are no grounds under Article 85(1) or Article 86 of the Treaty for action on its part in respect of an agreement, decision or concerted practice. **[1291]**

Article 4 – Result of procedures on complaint or on the Commission's own initiative

1. Where the Commission finds that there has been an infringement of Articles 85(1) or 86 of the Treaty, it may by decision require the undertakings or associations of undertakings concerned to bring such an infringement to an end.
Without prejudice to the other provisions of this Regulation, the Commission may address recommendations for termination of the infringement to the undertakings or associations of undertakings concerned before taking a decision under the preceding subparagraph.

2. If the Commission, acting on a complaint received, concludes that, on the evidence before it, there are no grounds for intervention under Articles 85(1) or 86 of the Treaty in respect of any agreement, decision or concerted practice, it shall take a decision rejecting the complaint as unfounded.

3. If the Commission, whether acting on a complaint received or on its own initiative, concludes that an agreement, decision or concerted practice satisfies the provisions of both Article 85(1) and 85(3) of the Treaty, it shall take a decision applying paragraph 3 of the said Article. Such a decision shall indicate the date from which it is to take effect. This date may be prior to that of the decision. **[1292]**

Article 5 – Application of Article 85(3) of the Treaty: Objections

1. Undertakings and associations of undertakings which wish to seek application of Article 85(3) of the Treaty in respect of agreements, decisions and concerted practices falling

within the provisions of paragraph 1 of the said Article to which they are parties shall submit applications to the Commission.

2. If the Commission judges an application admissible and is in possession of all the available evidence and no action under article 3 has been taken against the agreement, decision or concerted practice in question, then it shall publish as soon as possible in the Official Journal of the European Communities a summary of the application and invite all interested third parties and the Member States to submit their comments to the Commission within 30 days. Such publication shall have regard to the legitimate interest of undertakings in the protection of their business secrets.

3. Unless the Commission notifies applicants, within 90 days of the date of such publication in the Official Journal of the European Communities, that there are serious doubts as to the applicability of Article 85(3) of the Treaty, the agreement, decision or concerted practice shall be deemed exempt, in so far as it conforms with the description given in the application, from the prohibition for the time already elapsed and for a maximum of six years from the date of publication in the Official Journal of the European Communities.

If the Commission finds, after expiry of the 90-day time limit, but before expiry of the six-year period, that the conditions for applying Article 85(3) of the Treaty are not satisfied, it shall issue a decision declaring that the prohibition in Article 85(1) applies. Such decision may be retroactive where the parties concerned have given inaccurate information or where they abuse an exemption from the provisions of Article 85(1) or have contravened Article 86.

4. The Commission may notify applicants as referred to in the first subparagraph of paragraph 3; it shall do so if requested by a Member State within 45 days of the forwarding to the Member State of the application in accordance with Article 8(2). This request must be justified on the basis of considerations relating to the competition rules of the Treaty.

If it finds that the conditions of Article 85(1) and (3) of the Treaty are satisfied, the Commission shall issue a decision applying Article 85(3). The decision shall indicate the date from which it is to take effect. This date may be prior to that of the application.

[1293]

Article 6 – Duration and revocation of decisions applying Article 85(3)

1. Any decision applying Article 85(3) of the Treaty adopted under Articles 4 or 5 of this Regulation shall indicate the period for which it is to be valid; normally such period shall not be less than six years. Conditions and obligations may be attached to the decision.

2. The decision may be renewed if the conditions for applying Article 85(3) of the Treaty continue to be satisfied.

3. The Commission may revoke or amend its decision or prohibit specific acts by the parties:

(*a*) where there has been a change in any of the facts which were basic to the making of the decision; or
(*b*) where the parties commit a breach of any obligation attached to the decision; or
(*c*) where the decision is based on incorrect information or was induced by deceit; or
(*d*) where the parties abuse the exemption from the provisions of Article 85(1) of the Treaty granted to them by the decision.

In cases falling under subparagraphs (*b*), (*c*) or (*d*), the decision may be revoked with retroactive effect.   **[1294]**

Article 7 – Powers

Subject to review of its decision by the Court of justice, the Commission shall have sole power to issue decisions pursuant to Article 85(3) of the Treaty.

The authorities of the Member States shall retain the power to decide whether any case falls under the provisions of Article 85(1) or Article 86 of the Treaty, until such time as the Commission has initiated a procedure with a view to formulating a decision on the case in question or has sent notification as provided by the first subparagraph of Article 5(3) of this Regulation. **[1295]**

Article 8 – Liaison with the authorities of the Member States

1. The Commission shall carry out the procedures provided for in this Regulation in close and constant liaison with the competent authorities of the Member States; these authorities shall have the right to express their views on such procedures.

2. The Commission shall immediately forward to the competent authorities of the Member States copies of the complaints and applications and of the most important documents sent to it or which it sends out in the course of such procedures.

3. An Advisory Committee on Agreements and Dominant Positions in Air Transport shall be consulted prior to the taking of any decision following upon a procedure under Article 3 or of any decision under the second subparagraph of Article 5(3), or under the second subparagraph of paragraph 4 of the same Article or under Article 6. The Advisory Committee shall also be consulted prior to adoption of the implementing provisions provided for in Article 19.

4. The Advisory Committee shall be composed of officials competent in the sphere of air transport and agreements and dominant positions. Each Member State shall nominate two officials to represent it, each of whom may be replaced, in the event of his being prevented from attending, by another official.

5. Consultation shall take place at a joint meeting convened by the Commission; such a meeting shall be held not earlier than 14 days after dispatch of the notice convening it. In respect of each case to be examined, this notice shall be accompanied by a summary of the case, together with an indication of the most important documents, and a preliminary draft decision.

6. The Advisory Committee may deliver an opinion notwithstanding that some of its members or their alternates are not present. A report of the outcome of the consultative proceedings shall be annexed to the draft decision. It shall not be made public.

[1296]

Article 9 – Requests for information

1. In carrying out the duties assigned to it by this Regulation, the Commission may obtain all necessary information from the governments and competent authorities of the Member States and from undertakings and associations of undertakings.

2. When sending a request for information to an undertaking or association of undertakings, the Commission shall forward a copy of the request at the same time to the competent authority of the Member State in whose territory the head office of the undertaking or association of undertakings is situated.

3. In its request, the Commission shall state the legal basis and purpose of the request and also the penalties for supplying incorrect information provided for in Article 12(1)(*b*).

4. The owners of the undertakings or their representatives and, in the case of legal persons or of companies, firms or associations having no legal personality, the person

authorized to represent them by law or by their rules shall be bound to supply the information requested.

5. When an undertaking or association of undertakings does not supply the information requested within the time limit fixed by the Commission, or supplies incomplete information, the Commission shall by decision require the information to be supplied. The decision shall specify what information is required, fix an appropriate time limit within which it is to be supplied and indicate the penalties provided for in Article 12(1)(*b*) and Article 13(1)(*c*), as well as the right to have the decision reviewed by the Court of Justice.

6. At the same time the Commission shall send a copy of its decision to the competent authority of the Member State in whose territory the head office of the undertaking or association of undertakings is situated.   **[1297]**

Article 10 – Investigations by the authorities of the Member States

1. At the request of the Commission, the competent authorities of the Member States shall undertake the investigations which the Commission considers to be necessary under Article 11(1) or which it has ordered by decision adopted pursuant to Article 11(3). The officials of the competent authorities of the Member States responsible for conducting these investigations shall exercise their powers upon production of an authorization in writing issued by the competent authority of the Member State in whose territory the investigation is to be made. Such an authorization shall specify the subject matter and purpose of the investigation.

2. If so requested by the Commission or by the competent authority of the Member State in whose territory the investigation is to be made, Commission officials may assist the officials of the competent authority in carrying out their duties.   **[1298]**

Article 11 – Investigating powers of the Commission

1. In carrying out the duties assigned to it by this Regulation, the Commission may undertake all necessary investigations into undertakings and associations of undertakings. To this end the officials authorized by the Commission shall be empowered:

    (*a*) to examine the books and other business records:

    (*b*) to take copies of, or extracts from, the books and business records;

    (*c*) to ask for oral explanations on the spot;

    (*d*) to enter any premises, land and vehicles used by undertakings or associations of undertakings.

2. The authorized officials of the Commission shall exercise their powers upon production of an authorization in writing specifying the subject matter and purpose of the investigation and the penalties provided for in Article 12(1)(*c*) in cases where production of the required books or other business records is incomplete. In good time, before the investigation, the Commission shall inform the competent authority of the Member State, in whose territory the same is to be made, of the investigation and the identity of the authorized officials.

3. Undertakings and associations of undertakings shall submit to investigations ordered by decision of the Commission. The decision shall specify the subject matter and purpose of the investigation, appoint the date on which it is to begin and indicate the penalties provided for in Articles 12(1)(*c*) and 13(1)(*d*) and the right to have the decision reviewed by the Court of Justice.

4. The Commission shall take the decisions mentioned in paragraph 3 after consultation with the competent authority of the Member State in whose territory the investigation is to be made.

5. Officials of the competent authority of the Member State in whose territory the investigation is to be made may assist the Commission officials in carrying out their duties, at the request of such authority or of the Commission.

6. Where an undertaking opposes an investigation ordered pursuant to this Article, the Member State concerned shall afford the necessary assistance to the officials authorized by the Commission to enable them to make their investigation. To this end, Member States shall take the necessary measures after consultation of the Commission by 31 July 1989. **[1299]**

Article 12 — Fines

1. The Commission may, by decision, impose fines on undertakings or associations of undertakings of from 100 to 5 000 ECU where, intentionally or negligently:

    (a) they supply incorrect or misleading information in connection with an application pursuant to Article 3(2) or Article 5; or

    (b) they supply incorrect information in response to a request made pursuant to Article 9(3) or (5), or do not supply information within the time limit fixed by a decision adopted under Article 9(5); or

    (c) they produce the required books or other business records in incomplete form during investigations under Article 10 or Article 11, or refuse to submit to an investigation ordered by decision taken pursuant to Article 11(3).

2. The Commission may, by decision, impose fines on undertakings or associations of undertakings of from 1 000 to 1 000 000 ECU, or a sum in excess thereof but not exceeding 10% of the turnover in the preceding business year of the undertakings participating in the infringement, where either intentionally or negligently they:

    (a) infringe Article 85(1) or Article 86 of the Treaty; or

    (b) commit a breach of any obligation imposed pursuant to Article 6(1) of this Regulation.

In fixing the amount of the fine, regard shall be had both to the gravity and to the duration of the infringement.

3. Article 8 shall apply.

4. Decisions taken pursuant to paragraphs 1 and 2 shall not be of a penal nature.

5. The fines provided for in paragraph 2(a) shall not be imposed in respect of acts taking place after notification to the Commission and before its decision in application of Article 85(3) of the Treaty, provided they fall within the limits of the activity described in the notification.

However, this provision shall not have effect where the Commission has informed the undertakings or associations of undertakings concerned that, after preliminary examination, it is of the opinion that Article 85(1) of the Treaty applies and that application of Article 85(3) is not justified. **[1300]**

Article 13 — Periodic penalty payments

1. By decision, the Commission may impose periodic penalty payments on undertakings or associations of undertakings of from 50 ECU to 1 000 ECU per day, calculated from the date appointed by the decision, in order to compel them:

(a) to put an end to an infringement of Article 85(1) or Article 86 of the Treaty, the termination of which has been ordered pursuant to Article 4 of this Regulation;

(b) to refrain from any act prohibited under Article 6(3);

(c) to supply complete and correct information which has been requested by decision, taken pursuant to Article 9(5);

(d) to submit to an investigation which has been ordered by decision taken pursuant to Article 11(3).

2. When the undertakings or associations of undertakings have satisfied the obligation which it was the purpose of the periodic penalty payment to enforce, the Commission may fix the total amount of the periodic penalty payment at a lower figure than that which would result from the original decision.

3. Article 8 shall apply.   **[1301]**

Article 14 — Review by the Court of Justice

The Court of Justice shall have unlimited jurisdiction within the meaning of Article 172 of the Treaty to review decisions whereby the Commission has fixed a fine or periodic penalty payment; it may cancel, reduce or increase the fine or periodic penalty payment imposed.   **[1302]**

Article 15 — Unit of account

For the purpose of applying Articles 12 to 14, the ECU shall be adopted in drawing up the budget of the Community in accordance with Articles 207 and 209 of the Treaty.
                                                                             [1303]

Article 16 — Hearing of the parties and of third persons

1. Before refusing the certificate mentioned in Article 3(2), or taking decisions as provided for in Articles 4, 5(3) second sub-paragraph and 5(4), 6(3), 12 and 13, the Commission shall give the undertakings or associations of undertakings concerned the opportunity of being heard on the matters to which the Commission takes, or has taken, objection.

2. If the Commission or the competent authorities of the Member States consider it necessary, they may also hear other natural or legal persons. Applications by such persons to be heard shall be granted when they show a sufficient interest.

3. When the Commission intends to take a decision pursuant to Article 85(3) of the Treaty, it shall publish a summary of the relevant agreement, decision or concerted practice in the Official Journal of the European Communities and invite all interested third parties to submit their observations within a period, not being less than one month, which it shall fix. Publication shall have regard to the legitimate interest of undertakings in the protection of their business secrets.   **[1304]**

Article 17 — Professional secrecy

1. Information acquired as a result of the application of Articles 9 to 11 shall be used only for the purpose of the relevant request or investigation.

2. Without prejudice to the provisions of Articles 16 and 18, the Commission and the competent authorities of the Member States, their officials and other servants shall not disclose information of a kind covered by the obligation of prefessional secrecy and which has been acquired by them as a result of the application of this Regulation.

3. The provisions of paragraphs 1 and 2 shall not prevent publication of general information or of surveys which do not contain information relating to particular undertakings or associations of undertakings.   **[1305]**

Article 18 – Publication of decisions

1. The Commission shall publish the decisions which it adopts pursuant to Articles 3(2), 4, 5(3) second subparagraph, 5(4) and 6(3).

2. The publication shall state the names of the parties and the main contents of the decision; it shall have regard to the legitimate interest of undertakings in the protection of their business secrets.   **[1306]**

Article 19 – Implementing provisions

The Commission shall have the power to adopt implementing provisions concerning the form, content and other details of complaints pursuant to Article 3, applications pursuant to Articles 3(2) and 5 and the hearings provided for in Article 16(1) and (2).   **[1307]**

Article 20 – Entry into force

This Regulation shall enter into force on 1 January 1988.   **[1308]**

This Regulation shall be binding in its entirety and directly applicable in all Member States.

Done at Brussels, 14 December 1987.

ANNEX

LIST REFERRED TO IN ARTICLE 2

(a) The introduction or uniform application of mandatory or recommended technical standards for aircraft, aircraft parts, equipment and aircraft supplies, where such standards are set by an organisation normally accorded international recognition, or by an aircraft or equipment manufacturer;
(b) the introduction or uniform application of technical standards for fixed installations for aircraft, where such standards are set by an organisation normally accorded international recognition;
(c) the exchange, leasing, pooling, or maintenance of aircraft, aircraft parts, equipment or fixed installations for the purpose of operating air services and the joint purchase of aircraft parts, provided that such arrangements are made on a non-discriminatory basis;
(d) the introduction, operation and maintenance of technical communication networks, provided that such arrangements are made on a non-discriminatory basis;
(e) the exchange, pooling or training of personnel for technical or operational purposes;
(f) the organisation and execution of substitute transport operations for passengers, mail and baggage, in the event of breakdown/delay of aircraft, either under charter or by provision of substitute aircraft under contractual arrangements;
(g) the organisation and execution of successive or supplementary air transport operations, and the fixing and application of inclusive rates and conditions for such operations;
(h) the consolidation of individual consignments;
(i) the establishment or application of uniform rules concerning the structure and the conditions governing the application of transport tariffs, provided that such rules do not directly or indirectly fix transport fares and conditions;

(*j*) arrangements as to the sale, endorsement and acceptance of tickets between air carriers (interlining) as well as the refund, pro-rating and accounting schemes established for such purposes;

(*k*) the clearing and settling of accounts between air carriers by means of a clearing house, including such services as may be necessary or incidental thereto; the clearing and settling of accounts between air carriers and their appointed agents by means of a centralised and automated settlement plan or system, including such services as may be necessary or incidental thereto. **[1309]**

REGULATION (EEC) No 3976/87 OF THE COUNCIL
of 14 December 1987

on the application of Article 85(3) of the Treaty to certain categories of agreements and concerted practices in the air transport sector

THE COUNCIL OF THE EUROPEAN COMMUNITIES,

Having regard to the Treaty establishing the European Economic Community and in particular Article 87 thereof,

Having regard to the proposal from the Commission

Having regard to the opinions of the European Parliament

Having regard to the opinions of the Economic and Social Committee,

Whereas Council Regulation (EEC) No 3975/87 lays down the procedure for the application of the rules on competition to undertakings in the air transport sector; whereas Regulation No 17 of the Council lays down the procedure for the application of these rules to agreements, decisions and concerted practices other than those directly relating to the provision of air transport services;

Whereas Article 85(1) of the Treaty may be declared inapplicable to certain categories of agreements, decisions and concerted practices which fulfil the conditions contained in Article 85(3);

Whereas common provisions for the application of Article 85(3) should be adopted by way of Regulation pursuant to Article 87; whereas, according to Article 87(2)(*b*), such a Regulation must lay down detailed rules for the application of Article 85(3), taking into account the need to ensure effective supervision, on the one hand, and to simplify administration to the greatest possible extent, on the other; whereas, according to Article 87(2)(*d*), such a Regulation is required to define the respective functions of the Commission and of the Court of Justice;

Whereas the air transport sector has to date been governed by a network of international agreements, bilateral agreements between States and bilateral and multilateral agreements between air carriers; whereas the changes required to this international regulatory system to ensure increased competition should be effected gradually so as to provide time for the air transport sector to adapt;

Whereas the Commission should be enabled for this reason to declare by way of Regulation that the provisions of Article 85(1) do not apply to certain categories of agreements between undertakings, decisions by associations of undertakings and concerted practices;

Whereas it should be laid down under what specific conditions and in what circumstances the Commission may exercise such powers in close and constant liaison with the competent authorities of the Member States;

Whereas it is desirable, in particular, that block exemptions be granted for certain categories of agreements, decisions and concerted practices; whereas these exemptions should be granted for a limited period during which air carriers can adapt to a more competitive environment; whereas the Commission, in close liaison with the Member States, should be able to define precisely the scope of these exemptions and the conditions attached to them;

Whereas there can be no exemption if the conditions set out in Article 85(3) are not satisfied; whereas the Commission should therefore have power to take the appropriate measures where an agreement proves to have effects incompatible with Article 85(3); whereas the Commission should consequently be able first to address recommendations to the parties and then to take decisions;

Whereas this Regulation does not prejudice the application of Article 90 of the Treaty;

Whereas the Heads of State and Government, at their meeting in June 1986, agreed that the internal market in air transport should be completed by 1992 in pursuance of Community actions leading to the strengthening of its economic and social cohesion; whereas the provisions of this Regulation, together with those of Council Directive 87/601/EEC of 14 December 1987 on fares for scheduled air services between Member States and those of Council Decision 87/602/EEC of 14 December 1987 on the sharing of passenger capacity between air carriers on scheduled air services between Member States and on access for air carriers to scheduled air service routes betwen Member States, are a first step in this direction and the Council will therefore, in order to meet the objective set by the Heads of State and Government, adopt further measures of liberalization at the end of a three year initial period,

HAS ADOPTED THIS REGULATION:

Article 1

This Regulation shall apply to international air transport between Community airports.

[1310]

Article 2

1. Without prejudice to the application of Regulation (EEC) No 3975/87 and in accordance with Article 85(3) of the Treaty, the Commission may by regulation declare that Article 85(1) shall not apply to certain categories of agreements between undertakings, decisions of associations of undertakings and concerted practices.

2. The Commission may, in particular adopt such regulations in respect of agreements, decisions or concerted practices which have as their object any of the following:

- joint planning and coordination of the capacity to be provided on scheduled air services, insofar as it helps to ensure a spread of services at the less busy times of the day or during less busy periods or on less busy routes, so long as any partner may withdraw without penalty from such agreements, decisions or concerted practices, and is not required to give more than three months' notice of its intention not to participate in such joint planning and coordination for future seasons,
- sharing of revenue from scheduled air services, so long as the transfer does not exceed 1% of the poolable revenue earned on a particular route by the transferring partner, no costs are shared or accepted by the transferring partner and the transfer is made in compensation for the loss incurred by the receiving partner in scheduling flights at less busy times of the day or during less busy periods,
- consultations for common preparation of proposals on tariffs, fares and conditions for the carriage of passengers and baggage on scheduled services, on condition that consultations on this matter are voluntary, that air carriers will not be bound by their results and that the Commission and the Member States whose air carriers are concerned may participate as observers in any such consultations,
- slot allocation at airports and airport scheduling, on condition that the air carriers concerned shall be entitled to participate in such arrangements, that the national and multilateral procedures for such arrangements are transparent and that they take into account any constraints and distribution rules defined by national or international authorities and any rights which air carriers may have historically acquired,
- common purchase, development and operation of computer reservation systems relating to timetabling, reservations and ticketing by air transport undertakings, on condition that air carriers of Member States have access to such systems on equal terms, that participating carriers have their services listed on a non-discriminatory basis and also that any participant may withdraw from the system on giving reasonable notice,
- technical and operational ground handling at airports, such as aircraft push back, refuelling, cleaning and security,
- handling of passengers, mail, freight and baggage at airports,
- services for the provision of in-flight catering.
- [- consultations on cargo rates][1]

3. Without prejudice to paragraph 2, such Commission regulations shall define the categories of agreements, decisions or concerted practices to which they apply and shall specify in particular:

(a) the restrictions or clauses which may, or may not, appear in the agreements, decisions and concerted practices;

(b) the clauses which must be contained in the agreements, decisions and concerted practices, or any other conditions which must be satisfied.   **[1311]**

Article 3

Any regulation adopted by the Commission pursuant to Article 2 shall expire on [31 December 1992].[1]   **[1312]**

Article 4

Regulations adopted pursuant to Article 2 shall include a provision that they apply with retroactive effect to agreements, decisions and concerted practices which were in existence at the date of the entry into force of such regulations.   **[1313]**

Article 5

Before adopting a regulation, the Commission shall publish a draft thereof and invite all persons and organizations concerned to submit their comments within such reasonable time limit, being not less than one month, as the Commission shall fix.   **[1314]**

Article 6

The Commission shall consult the Advisory Committee on Agreements and Dominant Positions in Air Transport established by Article 8(3) of Regulation (EEC) No 3975/87 before publishing a draft Regulation and before adopting a Regulation,   **[1315]**

Article 7

Where the persons concerned are in breach of a condition or obligation which attaches to an exemption granted by a Regulation adopted pursuant to Article 2, the Commission may, in order to put an end to such a breach:

— address recommendations to the persons concerned, and
— in the event of failure by such persons to observe those recommendations, and depending on the gravity of the breach concerned, adopt a decision that either prohibits them from carrying out, or requires them to perform, specific acts or, while withdrawing the benefit of the block exemption which they enjoyed, grants them an individual exemption in accordance with Article 4(2) of Regulation (EEC) No 3975/87 or withdraws the benefit of the block exemption which they enjoyed.

2. Where the Commission, either on its own initiative or at the request of a Member State or of natural or legal persons claiming a legitimate interest, finds that in any particular case an agreement, decision or concerted practice to which a block exemption granted by a regulation adopted pursuant to Article 2(2) applies, nevertheless has effects which are incompatible with Article 85(3) or are prohibited by Article 86, it may withdraw the benefit of the block exemption from those agreements, decisions or concerted practices and take, pursuant to Article 13 of Regulation (EEC) No 3975/87, all appropriate measures for the purpose of bringing these infringements to an end.

3. Before taking a decision under paragraph 2, the Commission may address recommendations for termination of the infringement to the persons concerned.   **[1316]**

Article 8

The Council shall decide on the revision of this Regulation by [31 December 1992] on the basis of a Commission proposal to be submitted by [1 July 1992].[1]   **[1317]**

Article 9

This Regulation shall enter into force on 1 January 1988.   **[1318-51]**

This Regulation shall be binding in its entirety and directly applicable in all Member States.

Done at Brussels, 14 December 1987

AMENDMENTS
1 New indent in Article 2(2) and the dates in Articles 3 and 8 inserted by Council Regulation (EEC) No 2344/90 with effect from 12 August 1990.

DIRECTIVE No 87/601 OF THE COUNCIL
of 14 December 1987

on fares for scheduled air services between Member States

(revoked by Council Regulation (EEC) No 2342/90, post)

DECISION No 87/602 OF THE COUNCIL
of 14 December 1987

on the sharing of passenger capacity between air carriers on scheduled air services between Member States and on access for air carriers to scheduled air-service routes between Member States

(revoked by Council Regulation (EEC) No 2343/90, post)

REGULATION (EEC) No 2671/88 OF THE COMMISSION
of 26 July 1988[1]

on the application of Article 85(3) of the Treaty to certain categories of agreements between undertakings, decisions of associations of undertakings and concerted practices concerning joint planning and coordination of capacity, sharing of revenue and consultations on tariffs on scheduled air services and slot allocation at airports

NOTE
1 This text of the Regulation incorporates the corrigendum published by the Commission in OJ No L 66, 10.3.89, p. 39.

THE COMMISSION OF THE EUROPEAN COMMUNITIES,
Having regard to the Treaty establishing the European Economic Community,
Having regard to Council Regulation (EEC) No 3976/87 of 14 December 1987 on the application of Article 85(3) of the Treaty to certain categories of agreements and concerted practices in the air transport sector, and in particular Article 2 thereof,
Having published a draft of this Regulation,
Having consulted the Advisory Committee on Agreements and Dominant Positions in Air Transport,
Whereas

(1) Regulation (EEC) No 3976/87 empowers the Commission to apply Article 85(3) of the Treaty by regulation to certain categories of agreements, decisions or concerted practices relating directly or indirectly to the provision of air transport services.

(2) Agreements, decisions or concerted practices concerning joint planning and coordination of capacity, sharing of revenue, consultations on tariffs and slot allocation at airports are liable to restrict competition and affect trade between Member States.

(3) Agreements concerning joint planning and coordination of capacity can help ensure the maintenance of services at less busy times of the day, during less busy periods or on less busy routes, thus benefiting air transport users. However, no air carrier should be bound by each agreement or concerted practice but must be free to change its planned services unilaterally. Nor must they prevent carriers deploying extra capacity. Any clauses concerning extra flights must not require prior approval in the event of deviation or involve financial penalties. Agreements must also allow parties to withdraw from them at reasonably short notice.

(4) Agreements on the sharing of revenue may encourage airlines to provide a service on a route during less busy periods, thereby improving the service to air transport users. To be eligible for exemption under Article 85(3), however, revenue sharing must be kept within limits such that it does not affect the competitiveness of more efficient carriers. It must also be clearly related—route by route, and not merely in aggregate, because each route has its specific features—to improvements in the services covered by the agreement.

(5) Council Directive 87/601/EEC of 14 December 1987 on fares for scheduled air services between Member States has laid down a new procedure for the establishment of air fares, which is a step towards an increase in price competition in air transport. The procedure restricts the possibility of innovative and competitive fare proposals by air carriers being blocked. Hence, competition may not be eliminated under these arrangements and consumers will benefit from them. Consultations on tariffs between air carriers may therefore be permitted, provided that participation in such consultations is optional, that they do not lead to an agreement in respect of tariffs or related conditions and that in the interests of transparency the Commission and the Member States concerned can send observers to them.

(6) Agreements on slot allocation at airports and airport scheduling can improve the utilization of airport capacity and airspace, facilitate air traffic control and help spread out the supply of air transport services from the airport. However, to provide a satisfactory degree of security and transparency, such arrangements can only be accepted if all the air carriers concerned can participate in the negotiations, and if the allocation is made on a non-discriminatory and transparent basis.

(7) In accordance with Article 4 of Regulation (EEC) No 3976/87, this Regulation should apply with retroactive effect to agreements, decisions and concerted practices in existence on the date of entry into force of this Regulation, provided that they meet the conditions for exemption set out in this Regulation.

(8) Under Article 7 of Regulation (EEC) No 3976/87, this Regulation should also specify the circumstances in which the Commission may withdraw the block exemption in individual cases.

(9) No applications under Articles 3 or 5 of Council Regulation (EEC) No 3975/874 need be made in respect of agreements automatically exempted by this Regulation. However, when real doubt exists, undertakings may request the Commission to declare whether their agreements comply with this Regulation.

(10) The Regulation is without prejudice to the application of Article 86 of the Treaty,
HAS ADOPTED THIS REGULATION:

TITLE I

EXEMPTIONS

Article 1

Pursuant to Article 85(3) of the Treaty and subject to the provisions of this Regulation, it is hereby declared that Article 85(1) of the Treaty shall not apply to agreements between undertakings in the air transport sector, decisions by associations of such undertakings and concerted practices between such undertakings which have as their purpose one or more of the following:

— joint planning and coordination of the capacity to be provided on scheduled international air services between Community airports,
— sharing of revenue from scheduled international air services between Community airports,
— the holding of consultations for the joint preparation of proposals on tariffs for the carriage of passengers and baggage on scheduled international air services between Community airports,
— slot allocation and airport scheduling in so far as they concern international air services between airports in the Community.   **[1352]**

TITLE II

SPECIAL PROVISIONS

Article 2 — Special provisions for agreements on joint planning and coordination of capacity

The exemption concerning joint planning and coordination of the capacity to be provided on scheduled air services shall apply only if:

(a) the agreements, decisions and concerted practices do not bind air carriers to the results of the planning and coordination;

(b) the planning and coordination are intended to ensure a satisfactory supply of services at less busy times of the day, during less busy periods or on less busy routes;

(c) the agreements, decisions and concerted practices do not include arrangements such as to limit in advance, directly or indirectly, the capacity to be provided by the participants or to share capacity.

(d) the agreements, decisions and concerted practices do not prevent carriers taking part in the planning and coordination from changing their planned services, both with respect to capacity and schedules, without incurring penalties and without being required to obtain the prior approval of the other participants;

(e) the arrangements, decisions and concerted practices do not prevent carriers from withdrawing from the planning and coordination for future seasons without penalty, on giving notice of not more than three months to that effect;

(f) the agreements, decisions and concerted practices do not seek to influence the capacity provided or schedules adopted by carriers not participating in them.
                                                                                         [1353]

Article 3 — Special provisions for agreements for the sharing of revenue from scheduled air services

1. The exemption concerning the sharing of revenue from scheduled air services shall apply only if:

(a) the transfer of revenue is made in compensation for the loss incurred by the receiving partner in scheduling flights at less busy times of the day, or during less busy periods in a particular traffic season;

(b) the transfer can be made in only one direction, which is to be determined in advance when the agreement is concluded for the season in question

(c) the transfer does not exceed 1% of the revenue earned by the transferring partner on the route concerned, after deducting 20% of that revenue as a contribution to costs;

(d) neither partner bears any of the costs incurred by the other partner

(e) the agreement contains no provision which would impede either carrier from providing additional capacity, whether such impediment is financial or through a procedure for allocating such capacity.

2. Where the agreement covers several routes, the transfer of revenue shall be determined route by route and all the conditions referred to in paragraph 1 shall be satisfied individually for each route (city pair or, where points are combined, group of cities).

[1354]

Airports serving the same city shall be same point.

Article 4 – Special provisions for agreements on consultations on tariffs

1. The exemption concerning the holding of consultations on tariffs shall apply only if:

(a) the consultations are solely intended to prepare jointly tariff proposals covering scheduled air fares to be paid by members of the public directly to a participating air carrier or to its authorized agents for carriage as passengers with their accompanying baggage on a scheduled service and the conditions under which those fares apply, in application of Article 4 of Directive 87/601/EEC;

(b) the consultations only concern tariffs subject to approval by the aeronautical authorities of the Member States concerned, and do not extend to the capacity for which such tariffs are to be available;

(c) the tariffs which are the subject of the consultations are applied by participating air carriers without discrimination on grounds of passengers' nationality or place of residence within the Community;

(d) participation in the consultations is voluntary and open to any air carrier who operates or has applied to operate on the route concerned;

(e) any draft tariff proposals which may result from the consultations are not binding on participants, that is to say, following the consultations the participants retain the right to act independently, both in putting forward tariff proposals for approval independently of the other participants and in freely applying such tariffs after they have been approved;

(f) the consultations do not entail agreement on agents' remuneration or other elements of the tariffs discussed;

(g) in respect of each tariff which was the subject of the consultations, each participant informs the Commission without delay of its submission to the aeronautical authorities of the Member States concerned.

2. (a) The Commission and the Member States concerned shall be entitled to send observers to tariff consultations, whether bilateral or multilateral. For this purpose, air carriers shall give the Member States concerned and the Commission the same notice as is given to participants, but not less than 10 days' notice, of the date, venue and subject-matter of the consultations.

(b) Such notice shall be given

(i) to the Member States concerned according to procedures to be established by the competent authorities of those Member States;

(ii) to the Commission according to procedures to be published from time to time in the Official Journal of the European Communities.

(c) A full report on the consultations shall be submitted to the Commission by or on behalf of the air carriers involved at the same time as it is submitted to participants, but not later than six weeks after the consultations were held.

[1355]

Article 5 – Special provisions for agreements on slot allocation and airport scheduling

1. The exemption concerning slot allocation and airport scheduling shall apply only if:

   (a) The consultations on slot allocation and airport scheduling are open to all air carriers having expressed an interest in the slots which are the subject of the consultations;

   (b) Any rules of priority established are neither directly nor indirectly related to carrier identity or nationality or category of service and take into account constraints or air traffic distribution rules laid down by competent national or international authorities. Such rules of priority may take account of rights acquired by air carriers through the use of particular slots in the previous corresponding season;

   (c) The rules of priority established shall be made available on request to any interested party;

   (d) The rules of priority shall be applied without discrimination, that is to say that the rules shall not prevent each carrier having an equal right to slots for its services.

2. (a) The Commission and the Member States concerned shall be entitled to send observers to consultations on slot allocation and airport scheduling held in the context of a multilateral meeting in advance of each season. For this purpose, air carriers shall give the Member States concerned and the Commission the same notice as is given to participants, but not less than 10 days' notice, of the date, venue and subject-matter of the consultations.

   (b) Such notice shall be given

      (i) to the Member States concerned according to procedures to be established by the competent authorities of those Member States;

      (ii) to the Commission according to procedures to be published from time to time in the Official Journal of the European Communities.   **[1356]**

Article 6

Any air carrier claiming the benefit of this Regulation must be able at all times to demonstrate to the Commission, on request, that the conditions of Articles 2 to 5 are fulfilled.

[1357]

TITLE III

MISCELLANEOUS PROVISIONS

Article 7

The Commission may withdraw the benefit of this Regulation, pursuant to Article 7 of Regulation (EEC) No 3976/87, where it finds in a particular case that an agreement, decision or concerted practice exempted under this Regulation nevertheless has certain effects which are incompatible with the conditions laid down by Article 85(3) or are prohibited by Article 86 of the Treaty.   **[1358]**

Article 8

This Regulation shall enter into force on the day following its publication in the Official Journal of the European Communities.

It shall apply with retroactive effect to agreements, decisions and concerted practices which were in existence at the date of is entry into force, from the time when the conditions of application of this Regulation were fulfilled.

It shall expire on 31 January 1991.   **[1359]**

This Regulation shall be binding in its entirety and directly applicable in all Member States.

Done at Brussels, 26 July 1988.

REGULATION (EEC) No 2672/88 OF THE COMMISSION
of 26 July 1988

on the application of Article 85(3) of the Treaty to certain categories of agreements between undertakings, relating to computer reservation systems for air transport services

THE COMMISSION OF THE EUROPEAN COMMUNITIES,

Having regard to the Treaty establishing the European Economic Community,

Having regard to Council Regulation (EEC) No 3976/87 of 14 December 1987 on the application of Article 85(3) of the Treaty to certain categories of agreements and concerted practices in the air transport sector, and in particular to Article 2 thereof,

Having published a draft of this Regulation

Having consulted the Advisory Committee on Agreements and Dominant Positions in Air Transport,

Whereas

(1) Regulation (EEC) 3976/87 empowers the Commission to apply Article 85(3) of the Treaty by regulation to certain categories of agreements, decisions and concerted practices relating directly or indirectly to the provision of air transport services.

(2) Agreements for the common purchase, development and operation of computer reservation systems relating to time-tabling, reservations and ticketing are liable to restrict competition and affect trade between Member States.

(3) Computer reservation systems can render useful services to air carriers, travel agents and air travellers alike by giving ready access to up-to-date and detailed information in particular about flight possibilities, fare options and seat availability. They can also be used to make reservations and in some cases to print tickets and issue boarding passes. They thus help the air traveller to exercise choice on the basis of fuller information in order to meet his travel needs in the optimal manner. However, in order for these benefits to be obtained, flight schedules and fare displays must be as compete and unbiased as possible.

(4) The CRS market is such that few individual European undertakings could on their own make the investment and achieve the economies of scale required to compete with the more advanced existing systems. Cooperation in this field should therefore be permitted. A block exemption should therefore be granted for such cooperation.

(5) The cooperation should not allow the parent carriers to create undue advantages for themselves and thereby distort competition. It is therefore necessary to ensure that no discrimination exists between parent carriers and participating carriers with regard in particular to access and neutrality of display. The block exemption should be subject to conditions which will ensure that all air carriers can participate in the systems on a non-discriminatory basis as regards access, display,

information loading and fees. Moreover, in order to maintain competition in an oligopolistic market subscribers must be able to switch from one system to another at short notice and without penalty, and system vendors and air carriers must not act in ways which would restrict competition between systems.

(6) In accordance with Article 4 of Regulation (EEC) No 3976/87 this Regulation should apply with retroactive effect to agreements in existence on the date of entry into force of this Regulation provided that they meet the conditions for exemption set out in this Regulation.

(7) Under Article 7 of Regulation (EEC) No 3976/87, this Regulation should also specify the circumstances in which the Commission may withdraw the block exemption in individual cases.

(8) Agreements which are exempted automatically by this Regulation need not be notified under Council Regulation No 17. However, when real doubt exists, undertakings may request the Commission to declare whether their agreements comply with this Regulation.

(9) This Regulation is without prejudice to the application of Article 86 of the Treaty,
HAS ADOPTED THIS REGULATION:

Article 1 – Exemptions

Pursuant to Article 85(3) of the Treaty and subject to the conditions set out in Articles 3 to 10 of this Regulation, it is hereby declared that Article 85(1) of the Treaty shall not apply to agreements between undertakings the purpose of which is one or more of the following:

(a) to purchase or develop a CRS in common
(b) to create a system vendor to market and operate the CRS;
(c) to regulate the provision of distribution facilities by the system vendor or by distributors.

The exemption shall apply only to the following obligations:

(i) an obligation not to engage directly or indirectly in the development, marketing or operation of another CRS;

(ii) an obligation on the system vendor to appoint parent carriers or participating carriers as distributors in respect of all or certain subscribers in a defined area of the common market;

(iii) an obligation on the system vendor to grant a distributor exclusive rights to solicit all or certain subscribers in a defined area of the common market; or

(iv) an obligation on the system vendor not to allow distributors to sell distribution facilities provided by other system vendors. **[1360]**

Article 2 – Definitions

For the purposes of this Regulation

— "Computer reservation system" or "CRS" means a computerized system containing information about air carrier schedules, fares, seat availability and related services, through which reservations can be made or tickets issued or both.

— "Distribution facilities" means facilities provided by a system vendor for the display of information to subscribers about air carrier schedules, fares, seat availability, for making reservations or issuing tickets or both, and for providing any other related services.

— "Distributor" means an undertaking which is authorized by the system vendor to provide distribution facilities to subscribers.

— "Parent carrier" means an air carrier which is a system vendor or which directly or indirectly, alone or jointly with others owns or controls a system vendor.

— "Participating carrier" means an air carrier which has an agreement with a system vendor for the display of its flight schedules, fares or seat availability or for reservations to be made or tickets to be issued through the CRS for the sale of air transport

services to members of the public. To the extent that a parent carrier uses its own CRS distribution facilities it is considered a participating carrier.
— "Subscriber" means an undertaking other than a participating carrier, using a CRS within the Community under contract or other arrangement with a system vendor or a distributor for the sale of air transport services to members of the public.
— "System vendor" means an undertaking which operates a CRS.   **[1361]**

Article 3 — Access

1. The system vendor shall, within the available capacity, offer any air carrier the opportunity to become a participating carrier. The system vendor shall not require acceptance of supplementary obligations which, by their nature or according to commercial usage, have no connection with participation in the CRS.

2. Distribution facilities provided by the system vendor shall be offered to all participating carriers without discrimination.

3. A participating carrier shall have the right to terminate his contract with the system vendor without penalty on giving notice which shall not exceed six months to expire no earlier than the end of the first year.   **[1362]**

Article 4 — Display

1. Participating carriers shall be entitled to have their schedules, fares and availability displayed in a neutral display identified as such. This display shall be without discrimination, in particular as regards the order in which information is presented, which shall not be based on any factor directly or indirectly relating to carrier identity.

2. The system vendor shall not intentionally or negligently display inaccurate or misleading information.

3. The methodologies used for the ranking and presentation of information displayed by the CRS shall be made available to interested parties on request.   **[1363]**

Article 5 — Information loading

The system vendor shall not discriminate between participating carriers in the care and timeliness of information loading.   **[1364]**

Article 6 — Fees

Any fee charged by the system vendor shall be non-discriminatory and reasonably related to the cost of the service provided and shall in particular be the same for the same level of service.   **[1365]**

Article 7 — Reciprocity

1. The conditions laid down in Articles 3 to 6 shall not apply to a system vendor in respect of an air carrier that is a parent carrier owning or controlling another CRS, to the extent that such other CRS does not offer equivalent treatment to parent carriers owning or controlling the CRS subject to this Regulation.

2. The system vendor proposing to avail itself of the provisions of paragraph 1 must notify the Commission of its intentions and the reasons therefor at least 14 days in advance of such action.   **[1366]**

Article 8—Contracts with subscribers

1. A subscriber shall have a right to terminate his contract with the system vendor or distributor without penalty on giving notice which shall not exceed three months to expire no earlier than the end of the first year.

2. The system vendor or distributor shall not require a subscriber to sign an exclusive contract, nor directly or indirectly prevent a subscriber from subscribing to or using another CRS. **[1367]**

Article 9—Obligations of parent carriers

A parent carrier shall not link commissions or other incentives to subscribers for the sale of tickets on its air transport services to the utilization by the subscribers of the CRS of which it is a parent carrier. **[1368]**

Article 10—Competition between system vendors

The system vendor shall not enter into any agreement or engage in a concerted practice with other system vendors with the object or effects partitioning the market. **[1369]**

Article 11

The Commission may withdraw the benefit of this Regulation, pursuant to Article 7 of Regulation (EEC) No 3976/87, where it finds in a particular case that an agreement exempted by this Regulation nevertheless has certain effects which are incompatible with the conditions laid down by Article 85(3) or which are prohibited by Article 86 of the Treaty, and in particular where

   (i) the agreement hinders the maintenance of effective competition in the market for computer reservation systems
  (ii) the agreement has the effect of restricting competition in the air transport or travel-related markets
 (iii) the system vendor directly or indirectly imposes unfair prices, fees or charges on subscribers or on participating carriers
 (iv) the system vendor or distributor refuses to enter into a contract with a subscriber for the use of a CRS without an objective and legitimate reason of a technical or commercial nature
  (v) a parent carrier who holds a dominant position within the common market or in a substantial part of it refuses to participate in the distribution facilities provided by a competing CRS without an objective and legitimate reason of a technical or commercial nature. **[1370]**

Article 12

This Regulation shall enter into force on the day of its publication in the Official Journal of the European Communities.

It shall apply with retroactive effect to agreements which were in existence at the date of its entry into force, from the time when the conditions of application of this Regulation were fulfilled.

It shall expire on, 31 January 1991. **[1371]**

This Regulation shall be binding in its entirety and directly applicable in all Member States.

Done at Brussels, 26 July 1988.

REGULATION (EEC) No 2673/88 OF THE COMMISSION
of 26 July 1988[1]

on the application of Article 85(3) of the Treaty to certain categories of agreements between undertakings decisions of associations of undertakings and concerted practices concerning ground handling services

NOTE

1 This text of the Regulation incorporates the corrigendum published by the Commission in OJ No L 66, 10.3.89. p. 39.

THE COMMISSION OF THE EUROPEAN COMMUNITIES,

Having regard to the Treaty establishing the European Economic Community,

Having regard to Council Regulation (EEC) No 3976/87 of 14 December 1987 on the application of Article 85(3) of the Treaty to certain categories of agreements and concerted practices in the air transport sector, and in particular Article 2 thereof,

Having published a draft of this Regulation,

Having consulted the Advisory Committee on Agreements and Dominant Positions in Air Transport,

Whereas

(1) Regulation (EEC) No 3976/87 empowers the Commission to apply Article 85(3) of the Treaty by regulation to certain categories of agreements, decisions and concerted practices relating directly or indirectly to the provision of air transport services.

(2) Agreements, decisions or concerted practices concerning ground handling services provided either by air carriers or specialized undertakings, such as technical and operational ground handling, handling of passengers, mail, freight and baggage, and services for the provision of in-flight catering, are liable in certain circumstances to restrict competition and affect trade between Member States. It is appropriate, in the interests of legal certainty for the undertakings concerned, to define a category of agreements which, although not generally restrictive of competition, may benefit from an exemption in the event that, because of particular economic or legal consequences, they should fall within the scope of Article 85(1).

(3) Such agreements, decisions or concerted practices may produce economic benefits, in so far as they help to ensure that services of a high standard are provided with continuity and at reasonable cost, and both air carriers and air transport users share in those benefits.

(4) However, it is necessary to attach conditions to the exemption of such agreements, decisions and concerted practices to ensure that they do not contain restrictions that are not indispensable for the optimal provision of the services, and that they do not lead to the elimination of competition with respect of those services.

(5) The exemption granted by the Regulation must therefore be subject to the condition that the agreements do not oblige air carriers to obtain services exclusively from a particular supplier, that the supply of the services is not tied to the conclusion of contracts for other goods or services, that each airline is free to choose from the range of services offered to it those which best meet its needs, that the rates charged are reasonable for the services actually provided and that air carriers are free to withdraw from the agreements without penalty upon simple notice of not more than three months to that effect.

(6) In accordance with Article 4 of Regulation (EEC) No 3976/87, this Regulation should apply with retroactive effect to agreements, decisions and concerted practices in existence on the date of entry into force of this Regulation provided that they meet the conditions for exemption set out in this Regulation.

(7) Under Article 7 of Regulation (EEC) No 3976/87, this Regulation should also specify the circumstances in which the Commission may withdraw the block exemption in individual cases.

(8) Agreements, decisions and concerted practices that are exempted automatically by this Regulation need not be notified under Council Regulation No 17. However, when real doubt exists undertakings may request the Commission to declare whether their agreements comply with this Regulation.

(9) This Regulation is without prejudice to the application of Article 86 of the Treaty,

HAS ADOPTED THIS REGULATION:

Article 1

Pursuant to Article 85(3) of the Treaty and subject to the provisions of Article 3 of this Regulation, it is hereby declared that Article 85(1) of the Treaty shall not apply to agreements, decisions or concerted practices to which only two undertakings are party and which deal only with the supply by one party of services referred to in Article 2 to an air carrier at an airport in the Community open to international air traffic. **[1372]**

Article 2

The exemption granted under Article 85(3) of the Treaty shall apply to the following services:

1. all technical and operational services generally provided on the ground at airports, such as the provision of the necessary flight documents and information to crews, apron services, including loading and unloading, safety, aircraft servicing and refuelling, and operations before take-off;
2. all services connected with the handling of passengers, mail, freight and baggage, such as information to passengers and visitors, the handling of passengers and their baggage before departure and after arrival and the handling and storage of freight and mail in conjunction with the postal services;
3. all services for the provision of in-flight catering, including the preparation, storage and delivery of meals and supplies to aircraft and the maintenance of catering equipment. **[1373]**

Article 3

The exemption shall apply only if:

1. the agreements, decisions or concerted practices do not oblige an air carrier to obtain any or all of the ground handling services referred to in Article 2 exclusively from a particular supplier;
2. the supply of the ground handling services referred to in Article 2 is not tied to the conclusion of contracts for or acceptance of other goods or services which, by their nature or according to commercial usage, have no connection with the services referred to in Article 2 or to the conclusion of a similar contract for the supply of services at another airport;
3. the agreements, decisions or concerted practices do not prevent an air carrier from choosing from the range of ground handling services offered by a particular supplier those it wants to take from that supplier and do not deny it the right to procure similar or other services from another supplier or to provide them itself;
4. the supplier of the ground handling services does not impose, directly or indirectly, prices or other conditions which are unreasonable and which, in particular, bear no reasonable relation to the cost of the services provided;
5. the supplier of the ground handling services does not apply dissimilar conditions to equivalent transactions with different customers;
6. any air carrier is able to withdraw from the agreement with the supplier without penalty, on giving notice of not more than three months to that effect.

[1374]

Article 4

The Commission may withdraw the benefit of this Regulation, pursuant to Article 7 of Regulation (EEC) No 3976/87, where it finds in a particular case that an agreement, decision or concerted practice exempted under this Regulation nevertheless has certain effects which are incompatible with the conditions laid down by Article 85(3) or are prohibited by Article 86 of the Treaty.   **[1375]**

Article 5

This Regulation shall enter into force on the day following its publication in the Official Journal of the European Communities.

It shall apply with retroactive effect to agreements, decisions and concerted practices which were in existence at the date of its entry into force, from the time when the conditions of application of this Regulation were fulfilled.

It shall expire on 31 January 1991.   **[1376]**

This Regulation shall be binding in its entirety and directly applicable in all Members States.

Done at Brussels, 26 July 1988.

REGULATION (EEC) No 4087/88 OF THE COMMISSION
of 30 November 1988

on the application of Article 85(3) of the Treaty to categories of franchise agreements

THE COMMISSION OF THE EUROPEAN COMMUNITIES,

Having regard to the Treaty establishing the European Economic Community,

Having regard to Council Regulation No 19/65/EEC of 2 March 1965 on the application of Article 85(3) of the Treaty to certain categories of agreements and concerted practices as last amended by the Act of Accession of Spain and Portugal, and in particular Article 1 thereof,

Having published a draft of this Regulation,

Having consulted the Advisory Committee on Restrictive Practices and Dominant Positions, Whereas:

(1) Regulation No 19/65/EEC empowers the Commission to apply Article 85(3) of the Treaty by Regulation to certain categories of bilateral exclusive agreements falling within the scope of Article 85(1) which either have as their object the exclusive distribution or exclusive purchase of goods, or include restrictions imposed in relation to the assignment or use of industrial property rights.

(2) Franchise agreements consist essentially of licences of industrial or intellectual property rights relating to trade marks or signs and know-how, which can be combined with restrictions relating to supply or purchase of goods.

(3) Several types of franchise can be distinguished according to their object: industrial franchise concerns the manufacturing of goods, distribution franchise concerns the sale of goods, and service franchise concerns the supply of services.

(4) It is possible on the basis of the experience of the Commission to define categories of franchise agreements which fall under Article 85(1) but can normally by regarded as satisfying the conditions laid down in Article 85(3). This is the case for franchise agreements whereby one of the parties supplies goods or provides services to end users. On the other hand, industrial franchise agreements should not be covered by this Regulation. Such agreements, which usually govern relationships between producers, present different characteristics than the other types of franchise. They consist of manufacturing licences based on patents and/or technical know-how, combined with trade-mark licences. Some of them may benefit from other block exemptions if they fulfil the necessary conditions.

(5) This Regulation covers franchise agreements between two undertakings, the franchisor and the franchisee, for the retailing of goods or the provision of services to end users, or a combination of these activities, such as the processing or adaptation of goods to fit specific needs of their customers. It also covers cases where the relationship between franchisor and franchisees

is made through a third undertaking, the master franchisee. It does not cover wholesale franchise agreements because of the lack of experience of the Commission in that field.

(6) Franchise agreements as defined in this Regulation can fall under Article 85(1). They may in particular affect intra-Community trade where they are concluded between undertakings from different Member States or where they form the basis of a network which extends beyond the boundaries of a single Member State.

(7) Franchise agreements as defined in this Regulation normally improve the distribution of goods and/or the provision of services as they give franchisors the possibility of establishing a uniform network with limited investments, which may assist the entry of new competitors on the market, particularly in the case of small and medium-sized undertakings, thus increasing inter-brand competition. They also allow independent traders to set up outlets more rapidly and with higher chance of success than if they had to do so without the franchisor's experience and assistance. They have therefore the possibility of competing more efficiently with large distribution undertakings.

(8) As a rule, franchise agreements also allow consumers and other end users a fair share of the resulting benefit, as they combine the advantage of a uniform network with the existence of traders personally interested in the efficient operation of their business. The homogeneity of the network and the constant cooperation between the franchisor and the franchisees ensures a constant quality of the products and services. The favourable effect of franchising on inter-brand competition and the fact that consumers are free to deal with any franchisee in the network guarantees that a reasonable part of the resulting benefits will be passed on to the consumers.

(9) This Regulation must define the obligations restrictive of competition which may be included in franchise agreements. This is the case in particular for the granting of an exclusive territory to the franchisees combined with the prohibition on actively seeking customers outside that territory, which allows them to concentrate their efforts on their allotted territory. The same applies to the granting of an exclusive territory to a master franchisee combined with the obligation not to conclude franchise agreements with third parties outside that territory. Where the franchisees sell or use in the process of providing services, goods manufactured by the franchisor or according to its instructions and/or bearing its trade mark, an obligation on the franchisees not to sell, or use in the process of the provision of services, competing goods, makes it possible to establish a coherent network which is identified with the franchised goods. However, this obligation should only be accepted with respect to the goods which form the essential subject-matter of the franchise. It should notably not relate to accessories or spare parts for these goods.

(10) The obligations referred to above thus do not impose restrictions which are not necessary for the attainment of the abovementioned objectives. In particular, the limited territorial protection granted to the franchisees is indispensable to protect their investment.

(11) It is desirable to list in the Regulation a number of obligations that are commonly found in franchise agreements and are normally not restrictive of competition and to provide that if, because of the particular economic or legal circumstances, they fall under Article 85(1), they are also covered by the exemption. This list, which is not exhaustive, includes in particular clauses which are essential either to preserve the common identity and reputation of the network or to prevent the know-how made available and the assistance given by the franchisor from benefiting competitors.

(12) The Regulation must specify the conditions which must be satisfied for the exemption to apply. To guarantee that competition is not eliminated for a substantial part of the goods which are the subject of the franchise, it is necessary that parallel imports remain possible. Therefore, cross deliveries between franchisees should always be possible. Furthermore, where a franchise network is combined with another distribution system, franchisees should be free to obtain supplies from authorized distributors. To better inform consumers, thereby helping to ensure that they receive a fair share of the resulting benefits, it must be provided that the franchisee shall be obliged to indicate its status as an independent undertaking, by any appropriate means which does not jeopardize the common identity of the franchised network. Furthermore, where the franchisees have to honour guarantees for the franchisor's goods, this obligation should also apply to goods supplied by the franchisor, other franchisees or other agreed dealers.

(13) The Regulation must also specify restrictions which may not be included in franchise agreements if these are to benefit from the exemption granted by the Regulation, by virtue of the fact that such provisions are restrictions failing under Article 85(1) for which there is no general presumption that they will lead to the positive effects required by Article 85(3). This applies in particular to market sharing between competing manufacturers, to clauses unduly limiting the franchisees choice of suppliers or customers, and to cases where the franchisee is restricted

in determining its prices. However, the franchisor should be free to recommend prices to the franchisees, where it is not prohibited by national laws and to the extent that it does not lead to concerted practices for the effective application of these prices.

(14) Agreements which are not automatically covered by the exemption because they contain provisions that are not expressly exempted by the Regulation and not expressly excluded from exemption may nonetheless generally be presumed to be eligible for application of Article 85(3). It will be possible for the Commission rapidly to establish whether this is the case for a particular agreement. Such agreements should therefore be deemed to be covered by the exemption provided for in this Regulation where they are notified to the Commission and the Commission does not oppose the application of the exemption within a specified period of time.

(15) If individual agreements exempted by this Regulation nevertheless have effects which are incompatible with Article 85(3), in particular as interpreted by the administrative practice of the Commission and the case law of the Court of Justice, the Commission may withdraw the benefit of the block exemption. This applies in particular where competition is significantly restricted because of the structure of the relevant market.

(16) Agreements which are automatically exempted pursuant to this Regulation need not be notified. Undertakings may nevertheless in a particular case request a decision pursuant to Council Regulation No 17 as last amended by the Act of Accession of Spain and Portugal.

(17) Agreements may benefit from the provisions either of this Regulation or of another Regulation, according to their particular nature and provided that they fulfil the necessary conditions of application. They may not benefit from a combination of the provisions of this Regulation with those of another block exemption Regulation.

HAS ADOPTED THIS REGULATION:

Article 1

1. Pursuant to Article 85(3) of the Treaty and subject to the provisions of this Regulation, it is hereby declared that Article 85(1) of the Treaty shall not apply to franchise agreements to which two undertakings are party, which include one or more of the restrictions listed in Article 2.

2. The exemption provided for in paragraph 1 shall also apply to master franchise agreements to which two undertakings are party. Where applicable, the provisions of this Regulation concerning the relationship between franchisor and franchisee shall apply mutatis mutandis to the relationship between franchisor and master franchisee and between master franchisee and franchisee.

3. For the purposes of this Regulation

(a) "franchise" means a package of industrial or intellectual property rights relating to trade marks, trade names, shop signs, utility models, designs, copyrights, know-how or patents, to be exploited for the resale of goods or the provision of services to end users;

(b) "franchise agreement" means an agreement whereby one undertaking, the franchisor, grants the other, the franchisee, in exchange for direct or indirect financial consideration, the right to exploit a franchise for the purposes of marketing specified types of goods and/or services; it includes at least obligations relating to:

— the use of a common name or shop sign and a uniform presentation of contract premises and/or means of transport,
— the communication by the franchisor to the franchisee of know-how,
— the continuing provision by the franchisor to the franchisee of commercial or technical assistance during the life of the agreement;

(c) "master franchise agreement" means an agreement whereby one undertaking, the franchisor, grants the other, the master franchisee, in exchange for direct or indirect financial consideration, the right to exploit a franchise for the purposes of concluding franchise agreements with third parties, the franchisees;

(d) "franchisor's goods" means goods produced by the franchisor or according to its instructions, and/or bearing the franchisor's name or trade mark;

(e) "contract premises" means the premises used for the exploitation of the franchise or, when the franchise is exploited outside those premises, the base from which the franchisee operates the means of transport used for the exploitation of the franchise (contract means of transport);

(f) "know-how" means a package of non-patented practical information, resulting from experience and testing by the franchisor, which is secret, substantial and identified;

(g) "secret" means that the know-how, as a body or in the precise configuration and assembly of its components, is not generally known or easily accessible; it is not limited in the narrow sense that each individual component of the know-how should be totally unknown or unobtainable outside the franchisor's business;

(h) "substantial" means that the know-how includes information which is of importance for the sale of goods or the provision of services to end users, and in particular for the presentation of goods for sale, the processing of goods in connection with the provision of services, methods of dealing with customers, and administration and financial management; the know-how must be useful for the franchisee by being capable, at the date of conclusion of the agreement, of improving the competitive position of the franchisee, in particular by improving the franchisee's performance or helping it to enter a new market;

(i) "identified" means that the know-how must be described in a sufficiently comprehensive manner so as to make it possible to verify that it fulfils the criteria of secrecy and substantiality; the description of the know-how can either be set out in the franchise agreement or in a separate document or recorded in any other appropriate form. **[1377]**

Article 2

The exemption provided for in Article 1 shall apply to the following restrictions of competition:

(a) an obligation on the franchisor, in a defined area of the common market, the contract territory, not to

— grant the right to exploit all or part of the franchise to third parties,
— itself exploit the franchise, or itself market the goods or services which are the subject-matter of the franchise under a similar formula.
— itself supply the franchisor's goods to third parties;

(b) an obligation on the master franchisee not to conclude franchise agreements with third parties outside its contract territory;

(c) an obligation on the franchisee to exploit the franchise only from the contract premises;

(d) an obligation on the franchisee to refrain, outside the contract territory, from seeking customers for the goods or the services which are the subject-matter of the franchise;

(e) an obligation on the franchisee not to manufacture, sell or use in the course of the provision of services, goods competing with the franchisor's goods which are the subject-matter of the franchise; where the subject-matter of the franchise is the sale or use in the course of the provision of services both certain types of goods and spare parts or accessories therefor, that obligation may not be imposed in respect of these spare parts or accessories. **[1378]**

Article 3

1. Article 1 shall apply notwithstanding the presence of any of the following obligations on the franchisee, in so far as they are necessary to protect the franchisor's industrial or intellectual property rights or to maintain the common identity and reputation of the franchised network:

(*a*) to sell, or use in the course of the provision of services, exclusively goods matching minimum objective quality specifications laid down by the franchisor;

(*b*) to sell, or use in the course of the provision of services, goods which are manufactured only by the franchisor or by third parties designated by it, where it is impracticable, owing to the nature of the goods which are the subject-matter of the franchise, to apply objective quality specifications;

(*c*) not to engage, directly or indirectly, in any similar business in a territory where it would compete with a member of the franchised network, including the franchisor; the franchisee may be held to this obligation after termination of the agreement, for a reasonable period which may not exceed one year, in the territory where it has exploited the franchise;

(*d*) not to acquire financial interests in the capital of a competing undertaking, which would give the franchisee the power to influence the economic conduct of such undertaking;

(*e*) to sell the goods which are the subject-matter of the franchise only to end users, to other franchisees and to resellers within other channels of distribution supplied by the manufacturer of these goods or with its consent;

(*f*) to use its best endeavours to sell the goods or provide the services that are the subject-matter of the franchise, to offer for sale a minimum range of goods, achieve a minimum turnover, plan its orders in advance, keep minimum stocks and provide customer and warranty services;

(*g*) to pay to the franchisor a specified proportion of its revenue for advertising and itself carry out advertising for the nature of which it shall obtain the franchisor's approval.

2. Article 1 shall apply notwithstanding the presence of any of the following obligations on the franchisee:

(*a*) not to disclose to third parties the know-how provided by the franchisor; the franchisee may be held to this obligation after termination of the agreement;

(*b*) to communicate to the franchisor any experience gained in exploiting the franchise and to grant it, and other franchisees, a non-exclusive licence for the know-how resulting from that experience;

(*c*) to inform the franchisor of infringements of licensed industrial or intellectual property rights, to take legal action against infringers or to assist the franchisor in any legal actions against infringers:

(*d*) not to use know-how licensed by the franchisor for purposes other than the exploitation of the franchise; the franchisee may be held to this obligation after termination of the agreement;

(*e*) to attend or have its staff attend training courses arranged by the franchisor;

(*f*) to apply the commercial methods devised by the franchisor, including any subsequent modification thereof, and use the licensed industrial or intellectual property rights;

(*g*) to comply with the franchisor's standards for the equipment and presentation of the contract premises and/or means of transport;

(*h*) to allow the franchisor to carry out checks of the contract premises and/or means of transport, including the goods sold and the services provided, and the inventory and accounts of the franchisee;

(*i*) not without the franchisor's consent to change the location of the contract premises;

(*j*) not without the franchisor's consent to assign the rights and obligations under the franchise agreement.

3. In the event that, because of particular circumstances, obligations referred to in paragraph 2 fall within the scope of Article 85(1), they shall also be exempted even if they are not accompanied by any of the obligations exempted by Article 1. **[1379]**

Article 4

The exemption provided for in Article 1 shall apply on condition that:

(*a*) the franchisee is free to obtain the goods that are the subject-matter of the franchise from other franchisees; where such goods are also distributed through another network of authorized distributors, the franchisee must be free to obtain the goods from the latter;

(*b*) where the franchisor obliges the franchisee to honour guarantees for the franchisor's goods, that obligation shall apply in respect of such goods supplied by any member of the franchised network or other distributors which give a similar guarantee, in the common market;

(*c*) the franchisee is obliged to indicate its status as an independent undertaking; this indication shall however not interfere with the common identity of the franchised network resulting in particular from the common name or shop sign and uniform appearance of the contract premises and/or means of transport.

[1380]

Article 5

The exemption granted by Article 1 shall not apply where:

(*a*) undertakings producing goods or providing services which are identical or are considered by users as equivalent in view of their characteristics, price and intended use, enter into franchise agreements in respect of such goods or services;

(*b*) without prejudice to Article 2(e) and Article 3(1)(b), the franchisee is prevented from obtaining supplies of goods of a quality equivalent to those offered by the franchisor;

(*c*) without prejudice to Article 2(e), the franchisee is obliged to sell, or use in the process of providing services, goods manufactured by the franchisor or third parties designated by the franchisor and the franchisor refuses, for reasons other than protecting the franchisor's industrial or intellectual property rights, or maintaining the common identity and reputation of the franchised network, to designate as authorized manufacturers third parties proposed by the franchisee;

(*d*) the franchisee is prevented from continuing to use the licensed know-how after termination of the agreement where the know-how has become generally known or easily accessible, other than by breach of an obligation by the franchisee;

(*e*) the franchisee is restricted by the franchisor, directly or indirectly, in the determination of sale prices for the goods or services which are the subject-matter of the franchise; without prejudice to the possibility for the franchisor of recommending sale prices;

(*f*) the franchisor prohibits the franchisee from challenging the validity of the industrial or intellectual property rights which form part of the franchise, without prejudice to the possibility for the franchisor of terminating the agreement in such a case;

(*g*) franchisees are obliged not to supply within the common market the goods or services which are the subject-matter of the franchise to end users because of their place of residence. **[1381]**

Article 6

1. The exemption provided for in Article 1 shall also apply to franchise agreements which fulfil the conditions laid down in Article 4 and include obligations restrictive of competition which are not covered by Articles 2 and 3(3) and do not fall within the scope of Article 5, on condition that the agreements in question are notified to the Commission in accordance with the provisions of Commission Regulation No 27 and that the Commission does not oppose such exemption within a period of six months.

2. The period of six months shall run from the date on which the notification is received by the Commission. Where, however, the notification is made by registered post, the period shall run from the date shown on the postmark of the place of posting.

3. Paragraph 1 shall apply only if:

   (*a*) express reference is made to this Article in the notification or in a communication accompanying it; and
   (*b*) the information furnished with the notification is complete and in accordance with the facts.

4. The benefit of paragraph 1 can be claimed for agreements notified before the entry into force of this Regulation by submitting a communication to the Commission referring expressly to this Article and to the notification. Paragraphs 2 and 3(b) shall apply mutatis mutandis.

5. The Commission may oppose exemption. It shall oppose exemption if it receives a request to do so from a Member State within three months of the forwarding to the Member State of the notification referred to in paragraph 1 or the communication referred to in paragraph 4. This request must be justified on the basis of considerations relating to the competition rules of the Treaty.

6. The Commission may withdraw its opposition to the exemption at any time. However, where that opposition was raised at the request of a Member State, it may be withdrawn only after consultation of the Advisory Committee on Restrictive Practices and Dominant Positions.

7. If the opposition is withdrawn because the undertakings concerned have shown that the conditions of Article 85(3) are fulfilled, the exemption shall apply from date of the notification.

8. If the opposition is withdrawn because the undertakings concerned have amended the agreement so that the conditions of Article 85(3) are fulfilled, the exemption shall apply from the date on which the amendments take effect.

9. If the Commission opposes exemption and its opposition is not withdrawn, the effects of the notification shall be governed by the provisions of Regulation No 17. **[1382]**

Article 7

1. Information acquired pursuant to Article 6 shall be used only for the purposes of this Regulation.

2. The Commission and the authorities of the Member States, their officials and other servants shall not disclose information acquired by them pursuant to this Regulation of a kind that is covered by the obligation of professional secrecy.

3. Paragraphs 1 and 2 shall not prevent publication of general information or surveys which do not contain information relating to particular undertakings or associations of undertakings. **[1383]**

Article 8

The Commission may withdraw the benefit of this Regulation, pursuant to Article 7 of Regulation No 19/65/EEC, where it finds in a particular case that an agreement exempted by this Regulation nevertheless has certain effects which are incompatible with the conditions laid down in Article 85(3) of the Treaty, and in particular where territorial protection is awarded to the franchisee and:

(a) access to the relevant market or competition therein is significantly restricted by the cumulative effect of parallel networks of similar agreements established by competing manufacturers or distributors;

(b) the goods or services which are the subject-matter of the franchise do not face, in a substantial part of the common market, effective competition from goods or services which are identical or considered by users as equivalent in view of their characteristics, price and intended use;

(c) the parties, or one of them, prevent end users, because of their place of residence, from obtaining, directly or through intermediaries, the goods or services which are the subject-matter of the franchise within the common market, or use differences in specifications concerning those goods or services in different Member States, to isolate markets;

(d) franchisees engage in concerted practices relating to the sale prices of the goods or services which are the subject-matter of the franchise;

(e) the franchisor uses its right to check the contract premises and means of transport, or refuses its agreement to requests by the franchisee to move the contract premises or assign its rights and obligations under the franchise agreement, for reasons other than protecting the franchisor's industrial or intellectual property rights, maintaining the common identity and reputation of the franchised network or verifying that the franchisee abides by its obligations under the agreement.

[1384]

Article 9

This Regulation shall enter into force on 1 February 1989.
It shall remain in force until 31 December 1999.   **[1385]**

This Regulation shall be binding in its entirety and directly applicable in all Member States.

Done at Brussels, 30 November 1988.

REGULATION (EEC) No 4260/88 OF THE COMMISSION
of 16 December 1988

on the communications, complaints and applications and the hearings provided for in Council Regulation (EEC) No 4056/86 laying down detailed rules for the application of Articles 85 and 86 of the Treaty to maritime transport

THE COMMISSION OF THE EUROPEAN COMMUNITIES,

Having regard to the Treaty establishing the European Economic Community,

Having regard to Council Regulation (EEC) No 4056/86 of 22 December 1986 laying down detailed rules for the application of Articles 85 and 86 of the Treaty to maritime transport, and in particular Article 26 thereof,

Having regard to the opinion of the Advisory Committee on Agreements and Dominant Positions in the field of Maritime Transport.

Whereas, pursuant to Article 26 of Regulation (EEC) No 4056/86, the Commission is empowered to adopt implementing provisions concerning the scope of the obligation of communication pursuant to Article 5(5), the form, content and other details of complaints pursuant to Article 10 and of applications pursuant to Article 12 and the hearings provided for in Article 23(1) and (2) of that Regulation;

Whereas the obligation of communication to the Commission of awards at arbitration and recommendations by conciliators provided for in Article 5(5) of Regulation (EEC) No 4056/86 concerns the settlement of disputes relating to the practices of conferences referred to in Articles 4 and 5(2) and (3) of that Regulation; whereas it seems appropriate to make the procedure for this notification as simple as possible; whereas it is appropriate, therefore, to provide for notifications to be made in writing, attaching the documents containing the text of the awards and recommendations concerned;

Whereas complaints pursuant to Article 10 of Regulation (EEC) No 4056/86 may make it easier for the Commission to take action for infringement of Articles 85 and 86 of the EEC Treaty in the field of maritime transport; whereas it would consequently seem appropriate to make the procedure for submitting complaints as simple as possible; whereas it is appropriate, therefore, to provide for complaints to be submitted in one written copy, the form, content and details being left to the discretion of the complainants;

Whereas the submission of the applications pursuant to Article 12 of Regulation (EEC) No 4056/86 may have important legal consequences for each undertaking which is a party to an agreement, decision or concerted practice; whereas each undertaking should, therefore, have the right to submit such applications to the Commission; whereas, on the other hand, if an undertaking makes use of that right, it must so inform the other undertakings which are parties to the agreement, decision or concerted practice, in order that they may protect their interests;

Whereas it is for the undertakings and associations of undertakings to inform the Commission of the facts and circumstances in support of the applications submitted in accordance with Article 12 of Regulation (EEC) No 4056/86;

Whereas it is desirable to prescribe that forms be used for applications in order, in the interest of all concerned, to simplify and expedite examination thereof by the competent departments;

Whereas in most cases the Commission will in the course of the procedure for the hearings provided for in Article 23(1) and (2) of Regulation (EEC) No 4056/86 already be in close touch with the participating undertakings or associations of undertakings and they will accordingly have the opportunity of making known their views regarding the objections raised against them;

Whereas in accordance with Article 23(1) and (2) of Regulation (EEC) No 4056/86 and with the rights of the defence, the undertakings and associations of undertakings concerned must have the right on conclusion of the procedure to submit their comments on the whole of the objections raised against them which the Commission proposes to deal with in its decisions;

Whereas persons other than the undertakings or associations of undertakings which are involved in the procedure may have an interest in being heard; whereas, pursuant to the second sentence of Article 23(2) of Regulation (EEC) No 4056/86, such persons should have the opportunity of being heard if they apply and show that they have a sufficient interest;

Whereas it is desirable to enable persons who pursuant to Article 10 of Regulation (EEC) No 4056/86 have lodged a complaint to submit their comments where the Commission considers that on the basis of the information in its possession there are insufficient grounds for action;

Whereas the various persons entitled to submit comments must do so in writing, both in their own interest and in the interests of good administration, without prejudice to an oral procedure where appropriate to supplement the written procedure;

Whereas it is necessary to define the rights of persons who are to be heard, and in particular the conditions upon which they may be represented or assisted and the setting and calculation of time limits;

Whereas the Advisory Committee on Restrictive Practices and Dominant Positions in Maritime Transport delivers its opinion on the basis of a preliminary draft Decision; whereas it must therefore be consulted concerning a case after the inquiry in that case has been completed; whereas such consultation does not prevent the Commission from re-opening an inquiry if need be,

HAS ADOPTED THIS REGULATION:

SECTION I

NOTIFICATION, COMPLAINTS AND APPLICATIONS

Article 1 — Notifications

1. Awards at arbitration and recommendations by conciliators accepted by the parties shall be notified to the Commission when they concern the settlement of disputes relating to the practices of conferences referred to in Articles 4 and 5(2) and (3) of Regulation (EEC) No 4056/86.

2. The obligation of notification applies to any party to the dispute resolved by the award or recommendation.

3. Notifications shall be submitted forthwith by registered letter with an acknowledgement of receipt or shall be delivered by hand against receipt. They shall be written in one of the official languages of the Community.

Supporting documents shall be either originals or copies. Copies must be certified as true copies of the original. They shall be submitted in their original language. Where the original language is not one of the official languages of the Community, a translation in one of the official languages shall be attached.

4. When representatives of undertakings, of associations of undertakings, or of natural or legal persons sign such notifications, they shall produce written proof that they are authorized to act. **[1386]**

Article 2 — Complaints

1. Complaints pursuant to Article 10 of Regulation (EEC) No 4056/86 shall be submitted in writing in one of the official languages of the Community, their form, content and other details being left to the discretion of complainants.

2. Complaints may be submitted by:

    (*a*) Member States

    (*b*) natural or legal persons who claim a legitimate interest.

3. When representatives of undertakings, of associations of undertakings, or of natural or legal persons sign such complaints, they shall produce written proof that they are authorized to act. **[1387]**

Article 3 — Persons entitled to submit applications

1. Any undertaking which is party to agreements, decisions or practices of the kind described in Article 85(1) of the Treaty may submit an application under Article 12 of Regulation (EEC) No 4056/86. Where the application is submitted by some but not all of the undertakings concerned, they shall give notice to the others.

2. Where applications under Article 12 of Regulation (EEC) No 4056/86 are signed by representatives of undertakings, of associations of undertakings, or of natural or legal persons, such representatives shall produce written proof that they are authorized to act.

3. Where a joint application is submitted, a joint representative shall be appointed. **[1388]**

Article 4 — Submission of applications

1. Applications pursuant to Article 12 of Regulation (EEC) No 4056/86 shall be submitted on Form MAR shown in Annex I.

2. Several participating undertakings may submit an application on a single form.

3. Applications shall contain the information requested in the form.

4. Fourteen copies of each application and of the supporting documents shall be submitted to the Commission.

5. The supporting documents shall be either originals or copies. Copies must be certified as true copies of the original.

6. Applications shall be in one of the official languages of the Community. Supporting documents shall be submitted in their original language. Where the original language is not one of the official languages, a translation in one of the official languages shall be attached.

7. The date of submission of an application shall be the date on which it is received by the Commission. Where, however, the application is sent by registered post, it shall be deemed to have been received on the date shown on the postmark of the place of posting.

8. Where an application submitted pursuant to Article 12 of Regulation (EEC) No 4056/86 falls outside the scope of that Regulation, the Commission shall without delay inform the applicant that it intends to examine the application under the provisions of such other Regulation as is applicable to the case; however, the date of submission of the application shall be the date resulting from paragraph 7. The Commission shall inform the applicant of its reasons and fix a period for him to submit any comments in writing before it conducts its appraisal pursuant to the provisions of that other Regulation.   **[1389]**

SECTION II

HEARINGS

Article 5

Before consulting the Advisory Committee on Agreements and Dominant Positions in the field of Maritime Transport, the Commission shall hold a hearing pursuant to Article 23(1) of Regulation (EEC) No 4056/86.   **[1390]**

Article 6

1. The Commission shall inform undertakings and associations of undertakings in writing of the objections raised against them. The communication shall be addressed to each of them or to a joint agent appointed by them.

2. The Commission may inform the parties by giving notice in the *Official Journal of the European Communities*, if from the circumstances of the case this appears appropriate, in particular where notice is to be given to a number of undertakings but no joint agent has been appointed. The notice shall have regard to the legitimate interest of the undertakings in the protection of their business secrets.

3. A fine or a periodic penalty payment may be imposed on an undertaking or association of undertakings only if the objections were notified in the manner provided for in paragraph 1.

4. The Commission shall, when giving notice of objections, fix a period within which the undertakings and associations of undertakings may inform the Commission of their views.   **[1391]**

Article 7

1. Undertakings and associations of undertakings shall, within the appointed period, make known in writing their views concerning the objections raised against them.

2. They may in their written comments set out all matters relevant to their defence.

3. They may attach any relevant documents in proof of the facts set out. They may also propose that the Commission hear persons who may corroborate those facts.

[1392]

Article 8

The Commission shall in its Decision deal only with those objections raised against undertakings and associations of undertakings in respect of which they have been afforded the opportunity of making known their views. **[1393]**

Article 9

If natural or legal persons showing a sufficient interest apply to be heard pursuant to Article 23(2) of Regulation (EEC) No 4056/86 the Commission shall afford them the opportunity of making known their views in writing within such period as it shall fix.

[1394]

Article 10

Where the Commission, having received a complaint pursuant to Article 10 of Regulation (EEC) No 4056/86, considers that on the basis of the information in its possession there are insufficient grounds for acting on the complaint, it shall inform the persons who submitted the complaint of its reasons and fix a period for them to submit any further comments in writing. **[1395]**

Article 11

1. The Commission shall afford to persons who have so requested in their written comments the opportunity to put forward their arguments orally, if those persons show a sufficient interest or if the Commission proposes to impose on them a fine or periodic penalty payment.

2. The Commission may likewise afford to any other person the opportunity of orally expressing his views. **[1396]**

Article 12

1. The Commission shall summon the persons to be heard to attend on such date as it shall appoint.

2. It shall forthwith transmit a copy of the summons to the competent authorities of the Member States, who may appoint an official to take part in the hearing. **[1397]**

Article 13

1. Hearings shall be conducted by the persons appointed by the Commission for that purpose.

2. Persons summoned to attend shall either appear in person or be represented by legal representatives or by representatives authorized by their constitution. Undertakings

and associations of undertakings may moreover be represented by a duly authorized agent appointed from among their permanent staff.

Persons heard by the Commission may be assisted by lawyers or university teachers who are entitled to plead before the Court of Justice of the European Communities in accordance with Article 17 of the Protocol on the Statute of the Court, or by other qualified persons.

3. Hearings shall not be public. Persons shall be heard separately or in the presence of other persons summoned to attend. In the latter case, regard shall be had to the legitimate interest of the undertakings in the protection of their business secrets.

4. The essential content of the statements made by each person heard shall be recorded in minutes which shall be read and approved by him.   **[1398]**

Article 14

Without prejudice to Article 6(2), information and summonses from the Commission shall be sent to the addresses by registered letter with acknowledgement of receipt, or shall be delivered by hand against receipt.   **[1399]**

Article 15

1. In fixing the periods provided for in Articles 4(8), 6, 9 and 10, the Commission shall have regard both to the time required for preparation of comments and to the urgency of the case. A period shall be not less than two weeks; it may be extended.

2. Periods shall run from the day following receipt of a communication or delivery thereof by hand.

3. Written comments must reach the Commission or be dispatched by registered letter before expiry of the period. Where the period would expire on a Sunday or a public holiday, it shall be extended up to the end of the next following working day. For the purpose of calculating the extension, public holidays shall, in cases where the relevant date is the date of receipt of written comments, be those set out in Annex II to this Regulation, and in cases where the relevant date is the date of dispatch, those appointed by law in the country of dispatch.   **[1400]**

Article 16

This Regulation shall enter into force on the day following its publication in the *Official Journal of the European Communities*.   **[1401]**

This Regulation shall be binding in its entirety and directly applicable in all Member States.

Done at Brussels, 16 December 1988.

ANNEX I

This form must be accompanied by an annex containing the information specified in the attached Complementary Note[1]

The form and annex must be supplied in fourteen copies (two for the Commission and one for each Member State). Supply three copies of any relevant agreement and one copy of other supporting documents.

FORM MAR

Please do not forget to complete the Acknowledgement of Receipts annexed.

If space is insufficient, please use extra pages, specifying to which item on the form they relate.

TO THE COMMISSION OF THE EUROPEAN COMMUNITIES

Directorate-General for Competition
200, rue de la Loi
B-1049 Brussels

Application under Article 12 of Council Regulation No 4056/86 of 22 December 1986 with a view to obtaining a decision under Article 85(3) of the Treaty establishing the European Economic Community.

Identity of the parties

1. *Identity of applicant*

   Full name and address, telex and facsimile numbers, and brief description of the undertakings(s) or association(s) of undertakings submitting the application.

   For partnerships, sole traders or any other unincorporated body trading under a business name, give, also, the name, forename(s) and address of the proprietor(s) or partner(s).

   Where an application is submitted on behalf of some other person (or is submitted by more than one person) the name, address and position of the representative (or joint representative) must be given, together with proof of his authority to act. Where an application or notification is submitted by or on behalf of more than one person they should appoint a joint representative. (Article 3(2) and (3) of Commission Regulation No 4260/88).

NOTE
1 The Complementary Note follows the text of Commission Regulation (EEC) No. 4261/88, post

2. *Identity of any other parties*

Full name and address and brief description of any other parties to the agreement, decision or concerted practice (hereinafter referred to as "the arrangments").

State what steps have been taken to inform these other parties of this application.

(This information is not necessary in respect of standard contracts which an undertaking submitting the application has concluded or intends to conclude with a number of parties.)

Purpose of this application
(see Complementary Note)

(Please answer yes or no to the question)

Would you be satisfied with a comfort letter? (See the end of Section VII of the Complementary Note).

The undersigned declare that the information given above and in the . . . pages annexed hereto is correct to the best of their knowledge and belief, that all estimates are identified as such and are their best estimates of the underlying facts and that all the opinions expressed are sincere. They are aware of the provision of Article 19(1)(a) of Regulation (EEC) No 4056/86 (see attached Complementary Note).[1]

Place and date . . . .

Signatures: . . . .

. . . .

. . . .

COMMISSION
OF THE
EUROPEAN COMMUNITIES

Brussels: ....

Directorate-General for Competition

To

ACKNOWLEDGEMENT OF RECEIPT

(This form will be returned to the address inserted above if the top half is completed in a single copy by the person lodging it.)

Your application dated: ....

....

concerning: ....

Your reference: ....

Parties:

1. ....

2. .... and others

(There is no need to name the other undertakings party to the arrangement.)

___

(To be completed by the Commission.)

was received on: ....

and registered under No IV/MAR/ ....

Please quote the above number in all correspondence.

___

Provisional address: *Telephone:*   *Telex:*   *Telegraphic address:*
200, rue de la Loi   Direct line: 235 . . . .   COMEU B 21877   COMEUR Brussels
B-1049 Brussels   Telephone exchange: 235 11 11

[1402]

REGULATION (EEC) No 4261/88 OF THE COMMISSION
of 16 December 1988

on the complaints, applications and hearings provided for in Council Regulation (EEC) No 3975/87 laying down the procedure for the application of the rules on competition to undertakings in the air transport sector

THE COMMISSION OF THE EUROPEAN COMMUNITIES,

Having regard to the Treaty establishing the European Economic Community,

Having regard to Council Regulation (EEC) No 3975/87 of 14 December 1987 laying down the procedure for the application of the rules on competition to undertakings in the air transport sector and in particular Article 19 thereof,

Having regard to the opinion of the Advisory Committee on Agreements and Dominant Positions in Air Transport,

Whereas, pursuant to Article 19 of Regulation (EEC) No 3975/87, the Commission is empowered to adopt implementing provisions concerning the form, content and other details of complaints pursuant to Article 3(1) and of applications pursuant to Article 3(2) and 5 and the hearings provided for in Article 16(1) and (2) of that Regulation;

Whereas complaints pursuant to Article 3(1) of Regulation (EEC) No 3975/87 may make it easier for the Commission to take action for infringement of Articles 85 and 86 of the EEC Treaty in the field of air transport; whereas it would consequently seem appropriate to make the procedure for submitting complaints as simple as possible; whereas it is appropriate, therefore, to provide for complaints to be submitted in one written copy, the form, content and details being left to the discretion of the complainants;

Whereas the submission of the applications pursuant to Articles 3(2) and 5 of Regulation (EEC) No 3975/87 may have important legal consequences for each undertaking which is a party to an agreement, decision or concerted practice; whereas each undertaking should, therefore, have the right to submit such applications to the Commission; whereas, on the other hand, if an undertaking makes use of that right, it must so inform the other undertakings which are parties to the agreement, decision or concerted practice, in order that they may protect their interests;

Whereas it is for the undertakings and associations of undertakings to inform the Commission of the facts and circumstances in support of the applications submitted in accordance with Articles 3(2) and 5 of Regulation (EEC) No 3975/87;

Whereas it is desirable to prescribe that forms be used for applications in order, in the interest of all concerned, to simplify and expedite examination thereof by the competent departments;

Whereas in most cases the Commission will in the course of the procedure for the hearings provided for in Article 16(1) and (2) of Council Regulation (EEC) No 3975/87 already be in close touch with the participating undertakings or associations of undertakings and they will accordingly have the opportunity of making known their views regarding the objections raised against them;

Whereas in accordance with Article 16(1) and (2) of Regulation (EEC) No 3975/87 and with the rights of the defence, the undertakings and associations of undertakings concerned must have the right on conclusion of the procedure to submit their comments on the whole of the objections raised against them which the Commission proposes to deal with in its decisions;

Whereas persons other than the undertakings or associations of undertakings which are involved in the procedure may have an interest in being heard; whereas, by the second sentence of Article 16(2) of Regulation (EEC) No 3975/87, such persons must have the opportunity of being heard if they apply and show that they have a sufficient interest;

Whereas it is desirable to enable persons who pursuant to Article 3(1) of Regulation (EEC) No 3975/87 have lodged a complaint to submit their comments where the Commission considers that on the basis of the information in its possession there are insufficient grounds for action;

Whereas the various persons entitled to submit comments must do so in writing, both in their own interest and in the interests of good administration, without prejudice to an oral procedure where appropriate to supplement the written procedure;

Whereas it is necessary to define the rights of persons who are to be heard, and in particular the conditions upon which they may be represented or assisted and the setting and calculation of time limits;

Whereas the Advisory Committee on Restrictive Practices and Dominant Positions in Air Transport delivers its opinion on the basis of a preliminary draft decision; whereas it must therefore be consulted

concerning a case after the inquiry in that case has been completed; whereas such consultation does not prevent the Commission from re-opening an inquiry if need be,
HAS ADOPTED THIS REGULATION:

SECTION I

COMPLAINTS AND APPLICATIONS

Article 1 – Complaints

1. Complaints pursuant to Article 3(1) of Regulation (EEC) No 3975/87 shall be submitted in writing in one of the official languages of the Community, their form, content and other details being left to the discretion of complainants.

2. Complaints may be submitted by:

(*a*) Member States
(*b*) natural or legal persons who claim a legitimate interest.

3. When representatives of undertakings, of associations of undertakings, or of natural or legal persons sign such complaints, they shall produce written proof that they are authorized to act.   **[1403]**

Article 2 – Persons entitled to submit applications

1. Any undertaking which is party to agreements, decisions or practices of the kind described in Articles 85(1) and 86 of the Treaty may submit an application under Articles 3(2) and 5 of Regulation (EEC) No 3975/87. Where the application is submitted by some but not all of the undertakings concerned, they shall give notice to the others.

2. Where applications under Articles 3(2) and 5 of Regulation (EEC) No 3975/87 are signed by representatives of undertakings, of associations of undertakings, or of natural or legal persons, such representatives shall produce written proof that they are authorized to act.

3. Where a joint application is submitted, a joint representative shall be appointed.
                                                           [1404]

Article 3 – Submission of applications

1. Applications pursuant to Articles 3(2) and 5 of Regulation (EEC) No 3975/87 shall be submitted on Form AER shown in Annex I.

2. Several participating undertakings may submit an application on a single form.

3. Applications shall contain the information requested in the form.

4. Fourteen copies of each application and of the supporting documents shall be submitted to the Commission.

5. The supporting documents shall be either originals or copies. Copies must be certified as true copies of the original.

6. Applications shall be in one of the official languages of the Community. Supporting documents shall be submitted in their original language. Where the original language is not one of the official languages, a translation in one of the official languages shall be attached.

7. The date of submission of an application shall be the date on which it is received by the Commission. Where, however, the application is sent by registered post, it shall be deemed to have been received on the date shown on the postmark of the place of posting.

8. Where an application submitted pursuant to Article 3(2) and 5 of Regulation (EEC) No 3975/87 falls outside the scope of that Regulation, the Commission shall without delay inform the applicant that it intends to examine the application under the provisions of such other Regulation as is applicable to the case; however, the date of submission of the application shall be the date resulting from paragraph 7. The Commission shall inform the applicant of its reasons and fix a period for him to submit any comments in writing before it conducts its appraisal pursuant to the provisions of that other Regulation.   **[1405]**

SECTION II

HEARINGS

Article 4

Before consulting the Advisory Committee on Agreements and Dominant Positions in Air Transport, the Commission shall hold a hearing pursuant to Article 16(1) of Regulation (EEC) No 3975/87.   **[1406]**

Article 5

1. The Commission shall inform undertakings and associations of undertakings in writing of the objections raised against them. The communication shall be addressed to each of them or to a joint agent appointed by them.

2. The Commission may inform the parties by giving notice in the Official Journal of the European Communities, if from the circumstances of the case this appears appropriate, in particular where notice is to be given to a number of undertakings but no joint agent has been appointed. The notice shall have regard to the legitimate interest of the undertakings in the protection of their business secrets.

3. A fine or a periodic penalty payment may be imposed on an undertaking or association of undertakings only if the objections were notified in the manner provided for in paragraph 1.

4. The Commission shall, when giving notice of objections, fix a period within which the undertakings and associations of undertakings may inform the Commission of their views.   **[1407]**

Article 6

1. Undertakings and associations of undertakings shall within the appointed period, make known in writing their views concerning the objections raised against them.

2. They may in their written comments set out all matters relevant to their defence.

3. They may attach any relevant documents in proof of the facts set out. They may also propose that the Commission hear persons who may corroborate those facts.   **[1408]**

Article 7

The Commission shall in its decision deal only with those objections raised against undertakings and associations of undertakings in respect of which they have been afforded the opportunity of making known their views.   **[1409]**

Article 8

If natural or legal persons showing a sufficient interest apply to be heard pursuant to Article 16(2) of Regulation (EEC) No 3975/87 the Commission shall afford them the opportunity of making known their views in writing within such period as it shall fix.

[1410]

Article 9

Where the Commission, having received a complaint pursuant to Article 3(1) of Regulation (EEC) No 3975/87 considers that on the basis of the information in its possession there are insufficient grounds for acting on the complaint, it shall inform the persons who submitted the complaint of its reasons and fix a period for them to submit any further comments in writing. **[1411]**

Article 10

1. The Commission shall afford to persons who have so requested in their written comments the opportunity to put forward their arguments orally, if those persons show a sufficient interest or if the Commission proposes to impose on them a fine or periodic penalty payment.

2. The Commission may likewise afford to any other person the opportunity of orally expressing his views. **[1412]**

Article 11

1. The Commission shall summon the persons to be heard to attend on such date as it shall appoint.

2. It shall forthwith transmit a copy of the summons to the competent authorities of the Member States, who may appoint an official to take part in the hearing.

[1413]

Article 12

1. Hearings shall be conducted by the persons appointed by the Commission for that purpose.

2. Persons summoned to attend shall either appear in person or be represented by legal representatives or by representatives authorized by their constitution. Undertakings and associations of undertakings may moreover be represented by a duly authorized agent appointed from among their permanent staff.

Persons heard by the Commission may be assisted by lawyers or university teachers who are entitled to plead before the Court of Justice of the European Communities in accordance with Article 17 of the Protocol on the Statute of the Court, or by other qualified persons.

3. Hearings shall not be public. Persons shall be heard separately or in the presence of other persons summoned to attend. In the latter case, regard shall be had to the legitimate interest of the undertakings in the protection of their business secrets.

4. The essential content of the statements made by each person heard shall be recorded in minutes which shall be read and approved by him. **[1414]**

Article 13

Without prejudice to Article 5(2), information and summonses from the Commission shall be sent to the addressees by registered letter with acknowledgement of receipt, or shall be delivered by hand against receipt.   **[1415]**

Article 14

1. In fixing the periods provided for in Articles 3(8), 5, 8 and 9, the Commission shall have regard both to the time required for preparation of comments and to the urgency of the case. A period shall be not less than two weeks; it may be extended.

2. Periods shall run from the day following receipt of a communication or delivery thereof by hand.

3. Written comments must reach the Commission or be dispatched by registered letter before expiry of the period. Where the period would expire on a Sunday or a public holiday, it shall be extended up to the end of the next following working day. For the purpose of calculating the extension, public holidays shall, in cases where the relevant date is the date of receipt of written comments, be those set out in Annex II to this Regulation, and in cases where the relevant date is the date of dispatch, those appointed by law in the country of dispatch.   **[1416]**

Article 15

This Regulation shall enter into force on the day following its publication in the Official Journal of the European Communities.   **[1417]**

This Regulation shall be binding in its entirety and directly applicable in all Member States.

Done at Brussels, 16 December 1988.

COMPLEMENTARY NOTE

Contents

I	Purpose of Community rules on competition
II	Negative Clearance
III	Decisions applying Article 85(3)
IV	Purpose of the forms
V	Nature of the forms
VI	The need for complete and accurate information
VII	Subsequent procedure
VIII	Secrecy
IX	Further information and headings to be used in Annex to forms

Annex 1 Text of Articles 85 and 86 of the EEC Treaty
Annex 2 List of relevant Acts
Annex 3 List of Member States and Commission Press and Information Offices within the Community

Additions or alterations to the information given in these Annexes will be published by the Commission from time to time.

NB: Any undertaking uncertain about how to complete an application or wishing further explanation may contact the Directorate-General for Competition (DG IV) in Brussels. Alternatively, any Commission Information Office (those in the Community are listed in Annex 3) will be able to obtain guidance or indicate an official in Brussels who speaks the preferred official Community language.

I. Purpose of Community rules on competition

The purpose of these rules is to prevent the distortion of competition in the common market by monopolies or restrictive practices; they apply to any enterprise trading directly or indirectly in the common market wherever established. Article 85(1) of the Treaty establishing the European Economic Community (the text of Articles 85 and 86 is reproduced in Annex 1 to this note) prohibits restrictive agreements or concerted practices which may affect trade between Member States, and Article 85(2) declares contracts or other otherwise legally binding arrangements containing such restrictions void (although the European Court of Justice has held that if restrictive terms of contracts are severable, only those terms are void); Article 85(3), however, gives the Commission power to exempt practices with beneficial effects. Article 86 prohibits the abuse of a dominant position. The original procedures for implementing these Articles, which provide for "negative clearance" and a declaration applying Article 85(3), were laid down for the maritime transport sector in Regulation (EEC) No 4056/86 and for the air transport sector in Regulation (EEC) No 3975/87 (the references to these and all other acts mentioned in this note or relevant to applications made on the Forms are listed in Annex 2 to this note).

[1418]

II. Negative Clearance

The negative clearance procedure has been provided only for the air transport sector. Its purpose is to allow businesses ("undertakings") to ascertain whether or not the Commission considers that any of their arrrangements or behaviour are prohibited under Articles 85(1) or 86 of the Treaty. (It is governed by Article 3 of Regulation (EEC) No 3975/87.) Clearance takes the form of a decision by the Commission certifying that, on the basis of the facts in its possession, there are no grounds under Articles 85(1) or 86 of the Treaty for action on its part in respect of the arrangements or behaviour.

Any party may apply for negative clearance, even without the consent (but not without the knowledge) of other parties to arrangements. There would be little point in applying, however, where arrangements or behaviour clearly do not fall within the scope of Article 85(1) or Article 86. Nor is the Commission obliged to give negative clearance — Article 3(2) of Regulation (EEC) No 3975/87 states that " — the Commission may certify — " The Commission does not usually issue negative clearance decisions in cases which, in its opinion, so clearly do not fall within the scope of the prohibition of Article 85(1) that there is no reasonable doubt for it to resolve by such a decision. **[1419]**

III Decision applying Article 85(3)

The application for a decision applying Article 85(3) allows undertakings to enter into arrangements which, in fact, offer economic advantages even though they restrict competition. (It is governed by Articles 12 and 13 of Regulation (EEC) No 4056/86 and 4, 5 and 6 of Regulation (EEC) No 3975/87). Upon such application the Commission may take a decision declaring Article 85(1) to be inapplicable to the arrangements described in the decision. The Commission is required to specify the period of validity of any such decision, it can attach conditions and obligations and it can amend or revoke decisions or prohibit specified acts by the parties in certain circumstances notably if the decisions were based on incorrect information or if there is any material change in the facts.

Any party may submit an application even without the consent (but not without the knowledge) of other parties.

Regulations (EEC) No 4056/86 and (EEC) No 3975/87 provide for an "opposition procedure" under which applications can be handled expeditiously. If an application is admissible under the relevant Regulation, if it is complete and if the arrangement which is the subject of the application has not given rise to a complaint or to an own-initiation proceeding, the Commission publishes a summary of the request in the Official Journal of the European Communities and invites comments from interested third parties and from Member States. Unless the Commission notifies applicants within 90 days of the date of such publication that there are serious doubts as to the applicability of Article 85(3) the arrangement will be deemed exempt for the time already elapsed and for a maximum of six years from the date of publication. Where the Commission does notify applicants that there are serious doubts, the applicable procedure is outlined in point VII of this Complementary Note.

In the air transport sector, the Commission intends to adopt a number of Regulations declaring that Article 85(1) does not apply to categories of agreements.

A decision applying Article 85(3) may have retroactive effect. Should the Commission find that arrangements in respect of which the application was submitted are indeed prohibited by Article 85(1) and cannot benefit from the application of Article 85(3) and, therefore, take a decision condemning them, the parties are nevertheless protected, from the date of application, against fines for any infringement described in the application (Articles 19(4) of Regulation (EEC) No 4056/86 and 12(5) of Regulation (EEC) No 3975/87).   **[1420]**

IV. Purpose of the forms

The purpose of Form AER is to allow undertakings, or associations of undertakings, wherever situated, to apply to the Commission for negative clearance for arrangements or behaviour, or to apply to have them exempted from the prohibition of Article 85(1) of the Treaty by virtue of Article 85(3). The form allows undertakings applying for negative clearance to apply, at the same time, in order to obtain a decision applying Article 85(3). It should be noted that only an application in order to obtain a decision applying Article 85(3) affords immunity from fines. Form MAR only provides for an application for a decision under Article 85(3).

To be valid, applications in respect of maritime transport must be made on Form MAR (by virtue of Article 4 of Regulation No 4260/88) and in respect of air transport on Form AER (by virtue of Article 3 of Regulation No 4261/88).   **[1421]**

V. Nature of the Forms

The forms consist of a single sheet calling for the identity of the applicant(s) and of any other parties. This must be supplemented by further information given under the headings and references detailed below (see IX). For preference the paper used should be A4 (21×29.7 cm — the same size as the form) but must not be bigger. Leave a margin of at least 25 mm or one inch on the left hand side of the page and, if you use both sides, on the right hand side of the reverse.   **[1422]**

VI. The need for complete and accurate information

It is important that applicants give all the relevant facts. Although the Commission has the right to seek further information from applicants or third parties, and is obliged to publish a summary of the application before granting negative clearance or a decision applying Article 85(3), it will usually base its decision on the information provided by the applicant. Any Decision taken on the basis of incomplete information could be without effect in the case of a negative clearance, or voidable in that of a declaration applying Article 85(3). For the same reason it is also important to inform the Commission of any material changes to your arrangements made after your application.

Complete information is of particular importance in order to benefit from the application of Article 85(3) by means of the opposition procedure. This procedure can only apply where the Commission "is in possession of all the available evidence".

Moreover, you should be aware that Articles 19(1)(*a*) of Regulation (EEC) No 4056/86 and 12(1)(*a*) of Regulation (EEC) No 3975/87 enable the Commission to impose fines of from Ecu 100 to Ecu 5 000 on undertakings or associations of undertakings where, intentionally or negligently, they supply incorrect or misleading information in connection with an application.

The key words here are "incorrect or misleading information". However, it often remains a matter of judgement how much detail is relevant; the Commission accepts estimates where accurate information is not readily available in order to facilitate applications; and the Commission calls for opinions as well as facts.

You should therefore note that the Commission will use these powers only where applicants have, intentionally or negligently, provided false information or grossly inaccurate estimates or suppressed readily available information or estimates, or have deliberately expressed false opinions in order to obtain negative clearance or a declaration applying Article 85(3). **[1423]**

VII. Subsequent procedure

The application is registered in the Registry of the Directorate-General for Competition (DG IV). The date of receipt by the Commission (or the date of posting if sent by registered post) is the effective date of the submission. The application might be considered invalid if obviously incomplete or not on the obligatory form.

Further information might be sought from the applicants or from third parties, and suggestions might be made as to amendments to the arrangements that might make them acceptable.

An application for a decision under Article 85(3) may be opposed by the Commission either because the Commission does not agree that the arrangements should benefit from Article 85(3) or to allow for more information to be sought.

If, after examination, the Commission intends to issue a decision applying-Article 85(3), it is obliged to publish a summary of the application in the Official Journal of the European Communities and invite comments from third parties. Subsequently, a preliminary draft Decision has to be submitted to and discussed with the Advisory Committee on Restrictive Practices and Dominant Positions in Air Transport or in Maritime Transport — they will already have received a copy of the application. Only then, and providing nothing has happened to change the Commission's intention, can it adopt a decision.

Sometimes files are closed without any formal decision being taken, for example because it is found that the arrangements are already covered by a block exemption, or because the applicants are satisfied by a less formal letter from the Commission's departments (sometimes called a "comfort letter") indicating that the arrangements do not call for any action by the Commission, at least in present circumstances. Although not a Commission decision, a comfort letter indicates how the Commission's departments view the case on the facts currently in their possession which means that the Commission could if necessary — if, for example, it were to be asserted that a contract was void under Article 85(2) — take an appropriate decision. **[1424]**

VIII. Secrecy

The Commission and Member States are under a duty not to disclose information of the kind covered by the obligation of professional secrecy. On the other hand the Commission has to publish a summary of your application, should it intend to grant it, before taking the relevant decision. In this publication, the Commission " — shall have regard to the legitimate interest of undertakings in the protection of their business secrets". In this connection, if you believe that your interests would be harmed if any of the information you are asked to supply were to be published or otherwise divulged to other parties, please put all such information in a second annex, with each page clearly marked "Business Secrets"; in the principal annex, under any affected heading state "see second annex" or "also see second annex"; in the second annex repeat the affected heading(s) and reference(s) and give the information you do not wish to have published, together with your reasons for this. Do not overlook the fact that the Commission may have to publish a summary of your application.

Before publishing a summary of your application, the Commission will show the under-takings concerned a copy of the proposed text.   **[1425]**

IX. Further information and headings to be used in the Annex to the forms

The further information is to be given under the following headings and reference numbers. Wherever possible, give exact information. If this is not readily available, give your best estimate, and identify what you give as an estimate. If you believe any detail asked for to be unavailable or irrelevant, please explain why. This may, in particular, be the case if one party is notifying arrangements alone without the cooperation of other parties. Do not overlook the fact that Commission officials are ready to discuss what detail is relevant (see the nota bene at the beginning of this complementary note).

1. *Brief description*
Give a brief description of the arrangements or behaviour (nature, purpose, date(s) and duration) — (full details are requested below).

2. *Market*
The nature of the transport services affected by the arrangements or behaviour. A brief description of the structure of the market (or markets) for these services, e.g. who sells in it, who buys in it, its geographical extent, the turnover in it, how competitive it is, whether it is easy for new suppliers to enter the market, whether there are substitute services. If you are submitting a standard contract, say how many you expect to conclude. If you know of any studies of the market, it would be helpful to refer to them.

3. *Fuller details of the party or parties*
3.1 Do any of the parties form part of a group of companies? A group relationship is deemed to exist where a firm
— owns more than half the capital or business assets, or
— has the power to exercise more than half the voting rights, or
— has the power to appoint more than half the members of the supervisory board, board of directors or bodies legally representing the undertaking, or
— has the right to manage the affairs of another.
If the answer is yes, give:
— the name and address of the ultimate parent company;
— a brief description of the business of the group (and, if possible, one copy of the last set of group accounts);
— the name and address of any other company in the group competing in a market affected by the arrangements or in any related market, that is to say any other company competing directly or indirectly with the parties ("relevant associated company").
3.2. The most recently available total turnover of each of the parties, and, as the case may be, of the group of which it forms part (it could be helpful also if you could provide one copy of the last set of accounts).
3.3. The sales or turnover of each party in the services affected by the arrangements in the Community and worldwide. If the turnover in the Community is material (say more than a 5% market share), please also give figures for each Member State, and for previous years (in order to show any significant trends), and give each party's sales targets for the future. Provide the same figures for any relevant associated company. (Under this heading, in particular, your best estimate might be all that you can readily supply.)
3.4. In relation to the market (or markets) for the services described at 2 above, give, for each of the sales or turnover figures in 3.3, your estimate of the market share it represents.

3.5. If you have a substantial interest falling short of control (more than 25% but less than 50%) in some other company competing in a market affected by the arrangements, or if some other such company has a substantial interest in yours, give its name and address and brief details.

4. *Full details of the arrangements*

4.1. If the contents are reduced to writing give a brief description of the purpose of the arrangements and attach three copies of the text (except that purely technical descriptions may be omitted; in such cases, however, indicate parts omitted).

If the contents are not, or are only partially, reduced to writing, give a full description.

4.2. Detail any provisions contained in the arrangements which may restrict the parties in their freedom to take independent commercial decisions, for example regarding:
 — buying or selling prices, discounts or other trading conditions
 — the nature, frequency or capacity of services to be offered
 — technical development or investment
 — the choice of markets or sources of supply
 — purchases from or sales to third parties
 — whether to apply similar terms for the supply of equivalent services
 — whether to offer different services separately or together.

4.3. State between which Member States trade may be affected by the arrangements, and whether trade between the Community and any third countries is affected.

5. *Reasons for negative clearance*

If you are applying for negative clearance state, under the reference:

5.1. why, i.e. state which provision or effects of the arrangements or behaviour might, in your view, raise questions of compatibility with the Community's rules of competition. The object of this subheading is to give the Commission the clearest possible idea of the doubts you have about your arrangements or behaviour that you wish to have resolved by a negative clearance decision.

Then, under the following two references, give a statement of the relevant facts and reasons as to why you consider Articles 85(1) or 86 to be inapplicable, i.e.

5.2. why the arrangements do not have the object or effect of preventing, restricting or distorting competition within the common market to any appreciable extent, or why your undertaking does not have or its behaviour does not abuse a dominant position;

and/or

5.3. why the arrangements or behaviour are not such as may affect trade between Member States to any appreciable extent.

6. *Reasons for a decision applying Article 85(3)*

If you are requesting a decision applying Article 85(3), even if only as a precaution, explain how:

6.1. the arrangements contribute to improving production or distribution, and/or promoting technical or economic progress;

6.2. a proper share of the benefits arising from such improvement or progress accrues to consumers;

6.3. all restrictive provisions of the arrangements are indispensable to the attainment of the aims set out under 6.1 above;

6.4. the arrangements do not eliminate competition in respect of a substantial part of the services concerned.

7. *Other information*

7.1. Mention any earlier proceedings or informal contacts, of which you are aware, with the Commission and any earlier proceedings with any national authorities or courts even indirectly concerning these arrangements or this behaviour.

7.2. Give any other information presently available that you think might be helpful in allowing the Commission to appreciate whether there are any restrictions contained in the agreement, or any benefits that might justify them.

7.3. State whether you intend to produce further supporting facts or arguments not yet available and, if so, on which points.

7.4. State, with reasons, the urgency of your application. **[1426]**

ANNEX 1

TEXT OF ARTICLES 85 AND 86 OF THE EEC TREATY

[Reproduced at paras **[1000]** – **[1001]**, *ante]* **[1427]**

ANNEX 2

LIST OF RELEVANT ACTS

(as of 1 September 1988)

(If you think it possible that your arrangements do not need to be notified by virtue of any of these Regulations or notices it may be worth your while to obtain a copy.)

Implementing Regulations

Council Regulation (EEC) No 4056/86 of 22 December 1986 laying down detailed rules for the application of Articles 85 and 86 of the Treaty to maritime transport (OJ No L 378, 31. 12. 1986, p. 4).

Commission Regulation (EEC) No 4260/88 of 26 July 1988 on the scope of the obligation of communication; the form, content and other details of complaints and of applications, and the hearings provided for in Council Regulation (EEC) No 4056/86 of 22 December 1986 laying down detailed rules for the application of Articles 85 and 86 of the Treaty to maritime transport (OJ No L 378, 31. 12. 1986, p. 4).

Council Regulation (EEC) No 3975/87 of 14 December 1987 laying down the procedure for the application of the rules on competition to undertakings in the air transport sector (OJ No 374, 31. 12. 1987, p. 1).

Commission Regulation (EEC) No 4261/88 of 16 December 1988 on the form, content and other details of complaints and of applications, and the hearings provided for in Council Regulation (EEC) No 3975/87 laying down the procedure for the application of the rules of competition to undertakings in the air transport sector (OJ No L 376, 31. 12. 1988, p. 10).

Regulations granting block exemption in respect of a wide range of agreements

Commission Regulation (EEC) No 2671/88 of 26 July 1988 on the application of Article 85(3) of the Treaty to certain categories of agreements between undertakings, decisions of associations of undertakings and concerted practices concerning joint planning and coordination of capacity, sharing of revenue and consultations on tariffs on scheduled air services and slot allocation at airports (OJ No L 239, 30. 8. 1988, p. 9).

Commission Regulation (EEC) No 2672/88 of 26 July 1988 on the application of Article 85(3) of the Treaty to certain categories of agreements between undertakings relating to computer reservation systems for air transport services (OJ No L 239, 30. 8. 1988, p. 13).

Commission Regulation (EEC) No 2673/88 of 26 July 1988 on the application of Article 85(3) of the Treaty to certain categories of agreements between undertakings, decisions of associations of undertakings and concerted practices concerning ground handling services (OJ No L 239, 30. 8. 1988, p. 17).

Commission Notices of a general nature

Commission notice on agreements, decisions and concerted practices of minor importance which do not fall under Article 85(1) of the Treaty (OJ No C231, 12. 9. 1986, p. 2) – in the main, those where the parties share less than 5% of the market between them, and a combined annual turnover of less than ECU 200 million. **[1428]**

ANNEX 3

LIST OF MEMBER STATES AND COMMISSION PRESS AND INFORMATION OFFICES WITHIN THE COMMUNITY

(as of 1 January 1986)

The Member States as at the date of this Annex are: Belgium, Denmark, France, Germany, Greece, Ireland, Italy, Luxembourg, the Netherlands, Portugal, Spain and the United Kingdom.

The addresses of the Commission's Press and Information Offices in the Community are:

BELGIUM
Rue Archimède 73,
B-1040 Bruxelles
Tel. 23511 11

DENMARK
Højbrohus
Østergade 61
Postbox 144
DK-1004 Kobenhavn K
Tel. 14 41 40

FRANCE
61, rue des Belles-Feuilles
F-75782 Paris, Cedex 16
Tel. (1) 45 01 58 85

CMC1/Bureau 320
2, rue Henri Barbusse
F-13241 Marseille, Cedex 01
Tel. 91 08 62 02

FEDERAL REPUBLIC OF GERMANY
Zitelmannstrasse 22
D-5300 Bonn
Tel. 23 80 41

Kurfürstendamm 102
D-1000 Berlin 31
Tel. 8924028

Erhardtstrasse 27
D-8000 München
Tel. 23 99 29 00

GREECE
2 Vassilissis Sofias
TK 1602
GR-Athina 134
Tel. 724 39 82/724 39 83/724 39 84

IRELAND
39 Molesworth Street
IRL-Dublin 2
Tel. 71 22 44

ITALY
Via Poli 29
1-00187 Roma
Tel. 678 97 22

Corso Magenta 61
1-20123 Milano
Tel. 8015 05/6/7/8

LUXEMBOURG
Bâtiment Jean Monnet
Rue Alcide de Gasperi
L-2920 Luxembourg
Tel. 430 11

NETHERLANDS
Korte Vijverberg 5
NL-2513 AB Den Haag
Tel. 46 93 26

PORTUGAL
Rue do Sacramento à Lapa 35
P-1200 Lisboa
Tel. 60 21 99

SPAIN
Calle de Serrano 41
5a Planta
E-1 Madrid
Tel. 435 17 00

UNITED KINGDOM
8 Storey's Gate
UK-London SWIP 3AT
Tel. 222 8122

Windsor House
9/15 Bedfort Street
UK-Belfast BT2 7EG
Tel. 407 08

4 Cathedral Road
UK-Cardiff CF1 9SG
Tel. 3716 31

7 Alva Street
UK-Edinburgh EH2 4PH
Tel. 225 20 58

ANNEX II

(List of public holidays)

New Year   1 Jan
Good Friday
Easter Saturday
Easter Monday
Labour Day   1 May
Schuman Plan Day   9 May
Ascension Day
Whit Monday
Belgian National Day   21 July
Assumption   15 Aug
All Saints   1 Nov
All Souls   2 Nov
Christmas Eve   24 Dec
Christmas Day   25 Dec
The day following Christmas Day   26 Dec
New Year's Eve   31 Dec   **[1429]**

ANNEX I

This form must be accompanied by an annex containing the information specified in the attached Complementary Note¹

This form must be accompanied by an annex containing the information specified in the attached Complementary Note¹

The form and annex must be supplied in fourteen copies (two for the Commission and one for each Member State). Supply three copies of any relevant agreement and one copy of other supporting documents.

FORM AER

Please do not forget to complete the Acknowledgement of Receipt annexed.

If space is insufficient, please use extra pages, specifying to which item on the form they relate.

TO THE COMMISSION OF THE EUROPEAN COMMUNITIES

Directorate-General for Competition
200, rue de la Loi
B-1049 Brussels

A. Application for negative clearance pursuant to Article 3(2) of Council Regulation No 3975/87 of 14 December 1987 relating to implementation of Article 85(1) or of Article 86 of the Treaty establishing the European Economic Community.

B. Application under Article 5 of Council Regulation No 3975/87 of 14 December 1987 with a view to obtaining a decision under Article 85(3) of the Treaty establishing the European Economic Community.

Identity of the parties

1. *Identity of applicant*

   Full name and address, telex and facsimile numbers, and brief description of the undertakings(s) or association(s) of undertakings submitting the application.

   For partnerships, sole traders or any other unincorporated body trading under a business name, give, also, the name, forename(s) and address of the proprietor(s) or partner(s).

   Where an application is submitted on behalf of some other person (or is submitted by more than one person) the name, address and position of the representative (or joint representative) must be given, together with proof of his authority to act. Where an application or notification is submitted by or on behalf of more than one person they should appoint a joint representative. (Article 2(2) and (3) of Commission Regulation No 4261/88).

2. *Identity of any other parties*

Full name and address and brief
description of any other parties to the
agreement, decision or concerted
practice (hereinafter referred to as "the
arrangments").

State what steps have been taken to
inform these other parties of this
application.

(This information is not necessary in
respect of standard contracts which an
undertaking submitting the application
has concluded or intends to conclude
with a number of parties.)

Purpose of this applications   *(Please answer yes or*
(see Complementary Note)   *no to the questions)*

Are you asking for negative clearance alone? (See Complementary Note—Section IV, end of first paragraph—for the
consequence of such a request.)

Are you applying for negative clearance, and also applying
for a decision under Article 85(3) in case the Commission
does not grant negative clearance?

Are you only applying for a decision under Article 85(3)?

Would you be satisfied with a comfort letter? (See the end
of Section VII of the Complementary Note).

The undersigned declare that the information given above and in the . . . pages
annexed hereto is correct to the best of their knowledge and belief, that all estimates
are identified as such and are their best estimates of the underlying facts and that
all the opinions expressed are sincere. They are aware of the provision of Article
12(1)(a) of Regulation (EEC) No 3975/86 (see attached Complementary Note).

Place and date . . . .

Signatures: . . . .

. . . .

. . . .

Write nothing in this margin

COMMISSION
OF THE
EUROPEAN COMMUNITIES

Brussels: ....

Directorate-General for Competition

```
┌─────────────────────────────┐
│ To                          │
│                             │
│                             │
│                             │
│                             │
│                             │
└─────────────────────────────┘
```

ACKNOWLEDGEMENT OF RECEIPT

(This form will be returned to the address inserted above if the top half is completed in a single copy by the person lodging it.)

Your application dated: ....
....
concerning: ....
Your reference: ....
Parties:
1. ....
2. .... and others
(There is no need to name the other undertakings party to the arrangement.)

_____

(To be completed by the Commission.)

was received on: ....

and registered under No IV/AER/ ....

Please quote the above number in all correspondence.

_____

Provisional address: *Telephone:*   *Telex:*   *Telegraphic address:*
200, rue de la Loi   Direct line: 235 . . . .   COMEU B 21877   COMEUR Brussels
B-1049 Brussels   Telephone exchange: 235 11 11

[1430]

REGULATION (EEC) NO 556/89 OF THE COMMISSION
of 30 November 1988

on the application of Article 85(3) of the Treaty to certain categories of know-how licensing agreements

THE COMMISSION OF THE EUROPEAN COMMUNITIES,

Having regard to the Treaty establishing the European Economic Community,

Having regard to Council Regulation No 19/65/EEC of 2 March 1965 on the application of Article 85(3) of the Treaty to certain categories of agreements and concerted practices, as last amended by the Act of Accession of Spain and Portugal, and in particular to Article 1 thereof,

Having published a draft of this Regulation,

After consulting the Advisory Committee on Restrictive Practices and Dominant Positions,

Whereas

(1) Regulation No 19/65/EEC empowers the Commission to apply Article 85(3) of the Treaty by Regulation to certain categories of bilateral agreements and concerted practices falling within the scope of Article 85(1) which include restrictions imposed in relation to the acquisition or use of industrial property rights, in particular patents, utility models, designs or trade marks, or to the rights arising out of contracts for assignment of, or the right to use, a method of manufacture or knowledge relating to the use or application of industrial processes.

The increasing economic importance of non-patented technical information (e.g. descriptions of manufacturing processes, recipes, formulae, designs or drawings), commonly termed "know-how", the large number of agreements currently being concluded by undertakings including public research facilities solely for the exploitation of such information (so-called "pure" know-how licensing agreements) and the fact that the transfer of know-how is, in practice, frequently irreversible make it necessary to provide greater legal certainty with regard to the status of such agreements under the competition rules, thus encouraging the dissemination of technical knowledge in the Community. In the light of experience acquired so far, it is possible to define a category of such know-how licensing agreements covering all or part of the common market which are capable of falling within the scope of Article 85(1) but which can normally be regarded as satisfying the conditions laid down in Article 85(3), where the licensed know-how is secret, substantial and identified in any appropriate form ("the know-how"). These definitional requirements are only intended to ensure that the communication of the know-how provides a valid justification for the application of the present Regulation and in particular for the exemption of obligations which are restrictive of competition.

A list of definitions for the purposes of this Regulation is set out in Article 1.

(2) As well as pure know-how agreements, mixed know-how and patent licensing agreements play an increasingly important role in the transfer of technology. It is therefore appropriate to include within the scope of this Regulation mixed agreements which are not exempted by Commission Regulation (EEC) No 2349/84 (Article 1, 2 or 4) and in particular the following:

— mixed agreements in which the licensed patents are not necessary for the achievement of the objects of the licensed technology containing both patented and non-patented elements; this may be the case where such patents do not afford effective protection against the exploitation of the technology by third parties;

— mixed agreements which, regardless of whether or not the licensed patents are necessary for the achievement of the objects of the licensed technology, contain obligations which restrict the exploitation of the relevant technology by the licensor or the licensee in Member States without patent protection, in so far and as long as such obligations are based in whole or in part on the exploitation of the licensed know-how and fulfil the other conditions set out in this Regulation.

It is also appropriate to extend the scope of this Regulation to pure or mixed agreements containing ancillary provisions relating to trade marks and other intellectual property rights where there are no obligations restrictive of competition other than those also attached to the know-how and exempted under the present Regulation.

However, such agreements, too, can only be regarded as fulfilling the conditions of Article 85(3) for the purposes of this Regulation where the licensed technical knowledge is secret, substantial and identified.

(3) The provisions of the present Regulation are not applicable to agreements covered by Regulation (EEC) No 2349/84 on patent licensing agreements.

(4) Where such pure or mixed know-how licensing agreements contain not only obligations relating to territories within the common market but also obligations relating to non-member countries, the presence of the latter does not prevent the present Regulation from applying to the obligations relating to territories within the common market.

However, where know-how licensing agreements for non-member countries or for territories which extend beyond the frontiers of the Community have effects within the common market which may fall within the scope of Article 85(1), such agreements should be covered by the Regulation to the same extent as would agreements for territories within the common market.

(5) It is not appropriate to include within the scope of the Regulation agreements solely for the purpose of sale, except where the licensor undertakes for a preliminary period before the licensee himself commences production using the licensed technology to supply the contract products for sale by the licensee. Also excluded from the scope of the Regulation are agreements relating to marketing know-how communicated in the context of franchising arrangements or to know-how agreements entered into in connection with arrangements such as joint ventures or patent pools and other arrangements in which the licensing of the know-how occurs in exchange for other licences not related to improvements to or new applications of that know-how, as such agreements pose different problems which cannot at present be dealt with in one Regulation (Article 5).

(6) Exclusive licensing agreements, i.e. agreements in which the licensor undertakes not to exploit the licensed technology in the licensed territory himself or to grant further licences there, may not be in themselves incompatible with Article 85(1) where they are concerned with the introduction and protection of a new technology in the licensed territory, by reason of the scale of the research which has been undertaken and of the increase in the level of competition, in particular inter-brand competition, and in the competitiveness of the undertakings concerned resulting from the dissemination of innovation within the Community.

In so far as agreements of this kind fall in other circumstances within the scope of Article 85(1), it is appropriate to include them in Article 1, in order that they may also benefit from the exemption.

(7) Both these and the other obligations listed in Article 1 encourage the transfer of technology and thus generally contribute to improving the production of goods and to promoting technical progress, by increasing the number of production facilities and the quality of goods produced in the common market and expanding the possibilities of further development of the licensed technology. This is true, in particular, of an obligation on the licensee to use the licensed product only in the manufacture of its own products, since it gives the licensor an incentive to disseminate the technology in various applications while reserving the separate sale of the licensed product to himself or other licensees. It is also true of obligations on the licensor and on the licensee to refrain not only from active but also from passive competition, in the licensed territory, in the case of the licensor, and in the territories reserved for the licensor or other licensees in the case of the licensee. The users of technologically new or improved products requiring major investment are often not final consumers but intermediate industries which are well informed about prices and alternative sources of supply of the products within the Community. Hence, protection against active competition only would not afford the parties and other licensees the security they needed, especially during the initial period of exploitation of the licensed technology when they would be investing in tooling up and developing a market for the product and in effect increasing demand.

In view of the difficulty of determining the point at which know-how can be said to be no longer secret, and the frequent licensing of a continuous stream of know-how, especially where technology in the industry is rapidly evolving, it is appropriate to limit to a fixed number of years the periods of territorial protection, of the licensor and the licensee from one another, and as between licensees, which are automatically covered by the exemption. Since, as distinguished from patent licenses, know-how licences are frequently negotiated after the goods or services incorporating the licensed technology have proved successful on the market, it is appropriate to take for each licensed territory the date of signature of the first licence agreement entered into for that territory by the licensor in respect of the same technology as the starting point for the permitted periods of territorial protection of the licensor and licensee from one another. As to the protection of a licensee from manufacture, use, active or passive sales by other licensees the starting point should be the date of signature of the first licence agreement entered into by the licensor within the EEC. The exemption of the territorial protection shall apply for the whole duration of such allowed periods as long as the know-how remains secret and substantial, irrespective of when the Member States in question joined the Community and provided that each of the licensees, the restricted as well as the protected one, manufactures the licensed product himself or has it manufactured.

Exemption under Article 85(3) of longer periods of territorial production, in particular to protect expensive and risky investment or where the parties were not already competitors before the grant of the licence, can only be granted by individual decision. On the other hand, parties are free to extend the term of their agreement to exploit any subsequent improvements and to provide for the payment of additional royalties. However, in such cases, further periods of territorial protection, starting from the date of licensing of the improvements to or new applications of the licensed technology are substantial and secret and not of significantly less importance than the technology initially granted or require new expensive and risky investment.

(8) However, it is appropriate in cases where the same technology is protected in some Member States by necessary patents within the meaning of recital 9 of Regulation (EEC) No 2349/84 to provide with respect to those Member States an exemption under this Regulation for the territorial protection of the licensor and licensee from one another and as between licensees against manufacture, use and active sales in each other's territory for the full life of the patents existing in such Member States.

(9) The obligations listed in Article 1 also generally fulfil the other conditions for the application of Article 85(3). Consumers will as a rule be allowed a fair share of the benefit resulting from the improvement in the supply of goods on the market. Nor do the obligations impose restrictions which are not indispensable to the attainment of the abovementioned objectives. Finally, competition at the distribution stage is safeguarded by the possibility of parallel imports, which may not be hindered by the parties in any circumstances. The exclusively obligations covered by the Regulation thus do not normally entail the possibility of eliminating competition in respect of a substantial part of the products in question. This also applies in the case of agreements which grant exclusive licences for a territory covering the whole of the common market where there is the possibility of parallel imports from third countries, or where there are other competing technologies on the market, since then the territorial exclusivity may lead to greater market integration and stimulate Community-wide inter-brand competition.

(10) It is desirable to list in the Regulation a number of obligations that are commonly found in know-how licensing agreements but are normally not restrictive of competition and to provide that in the event that because of the particular economic or legal circumstances they should fall within Article 85(1), they also would be covered by the exemption. This list, in Article 2, is not exhaustive.

(11) The Regulation must also specify what restrictions or provisions may not be included in know-how licensing agreements if these are to benefit from the block exemption. The restrictions, which are listed in Article 3, may fall under the prohibition of Article 85(1), but in their case there can be no general presumption that they will lead to the positive effects required by Article 85(3), as would be necessary for the granting of a block exemption, and consequently an exemption can be granted only on an individual basis.

(12) Agreements which are not automatically covered by the exemption because they contain provisions that are not expressly exempted by the Regulation and not expressly excluded from exemption, including those listed in Article 4(2) of the Regulation, may nonetheless generally be presumed to be eligible for application of the block exemption. It will be possible for the Commission rapidly to establish whether this is the case for a particular agreement. Such agreements should therefore be deemed to be covered by the exemption provided for in this Regulation where they are notified to the Commission and the Commission does not oppose the application of the exemption within a specified period of time.

(13) If individual agreements exempted by this Regulation nevertheless have effects which are incompatible with Article 85(3), the Commission may withdraw the benefit of the block exemption (Article 7).

(14) The list in Article 2 includes among others obligations on the licensee to cease using the licensed know-how after the termination of the agreement ("post-term use ban") (Article 2(1)(3)) and to make improvements available to the licensor (grant-back clause) (Article 2(1)(4)). A post-term use ban may be regarded as a normal feature of the licensing of know-how as otherwise the licensor would be forced to transfer his know-how in perpetuity and this could inhibit the transfer of technology. Moreover, undertakings by the licensee to grant back to the licensor a licence for improvements to the licensed know-how and/or patents are generally not restrictive of competition if the licensee is entitled by the contract to share in future experience and

inventions made by the licensor and the licensee retains the right to disclose experience acquired or grant licences to third parties where to do so would not disclose the licensor's know-how.

On the other hand, a restrictive effect on competition arises where the agreement contains both a post-term use ban and an obligation on the licensee to make his improvements to the know-how available to the licensor, even on a non-exclusive and reciprocal basis, and to allow the licensor to continue using them even after the expiry of the agreement. This is so because in such a case the licensee has no possibility of inducing the licensor to authorize him to continue exploiting the originally licensed know-how, and hence the licensee's own improvements as well, after the expiry of the agreement.

(15) The list in Article 2 also includes an obligation on the licensee to keep paying royalties until the end of the agreement independently of whether or not the licensed know-how has entered into the public domain through the action of third parties (Article 2(1) (7)). As a rule, parties do not need to be protected against the foreseeable financial consequences of an agreement freely entered into and should therefore not be restricted in their choice of the appropriate means of financing the technology transfer. This applies especially where know-how is concerned since here there can be no question of an abuse of a legal monopoly and, under the legal systems of the Member States, the licensee may have a remedy in an action under the applicable national law. Furthermore, provisions for the payment of royalties in return for the grant of a whole package of technology throughout an agreed reasonable period independently of whether or not the know-how has entered into the public domain, are generally in the interest of the licensee in that they prevent the licensor demanding a high initial payment up front with a view to diminishing his financial exposure in the event of premature disclosure. Parties should be free, in order to facilitate payment by the licensee, to spread the royalty payments for the use of the licensed technology over a period extending beyond the entry of the know-how into the public domain. Moreover, continuous payments should be allowed throughout the term of the agreement in cases where both parties are fully aware that the first sale of the product will necessarily disclose the know-how. Nevertheless, the Commission may, where it was clear from the circumstances that the licensee would have been able and willing to develop the know-how himself in a short period of time, in comparison with which the period of continuing payments is excessively long, withdraw the benefit of the exemption under Article 7 of this Regulation.

Finally, the use of methods of royalties calculation which are unrelated to the exploitation of the licensed technology or the charging of royalties on products whose manufacture at no stage includes the use of any of the licensed patents or secret techniques would render the agreement ineligible for the block exemption (Article 3(5)). The licensee should also be freed from his obligation to pay royalties, where the know-how becomes publicly known through the action of the licensor. However, the mere sale of the product by the licensor or an undertaking connected with him does not constitute such an action (Article 2(1)(7) and Article 3(5)).

(16) An obligation on the licensee to restrict his exploitation of the licensed technology to one or more technical fields of application ("fields of use") or to one or more product markets is also not caught by Article 85(1) (Article 2(1)8)). This obligation is not restrictive of competition since the licensor can be regarded as having the right to transfer the know-how only for a limited purpose. Such a restriction must however not constitute a disguised means of customer sharing.

(17) Restrictions which give the licensor an unjustified competitive advantage, such as an obligation on the licensee to accept quality specifications, other licences or goods and services that the licensee does not want from the licensor, prevent the block exemption from being applicable. However, this does not apply where it can be shown that the licensee wanted such specifications, licences, goods or services for reasons of his own convenience (Article 3(3)).

(18) Restrictions whereby the parties share customers within the same technological field of use or the same product market, either by an actual prohibition on supplying certain classes of customer or an obligation with an equivalent effect, would also render the agreement ineligible for the block exemption (Article 3(6)).

This does not apply to cases where the know-how licence is granted in order to provide a single customer with a second source of supply. In such a case a prohibition on the licensee from supplying persons other than the customer concerned may be indispensable for the grant of a licence to the second supplier since the purpose of the transaction is not to create an independent supplier in the market. The same applies to limitations on the quantities the licensee may supply to the customer concerned. It is also reasonable to assume that such restrictions contribute to improving the production of goods and to promoting technical progress by furthering the dissemination of technology. However, given the present state of experience of the Commission with respect to such clauses and the risk in particular that they might deprive the second supplier of the possibility of developing his own business in the fields covered by the agreement it is appropriate to make such clauses subject to the opposition procedure (Article 4(2)).

(19) Besides the clauses already mentioned, the list of restrictions precluding application of the block exemption in Article 3 also includes restrictions regarding the selling prices of the licensed product or the quantities to be manufactured or sold, since they limit the extent to which the licensee can exploit the licensed technology and particularly since quantity restrictions may have the same effect as export bans (Article 3(7) and (8)). This does not apply where a licence is granted for use of the technology in specific production facilities and where both a specific know-how is communicated for the setting-up, operation and maintenance of these facilities and the licensee is allowed to increase the capacity of the facilities or to set up further facilities for its own use on normal commercial terms. On the other hand, the licensee may lawfully be prevented from using the licensor's specific know-how to set up facilities for third parties, since the purpose of the agreement is not to permit the licensee to give other producers access to the licensor's know-how while it remains secret (Article 2(1)(12)).

(20) To protect both the licensor and the licensee from being tied into agreements whose duration may be automatically extended beyond their initial term as freely determined by the parties, through a continuous stream of improvements communicated by the licensor, it is appropriate to exclude agreements with such a clause from the block exemption (Article 3(10)). However, the parties are free at any time to extend their contractual relationship by entering into new agreements concerning new improvements.

(21) The Regulation should apply with retroactive effect to know-how licensing agreements in existence when the Regulation comes into force where such agreements already fulfil the conditions for application of the Regulation or are modified to do so (Articles 8 to 10). Under Article 4(3) of Regulation No 19/65/EEC, the benefit of these provisions may not be claimed in actions pending at the date of entry into force of this Regulation, nor may it be relied on as grounds for claims for damages against third parties.

(22) Agreements which come within the terms of Articles 1 and 2 and which have neither the object nor the effect of restricting competition in any other way need no longer be notified. Nevertheless, undertakings will still have the right to apply in individual cases for negative clearance under Article 2 of Council Regulation No 17 or for exemption under Article 85(3),

HAS ADOPTED THIS REGULATION:

Article 1

(1) Pursuant to Article 85(3) of the Treaty and subject to the provisions of this Regulation, it is hereby declared that Article 85(1) of the Treaty shall not apply to pure know-how licensing agreements and to mixed know-how and patent licensing agreements not exempted by Regulation (EEC) No 2349/84, including those agreements containing ancillary provisions relating to trademarks or other intellectual property rights, to which only two undertakings are party and which include one or more of the following obligations:

1. an obligation on the licensor not to license other undertakings to exploit the licensed technology in the licensed territory;

2. an obligation on the licensor not to exploit the licensed technology in the licensed territory himself;

3. an obligation on the licensee not to exploit the licensed technology in territories within the common market which are reserved for the licensor;

4. an obligation on the licensee not to manufacture or use the licensed product, or use the licensed process, in territories within the common market which are licensed to other licensees;

5. an oligation on the licensee not to pursue an active policy of putting the licensed product on the market in the territories within the common market which are licensed to other licensees, and in particular not to engage in advertising specifically aimed at those territories or to establish any branch or maintain any distribution depot there;

6. an obligation on the licensee not to put the licensed product on the market in the territories licensed to other licensees within the common market;

7. an obligation on the licensee to use only the licensor's trademark or the get-up determined by the licensor to distinguish the licensed product during the term of the agreement, provided that the licensee is not prevented from identifying himself as the manufacturer of the licensed products;

8. an obligation on the licensee to limit his production of the licensed product to the quantities he requires in manufacturing his own products and to sell the licensed product only as an integral part of or a replacement part for his own products or otherwise in connection with the sale of his own products, provided that such quantities are freely determined by the licensee.

(2) The exemption provided for the obligations referred to in paragraph 1(1), (2) and (3) shall extend for a period not exceeding for each licensed territory within the EEC 10 years from the date of signature of the first licence agreement entered into by the licensor for that territory in respect of the same technology.

The exemption provided for the obligations referred to in paragraph 1(4) and (5) shall extend for a period not exceeding 10 years from the date of signature of the first licence agreement entered into by the licensor within the EEC in respect of the same technology.

The exemption provided for the obligation referred to in paragraph 1(6) shall extend for a period not exceeding five years from the date of the signature of the first licence agreement entered into by the licensor within the EEC in respect of the same technology.

(3) The exemption provided for in paragraph 1 shall apply only where the parties have identified in any appropriate form the initial know-how and any subsequent improvements to it, which become available to the parties and are communicated to the other party pursuant to the terms of the agreement and for the purpose thereof, and only for as long as the know-how remains secret and substantial.

(4) In so far as the obligations referred to in paragraph 1(1) to (5) concern territories including Member States in which the same technology is protected by necessary patents, the exemption provided for in paragraph 1 shall extend for those Member States as long as the licensed product or process is protected in those Member States by such patents, where the duration of such protection exceeds the periods specified in paragraph 2.

(5) The exemption of restrictions on putting the licensed product on the market resulting from the obligations referred to in paragraph 1(2), (3), (5) and (6) shall apply only if the licensee manufactures or proposes to manufacture the licensed product himself or has it manufactured by a connected undertaking or by a subcontractor.

(6) The exemption provided for in paragraph 1 shall also apply where in a particular agreement the parties undertake obligations of the types referred to in that paragraph but with a more limited scope than is permitted by the paragraph.

(7) For the purposes of the present Regulation the following terms shall have the following meanings:

1. "know-how" means a body of technical information that is secret, substantial and identified in any appropriate form;

2. the term "secret" means that the know-how package as a body or in the precise configuration and assembly of its components is not generally known or easily accessible, so that part of its value consists in the lead-time the licensee gains when it is communicated to him; it is not limited to the narrow sense that each individual component of the know-how should be totally unknown or unobtainable outside the licensor's business;

3. the term "substantial" means that the know-how includes information which is of importance for the whole or a significant part of (i) a manufacturing process

or (ii) a product or service, or (iii) for the development thereof and excludes information which is trivial. Such know-how must thus be useful, i.e. can reasonably be expected at the date of conclusion of the agreement to be capable of improving the competitive position of the licensee, for example by helping him to enter a new market or giving him an advantage in competition with other manufacturers or providers of services who do not have access to the licensed secret know-how or other comparable secret know-how;

4. the term "identified" means that the know-how is described or recorded in such a manner as to make it possible to verify that it fulfils the criteria of secrecy and substantiality and to ensure that the licensee is not unduly restricted in his exploitation of his own technology. To be identified the know-how can either be set out in the licence agreement or in a separate document or recorded in any other appropriate form at the latest when the know-how is transferred or shortly thereafter, provided that the separate document or other record can be made available if the need arises;

5. "pure know-how licensing agreements" are agreements whereby one undertaking, the licensor, agrees to communicate the know-how, with or without an obligation to disclose any subsequent improvements, to another undertaking, the licensee, for exploitation in the licensed territory;

6. "mixed know-how and patent licensing agreements" are agreements not exempted by Regulation (EEC) No 2349/84 under which a technology containing both non-patented elements and elements that are patented in one or more Member States is licensed;

7. the terms "licensed know-how" or "licensed technology" means the initial and any subsequent know-how communicated directly or indirectly by the licensor to a licensee by means of pure or mixed know-how and patent licensing agreements; however, in the case of mixed know-how and patent licensing agreements the term "licensed technology" also includes any patents for which a licence is granted besides the communication of the know-how;

8. the term "the same technology" means the technology as licensed to the first licensee and enhanced by any improvements made thereto subsequently, irrespective of whether and to what extent such improvements are exploited by the parties or the other licensees and irrespective of whether the technology is protected by necessary patents in any Member States;

9. "the licensed products" are goods or services the production or provision of which requires the use of the licensed technology;

10. the term "exploitation" refers to any use of the licensed technology in particular in the production, active or passive sales in a territory even if not coupled with manufacture in that territory, or leasing of the licensed products;

11. "the licensed territory" is the territory covering all or at least part of the common market where the licensee is entitled to exploit the licensed technology;

12. "territory reserved for the licensor" means territories in which the licensor has not granted any licences and which he has expressly reserved for himself;

13. "connected undertakings" means

   (a) undertakings in which a party to the agreement, directly or indirectly;
   − owns more than half the capital or business assets, or
   − has the power to exercise more than half the voting rights, or
   − has the power to appoint more than half the members of the supervisory board, board of directors or bodies legally representing the undertaking, or
   − has the right to manage the affairs of the undertaking;

   (b) undertakings which directly or indirectly have in or over a party to the agreement the rights or powers listed in (a);

(c) undertakings in which an undertaking referred to in (b) directly or indirectly has the rights or powers listed in (a);

(d) undertakings in which the parties to the agreement or undertakings connected with them jointly have the rights or powers listed in (a): such jointly controlled undertakings are considered to be connected with each of the parties to the agreement.   **[1431]**

Article 2

(1) Article 1 shall apply notwithstanding the presence in particular of any of the following obligations, which are generally not restrictive of competition:

1. an obligation on the licensee not to divulge the know-how communicated by the licensor; the licensee may be held to this obligation after the agreement has expired;

2. an obligation on the licensee not to grant sub-licences or assign the licence;

3. an obligation on the licensee not to exploit the licensed know-how after termination of the agreement in so far and as long as the know-how is still secret;

4. an obligation on the licensee to communicate to the licensor any experience gained in exploiting the licensed technology and to grant him a non-exclusive licence in respect of improvements to or new applications of that technology, provided that

   (a) the licensee is not prevented during or after the term of the agreement from freely using his own improvements, in so far as these are severable from the licensor's know-how, or licensing them to third parties where licensing to third parties does not disclose the know-how communicated by the licensor that is still secret; this is without prejudice to an obligation on the licensee to seek the licensor's prior approval to such licensing provided that approval may not be withheld unless there are objectively justifiable reasons to believe that licensing improvements to third parties will disclose the licensor's know-how, and

   (b) the licensor has accepted an obligation whether exclusive or not, to communicate his own improvements to the licensee and his right to use the licensee's improvements which are not severable from the licensed know-how does not extend beyond the date on which the licensee's right to exploit the licensor's know-how comes to an end, except for termination of the agreement for breach by the licensee; this is without prejudice to an obligation on the licensee to give the licensor the option to continue to use the improvements after that date, if at the same time he relinquishes the post-term use ban or agrees, after having had an opportunity to examine the licensee's improvements, to pay appropriate royalties for their use;

5. an obligation on the licensee to observe minimum quality specifications for the licensed product or to procure goods or services from the licensor or from an undertaking designated by the licensor, in so far as such quality specifications, products or services are necessary for

   (a) a technically satisfactory exploitation of the licensed technology, or

   (b) for ensuring that the production of the licensee conforms to the quality standards that are respected by the licensor and other licensees,

   and to allow the licensor to carry out related checks;

6. obligations

   (a) to inform the licensor of misappropriation of the know-how or of infringements of the licensed patents, or (*b*) to take or to assist the licensor in taking legal action against such misappropriation or infringements,

provided that these obligations are without prejudice to the licensee's right to challenge the validity of the licensed patents or to contest the secrecy of the licensed know-how except where he himself has in some way contributed to its disclosure;

7. an obligation on the licensee, in the event of the know-how becoming publicly known other than by action of the licensor, to continue paying until the end of the agreement the royalties in the amounts, for the periods and according to the methods freely determined by the parties, without prejudice to the payment of any additional damages in the event of the know-how becoming publicly known by the action of the licensee in breach of the agreement;

8. an obligation on the licensee to restrict his exploitation of the licensed technology to one or more technical fields of application covered by the licensed technology or to one or more product markets;

9. an obligation on the licensee to pay a minimum royalty or to produce a minimum quantity of the licensed product or to carry out a minimum number of operations exploiting the licensed technology;

10. an obligation on the licensor to grant the licensee any more favourable terms that the licensor may grant to another undertaking after the agreement is entered into;

11. an obligation on the licensee to mark the licensed product with the licensor's name;

12. an obligation on the licensee not to use the licensor's know-how to construct facilities for third parties; this is without prejudice to the right of the licensee to increase the capacity of its facilities or to set up additional facilities for its own use on normal commercial terms, including the payment of additional royalties.   **[1432]**

Article 3

Articles 1 and 2(2) shall not apply where:

1. the licensee is prevented from continuing to use the licensed know-how after the termination of the agreement where the know-how has meanwhile become publicly known, other than by the action of the licensee in breach of the agreement;

2. the licensee is obliged either:

    (*a*) to assign in whole or in part to the licensor rights to improvements to or new applications of the licensed technology;

    (*b*) to grant the licensor an exclusive licence for improvements to or new applications of the licensed technology which would prevent the licensee during the currency of the agreement and/or thereafter from using his own improvements in so far as these are severable from the licensor's know-how, or from licensing them to third parties, where such licensing would not disclose the licensor's know-how that is still secret; or

    (*c*) in the case of an agreement which also includes a post-term use ban, to grant back to the licensor, even on a non-exclusive and reciprocal basis, licences for improvements which are not severable from the licensor's know-how, if the licensor's right to use the improvements is of a longer duration than the licensee's right to use the licensor's know-how, except for termination of the agreement for breach by the licensee;

3. the licensee is obliged at the time the agreement is entered into to accept quality specifications or further licences or to procure goods or services which he does not want, unless such licences, quality specifications, goods or services are

necessary for a technically satisfactory exploitation of the licensed technology or for ensuring that the production of the licensee conforms to the quality standards that are respected by the licensor and other licensees;

4. the licensee is prohibited from contesting the secrecy of the licensed know-how or from challenging the validity of licensed patents within the common market belonging to the licensor or undertakings connected with him, without prejudice to the right of the licensor to terminate the licensing agreement in the event of such a challenge;

5. the licensee is charged royalties on goods or services which are not entirely or partially produced by means of the licensed technology or for the use of know-how which has become publicly known by the action of the licensor or an undertaking connected with him;

6. one party is restricted within the same technological field of use or within the same product market as to the customers he may serve, in particular by being prohibited from supplying certain classes of user, employing certain forms of distribution or, with the aim of sharing customers, using certain types of packaging for the products, save as provided in Article 1(1)(7) and Article 4(2);

7. the quantity of the licensed products one party may manufacture or sell or the number of operations exploiting the licensed technology he may carry out are subject to limitations, save as provided in Article 1(1)(8) and Article 4(2);

8. one party is restricted in the determination of prices, components of prices or discounts for the licensed products;

9. one party is restricted from competing with the other party, with undertakings connected with the other party or with other undertakings within the common market in respect of research and development, production or use of competing products and their distribution, without prejudice to an obligation on the licensee to use his best endeavours to exploit the licensed technology and without prejudice to the right of the licensor to terminate the exclusivity granted to the licensee and cease communicating improvements in the event of the licensee's engaging in any such competing activities and to require the licensee to prove that the licensed know-how is not used for the production of goods and services other than those licensed;

10. the initial duration of the licensing agreement is automatically prolonged by the inclusion in it of any new improvements communicated by the licensor, unless the licensee has the right to refuse such improvements or each party has the right to terminate the agreement at the expiry of the initial term of the agreement and at least every three years thereafter;

11. the licensor is required, albeit in separate agreements, for a period exceeding that permitted under Article 1(2) not to license other undertakings to exploit the same technology in the licensed territory, or a party is required for periods exceeding those permitted under Articles 1(2) or 1(4) not to exploit the same technology in the territory of the other party or of other licensees;

12. one or both of the parties are required:

   (a) to refuse without any objectively justified reason to meet demand from users or resellers in their respective territories who would market products in other territories within the common market;

   (b) to make it difficult for users or resellers to obtain the products from other resellers within the common market, and in particular to exercise intellectual property rights or take measures so as to prevent users or resellers from obtaining outside, or from putting on the market in the licensed territory products which have been lawfully put on the market within the common market by the licensor or with his consent;

   or do so as a result of a concerted practice between them.   **[1433]**

Article 4

(1) The exemption provided for in Articles 1 and 2 shall also apply to agreements containing obligations restrictive of competition which are not covered by those Articles and do not fall within the scope of Article 3, on condition that the agreements in question are notified to the Commission in accordance with the provisions of Commission Regulation No 27 and that the Commission does not oppose such exemption within a period of six months.

(2) Paragraph 1 shall in particular apply to an obligation on the licensee to supply only a limited quantity of the licensed product to a particular customer, where the know-how licence is granted at the request of such a customer in order to provide him with a second source of supply within a licensed territory.

This provision shall also apply where the customer is the licensee and the licence, in order to provide a second source of supply, provides for the customer to make licensed products or have them made by a sub-contractor.

(3) The period of six months shall run from the date on which the notification is received by the Commission. Where, however, the notification is made by registered post, the period shall run from the date shown on the postmark of the place of posting.

(4) Paragraphs 1 and 2 shall apply only if

(a) express reference is made to this Article in the notification or in a communication accompanying it; and

(b) the information furnished with the notification is complete and in accordance with the facts.

(5) The benefit of paragraphs 1 and 2 may be claimed for agreements notified before the entry into force of this Regulation by submitting a communication to the Commission referring expressly to this Article and to the notification. Paragraphs 3 and 4(b) shall apply mutatis mutandis.

(6) The Commission may oppose the exemption. It shall oppose exemption if it receives a request to do so from a Member State within three months of the transmission to the Member State of the notification referred to in paragraph 1 or of the communication referred to in paragraph 5. This request must be justified on the basis of considerations relating to the competition rules of the Treaty.

(7) The Commission may withdraw the opposition to the exemption at any time. However, where the opposition was raised at the request of a Member State and this request is maintained, it may be withdrawn only after consultation of the Advisory Committee on Restrictive Practices and Dominant Positions.

(8) If the opposition is withdrawn because the undertakings concerned have shown that the conditions of Article 85(3) are fulfilled, the exemption shall apply from the date of notification.

(9) If the opposition is withdrawn because the undertakings concerned have amended the agreement so that the conditions of Article 85(3) are fulfilled, the exemption shall apply from the date on which the amendments take effect.

(10) If the Commission opposes exemption and the opposition is not withdrawn, the effects of the notification shall be governed by the provisions of Regulation No 17.

[1434]

Article 5

(1) This Regulation shall not apply to:

1. agreements between members of a patent of know-how pool which relate to the pooled technologies
2. know-how licensing agreements between competing undertakings which hold interests in a joint venture, or between one of them and the joint venture, if the licensing agreements relate to the activities of the joint venture.
3. agreements under which one party grants the other a know-how licence and the other party, albeit in separate agreements or through connected undertakings, grants the first party a patent, trademark or know-how licence or exclusive sales rights, where the parties are competitors in relation to the products covered by those agreements;
4. agreements including the licensing of intellectual property rights other than patents (in particular trademarks, copyright and design rights) or the licensing of software except where these rights or the software are of assistance in achieving the object of the licensed technology and there are no obligations restrictive of competition other than those also attached to the licensed know-how and exempted under the present Regulation.

(2) However, this Regulation shall apply to reciprocal licences of the types referred to in paragraph 1(3) where the parties are not subject to any territorial restriction within the common market on the manufacture, use or putting on the market of the products covered by the agreements or on the use of the licensed technologies.   **[1435]**

Article 6

This Regulation shall also apply to:

1. pure know-how agreements or mixed agreements where the licensor is not the developer of the know-how or the patentee but is authorized by the developer or the patentee to grant a licence or a sub-licence;
2. assignments of know-how or of know-how and patents where the risk associated with exploitation remains with the assignor, in particular where the sum payable in consideration of the assignment is dependent upon the turnover attained by the assignee in respect of products made using the know-how or the patents, the quantity of such products manufactured or the number of operations carried out employing the know-how or the patents;
3. pure know-how agreements or mixed agreements in which rights or obligations of the licensor or the licensee are assumed by undertakings connected with them.
[1436]

Article 7

The Commission may withdraw the benefit of this Regulation, pursuant to Article 7 of Regulation No 19/65/EEC, where it finds in a particular case that an agreement exempted by this Regulation nevertheless has certain effects which are incompatible with the conditions laid down in Article 85(3) of the Treaty, and in particular where:

1. such effects arise from an arbitration award;
2. the effect of the agreement is to prevent the licensed products from being exposed to effective competition in the licensed territory from identical products or products considered by users as equivalent in view of their characteristics, price and intended use;
3. the licensor does not have the right to terminate the exclusivity granted to the licensee at the latest five years from the date the agreement was entered into and at least annually thereafter if, without legitimate reason, the licensee fails to exploit the licensed technology or to do so adequately;
4. without prejudice to Article 1(1)(6), the licensee refuses, without objectively valid

reasons, to meet unsolicited demand from users or resellers in the territory of other licensees;

5. one or both of the parties

   (*a*) without objectively justified reason, refuse to meet demand from users or resellers in their respective territories who would market the products in other territories within the common market; or

   (*b*) make it difficult for users or resellers to obtain the products from other resellers within the common market, and in particular where they exercise intellectual property rights or take measures so as to prevent resellers or users from obtaining outside, or from putting on the market in the licensed territory products which have been lawfully put on the market within the common market by the licensor or with his consent;

6. the operation of the post-term use ban referred to in Article 2(1)(3) prevents the licensee from working an expired patent which can be worked by all other manufacturers;

7. the period for which the licensee is obliged to continue paying royalties after the know-how has become publicly known by the action of third parties, as referred to in Article 2(1)(7), substantially exceeds the lead time acquired because of the head-start in production and marketing and this obligation is detrimental to competition in the market;

8. the parties were already competitors before the grant of the licence and obligations on the licensee to produce a minimum quantity or to use his best endeavours as referred to in Article 2(1)(9) and Article 3(9) have the effect of preventing the licensee from using competing technologies.   **[1437]**

Article 8

(1) As regards agreements existing on 13 March 1962 and notified before 1 February 1963 and agreements, whether notified or not, to which Article 4(2)(2)(*b*) of Regulation No 17 applies, the declaration of inapplicability of Article 85(1) of the Treaty contained in this Regulation shall have retroactive effect from the time at which the conditions for application of this Regulation were fulfilled.

(2) As regards all other agreements notified before this Regulation entered into force, the declaration of inapplicability of Article 85(1) of the Treaty contained in this Regulation shall have retroactive effect from the time at which the conditions for application of this Regulation were fulfilled, or from the date of notification, whichever is the later.   **[1438]**

Article 9

If agreements existing on 13 March 1962 and notified before 1 February 1963 or agreements to which Article 4(2) (2)(*b*) of Regulation No 17 applies and notified before 1 January 1967 are amended before 1 July 1989 so as to fulfil the conditions for application of this Regulation, and if the amendment is communicated to the Commission before 1 October 1989 the prohibition in Article 85(1) of the Treaty shall not apply in respect of the period prior to the amendment. The communication shall take effect from the time of its receipt by the Commission. Where the communication is sent by registered post, it shall take effect from the date shown on the postmark of the place of posting.   **[1439]**

Article 10

(1) As regards agreements to which Article 85 of the Treaty applies as a result of the

accession of the United Kingdom, Ireland and Denmark, Articles 8 and 9 shall apply except that the relevant dates shall be 1 January 1973 instead of 13 March 1962 and 1 July 1973 instead of 1 February 1963 and 1 January 1967.

(2) As regards agreements to which Article 85 of the Treaty applies as a result of the accession of Greece, Articles 8 and 9 shall apply except that the relevant dates shall be 1 January 1981 instead of 13 March 1962 and 1 July 1981 instead of 1 February 1963 and 1 January 1967.

(3) As regards agreements to which Article 85 of the Treaty applies as a result of the accession of Spain and Portugal, Articles 8 and 9 shall apply except that the relevant dates shall be 1 January 1986 instead of 13 March 1962 and 1 July 1986 instead of 1 February 1963 and 1 January 1967.   **[1440]**

Article 11

(1) Information acquired pursuant to Article 4 shall be used only for the purposes of the Regulation.

(2) The Commission and the authorities of the Member States, their officials and other servants shall not disclose information acquired by them pursuant to this Regulation of the kind covered by the obligation of professional secrecy.

(3) The provisions of paragraphs 1 and 2 shall not prevent publication of general information or surveys which do not contain information relating to particular undertakings or associations of undertakings.   **[1441]**

Article 12

This Regulation shall enter into force on 1 April 1989.
It shall apply until 31 December 1999.   **[1442]**

This Regulation shall be binding in its entirety and directly applicable in all Member States.

Done at Brussels, 30 November 1988.

REGULATION (EEC) No 4064/89 OF THE COUNCIL
of 21 December 1989

on the control of concentrations between undertakings

THE COUNCIL OF THE EUROPEAN COMMUNITIES,

Having regard to the Treaty establishing the European Economic Community, and in particular Articles 87 and 235 thereof,

Having regard to the proposal from the Commission,

Having regard to the opinion of the European Parliament,

Having regard to the opinion of the Economic and Social Committee,

(1) Whereas, for the achievement of the aims of the Treaty establishing the European Economic Community, Article 3(f) gives the Community the objective of instituting "a system ensuring that competition in the common market is not distorted';

(2) Whereas this system is essential for the achievement of the internal market by 1992 and its further development;

(3) Whereas the dismantling of internal frontiers is resulting and will continue to result in major corporate reorganizations in the Community, particularly in the form of concentrations;

(4) Whereas such a development must be welcomed as being in line with the requirements of dynamic competition and capable of increasing the competitiveness of European industry, improving the conditions of growth and raising the standard of living in the Community;

(5) Whereas, however, it must be ensured that the process of reorganization does not result in lasting damage to competition; whereas Community law must therefore include provisions governing those concentrations which may significantly impede effective competition in the common market or in a substantial part of it;

(6) Whereas Articles 85 and 86, while applicable, according to the case-law of the Court of Justice, to certain concentrations, are not, however, sufficient to control all operations which may prove to be incompatible with the system of undistorted competition envisaged in the Treaty;

(7) Whereas a new legal instrument should therefore be created in the form of a Regulation to permit effective control of all concentrations from the point of view of their effect on the structure of competition in the Community and to be the only instrument applicable to such concentrations;

(8) Whereas this Regulation should therefore be based not only on Article 87 but, principally, on Article 235 of the Treaty, under which the Community may give itself the additional powers of action necessary for the attainment of its objectives, including with regard to concentrations on the markets for agricultural products listed in Annex II to the Treaty;

(9) Whereas the provisions to be adopted in this Regulation should apply to significant structural changes the impact of which on the market goes beyond the national borders of any one Member State;

(10) Whereas the scope of application of this Regulation should therefore be defined according to the geographical area of activity of the undertakings concerned and be limited by quantitative thresholds in order to cover those concentrations which have a Community dimension; whereas, at the end of an initial phase of the application of this Regulation, these thresholds should be reviewed in the light of the experience gained;

(11) Whereas a concentration with a Community dimension exists where the combined aggregate turnover of the undertakings concerned exceeds given levels worldwide and within the Community and where at least two of the undertakings concerned have their sole or main fields of activities in different Member States or where, although the undertakings in question act mainly in one and the same Member State, at least one of them has substantial operations in at least one other Member State; whereas that is also the case where the concentrations are effected by undertakings which do not have their principal fields of activities in the Community but which have substantial operations there;

(12) Whereas the arrangements to be introduced for the control of concentrations should, without prejudice to Article 90(2) of the Treaty, respect the principle of non-discrimination between the public and the private sectors; whereas, in the public sector, calculation of the turnover of an undertaking concerned in a concentration needs, therefore, to take account of undertakings making up an economic unit with an independent power of decision, irrespective of the way in which their capital is held or of the rules of administrative supervision applicable to them;

(13) Whereas it is necessary to establish whether concentrations with a Community dimension are compatible or not with the common market from the point of view of the need to maintain and develop effective competition in the common market; whereas, in so doing, the Commission must place its appraisal within the general framework of the achievement of the fundamental objectives referred to in Article 2 of the Treaty, including that of strengthening the Community's economic and social cohesion, referred to in Article 130a;

(14) Whereas this Regulation should establish the principle that a concentration with a Community dimension which creates or strengthens a position as a result of which effective competition in the common market or in a substantial part of it is significantly impeded is to be declared incompatible with the common market;

(15) Whereas concentrations which, by reason of the limited market share of the undertakings concerned, are not liable to impede effective competition may be presumed to be compatible with the common market; whereas, without prejudice to Articles 85 and 86 of the Treaty, an indication to this effect exists, in particular, where the market share of the undertakings concerned does not exceed 25% either in the common market or in a substantial part of it;

(16) Whereas the Commission should have the task of taking all the decisions necessary to establish whether or not concentrations with a Community dimension are compatible with the common market, as well as decisions designed to restore effective competition;

(17) Whereas to ensure effective control undertakings should be obliged to give prior notification

of concentrations with a Community dimension and provision should be made for the suspension of concentrations for a limited period, and for the possibility of extending or waiving a suspension where necessary; whereas in the interests of legal certainty the validity of transactions must nevertheless be protected as much as necessary;

(18) Whereas a period within which the Commission must initiate proceedings in respect of a notified concentration and periods within which it must give a final decision on the compatibility or incompatibility with the common market of a notified concentration should be laid down;

(19) Whereas the undertakings concerned must be afforded the right to be heard by the Commission when proceedings have been initiated; whereas the members of the management and supervisory bodies and the recognized representatives of the employees of the undertakings concerned, and third parties showing a legitimate interest, must also be given the opportunity to be heard;

(20) Whereas the Commission should act in close and constant liaison with the competent authorities of the Member States from which it obtains comments and information;

(21) Whereas, for the purposes of this Regulation, and in accordance with the case-law of the Court of Justice, the Commission must be afforded the assistance of the Member States and must also be empowered to require information to be given and to carry out the necessary investigations in order to appraise concentrations;

(22) Whereas compliance with this Regulation must be enforceable by means of fines and periodic penalty payments; whereas the Court of Justice should be given unlimited jurisdiction in that regard pursuant to Article 172 of the Treaty;

(23) Whereas it is appropriate to define the concept of concentration in such a manner as to cover only operations bringing about a lasting change in the structure of the undertakings concerned; whereas it is therefore necessary to exclude from the scope of this Regulation those operations which have as their object or effect the co-ordination of the competitive behaviour of undertakings which remain independent, since such operations fall to be examined under the appropriate provisions of the Regulations implementing Articles 85 and 86 of the Treaty; whereas it is appropriate to make this distinction specifically in the case of the creation of joint ventures;

(24) Whereas there is no co-ordination of competitive behaviour within the meaning of this Regulation where two or more undertakings agree to acquire jointly control of one or more other undertakings with the object and effect of sharing amongst themselves such undertakings or their assets;

(25) Whereas this Regulation should still apply where the undertakings concerned accept restrictions directly related and necessary to the implementation of the concentration;

(26) Whereas the Commission should be given exclusive competence to apply this Regulation, subject to review by the Court of Justice;

(27) Whereas the Member States may not apply their national legislation on competition to concentrations with a Community dimension, unless this Regulation makes provision therefor; whereas the relevant powers of national authorities should be limited to cases where, failing intervention by the Commission, effective competition is likely to be significantly impeded within the territory of a Member State and where the competition interests of that Member State cannot be sufficiently protected otherwise by this Regulation; whereas the Member States concerned must act promptly in such cases; whereas this Regulation cannot, because of the diversity of national law, fix a single deadline for the adoption of remedies;

(28) Whereas, furthermore, the exclusive application of this Regulation to concentrations with a Community dimension is without prejudice to Article 223 of the Treaty, and does not prevent the Member States from taking appropriate measures to protect legitimate interests other than those pursued by this Regulation, provided that such measures are compatible with the general principles and other provisions of Community law;

(29) Whereas concentrations not covered by this Regulation come, in principle, within the jurisdiction of the Member States; whereas, however, the Commission should have the power to act, at the request of a Member State concerned, in cases where effective competition could be significantly impeded within that Member State's territory;

(30) Whereas the conditions in which concentrations involving Community undertakings are carried out in non-member countries should be observed, and provision should be made for the possibility of the Council giving the Commission an appropriate mandate for negotiation with a view to obtaining non-discriminatory treatment for Community undertakings;

(31) Whereas this Regulation in no way detracts from the collective rights of employees as recognized in the undertakings concerned,

HAS ADOPTED THIS REGULATION:

Article 1—Scope

1. Without prejudice to Article 22 this Regulation shall apply to all concentrations with a Community dimension as defined in paragraph 2.

2. For the purposes of this Regulation, a concentration has a Community dimension where:

(a) the combined aggregate worldwide turnover of all the undertakings concerned is more than ECU 5 000 million; and

(b) the aggregate Community-wide turnover of each of at least two of the undertakings concerned is more than ECU 250 million,

unless each of the undertakings concerned achieves more than two-thirds of its aggregate Community-wide turnover within one and the same Member State.

3. The thresholds laid down in paragraph 2 will be reviewed before the end of the fourth year following that of the adoption of this Regulation by the Council acting by a qualified majority on a proposal from the Commission.   **[1443]**

Article 2—Appraisal of concentrations

1. Concentrations within the scope of this Regulation shall be appraised in accordance with the following provisions with a view to establishing whether or not they are compatible with the common market.

In making this appraisal, the Commission shall take into account:

(a) the need to maintain and develop effective competition within the common market in view of, among other things, the structure of all the markets concerned and the actual or potential competition from undertakings located either within or outwith the Community;

(b) the market position of the undertakings concerned and their economic and financial power, the alternatives available to suppliers and users, their access to supplies or markets, any legal or other barriers to entry, supply and demand trends for the relevant goods and services, the interests of the intermediate and ultimate consumers, and the development of technical and economic progress provided that it is to consumers' advantage and does not form an obstacle to competition.

2. A concentration which does not create or strengthen a dominant position as a result of which effective competition would be significantly impeded in the common market or in a substantial part of it shall be declared compatible with the common market.

3. A concentration which creates or strengthens a dominant position as a result of which effective competition would be significantly impeded in the common market or in a substantial part of it shall be declared incompatible with the common market.

[1444]

Article 3—Definition of concentration

1. A concentration shall be deemed to arise where:

(a) two or more previously independent undertakings merge, or

(b) — one or more persons already controlling at least one undertaking, or
— one or more undertakings

acquire, whether by purchase of securities or assets, by contract or by any other means, direct or indirect control of the whole or parts of one or more other undertakings.

2. An operation, including the creation of a joint venture, which has as its object or effect the co-ordination of the competitive behaviour of undertakings which remain independent shall not constitute a concentration within the meaning of paragraph 1(*b*).

The creation of a joint venture performing on a lasting basis all the functions of an autonomous economic entity, which does not give rise to co-ordination of the competitive behaviour of the parties amongst themselves or between them and the joint venture, shall constitute a concentration within the meaning of paragraph 1(*b*).

3. For the purposes of this Regulation, control shall be constituted by rights, contracts or any other means which, either separately or in combination and having regard to the considerations of fact or law involved, confer the possibility of exercising decisive influence on an undertaking, in particular by:

(*a*) ownership or the right to use all or part of the assets of an undertaking;

(*b*) rights or contracts which confer decisive influence on the composition, voting or decisions of the organs of an undertaking.

4. Control is acquired by persons or undertakings which:

(*a*) are holders of the rights or entitled to rights under the contracts concerned, or

(*b*) while not being holders of such rights or entitled to rights under such contracts, have the power to exercise the rights deriving therefrom.

5. A concentration shall not be deemed to arise where:

(*a*) credit institutions or other financial institutions or insurance companies, the normal activities of which include transactions and dealing in securities for their own account or for the account of others, hold on a temporary basis securities which they have acquired in an undertaking with a view to reselling them, provided that they do not exercise voting rights in respect of those securities with a view to determining the competitive behaviour of that undertaking or provided that they exercise such voting rights only with a view to preparing the disposal of all or part of that undertaking or of its assets or the disposal of those securities and that any such disposal takes place within one year of the date of acquisition; that period may be extended by the Commission on request where such institutions or companies can show that the disposal was not reasonably possible within the period set;

(*b*) control is acquired by an office-holder according to the law of a Member State relating to liquidation, winding up, insolvency, cessation of payments, compositions or analogous proceedings;

(*c*) the operations referred to in paragraph 1(*b*) are carried out by the financial holding companies referred to in Article 5(3) of the Fourth Council Directive 78/660/EEC of 25 July 1978 on the annual accounts of certain types of companies, as last amended by Directive 84/569/EEC provided however that the voting rights in respect of the holding are exercised, in particular in relation to the appointment of members of the management and supervisory bodies of the undertakings in which they have holdings, only to maintain the full value of those investments and not to determine directly or indirectly the competitive conduct of those undertakings. **[1445]**

Article 4 — Prior notification of concentrations

1. Concentrations with a Community dimension defined in this Regulation shall be notified to the Commission not more than one week after the conclusion of the agreement, or the announcement of the public bid, or the acquisition of a controlling interest. That week shall begin when the first of those events occurs.

2. A concentration which consists of a merger within the meaning of Article 3(1)(*a*) or in the acquisition of joint control within the meaning of Article 3(1)(*b*) shall be notified jointly by the parties to the merger or by those acquiring joint control as the case may be. In all other cases, the notification shall be effected by the person or undertaking acquiring control of the whole or parts of one or more undertakings.

3. Where the Commission finds that a notified concentration falls within the scope of this Regulation, it shall publish the fact of the notification, at the same time indicating the names of the parties, the nature of the concentration and the economic sectors involved. The Commission shall take account of the legitimate interest of undertakings in the protection of their business secrets.   **[1446]**

Article 5 — Calculation of turnover

1. Aggregate turnover within the meaning of Article 1(2) shall comprise the amounts derived by the undertakings concerned in the preceding financial year from the sale of products and the provision of services falling within the undertakings' ordinary activities after deduction of sales rebates and of value added tax and other taxes directly related to turnover. The aggregate turnover of an undertaking concerned shall not include the sale of products or the provision of services between any of the undertakings referred to in paragraph 4.

Turnover, in the Community or in a Member State, shall comprise products sold and services provided to undertakings or consumers, in the Community or in that Member State as the case may be.

2. By way of derogation from paragraph 1, where the concentration consists in the acquisition of parts, whether or not constituted as legal entities, of one or more undertakings, only the turnover relating to the parts which are the subject of the transaction shall be taken into account with regard to the seller or sellers.

However, two or more transactions within the meaning of the first subparagraph which take place within a two-year period between the same persons or undertakings shall be treated as one and the same concentration arising on the date of the last transaction.

3. In place of turnover the following shall be used:

(*a*)   for credit institutions and other financial institutions, as regards Article 1(2)(*a*), one-tenth of their total assets.

As regards Article 1(2)(*b*) and the final part of Article 1(2), total Community-wide turnover shall be replaced by one-tenth of total assets multiplied by the ratio between loans and advances to credit institutions and customers in transactions with Community residents and the total sum of those loans and advances.

As regards the final part of Article 1(2), total turnover within one Member State shall be replaced by one-tenth of total assets multiplied by the ratio between loans and advances to credit institutions and customers in transactions with residents of that Member State and the total sum of those loans and advances;

(*b*)   for insurance undertakings, the value of gross premiums written which shall comprise all amounts received and receivable in respect of insurance contracts issued by or on behalf of the insurance undertakings, including also outgoing reinsurance premiums, and after deduction of taxes and parafiscal contributions or levies charged by reference to the amounts of individual premiums or the total volume of premiums; as regards Article 1(2)(*b*) and the final part of Article 1(2), gross premiums received from Community residents and from residents of one Member State respectively shall be taken into account.

4. Without prejudice to paragraph 2, the aggregate turnover of an undertaking concerned within the meaning of Article 1(2) shall be calculated by adding together the respective turnovers of the following:

(a) the undertaking concerned;

(b) those undertakings in which the undertaking concerned, directly or indirectly:

- owns more than half the capital or business assets, or
- has the power to exercise more than half the voting rights, or
- has the power to appoint more than half the members of the supervisory board, the administrative board or bodies legally representing the undertakings, or
- has the right to manage the undertakings' affairs;

(c) those undertakings which have in the undertaking concerned the rights or powers listed in (b);

(d) those undertakings in which an undertaking as referred to in (c) has the rights or powers listed in (b);

(e) those undertakings in which two or more undertakings as referred to in (a) to (d) jointly have the rights or powers listed in (b).

5. Where undertakings concerned by the concentration jointly have the rights or powers listed in paragraph 4(b), in calculating the aggregate turnover of the undertakings concerned for the purposes of Article 1(2):

(a) no account shall be taken of the turnover resulting from the sale of products or the provision of services between the joint undertaking and each of the undertakings concerned or any other undertaking connected with any one of them, as set out in paragraph 4(b) to (e);

(b) account shall be taken of the turnover resulting from the sale of products and the provision of services between the joint undertaking and any third undertakings. This turnover shall be apportioned equally amongst the undertakings concerned. **[1447]**

Article 6 — Examination of the notification and initiation of proceedings

1. The Commission shall examine the notification as soon as it is received.

(a) Where it concludes that the concentration notified does not fall within the scope of this Regulation, it shall record that finding by means of a decision.

(b) Where it finds that the concentration notified, although falling within the scope of this Regulation, does not raise serious doubts as to its compatibility with the common market, it shall decide not to oppose it and shall declare that it is compatible with the common market.

(c) If, on the other hand, it finds that the concentration notified falls within the scope of this Regulation and raises serious doubts as to its compatibility with the common market, it shall decide to initiate proceedings.

2. The Commission shall notify its decision to the undertakings concerned and the competent authorities of the Member States without delay. **[1448]**

Article 7 — Suspension of concentrations

1. For the purposes of paragraph 2 a concentration as defined in Article 1 shall not be put into effect either before its notification or within the first three weeks following its notification.

2. Where the Commission, following a preliminary examination of the notification within the period provided for in paragraph 1, finds it necessary in order to ensure the full effectiveness of any decision taken later pursuant to Article 8(3) and (4), it may decide on its own initiative to continue the suspension of a concentration in whole or in part until it takes a final decision, or to take other interim measures to that effect.

3. Paragraphs 1 and 2 shall not prevent the implementation of a public bid which has been notified to the Commission in accordance with Article 4(1), provided that the acquirer does not exercise the voting rights attached to the securities in question or does so only to maintain the full value of those investments and on the basis of a derogation granted by the Commission under paragraph 4.

4. The Commission may, on request, grant a derogation from the obligations imposed in paragraphs 1, 2 or 3 in order to prevent serious damage to one or more undertakings concerned by a concentration or to a third party. That derogation may be made subject to conditions and obligations in order to ensure conditions of effective competition. A derogation may be applied for and granted at any time, even before notification or after the transaction.

5. The validity of any transaction carried out in contravention of paragraph 1 or 2 shall be dependent on a decision pursuant to Article 6(1)(*b*) or Article 8(2) or (3) or on a presumption pursuant to Article 10(6).

This Article shall, however, have no effect on the validity of transactions in securities including those convertible into other securities admitted to trading on a market which is regulated and supervised by authorities recognized by public bodies, operates regularly and is accessible directly or indirectly to the public, unless the buyer and seller knew or ought to have known that the transaction was carried out in contravention of paragraph 1 or 2. **[1449]**

Article 8 – Powers of decision of the Commission

1. Without prejudice to Article 9, all proceedings initiated pursuant to Article 6(1)(*c*) shall be closed by means of a decision as provided for in paragraphs 2 to 5.

2. Where the Commission finds that, following modification by the undertakings concerned if necessary, a notified concentration fulfils the criterion laid down in Article 2(2), it shall issue a decision declaring the concentration compatible with the common market.

It may attach to its decision conditions and obligations intended to ensure that the undertakings concerned comply with the commitments they have entered into vis-à-vis the Commission with a view to modifying the original concentration plan. The decision declaring the concentration compatible shall also cover restrictions directly related and necessary to the implementation of the concentration.

3. Where the Commission finds that a concentration fulfils the criterion laid down in Article 2(3), it shall issue a decision declaring that the concentration is incompatible with the common market.

4. Where a concentration has already been implemented, the Commission may, in a decision pursuant to paragraph 3 or by separate decision, require the undertakings or assets brought together to be separated or the cessation of joint control or any other action that may be appropriate in order to restore conditions of effective competition.

5. The Commission may revoke the decision it has taken pursuant to paragraph 2 where:

(*a*) the declaration of compatibility is based on incorrect information for which one of the undertakings is responsible or where it has been obtained by deceit; or

(*b*) the undertakings concerned commit a breach of an obligation attached to the decision.

6. In the cases referred to in paragraph 5, the Commission may take a decision under paragraph 3, without being bound by the deadline referred to in Article 10(3). **[1450]**

Article 9 — Referral to the competent authorities of the Member States

1. The Commission may, by means of a decision notified without delay to the undertakings concerned and the competent authorities of the other Member States, refer a notified concentration to the competent authorities of the Member State concerned in the following circumstances.

2. Within three weeks of the date of receipt of the copy of the notification a Member State may inform the Commission, which shall inform the undertakings concerned, that a concentration threatens to create or to strengthen a dominant position as a result of which effective competition would be significantly impeded on a market, within that Member State, which presents all the characteristics of a distinct market, be it a substantial part of the common market or not.

3. It the Commission considers that, having regard to the market for the products or services in question and the geographical reference market within the meaning of paragraph 7, there is such a distinct market and that such a threat exists, either:

    (*a*) it shall itself deal with the case in order to maintain or restore effective competition on the market concerned; or

    (*b*) it shall refer the case to the competent authorities of the Member State concerned with a view to the application of that State's national competition law.

If, however, the Commission considers that such a distinct market or threat does not exist it shall adopt a decision to that effect which it shall address to the Member State concerned.

4. A decision to refer or not to refer pursuant to paragraph 3 shall be taken:

    (*a*) as a general rule within the six-week period provided for in Article 10(1), second subparagraph, where the Commission, pursuant to Article 6(1)(*b*), has not initiated proceedings or

    (*b*) within three months at most of the notification of the concentration concerned where the Commission has initiated proceedings under Article 6(1)(*c*), without taking the preparatory steps in order to adopt the necessary measures under Article 8(2), second subparagraph,. (3) or (4) to maintain or restore effective competition on the market concerned.

5. If within the three months referred to in paragraph 4(*b*) the Commission, despite a reminder from the Member State concerned, has not taken a decision on referral in accordance with paragraph 3 nor has taken the preparatory steps referred to in paragraph 4(*b*), it shall be deemed to have taken a decision to refer the case to the Member State concerned in accordance with paragraph 3(*b*).

6. The publication of any report or the announcement of the findings of the examination of the concentration by the competent authority of the Member State concerned shall be effected not more than four months after the Commission's referral.

7. The geographical reference market shall consist of the area in which the undertakings concerned are involved in the supply and demand of products or services, in which the conditions of competition are sufficiently homogeneous and which can be distinguished from neighbouring areas because, in particular, conditions of competition are appreciably different in those areas. This assessment should take account in particular of the nature and characteristics of the products or services concerned, of the existence of entry barriers or of consumer preferences, of appreciable differences of the undertakings' market shares between the area concerned and neighbouring areas or of substantial price differences.

8. In applying the provisions of this Article, the Member State concerned may take only the measures strictly necessary to safeguard or restore effective competition on the market concerned.

9. In accordance with the relevant provisions of the Treaty, any Member State may appeal to the Court of Justice, and in particular request the application of Article 186, for the purpose of applying its national competition law.

10. This Article will be reviewed before the end of the fourth year following that of the adoption of this Regulation.   **[1451]**

Article 10 — Time limits for initiating proceedings and for decisions

1. The decisions referred to in Article 6(1) must be taken within one month at most. That period shall begin on the day following that of the receipt of a notification or, if the information to be supplied with the notification is incomplete, on the day following that of the receipt of the complete information.

That period shall be increased to six weeks if the Commission receives a request from a Member State in accordance with Article 9(2).

2. Decisions taken pursuant to Article 8(2) concerning notified concentrations must be taken as soon as it appears that the serious doubts referred to in Article 6(1)(c) have been removed, particularly as a result of modifications made by the undertakings concerned, and at the latest by the deadline laid down in paragraph 3.

3. Without prejudice to Article 8(6), decisions taken pursuant to Article 8(3) concerning notified concentrations must be taken within not more than four months of the date on which proceedings are initiated.

4. The period set by paragraph 3 shall exceptionally be suspended where, owing to circumstances for which one of the undertakings involved in the concentration is responsible, the Commission has had to request information by decision pursuant to Article 11 or to order an investigation by decision pursuant to Article 13.

5. Where the Court of Justice gives a Judgment which annuls the whole or part of a Commission decision taken under this Regulation, the periods laid down in this Regulation shall start again from the date of the Judgment.

6. Where the Commission has not taken a decision in accordance with Article 6(1)(b) or (c) or Article 8(2) or (3) within the deadlines set in paragraphs 1 and 3 respectively, the concentration shall be deemed to have been declared compatible with the common market, without prejudice to Article 9.   **[1452]**

Article 11 — Requests for information

1. In carrying out the duties assigned to it by this Regulation, the Commission may obtain all necessary information from the Governments and competent authorities of the Member States, from the persons referred to in Article 3(1)(b), and from undertakings and associations of undertakings.

2. When sending a request for information to a person, an undertaking or an association of undertakings, the Commission shall at the same time send a copy of the request to the competent authority of the Member State within the territory of which the residence of the person or the seat of the undertaking or association of undertakings is situated.

3. In its request the Commission shall state the legal basis and the purpose of the request and also the penalties provided for in Article 14(1)(c) for supplying incorrect information.

4. The information requested shall be provided, in the case of undertakings, by their owners or their representatives and, in the case of legal persons, companies or firms,

or of associations having no legal personality, by the persons authorized to represent them by law or by their statutes.

5. Where a person, an undertaking or an association of undertakings does not provide the information requested within the period fixed by the Commission or provides incomplete information, the Commission shall by decision require the information to be provided. The decision shall specify what information is required, fix an appropriate period within which it is to be supplied and state the penalties provided for in Articles 14(1)(c) and 15(1)(a) and the right to have the decision reviewed by the Court of Justice.

6. The Commission shall at the same time send a copy of its decision to the competent authority of the Member State within the territory of which the residence of the person or the seat of the undertaking or association of undertakings is situated.   **[1453]**

Article 12 – Investigations by the authorities of the Member States

1. At the request of the Commission, the competent authorities of the Member States shall undertake the investigations which the Commission considers to be necessary under Article 13(1), or which it has ordered by decision pursuant to Article 13(3). The officials of the competent authorities of the Member States responsible for conducting those investigations shall exercise their powers upon production of an authorization in writing issued by the competent authority of the Member State within the territory of which the investigation is to be carried out. Such authorization shall specify the subject matter and purpose of the investigation.

2. If so requested by the Commission or by the competent authority of the Member State within the territory of which the investigation is to be carried out, officials of the Commission may assist the officials of that authority in carrying out their duties.

[1454]

Article 13 – Investigative powers of the Commission

1. In carrying out the duties assigned to it by this Regulation, the Commission may undertake all necessary investigations into undertakings and associations of undertakings.
   To that end the officials authorized by the Commission shall be empowered:

    (a) to examine the books and other business records;
    (b) to take or demand copies of or extracts from the books and business records;
    (c) to ask for oral explanations on the spot;
    (d) to enter any premises, land and means of transport of undertakings.

2. The officials of the Commission authorised to carry out the investigations shall exercise their powers on production of an authorization in writing specifying the subject matter and purpose of the investigation and the penalties provided for in Article 14(1)(d) in cases where production of the required books or other business records is incomplete. In good time before the investigation, the Commission shall inform, in writing, the competent authority of the Member State within the territory of which the investigation is to be carried out of the investigation and of the identities of the authorized officials.

3. Undertakings and associations of undertakings shall submit to investigations ordered by decision of the Commission. The decision shall specify the subject matter and purpose of the investigation, appoint the date on which it shall begin and state the penalties provided for in Articles 14(1)(d) and 15(1)(b) and the right to have the decision reviewed by the Court of Justice.

4. The Commission shall in good time and in writing inform the competent authority of the Member State within the territory of which the investigation is to be carried out

of its intention of taking a decision pursuant to paragraph 3. It shall hear the competent authority before taking its decision.

5. Officials of the competent authority of the Member State within the territory of which the investigation is to be carried out may, at the request of that authority or of the Commission, assist the officials of the Commission in carrying out their duties.

6. Where an undertaking or association of undertakings opposes an investigation ordered pursuant to this Article, the Member State concerned shall afford the necessary assistance to the officials authorized by the Commission to enable them to carry out their investigation. To this end the Member States shall, after consulting the Commission, take the necessary measures within one year of the entry into force of this Regulation.

[1455]

Article 14 — Fines

1. The Commission may by decision impose on the persons referred to in Article 3(1)(*b*), undertakings or associations of undertakings fines of from ECU 1 000 to 50 000 where intentionally or negligently:

   (*a*) they fail to notify a concentration in accordance with Article 4;
   (*b*) they supply incorrect or misleading information in a notification pursuant to Article 4;
   (*c*) they supply incorrect information in response to a request made pursuant to Article 11 or fail to supply information within the period fixed by a decision taken pursuant to Article 11;
   (*d*) they produce the required books or other business records in incomplete form during investigations under Article 12 or 13, or refuse to submit to an investigation ordered by decision taken pursuant to Article 13.

2. The Commission may by decision impose fines not exceeding 10% of the aggregate turnover of the undertakings concerned within the meaning of Article 5 on the persons or undertakings concerned where, either intentionally or negligently, they;

   (*a*) fail to comply with an obligation imposed by decision pursuant to Article 7(4) or 8(2), second subparagraph;
   (*b*) put into effect a concentration in breach of Article 7(1) or disregard a decision taken pursuant to Article 7(2);
   (*c*) put into effect a concentration declared incompatible with the common market by decision pursuant to Article 8(3) or do not take the measures ordered by decision pursuant to Article 8(4).

3. In setting the amount of a fine, regard shall be had to the nature and gravity of the infringement.

4. Decisions taken pursuant to paragraphs 1 and 2 shall not be of criminal law nature.

[1456]

Article 15 — Periodic penalty payments

1. The Commission may by decision impose on the persons referred to in Article 3(1)(*b*), undertakings or associations of undertakings concerned periodic penalty payments of up to ECU 25 000 for each day of delay calculated from the date set in the decision, in order to compel them:

   (*a*) to supply complete and correct information which it has requested by decision pursuant to Article 11;

(b) to submit to an investigation which it has ordered by decision pursuant to Article 13.

2. The Commission may by decision impose on the persons referred to in Article 3(1)(b) or on undertakings periodic penalty payments of up to ECU 100 000 for each day of delay calculated from the date set in the decision, in order to compel them:

    (a) to comply with an obligation imposed by decision pursuant to Article 7(4) or 8(2), second subparagraph, or

    (b) to apply the measures ordered by decision pursuant to Article 8(4).

3. Where the persons referred to in Article 3(1)(b), undertakings or associations of undertakings have satisfied the obligation which it was the purpose of the periodic penalty payment to enforce, the Commission may set the total amount of the periodic penalty payments at a lower figure than that which would arise under the original decision.

[1457]

Article 16 – Review by the Court of Justice

The Court of Justice shall have unlimited jurisdiction within the meaning of Article 172 of the Treaty to review decisions whereby the Commission has fixed a fine or periodic penalty payments; it may cancel, reduce or increase the fine or periodic penalty payments imposed. **[1458]**

Article 17 – Professional secrecy

1. Information acquired as a result of the application of Articles 11, 12, 13 and 18 shall be used only for the purposes of the relevant request, investigation or hearing.

2. Without prejudice to Articles 4(3), 18 and 20, the Commission and the competent authorities of the Member States, their officials and other servants shall not disclose information they have acquired through the application of this Regulation of the kind covered by the obligation of professional secrecy.

3. Paragraphs 1 and 2 shall not prevent publication of general information or of surveys which do not contain information relating to particular undertakings or associations of undertakings. **[1459]**

Article 18 – Hearing of the parties and of third persons

1. Before taking any decision provided for in Articles 7(2) and (4), Article 8(2), second subparagraph, and (3) to (5), and Articles 14 and 15, the Commission shall give the persons, undertakings and associations of undertakings concerned the opportunity, at every stage of the procedure up to the consultation of the Advisory Committee, of making known their views on the objections against them.

2. By way of derogation from paragraph 1, a decision to continue the suspension of a concentration or to grant a derogation from suspension as referred to in Article 7(2) or (4) may be taken provisionally, without the persons, undertakings or associations of undertakings concerned being given the opportunity to make known their views beforehand, provided that the Commission gives them that opportunity as soon as possible after having taken its decision.

3. The Commission shall base its decision only on objections on which the parties have been able to submit their observations. The rights of the defence shall be fully respected in the proceedings. Access to the file shall be open at least to the parties directly involved, subject to the legitimate interest of undertakings in the protection of their business secrets.

4. Insofar as the Commission or the competent authorities of the Member States deem it necessary, they may also hear other natural or legal persons. Natural or legal persons showing a sufficient interest and especially members of the administrative or management bodies of the undertakings concerned or the recognized representatives of their employees shall be entitled, upon application, to be heard.   **[1460]**

Article 19 — Liaison with the authorities of the Member States

1. The Commission shall transmit to the competent authorities of the Member States copies of notifications within three working days and, as soon as possible, copies of the most important documents lodged with or issued by the Commission pursuant to this Regulation.

2. The Commission shall carry out the procedures set out in this Regulation in close and constant liaison with the competent authorities of the Member States, which may express their views upon those procedures. For the purposes of Article 9 it shall obtain information from the competent authority of the Member State as referred to in paragraph 2 of that Article and give it the opportunity to make known its views at every stage of the procedure up to the adoption of a decision pursuant to paragraph 3 of that Article; to that end it shall give it access to the file.

3. An Advisory Committee on concentrations shall be consulted before any decision is taken pursuant to Article 8(2) to (5), 14 or 15, or any provisions are adopted pursuant to Article 23.

4. The Advisory Committee shall consist of representatives of the authorities of the Member States. Each Member State shall appoint one or two representatives; if unable to attend, they may be replaced by other representatives. At least one of the representatives of a Member State shall be competent in matters of restrictive practices and dominant positions.

5. Consultation shall take place at a joint meeting convened at the invitation of and chaired by the Commission. A summary of the case, together with an indication of the most important documents and a preliminary draft of the decision to be taken for each case considered, shall be sent with the invitation. The meeting shall take place not less than 14 days after the invitation has been sent. The Commission may in exceptional cases shorten that period as appropriate in order to avoid serious harm to one or more of the undertakings concerned by a concentration.

6. The Advisory Committee shall deliver an opinion on the Commission's draft decision, if necessary by taking a vote. The Advisory Committee may deliver an opinion even if some members are absent and unrepresented. The opinion shall be delivered in writing and appended to the draft decision. The Commission shall take the utmost account of the opinion delivered by the Committee. It shall inform the Committee of the manner in which its opinion has been taken into account.

7. The Advisory Committee may recommend publication of the opinion. The Commission may carry out such publication. The decision to publish shall take due account of the legitimate interest of undertakings in the protection of their business secrets and of the interest of the undertakings concerned in such publication's taking place.

[1461]

Article 20 — Publication of decisions

1. The Commission shall publish the decisions which it takes pursuant to Article 8(2) to (5) in the Official Journal of the European Communities.

2. The publication shall state the names of the parties and the main content of the decision; it shall have regard to the legitimate interest of undertakings in the protection of their business secrets. **[1462]**

Article 21 – Jurisdiction

1. Subject to review by the Court of Justice, the Commission shall have sole jurisdiction to take the decisions provided for in this Regulation.

2. No Member State shall apply its national legislation on competition to any concentration that has a Community dimension.

The first subparagraph shall be without prejudice to any Member State's power to carry out any enquiries necessary for the application of Article 9(2) or after referral, pursuant to Article 9(3), first subparagraph, indent (*b*), or (5), to take the measures strictly necessary for the application of Article 9(8).

3. Notwithstanding paragraphs 1 and 2, Member States may take appropriate measures to protect legitimate interests other than those taken into consideration by this Regulation and compatible with the general principles and other provisions of Community law.

Public security, plurality of the media and prudential rules shall be regarded as legitimate interests within the meaning of the first subparagraph.

Any other public interest must be communicated to the Commission by the Member State concerned and shall be recognized by the Commission after an assessment of its compatibility with the general principles and other provisions of Community law before the measures referred to above may be taken. The Commission shall inform the Member State concerned of its decision within one month of that communication. **[1463]**

Article 22 – Application of the Regulation

1. This Regulation alone shall apply to concentrations as defined in Article 3.

2. Regulations No 17, (EEC) No 1017/68, (EEC) No 4056/86 and (EEC) No 3975/87 shall not apply to concentrations as defined in Article 3.

3. If the Commission finds, at the request of a Member State, that a concentration as defined in Article 3 that has no Community dimension within the meaning of Article 1 creates or strengthens a dominant position as a result of which effective competition would be significantly impeded within the territory of the Member State concerned it may, insofar as the concentration affects trade between Member States, adopt the decisions provided for in Article 8(2), second subparagraph, (3) and (4).

4. Articles 2(1)(*a*) and (*b*), 5, 6, 8 and 10 to 20 shall apply. The period within which proceedings may be initiated pursuant to Article 10(1) shall begin on the date of the receipt of the request from the Member State. The request must be made within one month at most of the date on which the concentration was made known to the Member State or effected. This period shall begin on the date of the first of those events.

5. Pursuant to paragraph 3 the Commission shall take only the measures strictly necessary to maintain or restore effective competition within the territory of the Member State at the request of which it intervenes.

6. Paragraphs 3 to 5 shall continue to apply until the thresholds referred to in Article 1(2) have been reviewed. **[1464]**

Article 23 – Implementing provisions

The Commission shall have the power to adopt implementing provisions concerning the form, content and other details of notifications pursuant to Article 4, time limits pursuant to Article 10, and hearings pursuant to Article 18.   **[1465]**

Article 24 – Relations with non-member countries

1. The Member States shall inform the Commission of any general difficulties encountered by their undertakings with concentrations as defined in Article 3 in a non-member country.

2. Initially not more than one year after the entry into force of this Regulation and thereafter periodically the Commission shall draw up a report examining the treatment accorded to Community undertakings, in the terms referred to in paragraphs 3 and 4, as regards concentrations in non-member countries. The Commission shall submit those reports to the Council, together with any recommendations.

3. Whenever it appears to the Commission, either on the basis of the reports referred to in paragraph 2 or on the basis of other information, that a non-member country does not grant Community undertakings treatment comparable to that granted by the Community to undertakings from that non-member country, the Commission may submit proposals to the Council for an appropriate mandate for negotiation with a view to obtaining comparable treatment for Community undertakings.

4. Measures taken under this Article shall comply with the obligations of the Community or of the Member States, without prejudice to Article 234 of the Treaty, under international agreements, whether bilateral or multilateral.   **[1466]**

Article 25 – Entry into force

1. This Regulation shall enter into force on 21 September 1990.

2. This Regulation shall not apply to any concentration which was the subject of an agreement or announcement or where control was acquired within the meaning of Article 4(1) before the date of this Regulation's entry into force and it shall not in any circumstances apply to any concentration in respect of which proceedings were initiated before that date by a Member State's authority with responsibility for competition.   **[1467]**

This Regulation shall be binding in its entirety and directly applicable in all Member States.

Done at Brussels, 21 December 1989.

NOTE
   This text follows the republished version of the Regulation which appeared in the Official Journal on the 21 September 1990 (No L257/14), except for the substitution of "concentration" for "consideration" in the first sentence of Article 21(2).

COMMISSION NOTICE
of 24 December 1962

on exclusive dealing contracts with commercial agents[1]

I. The Commission considers that contracts made with commercial agents in which those agents undertake, for a specified part of the territory of the common market,

—to negotiate transactions on behalf of an enterprise,

or

—to conclude transactions in the name and on behalf of an enterprise,

or

—to conclude transactions in their own name and on behalf of this enterprise,

do not fall under the prohibition in Article 85(1) of the Treaty.

It is essential in this case that the contracting party, described as a commercial agent, should, in fact, be such, by the nature of his functions, and that he should neither undertake nor engage in activities proper to an independent trader in the course of commercial operations. The Commission regards as the decisive criterion which distinguishes the commercial agent from the independent trader, the agreement — express or implied — which deals with responsibility for the financial risks bound up with the sale or with the performance of the contract. Thus the Commission's assessment is not governed by the name used to describe the representative. Except for the usual *del credere* guarantee, a commercial agent must not by the nature of his functions assume any risk resulting from the transaction. If he does assume such risks, his function becomes economically akin to that of an independent trader and he must therefore be treated as such for the purposes of the rules of competition. In such a situation, the exclusive dealing contracts must be regarded as agreements made with independent traders.

The Commission considers that there is particular reason to assume that the function performed is that of an independent trader where the contracting party described as a commercial agent:

— is required to keep or does in fact keep, as his own property, a considerable stock of the products covered by the contract, or
— is required to organise, maintain or ensure at his own expense a substantial service to customers free of charge, or does in fact organise, maintain or ensure such a service, or
— can determine or does in fact determine prices or terms of business.   **[1468]**

II. Unlike the contracts with commercial agents covered here, exclusive dealing contracts with independent traders may well fall within Article 85(1). In the case of such exclusive contracts the restriction of competition lies either in the limitation of supply, when the vendor undertakes to supply a given product to one purchaser only, or in the limitation of demand, when the purchaser undertakes to obtain a given product from only one vendor. Where there are reciprocal undertakings competition is being restricted by both parties. The question whether a restriction of competition of this nature may affect trade between Member States depends on the circumstances of the particular case.

On the other hand, the Commission takes the view that the test for prohibition under Article 85(1) is not met by exclusive dealing contracts with commercial agents, since these contracts have neither the object nor the effect of preventing, restricting or distorting competition within the common market. The commercial agent only performs an auxiliary function in the market for goods. In that market he acts on the instructions and in the interest of the enterprise on whose behalf he is operating. Unlike the independent trader, he himself is neither a purchaser nor a vendor, but seeks purchasers or vendors in the interest of the other party to the contract, who is the person doing the buying or selling. In this type of exclusive dealing contract, the selling or buying enterprise does not cease to be a competitor; it merely uses an auxiliary, i.e. the commercial agent, to distribute or acquire products on the market.

The legal status of commercial agents is determined, more or less uniformly, by statute law in most of the Member States and by case law in others. The characteristic feature which all commercial agents have in common is their function as auxiliaries in the transaction of business. The powers of commercial agents are subject to the civil law provisions of agency. Within the limits of these provisions, the other party to the contract — who is the person selling or buying — is free to decide the product and the territory in respect of which he is willing to give these powers to his agent.

In addition to the competitive situation on the markets where the commercial agent functions as an auxiliary for the other party to the contract, the particular market on which the commercial agents offer their services for the negotiation or conclusion of transactions has to be considered. The obligation assumed by the agent — to work exclusively for one principal for a certain period of time — entails a limitation of supply on that market; the obligation assumed by the other party to the contract — to appoint him sole agent for a given territory — involves a limitation of demand on the market. Nevertheless, the Commission views these restrictions as a result of the special obligation between the commercial agent and his principal to protect each other's interests and therefore considers that they involve no restriction of competition.

The object of this Notice is to give enterprises some indication of the considerations by which the Commission will be guided when interpreting Article 85(1) of the Treaty and applying it to exclusive dealing contracts with commercial agents. The situation having thus been clarified, it will as a general rule no longer be useful for enterprises to obtain negative clearance for the agreements mentioned, nor will it be necessary to have the legal position established through a Commission decision on an individual case; this also means that notification will no longer be necessary for agreements of this type. This Notice is without prejudice to any interpretation that may be given by other competent authorities and in particular by the courts.   [1469]

NOTE
1 OJ 134, 24.12.1962, p. 2921.

COMMISSION NOTICE
of 29 July 1968

concerning Agreements, Decisions and concerted practices in the field of co-operation between enterprises[1]

Questions are frequently put to the Commission of the European Communities on the attitude it intends to take up, for purposes of implementation of the competition rules contained in the Treaties of Rome and Paris, with regard to co-operation between enterprises.

In this Notice, it endeavours to provide guidance which, though it cannot be exhaustive, may prove useful to enterprises in the correct interpretation, in particular, of Article 85(1) of the EEC Treaty and Article 65(1) of the ECSC Treaty.

I. The Commission welcomes co-operation among small and medium-sized enterprises where such co-operation enables them to work more efficiently and increase their productivity and competitiveness on a larger market. While considering that its duty is to facilitate co-operation among small and medium-sized enterprises in particular the Commission recognises that co-operation among large enterprises, too, can be economically desirable without presenting difficulties from the angle of competition policy.

Article 85(1) of the Treaty establishing the European Economic Community (EEC Treaty) and Article 65(1) of the Treaty establishing the European Coal and Steel Community (ECSC Treaty) provide that all agreements, decisions and concerted practices (hereafter referred to as "agreements") which have as their object or effect the prevention, restriction or distortion of competition within the common market (hereafter referred to as "restraints of competition") are prohibited as incompatible with the common market; under Article 85(1) of the EEC Treaty this applies, however, only if such agreements may affect trade between Member States.

The Commission feels that, in the interests of the small and medium-sized enterprises in particular, it should give some indication of the considerations by which it will be guided when interpreting Article 85(1) of the EEC Treaty and Article 65(1) of the ECSC Treaty and applying them to certain co-operation arrangements between enterprises, and should indicate which of these arrangements in its opinion do not come under these provisions. This Notice applies to all enterprises, irrespective of their size.

There may also be forms of co-operation between enterprises other than those listed below which are not prohibited by Article 85(1) of the EEC Treaty or Article 65(1) of the ECSC Treaty. This applies in particular if the market position of the enterprises co-operating with each other is in the aggregate too weak for the co-operation agreement between them to lead to an appreciable restraint of competition in the common market and — where the agreements fall within the scope of Article 85 of the EEC Treaty — to affect trade between Member States.

It is also pointed out that other forms of co-operation between enterprises or agreements containing additional clauses, to which the rules of competition of the Treaties apply, can be exempted pursuant to Article 85(3) of the EEC Treaty or be authorised pursuant to Article 65(2) of the ECSC Treaty.

The Commission intends to clarify rapidly, by means of suitable decisions in individual cases or by general notices, the status of the various forms of co-operation in accordance with the provisions of the Treaties.

No general statement can be made at this stage on the application of Article 86 of the EEC Treaty on the abuse of dominant positions within the common market or in a part of it. The same applies to Article 66(7) of the ECSC Treaty.

As a result of this Notice, as a general rule, it should no longer be useful for enterprises to obtain negative clearance, as defined by Article 2 of Regulation No 17, for the agreements listed, nor should it be necessary to have the legal position established through a Commission decision on an individual case. This also means that notification with this end in view will no longer be necessary for agreements of this type. However, if it is doubtful whether in an individual case an agreement between enterprises restricts competition or if other forms of co-operation between enterprises which, in the view of the enterprises, do not restrict competition are not listed here, the enterprises are free to apply, where the matter comes under Article 85(1) of the EEC Treaty, for negative clearance, or to file as a precautionary measure, where Article 65(1) of the ECSC Treaty is the relevant provision, an application on the basis of Article 65(2) of that Treaty.

This Notice is without prejudice to any interpretation to be given by the Court of Justice of the European Communities. **[1470]**

II. The Commission takes the view that the following agreements do not restrict competition.

1. Agreements having as their sole object:

    (*a*) An exchange of opinion or experience.
    (*b*) Joint market research,
    (*c*) The joint carrying out of comparative studies of enterprises or industries,
    (*d*) The joint preparation of statistics and calculation models.

Agreements whose sole purpose is the joint procurement of information which the various enterprises need to determine their future market behaviour freely and independently, or the use by each of the enterprises of a joint advisory body, do not have as their object or effect the restriction of competition. But if the freedom of action of the enterprises is restricted or if their market behaviour is co-ordinated either expressly or through concerted practices, there may be restraint of competition. This is in particular the case

where concrete recommendations are made or where conclusions are given such a form
that they induce at least some of the participating enterprises to behave in an identical
manner on the market.

The exchange of information may take place between the enterprises themselves or
through a body acting as an intermediary. It is, however, particularly difficult to distinguish between information which has no bearing on competition on the one hand and
behaviour in restraint of competition on the other, if there are special bodies which have
to register orders, turnover figures, investments and prices, so that it can as a rule not
be automatically assumed that Article 85(1) of the EEC Treaty or Article 65(1) of the
ECSC Treaty do not apply to them. A restraint of competition may occur in particular
on an oligopolistic market for homogeneous products.

In the absence of more far-reaching co-operation between the participating enterprises,
joint market research and comparative studies of different enterprises and industries to
collect information and ascertain facts and market conditions do not in themselves affect
competition. Other arrangements of this type, as for instance the joint establishment
of economic and structural analyses, so obviously do not affect competition that there
is no need to mention them specifically.

Calculation models containing specified rates of calculation must be regarded as
recommendations that may lead to restraints of competition.

2. Agreements having as their sole object:

    (*a*) Cooperation in accounting matters,
    (*b*) Joint provision of credit guarantees,
    (*c*) Joint debt-collecting associations,
    (*d*) Joint business or tax consultant agencies.

In such cases, the co-operation involved covers fields that are not concerned with the
supply of goods and services or the economic decisions of the enterprises taking part,
and thus does not lead to restraints of competition.

Cooperation in accounting matters is neutral from the point of view of competition
as it only assists in the technical handling of the accounting work. Nor is the creation
of credit guarantee associations affected by the competition rules, since it does not modify
the relationship between supply and demand.

Joint debt-collecting associations whose work is not confined to the collection of
outstanding payments in line with the intentions and conditions of the participating enterprises, or which fix prices or exert in any other way an influence on price formation,
may restrict competition. Application of uniform terms by all participating firms may
constitute a concerted practice, and the making of joint price comparisons may have
the same result. In this connection, no objection can be raised against the use of stan-
dardised printed forms; their use must, however, not be combined with an understanding
or tacit agreement on uniform prices, rebates or conditions of sale.

3. Agreements having as their sole object:

    (*a*) The joint implementation of research and development projects,
    (*b*) The joint placing of research and development contracts,
    (*c*) The sharing out of research and development projects among participating
        enterprises.

In the field of research, too, the mere exchange of experience and results serves for information only and does not restrict competition. It therefore need not be mentioned expressly.

Agreements on the joint execution of research work or the joint development of the
results of research up to the stage of industrial application do not affect the competitive
position of the parties. This also applies to the sharing of research fields and development work if the results are available to all participating enterprises.

However, if the enterprises enter into commitments which restrict their own research and development activity or the utilisation of the results of joint work so that they do not have a free hand with regard to their own research and development outside the joint projects, this may constitute an infringement of the Treaties' rules of competition. Where firms do not carry out joint research work, any contractual obligations or concerted practices binding them to refrain from research work of their own either completely or in certain sectors may result in a restraint of competition.

The sharing out of sectors of research without an understanding providing for mutual access to the results is to be regarded as a case of specialisation that may restrict competition.

There may also be a restraint of competition if agreements are concluded or corresponding concerted practices applied with regard to the practical exploitation of the results of research and development work carried out jointly, particularly if the participating enterprises undertake or agree to manufacture only the products or types of product developed jointly or to share out future production among themselves.

It is of the essence of joint research that the results should be exploited by the participating enterprises in proportion to their participation. If the participation of certain enterprises is confined to a specific sector of the joint research project or to the provision of only limited financial assistance, there is no restraint of competition—in so far as there has been any joint research at all—if the results of research are made available to these enterprises only in relation with the degree of their participation. There may, however, be a restraint of competition if certain participating enterprises are excluded from exploitation of the results, either entirely or to an extent not commensurate with their participation.

If the granting of licences to third parties is expressly or tacitly excluded, there may be a restraint of competition. However, the fact that research is carried out jointly warrants arrangements binding the enterprises to grant licences to third parties only by common agreement or by majority decision.

For the assessment of the compatibility of the agreement with the rules of competition, the legal status of the joint research and development work is immaterial.

4. Agreements which have as their sole object the joint use of production facilities and storing and transport equipment

These forms of co-operation do not restrict competition because they are confined to organisation and technical arrangements for the use of the facilities. There may be a restraint of competition if the enterprises involved do not bear the cost of utilisation of the installation of equipment themselves or if agreements are concluded or concerted practices applied regarding joint production or the sharing out of production or the establishment or running of a joint enterprise.

5. Agreements having as their sole object the setting up of consortia for the joint execution of orders, where the participating enterprises do not compete with each other as regards the work to be done or where each of them by itself is unable to execute the orders

Where enterprises do not compete with each other they cannot restrict competition between them by setting up consortia. This applies in particular to enterprises belonging to different industries but also to firms in the same industry to the extent that their contribution under the consortium consists only of goods or services which cannot be supplied by the other participating enterprises. It is not a question of whether the enterprises compete with each other in other sectors so much as whether in the light of the concrete circumstances of a particular case there is a possibility that in the foreseeable future they may compete with each other with regard to the products or services involved. If the absence of competition between the enterprises and the maintenance of this situation are based on agreements or concerted practices, there may be a restraint of competition.

But even in the case of consortia formed by enterprises which normally compete with each other there is no restraint of competition if the participating enterprises cannot execute a specific order by themselves. This applies in particular if, for lack of experience, specialised knowledge, capacity or financial resources, these enterprises, when working alone, have no chance of success or cannot finish the work within the required time-limit or cannot bear the financial risk.

Nor is there a restraint of competition if it is only by the setting up of a consortium that the enterprises are put in a position to make an attractive offer. There may, however, be a restraint of competition if the enterprises undertake to work solely in the framework of a consortium.

6. Agreements having as their sole object:

   (a) Joint selling arrangements,
   (b) Joint after-sales and repairs service, provided the participating enterprises are not competitors with regard to the products or services covered by the agreement.

As already explained in detail under heading 5, co-operation between enterprises cannot restrict competition if the firms are not in competition with each other.

Very often joint selling by small or medium-sized enterprises — even if they are competing with each other — does not entail an appreciable restraint of competition; it is, however, impossible to establish in this Notice any general criteria or to specify what enterprises may be deemed "small or medium-sized".

There is no joint after-sales and repair service if several manufacturers, without acting in concert with each other, arrange for an after-sales and repair service for their products to be provided by an enterprise which is independent of them. In such a case there is no restraint of competition even if the manufacturers are competitors.

7. Agreements having joint advertising as their sole object

Joint advertising is designed to draw the buyers' attention to the products of an industry or to a common brand; as such it does not restrict competition between the participating enterprises. However, if the participating enterprises are partly or wholly prevented, by agreements or concerted practices, from themselves advertising or if they are subjected to other restrictions, there may be a restraint of competition.

8. Agreements having as their sole object the use of a common label to designate a certain quality, where the label is available to all competitors on the same conditions

Such associations for the joint use of a quality label do not restrict competition if other competitors, whose products objectively meet the stipulated quality requirements, can use the label on the same conditions as the members. Nor do the obligations to accept quality control of the products provided with the label, to issue uniform instructions for use, or to use the label for the products meeting the quality standards constitute restraints of competition. But there may be restraint of competition if the right to use the label is linked to obligations regarding production, marketing, price formation or obligations of any other type, as is for instance the case when the participating enterprises are obliged to manufacture or sell only products of guaranteed quality. **[1471]**

NOTE
1 OJ C 75, 29.7.1968, p. 3, corrected by OJ C 84, 28.8.1968, p. 14.

COMMISSION NOTICE
of 18 December 1978

concerning its assessment of certain subcontracting agreements in relation to Article 85(1) of the EEC Treaty

1. In this notice the Commission of the European Communities gives its view as to subcontracting agreements in relation to Article 85(1) of the Treaty establishing the

European Economic Community. This class of agreement is at the present time a form of work distribution which concerns firms of all sizes, but which offers opportunities for development in particular to small and medium sized firms.

The Commission considers that agreements under which one firm, called "the contractor", whether or not in consequence of a prior order from a third party, entrusts to another, called "the subcontractor", the manufacture of goods, the supply of services or the performance of work under the contractor's instructions, to be provided to the contractor or performed on his behalf, are not of themselves caught by the prohibition in Article 85(1).

To carry out certain subcontracting agreements in accordance with the contractor's instructions, the subcontractor may have to make use of particular technology or equipment which the contractor will have to provide. In order to protect the economic value of such technology or equipment, the contractor may wish to restrict their use by the subcontractor to whatever is necessary for the purpose of the agreement. The question arises whether such restrictions are caught by Article 85(1). They are assessed in this notice with due regard to the purpose of such agreements, which distinguishes them from ordinary patent and know-how licensing agreements. **[1472]**

2. In the Commission's view, Article 85(1) does not apply to clauses whereby:

— technology or equipment provided by the contractor may not be used except for the purposes of the subcontracting agreement,
— technology or equipment provided by the contractor may not be made available to third parties,
— the goods, services or work resulting from the use of such technology or equipment may be supplied only to the contractor or performed on his behalf,

provided that and in so far as this technology or equipment is necessary to enable the subcontractor under reasonable conditions to manufacture the goods, to supply the services or to carry out the work in accordance with the contractor's instructions. To that extent the subcontractor is providing goods, services or work in respect of which he is not an independent supplier in the market.

The above proviso is satisfied where performance of the subcontracting agreement makes necessary the use by the subcontractor of:

— industrial property rights of the contractor or at his disposal, in the form of patents, utility models, designs protected by copyright, registered designs or other rights, or
— secret knowledge or manufacturing processes (know-how) of the contractor or at his disposal, or of
— studies, plans or documents accompanying the information given which have been prepared by or for the contractor, or
— dies, patterns or tools, and accessory equipment that are distinctively the contractor's,

which, even though not covered by industrial property rights nor containing any element of secrecy, permit the manufacture of goods which differ in form, function or composition from other goods manufactured or supplied on the market.

However, the restrictions mentioned above are not justifiable where the subcontractor has at his disposal or could under reasonable conditions obtain access to the technology and equipment needed to produce the goods, provide the services or carry out the work. Generally, this is the case when the contractor provides no more than general information which merely describes the work to be done. In such circumstances the restrictions could deprive the subcontractor of the possibility of developing his own business in the fields covered by the agreement. **[1473]**

3. The following restrictions in connection with the provision of technology by the contractor may in the Commission's view also be imposed by subcontracting agreements without giving grounds for objection under Article 85(1):

— an undertaking by either of the parties not to reveal manufacturing processes or other know-how of a secret character, or confidential information given by the other party during the negotiation and performance of the agreement, as long as the know-how or information in question has not become public knowledge,

— an undertaking by the subcontractor not to make use, even after expiry of the agreement, of manufacturing processes or other know-how of a secret character received by him during the currency of the agreement, as long as they have not become public knowledge,

— an undertaking by the subcontractor to pass on to the contractor on a non-exclusive basis any technical improvements which he has made during the currency of the agreement, or, where a patentable invention has been discovered by the subcontractor, to grant non-exclusive licences in respect of inventions relating to improvements and new applications of the original invention to the contractor for the term of the patent held by the latter.

This undertaking by the subcontractor may be exclusive in favour of the contractor in so far as improvements and inventions made by the subcontractor during the currency of the agreement are incapable of being used independently of the contractor's secret know-how or patent, since this does not constitute an appreciable restriction of competition.

However, any undertaking by the subcontractor regarding the right to dispose of the results of his own research and development work may restrain competition, where such results are capable of being used independently. In such circumstances, the subcontracting relationship is not sufficient to displace the ordinary competition rules on the disposal of industrial property rights or secret know-how.   **[1474]**

4. Where the subcontractor is authorized by a subcontracting agreement to use a specified trade mark, trade name or get up, the contractor may at the same time forbid such use by the subcontractor in the case of goods, services or work which are not to be supplied to the contractor.   **[1475]**

5. Although this notice should in general obviate the need for firms to obtain a ruling on the legal position by an individual Commission Decision, it does not affect the right of the firms concerned to apply for negative clearance as defined by Article 2 of Regulation No 17 or to notify the agreement to the Commission under Article 4(1) of that Regulation.

The 1968 notice on cooperation between enterprises,[1] which lists a number of agreements that by their nature are not to be regarded as anti-competitive, is thus supplemented in the subcontracting field. The Commission also reminds firms that, in order to promote co-operation between small and medium sized businesses, it has published a notice concerning agreements of minor importance which do not fall under Article 85(1) of the Treaty establishing the European Economic Community[2]

This notice is without prejudice to the view that may be taken of subcontracting agreements by the Court of Justice of the European Communities.   **[1476]**

NOTES
1 Notice concerning agreements, decisions and concerted practices relating to co-operation between enterprises (OJ No C 75, 29. 7. 1968, p. 3), ante.
2 See now Commission notice of 3 September 1986, post.

COMMISSION NOTICE
of 3 September 1986

on agreements of minor importance which do not fall under Article 85(1) of the Treaty establishing the European Economic Community

I

1. The Commission considers it important to facilitate co-operation between undertakings where such co-operation is economically desirable without presenting difficulties from the point of view of competition policy, which is particularly true of co-operation between small and medium-sized undertakings. To this end it published the "Notice concerning agreements, decisions and concerted practices in the field of co-operation between undertakings" listing a number of agreements that by their nature cannot be regarded as restraints of competition. Furthermore, in the Notice concerning its assessment of certain subcontracting agreements the Commission considered that this type of contract which offers opportunities for development, in particular, to small and medium-sized undertakings is not in itself caught by the prohibition in Article 85(1). By issuing the present Notice, the Commission is taking a further step towards defining the field of application of Article 85(1), in order to facilitate co-operation between small and medium-sized undertakings.

2. In the Commission's opinion, agreements whose effects on trade between Member States or on competition are negligible do not fall under the ban on restrictive agreements contained in Article 85(1). Only those agreements are prohibited which have an appreciable impact on market conditions, in that they appreciably alter the market position, in other words the sales or supply possibilities, of third undertakings and of users.

3. In the present Notice the Commission, by setting quantitative criteria and by explaining their application, has given a sufficiently concrete meaning to the concept "appreciable" for undertakings to be able to judge for themselves whether the agreements they have concluded with other undertakings, being of minor importance, do not fall under Article 85(1). The quantitative definition of "appreciable" given by the Commission is, however, no absolute yardstick; in fact, in individual cases even agreements between undertakings which exceed these limits may still have only a negligible effect on trade between Member States or on competition, and are therefore not caught by Article 85(1).

4. As a result of this Notice, there should no longer be any point in undertakings obtaining negative clearance, as defined by Article 2 of Council Regulation No 17, for the agreements covered, nor should it be necessary to have the legal position established through Commission decisions in individual cases; notification with this end in view will no longer be necessary for such agreements. However, if it is doubtful whether in an individual case an agreement appreciably affects trade between Member States or competition, the undertakings are free to apply for negative clearance or to notify the agreement.

5. In cases covered by the present Notice the Commission, as a general rule, will not open proceedings under Regulation No 17, either upon application or upon its own initiative. Where, due to exceptional circumstances, an agreement which is covered by the present Notice nevertheless falls under Article 85(1), the Commission will not impose fines. Where undertakings have failed to notify an agreement falling under Article 85(1) because they wrongly assumed, owing to a mistake in calculating their market share or aggregate turnover, that the agreement was covered by the present Notice, the Commission will not consider imposing fines unless the mistake was due to negligence.

6. This Notice is without prejudice to the competence of national courts to apply Article 85(1) on the basis of their own jurisdiction, although it constitutes a factor which such courts may take into account when deciding a pending case. It is also without prejudice

to any interpretation which may be given by the Court of Justice of the European Communities.   **[1477]**

II

7. The Commission holds the view that agreements between undertakings engaged in the production or distribution of goods or in the provision of services generally do not fall under the prohibition of Article 85(1) if:

  — the goods or services which are the subject of the agreement (hereinafter referred to as "the contract products") together with the participating undertakings' other goods or services which are considered by users to be equivalent in view of their characteristics, price and intended use, do not represent more than 5% of the total market for such goods or services (hereinafter referred to as "products") in the area of the common market affected by the agreement and
  — the aggregate annual turnover of the participating undertakings does not exceed 200 million ECU.

8. The Commission also holds the view that the said agreements do not fall under the prohibition of Article 85(1) if the abovementioned market share or turnover is exceeded by not more than one tenth during two successive financial years.

9. For the purposes of this Notice, participating undertakings are:

  (*a*) undertakings party to the agreement;
  (*b*) undertakings in which a party to the agreement, directly or indirectly,

      — owns more than half the capital or business assets or
      — has the power to exercise more than half the voting rights, or
      — has the power to appoint more than half the members of the supervisory board, board of management or bodies legally representing the under-takings, or
      — has the right to manage the affairs;

  (*c*) undertakings which directly or indirectly have in or over a party to the agree-ment the rights or powers listed in (*b*);
  (*d*) undertakings in or over which an undertaking referred to in (*c*) directly or indirectly has the rights or powers listed in (*b*).

Undertakings in which several undertakings as referred to in (*a*) to (*d*) jointly have, directly or indirectly, the rights or powers set out in (*b*) shall also be considered to be participating undertakings.

10. In order to calculate the market share, it is necessary to determine the relevant market. This implies the definition of the relevant product market and the relevant geographical market.

11. The relevant product market includes besides the contract products any other products which are identical or equivalent to them. This rule applies to the products of the participating undertakings as well as to the market for such products. The products in question must be interchangeable. Whether or not this is the case must be judged from the vantage point of the user, normally taking the characteristics, price and intended use of the goods together. In certain cases, however, products can form a separate market on the basis of their characteristics, their price or their intended use alone. This is true especially where consumer preferences have developed.

12. Where the contract products are components which are incorporated into another product by the participating undertakings, reference should be made to the market for the latter product, provided that the components represent a significant part of it. Where

the contract products are components which are sold to third undertakings, reference should be made to the market for the components. In cases where both conditions apply, both markets should be considered separately.

13. The relevant geographical market is the area within the Community in which the agreement produces its effects. This area will be the whole common market where the contract products are regularly bought and sold in all Member States. Where the contract products cannot be bought and sold in a part of the common market, or are bought and sold only in limited quantities or at irregular intervals in such a part, that part should be disregarded.

14. The relevant geographical market will be narrower than the whole common market in particular where:

— the nature and characteristics of the contract product, e.g. high transport costs in relation to the value of the product, restrict its mobility; or

— movement of the contract product within the common market is hindered by barriers to entry to national markets resulting from State intervention, such as quantitative restrictions, severe taxation differentials and non-tariff barriers, e.g. type approvals or safety standard certifications. In such cases the national territory may have to be considered as the relevant geographical market. However, this will only be justified if the existing barriers to entry cannot be overcome by reasonable effort and at an acceptable cost.

15. Aggregate turnover includes the turnover in all goods and services, excluding tax, achieved during the last financial year by the participating undertakings. In cases where an undertaking has concluded similar agreements with various other undertakings in the relevant market, the turnover of all participating undertakings should be taken together. The aggregate turnover shall not include dealings between participating undertakings.

16. The present Notice shall not apply where in a relevant market competition is restricted by the cumulative effects of parallel networks of similar agreements established by several manufacturers or dealers.

17. The present Notice is likewise applicable to decisions by associations of undertakings and to concerted practices. **[1478]**

REGULATION (EEC) No 2342/90 OF THE COUNCIL
of 24 July 1990

on fares for scheduled air services

THE COUNCIL OF THE EUROPEAN COMMUNITIES,

Having regard to the Treaty establishing the European Economic Community, and in particular Article 84(2) thereof,

Having regard to the proposal from the Commission,

Having regard to the opinion of the European Parliament,

Having regard to the opinion of the Economic and Social Committee,

Whereas it is important to adopt measures with the aim of progressively establishing the internal market over a period expiring on 31 December 1992 as provided for in Article 8a of the Treaty; whereas the internal market shall comprise an area without internal frontiers in which the free movement of goods, persons, services and capital is ensured;

Whereas Council Directive 87/601/EEC of 14 December 1987 on fares for scheduled air services between Member States made a first step towards the liberalization in respect of air fares, necessary to achieve the internal market in air transport; whereas the Council agreed to take further measures of liberalization;

Whereas it is appropriate to establish clear criteria according to which the Member States' authorities have to evaluate proposed air fares;

Whereas a system of double disapproval of air fares remains an objective to be achieved by 1 January 1993; whereas an important element in achieving further liberalization consists in gaining experience of this system during the interim period;

Whereas it is desirable to introduce a more flexible, simpler and more efficient system of zones within which air fares meeting particular conditions qualify for automatic approval by the aeronautical authorities of the States concerned;

Whereas, in the case of double approval and double disapproval of air fares, it is appropriate to provide for a procedure according to which Member States may ask the Commission to examine and decide on whether a proposed air fare conforms with the criteria laid down; whereas in case of excessively high or low air fares, the Commission must be able to suspend the application of an air fare during its examination;

Whereas, in the case of double approval of air fares, provision should be made for rapid consultation between Member States in the case of any disagreement and for procedures for settling such disagreements that are not resolved by consultations;

Whereas this Regulation replaces Directive 87/601/EEC; whereas it is therefore necessary to revoke that Directive;

Whereas it is desirable that the Council adopts further measures of liberalization in respect of air fares by 30 June 1992,

) HAS ADOPTED THIS REGULATION:

SCOPE AND DEFINITIONS

Article 1

This Regulation shall apply to criteria and procedures to be applied with respect to the establishment of scheduled air fares charged on routes between Member States.

[1479]

Article 2

For the purposes of this Regulation:

    (*a*) scheduled air fares means the prices to be paid in the applicable national currency for the carriage of passengers and baggage on scheduled air services and the conditions under which those prices apply, including remuneration and conditions offered to agency and other auxiliary services;

    (*b*) scheduled air service means a series of flights each possessing all the following characteristics:

        (i) it passes through the air space over the territory of more than one Member State;

        (ii) it is performed by aircraft for the transport of passengers or passengers and cargo and/or mail for remuneration, in such a manner that on each flight seats are available for individual purchase by members of the public (either directly from the air carrier or from its authorized agents);

        (iii) it is operated so as to serve traffic between the same two or more points, either:

            1. according to a published timetable; or

            2. with flights so regular or frequent that they constitute a recognizably systematic series;

    (*c*) flight means a departure from a specified airport towards a specified destination airport;

    (*d*) air carrier means an air transport enterprise with a valid operating licence from a Member State to operate scheduled air services;

(e) Community air carrier means:

   (i) an air carrier which has and continues to have its central administration and principal place of business in the Community, the majority of whose shares are and continue to be owned by Member States and/or nationals of Member States and which is and continues to be effectively controlled by such States or persons; or

   (ii) an air carrier which, at the time of adoption of this Regulation, although it does not meet the definition set out in (i):

     1. either has its central administration and principal place of business in the Community and has been providing scheduled or non-scheduled air services in the Community during the 12 months prior to adoption of this Regulation;

     2. or has been providing scheduled air services between Member States on the basis of third- and fourth-freedom traffic rights during the 12 months prior to adoption of this Regulation.

   The air carriers which meeet the criteria set out in this point (ii) are listed in Annex 1;

(f) a third-freedom traffic right means the right of an air carrier licensed in one State to put down, in the territory of another State, passengers, freight and mail taken up in the State in which it is licensed;

a fourth-freedom traffic right means the right of an air carrier licensed in one State to take on, in the territory of another State, passengers, freight and mail for off-loading in the State in which it is licensed;

a fifth-freedom traffic right means the right of an air carrier to undertake the air transport of passengers, freight and mail between two States other than the State in which it is licensed;

(g) States concerned means the Member States between which a scheduled air service is operated;

(h) zone of flexibility means a pricing zone as referred to in Article 4, within which air fares meeting the conditions in Annex II qualify for automatic approval by the aeronautical authorities of the States concerned. The limits of a zone are expressed as percentages of the reference fare;

(i) reference fare means the normal one way or return, as appropriate, economy air fare charged by a third- or fourth-freedom air carrier on the route in question; if more than one such fare exists, the arithmetic average of all such fares shall be taken unless otherwise bilaterally agreed; where there is no normal economy fare, the lowest fully flexible fare shall be taken. **[1480]**

CRITERIA

Article 3

1. Member States shall approve scheduled air fares of Community air carriers if they are reasonably related to the applicant air carrier's long-term fully-allocated relevant costs, while taking into account the need for a satisfactory return on capital and for an adequate cost margin to ensure a satisfactory safety standard.

2. In approving air fares pursuant to paragraph 1, Member States shall also take into account other relevant factors, the needs of consumers and the competitive market situation, including the fares of the other air carriers operating on the route and the need to prevent dumping.

3. Notwithstanding Article 4(4) and (5), Member States shall disapprove any fare that does not meet the terms of Article 4(3) and that is, in relation to the criteria defined in Article 3(1), excessively high to the disadvantage of users or unjustifiably low in view of the competitive market situation.

4. The fact that a proposed air fare is lower than that offered by another air carrier operating on the route shall not be sufficient reason for withholding approval.

5. A Member State shall permit a Community air carrier of another Member State operating a direct or indirect scheduled air service within the Community, having given due notice to the States concerned, to match an air fare already approved for scheduled services between the same city-pairs on the basis that this provision shall not apply to indirect air services which exceed the length of the shortest direct service by more than 20%. Member States may also permit a Community air carrier of another Member State operating a direct scheduled air service to match prices already accepted or published for a non-scheduled air service operated on the same route provided that both products are equivalent in terms of quality and conditions.

6. Only Community air carriers shall be entitled to introduce lower fares than the existing ones when they operate on the basis of third- and fourth-freedom traffic rights and, in the case of fifth-freedom traffic rights to introduce such lower fares only where they comply with Article 4(3).   **[1481]**

PROCEDURES

Article 4

1. Scheduled air fares shall be subject to approval by the Member States concerned. To this end, an air carrier shall submit its proposed air fares in the form prescribed by the aeronautical authorities of such Member States.

2. Aeronautical authorities shall not require air carriers to submit their fares in respect of routes within the Community more than 45 days before they come into effect.

3. (*a*) Until 31 December 1992, Member States shall, within zones of flexibility, permit third- and/or fourth-freedom and/or fifth-freedom air carriers to charge air fares of their own choice, subject to the respective conditions set out in Annex II and provided those air fares have been filed with the States concerned at least 21 days prior to the proposed date for their entry into force.

   (*b*) There shall be three zones of flexibility on any scheduled air services as follows:

   — a normal economy fare zone which shall extend from 95 to 105% of the reference fare,
   — a discount zone which shall extend from 94 to 80% of the reference fare,
   — a deep-discount zone which shall extend from 79 to 30% of the reference fare.

4. A fully flexible fare above 105% of the reference fare for a route within the Community shall be considered as approved unless, within 30 days of the date of its submission, both Member States have notified in writing their disapproval to the applicant air carrier, stating their reasons. The Member States shall also inform each other. At the request of either Member State, consultations shall take place between the States concerned within the 30-day period.

5. Until 31 December 1992, fares not complying with the terms of paragraphs 3 and 4 shall require approval by both States concerned. If neither of the Member States has expressed disapproval within 21 days of the date of submission of a fare, it shall be considered as approval.

6. A fare for a route within the Community, once approved, shall remain in force until it expires or is replaced. It may, however, be prolonged after its original date of expiry for a period not exceeding 12 months. **[1482]**

Article 5

1. A Member State which claims a legitimate interest in the route concerned may request the Commission to examine whether an air fare which does not meet the terms of Article 4(3) complies with Article 3(1) or whether a Member State has fulfilled its obligations under Article 3(3). The Commission shall forthwith inform the other Member State(s) involved and the air carrier concerned and give them the opportunity to submit their observations.

2. The Commission shall, within 14 days of receipt of a request under paragraph 1, decide whether the air fare shall remain in force during its examination.

3. The Commission shall give a decision on whether the air fare complies with Article 3(1) as soon as possible and in any event not later than two months after having received the request. This period may be prolonged to the extent necessary in order to obtain sufficient further information from the Member State concerned.

4. The Commission shall communicate its decision to the Member States and to the air carrier concerned.

5. Any Member State may refer the Commission's decision to the Council within a time limit of one month. The Council, acting by a qualified majority, may take a different decision within a period of one month. **[1483]**

CONSULTATION AND ARBITRATION SCHEME

Article 6

1. When a State concerned (the first State) decides, in accordance with Article 4(5), not to approve a scheduled air fare, it shall inform the other State concerned (the second State) in writing within 21 days of the fare being filed, stating its reasons.

2. If the second State disagrees with the decision of the first State, it shall so notify the first State within seven days of being informed, providing the information on which its decision is based, and request consultations. Each State shall supply all relevant information requested by the other. Either of the States concerned may request that the Commission be represented at the consultations.

3. If the first State has insufficient information to reach a decision on the fare, it may request the second State to enter into consultations before the expiry of the 21-day period prescribed in paragraph 1.

4. Consultations shall be completed within 21 days of being requested. If disagreements still persists at the end of this period, the matter shall be put to arbitration at the request of either of the States concerned. The two States concerned may agree to prolong the consultations or to proceed directly to arbitration without consultations.

5. Arbitration shall be carried out by a panel of three arbitrators unless the States concerned agree on a single arbitrator. The States concerned shall each nominate one member of the panel and seek to agree on the third member (who shall be a national of a third Member State and act as panel chairman). Alternatively they may nominate a single arbitrator. The appointment of the panel shall be completed within seven days. A panel's decisions shall be reached by a majority of votes.

6. In the event of failure by either State concerned to nominate a member of the panel or to agree on the appointment of a third member, the Council shall be informed forthwith and its President shall complete the panel within three days. In the event of the Presidency being held by a Member State which is party to the dispute, the President of the Council shall invite the Government of the next Member State due to hold the presidency and not party to the dispute to complete the panel.

7. The arbitration shall be completed within a period of 21 days of completion of the panel or nomination of the single arbitrator. The States concerned may, however, agree to extend this period. The Commission shall have the right to attend as an observer. The arbitrators shall make clear the extent to which the award is based on the criteria in Article 3.

8. The arbitration award shall be notified immediately to the Commission.

Within a period of 10 days, the Commission shall confirm the award, unless the arbitrators have not respected the criteria set out in Article 3 or the procedure laid down by the Regulation or the award does not comply with Community law in other respects.

In the absence of any decision within this period, the award shall be regarded as confirmed by the Commission. An award confirmed by the Commission shall become binding on the States concerned.

9. During the consultation and arbitration procedure, the relevant existing air fares shall be continued in force until the procedure has expired and any new fare has entered into force. **[1484]**

GENERAL PROVISIONS

Article 7

This Regulation shall not prevent Member States from concluding arrangements which are more flexible than the provisions of Article 4 or from maintaining such arrangements in force. **[1485]**

Article 8

At least once a year, the Commission shall consult on scheduled air fares and related matters with representatives of air transport user organizations in the Community, for which purpose the Commission shall supply appropriate information to the participants. **[1486]**

Article 9

In carrying out the duties assigned to it under this Regulation, the Commission may obtain all necessary information from the Member States and air carriers concerned. **[1487]**

Article 10

1. The Commission shall publish a report on the application of this Regulation by 31 May 1992 and every second year thereafter.

2. Member States and the Commission shall cooperate in implementing this Regulation, particularly as regards collection of information for the report referred to in paragraph 1.

3. Confidential information obtained in application of this Regulation shall be covered by professional secrecy. **[1488]**

Article 11

Where a Member State has concluded an agreement with one or more non-member countries which gives fifth-freedom rights for a route between Member States to an air carrier of a non-member country, and in this respect contains provisions which are incompatible with this Regulation, the Member State shall, at the first opportunity, take all appropriate steps to eliminate such incompatibilities. Until such time as the incompatibilities have been eliminated, this Regulation shall not affect the rights and obligations *vis-à-vis* non-member countries arising from such an agreement.   **[1489]**

Article 12

With a view to achieving the objective of a double-disapproval system for fares by 1 January 1993, the Council shall decide on the revision of this Regulation by 30 June 1992 at the latest, on the basis of a Commission proposal to be submitted by 31 May 1991.
                    [1490]

Article 13

Directive 87/601/EEC is hereby revoked.   **[1491]**

Article 14

This Regulation shall enter into force on 1 November 1990.   **[1492]**

This Regulation shall be binding in its entirety and directly applicable in all Member States.

Done at Brussels, 24 July 1990.

ANNEX I

AIR CARRIERS REFERRED TO IN ARTICLE 2(*e*)(ii)

The following air carriers meet the criteria referred to in Article 2(*e*)(ii) as long as they are recognized as a national carrier by the Member State which so recognizes them at the time of the adoption of this Regulation:
— Scandinavian Airlines System,
— Britannia Airways,
— Monarch Airlines.   **[1493]**

ANNEX II

CONDITIONS FOR DISCOUNT AND DEEP-DISCOUNT FARES

Discount zone

1. To qualify for the discount zone, a fare must meet the two following conditions:
— round or circle trip travel,

and

— reservation for the entire trip, ticketing and payment to be made at the same time, except that reservation for the return trip may be made at a later time; cancellation only permissible prior to departure of outbound travel and at a fee of at least 20%

of the price of the ticket; change of reservation only permissible at a fee equal to the difference between the fare paid and the next higher applicable fare.

Deep-discount zone

2. To qualify for the deep-discount zone, fares must meet the following conditions:

1. round or circle trip travel; and
2. any two of the following:

(a) minimum stay of not less than the "Sunday rule" or six days;
(b) (i) reservation for the entire trip, ticketing and payment to be made at the same time; cancellation or change of reservation only permissible prior to departure of outbound travel and at a fee of at least 20% of the price of the ticket;
or
(ii) mandatory advance purchase of not less than 14 days; reservation for the entire trip, ticketing and payment to be made at the same time; cancellation or change of reservation only permissible prior to departure of outbound travel and at a fee of at least 20% of the price of the ticket;
or
(iii) purchase of the ticket only permitted on the day prior to departure of outbound travel; reservation to be made separately for both the outbound and inbound journeys and only in the country of departure on the day prior to travel on the respective journeys;
(c) passenger to be aged not more than 25 years or not less than 60 years or father and/or mother with children aged not more than 25 years travelling together (minimum three persons);
(d) off-peak;
provided that:

1. the condition at (c) may not be combined with the condition at (d) alone; and
2. where the condition at (b)(i) is combined only with the conditions at (c) or (d), the zone of flexibility shall not extend below 40% of the reference fare.
[1494]

APPENDIX TO ANNEX II

1. Notes on the zonal scheme referred to in Article 4(3)(b) and (4)

(i) *Reference fare for 1990/91*
the reference fare referred to in Article 2(i) applicable on 1 September 1990.
(ii) *Reference fare for 1991/92*
the reference fare referred to in Article 2(i) applicable on 1 September 1991.

2. Definition of "off-peak"

An air carrier may designate certain flights as "off-peak" on the basis of commercial considerations.

When an air carrier wishes to use condition 2(2)(d), identification of the off-peak flights for each route shall be agreed between the aeronautical authorities of the Member States concerned on the basis of the proposal made by that air carrier.

On each route where the total activity of third- and fourth-freedom air carriers reaches a weekly average of 18 return flights, the air carrier concerned shall be allowed as a minimum to apply condition 2(2)(*d*) of annex II on up to 50% of its total daily flights, provided that the flights to which these conditions may be applied depart between 10.00 and 16.00 or between 21.00 and 06.00. **[1495]**

REGULATION (EEC) No 2343/90 OF THE COUNCIL
of 24 July 1990

on access for air carriers to scheduled intra-Community air service routes and on the sharing of passenger capacity between air carriers on scheduled air services between Member States

THE COUNCIL OF THE EUROPEAN COMMUNITIES,

Having regard to the Treaty establishing the European Economic Community, and in particular Article 84(2) thereof,

Having regard to the proposal from the Commission,

Having regard to the opinion of the European Parliament,

Having regard to the opinion of the Economic and Social Committee,

Whereas it is important to adopt measures with the aim of progressively establishing the internal market over a period expiring on 31 December 1992 as provided for in Article 8a of the Treaty; whereas the internal market shall comprise an area without internal frontiers in which the free movement of goods, persons, services and capital is ensured;

Whereas Decision 87/602/EEC made a first step towards the liberalization in respect of sharing of passenger capacity and access to the market, necessary to achieve the internal market in air transport; whereas the Council agreed to take further measures of liberalization at the end of a three-year initial period;

Whereas it is necessary to implement principles governing relations between States of registration and air carriers licensed in their territory by 1 July 1992 on the basis of common specifications and criteria;

Whereas arrangements for greater cooperation over the use of Gibraltar airport were agreed in London on 2 December 1987 by the Kingdom of Spain and the United Kingdom in a joint declaration by the Ministers of Foreign Affairs of the two countries, and such arrangements have yet to come into operation;

Whereas the development of the air traffic system in the Greek Islands and in the Atlantic Islands comprising the autonomous region of the Azores is at present inadequate and for this reason airports situated on these islands should be temporarily exempted from the application of this Regulation;

Whereas the infrastructure at Porto airport is still being expanded to enable it to cope with the growth in scheduled services; whereas, consequently, that airport should be exempted temporarily from the application of this Regulation until the expansion of this infrastructure is completed;

Whereas it is necessary to make special provision, under limited circumstances, for air services on new routes between regional airports and for public service obligations necessary for the maintenance of services to certain regional airports;

Whereas increased market access will stimulate the development of the Community air transport sector and give rise to improved services for users; whereas as a consequence it is necessary to introduce more liberal provisions concerning multiple designation, third-, fourth- and fifth-freedom traffic rights;

Whereas, taking into account problems relating to airport infrastructure, navigational aids and availability of slots, it is necessary to include certain limitations concerning the use of traffic rights;

Whereas the exercise of traffic rights has to be consistent with rules relating to safety, protection of the environment, allocation of slots and conditions concerning airport access and has to be treated without discrimination on grounds of nationality;

Whereas bilateral rules concerning capacity shares are not compatible with the principles of the internal market which should be completed by 1993 in the air transport sector; whereas therefore the bilateral restrictions must be diminished gradually;

Whereas it is especially important to encourage the development of inter-regional services in order to develop the Community network and to contribute to a solution of the problem of congestion at certain large airports; whereas, therefore, it is appropriate to have more liberal rules with respect to capacity sharing on these services;

Whereas in view of the relative importance for some Member States of non-scheduled traffic *vis-à-vis* scheduled traffic, it is necessary to take measures to alleviate its impact on the opportunities of carriers of Member States receiving such traffic; whereas the measures to be taken should not be aimed at limiting non-scheduled traffic or subjecting it to regulation;

Whereas, taking into account the competitive market situation, provision should be made to prevent unjustifiable economic effects on air carriers;

Whereas this Regulation replaces Directive 83/416/EEC, as last amended by Directive 89/463/EEC, and Decision 87/602/EEC; whereas it is therefore necessary to revoke that Directive and that Decision;

Whereas it is desirable that the Council adopt further measures of liberalization including cabotage in respect of market access and capacity sharing by 30 June 1992,

HAS ADOPTED THIS REGULATION:

SCOPE AND DEFINITIONS

Article 1

1. This Regulation concerns:

  (*a*) access to the market for Community air carriers;

  (*b*) the sharing of passenger capacity between the air carrier(s) licensed in one Member State and the air carrier(s) licensed in another Member State on scheduled air services between these States.

2. The application of this Regulation to the airport of Gibraltar is understood to be without prejudice to the respective legal positions of the Kingdom of Spain and the United Kingdom with regard to the dispute over sovereignty over the territory in which the airport is situated.

3. Application of the provisions of this Regulation to Gibraltar airport shall be suspended until the arrangements in the joint declaration made by the Foreign Ministers of the Kingdom of Spain and the United Kingdom on 2 December 1987 have come into operation. The Governments of Spain and the United Kingdom will so inform the Council on that date.

4. Airports in the Greek islands and in the Atlantic islands comprising the autonomous region of the Azores shall be exempted from the application of this Regulation until 30 June 1993. Unless otherwise decided by the Council, on a proposal of the Commission, this exemption shall apply for a further period of five years and may be continued for five years thereafter.

The airport of Porto shall be exempted from the application of this Regulation until 31 December 1992. This derogation shall be rescinded as soon as the Portuguese Republic judges that the economic conditions of the airport have improved.

To this end, the Portuguese Republic shall inform the Commission. The Commission shall communicate this information to the other Member States.   **[1496]**

Article 2

For the purposes of this Regulation:

  (*a*) air carrier means an air transport enterprise with a valid operating licence from a Member State to operate scheduled air services;

  (*b*) a third-freedom traffic right means the right of an air carrier licensed in one State to put down, in the territory of another State, passengers, freight and mail taken up in the State in which it is licensed;

  a fourth-freedom traffic right means the right of an air carrier licensed in one State to take on, in the territory of another State, passengers, freight and mail for off-loading in the State in which it is licensed;

  a fifth-freedom traffic right means the right of an air carrier to undertake the air transport of passengers, freight and mail between two States other than the State in which it is licensed;

(c) States concerned means the Member States between which a scheduled air service is operated;

(d) State of registration means the Member State in which the licence mentioned in paragraph (a) is issued;

(e) Community air carrier means:

(i) an air carrier which has and continues to have its central administration and principal place of business in the Community, the majority of whose shares are and continue to be owned by Member States and/or nationals of Member States and which is and continues to be effectively controlled by such States or persons, or

(ii) an air carrier which, at the time of adoption of this Regulation, although it does not meet the definition set out in (i):

1. either has its central administration and principal place of business in the Community and has been providing scheduled or non-scheduled air services in the Community during the 12 months prior to adoption of this Regulation;

2. or has been providing scheduled air services between Member States on the basis of third- and fourth-freedom traffic rights during the 12 months prior to adoption of this Regulation.

The air carriers which meet the criteria set out in this point (ii) are listed in Annex I;

(f) scheduled air service means a series of flights each possessing all the following characteristics:

(i) it passes through the air space over the territory of more than one Member State;

(ii) it is performed by aircraft for the transport of passengers or passengers and cargo and/or mail for remuneration, in such a manner that on each flight seats are available for individual purchase by members of the public (either directly from the air carrier or from its authorized agents);

(iii) it is operated so as to serve traffic between the same two or more points, either:

1. according to a published timetable; or

2. with flights so regular or frequent that they constitute a recognizably systematic series;

(g) flight means a departure from a specified airport towards a specified destination airport;

(h) multiple designation on a country-pair basis means the designation by a State of registration of two or more of the air carriers licensed by it to operate scheduled air services between its territory and that of another Member State;

(i) multiple designation on a city-pair basis means the designation by a State of registration of two or more of the air carriers licensed by it to operate a scheduled air service between an airport or airport system in its territory and an airport or airport system in the territory of another Member State;

(j) regional airport means any airport other than one listed in Annex II as a category 1 airport;

(k) airport system means two or more airports grouped together as serving the same city, as indicated in Annex II;

(l) capacity shall be expressed as the number of seats offered to the general public on a scheduled air service over a given period;

(*m*) capacity share means the share of a Member State expressed as a percentage of the total capacity calculated according to Article 11 in a bilateral relationship with another Member State excluding any capacity provided by fifth-freedom services;

(*n*) public service obligation means any obligation imposed upon an air carrier to take, in respect of any route which it is licensed to operate by a Member State, all necessary measures to ensure the provision of a service satisfying fixed standards of continuity, regularity and capacity which standards the carrier would not assume if it were solely considering its commercial interest.   **[1497]**

RELATIONS BETWEEN THE STATES OF REGISTRATION AND THEIR AIR CARRIERS

Article 3

1. This Regulation shall not affect the relationship between a Member State and air carriers licensed by that State regarding market access and capacity sharing.

2. The Council shall adopt, for implementation not later than 1 July 1992 on the basis of a Commission proposal concerning common specifications and criteria, to be submitted not later than 31 May 1991, rules governing the licensing of air carriers and route licensing.   **[1498]**

THIRD- AND FOURTH-FREEDOM TRAFFIC RIGHTS

Article 4

Subject to this Regulation, Community air carriers shall be permitted to exercise third- and fourth-freedom air services between airports or airport systems in one Member State and airports or airport systems in another Member State when these airports or airport systems are open for traffic between Member States or for international services.   **[1499]**

RELATIONS BETWEEN A MEMBER STATE AND AIR CARRIERS OF OTHER MEMBER STATES

Article 5

1. Subject to Article 6, a Member State shall authorize air carriers licensed in another Member State, which have been authorized by their State of registration, to

— exercise third- and fourth-freedom traffic rights as provided for in Article 4,
— use, within the Community, the same flight number for combined third- and fourth-freedom services.

2. Where an air carrier of one Member State has been licensed in accordance with this Article to operate a scheduled air service, the State of registration of that air carrier shall raise no objection to an application for the introduction of a scheduled air service on the same route by an air carrier of the other State concerned.

3. (*a*) A Member State, following consultations with other States concerned, may impose a public service obligation in respect of air services to a regional airport in its territory on a route which is considered vital for the economic development of the region in which the airport is located, to the extent necessary to ensure on that route the adequate provision of air services satisfying fixed standards of continuity, regularity, capacity and pricing which standards carriers would not assume if they were solely considering their commercial interest.

(*b*) The adequacy of air transport services shall be assessed having regard to:

  (i) the public interest;
  (ii) the possibility of having recourse to other forms of transport and the ability of such forms to meet the transport needs under consideration;
  (iii) the air fares and conditions which can be quoted to users.

(*c*) Notwithstanding paragraph 2, a Member State is not obliged to authorize more than one carrier to serve a route to which a public service obligation applies, provided the right to operate that service is offered by public tender for a period of up to three years to any air carrier with an operating licence issued in the States concerned and to any Community air carrier which, in accordance with Article 8, is entitled to exercise fifth-freedom traffic rights on the route. The submissions made by air carriers shall be communicated to the other States concerned and to the Commission.

(*d*) Subparagraph (*c*) shall not apply in any case in which the other Member State concerned proposes a satisfactory alternative means of fulfilling the same public service obligation.

(*e*) This paragraph shall not apply to routes with capacity of more than 30 000 seats per year.

4. Notwithstanding paragraph 2, a Member State, which has authorized one of the air carriers licensed by it to operate a passenger service on a new route between regional airports with aircraft of no more than 80 seats, is not obliged to authorize a reciprocal air service for a period of two years, unless it is operated with aircraft of no more than 80 seats, or it is part of a service operated under the terms of Article 7 in which not more than 80 seats are available for sale between the two regional airports in question, on each flight.

5. At the request of any Member State which considers that the development of a route is being unduly restricted by the terms of paragraphs 3 or 4, or on its own initiative or where disagreement arises regarding the application of paragraph 3, the Commission shall carry out an investigation and, on the basis of all relevant factors, shall take a decision within two months of commencing its investigation on whether paragraph 3 or 4 should continue to apply in respect of the route concerned.

6. The Commission shall communicate its decision to the Council and to the Member States. Any Member State may refer the Commission's decision to the Council within a time limit of one month. The Council, acting by a qualified majority, may take a different decision within a period of one month. **[1500]**

MULTIPLE DESIGNATION

Article 6

1. A Member State shall accept multiple designation on a country-pair basis by another Member State.

2. It shall also accept multiple designation on a city-pair basis:

  — from 1 January 1991, on routes on which more than 140 000 passengers were carried in the preceding year, or on which there are more than 800 return flights per annum,
  — from 1 January 1992, on routes on which more than 100 000 passengers were carried in the preceding year or on which there are more than 600 return flights per annum. **[1501]**

COMBINATION OF POINTS

Article 7

In operating scheduled air services to or from two or more points in another Member State or States other than its State of registration, a Community air carrier shall be permitted by the States concerned to combine scheduled air services and use the same flight number. Traffic rights between the combined points may be exercised according to Article 8. **[1502]**

COMBINATION OF POINTS

FIFTH-FREEDOM RIGHTS

Article 8

1. Community air carriers shall, in accordance with this Article, be permitted to exercise fifth-freedom traffic rights between combined points in two different Member States on the following conditions:

  (a) the traffic rights are exercised on a service which constitutes and is scheduled as an extension of a service from, or as a preliminary of a service to, their State of registration;
  (b) the air carrier cannot use, for the fifth-freedom service more than 50% of its seasonal seat capacity on the same third- and fourth-freedom service of which the fifth-freedom service constitutes the extension or the preliminary.

2. (a) The air carrier may, for a fifth-freedom service, use an aircraft which is different to but not larger than the aircraft which it uses for the third- and fourth-freedom service of which the fifth-freedom service is an extension or a preliminary.
  (b) When more than one fifth-freedom service is operated as an extension of or as a preliminary to a third- or fourth-freedom service, the capacity provision in paragraph 1(b) shall represent the aggregate seat capacity available for the carriage of fifth-freedom passengers on those fifth-freedom services.

3. An air carrier operating a fifth-freedom service in accordance with this Article shall furnish on request to the Member States involved all relevant information concerning:

  (a) the seasonal seat capacity on the third- and fourth-freedom service of which the fifth-freedom service constitutes the extension or the preliminary; and
  (b) in the case of fifth-freedom services to which Article 8(2)(b) applies, the seasonal capacity utilized on each service. **[1503]**

CONDITIONS FOR THE EXERCISE OF TRAFFIC RIGHTS

Article 9

This Regulation shall not affect a Member States' right to regulate without discrimination on grounds of nationality, the distribution of traffic between the airports within an airport system. **[1504]**

Article 10

1. Notwithstanding Article 5(2), the exercise of traffic rights is subject to published Community, national, regional or local rules relating to safety, the protection of the environment and the allocation of slots, and to the following conditions:

(*a*) the airport or airport system concerned must have sufficient facilities to accommodate the service;

(*b*) navigational aids must be sufficient to accommodate the service.

2. When the conditions in paragraph 1 are not met, a Member State may, without discrimination on grounds of nationality, impose conditions on, limit or refuse the exercise of those traffic rights. Before taking such a measure, a Member State shall inform the Commission and provide it with all the necessary elements of information.

3. Without prejudice to Article 9 and except with the agreement of the other Member State(s) concerned, a Member State shall not authorize an air carrier:

(*a*) to establish a new service; or

(*b*) to increase the frequency of an existing service

between a specific airport in its territory and another Member State for such time as an air carrier licensed by that other Member State is not permitted, on the basis of paragraphs 1 and 2, to establish a new service or to increase frequencies on an existing service to the airport in question, pending the adoption by the Council and the coming into force of a Regulation on a code of conduct on slot allocation based on the general principle of non-discrimination on the grounds of nationality.

4. At the request of any Member State, the Commission shall examine the application of paragraph 2 and/or paragraph 3 in any particular case and within one month decide whether the Member State may continue to apply the measure.

5. The Commission shall communicate its decision to the Council and to the Member States. Any Member State may refer the Commission's decision to the Council within a time limit of one month. The Council, acting by a qualified majority, may take a different decision within a period of one month. **[1505]**

SHARES OF CAPACITY

Article 11

1. From 1 November 1990, a Member State shall permit another Member State to increase its capacity share for any season by 7.5 percentage points compared to the situation during the previous corresponding season, it being understood that each Member State may in any event claim a capacity share of 60%.

2. The Council shall adopt, for implementation not later than 1 January 1993, on the basis of a Commission proposal to be submitted by 31 December 1991, provisions to abolish capacity sharing restrictions between Member States.

3. Capacity sharing limitations shall not apply to a service between regional airports irrespective of aircraft capacity.

4. In applying paragraph 1, unilateral cut-backs in capacity shall not be taken into account. In such cases, the basis for the calculation of capacity shares shall be the capacity offered in the previous corresponding seasons by the air carrier(s) of the Member State which has (have) reduced its (their) capacity. **[1506]**

Article 12

1. At the request of any Member State for which the application of Article 11 has led to serious financial damage for the air carrier(s) licensed by that Member State, the Commission shall carry out a review and, on the basis of all relevant factors, including the market situation, the financial position of the air carrier(s) concerned and the capacity

utilization achieved, shall take a decision on whether the capacity sharing on the routes to or from that State should be stabilized for a limited period.

2. At the request of a Member State whose scheduled air services are exposed to substantial competition from non-scheduled services and where a situation exists whereby the opportunities of carriers of that Member State to effectively compete in the market are unduly affected, the Commission, having examined all relevant factors, including the market situation and the capacity utilization achieved, and having consulted the other Member States concerned shall, within two months of having received the request, decide whether the 7.5 percentage points referred to in Article 11(1) shall be reduced for that bilateral relationship.

3. The Commission shall communicate its decision to the Council and to the Member States. Any Member State may refer the Commission's decision to the Council within a time limit of one month. The Council, acting by qualified majority, may take a different decision within a period of one month.   **[1507]**

GENERAL PROVISIONS

Article 13

1. This Regulation shall not prevent Member States from concluding between them arrangements which are more flexible than the provisions of Articles 6, 8 and 11 or from maintaining such arrangements in force.

2. The provisions of this Regulation shall not be used to make existing market access or capacity arrangements more restrictive.   **[1508]**

Article 14

1. The Commission shall publish a report on the implementation of this Regulation every two years and for the first time not later than 31 May 1992.

2. Member States and the Commission shall cooperate in implementing this Regulation, particularly as regards collection of information for the report referred to in paragraph 1.

3. Confidential information obtained in application of this Regulation shall be covered by professional secrecy.   **[1509]**

Article 15

The Council shall decide on the revision of this Regulation by 30 June 1992 at the latest, on the basis of a Commission proposal to be submitted by 31 May 1991.   **[1510]**

Article 16

Decision 87/602/EEC and Directive 83/416/EEC are hereby revoked.   **[1511]**

Article 17

This Regulation shall enter into force on 1 November 1990.   **[1512]**

This Regulation shall be binding in its entirety and directly applicable in all Member States.

Done at Brussels, 24 July 1990.

ANNEX I

AIR CARRIERS REFERRED TO IN ARTICLE 2(*e*)(ii)

The following air carriers meet the criteria referred to in Article 2(*e*)(ii) as long as they are recognized as national carriers by the Member State which so recognizes them at the time of the adoption of this Regulation:

- Scandinavian Airlines System,
- Britannia Airways,
- Monarch Airlines.

[1513]

ANNEX II

LIST OF CATEGORY 1 AIRPORTS

BELGIUM:	Brussels-Zaventem
DENMARK:	Copenhagen-Kastrup/Roskilde
FEDERAL REPUBLIC OF GERMANY:	Frankfurt-Rhein-Main, Düsseldorf-Lohausen, Munich-Riem
SPAIN:	Palma-Mallorca, Madrid-Barajas Malaga, Las Palmas
GREECE:	Athens-Hellinikon, Salonica-Micra
FRANCE:	Paris-Charles De Gaulle/Orly
IRELAND:	Dublin
ITALY:	Rome-Fiumicino/Ciampino, Milan-Linate/Malpensa
NETHERLANDS:	Amsterdam-Schiphol
PORTUGAL:	Lisbon, Faro
UNITED KINGDOM:	London-Heathrow/Gatwick/Stansted, Luton

[1514]

COMMUNICATION FROM THE GOVERNMENT OF THE FEDERAL REPUBLIC OF GERMANY

The Council has received the following communication from the Government of the Federal Republic of Germany:

When depositing its instruments of ratification of the Treaties establishing the European Communities, the Federal Republic of Germany declared that these Treaties applied equally to Land Berlin. It declared at the same time that the rights and responsibilities of France, the United Kingdom and the United States in respect of Berlin were unaffected. In view of the fact that civil aviation is one of the areas in which the said States have specifically reserved powers for themselves in Berlin, and following consultations with the Governments of these States, the Federal Republic of Germany states that the following Regulations are not applicable in Land Berlin:

- Council Regulation on fares for scheduled air services,
- Council Regulation on access for air carriers to scheduled intra-Community air service routes and on the sharing of passenger capacity between air carriers on scheduled air services between Member States,

— Council Regulation amending Regulation (EEC) No 3976/87 on the application
  of Article 85(3) of the Treaty to certain categories of agreements and concerted
  practices in the air transport sector.   **[1515]**

REGULATION (EEC) No 2367/90 OF THE COMMISSION
of 25 July 1990

**on the notifications, time limits and hearings provided for in Council Regulation
(EEC) No 4064/89 on the control of concentrations between undertakings**

THE COMMISSION OF THE EUROPEAN COMMUNITIES,
Having regard to the Treaty establishing the European Economic Community,
Having regard to Council Regulation (EEC) No 4064/89 of 21 December 1989 on the control
of concentrations between the undertakings, and in particular Article 23 thereof,
Having regard to Council Regulation No 17 of 6 February 1962, First Regulation implementing
Articles 85 and 86 of the Treaty as last amended by the Act of Accession of Spain and Portugal,
and in particular Article 24 thereof,
Having regard to Council Regulation (EEC) No 1017/68 of 19 July 1968 applying rules of competi-
tion to transport by rail, road and inland waterway as last amended by the Act of Accession of
Spain and Portugal, and in particular Article 29 thereof,
Having regard to Council Regulation (EEC) No 4056/86 of 22 December 1986 laying down detailed
rules for the application of Articles 85 and 86 of the Treaty to maritime transport and in particular
Article 26 thereof,
Having regard to Council Regulation (EEC) No 3975/87 of 14 December 1987 laying down detailed
rules for the application of the competition rules to undertakings in air transport and in particular
Article 19 thereof,
Having consulted the Advisory Committee on Concentrations, as well as the Advisory Committees
on Restrictive Practices and Monopolies in the Transport Industry, in Maritime Transport and in
Air Transport,

1. Whereas Article 23 of Regulation (EEC) No 4064/89 empowers the Commission to adopt
   implementing provisions concerning the form, content and other details of notifications pursuant
   to Article 4, time limits pursuant to Article 10, and hearings pursuant to Article 18;
2. Whereas Regulation (EEC) No 4064/89 is based on the principle of compulsory notification
   of concentrations before they are put into effect; whereas, on the one hand, a notification has
   important legal consequences which are favourable to the parties, while, on the other hand,
   failure to comply with the obligation to notify renders the parties liable to a fine and may also
   entail civil law disadvantages for them; whereas it is therefore necessary in the interests of legal
   certainty to define precisely the subject matter and content of the information to be provided
   in the notification;
3. Whereas it is for the parties concerned to make full and honest disclosure to the Commission of the facts and circumstances which are relevant for taking a decision on the notified
   concentration;
4. Whereas in order to simplify and expedite examination of the notification it is desirable to prescribe
   that a form be used;
5. Whereas since notification sets in motion legal time limits for initiating proceedings and for
   decisions, the conditions governing such time limits and the time when they become effective
   must also be determined;
6. Whereas rules must be laid down in the interests of legal certainty for calculating the time limits
   provided for in Regulation (EEC) No 4064/89; whereas in particular the beginning and end
   of the period and the circumstances suspending the running of the period must be determined;
   whereas the provisions should be based on the principles of Regulation (EEC, Euratom)
   No 1182/71 of 3 June 1971 determining the rules applicable to periods, dates and time limits,
   subject to certain adaptations made necessary by the exceptionally short legal time limits referred
   to above;
7. Whereas the provisions relating to the Commission's procedure must be framed in such way
   as to safeguard fully the right to be heard and the rights of defence;

8. Whereas the Commission will give the parties concerned, if they so request, an opportunity before notification to discuss the intended concentration informally and in strict confidence; whereas in addition it will, after notification, maintain close contact with the parties concerned to the extent necessary to discuss with them any practical or legal problems which it discovers on a first examination of the case and if possible to remove such problems by mutual agreement;

9. Whereas in accordance with the principle of the right to be heard, the parties concerned must be given the opportunity to submit their comments on all the objections which the Commission proposes to take into account in its decisions;

10. Whereas third parties having sufficient interest must also be given the opportunity of expressing their views where they make a written application;

11. Whereas the various persons entitled to submit comments should do so in writing, both in their own interest and in the interest of good administration, without prejudice to their right to request an oral hearing where appropriate to supplement the written procedure; whereas in urgent cases, however, the Commission must be able to proceed immediately to oral hearings of the parties concerned or third parties; whereas in such cases the persons to be heard must have the right to confirm their oral statements in writing;

12. Whereas it is necessary to define the rights of persons who are to be heard, to what extent they should be granted access to the Commission's file and on what conditions they may be represented or assisted;

13. Whereas it is also necessary to define the rules for fixing and calculating the time limits for reply fixed by the Commission;

14. Whereas the Advisory Committee on Concentrations shall deliver its opinion on the basis of a preliminary draft decision; whereas it must therefore be consulted on a case after the inquiry into that case has been completed; whereas such consultation does not, however, prevent the Commission from re-opening an inquiry if need be,

HAS ADOPTED THIS REGULATION:

SECTION I
NOTIFICATIONS

Article 1 – Persons entitled to submit notifications

1. Notifications shall be submitted by the persons or undertakings referred to in Article 4(2) of Regulation (EEC) No 4064/89.

2. Where notifications are signed by representatives of persons or of undertakings, such representatives shall produce written proof that they are authorized to act.

3. Joint notifications should be submitted by a joint representative who is authorized to transmit and to receive documents on behalf of all notifying parties. **[1516]**

Article 2 – Submission of notifications

1. Notifications shall be submitted in the manner prescribed by form CO as shown in Annex I. Joint notifications shall be submitted on a single form.

2. Twenty copies of each notification and fifteen copies of the supporting documents shall be submitted to the Commission at the address indicated in form CO.

3. The supporting documents shall be either originals or copies of the originals; in the latter case the notifying parties shall confirm that they are true and complete.

4. Notifications shall be in one of the official languages of the Community. This language shall also be the language of the proceeding for the notifying parties. Supporting documents shall be submitted in their original language. Where the original language is not one of the official languages, a translation into the language of the proceeding shall be attached. **[1517]**

Article 3 – Information to be provided

1. Notifications shall contain the information requested by form CO. The information must be correct and complete.

2. Material changes in the facts specified in the notification which the notifying parties know or ought to have known must be communicated to the Commission voluntarily and without delay.

3. Incorrect or misleading information shall be deemed to be incomplete information.

[1518]

Article 4 – Effective date of notifications

1. Subject to paragraph 2 notifications shall become effective on the date on which they are received by the Commission.

2. Subject to paragraph 3, where the information contained in the notification is incomplete in a material respect, the Commission shall without delay inform the notifying parties or the joint representative in writing and shall fix an appropriate time limit for the completion of the information; in such cases, the notification shall become effective on the date on which the complete information is received by the Commission.

3. The Commission may dispense with the obligation to provide any particular information requested by form CO where the Commission considers that such information is not necessary for the examination of the case.

4. The Commission shall without delay acknowledge in writing to the notifying parties or the joint representative receipt of the notification and of any reply to a letter sent by the Commission pursuant to paragraph 2 above.   **[1519]**

Article 5 – Conversion of notifications

1. Where the Commission finds that the operation notified does not constitute a concentration within the meaning of Article 3 of Regulation (EEC) No 4064/89 it shall inform the notifying parties or the joint representative in writing. In such a case, the Commission may, if requested by the notifying parties, as appropriate and subject to paragraph 2 below, treat the notification as an application within the meaning of Article 2 or a notification within the meaning of Article 4 or Regulation No 17, as an application within the meaning of Article 12 or a notification within the meaning of Article 14 or Regulation (EEC) No 1017/68, as an application within the meaning of Article 12 of Regulation (EEC) No 4056/86 or as an application within the meaning of Article 3(2) or of Article 5 of Regulation (EEC) No 3975/87.

2. In cases referred to in paragraph 1, second sentence, the Commission may require that the information given in the notification be supplemented within an appropriate time limit fixed by it in so far as this is necessary for assessing the operation on the basis of the abovementioned Regulations. The application or notification shall be deemed to fulfil the requirements of such Regulations from the date of the original notification where the additional information is received by the Commission within the time limit fixed.

[1520]

SECTION II
TIME LIMITS FOR INITIATING PROCEEDINGS AND FOR DECISIONS

Article 6 — Beginning of the time limit

1. The periods referred to in Article 10(1) of Regulation (EEC) No 4064/89 shall start at the beginning of the day following the effective date of the notification, within the meaning of Article 4(1) and (2) of this Regulation.

2. The period referred to in Article 10(3) of Regulation (EEC) No 4064/89 shall start at the beginning of the day following the day on which proceedings were initiated.

3. Where the first day of a period is not a working day within the meaning of Article 19, the period shall start at the beginning of the following working day.   **[1521]**

Article 7 — End of the time limit

1. The period referred to in the first subparagraph of Article 10(1) of Regulation (EEC) No 4064/89 shall end with the expiry of the day which in the month following that in which the period began falls on the same date as the day from which the period runs. Where such a day does not occur in that month, the period shall end with the expiry of the last day of that month.

2. The period referred to in the second sub-paragraph of Article 10(1) of Regulation (EEC) No 4064/89 shall end with the expiry of the day which in the sixth week following that in which the period began is the same day of the week as the day from which the period runs.

3. The period referred to in Article 10(3) of Regulation (EEC) No 4064/89 shall end with the expiry of the day which in the fourth month following that in which the period began falls on the same date as the day from which the period runs. Where such a day does not occur in that month, the period shall end with the expiry of the last day of that month.

4. Where the last day of the period is not a working day within the meaning of Article 19, the period shall end with the expiry of the following working day.

5. Paragraphs 2 to 4 above shall be subject to the provisions of Article 8.   **[1522]**

Article 8 — Addition of holidays

Where public holidays or other holidays of the Commission as defined in Article 19 fall within the periods referred to in Article 10(1) and in Article 10(3) of Regulation (EEC) No 4064/89, these periods shall be extended by a corresponding number of days.

[1523]

Article 9 — Suspension of the time limit

1. The period referred to in Article 10(3) of Regulation (EEC) No 4064/89 shall be suspended where the Commission, pursuant to Articles 11(5) or 13(3) of the same Regulation, has to take a decision because:

    (*a*) Information which the Commission has requested pursuant to Article 11(2) of Regulation (EEC) No 4064/89 from an undertaking involved in a concentration is not provided or not provided in full within the time limit fixed by the Commission;

    (*b*) an undertaking involved in the concentration has refused to submit to an investigation deemed necessary by the Commission on the basis of Article 13(1) of Regulation (EEC) No 4064/89 or to cooperate in the carrying out of such an investigation in accordance with the abovementioned provision;

(c) the notifying parties have failed to inform the Commission of material changes in the facts specified in the notification.

2. The period referred to in Article 10(3) of Regulation (EEC) No 4064/89 shall be suspended:

(a) in the cases referred to in subparagraph 1(a) above, for the period between the end of the time limit fixed in the request for information and the receipt of the complete and correct information required by decision;

(b) in the cases referred to in subparagraph 1(b) above, for the period between the unsuccessful attempt to carry out the investigation and the completion of the investigation ordered by decision;

(c) in the cases referred to in subparagraph 1(c) above, for the period between the occurrence of the change in the facts referred to therein and the receipt of the complete and correct information requested by decision or the completion of the investigation ordered by decision.

3. The suspension of the time limit shall begin on the day following that on which the event causing the suspension occurred. It shall end with the expiry of the day on which the reason for suspension is removed. Where such day is not a working day within the meaning of Article 19, the suspension of the time limit shall end with the expiry of the following working day.   **[1524]**

Article 10 – Compliance with the time limit

The time limits referred to in Article 10(1) and (3) of Regulation (EEC) No 4064/89 shall be met where the Commission has taken the relevant decision before the end of the period. Notification of the decision to the undertakings concerned must follow without delay.   **[1525]**

SECTION III

HEARING OF THE PARTIES AND OF THIRD PARTIES

Article 11 – Decisions on the suspension of concentrations

1. Where the Commission intends to take a decision under Article 7(2) of Regulation (EEC) No 4064/89 or a decision under Article 7(4) of that Regulation which adversely affects the parties, it shall, pursuant to Article 18(1) of that Regulation, inform the parties concerned in writing of its objections and shall fix a time limit within which they may make known their views.

2. Where the Commission pursuant to Article 18(2) of Regulation (EEC) No 4064/89 has taken a decision referred to in paragraph 1 provisionally without having given the parties concerned the opportunity to make known their views, it shall without delay and in any event before the expiry of the suspension send them the text of the provisional decision and shall fix a time limit within which they may make known their views. Once the parties concerned have made known their views, the Commission shall take a final decision annulling, amending or confirming the provisional decision. Where the parties concerned have not made known their view within the time limit fixed, the Commission's provisional decision shall become final with the expiry of that period.

3. The parties concerned shall make known their views in writing or orally within the time limit fixed. They may confirm their oral statements in writing.   **[1526]**

Article 12 – Decisions on the substance of the case

1. Where the Commission intends to take a decision pursuant to Article 8(2), second subparagraph, Article 8(3), (4) and (5), Article 14 or Article 15 of Regulation (EEC) No 4064/89, it shall, before consulting the Advisory Committee on Concentrations, hold a hearing of the parties concerned pursuant to Article 18 of that Regulation.

2. The Commission shall inform the parties concerned in writing of its objections. The communication shall be addressed to the notifying parties or to the joint representative. The Commission shall, when giving notice of objections, fix a time limit within which the parties concerned may inform the Commission of their views.

3. Having informed the parties of its objections, the Commission shall upon request give the parties concerned access to the file for the purposes of preparing their observations. Documents shall not be accessible in so far as they contain business secrets of other parties concerned or of third parties, or other confidential information including sensitive commercial information the disclosure of which would have a significant adverse effect on the supplier of such information or where they are internal documents of the authorities.

4. The parties concerned shall, within the time limit fixed, make known in writing their views on the Commission's objections. They may in their written comments set out all matters relevant to the case and may attach any relevant documents in proof of the facts set out. They may also propose that the Commission hear persons who may corroborate those facts. **[1527]**

Article 13 – Oral hearings

1. The Commission shall afford parties concerned who have so requested in their written comments the opportunity to put forward their arguments orally, if those persons show a sufficient interest or if the Commission proposes to impose a fine or periodic penalty payment on them. It may also in other cases afford the parties concerned the opportunity of expressing their views orally.

2. The Commission shall summon the persons to be heard to attend on such date as it shall appoint.

3. It shall forthwith transmit a copy of the summons to the competent authorities of the Member States, who may appoint an official to take part in the hearing.

[1528]

Article 14 – Hearings

1. Hearings shall be conducted by persons appointed by the Commission for that purpose.

2. Persons summoned to attend shall either appear in person or be represented by legal representatives or representatives authorized by their constitution. Undertakings and associations of undertakings may be represented by a duly authorized agent appointed from among their permanent staff.

3. Persons heard by the Commission may be assisted by lawyers or university teachers who are entitled to plead before the Court of Justice of the European Communities in accordance with Article 17 of the Protocol on the Statute (EEC) of the Court of Justice, or by other qualified persons.

4. Hearings shall not be public. Persons shall be heard separately or in the presence of other persons summoned to attend. In the latter case, regard shall be had to the legitimate interest of the undertakings in the protection of their business secrets.

5. The statements made by each person heard shall be recorded. **[1529]**

Article 15 – Hearing of third parties

1. If natural or legal persons showing a sufficient interest, and especially members of the administrative or management organs of the undertakings concerned or recognized workers' representatives of those undertakings, apply in writing to be heard pursuant to the second sentence of Article 18(4) of Regulation (EEC) No 4064/89, the Commission shall inform them in writing of the nature and subject matter of the procedure and shall fix a time within which they may make known their views.

2. The third parties referred to in paragraph 1 above shall make known their views in writing or orally within the time limit fixed. They may confirm their oral statements in writing.

3. The Commission may likewise afford to any other third parties the opportunity of expressing their views.   **[1530]**

SECTION IV

MISCELLANEOUS PROVISIONS

Article 16 – Transmission of documents

1. Transmission of documents and summonses from the Commission to the addressees may be effected in any of the following ways:

    (*a*) delivery by hand against receipt;
    (*b*) registered letter with acknowledgement of receipt;
    (*c*) telefax with a request for acknowledgement of receipt;
    (*d*) telex.

2. Subject to Article 18(1), paragraph 1 above also applies to the transmission of documents from the parties concerned or from third parties to the Commission.

3. Where a document is sent by telex or by telefax, it shall be presumed that it has been received by the addressee on the day on which it was sent.   **[1531]**

Article 17 – Setting of time limits

1. In fixing the time limits provided for in Articles 4(2), 5(2), 11(1) and (2), 12(2) and 15(1), the Commission shall have regard to the time required for preparation of statements and to the urgency of the case. It shall also take account of public holidays in the country of receipt of the Commission's communication.

2. The day on which the addressee received a communication shall not be taken into account for the purpose of fixing time limits.   **[1532]**

Article 18 – Receipt of documents by the Commission

1. Subject to Article 4(1), notifications must be delivered to the Commission at the address indicated in form CO or have been dispatched by registered letter before expiry of the period referred to in Article 4(1) of Regulation (EEC) No 4064/89. Additional information requested to complete notifications pursuant to Article 4(2) or to supplement notifications pursuant to Article 5(2) of this Regulation must reach the Commission at the aforesaid or have been dispatched by registered letter before the expiry of the time limit fixed in each case. Written comments on Commission communications pursuant to Articles 11(1) and (2), 12(2) and 15(1) must be delivered to the Commission at the aforesaid address before the time limit fixed in each case.

2. Where the last day of a period referred to in paragraph 1 is a day by which documents must be received and that day is not a working day within the meaning of Article 19, the period shall end with the expiry of the following working day.

3. Where the last day of a period referred to in paragraph 1 is a day by which documents must be dispatched and that day is a Saturday, Sunday or public holiday in the country of dispatch, the period shall end with the expiry of the following working day in that country.   **[1533]**

Article 19 – Definition of Commission working days

The term "working days" in Articles 6(3), 7(4), 9(3) and 18(2) means all days other than Saturdays, Sundays, public holidays set out in Annex II and other holidays as determined by the Commission and published in the *Official Journal of the European Communities* before the beginning of each year.   **[1534]**

Article 20 – Entry into force

This Regulation shall enter into force on 21 September 1990.   **[1535]**

This Regulation shall be binding in its entirety and directly applicable in all Member States.

Done at Brussels, 25 July 1990.

ANNEX I

FORM CO RELATING TO THE NOTIFICATION OF A CONCENTRATION PURSUANT TO COUNCIL
REGULATION (EEC) No 4064/89

A. Introduction

This form specifies the information to be provided by an undertaking or undertakings when notifying the Commission of a concentration with a Community dimension. A "concentration" is defined in Article 3 and "Community dimension" by Article 1 of Regulation (EEC) No 4064/89.

Your attention is particularly drawn to Regulation (EEC) No 4064/89 and to Commission Regulation (EEC) No 2367/90. In particular you should note that:

(a) all information requested by this form must be provided. However if, in good faith, you are unable to provide a response to a question or can only respond to a limited extent on the basis of available information, indicate this and give reasons. If you consider that any particular information requested by this form may not be necessary for the Commission's examination of the case, you may ask the Commission to dispense with the obligation to provide that information, under Article 4(3) of Regulation (EEC) No 2367/90;

(b) unless all sections are completed in full or good reasons are given explaining why it has not been possible to complete unanswered questions (for example, because of the unavailability of information on a target company during a contested bid) the notification will be incomplete and will only become effective on the date on which all the information is received. The notification will be deemed to be incomplete if information is incorrect or misleading;

(c) incorrect or misleading information where supplied intentionally or negligently could make you liable to a fine.

B. Who must notify

In the case of a merger (within the meaning of Article 3(1)(*a*) of Regulation (EEC) No 4064/89 or the acquisition of joint control in a undertaking within the meaning of Article 3(1)(*b*) of Regulation (EEC) No 4064/89, the notification shall be completed jointly by the parties to the merger or by those acquiring joint control as the case may be.

In the case of the acquisition of a controlling interest in an undertaking by another, the acquirer must complete the notification.

In the case of a public bid to acquire an undertaking, the bidder must complete the notification.

Each party completing the notification is responsible for the accuracy of the information which it provides.

For the purposes of this form "the parties to the concentration" ("the parties") includes the undertaking in which a controlling interest is being acquired or which is the subject of a public bid.

C. Supporting documentation

The completed notification must be accompanied by the following:

(*a*) copies of the final or most recent versions of all documents bringing about the concentration, whether by agreement between the parties concerned, acquisition of a controlling interest or a public bid;

(*b*) in a public bid, a copy of the offer document. If unavailable on notification it should be submitted as soon as possible and not later than when it is posted to shareholders;

(*c*) copies of the most recent annual reports and accounts of all the parties to the concentration;

(*d*) copies of reports or analyses which have been prepared for the purposes of the concentration and from which information has been taken in order to provide the information requested in sections 5 and 6;

(*e*) a list and short description of the contents of all other analyses, reports, studies and surveys prepared by or for any of the notifying parties for the purpose of assessing or analysing the proposed concentration with respect to competitive conditions, competitors (actual and potential), and market conditions. Each item in the list must include the name and position held of the author.

D. How to notify

The notification must be completed in one of the official languages of the European Community. This language shall thereafter be the language of the proceeding for all notifying parties.

The information requested by this form is to be set out using the sections and paragraph numbers of the form.

Supporting documents shall be submitted in their original language; where this is not an official language of the Community they shall be translated, into the language of the proceeding (Article 2(4) of Regulation (EEC) No 2367/90).

The supporting documents may be originals or copies of the originals. In the latter case the notifying party shall confirm that they are true and complete.

The financial data requested in Section 2.4 below must be provided in Ecus at the average conversion rates prevailing for the years or other period in question.

Twenty copies of each notification and fifteen copies of all supporting documents must be provided.

The notification should be sent to:

Commission of the European Communities,
Directorate General for Competition (DG IV),
Merger Task Force (Cort. 150),
200, rue de la Loi,
B-1049 Brussels;

or be delivered by hand during normal Commission working hours at the following address:

Commission of the European Communities,
Directorate General for Competition (DG IV),
Merger Task Force,
150, avenue de Cortenberg,
B-1040 Brussels.

E. Secrecy

Article 214 of the Treaty and Article 17(2) of Regulation (EEC) No 4064/89 require the Commission and the Member States, their officials and other servants not to disclose information they have acquired through the application of the Regulation of the kind covered by the obligation of professional secrecy. The same principle must also apply to protect confidentiality as between notifying parties.

If you believe that your interests would be harmed if any of the information you are asked to supply was to be published or otherwise divulged to other parties, submit this information separately with each page clearly marked "Business secrets". You should also give reasons why this information should not be divulged or published.

In the case of mergers or joint acquisitions, or in other cases where the notification is completed by more than one of the parties, business secrets may be submitted under separate cover, and referred to in the notification as an annex. In such cases the notification will be considered complete on receipt of all the annexes.

F. References

All references contained in this form are to the relevant articles and paragraphs of Council Regulation (EEC)   **[1536]**

SECTION 1

1.1. *Information on notifying party (or parties)*
       Give details of:

1.1.1. name and address of undertaking,

1.1.2. nature of the undertaking's business,

1.1.3. name, address, telephone, fax and/or telex of, and position held by, the person to be contacted.

1.2. *Information on other parties to the concentration*[1, 2]
       For each party to the concentration (except the notifying party) give details of:

1.2.1. name and address of undertaking,

1.2.2 nature of the undertaking's business,

1.2.3. name, address, telephone, fax and/or telex of, and position held by, the person to be contacted.

1.3.   *Address for service*
       Give an address in Brussels if available to which all communications may be made
       and documents delivered in accordance with Article 1(4) of Commission Regulation
       (EEC) No 2367/90.

1.4.   *Appointment of representatives*
       Article 1(2) of Commission Regulation (EEC) 2367/90 states that where notifica-
       tions are signed by representatives of undertakings, such representatives shall
       produce written proof that they are authorized to act. Such written authorization
       must accompany the notification and the following details of the representatives
       of the notifying party or parties and other parties to the concentration are to be
       given below:

1.4.1. is this a joint notification?

1.4.2. if "yes", has a joint representative been appointed?
       if "yes", please give the details requested in 1.4.3 to 1.4.6 below;
       if "no", please give details of the representatives who have been authorized to
       act for each of the parties to the concentration indicating who they represent;

1.4.3. name of representative;

1.4.4. address of representative;

1.4.5. name of person to be contacted (and address if different from 1.4.4.);

1.4.6. telephone, telefax and/or telex.   **[1537]**

SECTION 2 – Details of the concentration

2.1.   Briefly describe the nature of the concentration being notified. In doing so state:

       — whether the proposed concentration is a full legal merger, an acquisition, a
         concentrative joint venture or a contract or other means conferring direct or
         indirect control within the meaning of Article 3(3);
       — whether the whole or parts of parties are subject to the concentration;
       — whether any public offer for the securities of one party by another has the support
         of the former's supervisory boards of management or other bodies legally repre-
         senting the party concerned.

2.2.   List the economic sectors involved in the concentration.

2.3.   Give a brief explanation of the economic and financial details of the concentration.
       In doing so provide, where relevant, information about the following:

       — any financial or other support received from whatever source (including public
         authorities) by any of the parties and the nature and amount of this support,
       — the proposed or expected date of any major events designed to bring about the
         completion of the concentration,
       — the proposed structure of ownership and control after the completion of the
         concentration.

2.4.   For each of the parties, the notifying party shall provide the following data for
       the last three financial years:

2.4.1. worldwide turnover[3],

2.4.2. Community-wide turnover[4, 5],

2.4.3. turnover in each Member State[4, 5].

2.4.4. the Member State, if any, in which more than two-thirds of Community-wide turnover is achieved[4, 5],

2.4.5. profits before tax worldwide[6],

2.4.6. number of employees worldwide[7].　　　　　　　　　　　　　　　　**[1538]**

SECTION 3 – Ownership and control[7]

For each of the parties provide a list of all undertakings belonging to the same group. This list must include:

3.1.　　all undertakings controlled by the parties, directly or indirectly, within the meaning of Article 3(3);

3.2.　　all undertakings or persons controlling the parties directly or indirectly within the meaning of Article 3(3);

3.3.　　for each undertaking or person identified in 3.2 above, a complete list of all undertakings controlled by them directly or indirectly, within the meaning of Article 3(3).

For each entry to the list the nature and means of control shall be specified;

3.4.　　provide details of acquisitions made during the last three years by the groups identified above, of undertakings active in affected markets as defined in section 5 below.

The information sought in this section may be illustrated by the use of charts or diagrams where this helps to give a better understanding of the pre-concentration structure of ownership and control of the undertakings.　　　　　　　　　　　　**[1539]**

SECTION 4 – Personal and financial links

With respect to each undertaking or person disclosed in response to Section 3 provide:

4.1.　　a list of all other undertakings which are active on affected markets (affected markets are defined in section 5) in which the undertakings of the group hold individually or collectively 10% or more of the voting rights or issued share capital. In each case state the percentage held;

4.2.　　a list of all other undertakings which are active on affected markets in which the persons disclosed in response to Section 3 hold 10% or more of the voting rights or issued share capital. In each case state the percentage held;

4.3.　　a list for each undertaking of the members of their boards of management who are also members of the boards of management or of the supervisory boards of any other undertaking, which is active on affected markets; and (where applicable) for each undertaking a list of the members of their supervisory boards who are also members of the boards of management of any other undertaking which is active on affected markets;
　　　　in each case stating the name of the other undertaking and the position held.

Information provided here may be illustrated by the use of charts or diagrams where this helps to give a better understanding.　　　　　　　　　　　　　**[1540]**

SECTION 5 – Information on affected markets

The notifying party shall provide the data requested having regard to the following definitions:

Product markets

A relevant product market comprises all those products and/or services which are regarded as interchangeable or substitutable by the consumer, by reason of the products' characteristics, their prices and their intended use.

A relevant product market may in some cases be composed of a number of individual product groups. An individual product group is a product or small group of products which present largely identical physical or technical characteristics and are fully interchangeable. The difference between products within the group will be small and usually only a matter of brand and/or image. The product market will usually be the classification used by the undertaking in its marketing operations.

Relevant geographic market

The relevant geographic market comprises the area in which the undertakings concerned are involved in the supply of products or services, in which the conditions of competition are sufficiently homogeneous and which can be distinguished from neighbouring areas because, in particular, conditions of competition are appreciable different in those areas.

Factors relevant to the assessment of the relevant geographic market include the nature and characteristics of the products or services concerned, the existence of entry barriers or consumer preferences, appreciable differences of the undertakings' market shares between neighbouring areas or substantial price differences.

Affected markets

Affected markets consist of relevant product markets or individual product groups, in the Common Market or a Member State or, where different, in any relevant geographic market where:

    (*a*) two or more of the parties (including undertakings belonging to the same group as defined in Section 3) are engaged in business activities in the same product market or individual product group and where the concentration will lead to a combined market share of 10% or more. These are horizontal relationships; or

    (*b*) any of the parties (including undertakings belonging to the same group as defined in Section 3) is engaged in business activities in a product market which is upstream or downstream of a product market or individual product group in which any other party is engaged and any of their market shares is 10% or more, regardless of whether there is or is not any existing supplier/customer relationship between the parties concerned. These are vertical relationships.

I. *Explanation of the affected relevant product markets*

    5.1. Describe each affected relevant product market and explain why the products and/or services in these markets are included (any why others are excluded) by reason of their characteristics, their prices and their intended use.

    5.2. List the individual product groups defined internally by your undertaking for marketing purposes which are covered by each relevant product market described under 5.1 above.

II. *Market data on affected markets*

For each affected relevant product market and, where different, individual product group, for each of the last three financial years:

(*a*) for the Community as a whole;

(*b*) individually for each Member State where the parties (including undertakings belonging to the same group as defined in Section 3) do business;

(*c*) and where different, for any relevant geographic market, provide the following:

5.3. an estimate of the value of the market and, where appropriate, of the volume (for example in units shipped or delivered) of the market[8]. If available, include statistics prepared by other sources to illustrate your answers. Also provide a forecast of the evolution of demand on the affected markets;

5.4. the turnover of each of the groups to which the parties belong (as defined in Section 3);

5.5. an estimate of the market share of each of the groups to which the parties belong;

5.6. an estimate of the market share (in value and where appropriate volume) of all competitors having at least 10% of the geographic market under consideration. Provide the name, address and telephone number of these undertakings;

5.7. a comparison of prices charged by the groups to which the parties belong in each of the Member States and a similar comparison of such price levels between the Community and its major trading partners (eg the United States, Japan and EFTA);

5.8. an estimate of the value (and where appropriate volume) and source of imports to the relevant geographic market;

5.9. the proportion of such imports that are derived from the groups to which the parties belong;

5.10. an estimate of the extent to which any of these imports are affected by any tariff or non-tariff barriers to trade.

III. *Market data on conglomerate aspects*

In the absence of horizontal or vertical relationships, where any of the parties (including undertakings belonging to the same group as defined in Section 3) holds a market share of 20% or more for any product market or individual product group, provide the following information:

5.11. a description of each relevant product market and explain why the products and/or services in these markets are included (and why others are excluded) by reason of their characteristics, their prices and their intended use;

5.12. a list of the individual product groups defined internally by your undertaking for marketing purposes which are covered by each relevant product market described;

5.13. an estimate of the value of the market and the market shares of each of the groups to which the parties belong for each affected relevant product market and, where different, individual product group, for the last financial year:

(a) for the Community as a whole;

(b) individually for each Member State where the groups to which the parties belong do business;

(c) and where different, for any relevant geographic market.

In each response in Section 5 the notifying party shall explain the basis of the estimates used or assumptions made.   **[1541]**

SECTION 6 – General conditions in affected markets

The following information shall be provided in relation to the affected relevant product markets and, where different, affected individual product groups:

Record of market entry

6.1.   Over the last five years (or a longer period if this is more appropriate) has there been any significant entry to these markets in the Community? If the answer is "yes", provide information on these entrants, estimating their current market shares.

6.2.   In the opinion of the notifying party are there undertakings (including those at present operating only in extra-Community markets) that could enter the Community's markets? If the answer is "yes", provide information on these potential entrants.

6.3.   In the opinion of the notifying party what is the likelihood of significant market entry over the next five years?

Factors influencing market entry

6.4.   Describe the various factors influencing entry into affected markets that exist in the present case, examining entry from both a geographical and product viewpoint. In so doing take account of the following where appropriate:

  — the total costs of entry (capital, promotion, advertising, necessary distribution systems, servicing etc) on a scale equivalent to a significant viable competitor, indicating the market share of such a competitor;

  — to what extent is entry to the markets influenced by the requirement of government authorization or standard setting in any form? Are there any legal or regulatory controls on entry to these markets?

  — to what extent is entry to the markets influenced by the availability of raw materials?

  — to what extent is entry to the markets influenced by the length of contracts between an undertaking and its suppliers and/or customers?

  — describe the importance of licensing patents, know-how and other rights in these markets.

Vertical integration

6.5.   Describe the nature and extent of vertical integration of each of the parties.

Research and development

6.6   Give an account of the importance of research and development in the ability of a firm operating on the relevant market to compete in the long term. Explain the nature of the research and development in affected markets carried out by the undertakings to the concentration.

In so doing take account of the following where appropriate:

— the research and development intensities[9] for these markets and the relevant research and development intensities for the parties concerned;
— the course of technological development for these markets over an appropriate time period (including developments in products and/or services, production processes, distribution systems etc);
— the major innovations that have been made in these markets over this time period and the undertakings responsible for these innovations;
— the cycle of innovation in these markets and where the parties are in this cycle of innovation;
— describe the extent to which the parties concerned are licensees or licensors of patents, know-how and other rights in affected markets.

Distribution and service systems

6.7. Explain the distribution channels and service networks that exist on the affected markets. In so doing take account of the following where appropriate:

— the distribution systems prevailing on the market and their importance. To what extent is distribution performed by third parties and/or undertakings belonging to the same group as the parties as disclosed in Section 3?
— the service networks (for example maintenance and repair) prevailing and their importance in these markets. To what extent are such services performed by third parties and/or undertakings belonging to the same group as the parties as disclosed in Section 3?

Competitive environment

6.8. Give details (names, addresses and contacts) of the five largest suppliers to the notifying parties and their individual share of the purchases of the notifying parties.

6.9. Give details (names, addresses and contacts) of the five largest customers of the notifying parties and their individual share of the sales of the notifying parties.

6.10. Explain the structure of supply and demand in affected markets. This explanation should allow the Commission further to appreciate the competitive environment in which the parties carry out their business. In so doing take account of the following where appropriate:

— the phases of the markets in terms of, for example, take-off, expansion, maturity and decline. In the opinion of the notifying party, where are the affected products in these phases?
— the structure of supply. Give details of the various identifiable categories that comprise the supply side and describe the "typical supplier" of each category;
— the structure of demand. Give details of the various identifiable groups that comprise the demand side and describe the "typical customer" of each group;
— whether public authorities, government agencies or state enterprises or similar bodies are important participants as sources of supply or demand. In any instance where this is so give details of this participation;
— the total Community-wide capacity for the last three years. Over the period what proportion of this capacity is accounted for by the parties and what have been their rates of capacity utilization?

Cooperative agreements

6.11. To what extent do cooperative agreements (horizontal and/or vertical) exist in the affected markets?

6.12. Give details of the most important cooperative agreements engaged in by the parties in the affected markets, such as licensing agreements, research and development, specialization, distribution, long-term supply and exchange of information agreements.

Trade associations

6.13. List the names and addresses of the principal trade associations in the affected markets.

Worldwide context

6.14. Describe the worldwide context of the proposed concentration indicating the position of the parties in this market.

SECTION 7 – General matters

7.1. Describe how the proposed concentration is likely to affect the interests of intermediate and ultimate consumers, and the development of technical progress.

7.2. In the event that the Commission finds that the operation notified does not constitute a concentration within the meaning of Article 3 of Regulation (EEC) No 4064/89, do you request that it be treated as an application within the meaning of Article 2 or a notification within the meaning of Article 4 of Regulation No 17, as an application within the meaning of Article 12 or a notification within the meaning of Article 14 of Regulation (EEC) No 1017/68, as an application within the meaning of Article 12 of Regulation (EEC) No 4056/86 or as an application within the meaning of Article 3(2) or Article 5 of Regulation (EEC) No 3975/87?   **[1542]**

SECTION 8 – Declaration

The notification must conclude with the following declaration which is to be signed by or on behalf of all the notifying parties.

The undersigned declare that the information given in this notification is correct to the best of their knowledge and belief, that all estimates are identified as such and are their best estimates of the underlying facts and that all the opinions expressed are sincere.

They are aware of the provisions of Article 14(1)(*b*) of Regulation (EEC) No 4064/89.

Place and date:

Signatures: **[1543]**

NOTES

1 A concentration is defined in Article 3.

2 This includes the target company in the case of a contested bid, in which case the details should be completed as far as is possible.

3 See Article 5 for the definition of turnover and note the special provisions for credit, insurance, other financial institutions and joint undertakings.

For insurance undertakings, credit and other financial institutions, Community-residents and residents of a Member State are defined as natural or legal persons having their residence in a Member State, thereby following the respective national legislation. The corporate customer is to be treated as resident in the country in which it is legally incorporated. For the calculation of turnover, the notifying party should also refer to the examples: guidance note I for credit and other financial institutions; guidance note II for insurance undertakings; guidance note III for joint undertakings.

4 See guidance note IV for the calculation of turnover in one Member State with respect to Community-wide turnover.

5 "Profits before tax" shall comprise profit on ordinary activities before tax on profit.

6 Employees shall comprise all persons employed in the enterprise who have a contract of employment and receive remuneration.

7 See Article 3(3) to (5).

8 The value and volume of a market should reflect output less exports plus imports for the geographic market under consideration.

9 Research and development intensity is defined as research and development expenditure as a proportion of turnover.

GUIDANCE NOTE I*

CALCULATION OF TURNOVER FOR CREDIT AND OTHER FINANCIAL INSTITUTIONS

(Article 5(3)(*a*))

For the calculation of turnover for credit institutions and other financial institutions, we give the following example (proposed merger between bank A and bank B)

I. Consolidated balance sheets

(in million ecu)

Assets	Bank A	Bank B
Loans and advances to credit institutions	20 000	1 000
—to credit institutions within the Community:	(10 000)	(500)
—to credit institutions within one (and the same) Member State X:	(5 000)	(500)
Loans and advances to customers	60 000	4 000
—to Community residents:	(30 000)	(2 000)
—to residents of one (and the same) Member State X:	(15 000)	(500)
Other assets:	20 000	1 000
Total assets:	100 000	6 000

II. Calculation of turnover

In place of turnover, the following figures shall be used:

	Bank A	Bank B
1. *Aggregate worldwide turnover* is replaced by one-tenth of total assets: the total sum of which is more than ECU 5 000 million.	10 000	600

2. *Community-wide turnover*

is replaced by, for each bank, one-tenth of total assets multiplied by the ratio between loans and advances to credit institutions and customers within the Community; to the total sum of loans and advances to credit institutions and customers.

	Bank A	Bank B
This is calculated as follows: one-tenth of total assets:	10 000	600
which is multiplied for each bank by the ratio between: loans and advances to credit institutions and customers	10 000	500
within the Community	30 000	2 000
	40 000	2 500

and
the total sum of loans and advances to credit institutions	20 000	1 000
and customers	60 000	4 000
	80 000	5 000

For
Bank A: 10 000 multiplied by (40 000:80 000) = 5 000
Bank B: 600 multiplied by (2 000: 5 000) =   300
which exceeds ECU 250 million for each of the banks.

3. *Total turnover within one (and the same) Member State X*

	Bank A	*Bank B*
is replaced by one-tenth of total assets:	10 000	600

which is multiplied for each bank by the ratio between loans and advances to credit institutions and customers within one and the same Member State X; to the total sum of loans and advances to credit institutions and customers.

	Bank A	*Bank B*
This is calculated as follows:		
loans and advances to credit institutions and customers	5 000	500
with one (and the same) Member State X	15 000	500
	20 000	1 000

and
the total sum of loans and advances to credit institutions and customers	80 000	5 000

For
Bank A: 10 000 multiplied by (20 000:80 000) = 2 500
Bank B: 600 multiplied by (1 000: 5 000) =   120

Result:
50% of bank A's and 40% of bank B's Community-wide turnover are achieved in one (and the same) Member State X.

III. Conclusion

Since

    (*a*) the aggregate worldwide turnover of bank A plus bank B is more than ECU 5 000 million;

    (*b*) the Community-wide turnover of each of the banks is more than ECU 250 million; and

    (*c*) each of the banks achieve less than two-thirds of its Community-wide turnover in one (and the same) Member State,

the proposed merger would fall under the scope of the Regulation.   **[1544]**

NOTE
  * In the following guidance notes, the terms "institution" or "undertaking" are used subject to the exact delimitation in each case.

GUIDANCE NOTE II

CALCULATION OF TURNOVER FOR INSURANCE UNDERTAKINGS
(Article 5(3)(*a*))

For the calculation of turnover for insurance undertakings, we give the following example (proposed concentration between insurances A and B):

I. Consolidated profit and loss account

(in million ecu)

Income	Insurance A	Insurance B
Gross premiums written	5 000	300
—gross premiums received from Community residents:	(4 500)	(300)
—gross premiums received from residents of one (and the same) Member State X:	(3 600)	(270)
Other income:	500	50
Total income:	5 500	350

II. Calculation of turnover

1. *Aggregate worldwide turnover*
is replaced by the value of gross premiums written worldwide, the sum of which is ECU 5 300 million.
2. *Community-wide turnover*
is replaced, for each insurance undertaking, by the value of gross premiums written with Community residents. For each of the insurance undertakings, this amount is more than ECU 250 million.
3. *Turnover within one (and the same) Member State X*
is replaced, for insurance undertaking, by the value of gross premiums written with residents of one (and the same) Member State X.
For insurance A, it achieves 80% of its gross premiums written with Community residents within Member State X, whereas for insurance B, it achieves 90% of its gross premiums written with Community residents in that Member State X.

III. Conclusion

Since

    (a) the aggregate worldwide turnover of insurances A and B, as replaced by the value of gros premiums written worldwide, is more than ECU 5 000 million;

    (b) for each of the insurance undertakings, the value of gross premiums written with Community residents is more than ECU 250 million; but

    (c) each of the insurance undertakings achieves more than two-thirds of its gross premiums written with Community residents in one (and the same) Member State X,

the proposed concentration would not fall under the scope of the Regulation. **[1545]**

GUIDANCE NOTE III

CALCULATION OF TURNOVER FOR JOINT UNDERTAKINGS

A. *CREATION OF A JOINT UNDERTAKING* (Article 3(2))

In a case where two (or more) undertakings create a joint undertaking that constitutes a concentration, turnover is calculated for the undertakings concerned.

B. *EXISTENCE OF A JOINT UNDERTAKING* (Article 5 (5))

For the calculation of turnover in case of the existence of a joint undertaking C between two undertakings A and B concerned in a concentration, we give the following example:

I. Profit and loss accounts

(in million ecu)

Turnover	Undertaking A	Undertaking B
Sales revenues worldwide	10 000	2 000
— Community	(8 000)	(1 500)
— Member State Y	(4 000)	(900)

(in million ecu)

Turnover	Joint undertaking C	
Sales revenues worldwide	100	
— with undertaking A		(20)
— with undertaking B		(10)
Turnover with third undertakings	70	
— Community-wide		(60)
— in Member State Y		(50)

II. Consideration of the joint undertaking

(a) The undertaking C is jointly controlled (in the meaning of Article 3(3) and (4)) by the undertakings A and B concerned by the concentration, irrespective of any third undertaking participating in that undertaking C.

(b) The undertaking C is not consolidated by A and B in their profit and loss accounts.

(c) The turnover of C resulting from operations with A and B shall not be taken into account.

(d) The turnover of C resulting from operations with any third undertaking shall be apportioned equally amongst the undertakings A and B, irrespective of their individual shareholdings in C.

(e) Any joint undertaking existing between one of the undertakings concerned and any third undertaking shall (unless already consolidated) not be taken into account.

III. Calculation of turnover

(a) Undertaking A's aggregate worldwide turnover shall be calculated as follows: ECU 10 000 million and 50% of C's worldwide turnover with third undertakings (i.e. ECU 35 million), the sum of which is ECU 10 035 million.
Undertaking B's aggregate worldwide turnover shall be calculated as follows: ECU 2 000 million and 50% of C's worldwide turnover with third undertakings (i.e. ECU 35 million), the sum of which is ECU 2 035 million.

(*b*) The aggregate worldwide turnover of the undertakings concerned is ECU 12 070 million.

(*c*) Undertaking A achieves ECU 4 025 million with Member State Y (50% of C's turnover in this Member State taken into account), and a Community-wide turnover of ECU 8 030 million (including 50% of C's Community-wide turnover);

and undertaking B achieves ECU 925 million within Member State Y (50% of C's turnover in this Member State taken into account), and a Community-wide turnover of ECU 1 530 million (including 50% of C's Community-wide turnover).

IV. Conclusion

Since

(*a*) the aggregate worldwide turnover of undertakings A and B is more than ECU 5 000 million,

(*b*) each of the undertakings concerned by the concentration achieves more than ECU 250 million within the Community,

(*c*) each of the undertakings concerned (undertaking A 50.1% and undertaking B 60.5%) achieves less than two-thirds of its Community-wide turnover in one (and the same) Member State Y,

the proposed concentration would fall under the scope of the Regulation.   **[1546]**

GUIDANCE NOTE IV

APPLICATION OF THE TWO-THIRDS RULE
(Article 1)

For the application of the two-thirds rule for undertakings, we give the following examples (proposed concentration between undertakings A and B):

I. Consolidated profit and loss account

EXAMPLE 1

(in million ecu)

Turnover	Undertaking A	Undertaking B
Sales revenues worldwide	10 000	500
— within the Community:	(8 000)	(400)
— in Member State X:	(6 000)	(200)

EXAMPLE 2(a)

(in million ecu)

Turnover	Undertaking A	Undertaking B
Sales revenues worldwide	4 800	500
— within the Community:	(2 400)	(400)
— in Member State X:	(2 100)	(300)

EXAMPLE 2(b)
same figures as in example 2(*a*), BUT undertaking B achieves ECU 300 million in Member State Y.

II. Application of the two-thirds rule

EXAMPLE 1

1. *Community-wide turnover*
   is, for undertaking A, ECU 8 000 million and for undertaking B ECU 400 million.
2. *Turnover in one (and the same) Member State X*
   is, for undertaking A (ECU 6 000 million), 75% of its Community-wide turnover and
   is, for undertaking B (ECU 200 million), 50% of its Community-wide turnover.
3. *Conclusion*
   In this case, although undertaking A achieves more than two-thirds of its Community-wide turnover in Member State X, the proposed concentration would fall under the scope of the Regulation due to the fact that undertaking B achieves less than two-thirds of its Community-wide turnover in Member State X.

EXAMPLE 2(a)

1. *Community-wide turnover*
   of undertaking A is ECU 2 4000 million and of undertaking B, ECU 400 million.
2. *Turnover in one (and the same) Member State X*
   is, for undertaking A, ECU 2 100 million (i.e. 87.5% of its Community-wide turnover); and, for undertaking B, ECU 300 million (i.e. 75% of its Community-wide turnover).
3. *Conclusion*
   In this case, each of the undertakings concerned achieves more than two-thirds of its Community-wide turnover in one (and the same) Member State X; the proposed concentration would not fall under the scope of the Regulation.

EXAMPLE 2(b)

Conclusion

In this case, the two-thirds rule would not apply due to the fact that undertakings A and B achieve more than two-thirds of their Community-wide turnover in different Member States X and Y. Therefore, the proposed concentration would fall under the scope of the Regulation.   **[1547]**

ANNEX II

HOLIDAYS IN 1990

	B	DK	D	GR	E	F	IRL	I	L	NL	P	UK
New Year: 1. 1.	X	X	X	X	X	X	X	X	X	X	X	X
New Year: 2. 1.												X[1]
Carnival Monday: 26. 2.			X									
St. Patrick: 19. 3.							X					X[2]
Maundy Thursday: 12. 4.		X			X							
Good Friday: 13. 4.		X	X	X	X		X			X	X	X
Easter Monday: 16. 4.	X	X	X	X		X	X	X	X	X		X
Anniversary of the Liberation: 25. 4.								X				
Liberty Day: 25. 4.											X	
The Queen's Birthday: 30. 4.										X		
Labour Day: 1. 5.	X		X	X	X	X		X	X		X	
May holiday: 7. 5.												X
Armistice 1945: 8. 5.						X						
General Prayer Day: 11. 5.		X										
Ascension: 24. 5.	X	X	X			X			X	X		
Spring holiday: 28. 5.												X
Whit Monday: 4. 6.	X	X	X	X		X			X	X		
Constitution Day: 5. 6.		X										
Corpus Christi: 14. 6.			X[3]								X	
Orangeman's Day: 12. 7.												X[2]
St. James: 24. 7.					X							
First Monday in August: 6. 8.							X					X[1]
Friedensfest: 8. 8.			X[4]									
Assumption: 15. 8.	X		X[5]	X	X	X		X	X		X	
Summer Bank holiday: 27. 8.												X
Republic Day: 5.10.											X	
National holiday: 12.10.					X							
Bank holiday: 29.10.							X					
All Saints: 1.11.	X		X[6]		X	X		X	X		X	
All Souls: 2.11.	X											
Dynasty Day: 15.11.	X											
Repentance Day: 21.11.			X									
Constitution Day: 6.12.					X							
Christmas: 25.12.	X	X	X	X	X	X	X	X	X	X	X	X
Second day of Christmas: 26.12.	X	X	X	X			X	X	X	X		X

NOTES
1 Scotland.
2 Northern Ireland.
3 Baden-Württemberg, Bayern, Hessen, Nordrhein-Westfalen, Rheinland-Pfalz, Saarland.
4 City of Augsburg (Bayern).
5 Saarland and Bayern, Bayern, public holiday in administrative districts with a predominantly Catholic population.
6 Baden-Württemberg, Bayern, Nordrhein-Westfalen, Rheinland-Pfalz, Saarland.

COMMISSION

New Year's Day	1 January
Day after New Year's Day	2 January
Holy/Maundy Thursday	12 April
Good Friday	13 April
Easter Monday	16 April
Labour Day	1 May
Anniversary of the declaration by Robert Schuman	9 May
Ascension Day	24 May
Day after Ascension Day	25 May
Whit Monday	4 June
Assumption Day	15 August
All Saints Day	1 November
All Souls Day	2 November
Christmas	24 December
	25 December
	26 December
	27 December
	28 December
	29 December
	30 December
	31 December

[1548]

COMMISSION NOTICE

regarding restrictions ancillary to concentrations

I. INTRODUCTION

1. Council Regulation (EEC) No 4064/89 of 21 December 1989 on the control of concentrations between undertakings ("the Regulation") states in its 25th recital that its application is not excluded where the undertakings concerned accept restrictions which are directly related and necessary to the implementation of the concentration, hereinafter referred to as "ancillary restrictions". In the scheme of the Regulation, such restrictions are to be assessed together with the concentration itself. It follows, as confirmed by Article 8(2), second subparagraph, last sentence of the Regulation, that a decision declaring the concentration compatible also covers these restrictions. In this situation, under the provisions of Article 22, paragraphs 1 and 2, the Regulation is solely applicable, to the exclusion of Regulation No 17 as well as Regulations (EEC) No 1017/68, (EEC) No 4056/86 and (EEC) No 3975/87. This avoids parallel Commission proceedings, one concerned with the assessment of the concentration under the Regulation, and the other

aimed at the application of Articles 85 and 86 to the restrictions which are ancillary to the concentration.

2. In this notice, the Commission sets out to indicate the interpretation it gives to the notion of "restrictions directly related and necessary to the implementation of the concentration". Under the Regulation such restrictions must be assessed in relation to the concentration, whatever their treatment might be under Articles 85 and 86 if they were to be considered in isolation or in a different economic context. The Commission endeavours, within the limits set by the Regulation, to take the greatest account of business practice and of the conditions necessary for the implementation of concentrations.

This notice is without prejudice to the interpretation which may be given by the Court of Justice of the European Communities. **[1549]**

II. PRINCIPLES OF EVALUATION

3. The "restrictions" meant are those agreed on between the parties to the concentration which limit their own freedom of action in the market. They do not include restrictions to the detriment of third parties. If such restrictions are the inevitable consequence of the concentration itself, they must be assessed together with it under the provisions of Article 2 of the Regulation. If, on the contrary, such restrictive effects on third parties are separable from the concentration they may, if appropriate, be the subject of an assessment of compatibility with Articles 85 and 86 of the EEC Treaty.

4. For restrictions to be considered "directly related" they must be ancillary to the implementation of the concentration, that is to say subordinate in importance to the main object of the concentration. They cannot be substantial restrictions wholly different in nature from those which result from the concentration itself. Neither are they contractual arrangements which are among the elements constituting the concentration, such as those establishing economic unity between previously independent parties, or organizing joint control by two undertakings of another undertaking. As integral parts of the concentration, the latter arrangements constitute the very subject matter of the evaluation to be carried out under the Regulation.

Also excluded, for concentrations which are carried out in stages, are the contractual arrangements relating to the stages before the establishment of control within the meaning of Article 3, paragraphs 1 and 3 of the Regulation. For these, Articles 85 and 86 remain applicable as long as the conditions set out in Article 3 are not fulfilled.

The notion of directly related restrictions likewise excludes from the application of the Regulation additional restrictions agreed at the same time which have no direct link with the concentration. It is not enough that the additional restrictions exist in the same context as the concentration.

5. The restrictions must likewise be "necessary to the implementation of the concentration", which means that in their absence the concentration could not be implemented or could only be implemented under more uncertain conditions, at substantially higher cost, over an appreciably longer period or with considerably less probability of success. This must be judged on an objective basis.

6. The question of whether a restriction meets these conditions cannot be answered in general terms. In particular as concerns the necessity of the restriction, it is proper not only to take account of its nature, but equally to ensure, in applying the rule of proportionality, that its duration and subject matter, and geographic field of application, do not exceed what the implementation of the concentration reasonably requires. If alternatives are available for the attainment of the legitimate aim pursued, the undertakings must choose the one which is objectively the least restrictive of competition.

These principles will be followed and further developed by the Commission's practice in individual cases. However, it is already possible, on the basis of past experience, to indicate the attitude the Commission will take to those restrictions most commonly encountered in relation to the transfer of undertakings or parts of undertakings, the division of undertakings or of their assets following a joint acquisition of control, or the creation of concentrative joint ventures. **[1550]**

III. EVALUATION OF COMMON ANCILLARY RESTRICTIONS IN CASES OF THE TRANSFER OF AN UNDERTAKING

A. Non-competition clauses

1. Among the ancillary restrictions which meet the criteria set out in the Regulation are contractual prohibitions on competition which are imposed on the vendor in the context of a concentration achieved by the transfer of an undertaking or part of an undertaking. Such prohibitions guarantee the transfer to the acquirer of the full value of the assets transferred, which in general include both physical assets and intangible assets such as the goodwill which the vendor has accumulated or the know-how he has developed. These are not only directly related to the concentration, but are also necessary for its implementation because, in their absence, there would be reasonable grounds to expect that the sale of the undertaking or part of an undertaking could not be accomplished satisfactorily. In order to take over fully the value of the assets transferred, the acquirer must be able to benefit from some protection against competitive acts of the vendor in order to gain the loyalty of customers and to assimilate and exploit the know-how. Such protection cannot generally be considered necessary when *de facto* the transfer is limited to physical assets (such as land, buildings or machinery) or to exclusive industrial and commerical property rights (the holders of which could immediately take action against infringements by the transferor of such rights).

However, such a prohibition on competition is justified by the legitimate objective sought of implementing the concentration only when its duration, its geographical field of application, its subject matter and the persons subject to it do not exceed what is reasonably necessary to that end.

2. With regard to the acceptable duration of a prohibition on competition, a period of five years has been recognized as appropriate when the transfer of the undertaking includes the goodwill and know-how, and a period of two years when it includes only the goodwill. However, these are not absolute rules; they do not preclude a prohibition of longer duration in particular circumstances, where for example the parties can demonstrate that customer loyalty will persist for a period longer than two years or that the economic life cycle of the products concerned is longer than five years and should be taken into account.

3. The geographic scope of the non-competition clause must be limited to the area where the vendor had established the products or services before the transfer. It does not appear objectively necessary that the acquirer be protected from competition by the vendor in territories which the vendor had not previously penetrated.

4. In the same manner, the non-competition clause must be limited to products and services which form the economic activity of the undertaking transferred. In particular, in the case of a partial transfer of assets, it does not appear that the acquirer needs to be protected from the competition of the vendor in the products or services which constitute the activities which the vendor retains after the transfer.

5. The vendor may bind himself, his subsidiaries and commercial agents. However, an obligation to impose similar restrictions on others would not qualify as an ancillary restriction. This applies in particular to clauses which would restrict the scope for resellers or users to import or export.

6. Any protection of the vendor is not normally an ancillary restriction and is therefore to be examined under Articles 85 and 86 of the EEC Treaty. **[1551]**

B. Licences of industrial and commercial property rights and of know-how

1. The implementation of a transfer of an undertaking or part of an undertaking generally includes the transfer to the acquirer, with a view to the full exploitation of the assets transferred, of rights to industrial or commercial property or know-how. However, the vendor may remain the owner of the rights in order to exploit them for activities other than those transferred. In these cases, the usual means for ensuring that the acquirer will have the full use of the assets transferred is to conclude licensing agreements in his favour.

2. Simple or exclusive licences of patents, similar rights or existing know-how can be accepted as necessary for the completion of the transaction, and likewise agreements to grant such licences. They may be limited to certain fields of use, to the extent that they correspond to the activities of the undertaking transferred. Normally it will not be necessary for such licences to include territorial limitations on manufacture which reflect the territory of the activity transferred. Licences may be granted for the whole duration of the patent or similar rights or the duration of the normal economic life of the know-how. As such licences are economically equivalent to a partial transfer of rights, they need not be limited in time.

3. Restrictions in licence agreements, going beyond what is provided above, fall outside the scope of the Regulation. They must be assessed on their merits according to Article 85(1) and (3). Accordingly, where they fulfil the conditions required, they may benefit from the block exemptions provided for by Regulation (EEC) No 2349/84 on patent licences or Regulation (EEC) No 559/89 on know-how licences.

4. The same principles are to be applied by analogy in the case of licences of trade-marks, business names or similar rights. There may be situations where the vendor wishes to remain the owner of such rights in relation to activities retained, but the acquirer needs the rights to use them to market the products constituting the object of activity of the undertaking or part of an undertaking transferred.

In such circumstances, the conclusion of agreements for the purpose of avoiding confusion between trademarks may be necessary. **[1552]**

C. Purchase and supply agreements

1. In many cases, the transfer of an undertaking or part of an undertaking can entail the disruption of traditional lines of internal procurement and supply resulting from the previous integration of activities within the economic entity of the vendor. To make possible the break up of the economic unity of the vendor and the partial transfer of the assets to the acquirer under reasonable conditions, it is often necessary to maintain, at least for a transitional period, similar links between the vendor and the acquirer. This objective is normally attained by the conclusion of purchase and supply agreements between the vendor and the acquirer of the undertaking or part of an undertaking. Taking account of the particular situation resulting from the break up of the economic unity of the vendor such obligations, which may lead to restrictions of competition, can be recognized as ancillary. They may be in favour of the vendor as well as the acquirer.

2. The legitimate aim of such obligations may be to ensure the continuity of supply to one or other of the parties of products necessary to the activities retained (for the vendor) or taken over (for the acquirer). Thus, there are grounds for recognizing, for a transitional period, the need for supply obligations aimed at guaranteeing the quantities previously supplied within the vendor's integrated business or enabling their adjustment in accordance with the development of the market.

Their aim may also be to provide continuity of outlets for one or the other of the parties, as they were previously assured within the single economic entity. For the same reason, obligations providing for fixed quantities, possibly with a variation clause, may be recognized as necessary.

3. However, there does not appear to be a general justification for exclusive purchase or supply obligations. Save in exceptional circumstances, for example resulting from the absence of a market or the specificity of products, such exclusivity is not objectively necessary to permit the implementation of a concentration in the form of a transfer of an undertaking or part of an undertaking.

In any event, in accordance with the principle of proportionality, the undertakings concerned are bound to consider whether there are no alternative means to the ends pursued, such as agreements for fixed quantities, which are less restrictive than exclusivity.

4. As for the duration of procurement and supply obligations, this must be limited to a period necessary for the replacement of the relationship of dependency by autonomy in market. The duration of such a period must be objectively justified.   **[1553]**

IV. EVALUATION OF ANCILLARY RESTRICTIONS IN THE CASE OF A JOINT ACQUISITION

1. As set out in the 24th recital, the Regulation is applicable when two or more undertakings agree to acquire jointly the control of one or more other undertakings, in particular by means of a public tender offer, where the object or effect is the division among themselves of the undertakings or their assets. This is a concentration implemented in two successive stages; the common strategy is limited to the acquisition of control. For the transaction to be concentrative, the joint acquisition must be followed by a clear separation of the undertakings or assets concerned.

2. For this purpose, an agreement by the joint acquirers of an undertaking to abstain from making separate competing offers for the same undertaking, or otherwise acquiring control, may be considered an ancillary restriction.

3. Restrictions limited to putting the division into effect are to be considered directly related and necessary to the implementation of the concentration. This will apply to arrangements made between the parties for the joint acquisition of control in order to divide among themselves the production facilities or the distribution networks together with the existing trademarks of the undertaking acquired in common. The implementation of this division may not in any circumstances lead to the coordination of the future behaviour of the acquiring undertakings.

4. To the extent that such a division involves the break up of a pre-existing economic entity, arrangements that make the break up possible under reasonable conditions must be considered ancillary. In this regard, the principles explained above in relation to purchase and supply arrangements over a transitional period in cases of transfer of undertakings should be applied by analogy.   **[1554]**

V. EVALUATION OF ANCILLARY RESTRICTIONS IN CASES OF CONCENTRATIVE JOINT
    VENTURES WITHIN THE MEANING OF ARTICLE 3(2) SUBPARAGRAPH 2 OF THE
    REGULATION

This evaluation must take account of the characteristics peculiar to concentrative joint ventures, the constituent elements of which are the creation of an autonomous economic entity exercising on a long-term basis all the functions of an undertaking, and the absence of coordination of competitive behaviour between the parent undertakings and between them and the joint venture. This condition implies in principle the withdrawal of the parent undertakings from the market assigned to the joint venture and, therefore, their disappearance as actual or potential competitors of the new entity. **[1555]**

A. Non-competition obligations

To the extent that a prohibition on the parent undertakings competing with the joint venture aims at expressing the reality of the lasting withdrawal of the parents from the market assigned to the joint venture, it will be recognized as an integral part of the concentration. **[1556]**

B. Licences for industrial and commercial property rights and know-how

The creation of a new autonomous economic entity usually involves the transfer of the technology necessary for carrying on the activities assigned to it, in the form of a transfer of rights and related know-how. Where the parent undertakings intend nonetheless to retain the property rights, particularly with the aim of exploitation in other fields of use, the transfer of technology to the joint venture may be accomplished by means of licences. Suh licences may be exclusive, without having to be limited in duration or territory, for they serve only as a substitute for the transfer of property rights. They must therefore be considered necessary to the implementation of the concentration. **[1557]**

C. Purchase and supply obligations

If the parent undertakings remain present in a market upstream or downstream of that of the joint venture, any purchase and supply agreements are to be examined in accordance with the principles applicable in the case of the transfer of an undertaking. **[1558]**

COMMISSION NOTICE

regarding the concentrative and cooperative operations under Council Regulation (EEC) No 4064/89 of 21 December 1989 on the control of concentrations between undertakings

I. INTRODUCTION

1. Article 3(1) of Council Regulation (EEC) No 4064/89 ("the Regulation") contains an exhaustive list of the factual circumstances which fall to be considered as concentrations. In accordance with the 23rd recital, this term refers only to operations that lead to a lasting change in the structures of the participating undertakings.

By contrast, the Regulation does not deal with operations whose object or effect is the coordination of the competitive activities of undertakings that remain independent of each other. Situations of this kind are cooperative in character. Accordingly, they fall to be assessed under the provisions of Regulations (EEC) No 17, (EEC) No 1017/68, No 4056/86 or No 3975/87. The same applies to an operation which includes both a lasting structural change and the coordination of competitive behaviour, where the two are inseparable.

If the structural change can be separated from the coordination of competitive behaviour, the former will be assessed under the Regulation and the latter, to the extent that it does not amount to an ancillary restriction within the meaning of Article 8(2), second subparagraph of the Regulation, falls to be assessed under the other Regulations implementing Articles 85 and 86 of the EEC Treaty.

2. The purpose of this notice is to define as clearly as possible, in the interests of legal certainty, concentrative and cooperative situations. This is particularly important in the case of joint ventures. The same issue is raised in other forms of association between undertakings such as unilateral or reciprocal shareholdings and common directorships, and of certain operations involving more than one undertaking, such as unilateral or reciprocal transfers of undertakings or parts of undertakings, or joint acquisition of an undertaking with a view to its division. In all these cases, operations may not fall within the scope of the Regulation, where their object or effect is the coordination of the competitive behaviour of the undertakings concerned.

3. This notice sets out the main considerations which will determine the Commission's view to what extent the aforesaid operations are or are not caught by the Regulation. It is not concerned with the assessment of these operations, whether under the Regulation or any other applicable provisions, in particular Articles 85 and 86 of the EEC Treaty.

4. The principles set out in this notice will be followed and further developed by the Commission's practice in individual cases. As the operations considered are generally of a complex nature, this notice cannot provide a definitive answer to all conceivable situations.

5. This notice is without prejudice to the interpretation which may be given by the Court of Justice or the Court of First Instance of the European Communities.

[1559]

II. Joint Ventures within Article 3 of the Regulation

6. The Regulation in Article 3(2) refers to two types of joint venture: those which have as their object or effect the coordination of the competitive behaviour of undertakings which remain independent (referred to as "cooperative joint ventures") and those which perform on a lasting basis all the functions of an autonomous economic entity and which do not give rise to coordination amongst themselves or between them and the joint venture (referred to as "concentrative joint ventures"). The latter are concentrations and as such are caught by the Regulation. Cooperative joint ventures fall to be considered under other regulations implementing Articles 85 and 86.   **[1560]**

A. Concept of joint venture

7. To define the term "joint venture" within the meaning of Article 3(2), it is necessary to refer to the provision of Article 3(1)(*b*) of the Regulation. According to the latter, JVs are undertakings that are jointly controlled by several other undertakings, the parent companies. In the context of the Regulation the term JV thus implies several characteristics:

[1561]

1. *Undertaking*

8. A JV must be an undertaking. That is to be understood as an organized assembly of human and material resources, intended to pursue a defined economic purpose on a long-term basis.   **[1562]**

2. *Control by other undertakings*

9. In the context of the Regulation, a JV is controlled by other undertakings. Pursuant to Article 3(3) of the Regulation control means the possibility of exercising, directly or indirectly, a decisive influence on the activities of the JV; whether this condition is fulfilled

can only be decided by reference to all the legal and factual circumstances of the individual case.

10. Control of a JV can be based on legal, contractual or other means, within which the following elements are especially important:

- ownership or rights to the use of all or some of the JV's assets,
- influence over the composition, voting or decisions of the managing or supervisory bodies of the JV,
- voting rights in the managing or supervisory bodies of the JV,
- contracts concerning the running of the JV's business. **[1563]**

3. *Joint control*

11. A JV under the Regulation is jointly controlled. Joint control exists where the parent companies must agree on decisions concerning the JV's activities, either because of the rights acquired in the JV or because of contracts or other means establishing the joint control. Joint control may be provided for in the JV's constitution (memorandum or articles of association). However, it need not be present from the beginning, but may also be established later, in particular by taking a share in an existing undertaking.

12. There is no joint control where one of the parent companies can decide alone on the JV's commercial activities. This is generally the case where one company owns more than half the capital or assets of the undertaking, has the right to appoint more than half of the managing or supervisory bodies, controls more than half of the votes in one of those bodies, or has the sole right to manage the undertaking's business. Where the other parent companies either have completely passive minority holdings or, while able to have a certain influence on the undertaking, cannot, individually or together, determine its behaviour, a relative majority of the capital or of the votes or seats on the decision-making bodies will suffice to control the undertaking.

13. In many cases, the joint control of the JV is based on agreements or concertation between the parent companies. Thus, a majority shareholder in a JV often extends to one or more minority shareholders a contractual right to take part in the control of the JV. If two undertakings each hold half of a JV, even if there is no agreement between them, both parent companies will be obliged permanently to cooperate so as to avoid reciprocal blocking votes on decisions affecting the JV's activity. The same applies to JV's with three or more parents, where each of them has a right of veto. A JV can even be controlled by a considerable number of undertakings that can together muster a majority of the capital or the seats or votes on the JV's decision-making bodies. However, in such cases, joint control can be presumed only if the factual and legal circumstances — especially a convergence of economic interests — support the notion of a deliberate common policy of the parent companies in relation to the JV.

14. If one undertaking's holding in another is, by its nature or its extent, insufficient to establish sole control, and if there is no joint control together with third parties, then there is no concentration within the meaning of Article 3(1)(*b*) of the Regulation. Articles 85 or 86 of the EEC Treaty may however be applicable on the basis of Regulation (EEC) No 17 or other implementing Regulations (see III.1). **[1564]**

B. Concentrative joint ventures

15. For a joint venture to be regarded as concentrative it must fulfil all the conditions of Article 3(2), subparagraph 2, which lays down a positive condition and a negative condition. **[1565]**

1. Positive condition: joint venture performing on a lasting basis all the functions of an autonomous economic entity

16. To fulfil this condition, a JV must first of all act as an independent supplier and buyer on the market. JVs that take over from their parents only specific partial responsibilities are not to be considered as concentrations where they are merely auxiliaries to the commercial activities of the parent companies. This is the case where the JV supplies its products or services exclusively to its parent companies, or when it meets its own needs wholly from them. The independent market presence can even be insufficient if the JV achieves the majority of its supplies or sales with third parties, but remains substantially dependent on its parents for the maintenance and development of its business.

17. A JV exists on a lasting basis if it is intended and able to carry on its activity for an unlimited, or at least for a long, time. If this is not the case there is generally no long-term change in the structures of the parent companies. More important than the agreed duration are the human and material resources of the JV. They must be of such nature and quantity as to ensure the JV's existence and independence in the long term. This is generally the case where the parent companies invest substantial financial resources in the JV, transfer an existing undertaking or business to it, or give it substantial technical or commercial know-how, so that after an initial starting-up period it can support itself by its own means.

18. A decisive question for assessing the autonomous character of the JV is whether it is in a position to exercise its own commercial policy. This requires, within the limits of its company objects, that it plans, decides and acts independently. In particular, it must be free to determine its competitive behaviour autonomously and according to its own economic interests. If the JV depends for its business on facilities that remain economically integrated with the parent companies' businesses, that weakens the case for the autonomous nature of the JV.

19. The JV's economic independence will not be contested merely because the parent companies reserve to themselves the right to take certain decisions that are important for the development of the JV, namely those concerning alterations of the objects of the company, increases or reductions of capital, or the application of profits. However, if the commercial policy of the JV remains in the hands of the parent undertakings, the JV may take on the aspect of an instrument of the parent undertakings' market interests. Such a situation will usually exist where the JV operates in the market of the parent undertakings. It may also exist where the JV operates in markets neighbouring, or upstream or downstream of, those of the parent undertakings.   **[1566]**

2. Negative condition: absence of coordination of competitive behaviour

20. Subject to what is said in the first paragraph of this notice a JV can only be considered to be concentrative within the meaning of Article 3(2), subparagraph 2 of the Regulation, if it does not have as its object or effect the coordination of the competitive behaviour of undertakings that remain independent of each other. There must not be such coordination either between the parent companies themselves or between any or all of them on the one hand and the JV on the other hand. Such coordination must not be an object of the establishment or operation of the JV, nor may it be the consequence thereof. The JV is not to be regarded as concentrative if as a result of the agreement to set up the JV or as a result of its existence or activities it is reasonably foreseeable that the competitive behaviour of a parent or of the JV on the relevant market will be influenced. Conversely, there will normally be no foreseeable coordination when all the parent companies withdraw entirely and permanently from the JV's market and do not operate on markets neighbouring those of the JV's.

21. Not every cooperation between parent companies with regard to the JV prevents a JV from being considered concentrative. Even concentrative JVs generally represent a means for parent companies to pursue common or mutually complementary interests. The establishment and joint control of a JV is, therefore, inconceivable without an understanding between the parent companies as concerns the pursuit of those interests. Irrespective of its legal form, such a concordance of interests is an essential feature of a JV.

22. As regards the relations of the parent undertakings, or any one of them, with the JV, the risk of coordination within the meaning of Article 3(2) will not normally arise where the parent undertakings are not active in the markets of the JV or in neighbouring or upstream or downstream markets. In other cases, the risk of coordination will be relatively small where the parents limit the influence they exercise to the JV's strategic decisions, such as those concerning the future direction of investment, and when they express their financial, rather than their market-oriented, interests. The membership of the JV's managing and supervisory bodies is also important. Common membership of the JV's and the parent companies' decision-making bodies may be an obstacle to the development of the JV's autonomous commercial policy.

23. The dividing line between the concordance of interests in a JV and a coordination of competitive behaviour that is incompatible with the notion of concentration cannot be laid down for all conceivable kinds of case. The decisive factor is not the legal form of the relationship between the parent companies and between them and the JV. The direct or indirect, actual or potential effects of the establishment and operation of the JV on market relationships, have determinant importance.

24. In assessing the likelihood of coordination of competitive behaviour, it is useful to consider some of the different situations which often occur:

   (a) JVs that take over pre-existing activities of the parent companies;
   (b) JVs that undertake new activities on behalf of the parent companies;
   (c) JVs that enter the parent companies' markets;
   (d) JVs that enter upstream, downstream or neighbouring markets.   **[1567]**

(a) JVs that take over pre-existing activities of the parent companies

25. There is normally no risk of coordination where the parent companies transfer the whole of certain business activities to the JV and withdraw permanently from the JV's market so that they remain neither actual nor potential competitors — of each other nor of the JV. In this context, the notion of potential competition is to be interpreted realistically, according to the Commission's established practice[1]. A presumption of a competitive relationship requires not only that one or more of the parent companies could re-enter the JV's market at any time: this must be a realistic option and represent a commercially reasonable course in the light of all objective circumstances.

26. Where the parent companies transfer their entire business activities to the JV, and thereafter act only as holding companies, this amounts to complete merger from the economic viewpoint.

27. Where the JV takes on only some of the activities that the parent companies formerly carried on independently, this can also amount to a concentration. In this case, the establishment and operation of the JV must not lead to a coordination of the parent companies' competitive behaviour in relation to other activities which they retain. Coordination of competitive behaviour between any or all of the parent companies and the JV must also be excluded. Such coordination is likely where there are close economic links between the areas of activity of the JV on one side and of the parent companies on the other. This applies to upstream, downstream and neighbouring product markets.

28. The withdrawal of the parent companies need not be simultaneous with the establishment of the JV. It is possible — so far as necessary — to allow the parent companies a short transitional period to overcome any starting-up problems of the JV, especially bottlenecks in production or supplies. This period should not normally exceed one year.

29. It is even possible for the establishment of a JV to represent a concentration situation where the parent companies remain permanently active on the JV's product or service market. In this case, however, the parent companies' geographic market must be different from that of the JV. Moreover, the markets in question must be so widely separated, or must present structures so different, that, taking account of the nature of the goods or services concerned and of the cost of (first or renewed) entry by either into the other's market, competitive interaction may be excluded.

30. If the parent companies' markets and the JV's are in different parts of the Community or neighbouring third countries, there is a degree of probability that either, if it has the necessary human and material resources, could extend its activities from the one market to the other. Where the territories are adjacent or very close to each other, this may even be assumed to be the case. At least in this last case, the actual allocation of markets gives reason to suppose that it follows from a coordination of competitive behaviour between parent companies and the JV.   **[1568]**

NOTE
1. See the Thirteenth Report (1983) on Competition Policy, point 55.

(b) JVs that undertake new activities on behalf of the parent companies

31. There is normally no risk of coordination in the sense described above where the JV operates on a product or service market which the parent companies individually have not entered and will not enter in the foreseeable future, because they lack the organizational, technical or financial means or because, in the light of all the objective circumstances, such a move would not represent a commercially reasonable course. An individual market entry will also be unlikely where, after establishing the JV, the parent companies no longer have the means to make new investments in the same field, or where an additional individual operation on the JV's market would not make commercial sense. In both cases there is no competitive relationship between the parent companies and the JV. Consequently, there is no possibility of coordination of their competitive behaviour. However, this assessment is only true if the JV's market is neither upstream nor downsteam of, nor neighbouring, that of the parent companies.

32. The establishment of a JV to operate in the same product or service market as the parent companies but in another geographic market involves the risk of coordination if there is competitive interaction between the parent companies' geographic market and that of the JV.   **[1569]**

(c) JVs that enter the parent companies' market

33. Where the parent companies, or one of them, remain active on the JV's market or remain potential competitors of the JV, a coordination of competitive behaviour between the parent companies or between them and the JV must be presumed. So long as this presumption is not rebutted, the Commission will take it that the establishment of the JV does not fall under Article 3(2), subparagraph 2 of the Regulation.   **[1570]**

(d) JVs that operate in upstream, downstream or neighbouring markets

34. If the JV is operating in a market that is upstream or downstream of that of the parent companies, then, in general, coordination of purchasing or, as the case may be,

sales policy between the parent companies is likely where they are competitors on the upstream or downstream market.

35. If the parent companies are not competitors, it remains to be examined whether there is a real risk of coordination of competitive behaviour between the JV and any of the parents. This will normally be the case where the JV's sales or purchases are made in substantial measure with the parent companies.

36. It is not possible to lay down general principles regarding the likelihood of coordination of competitive behaviour in cases where the parent companies and the JV are active in neighbouring markets. The outcome will depend in particular on whether the JV's and the parent companies' products are technically or economically linked, whether they are both components of another product or are otherwise mutually complementary, and whether the parent companies could realistically enter the JV's market. If there are no concrete opportunities for competitive interaction of this kind, the Commission will treat the JV as concentrative. **[1571]**

III. OTHER LINKS BETWEEN UNDERTAKINGS

1. Minority shareholdings

37. The taking of a minority shareholding in an undertaking can be considered a concentration within the meaning of Article 3(1)(*b*) of the Regulation if the new shareholder acquires the possibility of exercising a decisive influence on the undertaking's activity. If the acquisition of a minority shareholding brings about a situation in which there is an undertaking jointly controlled by two or more others, the principles described above in relation to JVs apply.

38. As long as the threshold of individual or joint decisive influence has not been reached, the Regulation is not in any event applicable. Accordingly, the assessment under competition law will be made only in relation to the criteria laid down in Articles 85 and 86 of the EEC Treaty and on the basis of the usual procedural rules for restrictive practices and abuses of dominant position.

39. There may likewise be a risk of coordination where an undertaking acquires a majority or minority interest in another in which a competitor already has a minority interest. If so, this acquisition will be assessed under Articles 85 and 86 of the EEC Treaty. **[1572]**

2. Cross-shareholding

40. In order to bring their autonomous and hitherto separate undertakings or groups closer together, company owners often cause them to exchange shareholdings in each other. Such reciprocal influences can serve to establish or to secure industrial or commercial cooperation between the undertakings or groups. But they may also result in establishing a "single economic entity". In the first case, the coordination of competitive behaviour between independent undertakings is predominant; in the second, the result may be a concentration. Consequently, reciprocal directorships and cross-shareholdings can only be evaluated in relation to their foreseeable effects in each case.

41. The Commission considers that two or more undertakings can also combine without setting up a parent-subsidiary relationship and without either losing its legal personality. Article 3(1) of the Regulation refers not only to legal, but also to economic concentrations. The condition for the recognition of a concentration in the form of a combined group is, however, that the undertakings or groups concerned are not only subject to a permanent, single economic management, but are also amalgamated into a genuine economic unit,

characterised internally by profit and loss compensation between the various undertakings within the groups and externally by joint liability. [1573]

3. Representation on controlling bodies of other undertakings

42. Common membership of managing or supervisory boards of various undertakings is to be assessed in accordance with the same principles as cross-shareholdings.

43. The representation of one undertaking on the decision-making bodies of another is usually the consequence of an existing shareholding. It reinforces the influence of the investing undertaking over the activities of the undertaking in which it holds a share, because it affords it the opportunity of obtaining information on the activities of a competitor or of taking an active part in its commercial decisions.

44. Thus, common membership of the respective boards may be the vehicle for the coordination of the competitive behaviour of the undertakings concerned, or for a concentration of undertakings within the meaning of the Regulation. This will depend on the circumstances of the individual case, among which the economic link between the shareholding and the personal connection must always be examined. This is equally true of unilateral and reciprocal relationships between undertakings.

45. Personal connections not accompanied by shareholdings are to be judged according to the same criteria as shareholding relationships between undertakings. A majority of seats on the managing or supervisory board of an undertaking will normally imply control of the latter; a minority of seats at least a degree of influence over its commercial policy, which may further entail a coordination of behaviour. Reciprocal connections justify a presumption that the undertakings concerned are coordinating their business conduct. A very wide communality of membership of the respective decision-making bodies — that is, up to half of the members or more — may be an indication of a concentration. [1574]

4. Transfers of undertakings or parts of undertakings

46. A transfer of assets or shares falls within the definition of a concentration, according to Article 3(1)(*b*) of the Regulation, if it results in the acquirer gaining control of all or of part of one or more undertakings. However, the situation is different where the transfer conferring control over part of an undertaking is linked with an agreement to coordinate the competitive behaviour of the undertakings concerned, or where it necessarily leads to or is accompanied by coordination of the business conduct of undertakings which remain independent. Cases of this kind are not covered by the Regulation: they must be examined according to Articles 85 and 86 of the EEC Treaty and under the appropriate implementing Regulations.

47. The practical application of this rule requires a distinction between unilateral and reciprocal arrangements. A unilateral acquisition of assets or shares strongly suggests that the Regulation is applicable. The contrary needs to be demonstrated by clear evidence of the likelihood of coordination of the parties' competitive behaviour. A reciprocal acquisition of assets or shares, by contrast, will usually follow from an agreement between the undertakings concerned as to their investments, production or sales, and thus serves to coordinate their competitive behaviour. A concentration situation does not exist where a reciprocal transfer of assets or shares forms part of a specialization or restructuring agreement or other type of coordination. Coordination presupposes in any event that the parties remain at least potential competitors after the exchange has taken place. [1575]

5. Joint acquisition of an undertaking with a view to its division

48. Where several undertakings jointly acquire another, the principles for the assessment of a joint venture are applicable, provided that within the acquisition operation, the period of joint control goes beyond the very short term. In this case the Regulation may or may not be applicable, depending on the concentrative or cooperative nature of the JV. If, by contrast, the sole object of the agreement is to divide up the assets of the undertaking and this agreement is put into effect immediately after the acquisition, then, in accordance with the 24th recital, the Regulation applies. **[1576–1999]**

APPENDIX

EC PROPOSALS

PROPOSAL FOR A REGULATION (EEC) OF THE COUNCIL

(Submitted by the Commission on 8 September 1989)

amending 3975/87 laying down the procedure for the application of the rules on competition to undertakings in the air transport sector

THE COUNCIL OF THE EUROPEAN COMMUNITIES

Having regard to the Treaty establishing the European Community, and in particular to Article 87 thereof,

Having regard to the proposal from the Commission,

Having regard to the opinion of the European Parliament.

Whereas Council Regulation (EEC) No 3975/87 formed part of a package of interrelated measures adopted by the Council as a first step towards completing the internal market in transport; whereas its scope was accordingly limited to international transport between Community airports;

Whereas, therefore, the Commission has no means at present of investigating directly cases of suspected infringement of Articles 85 and 86 of the Treaty in respect of air transport within a Member State or between a Community airport and an airport in a third country and lacks such powers to take decisions or impose penalties as are necessary for it to bring to an end infringements established by it;

Whereas practices which affect competition in these areas of air transport may affect trade between Member States; whereas it is therefore desirable that rules should be laid down under which the Commission, acting in close and constant liaison with the competent authorities of the Member States, may take the requisite measures for the application of Articles 85 and 86 of the Treaty to these areas of air transport;

Whereas there is a need to produce a secure and clear legal framework for international air transport between the Community and third countries and for domestic air transport within a Member State, while ensuring a coherent application of the competition rules; whereas therefore the scope of Regulation (EEC) No 3975/87 should be extended to those other areas of air transport;

Whereas, in view of the characteristics of international air transport between the Community and third countries, account should be taken of the fact that the provisions of Regulation (EEC) No 3975/87 may in some cases result in conflicts with the laws and rules of third countries or with provisions contained in international agreements between Member States and third countries applicable to services on the route or routes concerned; whereas provision should be made for appropriate action to be taken with a view to resolving such conflicts in accordance with Community interests and with Community obligations under international law,

HAS ADOPTED THIS REGULATION

Article 1

Regulation (EEC) No 3975/87 is amended as follows:

1. The second paragraph of Article 1 shall be deleted.
2. The following new Article shall be inserted:

> **"Article 18a — Conflicts of international law**
>
> 1. Where the application of this Regulation in a particular case is liable to lead to a conflict with provisions laid down by law, regulation or administrative action of a third country, the Commission shall, at the earliest opportunity, hold with the competent authorities of the country concerned consultations aimed at resolving the conflict. The Commission shall inform the Advisory Committee referred to in Article 8 of the outcome of these consultations.
>
> 2. Where the Commission finds that the application of this Regulation in a particular case is liable to lead to a conflict with the provisions of an international agreement between a Member State and a third country, it shall, after consulting the Advisory Committee referred to in Article 8, notify the Member State concerned of this finding. The Member State shall, within three months of the

receipt of such notification, inform the Commission of the measures it intends to take with a view to resolving the conflict.

3. Where agreements with third countries need to be negotiated by the Community, the Council, acting on a proposal by the Commission, shall authorise the Commission to open necessary negotiations." **[2000]**

Article 2

This Regulation shall enter into force on the day following its publication in the Official Journal of the European Communities. **[2001]**

This Regulation shall be binding in its entirety and directly applicable in all Member States.

PROPOSAL FOR A REGULATION (EEC) OF THE COUNCIL
(Submitted by the Commission on 8 September 1989)

on the application of Article 85(3) of the Treaty to certain categories of agreements and concerted practices in the air transport sector

THE COUNCIL OF THE EUROPEAN COMMUNITIES,
 Having regard to the Treaty establishing the European Economic Community, and in particular to Article 87 thereof,
 Having regard to the proposal from the Commission,
 Having regard to the opinion of the European Parliament,
 Whereas Council Regulation (EEC) No 3975/87, as amended by Regulation (EEC) No   lays down the procedure for the application of the rules on competition to undertakings in the air transport sector;
 Whereas Article 85(1) of the Treaty may be declared inapplicable to certain categories of agreements, decisions and concerted practices which fulfil the conditions contained in Article 85(3);
 Whereas common provisions for the application of Article 85(3) should be adopted by way of Regulation pursuant to Article 87(2)(b), such a Regulation must lay down detailed rules for the application of Article 85(3), taking into account the need to ensure effective supervision, on the one hand, and to simplify administration to the greatest possible extent, on the other; whereas, according to Article 87(2)(d), such a Regulation is required to define the respective functions of the Commission and of the Court of Justice;
 Whereas international air transport between the Community and third countries is at present governed by a network of international and bilateral agreements between Member States and third countries; whereas many of these agreements encourage or allow air carriers to cooperate in matters of commercial importance; whereas in observing these agreements air carriers should not infringe the Treaty's competition rules, which apply fully to all air transport activities within the scope of Community law; whereas the application of the competition rules must nevertheless take account of obligations under existing international treaties and of the desirability of settling international disputes by consultation and negotiation; whereas air carriers should be enabled to conduct their business within a framework of reasonable certainty in relation to competition rules;
 Whereas the Commission should therefore be enabled to declare by way of Regulation that the provisions of Article 85(1) do not apply to certain categories of agreements between undertakings, decisions by associations of undertakings and concerted practices;
 Whereas it is desirable, in particular, that block exemptions be granted for certain categories of agreements, decisions and concerted practices; whereas the Commission, in close liaison with the Member States, should be able to define precisely the scope of these exemptions and the conditions attached to them;
 Whereas there can be no exemption if the conditions set out in Article 85(3) are not satisfied; whereas the Commission should therefore have power to take the appropriate measures where an

agreement proves to have effects incompatible with Article 85(3); whereas the Commission should consequently be able first to address recommendations to the parties and then to take decisions; Whereas this Regulation does not prejudge the application of Article 90 of the Treaty,

HAS ADOPTED THIS REGULATION

Article 1

This Regulation shall apply to international air transport between the Community and third countries.   **[2002]**

Article 2

1. Without prejudice to the application of Regulation (EEC) No 3975/87 and in accordance with Article 85(3) of the Treaty, the Commission may be Regulation declare that Article 85(1) shall not apply to certain categories of agreements between undertakings, decisions of associations of undertakings and concerted practices on international air routes between the Community and one or more third countries.

2. The Commission may, in particular adopt such Regulations in respect of agreements, decisions or concerted practices which have as their object any one of the following:

– joint planning and coordination of the capacity on scheduled air services,
– sharing of revenue from scheduled air services,
– joint preparation of proposals on tariffs, fares, rates and conditions for the carriage of passengers, baggage and cargo on scheduled services,
– slot allocation at airports and airport scheduling.

3. Without prejudice to paragraph 2, such Commission Regulations shall define the categories of agreements, decisions or concerted practices to which they apply and shall specify in particular:

(*a*) the restrictions or clauses which may, or may not, appear in the agreements, decisions and concerted practices;
(*b*) the clauses which must be contained in the agreements, decisions and concerted practices, or any other conditions which must be satisfied;
(*c*) the routes to which they apply.   **[2003]**

Article 3

1. A Regulation pursuant to Article 2 shall apply for a specified period.

2. It may be repealed or amended where circumstances have changed with respect to any factor which was basic to its adoption; in such case, a period shall be fixed for modification of the agreements and concerted practices to which the earlier Regulation applies.

Article 4

Regulations adopted pursuant to Article 2 may include a provision that they apply with retroactive effect to agreements, decisions and concerted practices which were in existence at the date of the entry into force of such Regulations.   **[2004]**

Article 5

Before adopting a Regulation, the Commission shall publish a draft thereof and invite all persons and organisations concerned to submit their comments within such reasonable time limit, being not less than one month, as the Commission shall fix.   **[2005]**

Article 6

The Commission shall consult the Advisory Committee on Agreements and Dominant Positions in Air Transport established by Article 8(3) of Regulation (EEC) No 3975/87 before publishing any such draft Regulation and before adopting any such Regulation.

[2006]

Article 7

1. Subject to paragraph 4, where the persons concerned are in breach of a condition or obligation which attaches to an exemption granted by a Regulation adopted pursuant to Article 2, the Commission may, in order to put an end to such a breach:

— address recommendations to the persons concerned, and
— in the event of failure by such persons to observe those recommendations, and depending on the gravity of the breach concerned, adopt a decision that either prohibits them from carrying out, or requires them to perform, specific acts or, while withdrawing the benefit of the block exemption which they enjoyed, grants them an individual exemption in accordance with Article 4(2) of Regulation (EEC) No 3975/87 or withdraws the benefit of the block exemption which they enjoyed.

2. Subject to paragraph 4, where the Commission, either on its own initiative or at the request of a Member State or of natural or legal persons claiming a legitimate interest, finds that in any particular case an agreement, decision or concerted practice to which a block exemption granted by a Regulation adopted pursuant to Article 2(2) applies, nevertheless has effects which are incompatible with Article 85(3) or are prohibited by Article 86, it may withdraw the benefit of the block exemption from those agreements, decisions or concerted practices and take, pursuant to Article 13 of Regulation (EEC) No 3975/87, all appropriate measures for the purpose of bringing these infringements to an end.

3. Before taking any decision under paragraph 2, the Commission may address recommendations for termination of the infringement to the persons concerned.

4. To the extent that the situation referred to in paragraph 1 or in paragraph 2 results from provisions laid down by law, regulation or administrative action of a third country or from the provisions of an air service agreement between a Member State and a third country, the Commission shall, before withdrawing the benefit of the block exemption, take appropriate action as specified in Article 18a of Regulation (EEC) No 3975/87.

[2007]

Article 8

This Regulation shall enter into force on the day following its publication in the Official Journal of the European Communities.

[2008]

This Regulation shall be binding in its entirety and directly applicable in all Member States.

PROPOSAL FOR A REGULATION (EEC) OF THE COUNCIL
(Submitted by the Commission on 8 September 1989)

amending Regulation (EEC) 3976/87 on the application of Article 85(3) of the Treaty to certain categories of agreements and concerted practices in the air transport sector

THE COUNCIL OF THE EUROPEAN COMMUNITIES
Having regard to the Treaty establishing the European Economic Community, and in particular to Article 87 thereof,
Having regard to the proposal from the Commission,
Having regard to the opinion of the European Parliament,
Whereas the scope of Council Regulation (EEC) No 3976/87 was limited to international air transport between Community airports;
Whereas the Commission should be enabled to grant similar block exemptions for agreements between undertakings, decisions by associations of undertakings and concerted practices related to air transport within a Member State,
HAS ADOPTED THIS REGULATION

Article 1

The word "international" is deleted in Article 1 of Regulation (EEC) No 3976/87.
[2009]

Article 2

This Regulation shall enter into force on the day following its publication in the Official Journal of the European Communities.   **[2010]**

This Regulation shall be binding in its entirety and directly applicable in all Member States.

PROPOSAL FOR A REGULATION (EEC) OF THE COUNCIL
(Submitted by the Commission on 21 December 1989

on the application of Article 85(3) of the Treaty to certain categories of agreements, decisions and concerted practices in the insurance sector

THE COUNCIL OF THE EUROPEAN COMMUNITIES,
Having regard to the Treaty establishing the European Economic Community, and in particular Article 87 thereof,
Having regard to the proposal from the Commission,
Having regard to the opinion of the European Parliament,
Having regard to the opinion of the Economic and Social Committee,
Whereas Article 85(1) of the Treaty may, in accordance with Article 85(3), be declared inapplicable to categories of agreements, decisions and concerted practices which fulfil the conditions contained in Article 85(3);
Whereas the provisions for the implementation of Article 85(3) must be adopted by way of regulation pursuant to Article 87;
Whereas cooperation between undertakings in the insurance sector is, to a certain extent, desirable to ensure the proper functioning of this sector and may at the same time promote the interest of consumers;

Whereas exemptions under Article 85(3) cannot themselves affect Community and national provisions promoting the interests of consumers in this sector;

Whereas agreements, decisions and concerted practices serving such aims may, in so far as they fall within the prohibition contained in Article 85(1), be exempted therefrom under certain conditions; whereas this applies particularly to agreements, decisions and concerted practices relating to common risk premium tariffs based purely on collectively ascertained statistics or loss experience, standard policy conditions, common coverage of certain types of risks, the settlement of claims, the testing and acceptance of security devices, and registers of and information on aggravated risks;

Whereas in view of the large number of notifications submitted pursuant to Council Regulation No 17, as last amended by the Act of Accession of Spain and Portugal, it is desirable that in order to facilitate the task of the Commission it should be enabled to declare by way of regulation that the provisions of Article 85(1) do not apply to certain categories of agreements, decisions and concerted practices;

Whereas it should be laid down under which conditions the Commission, in close and constant liaison with the competent authorities of the Member State, may exercise such powers;

Whereas, pursuant to Article 6 of Regulation No 17, the Commission may provide that a decision taken in accordance with Article 85(3) of the Treaty shall apply with retroactive effect; whereas it is desirable that the Commission be empowered to issue regulations whose provisions are to the like effect;

Whereas, pursuant to Article 7 of Regulation No 17, agreements, decisions and concerted practices may, by decision of the Commission, be exempted from prohibition, in particular if they are modified in such manner that Article 85(3) applies to them; whereas it is desirable that the Commission be enabled to grant by regulation like exemption to such agreements, decisions and concerted practices if they are modified in such manner as to fall within a category defined in an exempting regulation;

Whereas the possibility cannot be excluded that, in a specific case, the conditions set out in Article 85(3) may not be fulfilled; whereas the Commission must have power to regulate such a case pursuant to Regulation No 17 by way of decision having effect for the future,

HAS ADOPTED THIS REGULATION

Article 1

1. Without prejudice to the application of Regulation No 17 the Commission may, by regulation and in accordance with Article 85(3) of the Treaty, declare that Article 85(1) shall not apply to categories of agreements between undertakings, decisions of associations of undertakings and concerted practices in the insurance sector which have as their object cooperation with respect to:

  (*a*) common risk premium tariffs based purely on collectively ascertained statistics or loss experience;
  (*b*) common standard policy condition;
  (*c*) the common coverage of certain types of risks;
  (*d*) the settlement of claims;
  (*e*) the testing and acceptance of security devices;
  (*f*) registers of and information on aggravated risks.

2. Such regulation shall define the categories of agreements, decisions and concerted practices to which it applies and shall specify in particular:

  (*a*) the restrictions or clauses which may, or may not, appear in the agreements, decisions and concerted practices;
  (*b*) the clauses which must be contained in the agreements, decisions and concerted practices or the other conditions which must be satisfied.   **[2011]**

Article 2

Any Regulation pursuant to Article 1 shall be made for a specified period.

It may be repealed or amended where circumstances have changed with respect to any of the facts which were basic to its being made; in such case, a period shall be fixed for modification of the agreements, decisions and concerted practices to which the earlier regulation applies. [2012]

Article 3

A regulation pursuant to Article 1 may provide that it shall apply with retroactive effect to agreements, decisions and concerted practices to which, at the date of entry into force of that regulation, a decision issued with retroactive effect pursuant to Article 6 of Regulation No 17 would have applied. [2013]

Article 4

1. A regulation pursuant to Article 1 may provide that the prohibition contained in Article 85(1) shall not apply, for such period as shall be fixed by that regulation, to agreements, decisions and concerted practices already in existence on 13 March 1962 which do not satisfy the conditions of Article 85(3), where:

— within six months from the entry into force of the regulation, they are so modified as to satisfy the said conditions in accordance with the provisions of the Regulation, and

— the modifications are brought to the notice of the Commission within the time limit fixed by the regulation.

The provisions of the first subparagraph shall apply in the same way to agreements, decisions and concerted practices existing at the date of accession of new Member States to which Article 85(1) applies by virtue of accession and which do not satisfy the conditions of Article 85(3).

2. Paragraph 1 shall apply to agreements, decisions and concerted practices which had to be notified before 1 February 1963, in accordance with Article 5 of Regulation No 17, only where they have been so notified before that date.

As regards agreements, decisions and concerted practices existing at the date of accession of new Member States to which Article 85(1) applies by virtue of accession and which had to be notified within six months from the date of accession in accordance with Articles 5 and 25 of Regulation No 17, paragraph 1 shall not apply unless they have been so notified within this period.

3. The benefit of the provisions laid down pursuant to paragraph 1 may not be claimed in actions pending at the date of entry into force of a regulation adopted pursuant to Article 1; neither may it be relied on as grounds for claims for damages against third parties. [2014]

Article 5

Before making a regulation, the Commission shall publish a draft thereof to enable all persons and organisations concerned to submit their comments within such time limit, being not less than one month, as the Commission shall fix. [2015]

Article 6

1. The Commission shall consult the Advisory Commitee on Restrictive Practices and Monopolies:

(*a*) before publishing a draft regulation:
(*b*) before adopting a regulation.

2. Except where otherwise provided by this Regulation, paragraphs 5 and 6 of Article

10 of Regulation No 17, relating to consultation with the Advisory Committee, shall apply; joint meetings with the Commission shall however take place not earlier than one month after dispatch of the notice convening them. **[2016]**

Article 7

Where the Commission, either on its own initiative or at the request of a Member State or of natural or legal persons claiming a legitimate interest, finds that in any particular case agreements, decisions and concerted practices to which a regulation made pursuant to Article 1 of this Regulation applies have nevertheless certain effects which are incompatible with the conditions laid down in Article 85(3), it may withdraw the benefit of application of that regulation and take a decision in accordance with Articles 6 and 8 of Regulation No 17, without any notification pursuant to Article 4(1) of Regulation No 17 being required. **[2017]**

This Regulation shall be binding in its entirety and directly applicable in all Member States.

PROPOSAL FOR A REGULATION (EEC) OF THE COUNCIL
(Presented by the Commission on 18 June 1990)

on the application of Article 85(3) of the Treaty to certain categories of agreements, decisions and concerted practices between shipping companies

THE COUNCIL OF THE EUROPEAN COMMUNITIES,
  Having regard to the Treaty establishing the European Economic Community, and in particular Article 87 thereof,
  Having regard to the proposal from the Commission,
  Having regard to the opinion of the European Parliament,
  Having regard to the opinion of the Economic and Social Committee,
  Whereas Article 85(1) of the Treaty may in accordance with Article 85(3) be declared inapplicable to categories of agreements, decisions and concerted practices which fulfil the conditions contained in Article 85(3);
  Whereas the provisions for the application of Article 85(3) should be adopted by way of Regulation pursuant to Article 87; whereas, according to Article 87(2)(*b*), such a Regulation must lay down detailed rules for the application of Article 85(3), taking into account the need to ensure effective supervision, on the one hand, and to simplify administration to the greatest possible extent on the other; whereas, according to Article 87(2)(*d*), such a Regulation is required to define the respective functions of the Commission and of the Court of Justice;
  Whereas liner shipping is a capital intensive industry; whereas containerization has increased pressures for cooperation and rationalisation; whereas the Community shipping industry needs to attain the necessary economies of scale in order to compete successfully on the world liner shipping market;
  Whereas joint service agreements between liner shipping companies with the aim of rationalising their operations by means of technical, operational and/or commercial arrangements (described in shipping circles as consortia) can help to provide the necessary means for improving the productivity of liner shipping services and promoting technical and economic progress;
  Whereas users of the shipping services offered by consortia can obtain a share of the benefits resulting from the improvements in productivity and service, by means of, inter alia, regularity, cost reductions derived from higher levels of capacity utilization, better service quality stemming from improved vessels and equipment, and efficient door-to-door transport;
  Whereas most consortia deal with multi-modal transport operations which fall partly within the scope of Council Regulation (EEC) No 4056/86 and partly under Council Regulation (EEC)

No 1017/68 and, insofar as containers are concerned, partly under Regulation No 17/62 of the Council;

Whereas the Commission should be enabled to declare by way of regulation that the provisions of Article 85(1) do not apply to certain categories of consortia agreements, decisions and concerted practices, in order to make it easier for undertakings to cooperate in ways which are economically desirable and without adverse effect from the point of view of competition policy;

Whereas the Commission, in close and constant liaison with the competent authorities of the Member States, should be able to define precisely the scope of these exemptions and the conditions attached to them;

Whereas consortia in liner shipping are a specialized and complex type of joint venture; whereas there is a great variety of different consortia agreements operating in different circumstances; whereas the scope, parties, activities or terms of consortia are frequently altered; whereas the Commission should therefore be given the responsibility of defining from time to time the consortia to which the group exemption should apply;

Whereas, in order to ensure that all the conditions of Article 85(3) are met it would be necessary to attach to the block exemption conditions to ensure in particular that a fair share of the benefits would be passed on to shippers and that competition is not eliminated;

Whereas under Article 11(4) of Council Regulation (EEC) No 4056/86, Article 11(4) of Council Regulation (EEC) No 1017/68, and Article 6 of Regulation No 17 of the Council, the Commission may provide that a decision taken in accordance with Article 85(3) of the Treaty shall apply wth retroactive effect; whereas it is desirable that the Commission be empowered to adopt, by regulation, provisions to the like effect;

Whereas notification of agreements, decisions and concerted practices falling within the scope of this regulation shall not be made compulsory, being primarily the responsibility of undertakings to see to it that they conform to the rules on competition, and in particular to the conditions laid down by regulation concerning liner shipping consortia;

Whereas there can be no exemption if the conditions set out in Article 85(3) are not satisfied; whereas the Commission should therefore have power to take the appropriate measures where an agreement proves to have effects incompatible with Article 85(3); whereas the Commission should consequently be able first to address recommendations to the parties and then to take decisions;

HAS ADOPTED THIS REGULATION

Article 1

1. Without prejudice to the applications of Regulation (EEC) No 4056/86, Regulation (EEC) No 1017/68 and Regulation No 17, the Commission may, by regulation and in accordance with Article 85(3) of the Treaty, declare that Article 85(1) shall not apply to categories of agreements between undertakings, decisions of associations of undertakings and concerted practices that have as their object to promote or establish cooperation in the joint operation of maritime transport services or of combined maritime and land transport services.

2. Such regulation shall define the categories of agreements, decisions and concerted practices to which it applies and shall specify the conditions and obligations under which, pursuant to Article 85(3) of the Treaty, they shall be considered exempted from the application of Article 85(1) of the Treaty. [2018]

Article 2

1. The Regulation pursuant to Article 1 shall be made for a specified period.

2. It may be repealed or amended where circumstances have changed with respect to any of the facts which were basic to its being made. [2019]

Article 3

The regulation adopted pursuant to Article 1 may include a provision that it applies with retroactive effect to agreements, decisions and concerted practices which were in existence at the date of entry into force of such regulation, provided they comply with the conditions established therein. **[2020]**

Article 4

Before adopting the regulation, the Commission shall publish a draft thereof to enable all persons and organizations concerned to submit their comments within such reasonable time limit, being not less than one month, as the Commission shall fix. **[2021]**

Article 5

1. Before publishing the draft regulation and before adopting the regulation the Commission shall consult:

   (a) The Advisory Committee on Agreements and Dominant Position in Maritime Transport established by Article 15(3) of Regulation (EEC) No 4056/86;
   (b) the Advisory Committee on Restrictive Practices and Monopolies in the Transport Industry established by Article 16(3) of Regulation (EEC) No 1017/68;
   (c) the Advisory Committee on Restrictive Practices and Monopolies established by Article 10(3) of Regulation 17.

2. Paragraphs 5 and 6 of said provisions, relating to consultation with the Advisory Committees, shall apply, it being understood that joint meetings with the Commission shall take place not earlier than one month after dispatch of the notice convening them. **[2022]**

Article 6

1. Where the persons concerned are in breach of a condition or obligation which attaches to an exemption granted by the Regulation adopted pursuant to Article 1, the Commission may, in order to put an end to such a breach:

   — address recommendations to the persons concerned, and
   — in the event of failure by such persons to observe those recommendations, and depending on the gravity of the breach concerned, adopt a decision that either prohibits them from carrying out, or requires them to perform, specific acts or, while withdrawing the benefit of the block exemption which they enjoyed, grants them an individual exemption in accordance with Article 11(4) of Regulation (EEC) No 4056/86, Article 11(4) of Regulation (EEC) No 1017/68 and Article 6 of Regulation No 17, as appropriate, or withdraws the benefit of the block exemption which they enjoyed.

2. Where the Commission, either on its own initiative or at the request of a Member State or of natural or legal persons claiming a legitimate interest, finds that in any particular case an agreement, decision or concerted practice to which the block exemption granted by the regulation adopted pursuant to Article 1 applies, nevertheless has effects which are incompatible with Article 85(3) or are prohibited by Article 86, it may withdraw the benefit of the block exemption from those agreements, decisions or concerted practices and take all appropriate measures for the purpose of bringing these infringements to an end, pursuant to Article 13 of Regulation (EEC) No 4056/86, Article 13 of Regulation (EEC) No 1017/68 and Article 8 of Regulation No 17, as appropriate.

3. Before taking a decision under paragraph 2, the Commission may address recommendations for termination of the infringement to the persons concerned. **[2023]**

Article 7

This Regulation shall enter into force on the day following its publication in the Official
Journal of the European Communities.   **[2024]**

This Regulation shall be binding in its entirety and directly applicable in all Member
States.

DRAFT REGULATION (EEC) OF THE COMMISSION

**on the application of Article 85(3) of the Treaty to certain categories of agreements,
decisions and concerted practices concerning joint planning and coordination of
capacity, consultations on passenger tariffs and cargo rates on scheduled air services
and slot allocation at airports**

THE COMMISSION OF THE EUROPEAN COMMUNITIES,
  Having regard to the Treaty establishing the European Economic Community,
  Having regard to Council Regulation (EEC) No 3976/87 of 14 Decemer 1987 on the application
of Article 85(3) to certain categories of agreements, decisions and concerted practices in the air
transport sector, as amended by . . ., and in particular Article 2 thereof,
  Having published a draft of this Regulation,
  Having consulted the Advisory Committee on Agreements and Dominant Positions in Air
Transport,
  Whereas:

(1) Council Regulation (EEC) No 3976/87 empowers the Commission to apply Article 85(3) of the
    Treaty by regulation to certain categories of agreements, decisions or concerted practices relating
    directly or indirectly to the provision of air transport services.
(2) Agreements, decisions or concerted practices concerning joint planning and coordination of
    capacity, consultations on tariffs and slot allocation at airports are liable to restrict competition
    and affect trade between Member States.
(3) Arrangements concerning joint planning and coordination of capacity can help ensure the main-
    tenance of services at less busy routes, and the development of onward connections thus benefitting
    air transport users. However, no air carrier should be bound by the results of such planning
    and coordination but must be free to change its planned services unilaterally. Nor must the
    planning and coordination prevent carriers deploying extra capacity. Any clauses concerning
    extra flights must not require the approval of the other parties or involve financial penalties.
    Agreements must also allow parties to withdraw from them at reasonably short notice.
(4) Consultations on passenger tariffs or cargo rates may contribute to the generalized acceptance
    of interlinable fares and rates to the benefit of air carriers as well as air transport users. However,
    consultations must not exceed the lawful purpose of facilitating interlining. Council Regulation
    . . . of . . . July 1990 . . . on fares for scheduled air services between Member States and Council
    Regulation . . . of . . . on the operation of scheduled air cargo services between Member States
    are a step towards the increase of price competition in air transport and restrict the possibility
    of innovative and competition passenger fares and cargo rates being blocked. Hence, competition
    may not be eliminated under these arrangements. Consultations on passenger tariffs and on
    cargo rates between air carriers may therefore be permitted for the present time, provided that
    the participation in such consultations is optional, that they do not lead to an agreement in
    respect of passenger tariffs or related conditions or of cargo rates, that air carriers participating
    in the consultation mechanism are in principle obliged to interline with all other participants,
    at their own tariffs for the tariff category being discussed, and that in the interests of transparency
    the Commission and the Member States concerned can send observers to them.
(5) Arrangements on slot allocation at airports and airport scheduling can improve the utilization
    of airport capacity and airspace, facilitate air traffic control and help spread out the supply
    of air transport services from the airport. However, for competition not to be eliminated, entry
    to congested airport must remain possible. In order to provide a satisfactory degree of security
    and transparency, such arrangements can only be accepted if all the air carriers concerned can

participate in the negotiations, and if the allocation is made on a non-discriminatory and transparent basis.

(6) In accordance with Article 4 of Council Regulation (EEC) No 3976/87, this Regulation should apply with retroactive effect to agreements, decisions and concerted practices in existence on the date of entry into force of this Regulation provided that they meet the conditions for exemption set out in this Regulation.

(7) Under Article 7 of Regulation (EEC) No 3976/87, this Regulation should also specify the circumstances in which the Commission may withdraw the block exemption in individual cases.

(8) No applications under Article 3 or 5 of Council Regulation (EEC) No 3975/87 need be made in respect of agreements automatically exempted by this Regulation. However, when real doubt exists, undertakings may request the Commission to declare whether their agreements comply with this Regulation.

(9) The Regulation is without prejudice to the application of Article 86 of the Treaty,
HAS ADOPTED THIS REGULATION

TITLE I – EXEMPTIONS

Article 1

Pursuant to Article 85(3) of the Treaty and subject to the provisions of this Regulation, it is hereby declared that Article 85(1) of the Treaty shall not apply to agreements between undertakings in the air transport sector, decisions by associations of such undertakings and concerted practices between such undertakings which have as their purpose one or more of the following:

– joint planning and coordination of the capacity to be provided on scheduled international air services between Community airports,
– the holding of consultations on tariffs for the carriage of passengers, with their baggage, on scheduled international air services between Community airports,
– the holding of consultations on rates for the carriage of freight on scheduled international air services between Community airports, or
– slot allocation and airport scheduling in so far as they concern international air services between airports in the Community. **[2025]**

TITLE II – SPECIAL PROVISIONS

Article 2 – Special provisions for joint planning and coordination of capacity

The exemption concerning joint planning and coordination of the capacity to be provided on scheduled air services shall apply only if:

(a) the agreements, decisions and concerted practices do not bind air carriers to the results of the planning and coordination;

(b) the planning and coordination are intended to ensure a satisfactory supply of services at less busy times of the day, during less busy periods or on less busy routes, or to establish schedules which will facilitate connections for passengers or freight between services operated by the participants;

(c) the agreements, decisions and concerted practices do not include arrangements such as to limit, directly or indirectly, the capacity to be provided by the participants or to share capacity;

(d) the agreements, decisions and concerted practices do not prevent carriers taking part in the planning and coordination from changing their planned services, both with respect to capacity and schedules, without incurring penalties and without being required to obtain the approval of the other participants;

(e) the agreements, decisions and concerted practices do not prevent carriers from withdrawing from the planning and coordination for future seasons without penalty, on giving notice of not more than three months to that effect;

(*f*) the agreements, decisions and concerted practices do not seek to influence the capacity provided or schedules adopted by carriers not participating in them.
[2026]

Article 3 – Special provisions for consultations on passenger tariffs and cargo rates

1. The exemption concerning the holding of consultations on passenger tariffs and cargo rates shall apply only if:

(*a*) the consultations are primarily intended to arrange interlining. For this purpose the participants may discuss passenger tariffs or cargo rates to be paid by air transport users directly to a participating air carrier or to its authorized agents, for carriage as passengers or for the airport-to-airport transport of freight on a scheduled service. The consultations shall not extend to the capacity for which such tariffs or rates are to be available;

(*b*) any air carrier participating in the consultations grants other air carriers authority to issue or complete transportation documents for carriage over its routes in accordance with its own tariffs or rates and with other applicable provisions, and grants other carriers authority to effect changes to its transportation documents in accordance with generally applicable procedures. This obligation shall apply only to the types of tariffs or rates and to the seasons which were the subject of the consultations, provided that an air carrier may refuse to grant this authority for objective and non-discriminatory reasons of a technical or commercial nature, in particular concerned with the creditworthiness of the air carrier to whom this authority is refused, of which that carrier must be notified in writing;

(*c*) the passenger tariffs or cargo rates which are the subject of the consultations are applied by participating air carriers without discrimination on grounds of passengers' nationality or place of residence or on grounds of origin of the freight within the Community;

(*d*) participation in the consultations is voluntary and open to any air carrier who operates or has applied to operate on the route concerned;

(*e*) the consultations are not binding on participants, that is to say, following the consultations the participants retain the right to act independently;

(*f*) the consultations do not entail agreement on agents' remuneration or other elements of the tariffs or rates discussed;

(*g*) in respect of each passenger tariff which was the subject of the consultation, each participant informs the Commission without delay of its submission to the aeronautical authorities of the Member States concerned.

2. (*a*) The Commission and the Member States concerned shall be entitled to send observers to tariff consultations, whether bilateral or multilateral. For this purpose, air carriers shall give the Member States concerned and the Commission the same notice as is given to participants, but not less than ten days' notice, of the date, venue and subject-matter of the consultations.

(*b*) Such notice shall be given:

(i) to the Member States concerned according to procedures to be established by the competent authorities of those Member States;

(ii) to the Commission according to procedures to be published from time to time in the *Official Journal of the European Communities*.

(*c*) A full report on these consultations shall be submitted to the Commission by or on behalf of the air carriers involved at the same time as it is submitted to participants, but not later than six weeks after these consultations were held.
[2027]

Article 4 — Special provisions for slot allocation and airport scheduling

1. The exemption concerning slot allocation and airport scheduling shall apply only if:

(a) the consultations on slot allocation and airport scheduling are open to all air carriers having expressed an interest in the slots which are the subject of the consultations;

(b) rules of priority are established which neither directly nor indirectly related to carrier identity or nationality take into account constraints or air traffic distribution rules laid down by competent national or international authorities and give due consideration to the needs of the travelling public and of the airport concerned. Such rules of priority may take account of rights acquired by air carriers through the use of particular slots in the previous corresponding season;

(c) the rules of priority established shall be made available on request to any interested party;

(d) the rules shall be applied without discrimination, that is to say that, subject to the rules, each carrier shall have an equal right to slots for its services;

(e) (i) if in the previous corresponding season there were no slots at an airport available for allocation during any (. . .) hour period, air carriers not using slots during that period, but having requested slots for that period during the previous corresponding season, shall have priority in the allocation of (. . .)% of newly created or vacant slots during that period to a maximum of (. . .) slots per carrier;

　　(ii) if in the previous corresponding season there were no slots at an airport available for allocation during any (. . .) hour period, and the operation of (i) has not caused the allocation to the carriers mentioned in (i) of at least (. . .) slots during that period, the air carriers holding on average more than (. . .) slot per day for two consecutive seasons will surrender as many slots as are required to enable re-allocation of at least (. . .) slot during a period to be specified, provided that a beneficiary of this re-allocation does not use the slots for services which have a lower priority under the rules applicable to that airport than any service during that period operated by the air carrier which surrendered the slot. This may be done by any objective way to decide which carrier or carriers will surrender the necessary slots. (e.g., proportionally, by lottery);

(f) air carriers participating in the consultations have access, at the latest at the time of the consultations, to:

　— lists of historical slots by air carrier and chronologically for all air carriers,
　— lists of requested slots (initial submissions) by air carriers and chronologically for all air carriers,
　— lists of allocated slots, and outstanding slot requests if different, by air carrier and chronologically for all air carriers,
　— lists of remaining slots available,
　— comparisons between requested slots and allocated slots by time interval and by carrier,
　— full details on the constraints being used in allocation,
　— if a request for slots is not accepted, the air carrier concerned shall be entitled to a statement of the reasons therefore.

2. (a) The Commission and the Member States concerned shall be entitled to send observers to consultations on slot allocation and airport scheduling held in the context of a multilateral meeting in advance of each season. For this purpose, air carriers shall give the Member States concerned and the Commission the same notice as is given to participants, but not less than ten days' notice, of the date, venue and subject-matter of consultations.

(b) such notice shall be given:

(i) to the Member States concerned according to procedures to be established by the competent authorities of those Member States;

(ii) to the Commission according to procedures to be published from time to time in the *Official Journal of the European Communities.* **[2028]**

TITLE III – MISCELLANEOUS PROVISIONS

Article 5

The Commission may withdraw the benefit of this Regulation, pursuant to Article 7 of Council Regulation (EEC) No 3976/87, where it finds in a particular case that an agreement, decision or concerted practice exempted by this Regulation nevertheless has certain effects which are incompatible with the conditions laid down by Article 85(3) or are prohibited by Article 86 of the Treaty. **[2029]**

Article 6

This Regulation shall enter into force on 1 February 1991 and expire on 31 December 1992.

It shall apply with retroactive effect to agreements, decisions and concerted practices in existence when it enters into force, from the time when the conditions of application of this Regulation were fulfilled. **[2030]**

This Regulation shall be binding in its entirety and directly applicable in all Member States.

DRAFT REGULATION (EEC) OF THE COMMISSION

on the application of Article 85(3) of the Treaty to certain categories of agreements between undertakings relating to computer reservation systems for air transport services

THE COMMISSION OF THE EUROPEAN COMMUNITIES,

Having regard to the Treaty establishing the European Economic Community,

Having regard to Council Regulation (EEC) No 3976/87 of 14 December 1987 on the application of Article 85(3) of the Treaty to certain categories of agreements and concerted practices in the air transport sector, as amended by . . ., and in particular Article 2 thereof,

Having published a draft of this Regulation,

Having consulted the Advisory Committee on Agreements and Dominant Positions in Air Transport,

Whereas:

(1) Council Regulation (EEC) No 3976/87 empowers the Commission to apply Article 85(3) of the Treaty by regulation to certain categories of agreements, decisions and concerted practices relating directly or indirectly to the provision of air transport services.

(2) Agreements for the common purchase, development and operation of computer reservation systems relating to timetabling, reservations and ticketing are liable to restrict competition and affect trade between Member States.

(3) Computer reservation systems can render useful services to air carriers, travel agents and air travellers alike by giving ready access to up-to-date and detailed information in particular about flight possibilities, fare options and seat availability. They can also be used to make reservations and in some cases to print tickets and issue boarding passes. They thus help the air traveller to exercise choice on the basis of fuller information in order to meet his travel needs in the optimal manner. However, in order for these benefits to be obtained, flight schedules and fares displays must be as complete and unbiased as possible.

(4) The CRS market is such that few individual European undertakings could on their own make the investment and achieve the economies of scale required to compete with the more advanced existing systems. Cooperation in this field should therefore be permitted. A block exemption should therefore be granted for such cooperation.

(5) In accordance with the code of conduct for computer reservation systems, cooperation should not allow the parent carriers to create undue advantages for themselves and thereby distort competition. It is therefore necessary to ensure that no discrimination exists between parent carriers and participating carriers with regard in particular to access and neutrality of display. The block exemption should be subject to conditions which will ensure that all air carriers can participate in the systems on a non-discriminatory basis as regards access, display, information loading and fees. Moreover, in order to maintain competition in an oligopolistic market, subscribers must be able to switch from one system to another at short notice and without penalty, and system vendors and air carriers must not act in ways which would restrict competition between systems.

(6) In accordance with Article 4 of Regulation (EEC) No 3976/87 this Regulation should apply with retroactive effect to agreements in existence on the date of entry into force of this Regulation provided that they meet the conditions for exemption set out in this Regulation.

(7) Under Article 7 of Regulation (EEC) No 3976/87, this Regulation should also specify the circumstances in which the Commission may withdraw the block exemption in individual cases.

(8) The agreements with are exempted automatically by this Regulation need not be notified under Council Regulation No 17. However, when real doubt exists, undertakings may request the Commission to declare whether their agreements comply with this Regulation.

(9) This Regulation is without prejudice to the application of Article 86 of the Treaty,
HAS ADOPTED THIS REGULATION

Article 1 — Exemptions

Pursuant to Article 85(3) of the Treaty and subject to the conditions set out in Articles 3 to 11 of this Regulation, it is hereby declared that Article 85(1) of the Treaty shall not apply to agreements between undertakings the purpose of which is one or more of the following:

(*a*) to purchase or develop a CRS in common; or
(*b*) to create a system vendor to market and operate the CRS; or
(*c*) to regulate the provision of distribution facilities by the system vendor or by distributors.

The exemption shall apply only to the following obligations:

(i) an obligation not to engage directly or indirectly in the development, marketing or operation of another CRS;
(ii) an obligation on the system vendor to appoint parent carriers or participating carriers as distributors in respect of all or certain subscribers in a defined area of the common market;
(iii) an obligation on the system vendor to grant a distributor exclusive rights to solicit all or certain subscribers in a defined area of the common market; or
(iv) an obligation on the system vendor not to allow distributors to sell distribution facilities provided by other system vendors. **[2031]**

Article 2 — Definitions

For the purposes of this Regulation:

—*"Computer reservation system (CRS)"* means a computerized system containing information about air carrier schedules, fares, seat availability and related services, provided by air carriers whether scheduled or not, and through which reservations can be made or tickets issued or both, to the extent that all or some of these services are made available to subscribers.

—*"Distribution facilities"* means facilities provided by a system vendor for the display of information to subscribers about air carrier schedules, fares, seat availability, for making reservations or issuing tickets or both, and for providing any other related services.

—*"Distributor"* means an undertaking which is authorized by the system vendor to provide distribution facilities to subscribers.

—*"Parent carrier"* means an air carrier which is a system vendor or which directly or indirectly, alone or jointly with others, owns or controls a system vendor.

—*"Participating carrier"* means an air carrier which has an agreement with a system vendor for the distribution of its services through a CRS. To the extent that a parent carrier uses the distribution facilities of its own CRS, it is considered a participating carrier.

—*"Subscriber"* means an undertaking other than a participating carrier, using a CRS within the Community under contract or other arrangement with a system vendor or a distributor for the sale of air transport services to members of the public.

—*"System vendor"* means any entity and its affiliates which is responsible for the operation of a CRS. [2032]

Article 3 – Access

1. A system vendor offering distribution facilities shall allow any air carrier the opportunity to participate, on an equal and non-discriminatory basis, in these facilities within the available capacity of the system concerned, subject to any technical constraints outside the control of the system vendor.

2. (*a*) A system vendor shall not:
   — attach unreasonable conditions to any contract with a participating carrier,
   — require the acceptance of supplementary conditions which, by their nature or according to commercial usage, have no connection with participation in its CRS and shall apply the same conditions for the same level of service.

   (*b*) A system vendor shall not make it a condition of participation in its CRS that a participating carrier may not at the same time be a participant in another system.

   (*c*) A participating carrier shall have the right to terminate his contract with a system vendor without penalty on giving notice which need not exceed six months, to expire no earlier than the end of the first year.

3. Loading and processing facilities provided by the system vendor shall be offered to all participating carriers without discrimination.

4. If the system vendor adds any improvement to the distribution facilities provided or the equipment used in the provision of the facilities, it shall offer these improvements to all participating carriers on the same terms and conditions, subject to current technical limitations. [2033]

Article 4 – Display

1. A system vendor shall provide a principal display and shall include therein data provided by participating carriers on schedules, fares and seats available for individual purchase in a clear and comprehensive manner and without discrimination or bias, in particular as regards the order in which information is presented.

2. A system vendor shall not intentionally or negligently display inaccurate or misleading information and, subject to Article 9(5), in particular:

   — the criteria to be used for ranking information shall not be based on any factor directly or indirectly relating to carrier identity and shall be applied on a non-discriminatory basis to all participating carriers,

—no discrimination on the basis of different airports serving the same city shall be exercised in constructing and selecting city-pairs. **[2034]**

Article 5 — Information loading

1. Participating carriers and others providing material for inclusion in a CRS shall ensure that the data submitted are comprehensive, accurate, non-misleading and transparent.

2. A system vendor shall not manipulate the material referred to in paragraph 1 in a manner that would lead to inaccurate, misleading or discriminatory information being provided.

3. A system vendor shall load and process data provided by participating carriers with equal care and timeliness, subject to the constraints of the loading method selected by individual participating carriers and to the standard formats used by the said vendor. **[2035]**

Article 6 — Fees

1. Any fee charged by a system vendor shall be non-discriminatory and reasonably related to the cost of the service provided and used, and shall, in particular, be the same for the same level of service.

2. A system vendor shall, on request, provide to interested parties details of current procedures, fees, systems facilities, editing and display criteria used. However, this provision does not oblige a system vendor to disclose proprietary information such as software programmes.

3. Any changes to fee levels, conditions or facilities offered and the basis therefore shall be communicated to all participating carriers and subscribers on a non-discriminatory basis. **[2036]**

Article 7 — Provision of information

A system vendor shall provide information, statistical or otherwise, generated by its CRS, other than that offered as an integral part of the distribution facilities, only as follows:

(a) information concerning individual bookings shall be made available on an equal basis to the air carrier or air carriers participating in the service covered by the booking;

(b) information in aggregate or anonymous form when made available on request to any air carrier shall be offered to all participating air carriers on a non-discriminatory basis;

(c) other information generated by the CRS shall be made available with the consent of the air carrier concerned and subject to any agreement between a system vendor and participating carriers;

(d) personal information concerning a consumer and generated by a travel agent shall be made available to others not involved in the transaction only with the consent of the consumer. **[2037]**

Article 8 — Reciprocity

1. The obligations of a system vendor under Articles 3 to 7 shall not apply in respect of a parent carrier of a third country to the extent that its CRS does not conform with this Regulation or does not offer Community air carriers equivalent treatment to that provided under this Regulation.

2. A system vendor or an air carrier proposing to avail itself of the provisions of paragraph 1 must notify the Commission of its intentions and the reasons therefore at least 14 days in advance of such action. In exceptional circumstances, the Commission may, at the request of the vendor or the air carrier concerned, grant a waiver from the 14-day rule.

3. Upon receipt of a notification, the Commission shall without delay determine whether discrimination within the meaning of paragraph 1 exists. If this is found to be the case, the Commission shall so inform all system vendors or the air carriers concerned in the Community as well as Member States. If discrimination within the meaning of paragraph 1 does not exist, the Commission shall so inform the system vendor or air carriers concerned. **[2038]**

Article 9 – Contracts with subscribers

1. A system vendor shall make any of the distribution facilities of a CRS available to any subscriber on a non-discriminatory basis.

2. A system vendor shall not require a subscriber to sign an exclusive contract, nor directly or indirectly prevent a subscriber from subscribing to, or using, any other system or systems.

3. A service enhancement offered to any other subscriber shall be offered by the system vendor to all subscribers on a non-discriminatory basis.

4. A system vendor shall not attach unreasonable conditions to any contract with a subscriber and, in particular, a subscriber may terminate his contract with a system vendor, without penalty, on giving notice which need not exceed three months to expire no earlier than the end of the first year.

5. A system vendor shall ensure, either through technical means or through the contract with the subscriber, that the principal display is provided for each individual transaction and that the subscriber does not manipulate material supplied by CRSs in a manner that would lead to inaccurate, misleading or discriminatory presentation of information to consumers. However, for any one transaction a subscriber may re-order data or use alternative displays to meet a preference expressed by a consumer.

6. A system vendor shall not impose any obligation on a subscriber to accept an offer of technical equipment, but may require the use of equipment compatible with its own system. **[2039]**

Article 10 – Relations with subscribers

1. A carrier shall not link the use of CRS of which it is parent or participating carrier by a subscriber with the receipt of any commission or other incentive for the sale of or issue of tickets for any of its air transport products.

2. A carrier shall not require use of CRS of which it is parent or participating carrier by a subscriber for any sale or issue of tickets for any air transport products provided either directly or indirectly by itself.

3. Paragraphs 1 and 2 shall be without prejudice to any condition which an air carrier may require of a travel agent when authorizing it to sell and issue tickets for its air transport products. **[2040]**

Article 11 – Competition between system vendors

The system vendor shall not enter into any agreement or engage in a concerted practice with other system vendors with the object or effect of partitioning the market.

[2041]

Article 12

The Commission may withdraw the benefit of this Regulation, pursuant to Article 7 of Regulation (EEC) No 3976/87, where it finds in a particular case that an agreement exempted by this Regulation nevertheless has certain effects which are incompatible with the conditions laid down by Article 85(3) or which are prohibited by Article 86 of the Treaty, and in particular where: **[2042]**

  (i) the agreement hinders the maintenance of effective competition in the market for computer reservation systems;
 (ii) the agreement has the effect of restricting competition in the air transport or travel related markets;
(iii) the system vendor directly or indirectly imposes unfair prices, fees or charges on subscribers or on participating carriers;
 (iv) the system vendor or distributor refuses to enter into a contract with a subscriber for the use of a CRS without an objective and non-discriminatory reason of a technical or commercial nature;
  (v) a parent carrier who holds a dominant position within the common market or in a substantial part of it, refuses to participate in the distribution facilities provided by a competing CRS without an objective and non-discriminatory reason of a technical or commercial nature;
 (vi) the system vendor denies participating carriers access to any facilities other than distribution facilities without an objective and non-discriminatory reason of a technical or commercial nature.

Article 13

This Regulation shall enter into force on 1 February 1991 and expire on 31 December 1992.
  It shall apply with retroactive effect to agreements which were in existence at the date of its entry into force, from the time when the conditions of application of this Regulation were fulfilled.   **[2043]**

This Regulation shall be binding in its entirety and directly applicable in all Member States.

DRAFT REGULATION (EEC) OF THE COMMISSION

on the application of Article 85(3) of the Treaty to certain categories of agreements, decisions and concerted practices concerning ground handling services

THE COMMISSION OF THE EUROPEAN COMMUNITIES,
  Having regard to the Treaty establishing the European Economic Community,
  Having regard to Council Regulation (EEC) No 3976/87 of 14 December 1987 on the application of Article 85(3) of the Treaty to certain categories of agreements and concerted practices in the air transport sector, amended by . . ., and in particular Article 2 thereof,
  Having published a draft of this Regulation,
  Having consulted the Advisory Committee on Agreements and Dominant Positions in Air Transport,
  Whereas:

(1) Council Regulation (EEC) No 3976/87 empowers the Commission to apply Article 85(3) of the Treaty by regulation to certain categories of agreements, decisions and concerted practices relating directly or indirectly to the provision of air transport services.

(2) Agreements, decisions or concerted practices concerning ground handling services provided either by air carriers or specialized enterprises, such as technical and operational ground handling, handling of passengers, mail, freight and baggage, and services for the provision of in-flight catering, are liable in certain circumstances to restrict competition and affect trade between Member States. It is appropriate, in the interests of legal certainty for the undertakings concerned, to define a category of agreements which, although not generally restrictive of competition, may benefit from an exemption in the event that, because of particular economic or legal circumstances, they sould fall within the scope of Article 85(1).

(3) Such agreements, decisions or concerted practices may produce economic benefits, in so far as they help to ensure services of a high standard provided with continuity and at reasonable cost, and both the air carriers and air transport users share in those benefits.

(4) However, it is necessary to attach conditions to the exemption of such agreements, decisions and concerted practices to ensure that they do not contain restrictions that are not indispensable for the optimal provision of the services, and that they do not lead to the elimination of competition to provide the services.

(5) The exemption granted by the Regulation must therefore be subject to the condition that the agreements do not oblige air carriers to obtain the services exclusively from a particular supplier, that the supply of the services is not tied to the conclusion of contracts for other goods or services, that each airline is free to choose from the range of services offered by a particular supplier those which best meet its needs, that the rates charged are reasonable for the services actually provided and that air carriers are free to withdraw from the agreements without penalty upon simple notice of not more than three months to that effect.

(6) In accordance with Article 4 of Council Regulation (EEC) No 3976/87, this Regulation should apply with retroactive effect to agreements, decisions and concerted practices in existence on the date of entry into force of this Regulation provided that they meet the conditions for exemption set out in this Regulation.

(7) Under Article 7 of Regulation (EEC) No 3976/87, this Regulation should also specify the circumstances in which the Commission may withdraw the block exemption in individual cases.

(8) Agreements, decisions and concerted practices that are exempted automatically by this Regulation need not be notified under Council Regulation No 17. However, when real doubt exists, undertakings may request the Commission to declare whether their arrangements comply with this Regulation.

(9) This Regulation is without prejudice to the application of Articles 86 and 90, in particular in situations where there is no competition for the provision of certain ground handling services at an airport,

HAS ADOPTED THIS REGULATION

Article 1

Pursuant to Article 85(3) of the Treaty and subject to the provisions of Article 3 of this Regulation, it is hereby declared that Article 85(1) of the Treaty shall not apply to agreements, decisions or concerted practices to which only two undertakings are party and which deal only with the supply by one party of services referred to in Article 2 to the other, an air carrier at an airport in the Community open to international air traffic.

[2044]

Article 2

The exemption granted under Article 85(3) of the Treaty shall apply to the following services:

 1. all technical and operational services generally provided on the ground at airports, such as the provision of the necessary flight documents and information to crews, apron services, including loading and unloading, safety, aircraft servicing and refuelling, and operations before take-off;

2. all services connected with the handling of passengers, mail, freight and baggage, such as information to passengers and visitors, the handling of passengers and their baggage before departure and after arrival, and the handling and storage of freight and mail in conjunction with the postal services;

3. all services for the provision of in-flight catering, including the preparation, storage and delivery of meals and supplies to aircraft and the maintenance of catering equipment. **[2045]**

Article 3

The exemption shall apply only if:

1. the agreements, decisions or concerted practices do not oblige the air carrier to obtain any or all of the ground handling services referred to in Article 2 exclusively from a particular supplier;

2. the supply of the ground handling services referred to in Article 2 is not tied to the conclusion of contracts for or acceptance of other goods or services which, by their nature or according to commercial usage, have no connection with the services referred to in Article 2 or to the conclusion of a similar contract for the supply of services at another airport;

3. the agreements, decisions or concerted practices do not prevent an air carrier from choosing from the range of ground handling services offered by a particular supplier those it wants to take from that supplier and do not deny it the right to procure similar or other services from another supplier or to provide them itself;

4. the supplier of the ground handling services does not impose, directly or indirectly, prices or other conditions and which, in particular, bear no reasonable relation to the cost of the services provided;

5. the supplier of the ground handling services does not apply dissimilar conditions to equivalent transactions with different customers;

6. the air carrier is able to withdraw from the agreement with the supplier without penalty, on giving notice of not more than three months to that effect.

[2046]

Article 4

The Commission may withdraw the benefit of this Regulation, pursuant to Article 7 of Council Regulation (EEC) No 3976/87, where it finds in a particular case that an agreement, decision or concerted practice exempted by this Regulation nevertheless has certain effects which are incompatible with the conditions laid down by Article 85(3) or are prohibited by Article 86 of the Treaty. **[2047]**

Article 5

This Regulation shall enter into force on 1 February 1991 and expire on 31 December 1992.

It shall apply with retroactive effect to agreements, decisions and concerted practices in existence when it enters into force, from the time when the conditions of application of this Regulation were fulfilled. **[2048]**

This Regulation shall be binding in its entirety and directly applicable in all Member States.

INDEX

References are to paragraph number

1

CONCENTRATIONS BETWEEN UNDER-
TAKINGS – *continued*
joint acquisition of undertaking with view to
division, [1576]
joint ventures, [1560]–[1571]
absence of coordination of competitive
behaviour, [1567]
concentrative, [1565]–[1571]
concept, [1561]
control by other undertakings, [1563]
entering parent companies' market, [1570]
joint control, [1564]
operating in upstream, downstream or
neighbouring markets, [1571]
performing all functions of autonomous
entity, [1566]
taking over pre-existing activities of parent
companies, [1568]
undertaking, [1562]
undertaking new activities on behalf of
parent companies, [1569]
jurisdiction, [1463]
liaison with authorities of Member States,
[1461]
minority shareholdings, [1572]
notifications, [1516]–[1548]
control, [1539]
conversion, [1520]
declaration, [1543]
details of concentration, [1538]
effective date, [1519]
financial links, [1540]
form, [1536], [1537]
information to be provided, [1518]
ownership, [1539]
personal links, [1540]
persons entitled to submit, [1517]
submission, [1517]
oral hearings, [1528]
periodic penalty payments, [1457]
principles of evaluation, [1550]
prior notification, [1446]
professional secrecy, [1459]
publication of decisions, [1462]
receipt of documents by Commission, [1533]
referral to competent authorities of Member
State, [1451]
representation on controlling bodies of other
undertakings, [1574]
requests for information, [1453]
restrictions ancillary to, [1549]–[1558]
evaluation in case of joint acquisition, [1554]
evaluation in cases of concentrative joint
ventures, [1555]–[1558]
licences of industrial and commercial property rights and of know-how, [1552],
[1557]
non-competitive clauses, [1551], [1556]
purchase and supply agreements, [1553],
[1558]
review of decisions by Court of Justice, [1458]

CONCENTRATIONS BETWEEN UNDER-
TAKINGS – *continued*
setting of time limits, [1532]
suspension of, [1449]
suspension, decisions on, [1526]
suspension of time limit, [1524]
time limits for decisions, [1452], [1516]–[1548]
time limits for initiating proceedings, [1452]
transfers of undertakings, [1575]
transmission of documents, [1531]
two-thirds rule, application of, [1547]
CONNECTED PERSON
meaning, [50]
CONSUMER
meaning, [112]
CONTRACT OF EMPLOYMENT
meaning, [112]
CONTRACT VALUE BEFORE AID
meaning, [1271]
CO-OPERATION BETWEEN ENTERPRISES
notice concerning agreements, decisions and
concerted practices, [1470]–[1471]
COSTS
Restrictive Practices Court, [585], [618], [645]

D

DEALER
meaning, [218]
DESIGNATED SERVICES
meaning, [140]
DIRECTOR GENERAL OF FAIR TRADING,
[1], [116]
action in consequence of report of Commission, [68]
annual reports, [100]
convictions, notification to, [106]
duties as to investigation under Restrictive
Trade Practices Act 1976, [148]
false or misleading information supplied to,
[75]
functions in relation to merger situations, [56]
general functions, [2]
general power to require information, [13],
[15]
investigations
investment business, and, [264]
investment business, and, [263]
judgments, notification to, [106]
monopoly references by, [19]
notice of intended prosecution to, [105]
power to obtain information under Act of
1976, [163]
powers of Secretary of State in relation to
functions of, [12]
preliminary investigation of possible anti-
competitive practices, [229]
publication of information and advice, [99]
receipt of copies of reports, [66]
reports, [100]
special power to require information, [14],
[15]